RICHARD WAGNER.

RICHARD WAGNER

His Life, His Work, His Century

Martin Gregor-Dellin

Translated by J. Maxwell Brownjohn

A Helen and Kurt Wolff Book
Harcourt Brace Jovanovich, Publishers
San Diego / New York / London

Library of Congress Cataloging in Publication Data

Gregor-Dellin, Martin, 1926–
Richard Wagner, his life, his work, his century.

"A Helen and Kurt Wolff book."
Bibliography: p.
Includes index.
1. Wagner, Richard, 1813–1883. 2. Composers—
Germany—Biography. I. Title.
ML410.W1G73413 1983 782.1′092′4 [B] 82–15421
ISBN 0–15–177151–0

First published in Germany under the title
Richard Wagner: Sein Leben, Sein Werk, Sein Jahrhundert

Designed by Nancy Kirsh Sugihara

Printed in the United States of America
First American edition
B C D E

Contents

POSTLUDE
1882-1883

APPENDIX

Illustrations

All photographs were supplied by Dr. Dietrich Mack, Thurnau.

Translator's Note

Wagner's prose works are here referred to by the titles that have long been entrenched in Wagnerian literature, however quaintly some of them—*The Artwork of the Future,* for example, or "Herodom and Christianity"—may fall upon the modern ear. The titles of his operas and music dramas have been left in German. As for excerpts from his libretti, I have rendered them as far as possible into straightforward, intelligible English rather than essaying "literary" or metrical translations that might obscure their true meaning. I am indebted to numerous fellow translators, notably Geoffrey Skelton, Robert Jacobs, and George Bird, for providing clues to Cosima's sometimes cryptic diary entries and short cuts through the jungle of Wagner's prose. Even where my reading of the original differs from theirs, they have often blazed a valuable and time-saving trail.

J. Maxwell Brownjohn

PRELUDE

1813-1821

ALAIN ROBBE-GRILLET: *"In the long run, nothing is more fantastic than accuracy."*

Alarums and Excursions

———————◆◆———————

At Teplitz on Saturday, May 22, 1813, Goethe wrote a poem destined to serve as a bugbear to generations of German children. *Die wandelnde Glocke* tells the story of a little boy who persistently sneaks off into the fields instead of going to church. When his mother threatens that the bell will come to fetch him, he thinks she is pulling his leg. Then, to his horror, the bell comes waddling in pursuit. After a nightmare chase fraught with fears that the bell will entrap him, he turns back just in time. All ends well, but the shock lingers on. Thus, little though such warnings were needed in a world already filled with the clangor of alarm bells, the grand old man of German letters continued to haunt youngsters' dreams for years to come.

On the same day, a war baby was born in Leipzig. Were it not for the time, place, and surrounding circumstances, we could name the child, briefly state his ancestry and parentage, and skim through those first three or four youthful years that normally pass in such an uneventful and unremembered way. Not so here, for this life—the life of Richard Wagner—did more than skirt the course of history; the threads of history and of his own career were so closely entwined from the first that their correlation must be as carefully traced as if Wagner's life story were the drama of his age. Fortunate is the composer who can preface a narrative work in the grand manner with an overture compounded of all the ingredients

3

of his period and personality: exaltation and terror, the sublime and the atrocious, raging turmoil and oases of self-absorbed tranquillity, spirituality and greed, suffering and tumult. Exempt from nothing and embroiled in everything, Richard Wagner became the most controversial of household names—a figure as fiercely debated as the century that set the stage for our own disaster-ridden epoch.

It all began with a cannonade in which half of Europe took part. Not far from Wagner's birthplace, the bloodiest battles to have raged on German soil since the Thirty Years' and Seven Years' wars were fought by Russians, Cossacks, and Bashkirs; Prussians and Saxons; Hessians, Badeners, and Württembergers; Austrians and Hungarians; Swedes and French.

Dresden, then a city of just over 40,000 inhabitants, had been occupied on April 26 by the allied monarchs Friedrich Wilhelm of Prussia and Alexander of Russia. Although the king of Saxony had fled his capital, social life continued to thrive there. The Court Theater presented evening performances of Lessing's *Minna von Barnhelm*, in which the innkeeper's role was successfully played by Ludwig Geyer, a painter and author as well as an actor. A close friend of the Wagners of Leipzig, Geyer was unofficial guardian to their eldest son, Albert, who had just been confirmed at his secondary school in neighboring Meissen. Geyer would have liked to escort the boy home to Leipzig, but the tide of war intervened. His fears of renewed carnage on Saxon soil proved well founded. On May 21 and 22, after some weeks of wary confrontation, the opposing armies clashed at Bautzen. Napoleon won a Pyrrhic victory, losing 25,000 men and gaining nothing. The thunder of cannon died away, the gunsmoke dispersed, and a decisive battle between the massed armies seemed imminent when the Furies paused for breath and gave precedence to the Fates: At her home in the Brühl in Leipzig, Johanna Rosine Wagner, who was then thirty-four, went into labor.

*   *   *

Wilhelm Richard Wagner was born on May 22, 1813, in the Jewish quarter of a city under French occupation. He was the ninth child of Friedrich Wagner, a police officer.* His fourteen-year-old brother Albert was in Meissen; the younger children—Rosalie, Julius, Luise, Klara, Ottilie, and Theresia—had remained in Leipzig with their parents. Theresia, Richard's immediate senior, whom he always forgot to include in enumerations of his brothers and sisters, was not yet five when she died in 1814. Gustav, born in 1801, had died at the age of three. Given the current rate of infant mortality, the family had lost surprisingly few of its number—an indication that the Wagners enjoyed the modest comforts proper to a public servant's household. By middle-class standards, all the children prospered save Julius, who clearly lacked drive and strength of character.* That the tribulations of 1813 left the Wagner family unscathed was attributable to one man alone, Ludwig Geyer, and he was still in Dresden.

Richard was not christened at once—his autobiography errs on this point—either because his godparents were out of reach, or because his father, who was first in line for the post of police chief, was too preoccupied with the unstable situation—a mounting crime rate and frequent skirmishes between occupying troops and local inhabitants—to organize a family gathering. After waiting for an armistice to be concluded on June 4, the Wagners exchanged the distasteful atmosphere of the city for temporary quarters at Stötteritz, an attractive village situated two or three miles southeast of Leipzig and on slightly higher ground. It was there, at the hub of Napoleon's dispositions in the subsequent Battle of Leipzig, that Richard Wagner spent the first few weeks of his life in the care of a mother concerned for the welfare of her children and the safety of her husband, Friedrich, who hurried to and fro between Stötteritz, the Brühl, and police headquarters. It was also there, on June 18, that Friedrich Wagner celebrated his forty-third birthday —his last, as it turned out—in the best of health.

Whether or not the Wagners felt truly safe in their village retreat, Ludwig Geyer urged them—if he himself could not partake of "pleasant summer pastimes in delightful Stötteritz"—to join him at Teplitz in peaceful Bohemia. The Dresden branch of the Seconda Theater Company, to which Geyer belonged, had decided to move there after Napoleon reoccupied the Saxon capital, reintroduced Gallic pomp and circumstance into its theatrical and social functions, and thereby brought indigenous artistic activity to a standstill. "Napoleon has promised to transform Saxony into a paradise," Geyer, an acute and witty observer of the contemporary scene, wrote to his Leipzig friends. "The prospects are excellent indeed. We have been well-nigh stripped to our shirts, and the

fulfillment of his pledge will restore us entirely to a state of innocence."

But Napoleon's star was inexorably declining. Spain had risen
in revolt, and Wellington's expeditionary force was driving the
French from occupied territory. At Vitoria on June 21, Wellington
inflicted a grave defeat on Napoleon at the Iberian extremity of his
far-flung dominions. The French emperor was galvanized once
more. In July, he left Dresden to attend a review in Leipzig, where
he lodged at the Thomä House in Rathausplatz. This large and
imposing edifice, which Goethe refers to as "Apel's House," had
passed into the possession of an exchequer commissioner whose
unmarried daughter, Jeannette Thomä, ran it as a form of guesthouse available for state visits. Jeannette was a friend of the Wagners, in particular of Friederike, Friedrich Wagner's younger
sister. It was inevitable, therefore, that young Richard should one
day become acquainted with the celebrated suite of rooms where
former King Jerome of Westphalia had resided in 1809, and where
Napoleon now held court in demonstration of a power he no
longer wielded.

Napoleon's arrival in Rathausplatz ended the Wagners' sojourn
at Stötteritz. Friedrich Wagner was recalled to the city on urgent
police business, and Johanna Rosine went off to Teplitz without
him—a fact that did not come to light for a century and gave rise
to much speculation when confirmed by an entry dated July 21, 1813,
in the list of persons visiting the Bohemian spa. It must have been
a remarkable journey. To travel by coach through enemy lines at
a period of such uncertainty was no common undertaking, even
for a woman as courageous as Johanna Wagner. Although she
visited the thermal baths of Bohemia nearly every year, this arduous and not unhazardous wartime expedition suggests that Friedrich Wagner feared the worst for Leipzig and welcomed his wife's
absence. It is quite inconceivable that she would have left Richard,
who was only two months old, in the care of friends or of her
sister-in-law Friederike. He must therefore have exchanged cots
for the second time in his short life and been promenaded through
the grounds of the spa while Ludwig Geyer sought to allay
Johanna's misgivings. Geyer could have pointed out that Privy
Councillor and Minister of State von Goethe, too, was amusing
himself at Teplitz. Goethe, who did not take the war too seriously
and was little affected by the general ferment of patriotism, had

traveled there in April via Leipzig and Dresden. His journal lists the notables who had likewise escaped the "walking bell" of war and assembled at Teplitz to recuperate between battles.

But the summer lull was deceptive. The armistice expired. On August 10, Goethe left Teplitz and returned to Thuringia by way of Dresden, where he caught another glimpse of the French emperor.

On August 11, Austria declared war on Napoleon and all foreigners had to quit Bohemia within forty-eight hours. Ludwig Geyer and his company set off for Dresden. Johanna Wagner hastily packed her bags and returned to Leipzig, where Richard's belated christening took place on August 16. He was baptized in the same Thomaskirche where Johann Sebastian Bach had once played the organ.

Only days later, on August 22, the air was rent by cannon firing a salute to Napoleon, who had fought a battle at Löwenberg in Silesia. Shortly afterward, fighting shifted to the Dresden area.

On October 13, as the opposing armies drew closer to Leipzig, Napoleon's ally, the king of Saxony, moved into the Thomä House. On October 16, a Saturday, the Austrians set their right wing in motion. At about nine in the morning, they unleashed such a furious bombardment that windows shattered in the city itself. Then columns of assault troops hurled themselves at the French positions. The din of battle could now be heard in the center of Leipzig. By this time, the Wagners had no recourse but to stay put. Friedrich Wagner remained at his post while his wife and weeping children clustered around the cradle of Richard, who was not quite five months old.

When darkness brought the murderous engagement to an end, 20,000 dead and wounded were lying on the field of battle. The ensuing Sunday was relatively peaceful. On Monday, October 18, having received no answer to his armistice proposal, Napoleon resumed hostilities on a narrow front against an enemy twice his strength. On Tuesday morning, October 19, the allied assault on the suburbs began. A fire alarm was sounded in the Brühl. General Bertrand fell back on the road to Weissenfels, a southward withdrawal that almost sealed his emperor's fate. Bare-headed, Napoleon galloped through the city and escaped by the skin of his teeth. General Bennigsen pressed home the Russian attack on the Peterstor. Many lives were lost, and confusion in the city reached its

height when the Elster bridge in front of the Ranstädter Tor was
blown up too soon. King Friedrich August of Saxony was cor-
nered at the Thomä House and led off into captivity, his troops
having defected to the Prussians in mid-battle. Crown Prince Ber-
nadotte of Sweden, Count Langeron, and General Bennigsen entered the city by three different gates. The victors were welcomed
with martial music by troops from Saxony, Baden, and Hesse.
When the Swedish crown prince had dismounted in the marketplace, he was joined there by the czar of Russia and the king of
Prussia. Half an hour later, Emperor Franz I of Austria rode in
through the Grimmäisches Tor. The royal personages embraced
each other in a dignified manner appropriate to the occasion.
Though won, the war was not yet over, and they had no wish to
prolong it needlessly by delaying their pursuit of Napoleon. The
victors' preliminary discussion in Leipzig marketplace was a prelude to the Congress of Vienna.

*   *   *

Richard Wagner must have been treated to many highly colored
accounts of 1813, the year of his birth, by those in whom it had
aroused such hopes and fears: his aunt Friederike, his uncle Adolf
Wagner, Jeannette Thomä, his brothers and sisters, his Leipzig
friends and schoolteachers. Little though he retained of these
childhood yarns and seldom though he referred to them, the events
of 1813 had an intimate bearing on his life. His character was deeply
imprinted by the conditions that prevailed during his early years,
by the menacing proximity of war and the lingering sense of
insecurity that beset his family and friends.

For a start, the war deprived him of his father. Leipzig's hospi-
tals were overcrowded, sick and wounded men thronged its
churches and schools, horses' carcasses rotted outside its gates, and
many a corpse had not been recovered. Inevitably, epidemics raged
among the inhabitants of the war-scarred city. Being a guardian of
law and order, Friedrich Wagner could not desert his post. Early
in November, weakened by his exertions, he contracted typhus,
and on November 23, 1813, when Richard was exactly six months
old, he succumbed to the disease.

However hectic those first six months had been, the family was
now threatened with complete disintegration. Thirty-five years
old and ill-provided for, Johanna stood alone, or almost alone, in

the shadow of an uncertain future. Friedrich Wagner had left very little—not even a portrait of himself.* In the event, his vacant place as head of the family was assumed by Ludwig Geyer, who devoted the remainder of his life to the Wagner children's maintenance and upbringing. Wagner recalls in his autobiography, *My Life*, that Geyer had often been called on to deputize for his father "in the bosom of the family" during the latter's lifetime. Friedrich Wagner was a devotee of the theater, "and it seems that he [Geyer] often had to pacify the woman of the house [Johanna] when she complained, whether rightly or wrongly, of her husband's inconstancy."* It is improbable that Geyer, who was almost nine years younger than the stage-struck policeman and roughly Johanna's age, abused his friend's trust by overstepping the bounds of propriety, or Friedrich would never have sanctioned Johanna's lone excursion to Teplitz in time of war. The two men's friendship remained uncloudedly cordial until the day of Friedrich's death.

Hurrying to Leipzig to assist the harassed widow, Geyer took the closest interest in the fate of his dead friend's offspring. He saw to it that Albert soon returned to his boarding school at Meissen and prevailed on some Dresden families of his acquaintance to give Rosalie and Luise a temporary home. But for his good offices, it is unlikely that Johanna would have managed to provide for her children.

She received scant help from her brother-in-law Adolf, an earnest but uninspired scholar, author, and translator who never enjoyed any great popular success. Adolf was an unpractical and rather unworldly recluse. His prejudice against opera and the theater was insuperable. "For him who knows the actor's world," he lectured his nearest and dearest, "there is little need to discuss how much it enervates a person, rendering him empty and shallow." Drama on paper was one thing, the actual smell of greasepaint another. Not unnaturally, Adolf was far from gratified by Ludwig Geyer's intervention. He firmly disapproved of the idea that his dead brother's children should be prematurely exposed to the dangerous temptations of the theater, so he did his best to prevent the girls from being groomed for a stage career. His efforts were in vain, however. Just as he lacked the authority and financial resources that might have enabled him to help and influence his widowed sister-in-law, so he failed to produce any cogent arguments against the development of a closer relationship between her and an artist whose popularity, modesty, integrity, and good name were as widely acknowledged as those of Ludwig Geyer.

To his own regret and theirs, Geyer was at first obliged to tend the Leipzig family from a distance. He wrote letters whose decorous tone conveyed a proper regard for Johanna's feelings, sent his love to the children, and used language fit for anyone's eyes. Whether or not the formal *"Sie"* with which he still addressed her after so many years of friendship was a pure convention, Johanna had no need to keep his letters locked away. Geyer expressed concern over Albert's health—the family's misfortunes seemed endless—and later took an interest in his professional training. He also developed a special, though not unduly conspicuous, affection for Richard, the fatherless infant whom everyone regarded with such solicitude. Even before Christmas, Geyer referred in one of his letters to "the Cossack" and urged Johanna to light a pretty tree for him. "I should like to rough-and-tumble the boy around on my sofa a little," he wrote; and again, on January 14, 1814: "The Cossack's high spirits must be divine. For the first window he smashes, he shall get a silver medal." That day was a long way off, however, for the little boy, though lively, was frail in a way that branded him as a wartime child. Meanwhile, death continued to stalk the Wagners.

On January 18, 1814, Richard's four-year-old sister, Theresia, was carried off by an epidemic or a childish ailment of some kind. His paternal grandmother, Johanna Sophia, née Eichel, who was just short of seventy, also died before the month was up. Uncle Adolf, who had lived with her, joined his sister Friederike at the Thomä House and installed himself in a gloomy chamber overlooking the inner courtyard. There he sat surrounded by piles of books with a pointed felt cap on his head. Friederike, who had never married either, was fast developing into an old maid like her friend and constant verbal sparring partner, Jeannette Thomä, a plump creature given to wearing curly blond wigs. Now that Adolf had completed the party, the three of them inhabited the sumptuous guesthouse like a trio of spectral, Hoffmannesque apparitions.

Toward the end of February, Johanna Wagner sought a little respite from her domestic misfortunes by visiting Dresden to see Geyer and the two girls. We do not know if she took Richard with her, but she and Geyer became secretly betrothed. Although her year of mourning had many months to run, a union with the man who had already assumed the place of father and guardian could not be postponed indefinitely. What was more, Johanna possessed a firm and enduring basis for remarriage in the love and affection that had only been held in check—if at all—until now. When visiting Leipzig at Easter, Geyer was able to hold out the prospect of a speedy removal to Dresden. Thanks to an improvement in the Seconda Company's remuneration from public funds, he would soon be in a position to feed and house a family in befitting style. Geyer had become a court player.

The summer passed without further mishap, and in August, Johanna was able to leave her somewhat diminished but thriving brood of children to themselves. On August 28, 1814, she married her second husband at Pötewitz, near Zeitz. None too soon, either, because she was expecting another child. The family's move to Dresden took place toward the end of the year—the Congress of Vienna had opened in the meantime—and on February 26, 1815, in their new apartment on the corner of Moritzstrasse, Richard's half-sister, Cäcilie, was born.

Richard seemed finally to have found a permanent home, but his health gave constant cause for concern until he was well into his third year. His big head, with its silky hair and vivid blue eyes, sat perched on a far too frail little body with matchstick legs. Johanna later saddened Richard by confiding that there had been times when she gave him up for lost and wished him dead. All else apart, he suffered from a recurrent rash that sometimes developed into facial erysipelas. This persisted throughout his life, together with other ailments, some of them psychosomatic, such as chronic abdominal discomfort.

As for the profound mental stress to which he was subjected during his first three years of life, and which contributed to his physical susceptibilities as an adult, this has hitherto been given insufficient consideration. Unless its roots are laid bare, we cannot hope to understand the man he became; neither his fears nor his dualistic nature, neither his self-contradictory traits nor his reaction to what modern sociologists would call a determinate role. Even in default of any prior psychological knowledge, however, their origins may readily be discerned in the constant toings and froings of his early life and the frequency with which fears of death and deprivation afflicted him as a very young child. All his security fantasies were centered on the mother whose protection he in-

stinctively sought at crucial moments in his childhood, just as
everything suggests that his desire to take refuge in soft, caressing
fabrics—in silk, satin, and velvet—should be construed as an unconscious and instinctive urge to reproduce that all-encompassing
maternal warmth. He admitted to Cosima, for example, that certain silky fabrics produced an "electrifying" effect on his skin
similar to, though less pronounced than, the caressing touch of her
hand. Wagner's craving for the shelter and embrace of protective
femininity was such that mere contact with his sisters' clothing
and possessions in the nursery could set his heart pounding
fiercely, as he himself confesses in *My Life,* and that he would lie
down in a position that enabled him to feel the warmth of his
sisters' breath as they bent solicitously over his recumbent form.
He was forever devising novel and effective costumes and dis-
guises, much to the derision of his contemporaries, who used his
letters to a Viennese milliner as a weapon against him. It is clear
that Wagner was simply ritualizing and externalizing a condition
that should properly be defined as a complex: an unconscious and,
once implanted, irreversible craving to return to the sheltering
maternal lap; a reenactment born of the unfulfilled desire for love
which psychologists also encounter in deviant forms of sexuality.*
On January 24, 1869, Cosima noted in her diary: "Unfortunately,
Richard's passion for silks elicited a remark from me which I
should have done better to leave unsaid, because it provoked a
touch of ill humor." It appears that this subject was so taboo that
he resented her allusion to it—a fact that wholly supports our
present theory. If Wagner's predilection for "luxury" sometimes
assumed the character of a fetish, this was largely for the reasons
stated above. "If the world but knew," he once wrote to some
friends in his debt-ridden middle years, "what I am compensating
myself for!" He probably had no full conception of it himself.

But this is only one side of the coin. From a superficial aspect,
it would also seem that the rootlessness and turmoil of his earliest
phase of existence was echoed by the impermanence of his many
different abodes, almost all of which he chose as places to remain
in for a considerable time, if not for good. He was "home" at last,
he wrote at a period when Bayreuth lay well in the future; this
would really and truly be his last home of all—the one where he
meant to stay put. And stay put he did, until the deceptive air of
permanence was shattered by some sudden mishap or chain of

unforeseen developments—or, it would be truer to say, disrupted by something in his own unconscious. Unthinkingly obsessed with the translation of his ideas into reality, he was an artist who always formed such a Wagnerian assessment of his position— meaning ill considered as well as courageous—that the apparent constants in which he believed, like everyone within his orbit, could be utterly overthrown by a few minor factors. All this signifies is that, so far from being extraneous, the restlessness resided in himself. Something had inflicted a wound that refused to heal, and his sense of balance vis-à-vis reality was so early impaired that he either failed to recognize the defect or kept what he knew to himself.

This is not to say that he had no practical sense. He later developed an immense talent for organization, was never at a loss for ideas, designed buildings and institutions, and would happily have launched whole programs of political and social reform. However, a grasp of reality entails not only bright ideas but an eye for proportion—the wit to cooperate with things as they are and assess them in relation to one's own resources. As a child, Wagner attached cardboard clouds to chairs and threw a tantrum when he failed in his attempts to float on them. "I am still the same today," he told Cosima in 1871. "I cannot reconcile the real with the ideal." This is a key sentence. Although he meant it jocularly, there was a bitter underlying truth—one for which no remedy existed. In the child, all that was noticeable was physical frailty coupled with a lively, restless, and somewhat tearful disposition. Richard suffered from deep-seated fears and terrible nightmares that never entirely deserted him in later life. His favorite playmate was his little half-sister Cäcilie, whom he called Cilje. He bore the name Geyer, just as she did, until he reached the age of fourteen. Everyone addressed him as Richard Geyer, the name by which he was first introduced as a four-year-old tot to Carl Maria von Weber, who had been summoned to Dresden in 1816, became operatic director there in the following year, and was a frequent visitor to the Geyer home from then on.

Ludwig Geyer's new family soon acquired a congenial circle of friends. Cheerful by nature, though subject to occasional fits of melancholy, Geyer was an extremely gentle and kindhearted man. This did not, however, prevent him from impersonating the foulest and most abject villains on stage—characters such as Iago, Alba,

Franz Moor, Marinelli, and the President in Schiller's *Kabale und Liebe*—or playing the lead in *Die Waise und der Mörder* and *Die beiden Galeerensklaven*, blood-and-thunder dramas that little Richard, when he eventually saw them, found quite horrific. The critics were full of praise for Geyer's character acting and never omitted to publish expressions of regret when he failed to appear on stage. It was during these years that his diverse talents came to fruition. At Karlsbad in June and July 1817, he participated in public readings, or "declamations." He was also the author of plays in the Dresden Kotzebue genre such as *Das Mädchen aus der Fremde, Das Erntefest, Die neue Delila*—a satirical comedy written to mark Johanna's fortieth birthday on September 19, 1818, in which Geyer and Kriegsrat Georgi played the shepherds Damoetas and Philemon—and *Der bethlehemitische Kindermord* [*The Massacre of the Innocents*], whose principal character, the painter Klaus, was based on himself. Lastly, being unable to support the family by acting and writing alone, he devoted more time to painting and cultivated his reputation as a portraitist.

At Dresden, he not only painted the queen but created a stir at various exhibitions. While visiting Munich for a guest appearance in 1819, he was so swamped with commissions from the aristocracy that he had to seek temporary leave of absence from the theater. Competent at everything but brilliant at nothing, Geyer often lamented his lack of proper training. Having been compelled by poverty to cut short his studies, he tried to compensate by sheer hard work, a task that overtaxed his constitution.

Geyer pinned all his brightest hopes on Richard. He would gladly have adopted the boy and interested him in painting, but Richard showed no bent for it. Though eager to paint gigantic canvases at once—a characteristic trait!—he suffered from a regrettable inability to draw, so his stepfather gave up. It was different with the theater, which irresistibly attracted the boy and fired his imagination. When *Der Weinberg an der Elbe*, a Singspiel with music by Carl Maria von Weber, was performed to mark the return of King Friedrich August, Richard made his first stage appearance "as an angel all sewn up in tights, with wings on my back, in a graceful pose that was the product of laborious study." His fee for this engagement, he recalled, was a pretzel.

Natalie Bilz-Planer, the daughter of Richard Wagner's first wife,

Minna, claimed that four-year-old Richard also took part in Schiller's *Wilhelm Tell*, with Geyer as Tell and Klara as his eldest child. The baby of the family, who was on stage for only a moment, had one line to say—"Mother, I shall stay with you!"—but ran off in the wrong direction with a panic-stricken cry of "Kläre, if you're going, I'm going too!" Frau Bilz-Planer had heard such anecdotes from her mother, who in turn was told them by Richard's brothers and sisters.

Richard himself recalled playing another small part, this time in Kotzebue's *Menschenhass und Reue*. He further recalled grossly exaggerating its size to his teacher as an excuse for failing to do his homework.

This first taste of school, which is also mentioned in *My Life*, was probably just a brief and premature "guest appearance" at the school run by Karl Friedrich Schmidt, vice-cantor to the Court of Dresden, in 1817. In his schoolboy role, Richard did not distinguish himself by consistent endeavor. The family were forever casting around for better and more suitable courses of instruction. True, he was becoming noticeably more robust and turning into a much-admired performer of headstands and somersaults who "daily leaves the seat of his trousers on the fence," as his stepfather wrote to brother Albert, but he was certainly no infant prodigy or child of outstanding talent. What Richard most recalled of his early days in school were the trips between there and home and the well-known local eccentrics he encountered on the way.

Often, while walking down Ostra Allee toward the old opera house, he would hear someone playing the violin inside the walls of a mansion. Residing on the same street—not that Richard knew it—was a young philosopher who, on March 5, 1817, began to draft his magnum opus. It was here at Dresden that this thinker set forth "everything from which his whole philosophy sprang, gradually emerging as a lovely landscape does from morning mist." The name of this solitary man, who fathered a child by a Dresden girl but never married, was Arthur Schopenhauer. Living on the interest from inherited wealth, Schopenhauer savored the beauties of a city resplendent with works of art and places of interest: the celebrated art gallery, the castle, Chiaveri's Hofkirche, Bähr's Frauenkirche, Pöppelmann's Zwinger, the Brühlsche Terrassen, the porcelain collection, and the Japanese Palace with its huge library. Dresden, whose population had grown to 57,000 five years after the war, was one of the few cities north of the Alps with such a well-matured cultural feast to offer.

Ludwig Geyer's health began to fail at the end of 1819. He suffered from chronic colds and spells of prostration, and had clearly contracted tuberculosis. He paid a last visit to Breslau, where Albert had been engaged as a tenor by his friend Bieray, the theatrical director, and traveled in December 1820 to Leipzig. Here he stayed with Friederike and Adolf Wagner at the Thomä House, where Prince Karl Philipp zu Schwarzenberg, one of the strategists of the Battle of Leipzig, had died a month or two earlier. Geyer found "something ominous" about the place, and Johanna came to escort him home to Dresden. On February 24, 1821, by which time he had turned forty-one, Geyer attended a performace of *Der bethlehemitische Kindermord* in which thirteen-year-old Klara took part. At Easter, the family moved to a new apartment in the Jüdenhof, on the corner of Frauengasse.

Richard had meanwhile been entrusted to the care of Pastor Christian Wetzel at Possendorf, near Dresden, where it was intended that he should develop a thirst for knowledge, free from distracting influences, in the company of other boys. The pastor had a fifteen-year-old daughter, Concordia Caritas, whom Richard took to at once. Majestic, bushy-eyebrowed Wetzel was a man of wide interests—art, literature, and astronomy—and became Richard's first real teacher. In the evenings, he would regale the children with the adventures of Robinson Crusoe, and his readings from a biography of Mozart made as deep an impression on the new boy as did newspaper reports of the Greek War of Independence, which had broken out in 1821. The love of Greece that later prompted Wagner to apply himself to the mythology and history of ancient Hellas, an enthusiasm from which he derived lasting benefit, originated in his heartfelt sympathy for the Greeks in their struggle with the Turks.

On September 28, Geyer collapsed with chest pains at the family home in Dresden. Richard hurried back there on foot with the messenger who had brought word to Possendorf, covering the distance in three hours. Next day, to take her husband's mind off his sufferings, Johanna asked young Richard to show him what he had learned on the piano. After listening to an attempt at *Üb immer Treu und Redlichkeit* in the room next door, Geyer was heard to wonder feebly whether the boy might possibly have a talent for music.

He died the next morning. Johanna appeared in the night nursery, sobbing, with a special message "like a benediction" for each of the children. To Richard she said, "He hoped to make something of you." Eighteen-year-old Rosalie, who preserved her composure admirably in the days that followed, solemnly vowed to stand by her mother and adjured the younger children to help her. She took a special interest in Richard, whose longtime confidante and first artistic conscience she eventually became.

This latest calamity to befall the family was deeply felt by all. "Father" Geyer had been universally loved. Richard had lost a second father—the only one he ever knew—but which of the two had sired him?

*　　*　　*

Richard Wagner's paternity has been hotly debated by succeeding generations for longer than it deserves. Stripped of its polemical and political trappings, the question dissolves—genealogically speaking—into little more than thin air. All that imbues it with a controversial flavor is the assumption that Ludwig Geyer's forebears were Jewish or the supposition that Wagner believed them to be so, in which case his ideological contradictions can be neatly reinterpreted as an inferiority complex and his anti-Semitism as Jewish self-loathing. But this is nonsense. Why, for instance, would Wagner have loved "Father" Geyer in such a sentimental fashion, collected mementos of him, and positively boasted of them? Why would he have gazed at Geyer's portrait with adoration or insisted that the flyleaves of the four-volume, privately printed edition of *My Life* be symbolically adorned with a vulture [*Geier*]? Writing in 1888, nine months before his mind gave way completely, Nietzsche questioned in *Der Fall Wagner* whether Wagner had been German at all, but his denunciatory footnote— "A vulture [*Geyer*] is almost an eagle," meaning a Jew—was pure invention.

The Geyers, or Geiers, were a family with extensive ramifications in Thuringia and Saxony. The senior chaplain to the Electoral Court of Saxony who delivered the funeral address for Heinrich Schütz on November 17, 1672, and who carved himself a modest niche in musical history by virtue of this earliest biography of the great German composer, was a Martin Geier. A Baroness von Ulmann, whose mother belonged to the same clerical family, was married in 1717 to Heinrich Sigismund von Bülow, one of whose descendants was none other than Hans von Bülow, first husband of Wagner's second wife, Cosima.

Ludwig Geyer's immediate antecedents came from Eisleben, where they had been organists and cantors since the seventeenth century, and can be traced back to Benjamin Geyer, town musician and cantor of the Andreaskirche, who died in 1720.

Though not exactly handsome, Ludwig Geyer's face was interesting and full of character. He had auburn hair and a lowish forehead, almond-shaped eyes and a mobile mouth. Looking at him, even through the medium of a portrait, one is struck by the good nature and integrity that illumine his expressive, artistic features. What endeared him to other people, for all his character actor's art of dissimulation, were his sensitivity and even temper, his kindness and good breeding, and the exemplary unselfishness that so affected Wagner when he learned from his half-sister Cäcilie what Geyer had written in his letters to their mother. He was struck by the refined and erudite tone of those letters—not something for which the Wagners were noted—and regretted that he and his family had failed to maintain it. "I believe," he wrote to Cäcilie, "that I now see with absolute clarity, even though I cannot help finding it extremely difficult to convey my view of this relationship. To me, it is as though our father Geyer, by sacrificing himself on behalf of the entire family, thought he was repaying some form of debt." Wagner could explain it no other way, but did "debt" [the German word can also mean "guilt"] imply that Geyer had cuckolded his friend? Wasn't it enough that he felt a debt of gratitude for the intimacy, warmth, and affection with which the Wagners had deputized for a family of his own when he was still lonely and impoverished?

It cannot be denied that Geyer cut a curious figure in his bachelor role as a friend of the family, but nothing ever diminished or impaired the profound friendship and loyalty that existed between himself and Johanna's husband, hard as it is to reconcile their extreme differences in temperament: Ludwig Geyer, the citizen artist; and Friedrich Wagner, the brilliant, sophisticated public servant who dabbled in the theater.

Friedrich Wagner's forebears came from the other end of Saxony. Martin Wagner, a miner's son born at Freiburg in 1603, became a schoolmaster and moved in 1651 to Hohburg, where he additionally assumed the post of sacristan (or verger) and founded a line of teachers, cantors, and organists. From then on, a succession of Samuel and Emanuel Wagners lived in villages near Wurzen, whence their wives came, and spent their lives "singing, reading, and playing the organ, likewise ringing bells and setting clocks." The son of the last Samuel, Gottlob Friedrich Wagner, Richard's grandfather, was the first to aim for higher things but came to grief because of his capacity for indolence and a volatile disposition of which some elements may have been transmitted to his grandson. Born in 1736, Gottlob became a pupil at Leipzig's Thomasschule in 1755, so Richard also owed him his birthplace. In 1759, Gottlob enrolled at the university as a student of theology, but his devotion to that serious and moral subject lasted only thirteen semesters—a relatively long time, but not long enough. In 1765, he became the father of an illegitimate child whom he graciously acknowledged as his own. The mother of this child, which died in infancy, was a schoolmaster's daughter named Johanna Sophie Eichel. Gottlob's lapse put an end to his theological career, so he turned to more worldly pursuits and became an exciseman instead. He finally married Johanna Eichel in 1769, and their second child, Karl Friedrich, survived.

Karl Friedrich, who died too soon to complete his successful career in the public service, studied law and fulfilled the hopes that had never been realized by his father. He entered the police force, joined a Masonic lodge, and qualified for the most senior posts without ever quite abandoning his artistic proclivities and love of the theater. He took part in a performance of Goethe's *Die Mitschuldigen* at the Thomä House and is said to have been "not devoid of gallant ardor for the ladies of the theater." His ardor bore no fruit, fortunately, or Richard Wagner's intricate network of family relationships would have been more complex still. Friedrich paid many enthusiastic calls on the then-celebrated Friederike Wilhelmine Worthon, later Madame Hartwig, the first Johanna in Schiller's *Jungfrau von Orleans*, who was, at the turn of the century, a radiant young beauty of twenty-three. His enthusiasm was such that Johanna Rosine later complained to her children, jokingly, that she had often had to wait meals for him. When scolded by her, he invariably claimed to have been detained by paperwork and backed this story up by holding out his "ink-stained" fingers, "which, when submitted perforce to closer scrutiny, proved to be entirely clean."

Thus the young married couple led a somewhat easygoing existence. There is no proof, however, that Johanna, who was light-hearted but not irresponsible, repaid her husband for his artistic extravagances and escapades by consoling herself with the ever faithful Ludwig Geyer. Equally, the possibility cannot be altogether excluded. What of Richard Wagner? Did he believe that Geyer was his natural father? He denied it to Cosima, but that means little. He must, at the very least, have thought it possible.

To be blunt, the arguments against Geyer's paternity do not consist solely in his decorous letters to Johanna before and after her first husband's death. What also militates against it is the temperamental and artistic dissimilarity between the worthy Ludwig Geyer and Richard Wagner himself. Everything in the latter that was venturesome and theatrical—all his marks of genius—point to his descent from the Wagners. Physiognomic evidence, which has often been adduced, is scanty and inconclusive, especially as Richard may well have taken more after his mother than his father. In fact, almost nothing in his outward appearance could possibly connect him with Geyer. He bore an unmistakable resemblance to his elder brothers and sisters, to which may be added another striking fact: A photograph taken in middle age shows that Albert, Richard's eldest brother, was the spit and image of his grandson Wieland.

If this is so, and if speculation about his paternity has yielded such meager results, why not leave well alone? Why do writers on Wagner decline to lay the problem aside for good? The answer is simple: Despite his sparse allusions to the subject, Wagner could not set his own mind at rest. His doubts went too deep to be talked away and dispelled with mere words. Embodied in Siegfried's question—"My father, how did he look?"—and embedded in Wagner's unconscious, they pervaded his entire operatic *oeuvre*.

What *did* his father look like? If his father was Friedrich, Richard possessed no likeness of him and knew nothing about him save the little he had gleaned from his mother. But the question of his father's appearance had a second, somatic dimension. Wagner fought for personal identity throughout his life. At almost every level, *Der Ring des Nibelungen* derives its conflict from situations involving the problem of identity: All too often, someone is not who he appears to be or is taken for. And fathers? Nearly all Wagner's dramatic themes are prefaced by a father's death. This is so of his early verse tragedy *Leubald und Adelaïde*, and almost all the heroes of his major music dramas are sadly isolated figures: Tannhäuser, Lohengrin (the loneliest of all), Siegmund, Siegfried, Wotan (after his fashion), and Walther von Stolzing (an orphan like Parsifal). Tristan, Siegfried, and Parsifal are born after their fathers' death and "never knew" them, and almost all these heroes have a surrogate or foster father, such as Siegfried's weird Mime ("mime" being Geyer's professional designation).

Tristan, offspring of a dead father and a mother who died in childbirth, ponders on the "grave old air" that was borne to him on the evening breeze "when the child was told of his father's death." The picture becomes still clearer when we explore the musical context of all these central passages in the work. Ernest Newman called the long, unaccompanied cor anglais melody at the beginning of *Tristan*'s last act one of the strangest and most mournful ever devised by man. Siegmund in *Die Walküre* has more than one name for the father who bequeathed him nothing but an empty wolfskin. Siegfried questions Mime in the following exchange:

"Then tell me, who was my father?"

"I never saw him."

"But my mother spoke his name?"

"He was slain, that's all she said, and commended you, a fatherless child, to my care."

Of course she never spoke his name, but the orchestra makes a reference to Wotan. Questioned about his father, Parsifal replies, "I do not know." He was a warrior who fell in battle, but Parsifal's mother clearly left him in the dark by design. And again, nothing could be more moving than Tristan's guessing game with Kurwenal in the last act of *Tristan und Isolde:* where he has been, where he is, his doubts as to all certain knowledge of time and place, his thrice-repeated "that I cannot tell you." Only one cognitive truth exists, he says, and that is divine oblivion. Such was Wagner's response to a deep existential need—his means of escape.

On top of everything else, the mother to whom Wagner clung with every fiber of his being was also shrouded in mystical obscurity. Johanna was a delightful woman, touchingly solicitous of her children, endowed with practical insight and native wit, sensitive and mentally receptive, but also erratic and, for all her imagination, extremely ill educated. And this woman, who made an enduringly "remarkable" impression on all who met her, shrouded her background in mystery.

Johanna came from Weissenfels an der Saale, a town some twenty miles southwest of Leipzig on the road to Weimar, and had been born in Mariengasse, not far from the marketplace, in 1774. The daughter of a master baker named Pätz, she was educated at a boarding school in Leipzig, where she enjoyed the protection of a "high-born, fatherly friend." This person she identified as a prince of Weimar who had "deserved well" of her family at Weissenfels. Her education seems, as Wagner himself surmised, to have been curtailed by the sudden death of this same "fatherly friend."

Johanna must have maintained her connection with Leipzig, and presumably with its amateur dramatic companies, or Friedrich Wagner, then vice-registrar to the municipal courts, would never have met and married his baker's daughter from Weissenfels. On June 2, 1798, when she was twenty-three years old, he brought her home from the former ducal seat as his wife. Johanna disclaimed all knowledge of Goethe and Schiller until Friedrich pointed them out to her on the promenade at Bad Lauchstädt and chided her for her ignorance. Had she failed to learn her lessons —her German was appalling—or, perish the thought, been compelled to leave her Leipzig boarding school because of insufficient mental ability? Was her swiftly fading beauty all that remained?

By the time Richard could first remember her—almost twenty years later, for she bore him relatively late in life—she was permanently attired in a cap because of a head ailment. She spoke to him with great earnestness of poetry, music, and painting but never of the theater, and even threatened to curse him if he turned to the stage. Despite the ill feeling that resulted when he did—though she never made good her threat—Johanna continued to occupy his thoughts and dreams into old age, just as she surfaced in the spontaneous exclamations of his characters. "Away! To our mother! Away!" conveys a sentiment not limited to the Norns. "My mother, that I could forget my mother!" Parsifal upbraids himself in act 2, and there are few things in music more tender than the string accompaniment to Siegfried's vision of his mother when the "forest murmurs" begin in his own second act: "Like to the roe deer's must her bright eyes have shone, but lovelier by far!" Then we hear the ravishingly beautiful love-life motif,* in which, as in every passage linking love and death, the cellos play their spine-tingling part.

Of the credible oral and written testimony to Wagner's love for his mother, one letter he wrote to Johanna in Karlsbad on July 25, 1835, assumes special significance. "Only to you, dearest Mother," he wrote, "does my mind return with the sincerest love and deep-est emotion." But that was not all: "See, Mother, now that we are apart, I am so overwhelmed with feelings of gratitude for your glorious love for your child, which you lately showed again with such warmth and affection, that I should dearly like to write and talk of it to you in the fondest tones of a lover to his beloved. Ah, but far more than that, for is not the love of one's mother far more —far more unsullied than any other?"

This conveys a remarkable, textbook mother fixation which was bound to affect his relations with the opposite sex.* Wagner was attracted only by "attached" women. If the psychologists are to be believed, he suffered from the traumatic notion that he was depriv-ing someone else of a wife (mother). He was even tactless enough to make this clear to Cosima. He had never had an untouched woman in his life, he told her; none of them had ever been "new."

Within the basic framework of Wagner's love for the "attached" woman, in other words, his mother, Ludwig Geyer undoubtedly represented the "rival." Chained to his mother, Wagner suffered from what psychologists would term an "injured third party" requirement—a complex that impels its victims to seek the strang-est forms of escape and release. Psychologists further state that this generally occurs in the mother-fixated. It would appear that their fixation creates a block that renders it hard to find release in other loving relationships, so the unconscious manufactures an obstacle to their fulfillment: The love object is already taken.

Instructive in this context are the circumstances that induce the psychic complex of mother fixation and love of woman in Sieg-fried. While lying beneath the lime tree, he dreams of how his mother may have looked. The love-of-woman, or *"Weibes Wonne und Wert,"* motif from Loge's narrative in the second scene of *Das Rheingold* is recalled by the orchestra as he does so, and the whole thing erupts into words once more when Siegfried removes Brünnhilde's breastplate on the rock and fear flares up in his eyes for the very first time: "That is no man!" Most members of the audience are half-inclined to laugh at this point—after all, young men seldom give vent to such utterances—and tend to miss what comes next: "On whom shall I call for help? Mother, Mother! Remember me!" Thomas Mann detected in these lines "a blend of mythical unsophistication and psychological, indeed, psychoanalytical modernity."

There is no denying it. The youth who learns the meaning of fear through love and calls on his mother for help is articulating what Wagner's letter of July 1835 betrays: the dominant role of someone else—a woman—and a classic case of mother fixation.

Parsifal provides another glaring association of the maternal with the erotic. Describing Herzeleide's love for her son, Kundry asks, "Then, when her frenzied arm embraced you, were you perchance afraid of her kisses?" Nowhere else in pre-Freudian literature can one find such an overt reference to sexuality in early childhood. At the same time, everything in Parsifal himself, as in every other aspect of his story, strives toward deliverance and redemption. Although the scene-changing music for act 3 reverts to the mother-recollection motif, it does so with a different outcome and for a different purpose. Kundry falls dead at Parsifal's feet, but Parsifal survives. The son has come of age: No longer in need of redemption, he dispenses it himself. Wagner's own cure is not complete until the close of this final act. As Nietzsche wrote in *Der Fall Wagner*: "Wagner pondered on nothing more deeply than he did on redemption: His opera is the opera of redemption. In his work, someone is forever seeking to be redeemed—sometimes a man, sometimes a woman. That is his problem."

It was a problem with many roots, just as his quest for personal identity was born of many impulses, some of which we now know. With them, he entered life's halls of learning.

PART ONE

1821-1849

HANS MAYER: "*Richard Wagner's basic political ideas should on no account be construed as 'incidental' to his great musical-dramatic creations. Where Wagner is concerned, any such separation of the political from the 'purely artistic' spheres is automatically precluded in any case, because he deliberately aimed, above all, at a union between artistic form and ideological content. That was the very means by which he strove to differentiate drama and music drama from plain, traditional opera. In fact, even the major Wagnerian works are closely linked in intellectual content to the development of Richard Wagner the Young German, Young Hegelian, utopian socialist, and anarchic individualist.*"

Apprenticeship

———◆———

On the very day of Ludwig Geyer's death, Pastor Wetzel came to escort Richard back to Possendorf from Dresden, again on foot. A week later, a carriage pulled up outside the parsonage. Having just grown accustomed to Possendorf, the boy was to be uprooted once more. Karl Geyer, the dead man's younger brother, had come to collect him after attending the funeral in Dresden. It had been agreed that this step-uncle from Eisleben, a goldsmith to whom Richard's elder brother Julius had already been apprenticed, should now take charge of Richard's upbringing too.

The trip by mail coach from Dresden to Eisleben was the first real journey Richard could remember. During a halt on the way there, he kissed the scrawny old horses, filled with compassion and grateful to them for conveying him to the birthplace of Martin Luther, that upright man of whom Pastor Wetzel had told him such remarkable stories. He drove through the gates with high hopes, only to find that Eisleben was a shabby town that had lain wrapped in almost medieval slumber since the days of the great reformer.

Uncle Karl Geyer's home overlooked the marketplace and was rented from a soap manufacturer. Grandmother Geyer, who was still alive, shared her gloomy back room with some captive robin redbreasts. Her eldest son's death had to be concealed from her, a pretense in which Richard, too, was expected to join. He took off his mourning and talked to the ailing old woman as though Ludwig still existed—strangely enough, without difficulty. Uncle Karl sent him to a private school run by another cleric, Pastor Alt, who failed to rekindle his enthusiasm for work. Richard preferred to sit beside the old fountain, which consisted of a pig trough, or catch robins for Grandmother Geyer, whose reluctant pets were always flying off. She died soon afterward, so he was free to wear black again.

Displays by a troupe of acrobats in Eisleben marketplace made a deep impression on the eight-year-old boy, who watched their death-defying feats of agility with bated breath. Inspired by the sight of Kolter, a celebrated local tightrope walker, traversing the square on a rope suspended between two towers, he experimented in the backyard with a balancing pole and a homemade rope of his own. He never entirely lost this craze for acrobatics.

Some Hussars were garrisoned in the town. If their brass band had not launched so often into the huntsmen's chorus from *Der Freischütz,* nothing of the new era and its music would have come to Richard's ears during his nine months at Eisleben—nine months only, for his interlude there lasted no longer than the one at Possendorf. Karl Geyer got married in the summer of 1822 and could no longer keep him.

At first he was packed off to Leipzig to stay with Adolf and Friederike Wagner. His mother had never been entirely happy about Eisleben—in Uncle Adolf's view, because of her "muddle-headed and finicky plans" for Richard's education—so she now proposed entrusting him to her brother-in-law in Leipzig. Adolf refused, however. Writing to his nephew Albert, who was acting as Johanna's advocate, he complained that life had been such a hard taskmaster in recent years that his condition could be likened to that of a falling body whose weight increases in proportion to the distance it falls. Given his present need to collect his thoughts and husband his time, he could not, with the best will in the world, devote himself to Richard's upbringing.

On this occasion, therefore, Richard did not stay long in Leipzig. Little Jeannette Thomä, who had broken a leg and was in a sorry state, put him up in one of the vacant royal guest rooms. It had sumptuous, silk-lined walls and was hung with terrifying portraits —terrifying because they came to life as soon as Aunt Friederike, herself a tall, gaunt specter with a pointed chin, had conducted the boy to bed by lamplight. Haunted by nocturnal apparitions, he used to wake up bathed in sweat.

The same childish fears persisted at Dresden, where he was entered in the roll of the Kreuzschule on December 2, 1822, under the name Wilhelm Richard Geyer. Pieces of furniture acquired a life of their own in his mind's eye, and he developed a particular dread of some stone beer bottles arrayed on shelves against the wall. Their smooth exterior stimulated his imagination to such an extent that he fancied they were weird, grimacing devil-masks capable of changing shape from one moment to the next. He would do anything rather than climb the stairs alone at night because the staircase windows overlooked the shelves and their sinister occupants, and by day he always shut his eyes. Even when coming home from school at the age of nine, he used to ring the doorbell so that the maidservant could escort him upstairs.

It is clear from this mention of a maidservant that the Geyers were not badly off after Ludwig's death. The court player had left his widow a pension, his pictures were appreciating in value, and Rosalie contributed generously to household expenses out of her first professional fees. From 1824 on, moreover, Johanna had no further need to support Klara, her third daughter, who was engaged by the Italian Opera at Dresden and gained excellent notices for her debut in Rossini's *Cenerentola.* Klara had received a proper musical grounding from Mieksch, her singing teacher, and was, like Rosalie, a fair performer on the piano. It was through her that Carl Maria von Weber and the Italian castrato Sassaroli became regular visitors to the Geyer home, where they and Mieksch discussed the relative merits of German and Italian music. *Der Freischütz* had been staged at Dresden while Richard was still at Eisleben, and the warmth of its reception there was as unprecedented and long-lasting as it had been in Berlin. Richard was introduced to Weber as a youthful devotee of his much-acclaimed work. He listened quietly to the musicians' heated debates. Comparing Sassaroli, a potbellied giant with a shrill voice and a strident, explosive laugh, with the frail and gentle Weber, Richard did not find it hard to take sides. He developed a positive aversion to everything Italian, and even Mozart's Italian libretto spoiled his pleasure when Rosalie and Klara sang an extract from *Don Giovanni.*

He listened to music with voluptuous delight and always got as close as he could to any band, especially when it was playing one of his favorite pieces. His craze for imitating musical instruments began very early. One day he begged the price of some manuscript paper and copied out Weber's *Lützows wilde Jagd*—the first piece of music to flow from his pen. Johanna, who had given him the money grudgingly, was touched when she saw his painstaking efforts.

Ludwig Geyer had left him a toy theater for which he made himself some puppets, and at some point he started to write a play about knights of old. The opening scene of this gory melodrama fell into his sisters' hands, and their scornful laughter was terrible to hear. It may well have been a similar play that Cäcilie recalled him presenting during a summer excursion to Loschwitz, where the Geyers owned a cottage. The "Cossack" set up his miniature stage beside the steps on the castle hill. One birthday, probably his tenth, was made memorable by a sudden storm that swept the flimsy theater into the air, ripped the curtain to shreds, and scattered the puppets in all directions. The heavens opened, sending the audience scampering down the steps in search of shelter, but the bedraggled playwright continued his performance in a voice choked with tears, clasping the remains of his ruined theater in his arms. He eventually consented to be taken home, still weeping. For some time afterward, mutilated puppets would occasionally be discovered and returned to him by sympathetic playmates.

That was how it all began. It was his first theatrical rumpus, a characteristic clash with incalculable forces. Cäcilie recalled their mother saying that it certainly wouldn't be the last time a treat of his was spoiled, but "the sooner we learn such things, the better."

At a friend's home, Richard and some schoolmates tried to stage *Der Freischütz* with scenery devised by themselves. He was born for the theater, even though he felt no urge whatever to tread the boards himself and never for an instant contemplated a career as an actor, singer, producer, or musician. He had been repelled by the idea of becoming a "playactor," he confessed to Cosima on March 5, 1874. "The thought of appearing before an audience in makeup and getting myself applauded would have appalled me—it never even crossed my mind." In that case, what? He had only one model from the first: Carl Maria von Weber, who embodied all he thought worth emulating without as yet being able to define it. Despite his limping, essentially unimpressive exterior, Weber was a composer and conductor who combined musicianship and authority with the fame that transcends mere virtuosity. Weber's was a triumph of mind over matter. His operas helped audiences to conceive of a German quality in art. Richard, who regarded *his* work in that light, felt German—in Weber's sense—from then on.

Creation and presentation were the boy's twin ideals, but his practical musical ability was still very limited. Piano lessons with a classics tutor named Humann had availed him little. (His fingering remained eccentric all his life, though he could perform the most difficult pieces with expression.) For the present, he was governed by whim alone and happy enough at the age of twelve if he could prevail on his tutor to join him in a four-handed arrangement of one of Weber's overtures—not that this was the purpose of his lessons. Humann himself predicted that Richard would get nowhere.

At school, he applied himself eagerly to the study of Greek mythology and history. He was quick on the uptake but showed no enthusiasm for anything not immediately within his scope. At thirteen, he translated part of the *Odyssey*, read Moritz's *Götterlehre*, and tackled Creuzer's *Symbolik und Mythologie der alten Völker*, a book he was later to reread with profit. Although he treated grammar churlishly, the processes of translation and copying enabled him to discover a personal talent for creative writing. Shakespeare, too, provided a strong mental stimulus. Spurred on by a fondness for recitation (his teacher, a Professor Sillig, got him to recite Hector's death speech from the *Iliad* and Hamlet's famous soliloquy), he vented his poetic impulses in some high-flown stanzas on the death of a schoolfellow. When purged of their worst metaphorical excesses, these were actually printed and distributed—much to the amazement of Johanna, who felt convinced that her talented son was destined to be a poet. He then embarked, in turn, on a never-completed epic entitled *The Battle of Parnassus* and an equally stillborn tragedy dealing with the death of Odysseus. The latter was based on one of Hyginus's myths and inspired by a free version of the same by August Apel, the dramatist and writer of ghost stories.

Although Richard's school days were endowed with variety and entertainment by a lively set of friends, his state of health fluctuated. As soon as he became aware of the depression and nervous irritation that heralded a relapse, he would shun the company of others. The slightest change in the weather brought on facial erysipelas, a condition to which he also ascribed the periodic shedding of his eyebrows. His schoolfellows cannot have found it easy to cope with these alternating bouts of irascibility and exuberance, and the stupid ones among them must have detested him for his mordant sarcasm. Richard's mental unrest may have told him that he was on the verge of a crucial transition, one that could determine the entire course of his life. Alternatively, he may have been tormented by his very ignorance of himself and the future, by the slow progress of an internal development that could be either a natural prelude to greater things or its opposite, a misguided leap into the void. Then, in 1826, came another change in his circumstances—an undoubted change for the better where his family was concerned, but not, at least temporarily, in his own case.

Rosalie, who had become the family's chief breadwinner, secured a well-paid theatrical engagement in Prague, so Johanna moved there with Ottilie and Cäcilie. Richard was sent to lodge and board at Dresden with the family of a Dr. Böhme, whose sons he knew from school. Entering upon his adolescent years with little supervision, he gave up versifying and devoted himself to horseplay with the other boys. This state of affairs, which lasted for some time, determined his approach to confirmation classes in the following year and his attitude toward the Church and religion in general. Physically small and inconspicuous but inventive and quick-witted, he took the lead in every kind of schoolboy prank. Deprived of his sisters' gentle, civilizing company, he found himself attracted in quite another way to Dr. Böhme's grown-up daughters and their girlfriends. It was at this time that he first fell in love with a girl—Malchen Lehmann, alias the Amalie Hoffmann of *My Life*—whose appearance in her Sunday finery reduced him to "tongue-tied admiration." Richard basked in her proximity, shyly stroked her hair, and turned puce whenever she entered the room.

In the winter of 1826–27, he met two of Bohemia's most celebrated belles, who were to haunt his dreams for a long time to come. His mother collected him from Dresden and bore him off to Prague in bitter winter weather. Because she preferred to travel in a hired carriage rather than take the mail coach, the journey lasted three whole days. To the exotic charms of the Bohemian landscape, regional costumes, girl harpists, and Catholic Prague were added those of two young women who had made friends with Ottilie. One blond and the other raven-haired, but both pretty, pampered, and high-spirited, they were Jenny and Auguste Raymann, the illegitimate daughters of Count Jan Pachta of Pravonin. These creatures from another world turned young Richard's head completely.

At Prague, where the art-loving upper classes constituted a close-knit society and spent much time discussing modern German literature, Richard became superficially acquainted with the stories of E. T. A. Hoffmann. It is possible that his second and even more adventurous trip to Prague, undertaken only six months later, was prompted by Hoffmann's writings (which made a lasting impression on him) as well as by his hankering after Bohemia and the *beaux yeux* of Jenny and Auguste. He set off for Prague on foot, accompanied by his friend Rudolf Böhme, the son of his Dresden landlord. Parched and hungry, the two boys tramped the byways under a scorching summer sun. When they passed country inns, Richard would timidly sidle up to the coaches halted there and beg a coin or two, posing as an apprentice journeyman. At one of these hostelries, where they were often compelled by lack of funds to choose between bed and board, they met an itinerant harpist returning from Hanover to his native Prague. He wore a black velvet beret and trotted out his pet phrase, *non plus ultra*, at every opportunity. Richard managed to gain the eccentric musician's confidence sufficiently to borrow forty kreutzers from him on the strength of his mother's Prague address. After carousing with him into the small hours, the boys left him behind next morning, prostrated by overindulgence in Czernosek wine, and waited in vain for him to catch up with them. Weeks later, when the harpist called on Johanna to collect his money, he was disappointed to find that he had missed his two young friends.

While in Prague, Richard broached the subject of Beethoven to his sisters. Having become familiar with the E major overture to *Fidelio* and songs such as "Adelaïde," he found the music so memorable that he yearned to discuss it with them. He was as distressed to learn that Beethoven had recently died—on March 26—as he had been by the news of Weber's death in London the year before. Moody, diffident, and sensitive, the youthful visitor feasted his eyes on the beauties of Prague, human as well as scenic. Although he briefly reencountered the Raymann girls, they took little notice of their fourteen-year-old admirer. Looking back at the city from a hill when leaving, he was so overcome with grief that he flung himself to the ground and burst into tears.

That same summer, 1827, Richard joined a party of schoolfellows on an excursion from Dresden to Leipzig. Attired in student garb, they traveled down the Elbe by boat as far as Meissen and tramped on to Grimma, where carriages had been hired. At a village en route, where the youngsters were to spend the night in a large barn, a puppeteer presented an evening performance of *Genoveva* in the local tavern, using almost life-sized marionettes. The rustic spectators became incensed at the schoolboys' constant gibes and interjections; but Richard, who sided with the unsophisticated audience, was so moved by the traditional old play that he memorized whole scenes. Even as an elderly man he could still recall Count Palatine's dramatically delivered line: "O Golo, Golo! You told the Fool to tickle me behind so I feel it in front!"

At Leipzig, Uncle Adolf informed his nephew that a closet in the lobby of the Thomä House contained a substantial library that had been left by his father and now belonged to him. Richard eagerly took possession of the books. Renewed experience of the Thomä House and its pair of squabbling old maids was offset, this time, by a transformation in the streets outside, where students were proclaiming their political sentiments in matters of dress. To Richard, their Union colors and affected "swagger" seemed novel and fantastic. He noticed that the black beret, open-necked shirt, and long hair of the student associations—the traditional costume that had first impressed him as a child at Blasewitz—had disappeared "in the face of political persecution," as *My Life* so aptly puts it. He cherished a lifelong admiration for the Burschenschaft, the patriotic students' union originally formed in 1815, and his own beret was worn in memory of it, not in imitation of Dürer. The German Confederation kept such a tight and philistine curb on development in the German states that students found their twin outlets in bigotry and dissipation. This was what Richard first noticed at Leipzig, and he opted for the latter. Attracted by the fantastic and elitist aspect of the student clubs, he failed as yet to perceive their obtuse and unthinking side. Less concerned with content than with *Comment* and *Kommersbuch* [code of conduct and book of drinking songs], and animated by a new caste spirit that set them apart from the bourgeoisie, they aroused in many young people, as in Richard Wagner, an obscure longing to escape the constraints of school and home by becoming a student as speedily as possible. This sentiment was dangerously in tune with Richard's aversion to the "drier studies" and penchant for poetry, and the results soon became apparent.

Returning to Dresden, he left the Böhmes, moved to a garret, and embarked on *Leubald und Adelaïde*, a tragedy that had long been vaguely germinating in his mind. Inspired not only by the whole of Shakespeare's *oeuvre—Hamlet, Macbeth*, and *Lear* included—but also, in all probability, by Goethe's *Götz von Berlichingen*, it took its heroine's name from Beethoven's *Adelaïde*. Living on little more than his landlady's watery coffee, Richard let everything else slide. At the end of three months, when his studies had been neglected to an extent that made his position at the Kreuzschule untenable, he forestalled the school authorities by leaving. Under threat of punishment by the vice-principal, Baumgarten-Crusius, he claimed that his mother had summoned him home. He in turn persuaded her to allow him to move to Leipzig, where most of the family had just reassembled. His sister Luise, who had obtained a theatrical engagement there in 1827, was now married to Friedrich Brockhaus, the bookseller-publisher, and Johanna had returned from Prague with Ottilie and Cäcilie.

On January 21, 1828, after reaching Leipzig in time for Christmas, Richard enrolled at the Nikolaischule under the name Richard Wagner, which he retained from then on. He greatly resented being downgraded from the second to the third form and given easier meat than Homer to digest, and his spirit of rebellion was constantly sustained by arrogance and contempt for academic pedantry. He got on badly with his teachers from the start.

The address he gave them was "a staircase in the Pichhof, in front of the Hallisches Tor," this being a self-contained garret in his mother's house. He often passed his birthplace in the Brühl when walking into town, just as he also enjoyed walking and talking with Uncle Adolf, who had fled from Friederike and Jeannette Thomä in 1824 and now lived outside the Peterstor.

Richard's pride in his uncle was not without foundation. As a young man, Adolf Wagner had been presented to Schiller and complimented by him on his poetry. He had met Fichte at Jena and Tieck at Dresden, and had corresponded with Jean Paul. He had translated Sophocles, William Coxe, and Benjamin Franklin, written an introduction to *Caesar*, adapted Murray, contributed to Brockhaus's universal encyclopedia when it first appeared in 1812, and edited *Parnasso italiano*, an anthology of Italian poetry. The latter was dedicated to Goethe, who had sent him a silver cup in gratitude. One of Adolf's abiding services to literature was his fervent championship of Heinrich von Kleist, whom he called "a noble vessel of the German spirit" and defended against public obloquy after his suicide in an essay entitled "Über Mystizismus und Schwärmerei" ["On Mysticism and Enthusiasm"] (1812). Unfortunately, all these theoretical dissertations were couched in such convoluted language that even Richard, who shared his uncle's love of convolution, was taken aback by it. Adolf Wagner's pedantic and eccentric style had considerably detracted from his influence in the literary world. It occasionally attracted ridicule, a circumstance made all the more tragic and paradoxical by the fact that he himself took an independent line against the hidebound attitudes of German scholarship and poured scorn on petty philistinism in politics, religion, and education. The head beneath the pointed felt cap was full of smoldering resentment. Although Marburg University made Adolf a master of arts and doctor of philosophy in 1827, these honors were but poor and belated consolation for an utter dearth of response elsewhere.

The one person who listened to him admiringly and absorbed his influence, if only for a few years, was Richard. Wagner never tired, even in old age, of praising his uncle's gentle voice and noble, Goethean cast of mind. Adolf's literary models were exalted ones. He taught his nephew much of what he knew about Dante and the German classics, and his dissertations on Shakespeare were so vivid that Richard dreamed of meeting this idol in the flesh. Shakespeare was later joined by Beethoven. In Richard's eyes, they stood supreme, and he would dearly have liked to meet them both as a contemporary. Uncle Adolf read Shakespeare's plays aloud on their walks or recited passages from them by heart, inadvertently reinforcing his nephew's plan to complete *Leubald und Adelaïde*, the tragedy he had begun at Dresden, and stake his future on a single card.

Menaced by more trouble at school because of his persistent truancy, Richard needed confirmation of his literary gifts. He duly sent the bulky manuscript to Uncle Adolf and accompanied it with the news that he intended to leave school. Adolf was dumbfounded. Smitten with shame and dismay, he humorlessly informed Johanna of his share in her youngest son's aberration.

Richard drew an unexpected inference from this debacle: What his tragedy lacked was music of the kind composed by Beethoven for Goethe's *Egmont,* a copy of which he had found on his sister Luise's piano. Eager to learn the art of composition as quickly as possible, he borrowed Johann Bernhard Logier's *Methode des Generalbasses* from the lending library owned by Friedrich Wieck, who was soon to become Robert Schumann's teacher and father-in-law. He kept the book for so long that the charges amounted to more than he could pay—his first financial embarrassment. The family, to whom he was obliged to confess this debt, were quite as shocked by his foray into the field of music as they had been by his *Leubald* revelation.

But Richard was undaunted. If he could not attain his goal by way of the lending library, he would have to find another route. Secretly, he began to take music lessons from Christian Gottlieb Müller, then a Gewandhaus violinist and later director of music at Altenburg, who probably taught him the rudiments of conducting as well. Finding the tuition fees entailed much scrimping and saving, but his initial progress did not repay the effort. He was repelled by the aridity of routine instruction. To him, music was a demon, "a noble and mystical monster," which he identified with the work of Beethoven. It overwhelmed him with its power of dramatic expression, its spiritual vivacity and profundity. It was the language of form in motion, and he yearned—in some still undisclosed way—to wed it to words. Yet the ideal course had already been mapped out by E. T. A. Hoffmann in *Serapionsbrüder.* "To me," Hoffmann had written, "the only true opera seems one in which the music springs directly from the words, being a necessary product of the same." Wagner's Zurich essays on art continued to repeat this dictum almost word for word—until he repudiated it.

Cyprian's tale, "Der Kampf der Sänger," in *Serapionsbrüder* begins as follows: "At the season when spring and winter part company, on the night of the equinox, a man sat in his lonely chamber with Johann Christoph Wagenseil's book, *Von der Meistersinger holdseliger Kunst* [*Of the Mastersingers' Delightful Art*], open before him." Thus it was that young Richard met the earliest *Meistersinger* source—he read of the Mastersingers' berets, the greensward on which they assembled, and the Prize Song—before even coming to the next chapter, "Die Meistersänger auf der Wartburg," which begins: "It may have been in the year twelve hundred and eight that the noble landgrave of Thuringia, a zealous friend and stalwart patron of the fair art of singing, assembled six high masters of song at his court." There follow the names we know so well. Heinrich von Ofterdingen takes the place of Tannhäuser, but the persevering reader will soon come across Parcevall and Meister Klingsohr.

Small wonder that Richard seized so avidly on such reading matter, or that he showed little love for Christian Müller's austere lessons in harmony. He might have been called lazy, were it not that he reserved his diligence for other things. Time spent in listening with rapt attention to Beethoven's A Major Symphony and Mozart's *Requiem*, every note of which he absorbed, was the only time he did not consider wasted. His interest in the theater temporarily waned.

After the first performance of Heinrich Marschner's opera *Der Vampyr*, lack of interest on the part of the city fathers brought Director Küstner's regime to a somewhat inglorious end. Leipzig Theater closed down in May 1828. Richard's sister Luise had abandoned her stage career at the end of the season. Her husband Friedrich Brockhaus not only suffered his bride's impecunious relatives gladly but took a benevolent interest in his unruly young brother-in-law when the family council showed renewed concern about his progress.

Richard was singularly moved by Buonaventura Genelli's *Dionysus with the Muses of Apollo*, a painting owned by Friedrich Brockhaus. He met the artist soon afterward and never forgot him. It was also at the Brockhaus home that he made the acquaintance of Leah David, a Jewish banker's precociously beautiful daughter, and promptly lost his heart to her. He continued to idolize her until her future husband appeared on the scene. Although this quenched his ardor, Leah became the archetype of the whole string of adored but unattainable females who populated his life. The women with whom he enjoyed active sexual relations occupied another plane, like vessels of earthly as opposed to celestial love, until both erotic currents were belatedly merged in a single relationship.

For the fulfillment that love and art had temporarily denied him,

Richard substituted a friendship of the strangest kind. Having been powerfully attracted by the character of Kreisler, the brilliant but demented conductor in Hoffmann's *Phantasiestücke in Callots Manier*, he now identified Kreisler with a real-life Leipzig eccentric who displayed all the outward attributes of an artistic specter and musical original.

His name was Flachs, and it was his lanky build, lean face, and strange, convulsive mannerisms that first caught Richard's eye at open-air concerts. He conducted with spasmodic jerks of the head, puffing out his cheeks in what Richard took to be "demonic ecstasy." Flachs hailed from Dresden and knew all the musicians there, which provided him and Richard with a fund of conversation, and he was receptive enough to the young music lover's eager chatter to invite him home. Although most of the scores that littered his bachelor lodgings were worthless, one can readily imagine what treasures they must have seemed to hold in store for a youthful enthusiast. Invited back to the Geyer home for bread and cheese, Flachs persuaded the budding composer to play his earliest compositions—probably a D minor sonata and a D major quartet, neither of which survive—and further endeared himself by arranging one of Richard's airs for wind instruments. To Richard's boundless amazement, this piece was actually performed by the band at Kintschy's Swiss Chalet, a popular restaurant. His friendship with Flachs lasted no more than a year, an eternity in the life of a sixteen-year-old, but its intensity blinded him to the foolishness and feeble intellect of the man he later described as a musical "flax pole." It ended in disenchantment. Flachs, who had become ensnared by "a woman of dubious character," closed his doors to Richard in a fit of jealousy. Abruptly ashamed of his blindness, Richard shunned Flachs and his open-air concerts for some time to come.

In the summer of 1829, Richard set off on another of his long hikes. By way of Dessau, the small and idyllic ducal capital of Anhalt, he walked to Magdeburg, where his sister Klara was living with her husband of one year's standing, the singer Heinrich Wolfram. There he met another musical eccentric named Johann Christoph Kienlen, an ailing and alcoholic conductor whose sole reading matter was Goethe's *Faust* and whose sole topic of conversation Mozart. Kienlen's devotion to the latter was as vehement as his depreciation of Weber, whom he unfavorably compared with

Mozart at every turn. The German provinces teemed with musical oddities like Kienlen, who was nearing fifty and struck Richard as an elderly freak. Wolfram showed some of Richard's early compositions to Kienlen, who also composed. His amiable but emphatic verdict, delivered at an inn one night, was that he couldn't find a single point in their favor.

The richer by a copy of Beethoven's Quartet in E-flat Major, Opus 127, Richard left Magdeburg and returned home. There he immersed himself in Beethoven's scores and pursued his unsystematic musical studies to the exclusion of all else. When the full extent of his truancy emerged, as it very soon did, the family council prescribed what he had already begun in secret the previous fall: a course of study with Christian Müller. These lessons continued for nearly three years, from 1829 to 1831, and were, after all, to prove of considerable benefit.

Rosalie Wagner, who had returned to the newly established Leipzig Court Theater, urged her brother to take his studies seriously. Inspired in part by her reappearance on the scene, Richard had lately turned his attention to the stage. Heinrich Dorn had been appointed musical director, and meetings at the Brockhauses' and in Reichel's beer garden led to the development of friendly relations between Richard and the conductor-composer, who was only nine years his senior, and Dorn's younger stepbrother Louis Schindelmeisser.

The Court Theater opened on August 2, 1829, with a performance of *Julius Caesar* in which Rosalie spoke the prologue. On August 28, Goethe's eightieth birthday, the management experimented with a premiere of *Faust,* which ran for four and a half hours and turned out to be an unparalleled success. Rosalie, blond and slender, scored a major success of her own. A trifle mannered at first, she ended by captivating the audience with her natural and sensitive fusion of love, grief, and insanity. Richard's contemporary at the Nikolaischule, Franz Siegel, later editor of the *Dresdner Konstitutionelle Zeitung,* recalled that he used to keep a copy of Goethe's *Faust* under his school bench and covertly dip into it. He also broached the idea of a three-part drama of redemption entitled *Die Hexenküche mit dem Faust* [*The Witches' Kitchen and Faust*], in which Mephisto would ultimately—and thunderously—be engulfed: music of the spheres above, hellish uproar below. Siegel, whose chief recollection of Wagner was his waspish tongue, further recalled that he had seen Mozart's *Idomeneo* at the theater and found it tedious. "I pity the singers," he is reported to have said, "standing there all alone with their aria in front of the prompt box, and nothing around them but bare flats and an antique chair, or something of the sort, on which they aren't even allowed to sit."

He was far from bored by Auber's *La Muette de Portici*, first performed at Leipzig on September 28, 1829, in which Rosalie played the dumb girl. The opera's passionate evocation of patriotism impressed him as novel and revolutionary. Paying tribute to the composer on his death in 1871, he wrote that the novel feature of Auber's score was "its unwonted concision and drastic formal compression. The recitatives came storming at us like thunderbolts; the transition from them to the choral ensembles was tempestuous; and suddenly, in the midst of this raging turmoil, came vigorous pleas for prudence or renewed outcries; then more fierce exultation, murderous tumult, and interspersed with it, yet again, the moving entreaty of fear or an entire nation murmuring its prayers."

For all the long-term influence of Auber's music, all Wagner's previous musical experiences were surpassed by Beethoven's *Fidelio* with Wilhelmine Schröder-Devrient, then twenty-four, in the leading role. Her lively and dramatic style of interpretation set the pattern for his ideal fusion of singing and acting. Immediately after the performance, he wrote and delivered to her hotel a letter which she treasured for decades. His life had at last acquired meaning, he told her, and if she ever heard his name extolled she should remember that it was she who had made him what he vowed henceforth to become. He longed to write a work that would be worthy of her, and it deeply distressed him that he was not yet able to do so.

This glaring disproportion between self-assurance and immaturity—the hazy realization that his aims and potentialities were as yet unmatched by his abilities—became a challenge that steered his ambitions toward an ill-defined goal. Despite his undoubted failure to see that fulfillment takes time, the attributes of genius include a measure of patience, a willingness to gamble on oneself, an ability to turn one's back on failure, recoup one's energies, sleep off one's dissipations, and acquire a personal idiom that entails the mastery of one's resources, in music more than any other art. The order in which they are mastered may be arbitrary.

Wagner began by steeping himself in the works of Beethoven and copying them. Heinrich Dorn, who knew him well at this time, doubted whether any young composer had ever been more familiar with Beethoven's *oeuvre* than Wagner at eighteen.

Instrumentally, Wagner made little progress; academically, he spread himself too thin and had to quit the Nikolaischule at Easter 1830 because there was no prospect of his qualifying for a place at university. In order to become a student, as he very much wanted to do for reasons of life-style, he had to return to school. On June 16, 1830, he enrolled at the Thomasschule. That summer, on the advice of Müller, his harmony teacher, he took violin lessons with Robert Sipp, a member of the Gewandhaus orchestra, but only got as far as playing "certain variations in F major by Mayseder" before giving up. Recalling this interlude sixty years later, Sipp said, "He was quick to learn but idle and unwilling to practice. He was my worst pupil."

Thus, Wagner displayed none of Mozart's or Liszt's precocious brilliance. His childhood affords no scope for the fabrication of legends, nothing that would entitle a biographer to heroize him. The chaotic circumstances of his early years do not amount to an enigma. He was just a sensitive, delicate, talented boy—a poor pupil even in subjects for which he showed some aptitude and inclination.

But did that matter? Whatever he wished to grasp, he clearly grasped. By the time he was done, he had familiarized himself with the technique of every orchestral instrument save the harp. Receptive to a variety of influences, Wagner had just discovered something that smote him like a revelation: Beethoven's Ninth Symphony. He resolved on a course which, had he betrayed his intention, would have exposed him to ridicule.

A Prerevolutionary Awakening

O ur first seventeen years are half a lifetime. At seventeen, the individual experiences a second awakening. Only then can one see the world as it is and consciously reflect on what it demands and bestows.

In Wagner's case, it was the spirit of 1830 that exerted the first major influence on his intellectual outlook. That year marked the beginning of a period that culminated in the insurrections of 1848–49; and the new decade, which opened with a European upheaval on the grand scale, was undoubtedly more turbulent, eventful, and fraught with conflict than the one that preceded it.

The spark was struck in France. Strongly republican in its initial stages, the July Revolution of 1830 replaced the Bourbons with the "citizen king," Louis Philippe. It also engendered a bourgeois society that, with its classic, early capitalistic mode of production, gave rise to conflicts and antagonisms of its own.

News of the July Revolution spread like wildfire. Events in Paris were broadcast more rapidly than ever before. The *Leipziger Zeitung* printed special editions whose reports filled Wagner with a strange and unfamiliar sense of elation. "Sudden awareness of living at a time when such things were taking place could hardly have failed to make an extraordinary impression on a youth of seventeen," he wrote in *My Life*. He had not been much in favor of revolution until then. A recent spell of proofreading on the revised edition of Becker's *Weltgeschichte* for his publisher brother-in-law, Brockhaus, had acquainted him with the French Revolution of 1789 and its aftermath. The horrors of that revolution had wounded his sensibilities and filled him with "genuine distaste for its heroes." Now that he was summoned to share in the actuality of political developments—now, as it were, that Lafayette rode again through the streets of Paris and the Tuileries were stormed once more—he reacted differently. "For me, the historical process began from that day forward; and, of course, my sympathies lay wholly with the revolution, which I now regarded as a courageous, victorious national struggle, altogether unblemished by the frightful excesses of the first French Revolution. Because the whole of Europe was soon to be convulsed, to a greater or lesser extent, by revolutionary upheavals, and because several German states were affected thereby, my feverish suspense persisted for a considerable period; and I became alive, for the first time, to the foundations of those movements that I saw as struggles waged by the young and hopeful portion of mankind against the old and effete."

Reports reaching Leipzig from Poland, where a revolt in 1830–31 had led to clashes with the Russian army and spelled exile for many freedom fighters, provoked rioting by the city's students, a few of whom were arrested. Their release was demanded, and smoldering resentment against the police and local authorities vented itself in acts of summary justice and attacks on unpopular officials. One notorious brothel, which allegedly enjoyed a magistrate's personal protection, was ransacked. Wagner, who joined the mob, saw for himself how outbursts of popular fury have a habit of "degenerating into frenzy." He woke the next day "as if from some hideous nightmare." But for a torn scrap of red curtain material, which he had borne home in triumph, he would have doubted his frantic participation in the events of the previous night.

The situation in Leipzig took a more serious turn when factory workers rebelled against unpopular employers and started smashing machinery. The same young men who two days earlier had fought the police were now summoned by police chiefs and city councillors to protect private property. The various student clubs duly mustered on the campus and marched off to restore order. Brockhaus's steam presses were among the machines threatened with destruction, so student sentinels were stationed on his premises. Thanks to the kudos he enjoyed as brother-in-law to the liberal printer and publisher, Wagner wormed his way into the company of the university's foremost "bloods."

He later claimed—this, too, must have been in his "pseudostudent" period—to have belonged to a club named the Wupsia, whose members drank nothing but hard liquor and celebrated its foundation every week. Wagner was attracted to the tavern as well as the concert hall, but the two proved quite compatible, and his excursions into politics and public houses failed to vitiate his delight in music.

He had made such a thorough study of Beethoven's Ninth Symphony that he wrote to Schott's of Mainz offering an arrangement of it for solo piano. (This letter of October 6, 1830, is his earliest extant piece of correspondence.) The offer was not accepted, so he simply thrust his arrangement into Schott's hand at the next Easter trade fair. Although Schott did not publish it, he kept the manuscript and presented Wagner with a copy of the *Missa Solemnis* in return. Wagner also approached Breitkopf & Härtel and the Bureau de Musique (later C. F. Peters), offering his services as a proofreader and arranger. To Breitkopf he sent a piano arrangement of Haydn's 103rd Symphony, coupled with an assurance that it was accurate. The fruits of his partial diligence were not, however, accepted.

Wagner's compositions in 1830 included an overture to Schiller's *Braut von Messina,** another overture in C major, and what must undoubtedly have been his most singular orchestral piece, the long-lost overture in B-flat major whose presentation itself was remarkable. He set out to write it in different-colored inks—red, green, and black—in order to differentiate the instrumental groups and lend visual expression to a Beethovenesque battle of the elements. Flachsian in its blend of ingenuity and eccentricity, this device was frustrated by lack of green ink. The overture's most notable feature was that the melody was interrupted every fifth bar by a booming drumbeat from the "black" depths. Heinrich Dorn agreed to perform it despite the misgivings of Matthäi, his first violin. The rest of the orchestra wagged their heads and chuckled during rehearsals, and the tympanist, who was never sure of his beat, became thoroughly confused, but Dorn stuck to his guns and insisted that the work be performed as it stood. The "New Overture," as it was anonymously described in the program, was finally performed at a charity concert on December 24, 1830.

Before present-giving at the Brockhauses', Wagner hurried to the theater with his sister Ottilie. She sat in a box, he found a seat in the stalls. Unfortunately, any thematic interplay the work may have possessed went unnoticed. As the fatal drumbeat recurred with dogged regularity, so the audience became increasingly surprised and amused. Disbelief yielded to hilarity as they waited for every fifth beat. "I heard my neighbors calculating and signaling this recurrent effect in advance," the composer recalled. "The torments I suffered, knowing their calculations to be correct, defy description." It was a horrific experience for one who always strove to minimize the danger of predictability in his major works. In fact, the sound of his overture almost sent him into a swoon. When it ended, as it did quite abruptly, without a conventional finale, the audience neither clapped nor hissed; they simply sat there in baffled silence.

The next day, Wagner apologized to his teacher, Müller, and begged him to regard what had happened as "a frivolity"; the whole affair, he said, was a youthful aberration and would not be repeated. "Besides," he added, "I'm relying on the fact that no member of the public knows my name, so the matter will pass as unnoticed as it deserves to be." Capable of self-criticism, he was also quick to call on Heinrich Dorn. Despite Dorn's assurance that he had discerned real talent in the piece and found it unnecessary to change a single note, Wagner remained to be convinced that Dorn had not been playing a practical joke on him.

On February 23, 1831, even before the academic year ended, Wagner enrolled at Leipzig University as a student of music, and by the Easter vacation he was a member of the Saxonia Club, which held its drinking sessions at the Grüne Schenke [Green Saloon] every Wednesday and Saturday. Its membership included the rowdies whose acquaintance Wagner had made at his brother-in-law's house. An athletic young man named Gebhardt won Wagner's admiration because he could lift two companions in the air, one in each hand, and stop a cab by holding onto its wheel spokes. Another by the name of Schröter introduced Wagner to the prose and poetry of Heinrich Heine during afternoon sessions in the Rosenthal and Kintschy's Swiss Chalet. Schröter also taught him the flippant, affected mode of speech that passed in such company for supercilious elegance.

Wagner was soon in trouble with Degelow, a demonic-looking fellow, and Stelzer, nicknamed Lope, a seasoned campaigner of twenty semesters. Carried away with undergraduate exuberance, he challenged them to cross sabers after a ritual exchange of insults. This he did although he had never fought a duel himself, merely witnessed a messy fight in which, to his alarm, a lot of blood was shed.

The dates for his duels had already been fixed when the formidable Lope Stelzer escaped his creditors by joining a party of Polish refugees and fleeing westward, later to end up in Algeria with the Foreign Legion. That left Degelow. Not long before their appointed encounter, Degelow paid a brief visit to Jena, whence news soon came that he had been fatally wounded in a prior engagement with rapiers.

Twice spared, Wagner was now confronted by his first real passage of arms with an energetic swordsman named Tischer, who had been picked as a suitable opponent by Wagner's "senior," a Herr von Schönfeld. Wagner happened to be suffering from a rash that would have increased the danger of the wounds he was bound, as a novice, to sustain. Although this skin condition would have warranted a postponement, he did not report it. Apprehensive but resigned to his fate, he left home on the morning of the duel and made for the Brühl, where Herr von Schönfeld lived. He found him leaning out of a window, puffing at his pipe. "You can go home, lad," he was told. "It's all off—Tischer's in the hospital." Wagner's fellow "Saxon" had gotten blind drunk in a brothel the previous night and been thrown out, but not before the outraged ladies of the house had injured him in the most degrading manner. This meant not only suspension from the university but expulsion from the club. Wagner had been spared yet again. From then on, the budding libertine turned his back on the dueling ground and succumbed to a different but no less dangerous craze.

At freshmen's drinking sessions, where he once spent three days and nights without returning home, he made it a point of honor to be among the tailenders. Here he fell among boon companions who infected him with a mania for gambling. He now spent his time at the Landsknecht, trying to multiply his pocket money.

Any cash he won, he promptly lost again, so the febrile excitement of the card table continued to hold him in thrall for three whole months. No one could dissuade him from these nightly excursions. As unapproachable as a drug addict, he endured even Rosalie's contempt in torpid silence. His appetite for games of chance was further whetted by heavier losses that hit his pocket hard and encouraged attempts to recoup them. When these failed, he decided to win everything back in short order by increasing his stakes. Being authorized to collect his mother's pension money, he drew out her substantial monthly allowance and gambled it away in a single night. He knew he could never return home under such circumstances and had visions of ending up like Lope Stelzer, an outcast in foreign climes.

He staked his last thaler and won, staked his winnings and won again. A few more successes, and he had recovered Johanna's pension. Telling himself that this was his last night ever at cards, he staked and won yet again, forcing the bank to close. His winnings covered all his debts. Next morning he made a clean breast of things to his mother. He was cured at last. Gambling lost all its charms for him, and his frivolous phase came to an end. He was not incorrect in supposing, later on, that these futile dissipations had built up a "protective crust" around a core that "needed natural reinforcement if it were not to be prematurely weakened by producing before its time."

His eyes were suddenly opened to the "terrible, darker aspect of German student-club life": It bred insensitivity. On May 26, 1831, Russian military superiority destroyed Polish hopes of liberation at the Battle of Ostrolenka. While gloom descended on Poland's Saxon sympathizers, the "Saxons" continued to booze and bluster. Wagner abandoned them in quest of other friends, or, rather, he made his first real friend, Theodor Apel. The son of Johann Apel, the ghost-story writer, Theodor was two years older than Wagner and not without means. He studied law but remained true to the Muses and began to write poetry. It was Apel who encouraged Wagner's serious tendencies and dissuaded him from wasting any more of his time.

By the summer, Wagner had completed a piano sonata in B-flat major for four hands, later to be orchestrated. Inspired by Rosalie's playing of Gretchen in Goethe's *Faust*, he also wrote seven pieces which he revised in 1832. There are echoes of Schubert in them.

The soldiers' song, *Burgen mit hohen Mauern*, may be ranked with the average male-voice choir literature of the period, and Brandner's song, *Es war ein Ratt' im Kellernest*, is dramatically and structurally compact. In August, Wagner visited his mother, who was taking the waters near Aussig, and soon afterward he embarked on regular lessons in composition—the need for which he now accepted—with Theodor Weinlig, cantor of the Thomaskirche.

Born in 1780, Theodor Weinlig had studied at Bologna and was grounded, as an organist and composer, in the polyphonic tradition of the eighteenth century. Fortunately for Wagner, he did not regard the study of counterpoint and fugue as a pupil's straitjacket, but as an analytical and practical exercise in structural autonomy. He was the second major influence on Wagner after Ludwig Geyer. Weinlig died in 1842, so he did not live to see his pupil scale the heights, but the choral writing, cudgel motif fugato, and exquisite polyphony of the cobbler's shop quintet in *Die Meistersinger* are all a tribute to his teaching.

Wagner's first apprentice piece was an academically unoriginal and unremarkable piano sonata in B-flat major. Weinlig, to whom it was dedicated, was sufficiently satisfied to prevail on Breitkopf & Härtel to publish it in 1832, together with a polonaise in D major. Having completed this exercise, Wagner was given leave to compose something for his own pleasure. He surprised Weinlig by producing the piano Fantasia in F-sharp Minor, which he finished on November 27, 1831. Its main defect was length. Its keyboard composition is reminiscent in certain passages of Schubert, whose work Wagner had yet to digest, and of early Beethoven. Aphoristically studded with quasi recitatives that tended to run away with him, and with the rudiments of a variation technique that his insufficient mastery of the piano rendered definitely inferior to comparable early works by other composers, the Fantasia remains a colorful piece. More than that, its adumbration of certain themes and motifs lends it an anticipatory quality—as though an immature composer were listening to the future and hearing music that defied his present ability to record it in writing.*

On November 4, probably under Weinlig's supervision, Wagner produced the final version of his Overture in D Minor, which had originated in September. It was performed at a Christmas theater concert and given again at the Gewandhaus. On February 23, 1832, Wagner attended this performance with his sisters Rosalie and

Luise. Influenced by Beethoven's *Coriolan* Overture, the work compared quite favorably with overtures by Marschner and Lindpaintner. The audience applauded and Luise wept for joy. Wagner's summing up, a month before Goethe's death, was "Am emerging from my apprenticeship."

Everything had abruptly changed for the better. Wagner's mother received a visit from Weinlig. Past experience made her quail at the sight of him, but he had merely come to inform her that he had taught Richard all he could. When Johanna asked what she owed in tuition fees, the cantor of the Thomaskirche replied that it would be unbecoming to accept payment for the pleasure it had given him to instruct her son; Richard's diligence and the hopes he pinned on him would be recompense enough. To Wagner himself he said, "You will probably never write any fugues and canons; you have, however, acquired independence. You are now standing on your own two feet and conscious of your ability to produce the most skillful work, if you so require."

That winter, Leipzig fell prey to Poland fever. On January 8, 1832, remnants of the Polish rebel army were publicly acclaimed as they marched into the city. With them came General Joseph Bem, who had fought at the Battle of Ostrolenka, and Count Vincenz Tyskiewicz, a handsome and distinguished figure who was lionized when he appeared in the foyer of the Gewandhaus with a party of fellow expatriates, elegant in his braided jacket and red velvet cap.

Wagner, who was introduced to the count at the home of his sister, Luise Brockhaus, enjoyed his company almost daily for a time. Vincenz Tyskiewicz acquired an aura of tragedy in the young man's eyes because of an incident in his past: He confided to Luise that he had shot and killed his first wife. While visiting one of his castles in the Polish backwoods, he had been startled to see a ghostly figure outside his bedroom window. Under the impression that it was an intruder, he seized his gun and fired into the darkness—only to discover that his wife had been playing a practical joke on him. Count Tyskiewicz might have stepped out of a knightly epic. Beside him, all the other Polish heroes with whom the people of Leipzig exchanged fraternal kisses paled into insignificance. On May 3, the last eighteen Polish refugees in the city met to celebrate Constitution Day at an inn on the outskirts of Leipzig. Only the Polish Committee and Richard Wagner, the count's personal guest, were invited. The crescendo of tears and laughter, sorrow and rejoicing culminated in a drunken orgy, and Wagner later crystallized his impressions of the night in an overture entitled *Polonia*.

The force of Beethoven's example and Weinlig's influence may also be discerned in Wagner's Piano Sonata in A Major, which ends in a three-part fugue. The concluding fugato of the C Major Overture written in March 1832 betrays how closely he had studied Mozart's *Jupiter* Symphony. It earned him nothing but a conductor's debut at the Altes Schützenhaus, where he wielded the baton at a concert of the Euterpe Musical Society run by his former teacher, Christian Müller. In April, the celebrated Henriette Wüst sang a "Scena and Aria" of his at a Court Theater "declamation" presented by the veteran actor Solbrig. On the last day of the same month, the C Major Overture was repeated during a guest recital by Matilde Palazzesi, an Italian singer with the Dresden Opera, this time at the Gewandhaus itself. Leipzig concertgoers must by now have begun to think twice about this smart-aleck nineteen-year-old composer who kept assailing their ears with his five-finger exercises.

Was the C Major Symphony, which he started early in the summer, just another study, or something more? It contained "strettos, really diabolical stuff," but Wagner was shrewd enough not to overreach himself. He took the position adopted by early Beethoven, roughly that of his Second Symphony, though with cognizance of its successors up to the Seventh in A Major. To have modeled himself on late Beethoven would have been the megalomaniac presumption of a dilettante. Thanks to Wagner's self-restraint, his only symphony was also the only "old-fashioned" work of his youth, and one on which he could publicly expatiate without embarrassment, even in old age. If anything of himself could be detected in it, he wrote on New Year's Eve 1882, it would be the boundless self-confidence with which, even at that stage, he "worried about nothing" and kept himself "immune from the servility that came into vogue soon afterward and has since become irresistible to the Germans."

Wagner had scarcely completed the C Major Symphony, which he did in the space of six weeks, when he felt a renewed urge to travel. This time his destination was Vienna. He packed the symphony and his three finished overtures and set off by special mail coach with Count Tyskiewicz, who had decided to return to Galicia. After traveling by way of Dresden and Pirna, the two friends parted at Brünn [Brno] in Moravia, never to meet again. Wagner, who was obliged to call a halt there till next day, learned that cholera had broken out in the city.

A fermata hovers over this desolate night, which he spent fully dressed on his bed in the wing of a hotel—reason enough to dwell on it briefly.

Alone and forlorn in the unfamiliar capital of an unfamiliar country, compassed about by alien sounds and smells on a sultry night, he lay staring into the darkness. And as he lay there, drowsy but quaking with terror, the phantoms of his childhood—the evil spirits of disease and death—fastened their grip on him once more. He felt, or so it seemed to him afterward, as if a demon had lured him into a trap so as to destroy him without trace, without witnesses, in a foreign land. Cholera stood before him like a living creature, climbed into bed with him, slipped between the sheets and embraced him. His limbs turned to ice. Numb with fear, he gave himself up for lost.

Did his mind go back? Did his short life trickle through the hourglass of his imagination in a swift and bewildering succession of images? Did he wonder if this—these nineteen years—was all that life had granted him? One can picture him striving to resist this flood of recollections, only to find that times and places had become telescoped in his mind. His rootless, disrupted childhood would have reemerged from the darkness of its unremembered beginnings, with journeys in jolting carriages, clouds scudding overhead, incessant stimuli, lack of security and lasting orientation —lack of anything that seemed certain to endure for longer than a few weeks or months. His route through life was lined with faces, but none of them told him who he was. Most of them had faded and vanished in a succession of farewells and bereavements. His past was an unlit chaos despite its glaring colors and radiant skies. He would have remembered hot summer afternoons at Loschwitz; the flames he had gazed into until his cheeks smarted before stealing morsels of meat from the spit; the dusty roads and streets he had tramped, innumerable and indistinguishable; a kaleidoscope of flowers, animals, and gaily dressed dolls; the soft dresses of his sisters and the sweetness of their breath on his cheek as he drifted off to sleep. Nothing in his life had ever come to rest because he himself had not. There was the recurrent stab of pain when his feelings were hurt; the urge to hit back and inflict pain in return; the remorse and disgust he felt when he had injured some school-mate weaker than himself, when arrogance and a native inability to suffer fools gladly drove him to ridicule others. He took pleasure in offending his teachers and friends, relishing his sarcasm and the acid, polished insults that were the only weapon of an undersized boy with an intermittent inferiority complex. He would have remembered the ridicule he himself had swallowed; his shame when a senior declined to exchange toasts with him; his sexual humiliations, his desires and rebuffs; his solitary self-abuse and the stale, sad disenchantment of its aftermath; his cheap successes, gained by means of tricks and pranks and feats of acrobatic skill because he could not, like Gebhardt, lift two companions in the air, and had not won a duel or even fought one; and the dearly pur-chased satisfaction of having earned another kind of esteem by abusing his own intelligence. He had no friends of long standing. Apel was far away in Heidelberg, Tyskiewicz had left, and whom would he find at home if he returned? Had he at least regained Rosalie's love, and for how long? How could he persuade others of his worth if he himself were not convinced of it, if there were nothing that really accorded with his sense of self and no one with whom to discuss such an unendearing subject? All his wounds hurt at once—all his wounds and farewells. It was less than a year since he had reduced his mother to tears—his mother, who had financed this journey from which he might never return if the epidemic, the spirit of death, seized upon him now, on his way to strangers to whom his music meant nothing, alone and forlorn and menaced by cholera. All the fears of a lifetime descended on him like Goe-the's bell, entrapping him past hope of deliverance. He was haunted, afflicted, and—above all else—alone.

Next morning, to his utter surprise, he awoke from his night-mare feeling perfectly hale and hearty.

*   *   *

In Vienna, where he stayed for nearly six weeks, Hérold's opera *Zampa* pursued him from theater to concert hall to café. The summer days were as lovely as the nights of flowing wine were lively, but artistically they proved an unmitigated disappointment. Not only had Hérold usurped the place of Beethoven, but, at the Kärntnertor Theater, Wagner saw a boring, unimaginative production of Gluck's *Iphigénie en Tauride* that far from matched the picture he had gained of that composer's work and character from Hoffmann's story "Ritter Gluck." He was at least entertained at the Theater an der Wien by such extravaganzas as Johann Lembert's *Die Abenteuer Fortunats* and Ferdinand Raimund's *Der Bauer als Millionär*, which made a deep impression on him. He also saw the Cagliostro of light music, Johann Strauss, who trembled like a Pythian priestess on her sacred tripod at the start of each waltz and sent his audiences into raptures. Whenever he returned to his lodgings in Danhausergasse, however, Wagner felt intellectually starved. An attempt to get his D Minor Overture played at a "very poor" students' rehearsal at the Conservatoire failed for lack of interest.

In September, he moved on to Bohemia. After a roundabout trip by stagecoach, he reached Count Pachta's estate at Pravonin, some eight miles from Prague. Old enough at last for an amour, he planned to take advantage of the count's hospitality and form a romantic liaison with his daughters—or at least with one of them. He settled on Jenny, the dark-haired elder of the two, though *embarras du choix* prompted him to pay court to the blond Auguste as well. He did not, however, behave "suitably" because he forgot that, although they were illegitimate and called Raymann, Pachta's daughters had to groom themselves for marriages worthy of their social standing, so all their flirting and coquetry amounted to nothing. Perversely, he started lecturing them.

He inveighed against their superficiality, their poor taste, and their aristocratic suitors, all of whom he was quick to recognize for the dimwits they were. He accepted the girls' reproaches but never apologized, attributing his conduct to real or feigned jealousy. "Conceive of Jenny as an ideal of beauty and add to that my ardent imagination," he wrote to Apel when the whole thing was over, "and you know all." For Wagner, nothing worked without imagination. "In her beauty," he went on to confess, "my passion believed it saw all that could exalt her into a glorious apparition. My idealizing eye discerned in her all it wanted to discern, and that was the trouble." Wagner's love consisted, almost invariably, of volition and imagination. He wanted to love the products of his fancy. Although they usually bore little relation to reality, this did not prevent him from embracing them with the entirety of a soul that hungered for love.

On October 12, while seated beside Jenny at the piano, his feelings overflowed. To conceal his tears, he ran outside. Somehow, the sight of the evening star reminded him that he was still alive and had not died at Brünn. He resumed his seat at once and, in the grip of some nameless ecstasy, began to improvise on Theodor Apel's poem *Abendglocken*. Out of the blue, or out of the depths of his emotional turmoil, came the recollection of a theme preserved in his mind from an earlier reading of "Die Hochzeit" in J. G. G. Büsching's *Ritterzeit und Ritterwesen*. He at first thought the plot might do for a timeless novella. Set on the estate of a wealthy art lover, it would tell the story of a bride who inadvertently causes the death of an unwanted admirer and falls lifeless on his coffin when summoned to attend his funeral.

Wagner's days at Pravonin were numbered. He paid a visit to Prague with Jenny, who taught him how love can be killed— exactly how we do not know, but it must have shaken him profoundly, because he writes to Apel of a "deathly chill" and describes how he saw "the aura of spiritual beauty dissolve, hour by hour." Back at Pravonin, dashing cavaliers continued to court the girls in a most objectionable manner. Together with a confectioner named Hascha, one of Auguste's admirers, Wagner found himself condemned to a wallflower's role. One evening, when he tried to call on Jenny, her mother detained him in an anteroom while the two young ladies, dressed to kill, were flirting in the drawing room with the aristocratic beaux he detested so much. That settled it. Writing from Leipzig to Apel, who was studying at Heidelberg, he declared, "She was unworthy of my love!"

More productive than this hopeless passion were his conversations with the Prague composer Václav Tomašek and the director of the local Conservatoire, Dionys Weber, who told him much about Mozart's style of presentation. Because Wagner either disavowed his admiration for the late works of Beethoven or disguised it from the conservative old man, Weber accepted his C Major Symphony and performed it at the Conservatoire in November. "Wagner sneaked up on Dionys the director, the score in his garments," joked the actor Heinrich Moritz, who had befriended Wagner and introduced him to the young composer-conductor Johann Kittl.

It was at Moritz's home that Wagner began drafting a libretto for *Die Hochzeit* [*The Wedding*], which was to be his first opera. Restored to medieval times, it was "a nocturnal piece of the darkest hue" and powerfully influenced, no doubt, by the mood of Marschner's *Vampyr*. To seal the reconciliation between two feuding families, the head of one invites the son of the other, Cadolt, to attend his daughter Ada's wedding. When Cadolt's gaze falls on Ada, she is attracted to him just as Senta is to the Dutchman. "My husband, speak," she says, "who is the stranger?" (Senta to Daland: "My father, speak, who is the stranger?") The rest is inevitable. Cadolt climbs the castle keep that night and enfolds Ada in an impassioned embrace. She thrusts him away and, in so doing, pushes him off the balcony. The two families are about to resume their ancient feud because of Cadolt's supposed murder when Ada sinks, dying, upon the coffin containing his broken body.

Everything suggests that Ada is the faithless Jenny, who makes an unworthy match with the wrong man and blindly repulses him who truly loves her. The theme of accidental death, too, seems reminiscent of Count Tyskiewicz's shot in the dark. If so, it only underlines the indelible impression made on Wagner by personalities and stories of a demonic, Hoffmannesque character.

Back in Leipzig once more, he composed the opening numbers and showed them to Rosalie as proof of his industry. Rosalie was disappointed. She found the whole theme too gruesome and missed all the things he had deliberately omitted, such as operatic embellishments and light relief. Because he set so much store by her opinion and approval and wanted to please her at all costs, he destroyed everything he had thus far written except for a first-scene septet that Weinlig had praised for its singable qualities.

Wagner's return to Leipzig brought a new figure into his life. Six years his senior, Heinrich Laube was a shrewd, forthright Silesian, an idealist and aphorist, a visionary and ambitious man of letters, and a burning glass of the spirit of the age. When Europe was set in motion in 1830, Laube had become a champion of liberalism. He had just completed *Das neue Jahrhundert*, a well-meant novel brimming with high-minded clichés, and was at work on his next project, a trilogy entitled *Das Junge Europa*. Everything about him was "new" and "young." His ideas, by his own admission, were unadulteratedly "progressive": He preached the divine rapture of free love and pronounced the old morality dead. Soon after he arrived in Leipzig, where he lingered quite by chance on his way to the west, he had asked his partner at a ball in the Hôtel de Pologne if she didn't agree that the marriage laws should be changed. "What," she retorted, "this minute?" She turned out to be one of Wagner's sisters, either Luise, Friedrich Brockhaus's wife, or Ottilie, who had since attracted the attentions of Brockhaus's younger brother Hermann, a twenty-six-year-old Orientalist.

Laube bumped into the Wagner clan wherever he went—at the theater, among other places, where he got to know Rosalie, the eldest of the brood. He fell for her gentle, slightly spinsterish charms (she was already nearing thirty) and was captivated by her portrayal of *Faust*'s Gretchen. Then he met Richard and became a welcome visitor to the Wagner-Geyer home. "Do you think Richard will ever make anything of himself?" he was promptly asked by Johanna. Impressed by what he had seen and heard, Laube reassured her. He soon discovered that Wagner was a progressive too, not that their views always coincided. Laube identified himself with a Young Europe whose targets of abuse included Carl Maria von Weber as well as literary orthodoxy, hidebound classicism, sentimental romanticism, Goethe and Schiller, Tieck and Novalis. Wagner disagreed, but Laube's tirades against German romantic "humbug" in opera had a long-term effect on him.

Laube and Wagner regularly met at Kintschy's, the café in the Rosenthal. Here they were often joined by portly Gustav Schlesier, a Dresden schoolfriend of Wagner's, and the author of *Polenlieder*, Ernst Ortlepp from Naumburg, a Beethoven devotee and itinerant scholar who went to seed and later died in tragic circumstances.

Laube was forever trumpeting the virtues of a worldly religion centered on the enjoyment of life. Wilhelm Heinse, an author of the "Storm and Stress" era, was then in process of rediscovery. Laube gave Wagner a copy of his *Ardinghello und die glückseligen Inseln* to read, a novel whose commendation of sensuality was based on a philosophy of freedom, beauty, and strength. Wagner was enthralled by the erotic side of this secular creed, with which

he later blended other philosophical trace elements such as Feuerbach's atheistic sensualism. The Ardinghello of the novel, an ad-
venturer of many artistic talents, flees from Rome to found a
utopian state where womankind and free love are accorded their
due by "the power of enjoyment." Although this was calculated to
appeal to any youthful idealist, Wagner must have paid more attention to certain other pronouncements—for example, "All art is
the portrayal of totality for the power of imagination." This was
as imprecise as any theory of opera, but there was nothing to
prevent Wagner from trying it out and heeding Hoffmann's advice
at the same time. In this he was encouraged by Rosalie.

Taking Gozzi's *La donna serpente* as his framework, Wagner
promptly got rid of the snake into which the fairy transforms
herself because it was incompatible with his artistic scheme of
things. The convoluted plot, retold in Ossianic style, includes a
clash with the spirit world: A mortal man falls in love with an
immortal fairy and has difficulty in adapting himself to her
ethereal realm.

Heinrich Laube now tried, without success, to interest Wagner
in his libretto for an opera to be entitled *Kosciuszko*, which was
simply a dramatized biography of the Polish national hero. Wagner found it hard to explain to Laube why he had to be his own
librettist. He was gradually becoming aware of a specific method,
peculiar to himself, which required that words be written with an
eye to music, or, rather, that both should derive from a single
underlying dramatic and musical idea. Rosalie, too, advised him
against the *Kosciuszko* venture. He remained noncommittal on the
subject until a visit to Würzburg enabled him to transmit a tactful
long-range refusal by letter.

For the moment, he was fully preoccupied with the first Leipzig
performance of his C Major Symphony. Councillor Friedrich
Rochlitz had accepted it for the Gewandhaus but insisted on a
tryout by Gottlieb Müller's Euterpe Society at the Schneider Her-
berge, a cramped and dirty old hall, on December 15, 1832. Despite
this inauspicious setting and what Wagner himself described as a
"disgraceful" interpretation of his work, Clara Wieck wrote to
Robert Schumann on December 17 that her father had told her that
a symphony by Friedrich Schneider, previously performed at the
Gewandhaus, was by comparison like a freight wagon that takes
two days to get to Wurzen, driven by a boring old carter and

always keeping strictly to the same track. Wagner, on the other hand, "drives hell-for-leather in a gig, tumbling into the ditch every other minute, but would nonetheless have reached Wurzen in a single day, black and blue or not."

At the Gewandhaus concert on January 10, 1833, August Pohlenz conducted, thirteen-year-old Clara Wieck played a piano concerto, fifteen-year-old Livia Gerhard sang, and nineteen-year-old Richard Wagner's symphony earned him benevolent applause. The reviews were friendly and encouraging, and the young composer received the following tribute from the city's shrewdest critic: Great things could be expected of him when "the mechanics of music are operated by his spirit instead of his intellect." Against this, the choral composer Franz Otto wrote to his boyhood friend Schumann on February 19 claiming that Wagner's symphony had been an undeniable failure. Heinrich Laube, who had since taken over as editor of the daily *Zeitung für die elegante Welt,* let it be known after a while that, although Wagner's C Major Symphony displayed "brash and audacious intellectual vigor," it also contained such "virginal naivety" that he pinned great hopes on the young man's musical talents. He may still have believed that Wagner would set his *Kosciuszko* to music.

In January, Wagner was invited to conduct one of his overtures at a concert given by the Würzburg Musical Society. This guest appearance had been engineered by his brother Albert. He gratefully accepted the invitation, not intending to return to Leipzig for some time.

Prelude in the Lower Ranks

———◆———

Like his music dramas, Wagner's life was punctuated by romantic features and epic interludes. The curtain rises, and the still untrodden expanse before us shimmers in the expectant light of dawn. A horn sounds softly, summoning us to new beginnings whose tempestuous outcome cannot as yet be discerned. . . .

In January 1833, Wagner left Leipzig and set off for Würzburg to visit his brother, who was employed there as a singer, actor, and producer. He traveled by mail coach via Hof to Bamberg, where he reflected on Hoffmann's sojourn in that town and first heard of Kaspar Hauser. The foundling's story moved and fascinated him —we can well understand why—and he even developed the mistaken notion that Hauser had been pointed out to him. In fact, Hauser was then working as a clerk in the appeals court at Ansbach, where he died of a knife wound on December 17 of the same year. Hauser's strange story was real Wagnerian copy, and something of it undoubtedly found its way into Wagner's conception of orphaned, Parsifalesque heroes whose origins are shrouded in mystery.

He arrived in Würzburg, chilled to the bone after making the trip in an open-framed wagon, and was swiftly instructed by Albert in his duties as chorus master. In this capacity, he earned a monthly salary of ten gulden for the three-month season. In May, the company dispersed until September. While Albert was away giving a guest performance at Strasbourg, Wagner took care of his brother's three children and worked on the first act of *Die Feen*, as his fairy opera was to be called. He also made friends with Alexander Müller, a talented musician with a great gift for improvising on the piano. Much of his time with Müller was spent at a beer garden where he became embroiled, for the last time in his life, in a drunken brawl. Egged on by his boon companions, he yielded to insensate fury and hit an unpopular but inoffensive young man on the head.

That summer he engaged in two successive love affairs, both of which he mentions in *My Life*. These were the first items in a collection that extended as far as Friederike Meyer and other less notable conquests of the early 1860s.

Wagner became infatuated with a young member of the chorus, Therese Ringelmann, whom he coached in singing by some method that "remained a mystery" to him ever after. She was the uneducated daughter of a gravedigger, and he kept their relationship a secret from his friends. When she not only pressed for a proposal of marriage but gave him grounds for jealousy, he brought the affair to a brusque end.

His second inamorata, a girl of Italian extraction named Friederike Galvani, was engaged to the oboist of the Würzburg theater orchestra. Buoyed with Franconian wine and emboldened by the look in Friederike's dark eyes, Wagner detached her from her oboist at a rustic wedding and was gratified when his rival seemed to accept the situation. Strangely enough, the Galvani family never insisted that the young chorus master should formalize the new arrangement and tolerated his irregular status. This not being a scenario into which the role of the injured third party could suitably be incorporated, Wagner made no attempt to resolve the equivocal nature of a relationship that offended no one. His eventual departure from Würzburg was attended by "the most touching and tearful leavetaking."

On August 6, when Albert returned, Wagner was able to show him the score of the first act of *Die Feen*. A stern critic, Albert opined that singers would find his music hard to perform, however much he modified it, but that, if approached in the right frame of mind, it might prove quite effective. Wagner made some alterations, but only to maladroit passages.

Even in *Die Feen*, the twenty-year-old composer showed himself fully equal to the problems of form posed by a conventional "number opera" in respect to arias, duets, ensemble singing, and dramatic construction. Wherever the individual could not yet hold its own, he inserted the traditional. Despite some trivialities of an unintentionally comic nature, such as Arindal's "Give my wife, my wife back to me!" he succeeded in producing an overture whose dramatic vivacity and brilliant string-work make it well worth hearing today. Beneath the specifically Wagnerian musical idiom and motif technique, there is much that heralds the development of a "music dramatist" *sui generis*.

Selections from *Die Feen* were performed at a concert in December, and the work that was never staged in its composer's lifetime* was finally completed on January 6, 1834.

There was nothing now to keep Wagner in Würzburg. He turned down an offer to become musical director at Zurich and returned home via Nürnberg, where his sister Klara and her husband Heinrich Wolfram were engaged at the local theater. Arriving back in Leipzig on January 21, he offered *Die Feen* for performance there. The family rallied around. Friedrich Brockhaus took the score to Friedrich Sebalt Ringelhardt, director of the resurrected Stadttheater, who gave Rosalie the impression that he intended to pursue the matter. However, the final decision rested with his musical advisers, the singer and producer Franz Hauser and the conductor Ferdinand Stegmayer. In March, when Laube had already announced the production of Wagner's opera in the *Zeitung für die elegante Welt*, Hauser charged the impatient composer with ignorance of his medium, lack of thorough training, and excessive orchestration. He further advised him to model himself on Gluck and Haydn, his one regret being that Bach had written no operas.

Wagner made a surprisingly dignified and well-reasoned attempt to argue his case in writing. Having detailed his training and knowledge of strict style, he cited Weinlig's recommendation that even early and imperfect works be given a hearing because this served to test young artists and enhance their self-knowledge. Hauser, he said, was taking the easy way out. "You dislike my opera," he wrote. "More than that, you dislike my whole direction because you pronounce it contrary to your own views on art."

The production of the opera was provisionally deferred until August, though Ringelhardt was said to be ordering the sets and having the vocal parts copied. In October, despite Rosalie's insistence, a run-through was again postponed. Wagner had by now lost interest in *Die Feen*. Something intervened to make him stray from his "direction."

Laube had forgotten the *Kosciuszko* affair sufficiently to invite his young friend to contribute to his newspaper. It was now that Wagner read the first part of Laube's epistolary novel, *Das Junge Europa*, which was strongly influenced by Heinse's *Ardinghello*. Infected by its extravagant liberalism, he cast a few prejudices to the winds. Wasn't Germany just a very small part of the world? Had he evolved an unduly Germanic ideology of opera? "Having emerged from abstract mysticism," he wrote in his "Autobiographical Sketch" of 1843, "I learned to love material. Beauty of subject matter, wit, and intellect I regarded as noble things. Where my music was concerned, I discovered them both [sic] in the Italians and French." Even while attempting to get *Die Feen* staged, he had undergone one of the most remarkable changes that affected him at this period.

The immediate cause was Bellini, or, more properly, Wilhelmine Schröder-Devrient. For the second time, this artist touched a central nerve in Wagner. She was making a guest appearance at Leipzig as Romeo in Bellini's *I Capuleti ed i Montecchi*, and what her interpretation extracted from that musically and textually feeble work was enough to arouse doubts in Wagner, who still worshiped Weber, as to the choice of means that lead to major successes. In his first article for Laube's paper, "German Opera," which was published anonymously on June 10, 1834, he dissociated himself from excessive Germanness of any kind. Weber, a lyrical talent, had never learned to handle song, and his *Euryanthe* had been an aberration. "We have strayed ever farther from the road that Mozart took to the benefit of our dramatic music." Wagner pursued a similar line in "Pasticcio," an article written at Magdeburg for the November 1834 issue of Schumann's *Neue Zeitschrift für Musik*. He vehemently complained that "none has grasped the reality of warm, true life" and that "our modern romantic grotesques are nothing but foolish lay figures." These were sentiments that Laube himself might have penned. "Seize your opportunity!" Wagner adjured composers under the good German pseudonym "Canto Spianato."

Wagner now formed closer ties with Robert Schumann, his

moody senior by two years, than he had managed to do in 1830, when he had listened to Schumann playing his *Abegg* Variations in Heinrich Dorn's company. His poetry-writing friend Theodor Apel reappeared on the scene, too. High-spirited and financially well-endowed, Apel shared his love of music and disdain for philistinism.

In the middle of June, Wagner joined Apel on a six-week trip to Bohemia, his last really carefree bachelor excursion. Traveling in a conveyance of their own—hired, needless to say, by Apel—they spent two weeks in Teplitz, where they stayed at the König von Preussen and Apel took the waters. They dined on the Wilhelmsburg, waxed poetic during nocturnal drives back to the hotel, and got so drunk on Czernosek wine that they faked a noisy fracas and brought alarmed spectators thronging into the square below their window. One morning, while Apel was taking the waters, Wagner drove up the Judenberg for a solitary breakfast at the Gasthof zur Schlackenburg. Here he roughed out the scenario of his second opera, *Das Liebesverbot*, basing it on Shakespeare's *Measure for Measure* but reshaping the theme for his own ends.

Wagner was concerned, not with justice, but with the triumph of untrammeled sensuality over puritanical hypocrisy. Set in sixteenth-century Palermo, the opera tells how Friedrich, a German governor, prohibits public entertainments during the king's absence and prosecutes "misdemeanors of love" without adhering to his own moral code. What are probably the most startling lines in Wagner's libretto occur at the very beginning: "The German buffoon—come, laugh him to scorn. Let that be the whole answer: Send him back home to his snow, let him be chaste and sober there." For the rest, Young German sentiments make a brilliant showing and there are distant echoes of *La Muette de Portici* and the Sicilian Vespers, the popular insurrection of 1282.

In a mood of amorous exuberance, Wagner and Apel moved on to Prague, where they stayed for another two weeks at the Schwarzer Ross in Alte Allee. The happy days that followed were spiced with "a certain capricious desire for revenge": Wagner introduced his friend to Jenny and Auguste Raymann as a potential suitor. The girls, whose marriage plans had soon to be settled, were disconcerted by the change in Wagner. What surprised them most of all was his newfound role as a flippant comedian. No longer the stern moral tutor, he clowned around instead of lecturing them on aesthetics. Unfortunately, he infected Apel with his tomfoolery, so the poor girls were at a loss to know where they stood.

At the hotel one night, Wagner so far forgot himself as to induce his companions to sing the *Marseillaise*—an unwise proceeding in Metternich's political domain. Summoned to the police station next morning, he was kept waiting but allowed to go after answering a few vague and typically Austrian inquiries regarding the length of his intended stay in Prague. On another occasion, while dressing, he teetered from window to window along the hotel's second-floor cornice.

Upon his return to Leipzig, the family announced that he had been offered the musical directorship of the Magdeburg Theater Company, which was spending the summer season at Bad Lauchstädt. He owed the recommendation to Stegmayer, who doubtless saw it as one way out of his *Feen* dilemma. Feeling skeptical, Wagner set off at the end of July, little suspecting what a fateful encounter lay in store for him on the very day of his arrival.

* * *

Bad Lauchstädt, a small spa near Merseburg, southwest of Halle, was the former summer seat of the Dukes of Saxony-Merseburg. It had been rediscovered by Goethe as a venue for guest performances by his Weimar theater company. In 1803, Schiller's *Braut von Messina* had opened at the local theater, a small but tasteful timber building, and it was on the promenade that Friedrich Wagner had pointed out Goethe to his wife, Johanna. The place had gone to seed since then. The impresario and director of the Magdeburg company, Heinrich Bethmann, an inveterate bankrupt, roamed the streets in his dressing gown and nightcap. Thus attired, he greeted Wagner at his lodgings and introduced his wife, who was reclining on a sofa with her elderly lover, a bass named Kneisel, quite brazenly seated beside her. A conference was quickly convened with the producer, Wilhelm Schmale, who lodged in the same building, and a toothless old skeleton of a theater attendant. It transpired that Bethmann and his colleagues had no idea how they were going to put on Mozart's *Don Giovanni*, a performance of which was scheduled for the following Sunday, because the Merseburg town bandsmen were refusing to turn out for a rehearsal on Saturday. Under these inauspicious circumstances,

Wagner declined the appointment but requested lodgings for the night. At the door of the house to which he was directed, he bumped into one of the lodgers, who happened to be the company's juvenile lead. An exceptionally pretty girl with a prim and self-assured manner, she introduced herself as Minna Planer. Wagner took a room on the floor below hers, reconsidered his position, and informed the Bethmanns that he would conduct *Don Giovanni* after all.

Returning to Leipzig to collect his belongings, he learned that Heinrich Laube had fallen foul of the latest antiliberal campaign. Whichever of his writings was to blame, the authorities had ordered him out of Saxony. One of the "radicals" and "ultraliberals" to whom Laube had drawn attention in his *Zeitung für die elegante Welt* was the British parliamentarian and author Edward Bulwer-Lytton, whose novel *Rienzi* had just appeared in a German translation by Bärmann, and Theodor Apel had at once conceived the idea that it might make an opera.

Laube had more to fear in July 1834 than expulsion from Saxony. Apel was persuaded to harbor him at Ermlitz, his estate near Halle, but retracted his original promise for fear of serious consequences. Laube was arrested soon afterward and committed to a Berlin prison as a result of renewed inquiries into his former links with student associations. Meanwhile, Wagner had packed his things and retired to a Laubean "Little Europe" with a population of less than a thousand.

At Bad Lauchstädt, Wagner's artistic distaste was temporarily offset by the lure of the stage, an easygoing life-style, and the pleasure he derived from conducting. He bantered with the performers, made friends with a tenor named Friedrich Schmitt, the one person there whose conversation and intelligence he esteemed, and was undisputed cock of the walk with the ladies of the company. Although he had designs on the delightful *jeune première*, whose cool and demure exterior only spurred him on the more, his success with her did not prevent him from generously bestowing his favors elsewhere. After all, hadn't Laube written in praise of libertinism as well as liberty? Yes, indeed, the roué was a truly enviable mortal, and Wagner felt it behooved him to emulate the roué's "virtue of rapturous enjoyment"—the democratic way in which he spread happiness and sampled the world's pleasures wherever they presented themselves. As Laube had proclaimed in the first volume of *Das Junge Europa*, he alone rated as a truly mature student of the age who could "love art, science, good company, and women—Nature, so called—with all his heart and soul." Wagner persevered to the best of his ability. He drank, dallied, and philandered, and by August 12, when the company moved on to Rudolstadt in the Saale Valley, he had made his first forays into Cupid's garden. The ball had started rolling and the first clouds were gathering on the horizon of "Nature, so called." Theodor Apel came to fetch him, and the two of them demonstrated their superabundance of youthful energy on the last night at Lauchstädt by demolishing a large tiled stove.

At Rudolstadt, Wagner got down to work again, even though he conducted no actual performances and attended no Thuringian sausage barbecues. He completed the first movement of an E major symphony started at Lauchstädt but abandoned the second because he felt that Beethoven was the end of the symphonic line. He then took the libretto of *Das Liebesverbot* and versified it. Uppermost in his mind were his relations with Minna Planer, which had cooled, almost at the outset, because of his tender interest in a certain Toni with whom, he wrote to Apel in September, he was "still involved." Nevertheless, Minna continued to be a thorn in his side. One evening, having missed her, he sat outside her lodgings on a cold stone bench, stared into the dark and overcast sky, and wept—whether for her or himself remains uncertain.

* * *

Nearly four years older than Wagner, Christine Wilhelmine Planer possessed the typical heartbreaker's combination of reserve and coquetry. She charmed and captivated the opposite sex with wide, inquiring eyes, a small and petulant mouth that later turned wry, a dainty nose of classic contour, and a wealth of dark, wavy hair surmounting a rather low forehead. She cherished no great love for her profession, in which she just got by with a mediocre voice and an arsenal of practiced gestures. Minna's long-term objective was middle-class security. At Lauchstädt, to Wagner's chagrin, she was generally thought to be betrothed to a Herr von Otterstedt, but the latter was soon compelled to marry money. Minna's respectable, respect-inviting manner was designed to camouflage an unhappy background from herself and others. Born on September 5, 1809, she was the daughter of a mechanic and former army trumpeter named Gotthelf Planer (or Planert, to cite the spelling on her baptismal certificate). At fifteen, having known extreme poverty, she was seduced and then abandoned by Ernst Rudolf von Einsiedel, a captain in the king of Saxony's guards. Minna's mother concealed her pregnancy, sent the unfortunate girl to live with relations in the country, and brought up Minna's illegitimate daughter, Natalie, as her own. Thus Natalie, or "Netty," was treated throughout her life as Minna's sister, and Minna's will of 1865 was inaccurate inasmuch as it named her "sister," not her daughter, as her heir. Natalie's supposed relationship to the wife of a famous composer, of which she naturally made much, was later to cause Wagner a great deal of unpleasantness because his ill-educated and ultimately destitute "sister-in-law" became a millstone around his neck.

Ever since gaining some success on the stage, Minna had deliberately concealed her undeserved misfortune behind a mask of bourgeois respectability. Despite this, she yielded to the impatient young chorus master's advances even before leaving Lauchstädt.

Unless we blind ourselves to the truth, previous accounts of the affair amount to a cover-up. Neither were Wagner and Minna Planer united by love at first sight, as is sometimes claimed, nor did she virtuously keep him at arm's length until they declared their passion at Magdeburg the following year. It was a sexual liaison of the kind extolled by Laube, and Wagner's letters to Apel are evidence of its instability. As early as August, he must have asked Minna why she granted him her favors even though she did not love him and would never, in all probability, be capable of doing so. Her response, which Wagner relayed to Apel verbatim, was, "How can I help it if you're stronger than me and kiss me half to death?" Writing from Rudolstadt on September 15, 1834, Wagner urged his friend to visit him soon, and added: "You can have the Planer girl too—she has transfigured me quite sensually a couple of times—it made me feel splendid." So Minna was a trophy that belonged to his earthly paradise, and he was destined to atone like Tannhäuser—not until redeemed by an Elisabeth, but until the earthly and the celestial became one.

At Rudolstadt they quarreled seriously over the mysterious Toni. Then, after a spell at Bernburg, the Bethmann company returned to Magdeburg, where the season opened on October 12.

Magdeburg was a garrison town of nearly 60,000 inhabitants.

The theater, which was situated on the Breiter Weg, had an orchestra thirty-three strong, including four first violins. Though modestly equipped by contemporary standards, it boasted an ambitious repertoire. The program was so congested that Wagner was overcome with long-suppressed revulsion. He had no wish to be a "German philistine" any longer, he wrote to Apel; within two years he would have completed both his operas and had them performed everywhere. Then he would be off. He proposed to head for Italy and France in Apel's company and try his luck there. On November 26, he complained: "I am altogether bogged down in my wretched goings-on." This was all too true, for he was deeply in debt and not too choosy about the company he kept. He confesses in *My Life* that a young woman "of not unblemished reputation" was making a play for him. Her name was Christiani, née Wunsch, and she belonged to the theater. "I drag myself feebly along, struggling impotently to unleash my energies, chained to a pitiable existence. . . ." In short, Wagner was disgusted with himself. Dunned by wine merchants and tailors and unable to pay singers engaged at his own expense, he was duped by Bethmann again and again. Never a man to save or budget, he had fallen into the hands of moneylenders.

And Minna? She had been avoiding him, alarmed by his extravagant behavior, and was enjoying the attentions of sundry local aristocrats. This made him wild with jealousy, and his feelings of resentment were intensified, as he confesses in *My Life*, "by a recollection of my sufferings at the Pachta house in Prague." He could not give Minna up. What fascinated him about her and cast such an irresistible spell over him was her blend of maturity, experience, sphinxlike inscrutability, and reserve—qualities that he readily mistook for maternal superiority. Thanks to a kindly providence—or a malign stroke of fate—he suffered another attack of erysipelas in December. Minna not only played nurse but kissed him despite the rash around his mouth.

On New Year's Eve, Wagner invited every leading member of the company to a party at his lodgings. Minna was on her best behavior. She fended off the admirers he despised and sent Frau Christiani "into a fit" by making no secret of her regard for him.

A few nights later, he arrived back at the lodgings dead drunk. Minna procured him "the necessary remedies" and allowed him to sleep in her bed. When he woke in the morning, "the sunrise shed an ever-clearer light on what I saw as the beginning of an infinitely momentous period in my life"—a bourgeois sobering-up process complete with hangover. The couple shared a decorous breakfast and, later in the morning, went for an equally decorous stroll outside of town. In a letter to brother Albert dated February 4, 1835, Wagner spoke of becoming engaged.

What with debts, alcoholic remorse, and emotional ups and downs, Wagner found little time for artistic introspection. He quickly cobbled together *Beim Antritt des neuen Jahres*, a New Year's cantata with words by Wilhelm Schmale, using themes and motifs from earlier compositions, including the C Major Symphony. This he did effectively enough to secure it a second hearing, and at a theater concert on January 10, 1835, he happily conducted his overture to *Die Feen*, with its far softer string texture. Eventually, on January 23, he embarked on the composition of *Das Liebesverbot*, for which he devised some sweeping choral ensembles. By March 31, however, he had relapsed into apathy.

Not even four guest appearances in April by Wilhelmine Schröder-Devrient sufficed to fill the coffers of the Magdeburg Theater Company or redeem Wagner's hopeless financial position. He accordingly decided to give a benefit concert at the Hotel zur Stadt London on May 2, the main attraction, apart from another appearance by Schröder-Devrient, being Beethoven's symphonic tribute to Wellington, *The Battle of Vittoria*.

Although he had relied on the concert to pay off his creditors, the Magdeburgers let him down. Either because they disbelieved the unconfirmed reports that Schröder-Devrient would appear yet again, or because the tickets were overpriced, they stayed away in droves. The celebrated guest artist sang a scena and aria by Rastrelli and Beethoven's *Adelaïde* to a half-empty hall. The rest of the program was unbearably noisy, and anyone who had not been deafened by Wagner's *Columbus* Overture, with its augmented brass section, was put to flight by *The Battle of Vittoria*. To quote the principal witness himself: "The cannonades and musketry had been arranged with the utmost care, on both the French and English sides, by dint of expensive, specially constructed apparatus, and the drums and bugles had been doubled and trebled. Then began a battle more ferocious, no doubt, than any ever fought in a concert hall, for the orchestra hurled itself at the exiguous audience with such decisive numerical superiority that they ended by abandoning all resistance and actually took flight." Even Wilhelmine Schröder-Devrient, who was so attached to Magdeburg's young conductor that she gallantly stayed put in a seat near the front, fled from a renewed British assault and rushed out wringing her hands—the signal for a panic-stricken stampede by the rest of the audience. Next morning Wagner found his duns awaiting him in file outside the hotel. Had not Madame Gottschalk, "a trustful Jewess," stepped in and soothingly assured her fellow creditors that Herr Wagner came of a prosperous Leipzig family, the Battle of Vittoria might have been refought with a different outcome.

On May 5, the theater closed and the company dispersed. With nothing to show for his time at Magdeburg but a mass of debts and "an intelligent brown poodle," Wagner returned to Leipzig and the bitter humiliations that awaited him in the bosom of his family.

There followed several months of tedium and turbulence brightened only by periodic spells of self-delusion and a few excursions on business and pleasure. Minna visited Leipzig for three days, and Rosalie teased her brother for being so obviously in love. This he noticed, but not the misgivings with which his mother and eldest sister regarded the latest rival for his affections.

A brief trip to Friedrich Schneider's Dessau music festival confirmed Wagner's hatred of classicism but enabled him to obtain a visa, which, in view of his having evaded military service in Saxony, was later to serve as his sole means of identification in various foreign countries. Setting out for Dresden to see Minna, he met her and her sister Amalie halfway, persuaded them to turn back, and spent a few carefree days with them in the Saxon Alps —a lover's self-indulgence for which he felt he was atoning in years to come. Despite every warning sign to the contrary, he became convinced that he had "breathed life and soul" into Minna, and that things would always be as they had been during their idyll in the mountains.

He also visited Heinrich Laube, who was recovering from his imprisonment—in a somewhat chastened frame of mind—at Bad Kösen. Laube's *Liebesbriefe* had just been published, and Wagner enthusiastically hailed such dogmas as the following: "Is it not a grand idea to give the world as many inhabitants again by emancipating women? You should associate with Negro slaves and Jews." With mother and sister in tow, his own emancipated woman was on her way to Magdeburg, where a new season was in prospect. Wagner took heart again. Armed with promises of money from Bethmann, but no hard cash, he set off on a recruiting tour. His quest for new singers began in Bohemia. Traveling to Prague by way of Teplitz, he did not actually see the Raymann sisters but heard that Jenny and Auguste had become the mistresses of a count and a baron respectively. On July 26, after visiting Karlsbad and Eger [Cheb], he caught his first glimpse of Bayreuth, which made an agreeable impression on him in the evening sunlight. His destination was Nürnberg, where he hoped to persuade Klara and her husband, Heinrich Wolfram, to join the Magdeburg company.

One night, Wolfram took him to a Nürnberg tavern frequented by a master joiner named Lauermann who, to the derision of his drinking companions, fancied himself a singer. For fun, Wolfram introduced his brother-in-law as the famous Italian bass Lablache. Lauermann was so exhilarated by his supposed encounter with a star of such magnitude that he was twice induced to sing some trivial street ballads before being conveyed home, dead drunk, in a wheelbarrow. On their return to the tavern, his tormentors found the entrance blocked by a crowd of workmen whom the landlord had refused to admit. Fists flew, and the free-for-all continued until one of the pugilists was felled by a blow between the eyes. Then everyone scattered and peace returned to the darkened street. Wagner never forgot this nocturnal fracas, which helped to enrich the cudgel scene in *Die Meistersinger.* There may well be some of Lauermann in Beckmesser, and the Night Watchman he already knew from Leipzig.

Returning home, Wagner learned that Uncle Adolf had died on August 1. Adolf had rounded off his life's work with an Italian edition of the writings of Giordano Bruno and an edition of Robert Burns.

*   *   *

Wagner's second season at Magdeburg opened with Spohr's *Jèssonda,* Bellini's *Norma,* and a clash of personalities. Petty jealousies raged among the members of the poorly paid company. Minna, whose relations with Wagner were still unresolved, complained of losing parts to a rival actress. Herr von Otterstedt having retired from the scene, she presented his portrait of her* to a Herr von

Barby—a mysterious act of generosity that infuriated Wagner when he heard about it. The painting found its way back into her possession by equally mysterious means. She implored Wagner to be honest with her. Wagner gave the required pledge but did not balk at deceiving her. It was "scoundrelly" of him, he admitted to Apel, whose approval of Young German promiscuity had ceased to be quite as wholehearted as Wagner's own.

He soon received an unpleasant shock, for Minna took advantage of the company's rivalries to break her contract and join the Königstadt Theater in Berlin. Her departure had unforeseen consequences. Wagner fired off passionate love letters in which he begged her to return and vowed to marry her. She had no need to worry about a career, he assured her, because he would somehow support them both. "Open your heart!" he entreated, but it soon became clear that they were at cross purposes, even then. No matter what he wrote, she either misunderstood or proved incapable of expressing herself in return. Instead of making him think twice, her inadequate replies only brought forth more effusions couched in solemn, high-flown language. That fall he succumbed to the temptations of a petty bourgeois idyll. He discussed wedding plans with Minna's mother, who was keeping house at Magdeburg, and looked forward to swapping in-law visits with Amalie and her lover (whom she ended up not marrying). Apel was reassured: It almost seemed as if Wagner's wings were clipped. Together, they at last succeeded in persuading Minna to return. As soon as she was back, she and her mother drew Wagner into the family circle. She even took him to visit her little "sister" Natalie at a boarding school near Magdeburg.

Wagner was now toiling feverishly at *Das Liebesverbot* in the hope of paying off his debts. This least successful of all his works caused him sleepless nights, overstimulated his imagination, and brought on violent bouts of sweating. Completed in January 1836, *Das Liebesverbot* turned out to be Wagner at his weakest; indeed, it was a backward step compared to the C Major Symphony, which had told him more about himself.

Bethmann had sanctioned the production of Wagner's latest opera, shortly before the company broke up, on condition that he pay the proceeds of the first performance into the general exchequer and underwrite the costs of the second. When informed of this,

his mother expressed concern: "I am much reassured to hear that you have now determined to present your opera at Magdeburg under your own direction, but why, my good Richard, should you relinquish the bulk of the profits?"

He was left with ten days in which to rehearse—not even long enough for the singers to memorize his complicated libretto. The Magdeburg police lodged a last-minute objection to the title: To their ears, "The Ban on Love" sounded far too frivolous, especially with Easter in the offing, so Wagner renamed his work *Die Novize von Palermo.* Ringelhardt's subsequent refusal to present it at Leipzig also sprang from a suspicion that the theme was "immoral."

The premiere on March 29, 1836, proved to be no more than a "musical shadow play." No one present followed the plot, the tenor ad-libbed, the orchestra mercifully drowned everything, and the audience—more bewildered than impressed—remained indifferent.

The second performance, which should have reimbursed the composer for all his out-of-pocket expenses, was a complete fiasco. Fifteen minutes before curtain, no one could be seen in the stalls save the "trustful" Madame Gottschalk, her husband, and a lone Polish Jew. All financial considerations having been banished by the sight of an empty house, the artists seized this golden opportunity to settle some personal scores. Herr Pollert, the husband of the Isabella, assaulted her lover, Herr Schreiber, the Claudio of the opera, and bloodied his nose. Frau Pollert, who rushed at her spouse, was soundly slapped and had hysterics, whereupon the producer went out front to announce that, "owing to unforeseen circumstances," the performance had been canceled. Shortly afterward, Robert Schumann's *Neue Zeitschrift für Musik* was sent an unsigned article on the musical scene at Magdeburg and, more especially, on the inadequate production of Herr Wagner's new opera. Wagner's covering letter to Schumann commented, "They are all swine [*Scheisskerle*] here!"

The Magdeburg interlude was over. Minna left for Königsberg, hoping to obtain an engagement in a place that might additionally offer employment to her future husband. Wagner paid a visit to Leipzig, where the Gewandhaus had by now entered its Mendelssohn era. He had sent Mendelssohn the score of his C Major Symphony in April, doubtless with an eye to securing it another performance, but unwisely accompanied it with the words "As a gift." This caused bad blood because Mendelssohn hung onto his "gift" and did nothing about it. The loss of his score sowed the seeds of resentment in Wagner's breast.

He was also stung by the persistence with which his mother and eldest sister advised him against marriage. Rosalie's parting words —"Who knows when I shall see you again!"—were strangely ominous: She never did. His correspondence with Theodor Apel, too, ceased in May. Apel fell from his horse, was badly concussed, and went blind after two years of acute suffering.

For Wagner and Minna, their final days at Magdeburg were a gloomy time. While out walking, they heard the cries of a suicide who had jumped into the millstream. The drowning man reached for the rake they held out but was swept away before their eyes and never reappeared. On the day Minna left for Königsberg and the eve of Wagner's own departure for Berlin, he saw crowds streaming out of town to watch the execution of a soldier who had murdered his sweetheart. At lunch that day—his last at Magdeburg—Wagner heard gruesome accounts of how the man had been broken on the wheel. There in the German provinces, a composer whose artistic modernity guaranteed him an influence that was to endure far into the twentieth century heard a lingering echo of the darkest Middle Ages.

The Serious Side of Life

At Berlin, where Wagner arrived on May 18 and took a room at the Kronprinz on Königsstrasse, misfortune continued to dog him. False expectations, coupled with gullibility and a fear of loneliness, impelled him to burn his bridges. He began by relying on the threadbare promises of a certain Herr Cerf, real name Karl Friedrich Hirsch [*Hirsch = Cerf =* stag], director of the Königstadt Theater, an erstwhile horse trader whose business acumen had earned him the title "Commissioner." Long after he saw through him, Wagner described Cerf as "one of the most singular products of the Berlin population." Such was the man who now promised, not only that *Das Liebesverbot* would be staged in the very near future, but that Wagner would soon succeed Gläser, the existing kapellmeister. This encouraged Wagner to believe in his imminent ability to repay his Magdeburg creditors, notably the Gottschalks, who were far less "trustful" than they had been. In fact, the Königstadt Theater was heading for the rocks. Deserted by his business sense, Cerf was forced to close down on July 1. All Wagner's Berlin dreams had come to nothing.

Did he receive a summons from Minna? Did she lure him to her side with the promise of an appointment as musical director at Königsberg? Far from it. She promised him nothing, not even her hand in marriage. For three whole weeks she left his effusions

76

unanswered. The full extent of his dilemma now stood revealed: He could not endure loneliness. He was "pining," he wrote. He was so softhearted that solitude was destroying him, undermining his reason. As one who looked back on a "largely bitter childhood," he expected his adulthood to make up for it. With what? With the matrimonial haven of her person, with the security afforded by her body, which he so passionately embraced in his fevered dreams. And how did Minna reply? Tersely and evasively, she informed him that she did not yet wish their relationship known in Königsberg. At once he was smitten with doubt. At Berlin, he had made the acquaintance of an amiable Jewish businessman named Schwabe, who had, he learned for the first time, been Minna's lover. That she had given her portrait to Herr von Barby he could not forget but no longer held against her. She had now become his faithful and beloved Minna, as steadfastly devoted to him as Leonore to Florestan. His letters made no reference to music. The language that passed between them was of quite another kind, yet still he failed to grasp their incompatibility. He was sexually addicted to her, but what would become of their relationship once his addiction waned? Never mind: He had to follow her, had to possess her. There could be no question of returning to Leipzig— he was not one to retrace his steps—nor could he stay in Berlin. Laube and some other friends took up a collection for him. On July 7, 1836, armed with the sixty thalers that remained after paying his Berlin expenses, he left by coach for Königsberg and the unknown.

Königsberg Theater, whose opening in 1809 had been attended by Queen Luise of Prussia, was under the management of Anton Hübsch. The incumbent kapellmeister, Louis Schuberth, was really based at Riga, where the local theater had temporarily closed down. Additionally detained at Königsberg by a love affair, Schubert was too competent a conductor to be packed off to Riga and his wife for the newcomer's sake, so Hübsch could give Wagner no firm assurance as to when he would take over. Wagner, therefore, had to resign himself to part-time employment and the humiliations of supernumerary status. At Memel, where the Königsberg company was playing during August and September, he adopted a suggestion of Laube's and sketched out an opera based on Heinrich König's *Die hohe Braut*, a novel set during the Franco-

Italian conflict of 1793. He sent this outline to Eugène Scribe, the librettist of Meyerbeer's *Les Huguenots*, but received no immediate reply.

His return to Königsberg on October 1 was taken as the occasion for a double initiative by an eccentric local patron of the arts named Abraham Möller, whose admiration for Minna now embraced her lover as well. Möller, who habitually revered all newcomers as rising stars in the theatrical firmament, had generously subsidized them in his more prosperous days. He now pressed for Wagner's appointment as kapellmeister and encouraged him to marry Minna, not only because it might further the young man's career but also because both his new protégés might thus be induced to settle permanently in "Prussian Siberia." Wagner seems to have hesitated, partly because of the difficulty of obtaining a marriage license. He was still a minor under Prussian law; a formal application had to be filed at Magdeburg, and Minna required her parents' consent.

Meanwhile, the couple quarreled with increasing violence. Wagner jealously reproached Minna for her Berlin adventure with Schwabe. She retorted that he was claiming rights he did not possess and pointed out that she had refused more advantageous proposals of marriage than his in the past. Although he now saw through her show of propriety—a bourgeois shibboleth for which he cared nothing—physical attraction triumphed over portents of disaster.

While visiting the parsonage to have their marriage license endorsed on the very eve of their wedding, they quarreled in the hall and were not reconciled until the startled clergyman made his appearance. But this was not the only ill omen: Even their statements on the marriage license were inaccurate. Wagner gave his year of birth as 1812 to make it seem that he had attained his majority, while Minna deducted four whole years from her age, which was twenty-seven, and claimed to be a mere twenty-three.

On November 24, 1836, Wagner and his bride were married by Pastor Weiss at the little church in Tragheim with a gaudily attired congregation of theatrical folk in attendance. While the rings were being exchanged, Wagner had one of his daydreams. It was as if he were hovering overhead, watching himself being pulled in two different directions. The pastor alluded in his sermon to the dark days that doubtless lay in store for the couple and reminded them that they both had an unknown friend. Pricking up his ears at this apparent reference to a mysterious new patron, Wagner gazed eagerly at the clergyman, only to be informed that the unknown good Samaritan was Jesus Christ. His hopes had been dashed yet again.

The newlyweds moved into rooms at III Steindamm, on the corner of Monckenstrasse, a cold little middle-class apartment that defied all their efforts to heat it. At Christmas, Wagner made a maladroit attempt to apprise Minna of his desire for children.* He took a coat from her theatrical wardrobe, used a similar coat to dress up a doll intended to represent Natalie, and placed a cradle in front of it containing the future "little one." Minna took great exception to this broad hint and shut herself up in her room.

It is hardly surprising, under these circumstances, that Wagner's musical output at Königsberg should have amounted to so little. He composed a *Rule Britannia* Overture—a tribute to Britain in her capacity as an opponent of the Holy Alliance—but it suffered the fate of all his minor dedicatory works: Either they were not accepted, or they failed in performance. He also sketched the libretto for a two-act comic opera based on an episode from *The Thousand and One Nights—Männerlist grösser als Frauenlist, oder Die glückliche Bärenfamilie* [*Woman Outwitted by Man, or The Happy Bear Family*]—which he conceived with an eye to the Königsberg Theater's modest resources and was later to work on at Riga. He ridiculed the German nobility but probably had no real intention of using such a theme to emulate someone whom he naively or mistakenly associated with his Young German ideals, namely, Meyerbeer.

Dated February 4, 1837, his first letter to the operatic maestro, whom he later reviled, was curious enough in itself. He professed his devotion to the Franco-Italian school of opera whose resources Meyerbeer had employed in "resolving the German's problem," which was how to render his creations "universal."—"Shall I deny," he said, "that it was your very works that brought this novel course of action to my notice?" This was more than the mere adulation of a tyro soliciting patronage, and Meyerbeer must have been impressed by the nature of the young man's compliments. Wagner also got in touch with August Lewald, editor of the quarterly journal *Europa*, who reproduced the Carnival Song from *Das Liebesverbot* together with an article deploring the Germans' lack of appreciation for talented young composers.

On April 1, 1837, Wagner finally took up his duties as musical director of the Königsberg Theater. Minna had brought Natalie to live with them, and the eleven-year-old girl became a reluctant witness to violent scenes of jealousy—nightly squabbles that always ended with Minna in tears. Although his wife had much to answer for, Wagner often put himself in the wrong by berating her with undue volume and vehemence.

There was, for example, a local businessman named Dietrich who publicly bragged of Minna's regard for him. Told of this by the tenor Friedrich Schmitt, whom he had recruited for the Königsberg company, Wagner went with him to see Dietrich and vainly sought a showdown. Meanwhile, Natalie's memoirs record —without exaggeration, one suspects—that domestic strife reached a new pitch of intensity. On Minna's side it undoubtedly stemmed from a combination of pressures: keeping house, learning her parts, and staving off creditors with whom she had to engage in endless and, to her, degrading skirmishes. In giving her hysteria free rein, however, she startled and stunned Wagner with the strident vulgarity that showed through the cracks in her carefully cultivated veneer of bourgeois decorum. Eventually, she made good her threat to leave him. Arriving home from a rehearsal on the afternoon of May 31, he found her drawers and wardrobe empty. Minna had taken Natalie and run off with Dietrich.

Accompanied by Abraham Möller, Wagner pursued her in a mail coach as far as Elbing, where their money ran out. On June 3, after hurrying back home to replenish his funds, he set off in pursuit again. Dietrich, the seducer, had apparently returned to Königsberg. At Dresden, where Wagner found his faithless wife at her parents' humble abode, he fell on his knees beside her bed, swore repentance, and implored her to come back to him. That his presence was "unwelcome" to her parents is an understatement. Minna's mechanic father threatened to throw him out on his ear for having ill-treated her. Wagner now gave serious consideration to the possibility of a divorce but decided to make one more attempt to salvage his marriage by holding out the prospect of a secure middle-class existence. However misguided this may have been, he endured Minna's reproaches with an equanimity so remarkable that it smacked of resignation.

Wagner owed his next post to the good offices of Louis Schindelmeisser, a Leipzig friend who was Heinrich Dorn's stepbrother. Visiting Berlin in mid-June, he obtained an interview with Karl von Holtei, the director of the Riga Theater, who signed a contract with him. This earned him a friendlier reception from Minna, who had removed her wedding ring but readily joined him in lodgings at Blasewitz, a few miles outside Dresden, where her agitation seemed to subside. All that really prompted this reunion with her husband was a maintenance order against the Einsiedels, for which she required his signature.* For the moment, however, a deceptive calm prevailed. Of these four months at Blasewitz, nothing of note remains to be told save Wagner's increasing attraction to the subject of Rienzi.* In view of its historical magnitude, his thoughts immediately turned to Paris. He stepped up his correspondence with Scribe, who denied having received his outline for *Die hohe Braut*, and used Brockhaus's commercial mail service to send him the score of *Das Liebesverbot* accompanied by his best regards to Giacomo Meyerbeer.

Minna left Blasewitz on some pretext and returned to her parents. Only a few days later, on July 21, Wagner learned that she had bolted again. It was her one really blatant act of deception, and the ever-faithful Abraham Möller, who was a personal enemy of Dietrich's, promptly reported from Königsberg that the man had left there for Dresden. Little did Möller know what this news would provoke—or almost provoke. It is evident from three key words in Wagner's "Red Pocketbook" that he took a horsewhip and a brace of pistols and went at once to confront Dietrich at his Dresden hotel. Fortunately, Dietrich and Minna had already left for Hamburg.

Wagner sought sympathy and consolation from Ottilie and Hermann Brockhaus, his sister and brother-in-law, at their summer villa in Dresden's Grosser Garten. He avoided traveling to Berlin via his native Leipzig because he was too ashamed to face his mother and Rosalie.

In Berlin he saw Amalie Planer, whom he later engaged for Riga, and joined her in lamenting her sister's delinquent behavior. He then embarked from Lübeck on his very first sea voyage, only to be delayed at Travemünde on August 4 by unfavorable winds. It was a week before the ship could resume its journey and August 21 before Wagner arrived in Riga, where he was temporarily safe from the hostile attentions of his creditors.

*   *   *

To begin with, he was quite as bewildered by the Russian calendar, which was twelve days in arrears, as he was by the vaudeville taste of Karl von Holtei and his Riga theatergoers, most of whom belonged to the city's numerous German colony. Holtei had been keeping these free-spending patrons and supporters sweet with Singspiele such as *Lenore*. Works in a more serious vein he left to Heinrich Dorn, now Riga's director of church music, and Wagner had thenceforth to contend with Holtei's foolish but not unfounded charges of excessive operatic "solidity."

Wagner's theatrical ambitions had not as yet been blunted by practical experience, and what he achieved with an orchestra only twenty-four strong seems, by local standards, to have been prodigious. In later years, when the cellist Poorten, who himself came from Riga, asked Wagner how he had managed to conduct at all in the city's barn of a theater, the composer replied that three features of the "barn" had stuck in his mind: the steep, amphitheaterlike gradient of the stalls; the darkness of the auditorium; and the rather low-lying orchestra pit. He had resolved that, if he ever came to design a theater of his own, he would take these three factors into account.

After several weeks in the Livonian capital, Wagner received letters from Amalie Planer, giving a pitiful account of Minna's sick and sorry state of mind, and from Minna herself, who confessed her infidelity. Although he greeted Amalie's letter coolly, Minna's softened his heart. She had gained a true appreciation of her love for him, she wrote, and earnestly craved his forgiveness. According to Wagner, it was the first and last time she ever expressed such sentiments; it was also the one letter she (or Natalie) destroyed (a counterproductive act, because it might well have endeared her more to posterity). On October 19, Minna and Amalie arrived in Riga, where the couple celebrated their reunion and reconciliation. They agreed that Minna should abandon her stage career forever, though Holtei was pressing her to accept a new engagement.

Early in 1838, the Wagners and Amalie moved to a new and more spacious apartment in the suburb of Petersburg. This the sisters filled with the songs they remembered from their childhood—but not for long, because they soon fell out. Amalie accepted a proposal of marriage from a Russian cavalry officer, Captain (later General) Carl von Meck. For reasons never explained, she and Minna neither saw nor spoke to each other throughout the rest of their time in Riga.

Wagner had some peace at last. Though already preoccupied with *Rienzi* and other schemes, he carried out the bread-and-butter work required of him. This included arias for insertion in existing material and the melody for a national anthem in honor of Czar Nicholas's birthday, the success of which did not lessen his enthusiasm for the Polish cause. These pieces were applauded, but their frequent repetition displeased local connoisseurs. Wagner's self-admitted predilection for brass resulted, at a concert given on March 19, 1838, in a regrettable juxtaposition of the *Columbus* and *Rule Britannia* overtures and the *Nicholas* Anthem. Heinrich Dorn, to whom Wagner had formerly been close in his love of Beethoven, wrote a razor-edged review that caused Wagner great annoyance. Dorn began by stating, quite rightly, that Wagner kept his feet rooted in Beethoven but flailed his arms (as a conductor) in every musical direction. All well and good, said Dorn, because a hidebound kapellmeister who fanatically opposed every other genre of music spelled the ruin of any theater. "But to attempt to combine every possible style and manner in his own compositions, so as to endear himself to all parties, is the surest way of pleasing no one." Some of these shafts must have struck home. Even in the thick of the overture controversy, which earned him the hostility of Holtei and his set, he entered upon a process of inner transformation that continued throughout 1838.

This process entailed withdrawing into his shell. He states in *My Life* that "the anxieties attendant on my ardent youthful desires were in some manner subdued and allayed," and that his energies were thenceforth directed toward "the ideal goal . . . that was to be my sole guide through life." Although this provides renewed evidence of the fateful duality of body and soul that possessed him into late middle age, it also reveals how the forces released within him took precedence over the continuing "ordinary cares of life."

Apart from Bulwer-Lytton's novels, his reading matter during this period included Heinrich Heine's *Memoiren des Herrn von Schnabelewopski*, published in 1833. It was the first volume of *Salon* that introduced him to the tale of the Flying Dutchman and his accursed ship—not an ancient legend in this form, but one from which Heine's version had adopted all the ingredients that were bound to appeal to Wagner, notably the redemption by a woman's love and fidelity of a sea captain condemned to go ashore only once every seven years.

For the time being, Wagner let the subject drop. He toyed with the idea of emulating Heinrich Dorn, whose operetta *Der Schöffe von Paris* had gained a local success, and completing *Männerlist grösser als Frauenlist, oder Die glückliche Bärenfamilie*, which would have lent itself to presentation in a smallish provincial theater. Then he abandoned the idea and gave the libretto to Franz Löbmann, his "worthy but not overtalented" assistant conductor.

It is strange that the intrinsically unimportant libretto for *Bärenfamilie* has never been placed in its proper context: Not only was it an aftereffect of Laube's and Heine's influence, but also a pointer to the future. It was, coincidentally, the only time Wagner modeled a character so openly on a member of his own family—in this case, brother Julius, the peripatetic goldsmith.

Bärenfamilie tells how Julius Wander, a jeweler, boasts of being shrewder than any woman but is outwitted by a beautiful young girl, Leontine, who passes herself off as the daughter of Baron von Abendtau. By the time Julius realizes that the real Abendtau daughter is as ugly as sin, and that her "most prominent attraction" is a gigantic nose, there is no turning back: The baron insists that he fulfill his promise of marriage. Julius is saved in the nick of time by the appearance of a bear catcher, who turns out to be his long-lost father, because Abendtau refuses to marry his daughter off to a person of such low degree. Julius, who gets his Leontine, triumphantly extols his humble birth because it has brought him happiness and delivered him from a fate worse than death. The long-lost father theme need hardly surprise us, but Wagner's fierce attack on the nobility, among them a Baron von Nachtschatten [Nightshade] (Metternich's nickname was Fürst von Mitternacht [Prince Midnight]), foreshadows *Rienzi*. To Wagner, a champion of Young German ideals, the historical Rienzo's main charm lay in his humble origins and campaign against the aristocracy.

Wagner abandoned his *Bärenfamilie* farce after completing two scenes, apparently repelled by the prospect of composing still more music in the style of Auber. Instead, he focused all his energies on a work that exploded provincial notions of opera and was not designed for a theater such as Riga's. This decision anticipated his break with the circumstances under which he was currently living.

*   *   *

Bulwer-Lytton's novel *Rienzi* had been inspired by a little-known and wholly unpolitical play entitled *Rienzi: A Tragedy in Five Acts* by Mary Russell Mitford. Based on this piece but skillfully amplified, the novel contained dramatic highlights that lent themselves to use by Wagner. It was a historical drama on a grand scale. Born in 1313, Cola di Rienzo was the son of an innkeeper. Wagner's sole departure from the novel was to deprive him of the beloved whom Bulwer-Lytton had given him and substitute a sister, thereby leaving the "last tribune" free to fulfill his mission, the restoration of Rome's municipal autonomy, and play out his role as a celibate folk hero. The undoubted result of this was to overdraw a figure veiled in historical obscurity. Wagner's portrayal of Rienzi foreshadows his later heroes and the concepts of regeneration to be found in his very last works. This is the strongest aspect of the character, but the weakest of the opera and the most questionable of its received historical ideas. Wagner's operatic hymn to liberty glorifies the dictator, not the people. Transferred to the stage without idealization, *Rienzi* discloses other aspects as well, however. Regarded in this light, it enabled the better artist in Wagner to win through notwithstanding—the Wagner who always adopted a diverse approach and did not eschew any inherent criticism that might be leveled against him. With his arrogance and martial propensities, the abandoned redeemer is not merely an identification object.

When writing the libretto in the summer of 1838, Wagner deliberately neglected verse and diction because he wished the opera to subsist on its plot. In his experience, "fine verses" never enhanced the effect of music but prettified it in an untheatrical way. By the time he returned from a summer season at Mitau [Mitava] and began his orchestral sketch on August 7, one day after completing the libretto, any objective observer could have tagged *Rienzi* as a very long-term project—a cuckoo's egg of a grand opera hatched in a Wagnerian nest.

Hans von Bülow's humorous verdict on *Rienzi*—that it was Meyerbeer's best opera—is far from being as offensive as Wagner's first biographer, Carl Glasenapp, felt obliged to complain. Indeed, had Wagner died soon after completing the work—as he might well have done—it would doubtless have been regularly and enthusiastically revived, to this day, as the only Young German revolutionary opera ever written.*

Rehearsals of Etienne Méhul's *Joseph en Egypte* provided Wagner with a practical standard of comparison, even though the Riga Theater was too small to accommodate an orchestra of adequate size. In embarking on the first two acts of *Rienzi*, he injected a little life into the apartment in the Riga suburbs. Seated at his Bergmann piano before an audience of friends and acquaintances, he used to astound and enthrall them with his clumsy but dramatic renderings of work in progress, singing the heroic tenor passages to an accompaniment of snapping strings. All that interrupted his work during the winter of 1838–39 was a bout of typhoid fever, which encouraged some of his envious "friends" and secret rivals to believe that he was on his last legs.

He never really endeared himself to Riga society, though the subscription concerts he gave during his last winter in the city earned him a measure of public esteem. "As a conductor, Wagner achieved some notable results," wrote Dorn, who was destined to succeed him. He did so under circumstances that infuriated Wagner and unjustly branded him as the younger man's archenemy. Holtei, who left Riga in January 1839 after the death of his wife, had previously agreed with Dorn that he was to replace Wagner as kapellmeister. Though well-disposed toward Wagner, the theater's new director—the tenor Joseph Hoffmann—felt bound by this prior arrangement. Now that the aftereffects of Holtei's malign influence were fully apparent, Minna disclosed that he had made improper advances to her soon after her arrival in Riga—advances that had, of course, been indignantly rejected. Wagner, who took her word for this, explains Holtei's conduct in *My Life* by claiming that his attentions to pretty women were designed to mask his homosexual proclivities. These unfounded allegations, coupled with his animosity toward Dorn, bear witness to Wagner's chagrin at his first-ever formal dismissal. Being weary of the whole provincial scene, however, and having other things in mind, he construed his enforced departure at the end of the season as a stroke of fate—a signal to alter course—and greeted it with a touch of relief. *Rienzi* would solve all his problems, but first he must get to Paris.

He took advantage of four weeks of French lessons with a Monsieur Henriot to obtain from him a translation of the *Rienzi* libretto. As for his debts in Magdeburg, Königsberg, and Riga itself, he hoped to settle them with the proceeds from the sale of his household effects, Minna's fee for her farewell performance at the theater, and an advance of salary granted him by Hoffmann. Abraham Möller, who was visiting Riga, advised against this: He must spend the money on getting to Paris, where the certain success of his grand opera would enable him to clear all his debts at a stroke. By applying for a passport in Riga, where all such applications had by law to be advertised in the press, he would inevitably alert his creditors and delay his departure until the last thaler had been paid. He must therefore sneak across the Russo-Prussian border while at Mitau for the short summer season there. Wagner fell in with this somewhat hazardous escape plan, and Möller, the eccentric Königsberg Mephisto, who might have been smuggled into Wagner's life story by some adapter of the Faust theme, never to reappear, extended a helping hand once more.

Flight from Riga

N ot all of Wagner's many journeys are as well worth recording
as the one that began at Mitau on July 9, 1839, and ended in
Paris on September 17. It was attended by so much danger and
anxiety that it profoundly affected the outlook and imaginative
powers of a man who was naturally prone to emotional extremes.
We now know almost every detail of Wagner's flight, down to and
including the dimensions and specifications of the sailing ship
whose theatrical counterpart may well be Daland's vessel in *Der
Fliegende Holländer*.

Already fully laden, the special coach for Tilsit was piled high
at Mitau with Wagner's baggage—scores, tableware, candlesticks,
and all—one piece of which was later lost at sea. The catalog of
disasters began when no room could be found inside the coach for
Robber, his shaggy black Newfoundland dog. The poor beast accompanied the conveyance throughout most of the hot July day,
panting with exhaustion as it loped along the dusty highway, until
even Wagner's disgruntled fellow passengers were moved to pity.
The coach pulled up and the huge dog squeezed in between their
legs. On July 10, after traveling toward Tauroggen through the
forests, meadows, and lakes of Courland, Wagner and Minna
reached a point just short of the Russo-Prussian frontier. Here
they were met by Möller, who had turned up from Königsberg in

a small traveling carriage. They and their dog changed vehicles and were driven along bypaths to a thoroughly sinister-looking establishment that proved to be a smuggler's drinking den frequented after nightfall by Polish Jews of forbidding aspect. Awaiting them there was their guide, a friend of Möller's from a nearby Prussian estate. Möller then took his leave, manifestly perturbed at the dangers to which he had exposed them.

The frontier could only be crossed at night because Cossack sentries were posted every thousand paces and the intervening stretches were patrolled by pickets. The guide waited until sentry-changing time before setting off with his charges. Robber behaved admirably, walking to heel and never uttering a sound. At the foot of a hill, Wagner and his wife had to scramble across a ditch marking the frontier, but even then they were not out of danger because Russian patrols had orders to fire into Prussian territory. At length their guide conducted them to Möller's coachman, who had been waiting in a neighboring lane. They were then driven to a Prussian frontier village and reunited with Möller and their baggage at an inn. Wagner records that Möller, himself sick with anxiety, sprang out of bed to greet them "sobbing and rejoicing."

Next day Möller's carriage conveyed them through the Tilsit plain, past Labiau [Polessk], to Arnau, a village within sight of Königsberg. Here they spent the night at another small inn. Then, if not before, they realized that the dog's presence made it quite impossible for them to travel overland from Königsberg to Paris by mail coach or hired carriage. They therefore decided on a sea voyage via London. Möller went into Königsberg to inquire about passage while Wagner and Minna recovered from their exertions. He returned with the news that a merchant ship berthed at Pillau would shortly be sailing for London.

On July 14, after four days' rest, the party set off in a local conveyance "little better than a wagon." Wagner could not afford to pass through Königsberg itself for fear of his creditors, so the coachman took a northerly route around the city. After negotiating sundry byways, he ended up in a farmyard and, while attempting to turn his cumbersome vehicle, upset it. Möller came off lightly and Wagner was pitched into a dunghill, but Minna was pinned beneath the coach and badly bruised. Natalie claimed later that she had a miscarriage. Though impossible to confirm, this would certainly have been a matter of significance. All we know for sure is that she spent the night in pain at a neighboring farmhouse.

By way of Laath, Kummerau, Miedenau, and Fischhausen, the party reached the narrow headland at Pillau, where they dismounted at an inn beside the local lighthouse and Möller said good-bye. By dawn on July 19, the Wagners were safely aboard ship.

The *Thetis* was bound for London with a cargo of oats and dried peas. A merchant vessel, she belonged to a shipowner named Jakob P. Liedtke of Pillau, whose bills of lading survived—remarkably enough—for more than a century. This made it possible to check the accuracy of Wagner's memoirs.* He was correct in recalling that the captain's name was Wulff—R. Wulff, to be exact—and that the seaman who attracted Robber's insuperable dislike during the voyage was one Koske. Koske did, in fact, come from a well-known Pillau seafaring family of the same name. Wagner's statement that the schooner *Thetis* was an alarmingly small vessel, recorded nearly thirty years afterward, was just as accurate and far from exaggerated. With a displacement of 120 tons and a length of little more than 80 feet, she was small even by contemporary standards. She had two masts, both gaff-rigged, and three staysails, and boasted a wooden figurehead of the Greek sea goddess Thetis beneath her bowsprit.

Schooners of this size were then used almost exclusively for trading in the Baltic or plying between German ports in the Baltic and the North Sea. A voyage to London was exceptional, therefore, but with favorable winds should have taken no more than a week. Liedtke may either have trusted to the skill of his experienced master or told himself that nothing could go wrong in the month of July. Not that Wagner ever knew it: The full extent of the shipowner's recklessness became apparent just over nine years later, when the ill-starred *Thetis* sank in a storm, presumably with all hands.

The crew numbered seven—the captain and six seamen, of whom only Koske found a place in Wagner's memoirs because of his feud with Robber—and the vessel was poorly provisioned. The *Thetis* and her illegal passengers set sail on Friday, July 19, 1839, only to lie becalmed for several days. Wagner took advantage of the fine weather to read George Sand's *La dernière Aldini* on deck. On

July 25, the ship came in sight of land again. During this part of the passage, which took her past Copenhagen and Elsinore, Captain Wulff concealed the Wagners in the cable locker to preserve them from discovery by Danish customs officers, all vessels having been liable to pay dues since the imposition of the Continental Blockade.

Two days later, on July 27, a terrible storm blew up in the Skagerrak. The sound of the wind whistling in the *Thetis*'s rigging —a sound that operagoers have occasion to hear again—played so powerfully on Wagner's imagination that he thought he saw a ship loom up alongside and vanish into the murk. The legend of the Flying Dutchman, whose authenticity the seamen confirmed, took on color and reality in his mind. All hell broke loose overhead. For two whole days, Wagner lay seasick and numb with terror in the captain's cramped little cabin. The ship pitched and tossed, the wind howled, and breakers tore the sea nymph off the schooner's bow: The *Thetis* had lost her tutelary figurehead.

Captain Wulff saved his ship by running for shelter in a Norwegian fjord. The haven that loomed up ahead on July 29 was Sandvigen on Borøya, ten miles northeast of Arendal. (Daland: "Sandwike it is! Full well I know the bay.") Wagner was filled with delight and relief by the sight of the rugged coastline, the steadily moderating waves beyond which the fjord's chain of islands and beetling cliffs combined to form a solid rampart, and the tangible nature of the horizon. The seamen's "ship's cry" echoed from the towering walls of granite, and its rhythm was to underlie the sailors' chorus in Wagner's next opera—a motif brilliantly heralded by the overture. Although he did not understand the men's Low German dialect, he perfectly preserved the rhythm of their words.

Crew and passengers celebrated their deliverance in comfort at the mill on Sleibrevig; and on July 31, the *Thetis* left Sandvigen— or tried to. Still dogged by misfortune, and despite the presence of a pilot on board, the schooner fouled an invisible reef. Wulff, who feared that his vessel had sustained serious damage, was forced to turn back. The *Thetis* dropped anchor once more, and Wagner was invited to accompany the captain and two seamen on a boat trip to Tromsond, the nearest town of any size. While Wulff was arranging to have his ship inspected by the port authorities, Wagner went for a long walk across the moorland plateau. Here he drank in the barren majesty of a fjord-riven landscape whose dark, treeless, melancholy expanse merged imperceptibly with a gray and overcast sky: rocky highlands brooding beneath a Nordic Valhalla. . . . Minna was faint with anxiety by the time he returned in the ship's boat long after nightfall.

Finally, on August 1, the *Thetis* was able to resume her voyage across the North Sea. On Sunday, August 4, a strong north wind got up and drove the schooner swiftly before it. Two days later, however, the wind veered perilously and she found herself heading into a series of fierce squalls. This raging pandemonium, which surpassed anything the ship had previously undergone, lasted for another three days. At half-past two on the afternoon of the second day, Wednesday, a thunderstorm broke. Squalls and billows hurled the schooner in all directions, causing her to rear and plunge so violently that the Wagners thought their end had come. Indeed, Minna asked her husband to lash them together so that they would be united in death. The crew, who superstitiously took them to be the cause of their misfortunes, had long been casting malevolent glances in their direction. The tempest continued to rage until August 8. Having lost his bearings, Captain Wulff kept his glass trained on a vessel sailing some eight miles ahead. He saw in the nick of time that she had run aground on one of the sandbanks off the Dutch coast, and the *Thetis* hurriedly altered course.

At last, on August 9, Wulff sighted the English coast near Southwold and picked up a gray-haired, dependable-looking English pilot. The very look of him filled Wagner with a "religious sense of well-being"—prematurely, it turned out, because the following day brought a change in the weather. Struggling against a westerly gale, the *Thetis* had to claw her way through more sandbanks. Her travails did not cease until the night of August 12, when she dropped anchor at Gravesend in the Thames Estuary after completing a voyage of just over a thousand nautical miles in twenty-four days, of which twenty were spent at sea. She reached port in a somewhat battered condition, but her cargo of peas and oats was safe.

Wagner had had enough. It was his last voyage ever aboard a sailing ship. He, Minna, and Robber transferred to an ultramodern, newly commissioned steamer that put them ashore near London Bridge. They then proceeded by cab to the Horseshoe Tavern [actually, the Hoop and Horseshoe], a recommendation of Wulff's, and spent the night there. Next morning, armed with another recommendation volunteered by a little Jewish hunchback from Hamburg, they took a cab to the King's Arms boardinghouse in Old Compton Street. There the exhausted couple looked forward to a long and refreshing sleep, only to suffer a recurrence of seasickness when the bed seemed to swoop and soar beneath them.

The next week they spent recovering from their voyage and feasting their eyes on a metropolis such as neither of them had ever seen before. Wagner tried to look up Sir George Smart, the conductor of the Philharmonic Society, and the author and M.P. Edward Bulwer-Lytton, but neither was in London. He did, however, gain admission to the strangers' gallery of the House of Lords and witness a debate there. Among those taking part were the premier, Viscount Melbourne, Lord Brougham, and the Duke of Wellington. He was particularly impressed by the hero of the Peninsular War, who had later won the Battle of Waterloo in alliance with Blücher.

On August 20, Wagner and his wife and dog left the hub of the British Empire and crossed the Channel by steamer. During the crossing, he learned from a Mrs. Manson that Giacomo Meyerbeer was staying in Boulogne. Having been given a letter of recommendation to the celebrated composer, who happened to be a friend of hers, Wagner decided to linger a while in Boulogne and complete the second act of *Rienzi* before proceeding to Paris. On the morrow of his arrival, he drove out into the country and took lodgings at Le Petit Caporal, a wine merchant's house. Here he promptly set to work on his score in preparation for a visit to Meyerbeer.

Meyerbeer, who at forty-eight could pride himself on two big and remunerative operatic successes, *Robert le Diable* and *Les Huguenots*, gave his young confrere a cordial reception and sat through a reading of *Rienzi*'s first three acts. For his part, Wagner was agreeably impressed by the Berlin-born composer's mobile features. Meyerbeer looked through the first two acts of the score, which Wagner had finished on September 12, praised his fine handwriting, which he pronounced "peculiarly Saxon," and consented to write him some letters of introduction to the management of the Grand Opéra. He also introduced him to the composer Ignaz Moscheles and the pianist Marie Blahedka, both of whom were then in Boulogne, and Wagner was invited to their soirees. Encouraged by his social contacts with such prominent figures in the world of music, Wagner pinned increasing hopes on Paris and quickly forgot the perils and exertions of the previous two months. He wrote to his sister Cäcilie's fiancé, Eduard Avenarius, who ran the Paris branch of the Brockhaus publishing business, asking him to look for some lodgings. Then, on September 16, he blithely set off for the capital in a diligence, one of the express mail coaches operated by the French postal authorities.

When Wagner came within sight of Paris on Tuesday, September 17, he felt he was nearing his life's goal, his key to fame and the fulfillment of all his dreams. Utter disenchantment was to follow.

A German Musician in Paris

———◆———

Anyone describing the dismal poverty and desolation of Wagner's Parisian "apartments" could abandon himself to paraphrastic word-music were it not for a strange whiff of uncertainty—a hidden turning point in this chess game of a career that most biographers ascribe to a far later phase in its development. Richard Wagner's complex image—all that was paradoxical in his character, revolutionary in his art, equivocal in his cultural criticism; his turning away from "civilization" and its supersession by a new image of man derived from saga, not history—all this became crystallized here. It was now that the shape of things to come showed its face. After Wagner's first eighteen months in Paris, the die was cast.

The Wagners moved into an inexpensive *hôtel garni* on rue de la Tonnellerie, a side street off rue St. Honoré near the Marché des Innocents. Day and night, noise and foul smells drifted through the windows of the room from which Wagner set off to pay fruitless calls on those who might be willing to help him. He was almost grotesquely ingenuous. No one in Paris had time for a young German composer eager to conquer the world with a bundle of obscure or unfinished scores. Introductions he had, of course, but only to people who either forgot to keep appointments or listened patiently to Herr Vagnère expounding his ideas in fractured

French and left it at that. What was he to live on? What ever had inspired him to come in the first place?

Wagner reacted to his predicament with grim humor. "Dearest friend," he wrote to Avenarius, "my wife humbly requests you to send her, by the bearer of this, 10,000 francs. Should this not be immediately possible, she asks you at least to lend her your kindly coffee grinder for twelve hours, the same to be returned to you tomorrow morning." Avenarius, who in 1840 became his brother-in-law, had already lent him 350 francs—all he could afford. When Cäcilie, once Wagner's favorite sister, joined her new husband in Paris, these financial transactions caused considerable ill feeling.

Most of the friends Wagner made were also in need; the poor cleave only to the poor. Typical of these friends were a trio of down-at-heel idealists, cronies whom he never forgot and whose regular calls on her hospitality Minna was long-suffering enough to tolerate for years. They were happy to share a loaf of bread or bottle of wine in return—when they had one to spare, which was seldom—but spent most of their time waiting optimistically for the major breakthrough which their far more talented friend was bound to make in the end.

Wagner got to know the first of them, Gottfried Anders, through Avenarius. A forty-five-year-old librarian and music historian, he was a Rhineland aristocrat who had dropped his original surname and called himself Anders [Otherwise] for reasons of anonymity. Immensely knowledgeable, particularly on the subject of Beethoven, Anders was too unbusinesslike to have become more, during his years in Paris, than an occasional contributor to Maurice Schlesinger's *Gazette musicale* and a humble *employé* of the Bibliothèque Royale. Under Wagner's enlivening influence, he seemed to receive a new lease on life and offered to explore the Paris terrain for Wagner. It was a case of the blind leading the blind. Anders enlisted the aid of Samuel Lehrs, a Königsberg philologist who scraped together a living by helping to edit Didot's edition of the Greek classics and was destined to die of tuberculosis at the age of thirty-seven. Wagner, who formed "one of my life's most beautiful friendships" with the young Jewish scholar, was appreciative enough of his influence to commemorate him in his Paris short stories as "the German philologist."

Although Anders and Lehrs usually went around like Siamese twins in adversity, they turned up one day with the young Dresden painter Ernst Kietz, a boyishly scatterbrained, naively care-free and warmhearted character who brought some light relief into their bleak lives. A student of Delaroche, this ever-optimistic young artist had one regrettable thing in common with Anders and Lehrs, both of whom were far better educated: He was a congenital failure. His sense of humor made him excellent company, but he was feckless in the extreme, and his name has endured more on account of his friendship with Wagner than because of any personal achievement.

A little variety was injected into this penurious but devoted circle by Heinrich Laube's arrival in November 1839. Jailed for seven years in 1835, Laube had had his sentence commuted to eighteen months' "fortress detention"— a less rigorous form of imprisonment—and was permitted to spend them at Muskau, Prince Pückler's castle in Silesia. While in exile, he acquired a sympathetic new mistress, Iduna Budäus, the widow of a Leipzig physician, and it was with her that he set off to recuperate in Normandy, traveling via Paris, when released early in 1839. Having conducted a brisk correspondence with Heinrich Heine throughout this time, he now used Heine as an entrée into Parisian society, Meyerbeer included. In turn, he introduced Wagner to Heine and, very probably, to the painter Friedrich Pecht, another Delaroche pupil of whom Wagner had already heard through Kietz.

Pecht later recalled seeing "a youthfully handsome couple"— the Wagners—strolling toward him in the Salon Carré, the Louvre picture gallery. There was "something soft" about Wagner, "for all his intellectual vivacity, which was immediately perceptible." Although he seemed aloof and made "no really significant impression," this picture changed in stimulating company. Over dinner with the Laubes and Heines at Brocci's, the Italian restaurant on rue Lepelletier, near the Opéra, Wagner enthralled his listeners with an account of his eventful flight from Riga. Heine's delightful twenty-four-year-old wife, Mathilde, a childishly naive and amusing creature who had not long learned to read and write at a boarding school for girls, possessed a charm and gaiety that quite eclipsed the other two women. Frau Laube, though "highly intelligent," looked "somewhat faded" by comparison, and Minna's beauty had a sterile quality. Laube wrote in 1843 that Heine, "usually so nonchalant," had clasped his hands in prayer at Wagner's confident expectations of making his fortune in Paris.

Pecht was soon filled with admiration for Wagner's sparkling wealth of intellect, just as he felt sorry for Minna, who endured her trials in Paris with surprising fortitude. She concealed the miseries of her hand-to-mouth existence from the public gaze and accepted the need to pawn her theatrical wardrobe and remaining pieces of jewelry—even to the extent of allowing her husband to sell the pawn tickets themselves.

Pecht recalled that everyone marveled at the way in which, abject poverty notwithstanding, Wagner entertained his friends with anecdotes, outlined his ambitious plans, and held forth on music and musicians, displaying an almost incredible knowledge of the musical literature of every period. Pecht further recalled him discoursing at length on the technical development of musical instruments, a continuing process that "dated" a lot of music. Even Mozart, he declared, was "outmoded" in many respects.

This new relationship to the language of music symptomizes the evolutionary nature of Wagner's art, which first found expression in Paris. In advance of his own musical development, he already nursed dynamic conceptions of form that were influenced, not by grand opera, but by the dramatic principles underlying Beethoven's symphonic music. What had happened? Not as much, perhaps, as he himself alleged, for he had a knack of dramatizing the watersheds in his career after the event. On reencountering Beethoven's Ninth Symphony at a Conservatoire rehearsal in November 1839, he was so overwhelmed by Habeneck's assiduous reading of this music that a whole period of uncertainty fell away "as it were, into a deep abyss of shame and remorse." We are told in *My Life* that the immediate product of this mental upheaval was the first movement of a *Faust* symphony that he had sketched by December 13 and orchestrated by January 12, 1840.

This is not, however, beyond question. Habeneck's performance of the Ninth did not take place until March 1840, and Wagner probably backdated the rehearsals. He did, on the other hand, hear Hector Berlioz's dramatic symphony *Roméo et Juliette* at one of its two first performances on November 24 or December 1, so this may well have been the work that kindled his symphonic ambitions. It was not long, in any case, before he decided to abandon the idea of a complete symphony and stop short at a single movement. A letter to Meyerbeer dated January 18, 1840, announced that he had written a *Faust* Overture. Whatever the truth, this work represents a turning point in his musical development.

He was visited while composing it by Berlioz himself. Viewed in relation to the superficiality of the Parisian musical scene, the French composer made an immediate impression on Wagner, who found the *Symphonie Fantastique* "marvelous" and continued to regard Berlioz's work with mingled admiration and puzzlement for most of his life. By contrast, the Grand Opéra left him so wholly dissatisfied—his "Autobiographical Sketch" of 1843 pronounced its achievements "devoid of all genius"—that he seldom attended it.

*   *   *

Wagner informed Meyerbeer that he had written his *Faust* Overture "in anguish, and much afflicted by toothache." For anguish, read penury. He had hoped to earn some money and attention by setting a few French poems to music. He even had the French version of Heine's *Zwei Grenadiere* printed at his own expense for fifty francs; but to no avail: The singers he approached showed little interest. The words for his essays in songwriting* were probably found for him by Anders and Lehrs. They included texts by Hugo, Ronsard, Reboul, and Béranger, but only the anonymous *Dors, mon enfant, entre mes bras* possesses a charm that anticipates certain lyrical qualities in *Der Fliegende Holländer* and distinguishes it from the rest of Wagner's Parisian potboilers.

When none of his efforts bore fruit, he decided to fall back on work already completed, notably his sensual, sensational *Liebesverbot*. Cold-shouldered by the Grand Opéra and ignored by Anténor Joly, director of the Théâtre de la Renaissance, he now asked Meyerbeer to approach the latter direct and give *Das Liebesverbot* his personal recommendation. Wagner's letters to Meyerbeer over the next eighteen months—letters written in "ardent admiration" —make astonishing reading in the light of later developments.* "You alone can help by promising to write Joly an opera. Terrorism is the only means, and you alone, my revered master of all notes, can employ it. I have no hope of salvation in this world save from you." Or again: "The sense of gratitude that animates me in your regard, my generous protector, knows no bounds." Or even: "I shall be a true and faithful slave, for I frankly confess to having within me a servile nature. . . . Therefore buy me, Sir. You will not be making a wholly valueless purchase!" And finally: "Goethe is dead, and he was no musician anyway. I have no one left but you." On June 4, 1840, Wagner's awareness that he must not overdo things prompted him to apologize for the "degree of exaltation" with which he had overstepped the bounds of "delicacy and modesty." On December 29, however, despite all the disappointments he was later to lay at Meyerbeer's door, he wrote to Schumann: "Don't let Meyerbeer be disparaged so much; I owe the man everything, my imminent fame in particular." It was not until 1841, with fame continuing to elude him, that Wagner, under the curious and self-derisory pseudonym W. Freudenfeuer [*Feu de Joie*], began to fire off journalistic gibes to the effect that Meyerbeer owed his success to the venality of Parisian opera directors. Early in 1842, one of his "Letters from Paris" informed the readers of Schumann's *Neue Zeitschrift für Musik* that Halévy was not a "sly, deliberate trickster like Meyerbeer"—a phrase that Schumann tactfully changed to "*filou* [rogue] like M."

One undoubted trouble was that Meyerbeer had to spend most of his time out of Paris, and that little could be effected at long range. Thanks to his efforts, however, Wagner heard while at work on his orchestral sketch for the third act of *Rienzi* that Joly had changed his mind: The Théâtre de la Renaissance was to produce *Das Liebesverbot* after all.

It was Lehrs, of all people, who advised Wagner to leave the *hôtel garni* and rent some more comfortable lodgings on rue du Helder for 1,200 francs a year. This Wagner did on the strength of his impending success, arguing that no one got anywhere in Paris unless he put on a show of self-confidence. Wagner had taken yet another gamble on the future, and the odds were steadily lengthening. His first visitor after moving to rue du Helder on April 15, 1840, was Anders, who brought him the dismal news that the Théâtre de la Renaissance had gone bankrupt and was closing down.

The consequences of this were threefold. First, *Das Liebesverbot* remained finally and permanently "undiscovered," which at least exempted its composer from another professional defeat. Second, Wagner's disappointed companions in misfortune hinted to him that Meyerbeer had deliberately recommended the work to a moribund theater—a view that Wagner himself espoused, though without drawing any precipitate conclusions. Third and last, this debacle set the seal on a financial catastrophe to which Wagner alluded in a diary begun and abandoned that summer. "Every resource is exhausted," he wrote with quiet resignation. Part of the new apartment had to be sublet, and Minna was reduced to the status of a landlady and chambermaid. To Wagner's surprise, the *petites gens* of the neighborhood did not regard this as socially degrading.

But for Heinrich Laube, humiliating dependence on the charity of his creditors, large and small, coupled with the unlikelihood of ever settling all his debts at a stroke, would doubtless have driven Wagner to quit Paris earlier than he did. Laube, who had returned to Germany on February 4, 1840, persuaded a Leipzig Jewish patron of the arts named Axenfeld, among other wealthy friends, to underwrite the unknown young composer's expenses in Paris for another six months.

With ruin staring him in the face, Wagner divided his physical and mental energies between two separate projects. On June 4, 1840, while in the process of completing the third act of *Rienzi* and starting on the orchestral sketch for the fourth, he wrote to Meyerbeer asking him to interest the Grand Opéra in a less elaborate scheme: a one-act *Fliegender Holländer* designed to be a curtain raiser for a ballet performance. "Oh, give me some sign that you have not forgotten me," he wrote. Meyerbeer instructed his secretary to help the young man whose letters so touchingly demonstrated that talent and enthusiasm were not automatically rewarded with success. By July 26, Wagner was able to inform Meyerbeer, then staying at Bad Ems, that several numbers were ready for a hearing. Apart from the sailors' chorus and the song of the Dutchman's crew, these included the ballad from the second act, in which he believed he had "unwittingly set down the thematic germ of the entire music for the opera." Having produced a French synopsis of his *Vaisseau fantôme* prose sketch for Léon Pillet, the new director of the Grand Opéra, Wagner had it checked by Heinrich Heine and was amused to be told that Erik (who was still called Georg) should be described as Senta's *amant*, not her *amateur*.

Wagner saw a great deal of Heine at this period. He admired him, and there is no doubt that he adopted him as a literary model. It was as a writer, too, that Wagner first became known, contributing to Schlesinger's *Gazette musicale*, August Lewald's *Europa* (as W. Freudenfeuer!), and, during his last year in Paris, to Hofrat

Winkler's *Dresdener Abend-Zeitung*. Although he obtained more of his copy from Lehrs and Anders than from personal experience, the best of his pieces on the German musical scene and conditions in France—on art, music, and the theater—are fully up to the standards of Heine or Börne. Some of them leveled due criticism at the decadence and superficiality of the Parisian theater, but his article "German Music," written in the same year, betrays how closely his thoughts and hopes were still bound up with France. "Because the two nations are joining hands and imparting mutual strength," he wrote, "the basis of a great artistic epoch has, at all events, been laid. May this noble union never be dissolved, for one can conceive of no two peoples whose mingling and fraternization could produce greater and more perfect artistic results than the Germans and the French, the genius of each nation being entirely capable of supplying whatever is deficient in the other."

*   *   *

Although Wagner's articles earned him next to nothing and his sources of assistance in Leipzig had dried up, he refused to stop work on the last act and overture of *Rienzi*. His consequent financial collapse threatened utter ruin—distraint, eviction, and imprisonment for debt. On September 20, 1840, Wagner turned in despair to his blind boyhood friend, Theodor Apel, whom he had neglected for so long. "To avoid all semblance of hypocrisy, I shall at once set down at the head of this letter—my first to you in years —that which, being the selfish part, should properly be mentioned last: I am in the direst straits, and you are to help me!" In response to this awkward request, Apel sent all he could spare— 6 friedrichsdor, or 125 francs—via Laube, who aggravated Wagner's predicament by trying to raise more money elsewhere before forwarding Apel's gift and covering letter to Paris.

On October 25 and November 17, Minna wrote Apel another two begging letters, whose publication in the Burrell Collection (1950) caused an understandable flutter in biographical circles. The first letter stated that Wagner had that very day been imprisoned for debt. According to the second letter, his condition had been exacerbated by illness and she could not afford to nurse him. Both these tearfully eloquent missives had, in fact, been drafted for her by Wagner on scraps of paper. If we are to believe them, he spent the end of October and part of November in a debtors' prison, yet no word of his incarceration can be found in *My Life*. His other autobiographical writings are no less silent on the subject than his friends' memoirs. Was it shame that made him draw such a complete veil over this ultimate humiliation?

No objective approach to this question can afford to ignore such evidence as seems to conflict with the story of Wagner's imprisonment. His short story "A Pilgrimage to Beethoven" was written at this period, because the *Gazette musicale* published the first of its four installments on November 19. *My Life* tells us that he completed the score of *Rienzi* on the same day, not having started the orchestral sketch for the overture until October 23.* That he did all this work in prison is almost inconceivable. The sheets of paper on which the aforesaid letters were drafted came from notebooks of a type he continued to use, so he probably drafted them at home. Furthermore, a letter to Laube dated December 3 states that no one could have lived through any two days more frightful than the first and second of the current month. "With their last remaining pfennigs, my poor friends here have helped as best they can to postpone the threatened blow until the fifteenth next; that blow will spell immediate and irrevocable distraint and the loss of my personal freedom. I did not believe this, but I came within a hairbreadth of it, for as a foreigner I do not have access to all the customary means of appeal." In other words, imprisonment for debt had been deferred once more. As Werner Wolf, coeditor of Wagner's collected letters (1967), rightly comments, it seems improbable that Wagner would have described the first two days of December as the acme of frightfulness if he had been arrested previously. No one remains unscarred by that kind of experience. If it had embedded itself in his mind at twenty-seven, he would have dreamed of it in later life, just as he constantly dreamed of Paris, his debts, and Minna. At the very least, he would have mentioned it to such a trusted confidante as Cosima, yet her diaries contain no such reference.

Last but not least, on October 25, the day of his alleged imprisonment, he invited Kietz over for the evening (Anders and Lehrs too, no doubt) and tersely added, "It's important." Everything suggests that he used this occasion to enlist his friends in a plot to dramatize his pleas for help by feigning imprisonment. If he did, in fact, hoodwink Apel in this way, Wagner deserves far more discredit than any that might have accrued from the supposed discovery of his imprisonment for debt.

There is no doubt that his financial worries were becoming too much for him; that he felt deeply humiliated by his futile essays in fund raising and spent a good deal of time bemoaning his lot. He even went the rounds of his billholders, among them a cheese-monger, and tried to beg the postage for his *Rienzi* score.

Having abandoned all hope of placing *Rienzi* in Paris, he addressed a petition to the king of Saxony requesting its acceptance in Dresden and sent the original score to Baron von Lüttichau, intendant of the Court Theater. He survived the next few months by making piano arrangements of excerpts from Donizetti's *La Favorita* for Schlesinger, the music publisher at whose office he had a first—unfruitful—encounter with Franz Liszt. Wagner applied himself indefatigably to "this humiliating, albeit remunerative task as if it were a penance imposed for the expiation of past sins." To save fuel, he and Minna confined themselves throughout that winter to the bedroom, which also served as a drawing room, dining room, and study. Two short steps took him from his bed to his desk, from there to the dining table, and back to bed again. It was this unhealthy routine, he believed, that lay at the root of his chronic stomach trouble.

On New Year's Eve, the Wagners' irrepressible friends invaded their lodgings with surprise gifts of food and drink. Wagner got as drunk as only the very poor can. On the stroke of midnight, he mounted a chair, then sprang onto the table. From this vantage point he delivered an encomium on Zschokke's *Auswandererkolonie Maryland*, extemporized a humorous diatribe on the past failures of all present, and prophesied so rosy a future for them that they ended up on the floor, beside themselves with tipsy laughter. They were past going home by this time, so Minna had to put them up for the rest of the night.

*   *   *

During the year just ended, 1840, in which Wagner had experienced the total dependence of the penniless artist on the affluent, Pierre-Joseph Proudhon's *Qu'est-ce que la Propriété?* had been published in Paris. Wagner first became acquainted with Proudhon's basic principle—that property connotes theft—through Samuel Lehrs, who always had his finger on the literary pulse. He found it so thought-provoking that he never forgot the author's name; but he had no gift for the patient, painstaking assimilation of economic, scientific, and political theories. Most of what he retained consisted of slogans—conclusions devoid of reasoned argument. Hence, too, the frequent criticism that his writings mingle the true with the false, confusing terms whose meanings can vary widely according to the intellectual context in which they are used. What he first learned of Proudhon's views may have been that property meant the dispossessing of the weak by the strong, but that a simple reversal of roles through revolution did not in itself pave the way for social justice. Whatever the lengths to which Wagner carried his sociorevolutionary and anarchistic ideas, one thing is certain: Their seeds were sown in Paris by his experience of poverty and the loathing he felt for a corrupt artistic milieu that he considered representative of the state of society in general.

We can well imagine how an artist as beset by misfortune as Wagner must have felt, one morning at the end of March 1841, when Liszt received him in the drawing room of his hotel suite in Paris. Only two years older but already a famous virtuoso, Liszt dazzled and almost stupefied Wagner with the glamour that surrounded him. Wagner's poor French did not permit him to engage in conversation with the other guests, and all he could think of to say, when Liszt inquired how he could be of service, was that he had wished to make his acquaintance. Liszt had forgotten Laube's introduction. Striving to make musical small talk, Wagner asked if his gracious host knew Johann Loewe's *Erlkönig* as well as Schubert's. Liszt's reply—just to set the seal on a thoroughly embarrassing occasion—was in the negative.

Though unable to afford the rent of 25 rue du Helder any longer, Wagner gave notice a week too late and was compelled, to his horror, to retain the lease for another year. On April 29, 1841, having luckily found a family prepared to take the rooms off his hands for a few months, he moved to cheaper lodgings at Meudon, just outside Paris. His time there proved to be a milestone in his career.

M. Jadin, the Wagners' landlord at 3 avenue de Meudon, was one of the numerous eccentrics who seemed destined to cross the young composer's path. Well over seventy, Jadin was a Bourbon legitimist who wore wigs and gaily colored jabots on his sorties into town, bathed at night in a tub in his garden, and adorned the walls of the house with childish paintings perpetrated by himself. Unhappily, he also owned a collection of musical instruments, which he tried out morning and night. This was a nuisance, but Wagner had no option. Over a period of ten days—between May 18 and 28, 1841—he produced the original draft of *Der Fliegende Holländer*. The action still took place on the Scottish coast. Its removal to Norway—an act of self-identification—probably occurred just before the opera went into rehearsal, when Wagner had already given Laube his "Autobiographical Sketch," with its reference to his Norwegian adventure. Daland took the place of Donald and Georg became Erik, but Senta remained a felicitous choice of name for his heroine. It was, in fact, an invention of the composer. He must have remembered the Norwegian cry of *"Tjenta!"*—maidservant—and thought it an apt name for a self-sacrificing creature who, echoing the words of Beethoven's Leonore, "Whoe'er you be!" falls blindly in love with someone roaming the seven seas in quest of deliverance.

Meanwhile, Baron von Lüttichau had received an extremely generous letter of recommendation from Meyerbeer. Dated March 18, 1841, this informed the Dresden intendant that "Some of the passages he played to me I found imaginative and very dramatic in effect. May this young artist enjoy Your Excellency's protection and have occasion to see his fine talent more widely recognized." On June 29, Lüttichau approved the production of *Rienzi* at Dresden, and the news of its acceptance encouraged Wagner to get on with *Der Fliegende Holländer*. He kept the wolf from the door for the next few weeks by finally, on July 2, selling his *Vaisseau fantôme* sketch for 500 francs to the Grand Opéra, whose management commissioned the conductor Pierre Dietsch to make an opera out of it.

When Wagner's piano reached Meudon early in July, he dared not touch it for an entire day, so afraid was he that this hiatus in the creative process would have destroyed his inspiration. Apprehensively, he set to work. And then, quite suddenly, so he tells us in *My Life*, the music started to flow from his pen as though he had already composed the Helmsman's Song and the Spinning Chorus but forgotten to write them down. When, having done so, he realized that these pieces had only just taken shape in his mind, he became "quite delirious with joy."

It took him seven weeks, from July 11 to August 22, 1841, to complete his orchestral sketch for *Holländer*. With the exception of the overture, which he carried around in his head and wrote down in November, after moving back to Paris, the entire score came into being in less than four months. Ten years later, in his somewhat verbose *Communication to My Friends*, he commented at length on the importance of the opera's overall conception as regards his development into a music dramatist. "I now took a new road," he wrote, "—that of revolution against the contemporary world of art." At the time, however, he sensed little of this; he was evolving into an original genius unbeknown to himself.

On the Road to Music Drama

Der Fliegende Holländer

M usic may be stupid or intelligent. Its degree of stupidity or intelligence does not depend on complexity or originality of melodic inspiration; on freshness and novelty of idiom, execution, or technical preparation; on style or method; on richness or economy of presentation; and least of all on the intelligence or erudition of the composer. Brilliantly clever musicians have been known to write stupid music. Specific musical "intelligence" manifests itself in something that might be called the physiognomy of its "melos," defined by Wagner himself as "the singing soul of melody." Just as faces can be stupidly or intelligently beautiful in all classes of human society, so stupid and intelligent music exists at every level, from light music to opera, from small-scale chamber music to symphonies. Although this has to be heard and cannot be explained in words or print, musical intelligence may be negatively defined by what is fundamentally absent from works whose combination of melody and rhythm possesses beauty or subtlety, namely, *triviality*.

In that sense, discounting a few wholly uninspired occasional compositions, Wagner wrote nothing but intelligent music from *Der Fliegende Holländer* onward. This, it must be conceded, is as little open to proof by means of musical theory as is the structural perfection of a painting by the laws of mathematics and geometry. Nevertheless, the survival of Wagner's stage works, vulnerable as they are to changing times, may be attributed to the degree of musical intelligence that immunized them against decay. No matter how many and various the interpretations that may be placed upon their content and structure, none of them would have been preserved from gradual decline, nor from the "unperformability" built into them by their sheer dimensions, had it not been for the absence of triviality and wealth of expression that inform their musical language.

The very first bars of *Der Fliegende Holländer* signal a new departure. Although Wagner did not begin by writing the overture, its conception was complete and its dramatic structure mapped out in his mind. The dramatic essence of the work comes alive in every one of its musical ideas and dominates the stage. Although this does not make it a music drama in the real, dogmatic sense—a definition, it should be noted, that Wagner steadfastly rejected in this instance—it does attain the status of what Carl Dahlhaus calls a "scene opera," in which related elements combine, musically as well as dramatically, to form a coherent series of events. This is itself an illustrative category within the music-drama genre to the extent that, from the aspect of composition, nothing occurs without good reason or adequate motivation.

And all this descended on Wagner—out of the blue, as it were —when he had just brought *Rienzi* to a laborious conclusion and had only recently been struggling to secure a performance for the inferior *Das Liebesverbot*. With his gaze fixed on the forthcoming production of *Rienzi* at Dresden, he himself was quite unaware of what dawned on him later: that *Holländer* represented a watershed in his musical development. After Küstner of the Munich Court Theater had turned it down at the libretto stage, he recommended it to Berlin, almost casually, as "a minor work."

The prospect of outflanking Dresden by successfully launching *Holländer* in Berlin seemed far from remote because Wagner had again put his faith in God and Meyerbeer. On December 7, 1841, Meyerbeer noted in his diary: "Called on Redern [the Berlin intendant] to recommend the score of *Der Fliegende Holländer* by Richard Wagner." Predictably, reactions to its musical texture ranged from skepticism to consternation. The kapellmeister, Carl Hennig—possibly the first person to recognize the full extent of

Wagner's gifts on the strength of a score—was alone in describing it, in a report dated January 9, 1842, as a "brilliant and original" work.

From then on, *Holländer* sailed under two flags. Pierre Dietsch's setting of *Le Vaisseau fantôme* quickly ran aground.* Wagner's fee for parting with the draft scenario had been spent by September, even before he returned from Meudon to Paris. He resumed his paid labor for Schlesinger but developed an even firmer intention of going back to Germany, where Gottfried Semper's handsome new Dresden opera house had just been opened.

Meanwhile, Samuel Lehrs was exerting a strange but stimulating influence on him. The impoverished scholar, who had caught cold in his unheated lodgings and contracted tuberculosis, presciently drew him into discussions on the subject of death and immortality. This "concern with philosophical matters" made such an impression on Wagner that he mentions it in *My Life* and records his surprise at hearing Lehrs cast doubt on "survival after death." It may be surmised that Lehrs was already conversant with Ludwig Feuerbach's *Wesen des Christentums*, which had been published earlier that year. If so, this would be Wagner's earliest exposure to the author who, after Proudhon, most decisively influenced the basic idea of the *Ring*. The theory of the circulation of gold was now joined by the twin conceptions of an end to the gods and an earthly religion founded on human love.

It was at this stage that Wagner happened on the Tannhäuser story. He does not say where, but we know that its source was Heinrich Heine, whose "Tannhäuser, Eine Legende" had appeared in the third volume of *Salon* in 1837. Heine's was a frivolous version, of course, complete with a papal curse, a handsome tribute to Milady Venus, and a pilgrim hurrying back with remorseful enthusiasm to the Gardens of Pleasure, where his bleeding feet are kissed by the Mistress of Delights; in other words, an unremitting hymn to the senses. Needless to say, this was not Wagner's only source, any more than was the original text of 1521, in which the noble Danheuser is likewise cast out by Pope Urban IV and returns to his goddess's realm inside the magic mountain. Wagner's memoirs speak of a "folklore book" about Tannhäuser that did not exist, unless he was referring to *Die Sagen von Eisenach und der Wartburg, dem Hörselberg und Reinhardsbrunn*, a collection of Thuringian legends published by Ludwig Bechstein in 1835. Wagner interwove the legends of the Venusberg and the song contest, a combination that could not have been fortuitous. Bechstein's book, which embodied the first simultaneous presentation of both themes, neatly transferred the action to the Eisenach area. It not only related the stories in close conjunction but declared that Tannhäuser had lived in the days "when the noble Landgrave Hermann of Thuringia assembled at the Wartburg many bards who proudly vied with each other in song for prizes of great value." That may have been the crucial sentence.

For all Wagner's additions and all his variations on the theme of sin and atonement, Heine's glorification of sensual pleasure shows through in a telltale—that is to say, musical—fashion. It was because of this, and because Wagner's *Tannhäuser* is allied to Heine's by its provocative hymn to Venus, that both undisclosed sources acquired joint significance and must have put Wagner on the track of the splendid dramatic solution that enabled him to devise a new Tannhäuser myth. On the track only, for an essential ingredient was still missing: There was no woman at the court of Landgrave Hermann—no foil to Venus. Wagner's incorporation of a third stratum of legend was another great feat of originality, but the time for that was yet to come.

He was eager to know more and delve deeper into the background of his theme. Samuel Lehrs, whose brother taught classical philology at Königsberg, came to his aid once more. He brought Wagner a volume of the historical and literary proceedings of the Royal German Society of Königsberg for 1838, which contained a paper by Professor C. T. L. Lucas entitled "Über den Krieg von Wartburg." The professor's annotated late medieval account of the song contest supplied Wagner with the color and atmosphere he needed, but the same volume also carried a detailed résumé of the Lohengrin epic. Although this was more than Wagner could digest and assimilate at first reading, it opened his eyes to an entirely new world—a realm of myths and prophetic dreams which, though rooted somewhere in human history, were largely untrammeled by historical factors.

Was Paris a fit place in which to ponder, and possibly act, on such thematic perceptions? To begin with, Tannhäuser's gardens of delight were at most a refuge from the ugly world of poverty. It was not his renewed creative momentum that prompted Wagner to think seriously about setting a date for departure—he was generally indifferent to unpleasant surroundings—but concern for the fate of *Rienzi*. From Dresden came reports of delays and difficulties, even though chorus master Wilhelm Fischer and costume designer Ferdinand Heine, who were to become Wagner's staunchest allies there, had quietly persevered with their study of the work. Unless he went there himself, the whole project might well go back into the melting pot.

Was he homesick for Germany? That too, undoubtedly, as he concedes in *A Communication to My Friends:* "I was assailed by an emotional, nostalgic patriotism of which I had previously been quite unaware. This patriotism was devoid of political coloration, for my enlightenment was such, even then, that political Germany —in relation to political France, let us say—held not the least attraction for me." He had received unmistakable indications that the political situation had worsened, not improved, since his departure from Germany in 1837. In force since 1836, Saxony's law on general pre- and post-publication censorship had been steadily extended. Although the authorities applied it in a comparatively liberal way, *Rienzi* did not remain unscathed. Wagner, who was leniently treated at this juncture, had wherever possible to substitute "Roman" for "papal" throughout the libretto—and not merely because, in a country ruled by a Catholic dynasty, ecclesiastical subjects were taboo on the stage.* As for allusions to freedom, the censor allowed them to stand only in contexts relating to oppression by the *nobili*. Wherever they referred to the Church's obstruction of efforts to bring about Italian unity, he wielded his pencil.

Wagner readily accepted these changes wherever they left *Rienzi*'s stature and musical structure unimpaired. He also accepted the need for cuts, even to the extent of sending Fischer a computation of the opera's running time. Though detailed down to the last minute, this schedule was naturally rendered illusory, in the case of a work like *Rienzi*, by intermissions and applause.

Thus Wagner's last six months in Paris were spent, as it were, in another world. Despite the lasting sense of bitterness with which he took leave of the city, he did not despise French music. He continued to regard Berlioz as an intriguing phenomenon, and he preferred French opera to Italian, partly swayed, perhaps, by the charm of its melodious contralto arias. He admired Halévy and early Auber, though in one of his last really scintillating Paris articles, Wagner deeply deplored the latter's capitulation to easy success. Composing, he said, had become as much of a habit with Auber as lathering with a barber, and the maestro often lathered his public and left it at that. "This being so, audiences often emerge from his barbershop with their beards still long and have no recourse but to wipe the lather off, fragrant as it is, if they are unwilling to wait for it to evaporate by itself, which it generally does even before they get home."

Richard and Minna Wagner left Paris on April 7, 1842. Their journey to Dresden took five days. On reaching the Rhine, Wagner experienced some of the sensations described in Heine's *Deutschland, ein Wintermärchen*—the pounding heart and moist eyes of the returning exile. During the one sunlit hour on this excruciatingly cold and uncomfortable trip, he was entranced by the sight of the Wartburg looming over Eisenach. He promptly christened a neighboring ridge the Hörselberg and, as he drove along the valley below, visualized the setting for the third act of *Tannhäuser*.

Tannhäuser

After sleeping off the effects of his journey at the Gasthof zur Stadt Gotha, Wagner left Minna in Dresden on April 15, 1842, and traveled on to Leipzig. Here he found his family in surprisingly easy circumstances: his mother well provided for, his sister Ottilie the contented mother of two sons and wife of a prosperous Orientalist, and all the Wagner clan less temperamental than of yore. Because their ever-optimistic brother-in-law seemed unlikely to bring discredit on himself with *Rienzi*, Hermann and Friedrich Brockhaus volunteered to support him for six months by contributing another two hundred thalers, twenty of which they gave him on the spot.

At Dresden, where preparations for *Rienzi* were slowly getting under way, the prospects looked quite bright. Wagner was warmly welcomed on his arrival by Wilhelm Fischer, the kindly old chorus master, who had never met him before, and conditions at the theater seemed not unencouraging. The chief kapellmeister, Carl Gottlieb Reissiger, himself an ambitious and prolific composer, had established a German theater in the Weber tradition. This should be borne in mind, because Wagner's pen portrait of him is

the height of injustice. Although Reissiger was fifteen years older
—and a man of forty-five then rated as old and spent—and although he irritated Wagner by playing the well-schooled, well-
groomed gentleman musician, he was not incompetent and cannot
be accused of lapsing into "humdrum" performances. By 1842, he
had brought the theater orchestra up to an amazing standard of
execution. Among its seventy-odd musicians were virtuosi as outstanding as the Polish leader Joseph Lipinski; the cellists Dotzauer
and Kummer, who were celebrated teachers; the flautist Für-
stenau; the oboist Hiebendahl; the trumpeter Queisser; and the
horn player Lewy. The singers included Wilhelmine Schröder-
Devrient, still a magnificent performer though vocally somewhat
mannered and, if the truth be told, too corpulent and lacking in
youthful freshness for the part of Adriano; the famous soprano
Henriette Wüst; the ebullient tenor Joseph Tichatschek; and the
bass baritone Anton Mitterwurzer, one of the greatest of his day.

Wagner was back home at last in a place where he could work,
a snug and familiar environment where he planned to make his
mark. He was home, yes, but his letters during those first few
months are an unceasing lament for what he had lost, for Paris, for
the vanished joys of friendship—a hymn to the Lehrs-Anders-
Kietz trinity. The very mention of Cäcilie and Eduard Avenarius,
with whom Richard and Minna had eventually reestablished close
ties, was enough to bring tears to their eyes. Wagner assured Lehrs
that he would rather be "at the very end of the earth," poor but
merry, in the company of his fellow paupers. "I have no preference
from the geographical aspect, and discounting its handsome ranges
of hills, its valleys and forests, I am even repelled by my native
land. These Saxons are an accursed breed—unctuous, malleable,
maladroit, indolent, and coarse—what have I to do with them?" If
he really swore eternal allegiance to his country when crossing the
frontier, as he claims in his "Autobiographical Sketch," how did
he reconcile these conflicting sentiments? Perhaps the fault is ours
for taking him too literally.

Wagner was not alone in his poor opinion of the Saxons. Robert
Prutz, a heavily censored poet and democrat whose prerevolution-
ary lectures on current events were just as heavily attended, called
Dresden "the cake-eaters' Mecca" and its inhabitants "torpid
mouth-openers who still believe that everything happens 'outside'
just so that they can have an interesting newspaper to read every

morning over their wretched coffee." In her book on Bakunin, the historian Ricarda Huch declared: "In no country is the philistine class as numerous as in Germany, and in no city as conspicuous as in Dresden." Naturally enough, there were reasons for this state of affairs.

Saxony was a poor country. The 1840s brought famine to the Erzgebirge on a scale that would have been almost unthinkable elsewhere in Germany. In Dresden itself, unlike Leipzig, only a thin upper crust of aristocrats and burghers could be distinguished from the poverty-stricken mass of its seventy thousand inhabitants, whose standard of living was low.

The suppers Minna and her husband so often shared with Fischer at the Heine home consisted chiefly of potatoes and herrings. Wagner, who had sometimes not eaten all day, cherished a high regard for Frau Heine's gravy. He conveyed an impression of threadbare elegance. One of the Heine children recalled that he was wearing a pair of shabby kid gloves when he paid his first visit.

Minna badly needed medical treatment and baths because of incipient heart trouble. But for the fortunate fact that Ottilie and Luise had married into the affluent Leipzig middle class, neither Wagner nor his mother could have afforded a trip to Teplitz that summer.

The Wagners left for Bohemia on June 9, 1842, and took lodgings at a farmhouse in Schönau. Johanna started off the holiday elsewhere before moving in with them. She kept her distance at first —"she mutters to herself for hours on end," Wagner reported to the family—and only joined them for occasional walks. What happened then, and what Wagner wrote of his mother in correspondence, was indicative of so deep a rift between them that early chroniclers to the "court of Bayreuth" deliberately ignored it.

After returning to Dresden prematurely, Wagner wrote to Minna at the end of July that he reproached himself for having exposed her to his mother's nagging. He himself was better able to cope with it. Let her say what she pleased, he kept telling himself. He would tolerate her because she was his mother and because he knew she was fond of Minna despite everything; but her remarks left him cold. We might dismiss this as a sop to Minna, were it not for a letter to Cäcilie and her husband dated September 11, 1842, in which he expressly defended poor Minna, who was "profoundly hurt and indignant at Mother's utterly unprincipled behavior and quite unbridled whims," and endorsed her complaints about the sixty-four-year-old widow's stinginess, selfishness, and malice. "One must concede, I suppose, that she causes nothing but mischief in our family because of her strange propensity for distortion, misrepresentation, and gossip, with the result that all our brothers and sisters keep her at arm's length." Minna, he declared, could now understand what Cäcilie had suffered while living with their mother for so long. Wagner's further assertion that Johanna's "everlasting habit of talking in fine phrases and instructive metaphors" was "mostly quite unthinking" may well imply that the pious homilies that used sometimes to reduce her children to laughter after Geyer's death had degenerated into high-flown claptrap, and that her childish nature had become unstable. Wagner declined to be explicit about her "genuinely sordid tendencies."—"It has to be admitted, dear Cäcilie, that one cannot blame everything on Mother's age and past tribulations. The vagaries and resentments of old women may be explained in this way. When they degenerate into forgetfulness of all *dignity*, however, we are obliged to deplore a saddening exception."

This all sounds harsh and disillusioning, particularly to those whose idealized picture of the composer requires an unclouded mother-son relationship and a blithe maternal disposition. But we must take things as we find them and correct the picture accordingly. There have been few other men of genius who, like Wagner, were blessed with almost *nothing* save their natural gifts.

"We cannot truly say that we greatly enjoyed Teplitz," Wagner told Cäcilie in the same letter. His stay there was important nonetheless. On June 22, perhaps to escape his mother's company, he went off alone to Aussig on the Schreckenstein and roughed it for several nights at the local inn. The wooded hills of the Bohemian Forest revived his memories of the Wartburg area. One moonlit night, wrapped only in a sheet, he clambered around the ruins on the Schreckenstein. Another time, while ascending the Wostrai, he came across a goatherd piping a merry dance tune. Although he soon forgot it and did not make use of a cursory record he kept, he promptly visualized a band of pilgrims filing past the goatherd and down the valley. This combination of "merry pastoral dance" and "chorus of elderly pilgrims" gave birth, two years later, to one of the most lyrical and atmospheric scenes that ever came from Wagner's pen. He was also quick to devise melodic ideas for the Venusberg and the pilgrims' procession.

At this stage, the prose sketch for *Tannhäuser*, still entitled *Der Venusberg*, was more than twenty pages long. Wagner began it on the Schreckenstein on June 22, 1842, and completed the second version at Teplitz on July 8. It contained his third and last decisive modification of the original story: The saintly Elisabeth had appeared on the scene. He made her the landgrave's niece because the daughter-in-law of the legend could hardly have fulfilled the roles of love object, lover, and redeemer. In Venus and Elisabeth, Wagner had created the embodiments of earthly and celestial love between which Heinrich Tannhäuser was to waver like Heinrich Faust between hell and heaven. Only now did his obligatory redemption become feasible.

Just as in *Der Fliegende Holländer*, though in a somewhat more exemplary, idealistic, and ethereal fashion, Tannhäuser's spiritual salvation is accomplished by the self-sacrifice of a woman in love. Because the minnesingers at the Wartburg raise their voices in praise of love and not, as in every other version of the legend, of princes, Tannhäuser's hymn to Venus not only shocks and scandalizes his sterile band of fellow knights but becomes the focus of the entire work. Young Germany's "wholesome sensuality" had been fused with the yearning for redemption that continued to wield a powerful influence over Wagner until the very end—until *Parsifal* itself.

Some Dresden critics averred that Wagner had written *Tannhäuser* at the instigation of the Catholic party. This suspicion, which was voiced in a politically explosive situation, can only have been based on the false inference that Tannhäuser's despairing cry —"My salvation reposes in [the Virgin] Mary!"—constituted the ultimate and definitive message of the work. Elisabeth's intervention on behalf of the wavering sinner represented a third course: the reinstitution of an unspoiled, pristine Christian love to which courtly conventions, too, were anathema.

But the composer of *Tannhäuser*, himself a lifelong devotee of love, has left us yet another pretty arabesque on the subject of his hero's conversion "from Venus to the Virgin." While drafting his scenario in seclusion at Aussig, he went to inspect a madonna in the local church. His opinion of this Mengs copy of a Carlo Dolci original was that "had Tannhäuser seen it, I could well understand how he came to turn from Venus to Mary without being too much carried away by piety."

*   *   *

On returning to Dresden, Wagner began by taking stock of his financial position. The small apartment at 5 Waisenstrasse cost twelve thalers a month and his rented piano four. That left fourteen out of the Brockhaus brothers' monthly allowance of thirty thalers to live on, and he possessed only three shirts. Writing to Avenarius, he confided that he often felt like "bellowing" for the day when he and Minna would cease to be "respectably dressed beggars," and added: "Happy the man who can openly wear rags on his back!" Everything, he told himself, would have to change when *Rienzi* was unveiled.

Although rehearsals were now proceeding apace, thanks to the rapturous enthusiasm of the cast, everyday life at Dresden was "a cold, colorless tedium" compared to Paris. The potato- and herring-fed townsfolk were provincial German philistines whose newspapers hotly debated subjects such as the mischief caused by packs of marauding dogs and the doffing of hats in the street. Had it not been for wondrous reports about a forthcoming theatrical treat broadcast by musicians and singers, foremost among them Tichatschek, who was supremely happy with his part, an alleged first opera by a locally unknown composer would not have brought people flocking to the box office or created such a furor.

On the eve of the *Rienzi* premiere, Wagner met a lonely young sculptor named Gustav Kietz, the brother of his painter friend in Paris. A pupil of Ernst Rietschel's, he took to Wagner at once and became a shy but faithful devotee.

On Wagner's own submission, the trepidation with which he looked forward to the night of October 20, 1842, was as unique in his experience as the amazement that possessed him afterward. It was all too unreal, too much like a fairy tale, to merit belief. The audience went wild, and no one was more astonished at the effect of the first three acts than the composer himself, who took his curtain calls in a kind of trance. He regretted not having cut the work more drastically because it had already lasted four hours. Ten o'clock came and went before the fourth act even started. He mistook the applause for a "final act of courtesy" on the part of an audience that had heard enough and would now go home en masse. But there was no sign of an exodus, and Ferdinand Heine, who had prowled the house during intermissions, overheard some remarkable verdicts. German traditionalists and contrapuntists declared that Wagner's opera placed him in line of descent from the worthiest of masters; Italianists opined that he surpassed even the divine Donizetti. Like most successes, this one was based on a variety of misapprehensions. Wagner's own uncertainty testifies to that, because the public's perseverance left him "utterly perplexed." Everyone was so overwhelmed by the tragic conclusion of the fourth act that a stunned silence fell. When the curtain finally came down at a quarter to midnight, the applause continued for fifteen minutes. Moved by this thunderous ovation, the composer went off to celebrate with his nearest and dearest, only to find that every inn was closed. That night, Minna slipped some laurel leaves between his sheets.

Still mistrustful of what had happened when he woke the next morning, Wagner genuinely believed that the management would laugh the premiere off and abstain from any repetition of such an exhausting night's work. He slunk into the theater hell-bent on saving something from the wreck by making drastic cuts, but was dissuaded by messages from the management and protests from the performers. Tichatschek tearfully insisted that he would not allow Wagner to delete a single note of his part because it was "too heavenly."

Wagner was at last persuaded of his own success. "Triumph! Triumph!" he wrote to Paris. "The day has dawned!" His entire family, friends and relatives from Leipzig included, were summoned to witness the long-awaited breakthrough. They came by train. The seventy-mile stretch of track between Wagner's native city and Dresden, his second home, had been opened in 1839, while he was still abroad. To *Rienzi* by train . . . A new age had indeed dawned, but not, as yet, in musical history.

Robert Schumann, whom Wagner begged by letter to come, remained oddly aloof. Public disenchantment, too, set in after the third performance of *Rienzi*. In view of the opera's exceptional success, Baron von Lüttichau felt obliged to offer its composer an exorbitant fee—all of 300 thalers. (Tichatschek's silver armor alone had cost some 400.) Wagner's proceeds from *Rienzi* were insufficient even to pay off his Magdeburg creditors, whom he still owed 657 thalers.

Rienzi maintained its outward success despite an increase in ticket prices, but box-office sales declined when the "squalling brat"* was split into two parts, *Rienzis Grösse* [*Rienzi's Greatness*] and *Rienzis Fall* [*Rienzi's Downfall*], and presented on successive nights. This the Dresdeners condemned as sharp practice. They were happy enough to fork out when given their money's worth but objected to paying twice for a single opera; so the old arrangement was reinstituted with minor cuts, principally in the ballet and pantomime sequences.

Selections from *Rienzi* were included in benefit concerts for the veteran actress Sophie Schröder, Wilhelmine's mother, who recited Bürger's *Lenore*. They made very little impact, either at Leipzig or Berlin, partly because audiences were ignorant of their context. It was to the star of the Berlin concert, Wilhelmine Schröder-Devrient, that Wagner owed his first real conversation with Franz Liszt. The busy virtuoso, who had entirely forgotten their brief encounter in Paris, was jocularly reprimanded by Schröder-Devrient for his "contemptuous dismissal" of a struggling confrere. After sinking to the floor in an all-redeeming gesture of mock penitence, he set out to charm the younger man and thoroughly succeeded.

It was Schröder-Devrient, too, who helped to alleviate Wagner's financial worries by lending him 1,000 thalers early in 1843. Half of this sum he set aside for Magdeburg, the other half for Paris. Although the prima donna made him her confidant in affairs of the heart,* she never became his mistress. According to Cosima's diaries, he considered her too "played out," even in his Dresden kapellmeister years, but a hint of erotic tension persisted nonetheless. Once, in 1845, when he started to lecture her on her amours, she retorted, "What do you know about the subject, you marital cripple!" Schröder-Devrient, who was a divorcée, changed lovers frequently. Never a good judge of men, she became infatuated with a guards lieutenant named Döring. Her most faithful admirer, Lieutenant Hermann Müller, had to look on while his dashing rival pursued her from concert to concert and gambled away part of her fortune. In 1847, she left the Dresden stage and married Döring. She did not recognize him for what he was until she read the terms of their marriage contract: He had persuaded her to sign over all she possessed including her pension rights.

Wilhelmine Schröder-Devrient not only played godmother to *Rienzi* but became Wagner's first Senta and first Venus.

Because Berlin was still dragging its feet over *Der Fliegende Holländer*, the Dresden authorities pressed for an opportunity to premiere this opera too. Schröder-Devrient had to master her complicated role within a few weeks, which she did with much stamping of feet and many hysterical outbursts. Memorizing was not her only problem. Sensitive and susceptible as she was to members of the opposite sex, she proved incapable of devoting herself with sufficient ardor to the doomed Dutchman when confronted by Johann Michael Wächter, a squat bass baritone with a potbelly, stumpy legs, and beady little eyes. Filled with foreboding, Wagner hit on the idea of seating her current lover—not yet Döring but a Herr von Münchhausen—in the front row of the stalls, so that he would be in full view throughout the premiere on January 2, 1843. Schröder-Devrient gave a superlative performance, but to suggest that the evening was saved by her alone, or that *Holländer* was a total failure, is to subscribe to an overworked and unfounded myth. The first-night audience was wholly unprepared for a work that must, after *Rienzi*, have seemed rather puzzling. If the Dresdeners had not been gripped by the music and interested in the plot, they would have walked out, not filled the house for another three performances—even for Wagner's sake. Wagner was always honest in this respect and seldom given to self-delusion. Writing to Cäcilie Avenarius on January 5, 1843, he described his first-night success and added: "The second performance was yesterday, and such was my triumph that enthusiasm mounted still further. Again I was twice called out with the singers. The first time I let the singers go out on their own, but the audience would not rest until I myself had gone out alone in their wake."*

Wagner made a few subsequent changes. He composed some music for the transfiguration scene, refined the orchestration, and restored the ballad, which had been transposed into G minor for Schröder-Devrient, to its original key of A minor.

If *Der Fliegende Holländer* scored even a modest success, it did so despite its décor, which must have strained the imagination and dulled the eye with its utter lack of visual appeal. Act 1 employed the backdrop from Weber's *Oberon*, likewise the masts. The two ships came from the ballet *Der Seeräuber* [*The Pirate*], but no rugged cliffs were available. In act 2, the production enlisted Gretchen's room from Goethe's *Faust*, which had already been modified for use in the tragedy *Columbus*. The house in act 3 came from Schiller's *Wilhelm Tell*, and the ships, once again, from *Der Seeräuber*.

From this point of view the new opera was almost an unmitigated failure,* yet Wagner felt more grounds for pride than he had after the spectacular premiere of *Rienzi*. The comparatively friendly reception accorded to *Holländer* brought him satisfaction and filled him with confidence, even though the regrettably brief interval between the appearances of the two works could not fail to surprise people. This applied more to intellectuals than to straightforward opera lovers who cared little for matters of style. Most surprised of all was Heinrich Laube, who steadfastly put content before form. Laube opposed a system that in his estimation used politics merely as a pretext for art. He appealed for a progressive content, whereas Wagner skated away from it into a process of structural evolution. The crucial point is that both men meant quite different things when they spoke of content, and Laube knew little about music. Their controversy set the seal on Wagner's break with Young Germany and alienated Laube for good.

Worse still, and far more distressing in its effect on Wagner, was the reaction he got from someone who *did* know something about music. "Dearest friend," he wrote to Robert Schumann, "let us stick together. Who knows what good may come of this, especially as I hope that our artistic paths will meet after all." But Schumann steered clear of Dresden. He merely read Wagner's scores and discreetly intimated that what he himself discerned in *Der Fliegende Holländer* were "traces of Meyerbeer." He may have been right— in terms of the score alone—with regard to one or two phrases or melodic configurations, but he failed to perceive their relationship to the stage. Being devoid of theatrical instinct, he lacked the requisite power of imagination. The same went for *Tannhäuser*, which he at first condemned: Wagner was incapable of "writing or devising four consecutive bars of beautiful, hardly of good, music," he wrote to Mendelssohn. It was only when he had seen the opera that he took back much of what he had said and conceded that everything looked quite different on stage.

The effects of Schumann's allusion to Meyerbeer are hard to gauge, but it certainly made Wagner mistrustful of the shy, sensitive man whose faculties were so soon to fail. "To have drawn on that source would have sentenced my productive powers to death," he retorted. It is probable that his bitter hostility toward the much-acclaimed, much-decorated giant of the opera sprang from this insinuation that he was Meyerbeer's disciple—even his musical offspring—as well as his protégé. His breach with Eduard Hanslick was of similar origin. Wagner met the twenty-year-old law student and budding critic at a Marienbad guesthouse in the summer of 1845. Young Hanslick had been deeply impressed by *Rienzi* and *Der Fliegende Holländer*. Reviewing *Tannhäuser* in 1846, he accounted it "one of the most distinguished achievements we possess in this field" and ranked it with *Der Freischütz*, *Les Huguenots*, and Mendelssohn's *Ein Sommernachtstraum*. Wagner replied: "What puts us worlds apart is your high opinion of Meyerbeer. I say this with complete impartiality because Meyerbeer and I are on very friendly terms, and I have every reason to esteem him as a kindly, sympathetic person. But when I sum up all that repels me in operatic music making in the way of inward muddleheadedness and outward tedium, I lump it together under the heading 'Meyerbeer,' the more so because I discern in Meyerbeer's music a great gift for outward effect, which prevents art from nobly maturing in proportion as it seeks to satisfy by altogether repudiating inward emotions of every hue. He who strays into triviality has to pay for it in terms of his nobler nature, but he who deliberately seeks it out is fortunate, for he has to pay *nothing*."*

Laube, Schumann, Meyerbeer, Hanslick. . . . There is no doubt that Wagner held his own against them and was theoretically "right." What made the position so hopeless was his inability to take criticism in stride, and what put him in the wrong all his life was the spiteful way he responded to it. He also made the unpardonable mistake of crossing swords with his critics. Had he been a diplomatically skillful champion of his cause, he would have done what his artistic self-assurance as a composer always prompted him to do: to rely on his work and nothing else. Of his more venial errors, two were committed at Dresden in 1843.

* * *

The deaths of Joseph Rastrelli and Francesco Morlacchi had vacated the posts of (junior) musical director and royal court kapellmeister, the second of which ranked equal to that of Reissiger.

Wagner having by now won his spurs as a conductor, Lüttichau offered him each post in turn. On January 5, 1843, Wagner turned down a trial appointment at 1,200 thalers per annum on the grounds that he would require "authority in the fullest sense of the word" if he were to carry out far-reaching changes in the organization of the royal orchestra. By these he meant, among other things, improvements in the promotion and appointment of musicians and an end to humdrum performances, not the fundamental theatrical reforms for which he was to evolve plans in the years ahead. Not even Weber had been engaged without a one-year trial, but Wagner, who felt uneasy about the whole idea, was quite prepared to risk losing the appointment by imposing these exceptional conditions.

It was Weber's widow, Karoline, who tipped the scales by insisting that Wagner owed it to her husband to take the post. How, she asked, would she ever be able to face her husband in the hereafter if she had to report how poorly and slothfully Reissiger was administering his musical estate? Besides, Wagner had his wife's security to consider. By accepting the post he would be able to support her in due style.

Shock tactics were employed at a crucial meeting on February 2, 1843. At twelve noon, Wagner was ushered into the director's office, where the board of management solemnly announced that he had been appointed royal court kapellmeister for life at an annual salary of 1,500 thalers. Lüttichau and his colleagues tendered their congratulations. It was too late to back out now, even though Wagner realized that his career had taken "a fateful turn." After delivering an unctuous little speech, Lüttichau politely accompanied the new kapellmeister to his door, where Minna hugged him in a transport of delight.

Wagner was now the incumbent of a post that had been graced, two centuries earlier, by Heinrich Schütz, one of the foremost names in German musical history. Schütz's proud letters and memorandums to the electors of Saxony were to be memorably echoed by Wagner's own proposals for reform, which likewise deplored the social privations of a musician's life.

Writing to Lehrs on April 7, 1843, only a few days before his ailing friend's death, Wagner declared: "I have been plainly informed that I am expected to bring about a genuine artistic reorganization in the local world of music!" From now on, his demands in this respect provoked increasing friction with the theater's management and staff. This was not attributable to ill will on the part of Lüttichau, the erstwhile forester-in-chief who now held the ranks of privy councillor and gentleman of the bedchamber and was invested with full discretionary powers by the Crown. Lüttichau was neither a monster nor a rogue. He could even be warm and confiding, although Robert Prölss, the Dresden theatrical historian, does not credit him with the intellectual depth required for a great new upsurge of artistic activity—nor did he need it, given that his main responsibility was to balance the theater's books. Lüttichau was hard on performers who lacked audience appeal but tactful in his treatment of Wagner. A bushy-eyebrowed man with a Napoleonic habit of thrusting one hand inside his coat, he tended to regard the short, slender kapellmeister with an air of puzzlement, uncertain what strange ideas were brewing inside that impressive head with its lofty brow, lustrous eyes, and prominent chin. Glasenapp may well be right, for once, in surmising that Baron von Lüttichau had "a vague inkling of the superior importance of his kapellmeister that was not confined to their official relations."

Wagner states in *My Life* that his first audience with King Friedrich August II of Saxony, which was granted a few days after his installation, marked the zenith of his career at Dresden. "Thenceforward, anxiety reasserted itself in manifold ways."

Although his production of *Armide* found immediate favor with the royal family and earned him acclaim as a Gluck interpreter, complaints were soon heard. Joseph Lipinski, who objected to his tempi in Weber's *Euryanthe* and raised the matter with the management, promptly tried to undermine his position with Lüttichau and set the orchestra against him because of a disputed promotion. Last but not least, Wagner committed a pardonable but unfortunate blunder by taking the conductorship of Dresden's Liedertafel, or male-voice choral society, out of the hands of a Professor Löwe. This post, which he did not relinquish to Ferdinand Hiller until 1845, introduced him to his only lifelong friend, Dr. Anton Pusinelli, but was a constant source of trouble and vexation. His election attracted the hostility of the entire local musical establishment, which resented being passed over. The critic Julius Schladebach had also conducted a choral society and felt himself to be a "colleague."

Wagner failed to impress his enemies even by planning the biggest and most spectacular choral festival ever held in Germany. He laid aside the original draft of his *Tannhäuser* poem, which he had completed in April, and wrote the words and music of a *Liebesmahl der Apostel* [*Love-Feast of the Apostles*] to be performed in Dresden's Frauenkirche on July 6—"a kind of Ammergau play," as he described it to Cosima on July 17, 1879. Behind a choir twelve hundred strong he stationed an orchestra of a hundred musicians. Forty voices issuing from the dome of the church symbolized the Whitsuntide outpouring of the Holy Spirit—"Be comforted, for I am near"—whereupon the orchestra imitated the music of the spheres, and the disciples, gazing up in wonderment, broke into a chorus of "What tumult fills the air?" The church rang to the voices of the double choir, the harmonically progressive ninths and instrumental tremolos of the invisible orchestra. When it was all over, the massed choirs of Saxony felt indescribably elated at the effect they had produced. Schladebach and certain others, who were downright appalled, rightly protested that this was no glee club music.

Wagner completed the *Tannhäuser* poem on May 22, 1843, his thirtieth birthday, but the twin burdens of the theater and the choral society prevented him from making a start on the music. He tried to do so during the summer holidays, which he again spent at Teplitz-Schönau, but was distracted by the strange sense of unease that overcame him on reading Jacob Grimm's *Deutsche Mythologie*, and also by the abdominal cramps and twinges that were to plague him for the rest of his life. All he produced at Teplitz, where he arrived on July 19, were a few sketches for the Venusberg. He did not embark on the orchestral sketch for act 1 until November, having moved on October 1 to a new and more expensive apartment in Dresden's Ostra Allee. Act 2 was written in September and October, 1844, during a six-week stay at a vine-yard near Loschwitz, and act 3 in December. The score was not completed until April 3, 1845, after an entire winter's work.

At the premiere on October 19, 1845, which was sold out, the overture and the Venusberg music made little impact—"they were too novel for the audience," noted Gustav Kietz—but the septet at the close of the first act drew great applause and earned Wagner a curtain call. The second act went down better, though Kietz declared that Tannhäuser's account of his experiences in Rome and the opera's finale were largely unappreciated. The picture did not change until after the third performance. The gods were packed with young people, and audiences registered delighted approval after every act.

Tannhäuser's music carries an equivocal scent of roses and musk, and somehow the work was never quite finished despite Wagner's immediate alteration to the unintelligible finale, his numerous revisions, and the addition of the "pleasure grotto" music to the Paris version. He would doubtless have liked to iron out its inconsistencies and bring it into line with the musical ideas he had developed by 1860. On the other hand, much of the opera's charm stems from its diverse and disunited ingredients.

Tannhäuser was daring in its use of deceptive cadences and ambiguous chords such as the diminished seventh. The suspension in "Approach ye the shore," too, is startling. If, as usual, the sea is invisible at this point—and how could it be otherwise, in the environs of the Hörselberg?—this fairy song in a sensual hell seems, textually and musically, to anticipate the turn of the century in an aestheticist and formalist manner. It is pure *l'art pour l'art*, and accounts for Baudelaire's enthusiasm.

Dr. Richard Faust in Dresden

Politics

At this period, two men could often be seen walking the streets of Dresden deep in conversation. Any townsfolk prone to the fashionable belief that uncovering the head could be a health risk were absolved from raising their hats because the strollers took no notice of them. The taller of the two, August Röckel, was a powerfully built man with dark side-whiskers, long, thinning hair, and blue eyes magnified by a pair of glasses. His habitual tone of voice was subdued but vibrant with intensity. Despite the obvious respect with which he treated his companion, there was a commanding insistence about the way he addressed him. The term "Mephistophelean" could not, however, be applied to someone whom Liszt described as "a capital person—gentle, cultivated, and humane." The other man, who was clean-shaven and considerably shorter, with an imperiously tilted chin, would sometimes pause to emit a volley of oaths or a bellow of laughter. The Dresdeners called him their Dr. Richard Faust.

Shortly after his own installation, Wagner had succeeded in getting Röckel appointed to succeed Joseph Rastrelli as musical director, or assistant kapellmeister to himself. This he did over the opposition of Reissiger, who had also nominated a candidate, but Röckel was a Catholic and the Catholic Court of Saxony must have thought that two Protestant kapellmeisters were enough. In Röckel, Wagner acquired far more than an ally at the theater. Wagner never came as close to another fellow individualist or adopted his views more wholeheartedly, and Röckel repaid him with steadfast loyalty.

Born at Graz on December 1, 1814, August Röckel was a nephew of the composer Johann Nepomuk Hummel and the son of Joseph Röckel, a singer, conductor, and impresario who had been on friendly terms with Beethoven and had, in the course of a checkered career, sung the part of Florestan. Ever footloose, Röckel Sr. went to Paris in 1829, where he introduced the French to *Fidelio* and *Der Freischütz* with the aid of Wilhelmine Schröder-Devrient. In 1830, he summoned his sixteen-year-old son from Aachen to the French capital. Here, unlike Wagner, who had heard its echoes from afar, August Röckel witnessed the July Revolution firsthand. He not only made the personal acquaintance of Lafayette, Lafitte, and Marrast, but consorted with Spanish, Portuguese, and Polish refugees, whose stories filled him with outrage at the poverty, oppression, and injustice that reigned in most European countries.

The Röckels moved to England in 1832. Here August continued his musical training, the theatrical and practical aspect of which he learned from his father, but devoted himself with equal enthusiasm to the study of social reform movements. He read Robert Owen and Lammenais and was much impressed by the Chartists, who were campaigning for a democratic franchise that would enable social interests to be represented in Parliament. As one who had "matured under the liberal institutions of this country and been filled with their spirit," he must have felt doubly repelled by the constraints and provinciality of life in Germany when he returned there in 1838.

Röckel was the most thoroughgoing socialist and democrat ever to cross Wagner's path. He had reached the conclusion that society was founded on poverty and hunger, and that three out of every ten Germans were either in jail or living on charity, public assistance, or the proceeds of theft. The incarcerations and constitutional abuses that came to his ears when he returned to Germany, the stupefaction of masses drilled in blind and unquestioning obedience, the suppression of free speech, the infiltration of families by spies and informers—"in short, this whole morass of manifold abominations"—could not but fill a new arrival with "a sense of outrage barely intelligible to people who, having grown up in such ignominious conditions, were long inured to them and felt obliged to quell any vague, treasonable doubts that arose in their breasts as to the competence of those who perpetrated abuses of an inordinately shameless nature." This passage from Röckel's *Sachsens Erhebung und das Zuchthaus zu Waldheim* [*Saxony's Revolt and the Penitentiary at Waldheim*], published in 1865, is eloquent testimony to what he felt during this period.

Röckel found it as hard to gain a professional foothold as he did to adapt himself to political conditions. He accepted a junior conductorship at Bamberg, where he joined a set of South German liberals and was introduced to the writings of Ludwig Börne; but he did not remain long in this dead-end job. At Weimar, where the authorities at first denied him a resident's permit, he scraped together a living as a music teacher and in 1840 married a local actress related to Albert Lortzing, the Leipzig kapellmeister who had just achieved success with his opera *Zar und Zimmermann*. Röckel embarked on his Dresden appointment with high hopes whose collapse was to steer him in quite another direction. Because a musical director's salary of 600 thalers proved insufficient to support his rapidly growing family—he sired nine children—Röckel kept the wolf from the door by pawning his valuables and writing piano arrangements in his spare time. He showed so little aptitude for his official duties that he made a mess of his first few operatic performances and never rose to become more than a singing coach and deputy conductor. On the other hand, he was a brilliant pianist and score reader whose talents stood Wagner in good stead. He tinkered repeatedly with an opera of his own, *Farinelli*, but abandoned it in disgust on hearing *Rienzi*, *Holländer*, and *Tannhäuser*. Having once acknowledged Wagner's superiority in this field, he deemed it his duty to serve and assist him, communicate his own appreciation of Wagner's musical ideas to others, and temporarily offset Wagner's ignorance of modern political theory by discoursing on it during their long walks beside the Elbe. Although Wagner's own revolutionary writings reflect the entire range of socialist and anarchist ideas current at this period—from Proudhon, Lammenais, Mazzini, and Wilhelm Weitling to Max Stirner, whose *Der Einzige und sein Eigentum* [*The Individual and His Property*] appeared in 1845—it is doubtful that he himself actually read or studied any of these authors until 1849. The interest was his own, therefore, but the inspiration came from Röckel.

The one exception was Ludwig Feuerbach, in whom Röckel took little interest. Wagner, who recalled that his attention had been drawn to Feuerbach's works and ideas at Dresden by a German Catholic propagandist named Metzdorff, used the neo-Hegelian's atheistic ammunition in verbal skirmishes with Röckel and his friends at the Engelklub, Dresden's leading *café littéraire*.

We can still read what Röckel thought of the political situation in Saxony. Friedrich August II, a devout believer in the divine right of kings, was personally moderate and popular with his subjects. Although he stood by the 1831 Constitution, this had served to consecrate his absolute power, not curb it. "On the other hand, it had proved quite impossible to extract any concession or improvement from him in matters political. As soon as Minister von Lindenau, a humane and enlightened man, was compelled to give way before the growing strength of the reactionary party at court early in 1843, resistance to every demand of the age became steadily more obdurate and the arbitrary conduct of government and officialdom steadily more callous. When even the strictest application of censorship failed to curb journalistic comment sufficiently, numerous independent-minded journals were banned without more ado, and the ministry undertook to compensate the public for their closure with a series of newspapers tailored to its own point of view. As in the political field, so in religion, efforts were made to check all liberal tendencies and encourage infringements by the orthodox."

Röckel was here alluding to the religious controversy that had left its mark on *Tannhäuser*—a dispute which, although it extended far beyond the borders of Saxony, attained special intensity in a country ruled by a Catholic royal house. In October 1844, after conflicts within the Church had been aggravated by a proposal to exhibit the so-called Holy Coat at Trier, the Catholic priest Johannes Ronge repudiated the authority of the Vatican and published his decision in the press. Led by Ronge and Johannes Czersky, the German Catholic Campaign proceeded to attack papal autocracy, celibacy, and religious abuses. It split the Catholics of Saxony into two groups, pro-Roman and independent, and became the precursor of the Old Catholic movement whose spectacular reemergence in 1870 was viewed with sympathy by Wagner. The people of Saxony precipitately hailed Ronge as a national hero and a latter-day Luther. In the field of education, pressure exerted by orthodox clerics sparked off riots among the students of the Freiburger Akademie. Rightly or wrongly, responsibility for quelling the reformers was delegated to the king's brother, Duke Johann, an exceptionally zealous Catholic.

Disaster struck on August 12, 1845, after a Leipzig parade reviewed by Duke Johann in his capacity as commander in chief of the Communal Guard. Greeted with silence instead of the customary cheers, the heir to the throne cut the proceedings short and retired in high dudgeon to the Hôtel de Prusse. While he was lunching in a room at the rear of the building, cries of "Long live Ronge!" were heard in the street. The company of regular guardsmen stationed in front of the hotel promptly opened fire on the crowd, causing numerous casualties. At least fourteen bystanders were killed, among them an inoffensive scholar, and wounded women and children lay bleeding on the cobbles. Had it not been for the students of Leipzig, who prudently separated the militiamen from the regulars and disarmed them, and appeals for calm from Robert Blum, a political activist, the Leipzigers might well have provoked more slaughter by hurling themselves at the troops. Blum later delivered a funeral oration over the graves of the victims. No one ever established who had given the order to fire. When a deputation of Leipzig citizens came to request an official inquiry, Friedrich August was rash enough to send them packing. For the first time, something akin to opposition stirred in the popular mind.

Tannhäuser's first performance on October 19, 1845, occurred at the height of the public controversy occasioned by the Leipzig massacre. Small wonder that the work's apparent Catholicism aroused surprise, or that Wagner was deeply hurt and offended by the charge that he had written it on behalf of the Catholic party; that he, of all people, was on the side of the oppressors. He did, however, find people to support him. Even Professor Ernst Hähnel, the Dresden sculptor, was forced to concede that, viewed in the light of current issues, *Tannhäuser*'s disavowal of the Pope made him a German Catholic.

Debates between Röckel and Wagner, in which they were sometimes joined by the architect Gottfried Semper, the painter Friedrich Pecht—since returned from Paris—and other regular patrons of the Restaurant Engel, became more and more lively. Ludwig Feuerbach's *Grundsätze der Philosophie der Zukunft* [*Principles of the Philosophy of the Future*], published in 1843, had been followed in 1845 by his *Wesen der Religion* [*Nature of Religion*]. Feuerbach dismissed the Catholic controversy on the grounds that God is a creation of man—the consummate self-projected personality—and "the love of God" merely the everlasting human love that finds supreme confirmation in suffering. He was also reputed to have written that *sensuality* is the key to firsthand knowledge. To Wagner, who had already heard quite similar things from representatives of Young Germany, these statements seemed to blend. To him, Feuerbach meant primarily the urge for happiness, the struggle for an intelligible, palpable salvation that could genuinely be attained on earth. He duly based his idea of revolution on Feuerbach's eudaemonistic ethic. Revolution, insurrection, change. . . . Wagner construed them first and foremost as aids to the fulfillment of happiness; in fact, "the gospel of happiness" is a phrase that occurs in one of his revolutionary articles a few years later.

He even made an attempt to read Hegel's *Phänomenologie des Geistes* [*Phenomenology of Mind*], where he came across sentences such as the following: "It is not, incidentally, hard to perceive that our age is an age of birth and of transition to a new period." If he retained anything of the book, it was this.

Wherever Wagner went at this time, he spoke of God, liberty, and the evils of particularism. Once an idea had taken root in his mind, it tended to escape his lips at the first opportunity. While visiting Hermann Brockhaus at Leipzig in 1846 he met Laube and the composer Louis Spohr, who had endeared himself to Wagner by producing *Der Fliegende Holländer* at Kassel.* Wagner discoursed on political topics with a "sympathy and ardor" that surprised his companions. Spohr, a musical veteran with a warm regard for all things new, was especially pleased "because he [Wagner] spoke, of course, in an extremely liberal vein." The same night, Wagner attended a musical soiree in Spohr's honor at the home of Felix Mendelssohn. It was his last glimpse of either man.

The symptoms of Wagner's political commitment multiplied as time went by, although, in his singular new role as a Röckel adept and archliberal, he dissociated himself more and more strongly from those rhetoricians of progress, the Young Germans.* To one for whom the wind now blew from quite another direction, the Young Germans had become a bore, the more so because they continued to produce no art in tune with his own ideas.

In November 1846, Wagner invited a party of twelve to his home to celebrate the performance of Laube's play *Die Karlsschüler.* The painter Friedrich Pecht, who was present on this disastrous occasion, records that Wagner suddenly queried whether a dramatist who wrote about Schiller ought not to possess something of his hero's genius. When he aggravated this injury to Laube's literary self-esteem by dismissing the play as a "Scribean" tale of intrigue, no amount of toasts and expensive champagne could retrieve the situation, and the embarrassed guests dispersed.

Laube's mauling at the hands of Wagner, who stood poised on the threshold of fame and was growing arrogant, is attested by the Austrian author, socialist, and revolutionary Alfred Meissner, who had first met Wagner in September of the same year. He also describes a scene between Wagner and the new Dresden dramaturge Karl Gutzkow, with whom he went for an excursion in the country. "We talked a great deal during this first walk together, but only about politics. Richard Wagner considered the political situation ripe for fundamental change and thought it inevitable that there would be an upheaval in the near future. This transformation would proceed with ease and require only a few blows to be struck because our political and social structures were only outwardly stable. I still recall his precise words: that revolution had already been accomplished in the minds of all; that the new Germany was as complete as a casting and required but a single hammerblow on the clay mold to emerge. Gutzkow, who had meanwhile joined us, took the contrary view. He stressed the power of inertia—the strength of the old and fear of the new, the habitual deference and obedience of the masses, the spinelessness of the great majority—and gave vent, in his cautious way, to a host of doubts. Wagner lost his temper and cut the argument short in strong, ill-humored language."

Wagner's mood may have been exacerbated by his professional relations with Gutzkow, whose "dramaturgical" functions were vague and nominally covered opera as well as drama. This could not fail to create friction between the two men, and Wagner was loud in his complaints to Baron von Lüttichau that Gutzkow was trespassing on his preserves. After a hard day at the theater, he would come home to Minna, his dog Peps and parrot Papo, seething with fury and feeling that everything—in art as well as politics—was topsy-turvy and needed radical change.

His experiences outside Dresden were no more encouraging. He devotes much space in *My Life* to the weeks of disappointment he endured in Berlin during September and October, 1847, when *Rienzi* failed to score a success there. Everything depressed him, from the theater and his finances to the royal court, the weather, and politics. His conversations with the Breslau author Hermann Franck, a Dresden acquaintance of two years' standing whom he met again by chance in the Prussian capital, "assumed a peculiarly gloomy tone" because the king of Prussia had failed in his attempt to convene a representative assembly. "I was one of those," writes Wagner, "who had initially been disposed to attach a hopeful significance to this venture, but it was a very real shock to have the full personal and factual details of the affair elucidated for me by someone as well informed as Franck." All his hopes were banished by Franck's dispassionately expressed views on the Prussian state, on the German intelligentsia of whom it was "supposedly representative," and on the real nature of what was reputed to be "a model of order and good government." As one who had expected Prussia to contribute to the fruitful development of Germany, Wagner felt "plunged into chaos." Now that he had discovered the "hollowness" of the existing situation, any attempt to enlist the Prussian monarch's support for his artistic ideas—which were another matter altogether—struck him as absurd. It is this persistent mingling of the artistic and the political that makes it so hard to identify Wagner's motives for wanting revolution.

On November 23, 1847, while still depressed by his Berlin visit, he wrote an oft-cited letter to Ernst Kossak, the Berlin music critic. This, too, embodies a telltale change of tack. "Best of friends," wrote Wagner, "what avails all our preaching at the public? How greatly I deplore your taking so much trouble—and on my account, too! There is a dam to be breached here, and the name of the means to that end is revolution! A positive foundation must be attained. That which we consider good and right must become firmly and unalterably established; the bad that now prevails will then dissolve of itself into foolish, easily vanquished opposition. One sensible decision by the king of Prussia in regard to his Opera House, and all will instantly be well."

There are few better illustrations of the confusion that reigned in the mind of this "revolutionary in aid of the theater." Perhaps the only common denominator to which his ideas can be reduced is the philosophical egoism of Max Stirner—the blow for freedom struck by the individual for himself and, thus, for all. In 1851, Wagner tried to dispel the misunderstanding provoked by the above definition of his revolutionary aims. Part of the following sentence from *A Communication to My Friends* was carefully printed in wide-spaced type: "While reflecting on the possibility of effecting a fundamental change in our theatrical circumstances, I was driven quite automatically to a full appreciation *of the worthlessness of political and social conditions that could not, of themselves, produce artistic conditions in the public domain other than the very ones I was attacking.*"

Money

It is to Wagner's great credit that he found his musicians' salaries disgracefully inadequate, and one cannot fail to be shocked by a memorandum dated 1846 in which he describes how the best and most assiduous of his violinists have been laid low by ill health. He enumerates the "distressing tally" as follows: "*Kühne,* an excellent young violinist, has died of consumption; *Winterstein,* an exceptionally capable man, has been compelled by the manifest destruction of his health to tender his resignation in the prime of life; Chamber Musician *Franz* has performed no duties for nine months and will never, to all appearances, regain his health; Concertmaster *Morgenroth* has been unable to undertake any duties for nigh on a year; Chamber Musician *Lind* is persevering in his duties only by dint of extreme and most creditable efforts, and requires constant consideration." Such was the tone of Wagner's petition to Lüttichau, which remained unanswered for nearly a year and was then rejected.

Among the numerous changes and improvements demanded by Wagner were that basic salaries should be increased, instrumental sections augmented, discipline reinforced, and duties redistributed inside the theater and out. He further pressed for the introduction of orchestral concerts and insisted that every instrumentalist be given a chance to maintain his standard of performance by studying in private. Wagner's covering letter to Lüttichau, dated March 11, 1846, culminated in the statement that, under prevailing circumstances, the orchestra needed a spokesman who enjoyed the fullest confidence of the board of management. He therefore tendered his resignation.

This was risky, but Wagner always played for maximum stakes even when hovering on the brink of disaster. He had owed Wilhelmine Schröder-Devrient 1,000 thalers at 5 percent interest since early in 1843. His fee for conducting the Berlin premiere of *Holländer* in January 1844—100 ducats, or 300 thalers—had been used to repay his relatives, but the position would have been slightly less desperate had he refrained from taking a wild gamble.

Because Breitkopf & Härtel had offered him no down payment on his operatic scores and declined to pay a royalty on less than a hundred copies, he hit on the disastrous idea of marketing them himself. Wilhelmine Schröder-Devrient agreed to advance him part of the printing cost, so he commissioned C. F. Meser, the Dresden court music dealer, to publish the scores of *Rienzi* and *Holländer*. When the first installments fell due and Schröder-Devrient was invited to keep her part of the bargain, she confessed to Wagner that she had surrendered control of her affairs to her lover, the pernicious Lieutenant von Döring. Her money was invested and inaccessible, she told him: In short, she was either unable or unwilling to lend him any.

In desperation, Wagner turned to his three "private bankers": the ever faithful Anton Pusinelli, the oboist Hiebendahl, and the actor Hans Kriete. He negotiated a participatory contract with them—from which, needless to say, they never earned a groschen —and made up the balance by borrowing at an exorbitant rate of interest. Nearly all the theaters that were sent copies of *Rienzi* and *Holländer* promptly returned them, so the disaster ran its course. Hoping to offset his losses on these scores, Wagner spent another five hundred thalers on printing a hundred copies of *Tannhäuser*, which also remained unsold.

To make matters worse, Wilhelmine Schröder-Devrient suddenly and without offering any reason called in her four-year-old loan of a thousand thalers, plus interest. This move was inspired by her jealousy of Wagner's enchanting niece Johanna, whose promising career as a singer (she had played Elisabeth in *Tannhäuser*) was a source of irritation to the fading Venus. Wagner had no choice but to stave off ruin by asking the management for a loan of five thousand thalers—twice Reissiger's annual salary—from the theater's pension fund. This was granted on condition that he pay interest at 5 percent, take out a policy on his life to cover the full amount, and repay the principal in ten installments, starting in 1851. There was no alternative.

Relations with Minna, too, were becoming strained because Wagner found it hard to account for their permanent indebtedness. In April 1847, they took a somewhat cheaper apartment in the Palais Marcolini, in the Friedrichstadt quarter of Dresden, at an annual rent of only 100 thalers.

Lüttichau was not unnaturally surprised, therefore, when Wagner applied at the end of the year for a salary increase of five hundred thalers, which would have put him on a par with Reissiger. Even Lüttichau's patience had its limits. He forwarded the kapellmeister's petition to the king with the following statement of the case: "By virtue of his former sojourn in Paris, Wagner has acquired so lighthearted a view of life that he can probably be cured of it only by experiences as grave as those he is now undergoing in his present straitened circumstances—if, indeed, he can still extricate himself at all." Wagner, he went on, had failed to appreciate his good fortune in being appointed kapellmeister. Encouraged in his extravagant ideas by public acclaim, he had been misguided enough to suppose that his operas would prove as lucrative as Meyerbeer's in Paris and London. He had further been seduced into loss-making ventures by "the foolish notion of not relinquishing any profit from the publication of his works to the bookseller, but of diverting it to himself." Although it was doubtful whether Wagner's retention at Dresden justified "so exceptional a subvention," he had exerted himself "in particular instances" and given evidence of a laudable zeal that would render his departure "a matter for regret."

Wagner's request was granted on February 24, 1848, but with certain provisos. Lüttichau could not resist passing his "letter of recommendation" across the table and letting Wagner read it at his leisure. Many of the charges against him were well founded, but the sarcastic allusion to Paris was offensive and unjust. Wagner handed the letter back "in a daze," to use his own description. He had been granted the money, but at considerable cost to his pride.

Theatrical Maneuvers

Some artists are hotheads and revolutionaries with a total disregard for social conventions. Others have a natural bent for formal occasions and speechifying. In this respect as in every other, Wagner was brilliantly contradictory, as the events of 1843–49, in particular, made abundantly clear.

His first occasional composition at Dresden was a choral work for male voices to be performed at the unveiling of a monument to King Friedrich August I of Saxony designed by Rietschel. His first Palm Sunday concert, given after a very unsatisfactory visit to Hamburg, where he had conducted *Rienzi,* included Beethoven's *Pastoral* Symphony. It made as little impact as the first performance of his *Faust* Overture in the summer of 1844. The spectacle he staged in honor of the king's return from a visit to England was on quite a different scale. For this he had composed the words and music of an anthem entitled *Salute to the Beloved Friedrich August from His Faithful Subjects.*

Wagner had, in fact, arranged the welcoming ceremony without consulting Lüttichau, much to the latter's initial annoyance. On August 12, 1844, under the joint direction of Reissiger and Wagner, a hired steamer transported 200 singers and 106 instrumentalists to Pillnitz, near Dresden, where the ceremony unfolded on the grounds of the king's country seat. Reissiger beat time while Wagner took his place among the tenors. Everything went off splendidly. Friedrich August requested an encore of the last three verses, whereupon Wagner devised a "concerted evolution" which was executed with such "remarkable success" that he preened himself on it for years to come. He had the entire piece repeated, but only one verse was sung in the original crescent formation. The singers and instrumentalists then filed off in such a way that the strains of the anthem slowly faded upon the royal ear. "Thanks to my unparalleled efforts and omnipresent help, this withdrawal proceeded so smoothly that not the slightest faltering occurred in rhythm or delivery, and the whole thing could be accounted an assiduously rehearsed theatrical maneuver."

The showman in Wagner devised another theatrical maneuver of note on the occasion of Weber's reinterment in December 1844. The plan to transfer Weber's remains from St. Mary's Chapel in Moorfields, London, and rebury them in Dresden had at first met with strong official opposition. "Suppose Reissiger went off to take the waters and died at Karlsbad," was Lüttichau's unsympathetic comment. "We should then have to bear his body back in state to Dresden." Weber's homecoming, when it finally took place, was not the work of Wagner alone. He had inherited the project from Professor Löwe and enlisted the aid of the committee whose efforts took so long to bear fruit. Contemporary reports of the obsequies refer to him only as the composer of the funeral march and the male-voice chorus *Hebt an den Sang*. The funeral march was based on two motifs from *Euryanthe* and scored for eighty wind instruments. During rehearsals at the theater, Wagner tried it out for effect by clearing the stage and getting the musicians to circle him while playing. The male-voice chorus, which was written for the burial itself, acquired tonal coloring from its proximity in time to *Tannhäuser*, then nearing completion.

Weber's reinterment was delayed because the vessel carrying his coffin from Hamburg had become icebound on the Elbe at Wittenberg. Unable to continue their journey by river, Weber's ashes reached Dresden by train on the evening of December 14. Led by a thousand torchbearers, the cortege proceeded from the station to the chapel of the Catholic cemetery to the strains of Wagner's musical tribute. Here the coffin was greeted by Wilhelmine Schröder-Devrient, who emerged from the chapel bearing a laurel wreath. As she did so, Wagner recalled long afterward, the two of them—a man and a woman who had never quite been lovers— regarded one another "strangely." First to speak at the vault next morning was Director Schulz, the committee chairman. Then came Wagner, who was so carried away by the sound of his own voice that he seemed not only to hear but actually to see himself addressing the silent multitude. "I felt not the least bit nervous or distraught," he tells us in *My Life*, "except that, after one appropriate passage, there followed so disproportionately long a pause that those who saw me standing there with pensive, absent gaze did not know what to make of me. Only my own protracted silence and the breathless hush around me reminded me that I was there to speak, not listen. I promptly resumed my address and completed it with such fluency that the celebrated actor Emil Devrient pronounced himself remarkably impressed, not only as one who had attended a most moving funeral ceremony, but as a dramatic orator [in his own right]."

Theatrical maneuvers and self-dramatization. . . . Whenever Wagner was not harnessed to the mighty chariot of his music dramas, these subsidiary activities provided him with a safety valve, an outlet for excess pressure. They compensated him for an infinitely laborious creative process which, though its preliminary stages were dreamlike and almost unconscious, culminated in long hours of intense physical effort devoted to ruling manuscript paper, orchestrating, and copying out parts—a form of drudgery unenlivened over the years by any thrill of satisfaction.

Wagner expended vast amounts of energy on secondary spheres of activity, one of them being the mechanics of the theater. Discounting Schütz, no musician or composer before him had put so much effort into organization and presentation. While visiting Dresden for the production of his opera *La Vestale*, Spontini, who was overwhelmed by Wagner's professionalism, declared that he admired him so greatly that he would do his best to preserve him from the misfortune of pursuing his career as a dramatic composer. . . .

Productivity

On July 3, 1845, Wagner set off with his wife, dog, and parrot for a five-week holiday at Marienbad—his first since completing *Tannhäuser*—where he stayed at the Pension zum Kleeblatt. For reading matter, he took with him Georg Gervinus's history of German literature, Simrock and San Marte's translations of Wolfram von Eschenbach's epic poems *Parzival* and *Titurel*, and the anonymous *Lohengrin* epic with an introduction by Joseph von Görres. Vague preliminary plans for a Lohengrin drama had been germinating inside him since Paris, and at Teplitz, even before he wrote the music for *Tannhäuser*, Grimm's tales had reintroduced him to the Swan Knight theme, with its haunting vision of a silvery figure superimposed on the azure waves of a sea or river. Here in Bohemia, he was again overcome by a creative unease that nullified the beneficial effects of baths and glasses of mineral water. The doctors urgently advised him to abstain from physical and mental exertion. In avoiding the emotional stresses of the Lohengrin tragedy, he cured one evil with another: On one of his solitary walks, he mapped out the plot of *Die Meistersinger*.

He had come across pointers in this direction ever since his boyhood, even in Uncle Adolf's library. Now, in Gervinus, he encountered the story of Hans Sachs and the Marker. He was so tickled by the notion of reversing their roles and getting Sachs to penalize the Marker's infelicitous serenade by raising a chalk-marked shoe that he visualized the entire scene down to a concluding brawl modeled on the Nürnberg street fight that he himself had witnessed after impersonating Lablache for the benefit of Lauermann, the would-be singer. With this as a basis, he quickly devised the foregoing clash between the young Knight and the Marker (who had yet to be named). His lengthy prose sketch for all three acts of *Die Meistersinger* was written without interruption. The original draft is reproduced in his collected works, complete with a penciled addition that presumably dates from the Zurich period, when hopes of German unity had been dashed. These lines, which form the nub of Sachs's concluding address, read: *"Zerging' das heil'ge römische Reich in Dunst, uns bliebe doch die heil'ge deutsche Kunst"* ["Were the Holy Roman Empire to dissolve into mist, we still should have holy German art"]. This wording was retained in the Vienna drafts of 1861.

The framework was already complete, and it is surprising to observe how this German "national opera" evolved from a barbaric nucleus of aggression, violence, and "mob brutality" (Wapnewski). In its original form, the draft was a travesty of the *Tannhäuser* theme—Sachs versus the hidebound mastersingers, Tannhäuser versus the landgrave's hidebound entourage—and was intended as such. Having finished it, Wagner added the date, July 16, 1845, shelved it, and resumed his mineral baths.

But rest cures were not for him. Swiftly deserting the tub for the writing table, he began to map out most of the scenes for *Lohengrin.* He completed the prose version on August 3, after vainly trying to ward off one theme with another.

Taut as a bowstring with creative exhilaration, he was so intensely aware of his own vitality that he felt like a starving man confronted by a groaning board. According to the psychologist Otto Rank, he was merely fleeing from an unsatisfactory marriage into pubertal fantasies. Though poorly expressed, this contains an element of truth. Swamped by everyday routine, his marital relationship had cooled. Minna consoled herself with mineral baths while her husband poured out his need for love into a stage world where those impelled by ardent desire come close to self-destruction. Lohengrin glows with passion, Elsa trembles: the unattainable as a parable. Immersed in his bath, Wagner had quickly to forget the medieval poem before being able to regard these radiant apparitions as personified desires—Lohengrin "as typifying the true and only tragic subject, the tragedy of the vital element in modern times," as he puts it in *A Communication to My Friends*. A singular guise indeed for modernity! In fact, this opera deals with something that *does not work*—with preordained failure—and it is possible to see through the specious nature of Wagner's subsequent remarks: the projection of subjective states of mind construed as the vital element in modern times. At a distance of a few years, he could find no other way of accounting for the consuming passion that drove him to write *Lohengrin*. Lohengrin, he was to state in another context, was motivated by the quest for a woman to *believe* in him—a yearning to love and be loved, "to be understood through love."

Lohengrin is an artist's drama—art veiled in splendor, magic, and the miraculous—and its hero one who aspires to universal love and understanding in the guise of a woman. He is a third seeker after redemption in line of descent from Vanderdecken and Heinrich Tannhäuser. As for Elsa, she is sister to Senta in the impassioned defiance with which she conjures up something that at first exists purely in her imagination.

Where the music was concerned, Wagner was wise enough to let inspiration mature. In the early summer of 1846, when he had generously been granted another three months' leave of absence, he took himself off to Gross-Graupa, a village between Pillnitz and Pirna. It was here, between May 15 and July 30, that he roughly sketched the music for the entire work. Kietz and Bülow, who visited him at his rented house on the outskirts of the village, observed no signs of this gradual and tenuous creative process.

Back in Dresden, he began the orchestral sketch on September 9, starting at the end. By virtue of the motif that occurs in Lohengrin's account of the Grail, the third act proved to be the germ of the entire work. Such a method presupposes a high degree of structural awareness because elements of the whole must be present in its parts. Even if we concur with only half of Alfred Lorenz's findings, *Lohengrin*'s periodic formal arrangement seems positively constructivist.

But that was not its truly novel feature. When Thomas Mann rhapsodized about the "silver-blue beauty" of *Lohengrin*'s music, he was unwittingly defining the transition from *Tannhäuser* to *Lohengrin:* the discovery of *color*. In the latter work, Wagner explored the coloristic dimension of music and instrumentation.

He took a long time to complete the score, and even his work on the third act—the first to be tackled—was interrupted several times. Despite his preoccupation with death, Wagner never rushed things. His approach to composition took its deliberate tempo from a century accustomed to thinking on a grand scale. He banked on growing old and knew what the future could yet bring forth. "You dare to bark at the great Wagner?" he once demanded of Peps, his dog.

On October 31, 1846, he drafted a three-page scenario for a Barbarossa drama to be entitled *Friedrich I*. Although he temporarily abandoned it on the grounds that verse was "no use" in German, the subject continued to exercise his mind.

His labors on the orchestral sketch for *Lohengrin* during the summer of 1847 kept him in the highest of spirits. Friends visiting him in the garden behind the Palais Marcolini would sometimes find him perched, schoolboy fashion, in the fork of a tree. For the balcony scene in act 2, he now produced another of those psychologically telling passages for strings that prove him to be a master of musical delicacy. It was one of his great moments.

On January 1, 1848, he embarked on the full score of his last Dresden work. Then, on January 9, his mother died. After standing over Johanna's grave on an icy winter's morning, he had a long talk with Heinrich Laube, who had been very fond of her. They both deplored the failure of every noble endeavor to prevail over "the modern tendency to lapse utterly into worthlessness," though each man probably had his own idea of what this meant.

With his mother laid to rest, Wagner felt as if the last inward link between himself and his family—himself and Saxony—had been severed.

Monarchy or Republic?

In February 1848, Louis Philippe's "citizen monarchy" was overthrown and a republic proclaimed in Paris. The news was broken to Wagner during a rehearsal of Flotow's *Martha* by a triumphant August Röckel. Wagner himself remained skeptical. Although he regarded the revolution as a necessary "destruction of the physical shape of the present," he was slightly taken aback by it.

In Saxony, it was Leipzig that seized the initiative. On February 29 a citizens' assembly convened under the leadership of Robert Blum and Arnold Ruge and resolved to send a deputation to the king. This deputation was brusquely dismissed by the monarch on March 2, and feelings ran higher still. Although Interior Minister von Falkenstein resigned, Friedrich August stubbornly refused to accept that only concessions could avert the danger of a popular uprising. Delegates from six towns—Zwickau, Werdau, Crimmitschau, Meerane, Glauchau, and Waldenburg—were fobbed off with a promise to recall the Landtag, or representative assembly. Meantime, said the king, he could not bandy words with them. His parting shot: "I have nothing further to say to you save 'Farewell.' "

The Dresden authorities remained undismayed until it was announced, first by Leipzig and then by other cities, that their citizens were planning a concerted march on the capital. Ex-Minister von Lindenau persuaded the king to grant him an audience and explained how matters really stood. Friedrich August II, a downy-cheeked monarch who styled himself "the Beloved," was shocked to hear that Prussian troops had massed outside Leipzig on the orders of his cabinet but without his knowledge. This was such a blow to his pride that he curtly dismissed his cabinet on March 13 and appointed a new one composed of members of the opposition, with Baron von der Pfordten in charge of foreign, educational, and religious affairs. Government guarantees included the lifting of censorship, the introduction of trial by jury, electoral reform, and the abolition of feudal rights and tithes.

Having accomplished its semirevolution, Saxony cheered Friedrich August to the echo. On the night of March 13, Dresden was a sea of lights, and the king was applauded on sight. Coattails flapping, Wagner threaded his way excitedly through the crowds and stationed himself "wherever an especially hearty cheer might rejoice and appease the monarch's heart."

Röckel's verdict on these events was less enthusiastic. "The real changes effected by the March days in Saxony were confined to the removal of censorship and a change of ministers. As to the latter,

its results could not have been more advantageous to the Court."
No words need be wasted on Herr von der Pfordten, wrote
Röckel. He had later practiced in Bavaria what he tried to institute
in Saxony. "But let this be affirmed to the people of Saxony: Herr
v. d. Pfordten had deceived no one, least of all the democrats.
Universal mistrust pursued him from the first day on."

Bred by this mistrust, political associations sprang up throughout the country. Even while Saxony was celebrating its supposed
achievements, word came from Vienna that Metternich had been
overthrown. A few days later, on March 18, barricades went up in
Berlin and Frankfurt, and fierce fighting broke out. On March 31,
a German "preparliament" resolved to convene a national assembly invested with legislative powers.

Though not unconscious of these developments, Wagner was
preoccupied with his *Lohengrin* score, which he completed on
April 28. During the same March days that divided the century—
or at least its "preimperial" period—into two distinct parts, he
received some visitors of note. One was Franz Liszt, then in the
process of winding up his brilliant career as a virtuoso, who had
stopped off at Dresden on the way from Vienna to Weimar. The
other was Jessie, née Taylor, the wife of a Bordeaux wine merchant named Eugène Laussot. With Liszt, Wagner formed a lifelong, though sometimes turbulent, friendship. In twenty-year-old
Jessie Laussot, a shy but ardent admirer of his music, he acquired
his first real "Wagnerite" apart from Alwine Frommann of Berlin.
Jessie called on him escorted by Karl Ritter, an even younger
admirer. From then on, Ritter often visited Wagner in the company of Hans von Bülow, who wore the black, red, and gold
cockade of revolutionary Germany on his hat.

Revolutionary as his own inclinations were, Wagner's predomi-
nant concern was that the new movement had announced cuts in
the civil list and threatened to deprive the Court Theater of its
subsidies. In his political scheme of things, intellectuals were assigned the role of national redeemers. How, in that case, could he
accept that they, of all people, should suffer in consequence of the
latest developments? By May 11, he had completed a forty-page
"Plan for the Organization of a German National Theater in the
Kingdom of Saxony." This he submitted directly to the cabinet
office with a covering letter requesting an interview with ministers
Oberländer and Pfordten. Though revolutionary in tone, his plan

disarmingly claimed to be inspired by fear of revolution. In addition to proposing that the theater and orchestra be institutionally democratized, Wagner demanded that their financial position be guaranteed. The main points in his memorandum were as follows: that an association of dramatists and composers be formed; that the theatrical director be elected by serving personnel and by all the members of the aforesaid association; that a drama school and choral institute be established; that the orchestra be expanded and salaries increased; that an administrative council be appointed from among members of the orchestra; and finally, though Wagner deleted this passage when the document was reproduced in his collected writings, that authority be concentrated in the hands of a single kapellmeister who would occupy the post of intendant—himself, of course. "That's the crux of the matter!" Reissiger wrote in the margin of the document, when the cabinet referred it for appraisal to the existing board of management. Needless to say, the scheme was stillborn.

But the country was concerned with matters other than theatrical reform. Some idea of prevailing conditions may be gained from the newspapers of the day, which advised their readers to eat stale bread (because it is more filling) and published recipes for cockchafer soup, this being praised by a senior government physician for its highly nutritious properties.* So much for the social benefits conferred by the thirty-three years of peace that had elapsed since 1815.

On May 18, 1848, the German National Assembly convened at Frankfurt. Now that he had finished scoring *Lohengrin,* Wagner could not resist putting his oar in. On May 19, he wrote to the Saxon deputy Professor Wigard urging that the Frankfurt assembly resolve as follows: (1) that the existing German Bundestag be dissolved and the National Assembly become the sole constituent authority; (2) the immediate arming of a citizens' militia; (3) a defensive and offensive alliance with France; and (4) a measure of territorial reform under which German states with fewer than three and more than six million inhabitants would no longer be permitted. "The fate of the monarchs will depend upon their conduct: If they begin by being hostile and refractory, they must be arraigned, one and all, and the charge against them proved on entirely historical grounds." Only when these questions had been settled, said Wagner, could the assembly's constitutional labors commence. "Parliament must first completely revolutionize the individual states," he added. If Wigard could assent to this and steer the assembly in the requisite direction, it would redound to his everlasting credit. "Nothing less dramatic will attain our goal!"

Meanwhile, on May 15, a second revolt had broken out in Vienna. This compelled the authorities to summon a constituent assembly, and a third revolt on May 26 prevented the forces of reaction from dissolving the democratic committee. Wagner thereupon gave vent to "Greeting from Saxony to the Viennese," a poem he imprudently published in the *Allgemeine Österreichische Zeitung* on June 1. In fourteen stanzas, each of eight lines, he inveighed against overfed property owners who paid policemen and soldiers to guard their possessions, commended "the heroes of Vienna" for having "drawn the sword," and urged his fellow countrymen to follow suit. Before March of that year, the public expression of such sentiments would have cost him his job, if not his freedom.

Monarchy or republic? Now that this question was being more or less openly debated at Dresden, Wagner felt impelled to join in. Two major political associations had been formed. The Deutscher Verein, whose members included Eduard Devrient and Ernst Rietschel, advocated a constitutional monarchy. The Vaterlands-Verein, a republican pressure group, was composed of revolutionaries such as Röckel, Trützschler, Tzschirner, and Todt. Adolf von Trützschler, a Dresden lawyer, was one of its most radical representatives. Once, when Wagner made some allusion to the state, Trützschler retorted that he recognized no state, only society. Wagner, who took note of this remark, was later to reproach the Social Democrats on the grounds that all they, too, wanted was to gain control of the state.*

He plumped for the Vaterlands-Verein but contrived to be a republican without sawing through the royal branch on which his livelihood depended. In quest of a compromise, he wrote an article entitled "How Do Republican Endeavors Relate to Monarchy?" This piece, which approximated to Proudhon and unwittingly developed some of the socialist ideas expounded in 1843 by Wilhelm Weitling's *Evangelium des armen Sünders* [*Gospel of the Poor Sinner*], delighted Röckel so much that he persuaded Wagner to read it aloud at a meeting of the Vaterlands-Verein on June 14.

Wagner's address, which followed two insignificant tirades by other local speakers, lasted some twenty-five minutes. A distillation of all the ideas that had so far influenced him, it strongly dissociated itself from "that most fatuous and senseless doctrine" —communism—and from "the equal distribution of property and earnings." Although the Communist Manifesto had been published in February, it is doubtful whether Wagner had read it. He concealed the political gist of his speech behind an apologia for the royal house and a series of proposals for reform. These consisted in demands for "a people's militia destructive of all class distinctions" and for the abolition of the upper house and aristocratic privilege, the king himself being cast in the role of First Republican—an emancipated *primus inter liberos.* Wagner went on to inquire "the reason for all wretchedness in our present condition." This he identified as servitude to money, which "deformed the fine free will of man" into the most revolting passion—into avarice and usury. Happiness would be achieved only when there was a full exchange of abilities among as many employed persons as the land would support. "We shall recognize that human society is sustained, not by the supposed operation of money, but by that of its members." Somewhat vaguely, Wagner proclaimed that God would "enlighten us on the proper law whereby this principle shall be introduced into our lives. . . . Like an evil nightmare, this demonic concept of money shall leave us, with all its frightful retinue of overt and covert usury, bond-swindling, interest, and bankers' speculations. That will mean the full emancipation of the human race and the fulfillment of pure Christian doctrine." The consequence of thirty-three years of unbroken peace had been ruin and destitution, and unless the authorities acknowledged the rights bestowed on man by God, they would indeed hear the savage paean of communism at its crudest. "You think I threaten?" Wagner concluded. "No, I warn!"

This speech was reproduced by the *Dresdner Anzeiger,* unsigned but attributed to "A Member of the Vaterlands-Verein." All hell broke loose, and Eduard Devrient noted in his diary: "Thus does such a dreamer destroy his career!" Wagner had stirred up a hornets' nest. The monarchists took issue with his republican language, the republicans with his verbal obeisance to monarchy, the Communal Guard with his assertion that Saxony had "a standing army and a recumbent militia." Wagner's gibe, which spread like wildfire and was to demonstrate its accuracy in May 1849, caused so much gratuitous resentment that he was forced to apologize. As for those close to the throne, all they gathered was that he favored stripping aristocrats of their power and considered court toadies the root of all evil.

Advertisements were inserted in the *Dresdner Anzeiger* and other newspapers calling on Wagner to state his position in regard to the "anonymous" transcript. Readers' letters poured in, together with satirical poems accusing him of playing Faust or calling him "the little tin king." Perhaps the mildest rebuke of all appeared in the *Dresdner Journal* on June 17: "This fine vision, which reminds one of Lamartine, and sometimes, too, of Lamennais, is richer in problems than in solutions of the same." Röckel's idols stood revealed.

Having brought down this storm on his head—this crowning addition to the burdens of his existence in Dresden—Wagner stayed at home and suffered. Officious members of the orchestra went to Lüttichau and petitioned for his dismissal. Their request was opposed by Theodor Uhlig, a young violinist whose friendship with Wagner was of recent date but no less warm for that.

On June 18, Wagner tried to fend off disaster by writing Lüttichau a letter of self-justification in which he stated that his aim had been to dissuade the progressive party from violent excesses by dint of reasoned, moderate argument. The establishment of a republic need not entail the abolition of the monarchy. On the contrary, never had the Vaterlands-Verein heard a more wholehearted tribute to the king nor hailed one more fervently, so any offense caused by his initiative was based on a misapprehension. Pleading an incipient attack of gastric trouble, Wagner prefaced his letter by requesting two weeks' leave of absence.

Ever friendly, Eduard Devrient had drawn steadily closer to Wagner now that he was concentrating on his history of the German theater. Wagner urgently besought him to plead his case at court and consulted him several times before sending the king a personal letter dated June 21, 1848. This missive, which has only recently come to light, echoes his remarks to the Vaterlands-Verein, casts him in the role of a "mediator" between monarchists and republicans, and mingles self-defense with well-meant warnings. Despite its conventionally deferential tone, it cannot be interpreted as a piece of fawning opportunism. Wagner owned to a sense of "terrible anxiety" at the prospect of what might happen in the very near future. If he had given offense and done wrong, only the king could pronounce on the purity of his motives. He therefore awaited the royal verdict without fear.

Because Friedrich August preferred to play the incident down, there was no immediate response. "The king is saying nothing about the matter," Devrient noted in his diary, "—ignoring it, perhaps." Lüttichau dismissed a secret deputation from one section of the orchestra calling for Wagner's removal, whereupon Wagner thanked him effusively, even to the extent of addressing him as "Admirable Man" instead of "Excellency." He was being precipitate, because the intendant was clearly acting on instructions from the king, not from personal conviction.

But Wagner's political passions had far from subsided. He continued to debate matters vehemently with Eduard Devrient, who now counseled moderation. "He wants to destroy in order to rebuild," Devrient noted resignedly on June 21. "I want to transform the existing into a new world."

Wagner was preparing to make his debut on a stage that transcended the confines of the Court Theater, Dresden.

The Revolutionary

N ow thirty-five, Richard Wagner could no longer claim to be a
youthful hothead. He was a mature man in his middle years,
and fully responsible for all he said and did. Whatever his aims and
incentives, therefore, his part in the revolutionary events of
1848–49 was deliberate. He not only sought to minimize that involvement in *My Life* and elsewhere but muddled up the principal
features of his last year at Dresden so thoroughly that we must
reconstruct the chronology of the ensuing months. Only thus can
their seeming inconsistencies, their erratic twists and turns, be
translated into a coherent succession of personal, professional, and
political developments.

Having extended his sick leave, Wagner set off for Vienna early
in July 1848. The journey there was more in the nature of an escape
and not, as he claimed in his leave-of-absence request to Lüttichau,
an aid to mental and physical refreshment. Revolutionary Austria,
whose emperor had fled to Innsbruck, seemed to offer scope for his
plans for theater reform and prospects of fresh employment if his
existing livelihood were destroyed. Had either of these promises
been fulfilled, he would gladly have burned his bridges at once.

Flushed with wine and victory, and regardless of the fact that
the royalists' hold was far from broken, the Viennese were indulg-
ing in a midsummer's orgy of republicanism. The streets were
decked with flags and thronged with noisy, arguing, singing

crowds. Vienna, with its half-million inhabitants, impressed Wagner as a lovelier, livelier version of Paris. He took heart and trotted out his plans for a national theater based on the Dresden model.

Among the first people he approached were the dramatist Eduard von Bauernfeld and his friend Dr. Ludwig Frankl, editor of the *Sonntagsblätter*. He received a polite hearing and was provided with further introductions, but no one seemed to think the time had come to do anything definite. The *Abendzeitung* of July 20 reported Wagner's presence in Vienna and added: "He has devised an ingenious program for reorganizing the Viennese theater along the lines of a national institute and proposes to submit it to the Ministry of Education, which should then, in his opinion, refer it for appraisal to a committee of writers and musicians. Why, is there nothing to reorganize in Dresden?"

One of the suggested consultants was the dramatist Franz Grillparzer, who surprised Wagner by receiving him in his civil servant's uniform. Although he made a "very gentle impression," Grillparzer seemed disconcerted by his visitor's proposals. "While in Vienna," quipped the *Wiener Musikpresse*, "Kapellmeister Richard Wagner is composing a new opera: 'The Vermilion Republic.' "

Wagner also tried out his ideas on Professor Josef Fischhof of the Vienna Conservatoire, who showed him the manuscript of Beethoven's C Minor Piano Sonata, Opus III, but was—according to Hanslick—"not a little surprised to hear nothing from Wagner but political speeches, and nary a word about music." Fischhof introduced him to several representatives of the extreme left. These included the writer Friedrich Uhl, who took him along to a political club "of the most progressive tendencies," and Dr. Alfred Becher, a journalist and lawyer who was summarily shot by a firing squad on October 31, 1848, after counterrevolutionary forces had triumphed under the command of Field Marshal Prince zu Windischgraetz. Eduard Hanslick, too, spent an evening with Wagner at an open-air restaurant beside the Danube. "Wagner was all politics," Hanslick recalled. "He expected the victory of the Revolution to bring about a complete rebirth of art, society, and religion—a new theater and a new kind of music." Wagner himself hastened to assure everyone of his readiness to accept a post in the projected national institute provided he could sever his Dresden connections. Nobody took him up on his offer, however, and his plans for Vienna petered out even before the political tide turned.

Wagner's trip to Vienna was more than a failure. It exposed a wound that might otherwise have festered unseen: His marriage to Minna was on the verge of collapse. Minna must have reproached him bitterly for neglecting his duties and engaging in dangerous political activities. Even before leaving Vienna, he enlisted Devrient's services as a go-between and sent him a letter for delivery to Minna. This urged her to confide in "the excellent man" and proposed that they should both be guided by his advice. Wagner's covering letter to Devrient was not without discernment or remorse. For twelve long years, he wrote, his faithful spouse had borne the brunt of his misfortunes with patience, fortitude, and pride. However, she derived scant pleasure from his "few strokes of good fortune" because, knowing his true nature, she had never been able to trust him completely. Now she was threatening to succumb, and the fault was his for having too often disregarded her share in his fate. For his own part, he would not mind making a fresh start. Were he alone, he would proclaim himself an outlaw and fly wherever the wind carried him, but there was his wife to consider. "I am overcome by the most profound compassion for mankind when I reflect on that woman's devoted, sorrowful life." So what was he to do? Devrient did not know either. After paying Minna an abortive visit on July 21, he noted in his diary: "A volatile eccentric who always begins by aggravating matters and then, when it is too late, appeals for help."

Wagner returned to Dresden via Prague on July 22, having completed the last stage of the journey by river steamer. He discussed Viennese politics and his own bleak financial position with Devrient. On July 25, the latter called at the Wagners' home and made another attempt to reconcile them. "The woman is not so much unhappy as annoyed with him," he recorded in his diary, "and seems, as matters now stand, to be thinking more of herself than of him."

She had good reason, knowing that their social standing was in jeopardy, and that her husband was doing nothing to secure his livelihood.

Wagner failed to sell the rights of his three operas to Franz Liszt, who was too shrewd a judge of human nature to engage in business transactions between friends. During a brief visit to Weimar at the end of August, Wagner learned that the real reason for Liszt's surprising decision to settle down there was Princess Carolyne von Sayn-Wittgenstein, with whom he had formed a liaison in the preceding year.

Wagner now paid no heed to anything at Dresden. Instead of attending board meetings, which irked him, he devoted himself to private study. Friends spoke of his "Friedrichstadt exile."

He resumed work on his sketch for a five-act play about Friedrich Barbarossa.* Dated October 31, 1846, this brief outline had never entirely deserted his thoughts because of its political associations. He developed it but felt strangely averse to the thought of marshaling a series of historical facts. Then he was struck by a parallel between Friedrich I and the Nibelung myth. Was not the Hohenstaufen monarch a historical reincarnation of the heathen Siegfried? Had Wagner now applied himself to this historical hero, his play would have become a vast congeries of incidents. Why, on the other hand, did he not revert directly to the "youthfully handsome" figure that had come to him out of the mists of German legend? It was because the call of history was too pressing, and because Friedrich Barbarossa, too, was a partial embodiment of national aspirations, that he boldly turned back the page from history to myth and wrote *Die Wibelungen: Weltgeschichte aus der Saga* [*The Wibelungs: History out of Saga*]. By means of an etymological tightrope act, this essayistic fantasy transformed the Hohenstaufens into descendants of the Nibelungs. Wagner rejected the conventional theory that the Wibelings, or supporters of the Hohenstaufens, had taken their name from Waiblingen, Friedrich Barbarossa's Swabian birthplace, and identified them with the legendary Nibelungs. One little substitution, and Frederick Redbeard became a descendant of the divinely sired Siegfried, whose line had been extinguished by the end of the Hohenstaufens. Just as myth passed down into history, so had the Nibelungs' "ideal Hoard" become transmuted into that source of all social ills, "heritable property." The royal line was extinct, the Hoard degraded into filthy lucre, the people deprived of everything but song. Wagner had at last succeeded in reconciling socialism with the German sagas!

With the cultural eclecticism that made him an undoubted precursor of Oswald Spengler, he now proceeded to identify the Hoard with the Grail and declared that the "spiritual fusion of the Hoard with the Grail" had been consummated in the German mind. This not only linked the denouements of his redemption dramas (the story of Lohengrin and the Grail was still fresh in his memory) but introduced the most suspect element into his artistic cosmos: the savior-figure who insinuated himself into Wagner's works and staked their claim to conjure up visions of national recovery, regeneration, or whatever. Among Wagner's literary remains are some "concluding words" on his *Wibelungen* fantasy that seem to confirm this: "When shall you return, Friedrich, glorious Siegfried, and smite the evil, gnawing dragon of mankind?" What a hodgepodge of myth and history, art and politics, opera and revolution! (Rienzi, too, aspired to return.) If we relate this imploring cry to all Wagner's writings in the next few years, how are we to identify the dragon in every case? Quite clearly, any work that assumes a revelatory character by means of an artistic detour threatens to become ambivalent, suspect, and open to abuse.

But something altogether different was deleted from the first printing, as it was from Wagner's collected writings. A manuscript copy by Hans von Bülow, preserved in the National Archive at Bayreuth, contains a still-unpublished passage in which Wagner carried the etymological joke underlying his whole *Wibelungen* essay to crazy extremes. He related the name "Nibelungen" to German and Frankish forenames, allowed his imagination to roam via Gaul to Spain and Italy, and finally arrived at "Nabelon," alias Napoleon! What, he asked, if a last Nibelung had come from the south in quest of world dominion? "All the world's Welfs joined forces against him. . . ."

Wagner's *Wibelungen* essay was the root from which *Der Ring des Nibelungen* sprang. Only days or weeks after crossing this pons asinorum, he wrote *"Der Nibelungenmythus, als Entwurf zu einem Drama"* ["The Nibelung Myth as a Sketch for a Drama"], a complete and well-constructed plot for the entire *Ring* from which, so we are often told, only the downfall of the gods is missing.

But is it really? This spare and economical version of the *Ring* story states that Wotan himself cannot right the wrong that lurks in the depths of Nibelheim "without committing a fresh injustice: Only a free will, itself independent of the gods and capable of shouldering all guilt and atoning, can break the spell. . . ." The gods discern this capacity for free will in a man whom they rear "for an exalted destiny, that of discharging their own guilt, and their aim would be accomplished if they *destroyed themselves* by creating this man"; in other words, renounced their influence over a human mind. Why, then, should the burning of Valhalla have stemmed from another philosophical insight of later date? The gods' experiment fails and everything starts afresh. But since the gods are only figments of the human imagination—Wagner knew Feuerbach without as yet having read him--they have to disappear. The whole thing is merely a parable. Wagner's earliest plot for the *Ring* embodied the self-destruction of the gods. If he left them alive in the poem *Siegfrieds Tod*, it was for an obvious dramatic reason: They did not appear at all and had yet to disclose their guilt, the origins of which remained obscure. This, after all, was opera.

Wagner completed his prose version of the *Ring* plot, originally entitled *Die Nibelungensaga*, on October 4, 1848. This means that during the few weeks following his visit to Vienna, in August and September, 1848, he formed a complete mental picture of the towering edifice whose capstone—the last note of the *Ring* score— would not be laid until 1874. The plot was already what the *Ring* became, "a sociocritical picture of the age with a mythological structure" (Hans Mayer), and no one who has read *Die Wibelungen* would dispute that assertion.

* * *

The modern, sociocritical aspect of Wagner's essays was substantially influenced by his talks with August Röckel during the weeks he devoted to them. Röckel, who was becoming more and more galvanized by revolutionary ideas, had entered politics reluctantly but now began to agitate in earnest. Discussions with army officers such as Hermann Müller and Leo von Zychlinsky, some of them held in Wagner's garden behind the Palais Marcolini, prompted him to write a pamphlet setting forth the political significance of national militias and outlining plans for a Swiss-style military system to be adopted by all the German states. This he submitted to the Vaterlands-Verein, which printed and distributed it among the delegates to the Frankfurt assembly. Its publication resulted in Röckel's summary dismissal from the royal service.

To support his family, however inadequately, Röckel resorted to publishing. His *Volksblätter*, a weekly, first appeared on August 26, though nearly half its issues were confiscated on the spot. Röckel persuaded Wagner to write for this informative and well-edited periodical, but Wagner's actual contributions were less important than the fact that he humanely forbore to desert a friend who had fallen on hard times and compromised himself so deeply.

Pressure of work restricted the two men's intercourse to occasional walks. *My Life* presents a detailed account of the sort of topics they discussed on these outings. "He [Röckel] had already formed an extremely coherent picture of how to effect a complete transformation in the status of the middle class, as we commonly perceive it, by deducing the consequences of a total change in its social basis." Röckel presented his concept of labor in a form that Wagner later adopted himself, almost word for word. He predicted that all would merge themselves into a creative state in which work would cease to be a burden and become merely an occupation, because "each would participate in the requisite labor according to his strength and capacities." This he demonstrated by pointing out that "a field laboriously tilled by a single peasant was infinitely less productive than one cultivated by several persons along horticultural lines."

Heartened by these utopian excursions, which never failed to fill him with enthusiasm, Wagner was not too put out when subjected to another professional humiliation. On September 22, 1848, Dresden's royal orchestra celebrated its tercentenary. Reissiger was invested with the Knight's Cross of the Royal Saxon Civil Order of Merit; Wagner got nothing. At the gala concert, the new knight was deluged with applause while Wagner's fragment from *Lohengrin*, the finale of act 1, found little favor. He spent the whole day with the guest of honor, Heinrich Marschner, and the banquet that evening was also attended by Wilhelmine Schröder-Devrient. Wagner's toast to the royal orchestra, which made no mention of its history or of Heinrich Schütz, looked to the future and contained a conciliatory word for all, but he was already brooding on new prophecies of doom.

On October 15, Röckel's *Volksblätter* printed the first anonymous article that can be ascribed with certainty to Wagner, "Germany and Its Princes." This ceased to draw a distinction between the House of Wettin, Saxony's rulers, and other, more obnoxious, German dynasties. Why, it demanded, should penury, hardship, misery, and despair exist in the midst of plenty? Hadn't Saxony, a wealthy country inhabited by hardworking people, deserved a better fate? The fault lay not with Nature, but with the fact that men's labor did not receive its due reward. Six months had passed since the monarchs gave their pledges, and nothing had changed. Privilege still reigned supreme. "Awake," the article warned, "the eleventh hour has struck! Abandon your impotent, futile resistance. It can only visit *suffering* upon us and *ruin* upon *you.*" This was unvarnished language indeed, but no immediate inquiry was launched into the authorship of such predictions.

October 31 brought word of Vienna's bombardment, followed by the horrific news that the revolutionaries Blum, Becher, Jellinek, and Messenhauer had been murdered. Robert Blum came from Saxony. Had the Habsburgs shot a Saxon revolutionary as a favor to the Wettins? At Dresden, his funeral procession was joined by the liberal ministers of the March cabinet, paralyzed with fear of the masses and hamstrung by the king's aloof attitude.

During November, sanguinary clashes occurred in Berlin before the Prussian National Assembly was finally dissolved by Friedrich Wilhelm IV, who had not forgotten his humiliation that spring. Röckel thereupon wrote his "Open Letter to the Soldiers," a warning to the Prussian military to stand aside if matters came to a head in Saxony. He was promptly arrested but released three days later, bail of 10,000 thalers—a very substantial sum having been deposited through his lawyer by an anonymous landowner.

It was around this time that Wagner learned of the Dresden management's decision not to stage *Lohengrin* after all. Orders for the scenery had been canceled. Wagner's efforts to secure a revival of *Der Fliegende Holländer* had long since failed, and now came this fresh defeat: Dresden's resident composer could no longer expect to be premiered on his own home ground. Was Lüttichau simply getting back at him, as Wagner surmised, or were the authorities scared by the thought of Saxons and Thuringians taking up arms —at this of all times—in act 1? "Now is it time to guard the kingdom's honor. In east or west, the same be true for all. Let German lands array their martial hosts!" It must have appalled them to imagine King Heinrich hurling these words across the footlights when, in the streets outside, agitators were calling for a national militia. *Lohengrin*'s dramatic fervor was open to a different interpretation then than it has been in our own century.

After noting that the scenery for *Lohengrin* had been canceled, Wagner made the following pregnant entry in his "Annals," the

jottings he kept as a basis for his future autobiography: "At home
—break decided on."

* * *

Work on the *Nibelungen* drama had never been entirely discontinued during this period. The prose sketch was followed after
only a few weeks by *Siegfrieds Tod*, the poem that ultimately
formed the concluding part of the *Ring* and was written between
November 18 and 28, 1848.

Wagner began it with what was later embodied in act 1 of *Götterdämmerung*. This he really did against his better judgment, because
the plot had long been crystallized from start to finish. The upper
and lower worlds, the clans and their genealogies had already been
worked out, and no one need be surprised that Wagner one day
had to return to the bedrock of *Das Rheingold*. His main reason for
temporarily restricting himself to the concluding part was of a
psychological and creative nature. He balked at a long run-up and
wanted to make things easier for himself—too easy, for the retro-
grade process began at Dresden itself. Eduard Devrient shrewdly
pointed out that Brünnhilde's hostility toward Siegfried would be
incomprehensible without some previous indication of their mutual love. Wagner, who was quick to see the force of this argument,
wrote in the Norns' prologue and the cliff-top scene between
Brünnhilde and Siegfried.

Early in December, he gave a reading of *Siegfrieds Tod* at his
home in the presence of Gottfried Semper, Gustav Kietz, Wilhelm
Fischer, Ferdinand Heine and his son Wilhelm, Hans von Bülow,
and Karl Ritter. Although his circle of friends had somewhat
dwindled, Ferdinand Hiller's Wednesday soirees were still well
attended. Among those who now came to them were the liberal
Julius Fröbel, the philologist Hermann Köchly, whose revolutionary sympathies were steadily increasing, and the writer Gustav
Freytag, who vainly tried to interest Wagner in historical themes.

On the track of the "absolute," Wagner spent the winter reading
Hegel's *Lectures on the Philosophy of History*. He was brought face to
face with historical reality on January 10, 1849, when Saxony's
elected representatives met. The radical liberals (democrats and
republicans) had obtained 13,640 votes, the liberals 6,060. The con-
servatives were trounced so badly that they failed to win a single
parliamentary seat. Röckel had been elected to a small provincial

constituency and now enjoyed immunity, so the anonymous land-owner could retrieve his bail money. Parliament proceeded to demand recognition of the basic rights proclaimed by the Frank-furt assembly. Together with the adoption of the March Constitu-tion, this provoked a conflict which the German monarchs, acting in secret accord, skillfully fostered and exploited. And this, in turn, gave rise to a revolutionary situation that came to a head at an inopportune moment for Wagner.

Despite his populist and libertarian euphoria, Wagner could never at any stage in his life summon up the least enthusiasm for elections, popular assemblies, and parliamentary government—a respect in which he can be claimed as one of their own by left-wing extremists and right-wing authoritarians alike. He now reapplied himself to his favorite character, the revolutionary redeemer. This time the name was Jesus, not Siegfried. Wagner, the secret atheist who so often invoked the Almighty in his letters, wrote a detailed fifty-page sketch for a drama to be entitled *Jesus von Nazareth*, which portrayed Jesus purely as a social revolutionary. Its basic theme may be construed as follows: Because offenses against prop-erty presuppose a law of property, there can be no offense where no such law exists. Wagner eliminated Christ the symbol and made Jesus the man a victim of the shallow, infamous, abject sensuality of the Roman world, whose "worthlessness" he likened to that of the modern era. Judas and Barabbas forge plans for a Jewish revolt against the Romans, whereas Jesus, imbued with a Wagnerian urge to reject the unloving generality of mankind, is so incensed with life and so filled with yearning for redemption that he elects to die a self-sacrificial death. Apart from being identical with the philoso-phy of the suicides who now cremate themselves alive, this inter-mingling of early Christian, emancipatory, and social utopian ideas is precisely what Marx criticized in the so-called "true social-ists." It is possible, though not proven, that *Jesus von Nazareth* was inspired by personal knowledge, or at least public discussion, of *Das Leben Jesu* (1835–36) by the neo-Hegelian David Friedrich Strauss and of Wilhelm Weitling's *Evangelium des armen Sünders*, which had appeared in 1845. Röckel had studied Weitling closely, and the *Evangelium* contained chapters such as "Jesus Teaches the Abolition of Property," "Jesus Teaches the Abolition of Money," and "Jesus Is No Respecter of Property."

Wagner wrote ceaselessly. By February 10, 1849, he was back to politics again in Röckel's *Volksblätter*. In an anonymous article headed "Man and Existing Society," he flatly stated that 1848 had seen the start of a campaign by the former against the latter. The fighting in Austria and Prussia had served only to "clear the battlefield for that last and loftiest struggle." It was futile to oppose the said struggle because—and here is another apparent Hegelianism—no one could escape the pull of the current. "It lays hold of us notwithstanding, however secure our place of refuge; and all of us, the prince in his palace and the poor man in his cottage, must join forces in this great struggle, for we are all *men* and subject to the commandments of the *age*." The campaign against existing society had begun because society left to chance the individual's moral instruction and education, his mental and physical development. It was "the most sacred and sublime ever fought," for it was "the struggle of consciousness against chance, of mind against mindlessness, of morality against evil, of strength against weakness: It is the struggle for our destiny, our right, our happiness."

Two days later, on February 12, 1849, Wagner—unbeknown to Lüttichau—assembled the members of the orchestra at an inn, the Gasthof zum Lämmchen, and propounded his plans for reform. The management's reaction can be gauged from Secretary Winkler's minutes of a heated board meeting held on February 14. It took the form of an inquisition. Wagner was accused of having told his musicians that better times were coming, and that he would be of more help to them when they did. Conditions were as yet unfavorable, but the day would come when all present would be "liberated from them." Lüttichau declared that Wagner's words had sown the seeds of demoralization. He also humiliated the kapellmeister by charging him with dereliction of duty and professional negligence. What lends color to this reprimand is Wagner's own admission to Cosima that he had once been so engrossed in his work on *Tannhäuser* that he forgot to conduct Sunday morning Mass and did not realize it until reproved by a singer coming home from church. The minutes of the board meeting further record that Wagner was rebuked on the ruinous state of his finances. He not only conceded this but owned to feeling that he was out of place in his present post and would gladly have resigned if not restrained from so doing by "concern for his wife and his domestic position." It was conveyed to him that the board shared his sentiments and reserved the right to submit its findings to His Majesty. In despair, Wagner went running to Devrient, who noted: "The poor fellow was very crestfallen."

The one bright spot on Wagner's horizon at this period was a production of *Tannhäuser* at Weimar. This at last gained him recognition outside Dresden and sealed his friendship with Liszt, who wrote to him on February 26: "Once and for all, from now on account me one of your most zealous and devoted admirers. Whether near or far, depend on me and call on my services." It was a pledge he never broke.

*   *   *

Saxony's March cabinet, which had been able to fulfill only a small fraction of the promised reforms, resigned on February 24. The government was now headed by Baron Friedrich Ferdinand von Beust, an archconservative royalist whose appointment was far more consistent with the real balance of power. The political conflict on Saxony's northern border, too, entered a critical phase when the Prussian second chamber met on February 26.

The political rhymester in Wagner promptly came to life again. His poem *Die Not* [inadequately translated *Need*, for the word can mean anything from "emergency" to "destitution"] deserves a mention if only because its title became one of his central ideas. To him it connoted ultimate human necessity, a Freudian id—as Cosima's diaries bear witness—in the midst of suffering and stress. Intoxicated by the vision of a cleansing fire, Wagner called for the temples of Mammon to be reduced to ashes, complete with all the documentary appurtenances—the "papers and parchments"—of those whose income was unearned or gained by financial trickery. He wound up with a free paraphrase of the anarcho-Rousseauists: Life's happiness would blossom above the ruins; humanity, released from its chains, would survive in company with Nature.

During March, when Wagner composed this effusion, he made the acquaintance of a man who left an indelible impression on all who crossed his path. This was Mikhail Bakunin, the smoldering-eyed revolutionary, the leonine anarchist, savage and sensitive, obscurantist and idealistic, outlandish and imposing. Bakunin, who had fled from Bohemia in 1848, was living in Saxony under an assumed name. Before Easter, he moved from Leipzig to Dresden, where Röckel put him up for a few days and introduced him to Wagner. Bakunin, alias Dr. Schwarz, then rented a room in Wagner's neighborhood.

The bearded, corpulent, jovial giant was as irresistibly charming on the personal level as his political ideas were outré and alarming. Bakunin wanted to burn everything down without exception. "You won't need so many instruments then, and that will be excellent!" he told Wagner, with whom he quickly made friends. "Everything about him was colossal, and he was filled with primitive exuberance and strength," says *My Life*. For a while, Wagner was doubly disconcerted by "such frightful pronouncements" as Bakunin's doctrine of destruction because the Russian proved, on closer acquaintance, to be "a truly amiable, sensitive soul."

Mikhail Bakunin had studied Rousseau and Hegel and was personally acquainted with the leading socialists. His fondness for the German classics pervaded his nihilistic rodomontades like a sentimental undertone. He thought nothing of the French and expected little of the Germans, least of all a revolution that would sweep away all forms of political institution and render them superfluous. He predicted that Bohemia would soon rise in revolt, and that, failing the immediate destruction of everything in sight, the next step would be a union of German and Slav democrats and a confederation of European republics. Although Bakunin had believed that a revolutionary situation already existed in Prague, his hopes were quickly dashed by a visit to the city: His sole supporters there turned out to be a handful of callow students.

Röckel did not take long to recognize that, although he was a man endowed with "rare mental vigor and strength of character," Bakunin suffered from a lack of realism and excess of imagination that doomed him to be everlastingly disappointed by the actual state of political affairs.

Relations between Wagner and Bakunin were the acme of courtesy and consideration.* Monomaniacs though they were, the two men could listen to one another for hours on end. They made a strange and, for the space of a few weeks, inseparable pair. Bakunin was uninterested in Wagner's *Nibelungen* project and unenthusiastic about *Jesus von Nazareth*. He wished Wagner luck with its future development but urged him to portray Jesus as a weak character. He also advised him to ring the changes on a single set of phrases. The tenor was to sing "Off with his head!" the soprano "Hang him!" and the bass "Fire, fire!"

Bakunin took a great fancy to *Der Fliegende Holländer* when Wagner played and sang him the first few scenes. Although we are not told the reason, a glance at the Dutchman's opening monologue explains why. Its reference to "the annihilating blow wherewith the world comes crashing down" must surely have found a ready echo in the anarchist's mind.

Wagner conducted his last Palm Sunday concert, which included Beethoven's Ninth Symphony, on April 1. Bakunin had sneaked unnoticed into the previous day's rehearsal. When the last notes died away, he strode boldly up to the orchestra and called out to Wagner that, even if every other piece of music were destroyed in the coming conflagration, they must unite to preserve this symphony at the risk of their lives.

Meanwhile, the German Constitution had been adopted at Frankfurt on March 23. Friedrich Wilhelm IV of Prussia was elected emperor on March 28 but declined, on April 3, to accept the imperial crown from the hands of a parliamentary delegation. A few days later, on April 8, the *Volksblätter* published Wagner's most impassioned hymn to revolution, a rhapsodic and unbridled summons to the worm to turn at last.

The author pictured a tempest bearing down on "the hosts of the oppressed." To the terror of fearful generals and quaking cabinets, the Goddess of Revolution was at hand with a prophetic greeting for those in distress, who listened to it enraptured: "I shall destroy the dominion of the one over the many, of the dead over the living, of matter over mind. I shall shatter the power of the mighty, of law and of property." Revolutionary sentiments, then as now! "I shall destroy the existing order of things that divides united mankind into hostile nations, into powerful and weak, into privileged and deprived, into rich and poor, for its sole effect is to render us all unhappy. I shall destroy the order of things that makes millions the slaves of a few and those few the slaves of their own power, their own wealth. I shall destroy this order of things that divorces enjoyment from labor, makes labor a burden and enjoyment a vice, makes one person wretched by reason of deprivation and another by reason of affluence. I shall destroy this order of things that consumes men's energies in the service of dominion by the dead, of lifeless matter that keeps half of mankind in inactivity or useless activity, compelling hundreds of thousands of people to devote their vigorous youth to the maintenance of these vile conditions in the bustling but idle role of soldiers, civil servants, speculators, and moneymakers, while the other half has to sustain the whole disgraceful edifice by exerting itself to an inordinate degree and sacrificing all the joys of life."

Wagner omitted nothing from his catalog of spine-chilling predictions. The revolution would destroy "even unto the memory thereof" every trace of a lunatic system based on force, mendacity, care, hypocrisy, privation, sorrow, suffering, and betrayal. "Let all be destroyed that oppresses you and makes you suffer, and from the ruins of this old world let there arise a new, undreamed-of happiness." And so, as this operatic outburst reaches its finale, the poor and oppressed stand erect and proudly raise their heads. With rapture written on every ennobled countenance and glad cries of "I am a man!" they stream down into the valleys and plains and proclaim "the new gospel of happiness" to the entire world. . . .

Wagner had become a tocsin and mouthpiece of revolution. Although he claimed ignorance of political parties, his garden that April became the scene of discussions on the subject of arming the populace. According to Röckel's evidence at his trial, the participants included Röckel himself, Gottfried Semper, Dr. Munde, and lieutenants Schreiber, Erdmannsdorf, and Müller. No one saw anything unusual or objectionable in these conferences, following as they did upon the public formation of an Academic Legion* whose task was to assist the Communal Guard in maintaining peace and good order in the event of riots. Several such secret meetings were alleged to have taken place, some six weeks before fighting broke out, at the Friedrichstrasse home of a law student named Naumann, with Bakunin, Röckel, Semper, Wagner, and the aforementioned officers in attendance. Karl Wilhelm Oehme, a brass founder, later testified that Wagner and Röckel had instructed him to manufacture a considerable number of hand grenades prior to Easter 1849. These grenades, he said, were destined for Prague and delivered to the dispatch department of the *Dresdner Zeitung*. Oehme further stated that on May 4, Wagner had told him to fill them with explosives. Röckel denied all complicity in the hand-grenade affair. Surprising as it may seem, given that he was an honorable man who never wavered in his allegiance to a friend whom he shielded and exonerated on every other count, Röckel claimed that the order had been placed by Wagner alone. Oehme's statements have never been disproved. In retrospect, one is inclined—partly because of the Prague connection—to surmise that Wagner was acting on Bakunin's behalf. Bakunin made no comment when indicted. Wagner himself let slip not a word; or rather, he let slip only one, but its significance seems clear. Dated May 3, before the outbreak of hostilities, an entry in his "Annals" reads simply: "(Shrapnels [sic])."*

The atmosphere in Saxony during April 1849 was highly charged. There as elsewhere, people pinned great hopes on the adoption of the Reich Constitution, which secured the approval of twenty-eight German states. What invested the revolutionaries with such a sense of legitimacy was that the Saxon chambers, too, adopted it on April 12 and 14. Having done so, they waited for the king and his government to endorse the constitution and put it into effect. It was obstruction by Prussia and Hanover that brought matters to a head. Resolute left-wing opposition to Prussian government policy led on April 27 to the dissolution of the Prussian chamber, which was followed on April 30 by the dissolution of both Saxony's chambers by Friedrich August II. Such was the so-called "Princes' Plot" for which the ground had been prepared by a circular note dated April 28. Friedrich August simultaneously dismissed his cabinet, with the exception of Beust, Rabenhorst, and Zschinsky, so the country was effectively without a government. This was a clear infringement of the constitution, and messages poured in from all parts of Saxony imploring the king not to oppose the wishes of his people. But Friedrich August, the once-popular monarch with the meek expression and the childish, melancholy features, persisted in his stubborn and inflexible stand. Everything suggests that he was completely under the thumb of Beust, who wanted fighting to break out before the democrats could consolidate their hold throughout the country.

The opposition, which was unprepared for active hostilities, saw the writing on the wall. Wagner did, too. Röckel was no longer in Dresden, having fled to Prague as soon as the dissolution of parliament deprived him of immunity. Despite a ban on the *Volksblätter*, Wagner had already started collecting copy for the next issue and was determined to edit the periodical in Röckel's place.

By Wednesday, May 2, which was notable for what the *Dresdner*

Zeitung described as "barricade weather and revolutionary skies," the Prussian circular note had become public knowledge. General resentment was now intensified by rumors that Prussian troops were about to enter Saxony or had already done so. Wagner wrote to Röckel urging him to return to Dresden at once. He would be needed there because everything augured "a decisive conflict, if not with the king, then with Prussian troops; the only fear is that a revolution may break out too soon." This letter, which was later found in Röckel's possession, gravely compromised its author.

Preliminary musters were held early that afternoon by the Communal Guard, to which Wagner no longer belonged.* The same day, Dresden's city council and the College of Municipal Deputies —the last constitutional authorities left in the capital—formally requested the king to avert the threat to the country and decree that the Reich Constitution be "proclaimed law without delay or amendment." Their efforts were in vain. The disaster ran its course, and for clarity's sake we shall trace its progress day by day.*

* * *

Thursday, May 3. Beust's cabinet had indeed summoned military assistance from Prussia. The king placed his own forces on the alert. As for the local militia, the authorities virtually neutralized it that morning by parading its members, disarming them, and sending them home. The day was sultry, and the Elbe Valley was veiled in yellow mist. Toward midday, Wagner attended a committee meeting of the Vaterlands-Verein at which no firm decisions were reached. He was as depressed by the medley of scatterbrained views and proposals put forward as he was dismayed by "the intimidation to which advocates of democratic theories are subjected by the lower classes." He had left the meeting and was walking home, accompanied by a young painter named Kaufmann, when he suddenly heard a bell in the tower of the nearby Annakirche sound the alarm. "My God, it's started!" cried Kaufmann, and hurried off. (He later sought political asylum in Bern.)

In Wagner, the sound of the tocsin produced "the same phenomenon as that described by Goethe when he endeavors to explain the effect on his senses of the cannonade at Valmy." The whole square before him seemed bathed in a dark yellow, almost brownish light of the kind he had seen at Magdeburg during an eclipse of the sun. Filled with "unbridled satisfaction," he hit on the idea of securing Tichatschek's private arsenal for the Communal Guard. Tichatschek was away, so he advised the tenor's wife to relinquish his sporting guns to the Vaterlands-Verein in exchange for a receipt. This, too, leaked out and was later held against him.

That afternoon, an emergency meeting of city councillors appointed a committee to take defensive measures against foreign troops. Meanwhile, crowds had gathered outside the armory and were thronging Schlossgasse. A detachment of infantry opened fire without warning from the armory courtyard, inflicting four fatal casualties. Under a hail of stones from the mob and some musket fire from members of an athletic club who had hurried to the scene, the soldiers retreated into the armory.* One officer was killed and a number of men wounded. When a hastily mustered contingent of the Communal Guard turned up to pacify the infuriated townsfolk, the regulars opened fire on them with grapeshot, inflicting another twenty casualties.

Attracted to the armory by rumors of the bloodshed in progress there, Wagner met a wounded guardsman limping back and heard cries of "To the barricades!"

The defense committee had meanwhile given orders for barricades to be erected, and the city council twice sent deputations to the castle, where they joined forces with other delegates. After a long delay, the councillors were admitted. The following eyewitness account of this last appeal to the king was recorded by one Hugo Häpe: "In the most grievous agitation, these delegates prostrated themselves at his feet. They told him that his word now spelled the difference between life and death, but all to no avail. They suffered the same fate as that which had befallen them previously, just as it had a deputation of municipal councillors from Leipzig who had been with the king a short while before. Their representations and entreaties found no access to the king's heart: He could not break his word. Instead, many hearts are now breaking in death. . . ."

Swept along by the mob, Wagner reached the city hall, which was guarded by militiamen. Kietz, who was among them, noted: "Suddenly we saw Wagner coming across the Old Marketplace. Professor Rietschel, who was with us, called to him, 'Herr Kapellmeister, how are things in the city? Can you give us any news?'

Whereupon Wagner replied, 'Things are turning nasty!' and hurried on. Wagner did, in fact, manage to get into the council chamber, where he found everyone in confusion and disarray. Outside, the first corpse was being trundled past on an open wagon. At the sight of it, Wilhelmine Schröder-Devrient gave a shriek of horror and fury from the window of the Löwenapotheke.* The lawyer Samuel Tzschirner, a member of the defense committee, gave orders to sound the tocsin. This first death knell startled the combatants into a temporary truce.

Toward evening, Wagner strolled slowly back to Friedrichstadt past barricades made out of dismantled market stalls.

Friday, May 4. At about four in the morning, when the river valley was shrouded in mist, the king fled by steamer to the fortress of Königstein, accompanied by the queen and a retinue including the ministers Beust, Rabenhorst, and Zschinsky. Historians incline to Röckel's view that the king himself was in no danger, and that his "escape" was more an act of abduction on the part of ministers who wished to isolate him from the people. News of the rump government's flight spread through Dresden like wildfire. Early the same morning, Wagner went to the city hall, where the remaining members of parliament were forming a public safety committee. Delegates from the committee found every ministry deserted, however, so the barricades were manned. After a brief exchange of shots, the military agreed to a five-hour truce. At the same time, news arrived from Württemberg that the army there had enforced acceptance of the Reich Constitution by siding with the people. This confirmed the politicians of Saxony in their belief that a similar attitude could be induced in their own soldiers.

On calling at Ferdinand Heine's home later in the morning, Wagner met Wilhelmine Schröder-Devrient, who implored him to help stop the slaughter. He, too, was anxious to avoid bloodshed. Rather than abandon the country to the imponderables of revolutionary chaos, he favored constructing a united front based on legal, patriotic, and constitutional principles. In his view, this would be feasible if the Saxon Army joined the revolutionaries in repelling the Prussian invaders and forced the king to accept the Reich Constitution. Wagner hurried back to the city hall, where he met R. Römpler, the printer of Röckel's *Volksblätter,* and ordered some eighteen-inch strips of paper bearing the words "Are you with us against foreign troops?" These were duly printed and delivered to the city hall. Römpler's account reads: "Returning to the city hall about an hour later, I saw on my way there that the posters had been pasted all over the street corners and on the *inner* barricades. In the marketplace I again met Wagner and inquired if he had seen what use had been made of the posters. When he said no, I invited him to accompany me and see for himself. He was dumbfounded, and exclaimed, 'My God, who could have done such a stupid thing?' We then went together to Ostra Allee, where my business premises were. He waited until another two hundred posters had been run off, put them under his arm, and left the printshop. I followed him out to see what he intended doing. Then I saw him cross the barricade by the Old Opera House and walk *straight up to the soldiers* stationed in the castle square and on the Elbe bridge. There he distributed the aforesaid posters among the soldiers *with his own hands*. After that he proceeded to Brühlsche Terrasse. I lost sight of him but was subsequently informed that he had done the same thing there. One can only marvel that he was not arrested on the spot, or even shot, in the course of this enterprise." In Brühlsche Terrasse, Wagner ran into Gustav Kietz, gave him some posters, and told him to distribute them. The young sculptor was prevented from doing so by a captain who snatched them out of his hand but, fortunately for Kietz, called him a "misguided lad" and sent him on his way.

At noon, a provisional government was formed at the city hall. This comprised Karl Todt, a privy councillor; Otto Heubner of Freiburg, a district prefect and judge; and Tzschirner, the lawyer from Bautzen. To cheers and peals of bells, the newly elected representatives appeared on the balcony, where Professor Hermann Köchly* presented them to the crowd with great rhetorical finesse. Having been sworn in on the Reich Constitution, the provisional government issued a proclamation placing Saxony under the aegis of the states that had recognized the said constitution. It went on to remind Saxon troops that their sole duty was to uphold "the existing government and the unity and freedom of the German Fatherland." It was "Now or never. Freedom or slavery! Choose!" For the present, however, few positive steps could be taken. The bridges linking the old and new quarters of Dresden were controlled by artillery units loyal to the king, so there was nothing for it but to fortify the center of the city and wait.

Wagner now became acquainted with the grotesque side of such ill-organized revolts, with their alternation of mob hysteria and peaceful normality. That afternoon he saw Mikhail Bakunin strolling through the barricades, frock-coated and puffing at a cigar, in company with a young Galician violinist named Haimberger, who had exchanged his fiddle for a musket but flinched at the sound of every distant shot. Bakunin poured scorn on the whole insurrection. After a day spent studying maps in the city hall, he displayed the half amused, half sorrowful resignation of one who has turned up at the wrong party. Outside the city hall, Wagner was accosted by Gottfried Semper, who was posted there with a crack Communal Guard unit. Semper confessed that his conscience was troubling him. How, being a professor at the Royal Academy, could he reconcile his present activities with his status as a citizen? Wagner looked him straight in the eye and merely repeated the last word: "Citizen!"

It must have been while walking home on this warm and relatively peaceful spring evening that Wagner, so he tells us in *My Life*, devoted thought to his projected drama *Achilleus*. This was another Siegfried paraphrase inasmuch as one free individual— Achilles—renders the gods superfluous. Offered immortality by his mother, the goddess Thetis, the hero declines. Wagner's notes on the subject, made during 1848 and 1849, state that "Achilles' mother acknowledges that he is greater than the elements (gods). Man is the consummation of god. The eternal gods are the elements that first beget man. In man, therefore, creation is accomplished." This is one of the basic ideas of the *Ring*.

On reaching home, Wagner found some chance visitors: two nieces, the daughters of his sister Luise Brockhaus. He put everyone in the highest of spirits with his optimistic reports on the situation. Then he enjoyed a tranquil night's sleep—his last for a long time.

Saturday, May 5. Renewed negotiations between the provisional government and ministers Beust and Rabenhorst, who had returned to the New City the day before, bore no fruit at all. The king's representatives issued an unacceptable ultimatum calling for unconditional surrender and an admission of guilt. At this, hostilities were resumed and cannon began to bombard the Old City from emplacements inside the castle. Wagner reappeared at the city hall, where he recommended that Gottfried Semper be appointed to reinforce the existing barricades, which were amateurish affairs, and supervise the construction of new ones.

Someone who got to know Wagner during the insurrection was the young Austrian writer Ludwig Eckhardt, who had been arrested because of his *Polenlieder* in 1846 and had fled from Vienna to Dresden in 1848. Eckhardt came across Wagner in various parts of the city that day, "eagerly soliciting news and dispensing advice, and always with the excitement of one who is personally involved." Wagner realized how poorly equipped the rebels were. The provisional government, too, complained in a proclamation of "dereliction of duty by the majority of the local Communal Guard" and threatened coercive measures unless citizens showed greater alacrity in taking up arms. Intent on doing his own duty, Wagner climbed the 300-foot tower of the Kreuzkirche, the highest vantage point in the city. Snipers were firing on soldiers from the gallery, which itself was under fire from distant buildings. "Never fear, I'm immortal," Wagner is reported to have told a worried comrade. His task was to observe troop movements and report on them to the city hall. This he did by wrapping notes around stones and dropping them from the gallery to the street.

He remained all night in the tower of the Kreuzkirche, pursuing philosophical discussions with a schoolmaster from Döbeln, Dr. Wilhelm Berthold, who stood guard with him. Another eyewitness, Professor Thum of Reichenbach, recalled Wagner discoursing at length on the ancient and Christian philosophies of life, Dresden's royal orchestra, and the Leipzig concert hall, the Gewandhaus.

Sunday, May 6. When daylight came, Wagner observed rebel forces entering Dresden. At the same time, there were increasing signs that Prussian troops were concentrating in the New City: The "fraternal assistance" summoned by the king against his own people had arrived. Toward eleven o'clock, Wagner saw the Old Opera House go up in flames. Always regarded as a fire risk, it now burned like tinder, having allegedly been put to the torch for strategic reasons.* Wagner dispatched a messenger to Friedrichstadt for wine and snuff. The man returned with a message from Minna imploring him to return home. It was not until some seventy sharpshooters had assembled in the tower and bullets were whistling around his ears that Wagner yielded to *force majeure* and left the Kreuzkirche. He guided a platoon of Zittau insurgents to the old quarter and paid another visit to the city hall.

Shortly after midday, August Röckel finally arrived by mail coach from Prague. Without even catching a glimpse of his family, he went straight to the city hall. The utter lack of coordination and supervision that reigned there was all too obvious. Now that Prussian troops had taken a hand in the fighting, several buildings and barricades had been lost. Todt promptly set off for Frankfurt to request the National Assembly to mediate. Röckel and Wagner exchanged a final word and went their separate ways. Returning home, Wagner persuaded Minna that the threat to Friedrichstadt from Prussian troops was such that she must leave there at once. They agreed to meet next morning at a village outside the city, the plan being that Wagner should take Minna to his sister Klara at Chemnitz, where her husband, Heinrich Wolfram, had established a business.

Monday, May 7. It is not altogether certain whether Wagner left the city at eight that morning, as he mentions in a letter to Devrient on May 17, or whether *My Life* is correct in stating that he first had another meeting with Röckel and learned of the provisional government's plans to abandon the city and withdraw to the Erzgebirge. On foot, relishing the sound of birdsong and the sight of the peaceful countryside around him, he made his way to the rendezvous, where he rejoined Minna and hired a carriage. The direct routes to Chemnitz were either closed or choked with traffic, so they traveled via Tharandt and Freiberg. Meeting some reluctant militiamen on the way, Wagner urged them to reinforce the Dresden insurgents. At Oederan, just outside Chemnitz, he was stopped by a contingent of volunteers who took him for a deserter and allowed him to proceed only when he promised to return to Dresden the next morning. Unlike them, officers of the Chemnitz Communal Guard assumed that the kapellmeister must be an emissary from the provisional government. It was not until the evening of this eventful day that Wagner and his wife reached the Wolframs' house in Chemnitz.

Meanwhile, back in Dresden, Bakunin had apparently been pressing for a withdrawal from the capital to avoid further loss of life. What changed his mind was Heubner's noble and courageous bearing, which affected him so deeply that he proclaimed his intention of fighting on and standing by Heubner to the last.

At about eleven that night, Röckel sneaked out to the suburb of Plauen to guide a platoon of insurgents back to the Old City. He lost his way in the darkness and ran into a military patrol. Arrested on the spot, he was badly manhandled in the course of numerous interrogations.

Tuesday, May 8. Wagner headed back to Dresden in the morning, carrying a message from Freiberg for the city hall. He found the politicians there in the last stages of exhaustion, their faces imprinted with a mixture of fear and apathy. The city was past holding. Wagner remained for an hour and arranged to leave Dresden that night with Hermann Marschall von Bieberstein, a lawyer friend who had been appointed to travel by coach to Freiberg in the hope of strengthening the insurgents' position, if only outside the capital, by speeding the flow of reinforcements.

The provisional government, which still held out hopes of winning the battle in the open countryside, continued to issue calls to arms. The unity and freedom of the Fatherland, those most sacred possessions, must now, it proclaimed, be secured, "whether in urban barricade fighting or in pitched battle, or they will never be won."

By evening, after a day of house-to-house fighting, regular troops had penetrated to within a short distance of the Altmarkt and occupied Postplatz, where the Engelklub was situated. Bakunin, who suggested blowing up the city hall as a last heroic gesture, dropped the idea at Heubner's insistence. Fighting ceased when darkness fell.

Wednesday, May 9. At four in the morning, a signal from the tower of the Kreuzkirche told the insurgents that it was time to begin their surreptitious withdrawal. Wagner left the city with Marschall von Bieberstein and rode on ahead to Freiberg. Here the lawyer said good-bye. He eventually escaped to Switzerland, as did Todt from Frankfurt and Tzschirner—who had already deserted his post—from Dresden itself. Semper, Köchly, Eckhardt, Haimberger, and Hermann Müller all fled or emigrated a short time later, and nearly all of them met up again in Switzerland.

The evacuation of Dresden spelled the end of serious resistance to the loyalists. Any hope of being able to carry on the struggle in open country proved illusory. Columns of reinforcements dispersed when they encountered armed units retreating in the opposite direction, some of them in a haphazard and leaderless fashion.

At Freiberg, Wagner turned back once more and boarded a coach for Tharandt, hoping to discover more about the provisional government's plans. On the way there, he met the bulk of the Dresden insurgents, some two thousand armed men, with the carriages of the provisional government in their train. Heubner, now the effective head of government, was traveling with his aide, C. A. Martin, a senior post office official, Mikhail Bakunin, and Friedrich Semmig, a newspaper editor from Rochlitz. Wagner switched carriages and joined them. Bakunin, who had that morning denuded a Dresden avenue of timber for the construction of a barricade designed to cover the flanks of the retreating insurgents, seemed surprised that the townsfolk had so loudly bewailed the loss of their "lovely trees." According to Semmig, Wagner harangued his fellow passengers and kept shouting "War!" He described Wagner's flood of oratory as "one of my most stirring recollections of those terrible, tempestuous hours." All Wagner tells us is that he and Heubner eventually dismounted because the coachman, to Bakunin's malicious glee, kept complaining that his vehicle was overloaded.

Just outside Freiberg, they came upon some volunteers drawn up beside the road to salute them and receive further orders. In company with Heubner, Wagner inspected their ranks and was warmly greeted by an acquaintance from Dresden, a German Catholic priest named Metzdorff. Stationed on a neighboring hill was a small detachment of the Chemnitz Communal Guard. After representatives from this body had been sent to invite the provisional government to set up its headquarters at Chemnitz—a proposal that seemed in no way suspicious—the detachment wheeled and marched off.

Wagner accompanied Heubner on foot to his Freiberg home, where the rest of the party assembled for refreshment and consultation. Stephan Born, the Leipzig labor leader, recalled that Wagner ran to meet him with open arms, exclaiming that all was not yet lost—that the situation would be saved by the youth of the country. Exhausted, Wagner stretched out on a sofa and fell asleep at once. The room was deserted when he woke, so he hurried to the town hall. Here he found Heubner treating his fellow townsfolk to an impassioned speech from the balcony and publicly embraced him to the cheers of all present. At the insistence of the local authorities, however, Heubner and his party decided to leave

Freiberg and avail themselves of the invitation to set up their
provisional headquarters at Chemnitz.

The fact that Wagner escaped arrest during the next few hours
was attributable to one of those quirks of fate that always came to
his aid in the nick of time. Its consequences were momentous
enough to warrant a full description here. He announced his intention of going on *ahead* to Chemnitz and made his way to the staging
post. The mail coach was delayed, however, so he returned to the
town hall and Heubner's home, thinking that he might, after all,
reach Chemnitz more quickly by traveling with Heubner and his
party. He found both places deserted, and no one could tell him
where the others were. Hurrying back to the staging post, he
climbed aboard the mail coach just as it was about to leave. Unbeknown to him, he was setting off for Chemnitz *after* Heubner,
Bakunin, and Martin, not ahead of them. Heubner and his friends
were unaware that they had been lured into a trap by renegade
militiamen who, after issuing their spurious invitation, had gone
off to warn the civil and military authorities. On reaching the gates
of Chemnitz, Heubner formally stated his name and requested the
town councillors to call on him next day. He, Bakunin, and Martin
then repaired to an inn, where they retired to bed without posting
any form of guard. They woke to find themselves under arrest.

All that saved Wagner, who arrived on his own in the mail
coach, was that the informers had been keeping watch for
Heubner's carriage only. He alighted, went to a neighboring inn
—a different one, as luck would have it—and snatched a few hours'
sleep. Then, at five in the morning, he set off for his brother-in-
law's house. There he learned the details of his friends' arrest from
Heinrich Wolfram, but not until the afternoon, when Wolfram
returned from a spell of duty as a special constable. He had been
closely questioned by officers who had recognized Wagner outside
Freiberg and were furious at his having given them the slip.

Wolfram had some difficulty in persuading Wagner to leave at
once. Minna strongly opposed the idea because she believed in his
innocence, and Wagner himself, who felt he had done no wrong,
thought it inconceivable that any reprisals would be taken against
members of the provisional government or anyone involved in the
insurrection because their actions had been constitutionally legitimate. He even hoped at first to be able to resume his duties at
Dresden—once the storm had blown over—or at least to continue

to draw his salary on a temporary basis. This illusion was gradually dispelled by the actual course of events.

There is no doubt that, if arrested, he would have been sentenced to death like Heubner and Röckel—to name only two—and compelled to spend a decade or more in jail. This was confirmed by King Johann, who succeeded Friedrich August II in 1854, in a letter to the grand duke of Weimar. Wagner retorted that, if he had committed a crime, half the population of Saxony should also be brought to trial. He was not far wrong, but Friedrich August and his government thought otherwise. Among those indicted were thirty mayors, most exdeputies, and a number of priests and civil servants.

The loyalists lost thirty-one men of whom eight were Prussians and twenty-three Saxons. The insurgents' fatal casualties numbered a hundred and ninety-six, seven of them women. This was the official tally published by the *Dresdner Journal*, though the Prussian commander, Count von Waldersee, admitted that his men had thrown at least another fifty dead and captured rebels into the Elbe. Other victims of willful murder included a maid-servant, a Prince von Schwarzburg-Rudolstadt, who was attacked while confined to his hotel room with an eye complaint, some parliamentarians under a flag of truce, and the wounded inmates of a field hospital.

Wagner lay low till nightfall on May 10, when he boarded his brother-in-law's carriage. The coachman harnessed up, not knowing who his passenger was, and Wolfram escorted Wagner to Altenburg. From there Wagner took the mail coach to Weimar, where he arrived on May 13 and booked into the Hotel zum Erbprinzen. The same day, he went with Liszt to call on Princess Carolyne von Sayn-Wittgenstein. It seems that he temporarily concealed the full extent of his complicity in the Dresden uprising. "Be honest," Liszt said, "you've done something foolish!" But he firmly denied it.

Next morning Wagner attended an orchestral rehearsal of *Tannhäuser*, which several times moved him to tears of cathartic self-esteem.

Minna, who had returned to Dresden as soon as her husband left for Weimar, sent him an unreproachful letter full of dark forebodings. He replied on May 14 that his sole inference from what she had written was the warmth and purity of her love for him, but that she had never quite brought herself to appreciate the pressures he had "sighed under" or understand why he had been at odds with the world and become a revolutionary. "The Dresden revolution and its whole outcome have now taught me that I am anything but a true revolutionary: The very failure of the insurrection has shown me that a truly victorious revolutionary must proceed entirely without scruple. He cannot afford to think of wife and child, hearth and home: His sole endeavor must be destruction, and had the noble Heubner been prepared to act thus at Freiberg or Chemnitz, the revolution would have continued victorious." This hardly sounds like a recantation and is seldom quoted by those who wish the rest of Wagner's letter to serve as proof of a complete change of heart. "But people of our sort," he went on, "are not destined for this terrible task. We are revolutionaries only in order to *build* on fresh soil; it is *re-creation* that attracts us, not *destruction*, which is why we are not the people whom fate requires. These will arise from the very lowest dregs of society; we and our hearts can have nothing in common with them. You see? *Thus do I bid farewell to revolution.* . . ."

Minna soon received a visit from a Dresden police officer who informed her that he had orders to arrest her husband, but that he was empowered to hold the warrant in abeyance for three days and would gladly do so. Meanwhile, he advised her to write to him. If he returned, well and good; if not, he could stay where he was. From the look of it, even some members of the police force sympathized with Wagner and secretly welcomed his escape. He did not learn of this development at once because Minna's letters were sent care of Liszt, who had gone to Karlsruhe for three days.

On May 15, Wagner accompanied Liszt to Eisenach. While still aboard the train, he received an invitation from Grand Duchess Maria Pavlovna, the czar's sister, to visit Eisenach Castle that evening. Maria Pavlovna, who diplomatically feigned ignorance of his position, was all kindness and courtesy. The following day, Wednesday, Wagner paid a visit to the Wartburg, which was then unrestored, and refreshed his memories of the time he had driven past the massive castle seven years earlier, meditating on the Tannhäuser legend.

He returned to Weimar on Ascension Day, May 17, shortly before Liszt. On May 19, the *Dresdner Anzeiger* printed an ill-composed and inaccurate "Wanted" notice,* reports of which soon reached Weimar. Liszt urged Wagner to leave at once; and Liszt's friend Professor Siebert, a Jena physician who was also staying at the Erbprinz, advised him to seek temporary refuge and await further news at Magdala, on a government-owned farm run by J. Wernsdorf, an agriculturalist with democratic sympathies. Having sent for Minna, whom he insisted on seeing before he left Germany, Wagner set off on the three-hour journey to Magdala.

Minna was reluctant to join him there because she dreaded the finality of such a farewell meeting. Indeed, she told Eduard Devrient that if Wagner turned his back on Dresden, their marriage would be over. Gustav Kietz records that he visited her as soon as peace returned to the Saxon capital and the troops had been withdrawn. She sobbed out the story of Wagner's flight and protested his innocence, but what Kietz found most moving of all was the sound of the parrot in the next room squawking "Richard! Liberty!" throughout her sad recital.

PART TWO

———— ◆ ————

1849-1864

FRIEDRICH NIETZSCHE: *"Purely from the aspect of his value to Germany and German culture, Richard Wagner remains a big question mark, perhaps a German misfortune—fateful, at all events. But what does that matter? Is he not very much more than a German phenomenon? It would even seem to me that he belongs nowhere less than he does in Germany, where nothing is ready for him. Among Germans, his entire type is simply alien, peculiar, uncomprehended, incomprehensible."*

Crisis in Exile

The Zurich Essays

Herr Wernsdorf was privy to the real identity of the man who introduced himself at Magdala as "Professor Werder." On May 20, half hidden behind a barn door and some beer barrels, he and Wagner eavesdropped on a meeting of local would-be revolutionaries who had returned in disarray after marching off to Dresden. Their fervent expressions of sympathy for the rebels of Baden left Wagner and his host unmoved, and they quit their place of concealment feeling surfeited with shallow bombast.

Even Wernsdorf was struck by the coolness with which the Wagners greeted each other when Minna turned up the next day. It was clear that she thought her husband's conduct injudicious, to say the least. "Well," her manner seemed to convey, "you asked me to come, so I came. Take yourself off wherever you please. Personally, I'm going home right now." Although Wagner persuaded her to stay, the atmosphere on his thirty-sixth birthday was lugubrious in the extreme.

On May 23, acting on instructions received from Weimar, Wagner took a six-hour walk to Jena. Minna, who had gone on ahead, was waiting for him at the home of Professor Oskar Wolff, a friend of Liszt's. Here Wagner was given an out-of-date passport belonging to another academic, Professor Christian Widmann, a writer

and economist from Tübingen. On May 24, he finally said good-
bye to Minna. His official destination was Paris, not Zurich. He
had promised Liszt, who was financing his journey and had provided him with a small cash reserve, that he would seek his salvation in Paris and offer the Grand Opéra a new work. It is doubtful
whether he ever for a moment believed in this plan which Liszt,
Minna, and his Dresden friends conceived of as the solution to his
problems, even though he fell in with all their proposals on the
subject and used a series of subterfuges to keep their expectations
alive for as long as possible.

His Jena accomplices advised him against taking the direct route
to France through strife-torn Baden. It would be far safer, they
said, to head first for Switzerland by way of Bavaria, where all was
quiet again. This advice suited him admirably. He avoided the
railway stations and traveled south by mail coach via Rudolstadt,
Saalfeld, Coburg, Lichtenfels, and Nürnberg. On May 27, 1849, he
reached the gates of Lindau, where he was asked to surrender his
passport. He spent that night at a hotel, vainly trying to perfect
the sort of Swabian dialect spoken by Professor Widmann of Tübingen, in case he should be questioned about his personal particulars. It was a waste of time, fortunately, because his false and
invalid passport was returned without demur next morning.

Once on board a Swiss steamer, he felt safe at last. He crossed
Lake Constance in warm spring weather, feasting his eyes on the
Alpine panorama beyond, and landed at Rorschach, where he took
the express coach to Zurich. Here he hoped to enlist the aid of a
former Würzburg crony, Alexander Müller, who had been teaching music at Zurich since 1834. Müller, whom he called on early
next day, promptly introduced him to two cantonal secretaries
named Jakob Sulzer and Franz Hagenbuch. Through their good
offices, Wagner was, on May 30, issued with a passport valid for
Paris. This document possesses a certain importance because it is
our only attested guide to Wagner's height, which was 5 feet 5 1/2
inches.*

Wagner left Zurich the same night, Alexander Müller having
promised him shelter at his Rennweg home in case of need. On
June 2, after a brief stop at Strasbourg, he reached Paris. Although
it was not the city he had left ten years earlier, the musical scene
appeared to have changed little: If anything, he found it even more
ruled by money. Liszt's secretary Belloni, to whom he had been

referred, thought he could best help Wagner by approaching the writer Gustave Vaez on the subject of a new libretto. Wagner was not enthusiastic. He needed a translator, but the thought of having his nebulous ideas done over into French by Vaez did not boost his confidence in the project. From then on he left it to chance to foil his plans for a Paris production. For nearly a year, he again paid lip service to a half-lie—a pretense sustained purely for the benefit of his wife and friends.

Because cholera was raging in Paris—thirteen hundred people are reported to have succumbed in a single day—Wagner moved on June 8 to Rueil, just outside the capital, where Belloni and his family had also taken refuge. "A week in Paris was enough to show me what a monstrous mistake I had made," he wrote to Ferdinand Heine on November 18 of the same year. "Forgive me if I do not enlarge on the outrageous and worthless nature of artistic activity in Paris, especially in regard to opera." He could not have seen much of it. Instead of devoting thought to a new opera, as everyone expected him to, he spent his time at Rueil reading the works of Pierre-Joseph Proudhon, notably *Qu'est-ce que la Propriété?*, and Lamartine's *Histoire des Girondins.*

He now began to ponder on the relationship between art and revolution without betraying any such unruly ideas to Belloni or his kinsman, the mayor of Rueil, at whose home they took their meals. Wagner was deeply affected by evil tidings from Baden, where the insurgents had finally been quelled with the aid of Prussian troops. Among those taken prisoner was the Dresden attorney and Paulskirche deputy Adolf von Trützschler, whom Wagner knew from his days in the Vaterlands-Verein. On August 14, 1849, in flagrant violation of the law, Trützschler was tried by a Mannheim court-martial and summarily shot.

With no new work to offer and no market for any of his existing scores, Wagner became impatient to leave again. At the end of June, Liszt instructed Belloni to advance him 300 francs for traveling expenses, and on July 6, Wagner reappeared in Zurich, where he temporarily lodged with Alexander Müller. Even at this stage, he was determined to concentrate on his artistic ideals to the exclusion of all else, staving off outside pressure with the help of his friends. This provoked great friction with Minna, who refused to join him in Zurich unless he could guarantee her a regular income. She left his entreaties unanswered for so long that he wrote to Natalie imploring her to win her "sister" over. Minna found it depressing and ignominious that he should be unable to support her out of his own earnings. She had dreamed of seeing him at the head of the biggest royal orchestra in Germany, and all he could offer was the prospect of some lectures. On July 18, she wrote: "I trust you appreciate, my dear Richard, that my joining you will entail no mean sacrifice. What kind of future faces me now, and what can you offer me?" Little enough, in all conscience. Minna was right, of course, to remind him of his conjugal duties, but what she represented as a misfortune, to him meant liberation. He could never get over this misunderstanding, nor did his efforts to dispel it make any headway at all.

He was happy that summer in Switzerland. It is easy to imagine his relief at having severed the Gordian knot, escaped his debts and professional constraints—eluding a threat to his life and liberty. He never regretted what had happened, neither then nor later. "From the shore from which I have cast off, no new wind comes to fill my sails," he wrote to Ferdinand Heine that December, "—or at most some farts from Lüttichau and Winkler, but with such winds I no longer care to sail." He was not exaggerating when he wrote, two years later, in *A Communication to My Friends:* "I can find nothing to compare with the sense of well-being that pervaded me—once the first distressing effects had been overcome —when I felt free, free from the world of tormenting, ever-unfulfilled desires, free from the circumstances in which those desires had been my one devouring form of sustenance!" It was then, when the hunted outcast was absolved from further deference to "lies of any kind" and could proclaim his contempt for the world, that he felt "free through and through, hale and hearty," for the first time in his life.

He felt this even though he had no idea what to live on. Liszt could not help him ad infinitum because he was spending vast sums in supporting Princess Carolyne, whose income from Russia had been abruptly cut off at the instigation of her family. He continued to send him money nonetheless, settle his bills, and obtain subventions from the court theater at Weimar—once, even, from the Grand Duke himself, who chose to remain anonymous. Wagner's Swiss friends helped too, in their discreet and unobtrusive way, without ever asking for an IOU. They stood by him, but not from motives of personal affection alone. Their sense of solidarity with all outcasts and refugees was something quite new in Wagner's experience, and it reinforced his inclination to settle in Zurich for good.

Jakob Sulzer took such a keen and sometimes disputatious interest in the German émigré's plans because meeting Wagner had reminded him of his own neglected studies in the field of philosophy. Sulzer cared little for music, but this was soon to change. An earnest young man, he grew to admire the alien qualities of character that made Wagner so very different from himself. Despite Wagner's irritating traits, of which he was fully aware, Sulzer became one of his closest and staunchest friends.

Before long, Wagner was the focal point of a circle of art-loving intellectuals based on Sulzer's official residence. In addition to Alexander Müller and Franz Hagenbuch, the other cantonal secretary, these included Professor Ludwig Ettmüller, a white-bearded authority on the sagas; Bernhard Spyri, a youthful lawyer and newspaper editor; and Gottfried Keller's friend Wilhelm Baumgartner, a music teacher of no great professional ambition. After reading them his poem *Siegfrieds Tod* early in August, Wagner declared that he had never received a more attentive hearing from any male audience.

The authorities left Wagner entirely in peace, and by 1850 he had been deleted from the list of refugees liable to regular police checks.

It was at the *café littéraire* in Weinplatz, an expatriates' haunt, that Wagner underwent one of those peculiarly seminal experiences that were always associated in his mind with visual images. The vulgar wallpaper with its classical motifs reminded him of Genelli's *Dionysus with the Muses of Apollo*, the painting that had so much impressed him at the home of his brother-in-law Friedrich Brockhaus. He had a vivid recollection of it, and its personification of primordial beauty, grace, and strength initiated the train of thought from which there evolved his comprehensive theory of art, down to and including *The Artwork of the Future*.

Wagner's urge to write sprang from a combination of factors. In July, shortly after his return from Paris, Wilhelm Baumgartner had brought him a copy of Ludwig Feuerbach's *Gedanken über Tod und Unsterblichkeit* [*Reflections on Death and Immortality*], which Metzdorff, the German Catholic priest, had strongly recommended him to read at Dresden. He was deeply impressed, not

only by Feuerbach's social radicalism, but by his resolute athe-
ism.* If immortality were really reserved for great deeds and sublime works of art alone, Wagner could not but think it all the more
essential to preface any resumption of work on plans for mythological dramas by submitting the fundaments of his conception of
art to theoretical analysis and, at the same time, showing his true
political and philosophical colors.

Written at the end of July 1849, while he was still occupying a
small third-floor bedroom in Müller's apartment at 55 Rennweg,
Art and Revolution was a direct product of Proudhon's and Feuerbach's influence. It attacked Christianity's antisensualism and
blamed the artistic incapacity of the industrial age on its sociopolitical conditions. To the advantage of the wealthy, "God is
become Industry, which keeps the poor Christian worker alive
only until celestial market conditions bring about the gracious
necessity of releasing him into a better world." What Wagner's
essay characterized as the ideology of the rich—immoral activity
on the one hand, vicious inertia on the other—precisely foreshad-
owed two characters in the *Ring*, Alberich and Fafner, who personified these forms of behavior. Speaking of man's innate need for
art, Wagner went on to make his first reference to the alienation
of labor. Once the manual worker relinquished the product of his
labor, all that remained to him was its abstract value in terms of
money, and his activity could never transcend the workings of a
machine. "He regards it merely as toil, as dismal and bitter drudgery. This last is the lot of Industry's slaves. Our modern factories
present a wretched picture of utter human degradation: ceaseless
exertion, destructive of mind and body, devoid of love and enjoyment—often, too, almost devoid of purpose."

Many earlier students of Wagner were astonished to find him
writing such things in the middle of the nineteenth century, so it
became customary to suppress or ignore such passages in order, as
Glasenapp puts it, "to keep the principles of Wagner's theory free
from the often immature and inadequate ideas of contemporary
political liberalism"!

Scandalous and impermissible as this may seem to the modern
eye, we should be careful to avoid seizing too eagerly and indiscriminately on his stated views and accepting them at face value,
because they were compounded with an "anticivilizational" emotion of which more will be said in another context.

Nevertheless, *Art and Revolution* disposes of any idea that Wagner's political stance might have changed since the revolution. Even after his flight from Dresden, he continued to believe in "an impending upheaval in social conditions and a consequent improvement in the state of art."

The radicalism of this first essay was surpassed by a twelve-page fragment entitled "The Artistry of the Future," which was meant to form the second part of his treatise on revolution, art, and the future, but remained uncompleted and was never published during his lifetime. Under the heading "On the Principle of Communism," this declared: "Do you believe that history—the historical life of mankind—would cease with the end of our present condition and the inception of a new, communist world order? Quite the contrary, for true and distinct historical life will begin only with the cessation of what has hitherto been called the logic of history, which is really and essentially founded on fable, tradition, myth, and religion, on customs and institutions, justifications and assumptions that in no way rest ultimately on historical consciousness, but on (mainly arbitrary) figments of myth and imagination such as monarchy and heritable property." According to Wagner, the most consummate satisfaction of egoism, and its consequent abolition, was attainable only through its negation in communism. Science, he claimed, helped to induce an awareness of necessity while art displayed it to the human eye. He duly posited a sequence of superstitions leading up to "the truth": first polytheism; then Christianity, a necessary aberration; and finally communism, construed as a life devoted to science and art. (Who, one wonders, was to do the actual work?) Wagner expanded this fragment at irregular intervals by jotting down aphorisms of which the last was not added until April 1864, or shortly before he met Ludwig II. There is a recurrence of his pet idea, the justification of anarchy: "Liberty means tolerating no form of dominion over us that militates against our nature, our knowledge, and our desires. If we voluntarily establish a government that commands naught else but what we know and desire, it is superfluous and nonsensical.... To tolerate a government we assume not to know or desire what is right, however, is servile." Given that the passage in question is expressly headed "Anarchy," what else can it be but an argument in favor of *no* government?

"The most perfect condition on earth is that in which human

nature, infinitely enhanced by society, can evolve no desire that exceeds its capacity to fulfill the same." However much we may dismiss such ideas as the abstract fancies of an introspective musician, Wagner comes remarkably close to Marx's definition of the classless society.* He concludes with an almost verbatim echo of the Communist Manifesto: "A vast movement is striding through the world: It is the tempest of European revolution; all are taking part in it, and anyone who fails to promote it by pressing onward strengthens it by his resistance."

It is unlikely that we shall ever discover quite how Wagner came to articulate such extreme ideas, sometimes in the woolly language of a political dilettante, sometimes as if he were parroting a textbook on dialectical materialism. We can, however, inquire how much he actually knew about Karl Marx. Until now, the possibility that Wagner had some knowledge of Marx's ideas and writings has been flatly dismissed by the whole corpus of literature devoted to him. Marx was not represented in Wagner's libraries at Dresden and Bayreuth, nor does the name appear anywhere in his correspondence and memoirs. This suggests that Marx was utterly strange and unfamiliar to him. On the other hand, Wagner knew of Proudhon's ideas before he read his works. He also knew of Feuerbach before opening a single one of his books. And Marx? Had he never even heard of him? The mystery will be resolved in due course.

Wagner had intended *Art and Revolution* for the feature section of the Paris *National,* but it held no appeal for the French. Art was one thing, revolution another. On August 4, he sent the manuscript to Otto Wigand, a radical Leipzig publisher who correctly perceived that the author's notoriety might prove a commercial asset. The runaway kapellmeister was still talked of at princely courts and musical gatherings, though not on account of his operas, which remained an unfulfilled promise until *Lohengrin* became known.

Minna eventually left for Switzerland, determined to badger him into fulfilling that promise, and Wagner set off on foot to meet her at the beginning of September. He tramped through Toggenburg and Appenzell to St. Gallen and on to Rorschach, where Minna, who had noticeably aged in the interim, "poured cold water on his emotions" by threatening to go straight back to Dresden unless he treated her properly. She had come escorted by

Natalie, Peps the dog, and Papo the parrot. Natalie, a short, stout, ungainly girl who could not understand why her "sister" patronized her, became more and more refractory under Minna's eternal nagging. Peps, who was genuinely devoted to his master and never left his side, had such a sensitive nature that he howled and whimpered whenever someone addressed a friendly word to him. Papo's crowning achievement was to whistle themes from Beethoven symphonies.

Wagner lodged his peculiar ménage at Akazie, a house in Schanzengraben. On September 17, after his piano had arrived in company with a few packing cases filled with music and clothes, he moved into a ground-floor apartment at 182 Zeltweg, in the Hottingen quarter of Zurich.

Minna did not object to her husband's literary activities because his first pamphlet had earned a fee that encouraged them both to hope that further publications would yield still greater returns. He was now at work on *Die Nibelungen: Weltgeschichte aus der Sage,* and engaged in bringing his remarks on the Hoard into line with his latest Proudhonist findings. What he found considerably harder going than Proudhon or Feuerbach's *Gedanken über Tod und Unsterblichkeit* was the latter's *Wesen des Christentums.* Although he was almost defeated by its scope, it confirmed his belief that Feuerbach represented "the radical emancipation of the individual from the pressure of inhibiting ideas associated with faith in authority." He accordingly dedicated his next piece, *The Artwork of the Future,* to the philosopher who had long since renounced all worldly honors and now lived in seclusion at Bruckberg, a village near Nürnberg. Wagner's dedicatory letter of November 21 elicited a brief but cordial response from Feuerbach, who stated that he had read the essay with pleasure and found it incomprehensible that anyone should quarrel with it.

This second in the Zurich series of major essays on art (Glasenapp calls it "a product of genius" without citing a single word) contained further statements of a politically explosive nature. Wagner's friends were surprised to learn that modern states were the most unnatural of all human communities because they "came into being solely in consequence of external despotism, for example, dynastic family interests," and permanently harnessed together a certain number of people for a purpose which, if it had ever accorded with some common need, had ceased to do so in the course of time. Carried to its logical conclusion, this spelled the end of the Fatherland.

Industry, declared Wagner, was killing man "in order to employ him as a machine." Opposing utilitarianism, he predicted that "utilitarian man" would be redeemed by the "artistic man" of the future. (Once again, who was to produce?) He had at last discovered a key to the future's redemption by art: the new communal experience, the work of art by all and for all. Surprisingly, he concluded his treatise with *Wieland der Schmied*, the synopsis of an opera in which necessity ends by furnishing the hero with wings. The projected work, he wrote to Uhlig at the end of December, was intended to be merely "an aspect of revolution, a token of assent to destruction," for only destruction was needed now. If the time had come to "relentlessly stir the whole mess up," he was just the man, for "it is my business to make revolution wherever I go."

Reviewing *Siegfrieds Tod* in the light of *The Artwork of the Future*, Wagner found he had certain misapprehensions to dispel, even among his closest friends. "You say," he wrote to Ferdinand Heine on December 4, "that I have *insanely destroyed the bridge behind me*. You are wrong there. It was not I that destroyed the bridge. It collapsed with a tremendous crash of its own accord, because it was poorly and unsoundly constructed, and linked me to a shore on which, were I still living there, I should be deprived of all air to breathe. It was not I that wished to carry matters thus far; they carried themselves thus far, propelled by inherent and irresistible necessity."

Yet it was from Dresden's "airless shore" that a shaft of light now came to brighten Wagner's horizon. Frau Julie Ritter, the mother of his young admirer Karl, signified her willingness to make him an annual allowance of 500 thalers, or a third of the salary he had earned as a kapellmeister.

Soon after being widowed at Narva in 1840, Julie Ritter had moved with her daughter and two sons, Karl and Alexander, to Dresden, where her independent means enabled her to live in modest comfort. Wagner had met her only once, when he was invited to one of Karl's musical soirees. Although he did not stay long, there were tears of gratitude and emotion in her eyes when he left. Such was the woman who now extended her help to the exiled composer whom her sons and their fellow student, Hans von Bülow, admired and respected so deeply. "If experiences of this nature put any person in a good, noble, and cheerful frame of mind," Wagner wrote to Uhlig, "their effect on me at this particular juncture is truly beatific. Never before have I found the sense of freedom as beneficial as I do now, nor gained confirmation of the fact that freedom stems only from a loving relationship with others." Frau Ritter had intimated that she wished to join the Laussot family of Bordeaux in a relief operation. No precise details of this plan having yet arrived from Bordeaux, Wagner was in no hurry to leave for Paris and embark on another distasteful round of wire-pulling with Belloni's help.

All else apart, he was not in the best of health. The Hottingen apartment turned out to be so cold and damp that he developed rheumatism, which allegedly "went to his heart." He felt listless and depressed, even though the people of Zurich were now beginning to appreciate the caliber of the man who had come to live in their midst.

The musical needs of the city, which then had 33,000 inhabitants, were largely met by the Allgemeine Musik-Gesellschaft [Public Musical Society] and the Aktientheater, a commercial theater attached to the municipal casino. Neither institution would agree on a joint program, so the orchestral concerts, which generally employed the services of two dozen professionals and a dozen amateurs, were of a poor standard. The regular conductor, Franz Abt, was good at composing popular songs but quite unable to bring symphonic music to life. It was almost inevitable, therefore, that the committee of the Musical Society should get in touch with the expatriate kapellmeister, and that his impact on the musical life of a city like Zurich should have been considerable.

Even before Wagner's debut at a Musical Society concert on January 15—the music lovers of Zurich were enthralled by his reading of Beethoven's Seventh Symphony, which was unique in their experience—he had fallen into disfavor with the radical liberal *Neue Zürcher Zeitung*. This time through no fault of his own, he became embroiled in local politics. Bernhard Spyri, who was one of his closest friends and sang his praises at every turn, edited the conservative *Eidgenössische Zeitung*. This took Wagner's side, but it was a long time before the *Neue Zürcher Zeitung* would even deign to mention his name.

On January 28, 1850, Wagner informed Theodor Uhlig that he had completed his preliminary prose sketch for *Wieland der*

Schmied. How was he feeling, though? "Immensely foolish, for I am constantly striving, in the interests of my friends' good sense, to delude myself!" This was primarily a reference to Liszt, who persisted in believing that his operatic designs on Paris would succeed. Minna firmly denied in later years that she had browbeaten her husband into going to Paris while suffering from bronchitis and nervous tension. Be that as it may, his decision to go there was half prompted by her and half spontaneous. He could not have set off at a less opportune moment. Thanks to some unexplained misunderstanding, Belloni was away when Wagner reached Paris on January 31, and did not return throughout Wagner's fruitless six-week sojourn in lodgings at 59 rue de Provence.

This second visit to Paris was an even greater disaster than the first. Wagner made no headway at all. His hopes of getting the overtures to *Rienzi* and *Tannhäuser* performed at the Union Musicale were dashed when it suddenly transpired that insufficient rehearsal time remained before the end of the winter season. A reunion with Anders and Ernst Kietz only reminded him of past misfortunes and did nothing to raise his spirits. He attended a performance of Meyerbeer's latest box-office hit, *Le Prophète*, at the Grand Opéra, but was so infuriated when the Prophet's mother vented her grief "in the well-known series of inane roulades" that he walked out. At the end of February he wrote "Art and Climate" for the *Deutsche Monatsschrift*, a journal published in Stuttgart but edited in Zurich by a fellow refugee, Adolf Kolatschek. This article was a tirade against his "civilized" surroundings.

Then he received an invitation from Bordeaux. It was not his first communication from that quarter. A letter to Liszt dated February 6 mentions that he had been informed "tactfully, and by a third party" that a Madame Laussot of Bordeaux was willing to set aside an appreciable sum of money for him. The lady in question had learned of his plight from the Ritters of Dresden, made several contributions to his expenses, and requested a portrait of him, which Ernst Kietz painted. Once she had succeeded in overcoming the opposition of her family, or so it seemed, she approached Wagner direct.

Absolved from the need to pursue his operatic plans in Paris by her promise of continuing support and an invitation to Bordeaux, Wagner temporarily abandoned *Wieland der Schmied.*

The Jessie Laussot Interlude

What followed was like a dramatic action sequence spliced into a relatively uneventful motion picture. At this still immature stage, Wagner anticipated the Wesendonck and Bülow affairs, with their "injured third parties," by putting on a grotesque play of intrigue in which everyone deceived and hoodwinked everyone else.

As yet without any ulterior motive, Wagner wrote to his dear "Mienel" on March 13 informing her of his projected trip to the south. "Will you be cross with me if I tell you that I have come to a swift decision and finally accepted the most pressing and cordial invitation from my friends in Bordeaux—since they have sent me my traveling expenses—and that I shall accordingly leave for Bordeaux tomorrow morning? Were this family not in Bordeaux, and had they not provided for us during this time, I think I should no longer be alive!"

Wagner left Paris by diligence on March 14. On March 16, after an enjoyable journey by way of Orléans, Tours, and the Gironde, he reached Bordeaux and was made welcome at 38 cours du Jardin Public, the home of Eugène Laussot, wine merchant. It was hard at first to gauge the relations prevailing between its occupants: Laussot himself, a dapper but colorless *homme du monde* who reserved his occasional breaches of good manners for his wife; Jessie, pale, elegant, and youthfully attractive, her intelligent features initially set in a mask of sphinxlike reserve; and her mother, Ann Taylor, who soon turned out to be the spider in the web.

Jessie had been only sixteen when she attended the Dresden premiere of *Tannhäuser* during a visit to the Ritters, who were family friends. Her mother, the widow of a prosperous English lawyer, married her off to Eugène Laussot not long afterward. In 1848, Jessie paid another visit to Dresden. That, as we already know, was when she visited Wagner's home escorted by Karl Ritter. Ever since then, she had filled the vacuum of her barren, monotonous, and loveless life with an infatuation for Wagner's music. As soon as she heard that the composer she worshiped had fallen on hard times, she persuaded her family to assist him on a substantial scale. It was left to Ann Taylor to enlighten Wagner on the extent of the projected subsidy: Between them, the Taylor-Laussot ménage and the Ritters proposed to ease his financial burdens to the tune of 3,000 francs a year, 2,500 of which would be paid directly from Bordeaux in quarterly installments.

Wagner must have been so overwhelmed or astonished that he made no attempt to explore the motives underlying this act of generosity.

The Bordeaux trio lived on inherited wealth. Mrs. Taylor had not only refloated Eugène Laussot's bankrupt business but continued to keep the entire household going. She had clearly engaged in an affair with her son-in-law before marrying Jessie off to him. For this she atoned by tolerating and financing her daughter's whims, but only up to a point—and that was where Jessie and Wagner made a disastrous miscalculation. Had Wagner been discreet and observed the rules of middle-class etiquette, he would have remained on course financially for years to come. Instead, he followed the dictates of the "plot," and the drama unfolded. Twenty-one-year-old Jessie spoke fluent German; better still, she was a good listener. *Wieland der Schmied* appealed to her more than *Siegfrieds Tod,* and she promptly identified herself with the swan bride. To Wagner's surprise, she proved to be an accomplished pianist and delighted him with a performance of Beethoven's Piano Sonata in B-flat Major, Opus 106. When she sang to him, however, her shrill and strident voice so shocked his sensibilities that he urged her to confine herself to the keyboard. The trace of hysteria in her voice should have put him on his guard.

Eugène Laussot, who was bored by intelligent conversation, tended to leave them alone together even when he was not away on one of his frequent business trips, and Jessie's mother was too deaf to take much part in their discussions. It was not until Wagner witnessed a scene between Jessie and her husband that he discovered his common bond with her: They were both unhappily married, and he told her so. After her proposal that the family should abandon Bordeaux and the wine trade and move to Switzerland had fallen on stony ground, Jessie drew Wagner into a relationship whose intimacy fanned the flames of his wildest escapist dreams. Minna had just sent him one of her most bellicose epistles ever: She no longer chose to live at the side of a man who supported her on the charity of outsiders. They had come to the end of the road, she declared. From now on, he was to address her formally as *"Sie."*

Her declaration of war only strengthened Wagner's resolve to cast caution to the wind. He told Jessie that he intended to assign half his allowance to Minna and use the other half to "seek obliv-ion" in Greece or Asia Minor. With languishing sighs, Jessie hinted that she was ready to share his fate, throw off her marital chains, and follow him like Schwanhilde soaring into the blue with Wieland. Her pity for him seemed suddenly to have blossomed into erotic passion. Bewildered, agitated, and uncertain how to put his plan into effect, Wagner returned to Paris on April 5.

*   *   *

Thereafter, all those involved in this little drama acted with an instinctive lack of discretion that enhanced its theatrical impact and put weapons into their opponents' hands. Before long, the stage was bristling with naked blades.

Wagner had scarcely left Bordeaux when Jessie wrote Minna a letter. "Yes indeed, dear lady," she gushed, "we, your husband's admirers, are particularly concerned that he shall now live and write entirely as his heart bids him, and seek to work toward his great goal unhampered by external considerations. We are pre-pared to do anything in order to attain this end. Of that, dear lady, rest cordially assured." It was also their intention to comfort her, Minna Wagner, and help her forget her afflictions, which she had borne so steadfastly. Wagner's visit to Bordeaux had given them all great pleasure. They believed that his stay there had not been "disadvantageous" to him, and would gladly have had his wife there, too. . . .

Sincerity or hypocrisy? Had Wagner inspired the letter, or was he sustained by wholly unfounded expectations? Whatever the truth, Minna smelled a rat. Either then or later—we cannot be certain—she adorned Jessie's letter with the scribbled comment: "O false, treacherous creature!" As for Wagner, she left him in Paris without further news.

He had no idea what his next move should be. No arrangements had been made with Jessie, and he was too appalled by the prospect of Minna's recriminations to return to Zurich. Meanwhile, regard-less of the latest developments, Minna had complied with his wishes and moved to new quarters in Enge, on the left bank of the Zürichsee. It almost seemed that Wagner was recovering his bal-ance after the aberrations of the past few weeks.* He took a small room at an inn in Montmorency—kept by one Monsieur Homo, whose name amused him—where his "artistic instinct awoke once more." He reread his *Lohengrin* score and weighed the chances of getting it premiered somewhere. Ernst Kietz came to see him, and they spent some happy hours together. He was just beginning to enjoy his seclusion when he received a letter from Jessie informing him that she had decided to leave home and place herself under his protection.

It was probably this letter that made up his mind. He told Jessie that he planned to sail for Malta from Marseille on May 7 and take her with him to Asia Minor, traveling by way of Greece. As for her husband and mother, they should be led to believe that she was going to stay with the Ritters in Dresden. On April 16, Wagner wrote Minna a farewell letter couched in language that was intended, sadly but firmly, to bring about a final break between them.

"I am altogether alien to you," he wrote. "You see in me only awkwardnesses and eccentricities. You see in me only that which you find inexplicable, and nowhere find compensation for the suffering I cause you." Summarizing, he announced that the conflict between them was irreconcilable. She could not understand him and would only, at best, continue to delude herself about him. "Here is the only cure: to live apart!" He begged her most earnestly to accept half his annual allowance, which he still believed would be forthcoming, to help sustain her "wretched existence." It had been earned, so she need not feel ashamed of it. As to a divorce, he was against it. She would remain his wife in the eyes of the world. Since he was going abroad, she would have no difficulty in explaining his absence and making their separation seem natural. "May my courage not desert me!" he exclaimed with dark foreboding, and concluded with innumerable repetitions of "Farewell!" Abrim with self-pity, he wondered on paper how he would be able to endure being parted from her. "Farewell! Farewell! My wife! My dear old companion in misfortune!" We may safely assume that he wept as he wrote these words.

They smote Minna like a bolt from the blue. All she could think of, in her utter consternation, was how to get to Paris as quickly as possible. She armed herself with a letter from Sulzer and Baumgartner in which they jointly begged her husband to reconsider his decision and return to the fair city of Zurich, where his new lakeside home had been christened "Villa Rienzi." Their request was prompted, not by self-interest, but by a wish to prevent him from obstructing the course of his own destiny, which had already been "written in letters of fire."—"However your decision turns out, never forget that you will not find friends more faithful than those that await you in Zurich." This, undoubtedly, was Sulzer talking.

Wagner was in the process of sending his *Lohengrin* score to Weimar, hoping that Liszt might premiere it there, when Minna left Zurich on April 21. Still at Montmorency, he was alarmed on April 24 to hear that Minna had arrived in Paris and called on the bookseller Albert Franck to inquire his present address. He went into town at once, summoned Kietz to his hotel, and told him to inform Minna that he had already left. Kietz, who had been privy to Wagner's plans for some days, confessed to feeling "like the axis around which all the misery in the world revolves." After killing a little time, Kietz accompanied Minna to Montmorency on April 27, but Wagner had already, on the night of April 25, left for Geneva via Clermont-Tonnerre. Minna returned to Zurich, having accomplished nothing, while Wagner recuperated from his game of hide-and-seek at the Hôtel Byron in Villeneuve, at the eastern end of the Lake of Geneva. He was too exhausted to entertain any immediate idea of leaving for Asia Minor or anywhere else.

He did, however, summon up the energy to write two almost identical farewell letters to Minna and Kietz on May 4. In these he stated that he was that very day "leaving modern Europe for some time in order to visit Greece and the Orient." Surprisingly and gratifying enough—so he mendaciously assured his wife—sufficient funds for the fulfillment of this long-cherished ambition had been made available from London "by one of the most eminent English lawyers." His letter to Kietz was just as bogus. Kietz was clearly meant to show it to Minna, for whom he duly made a copy.

Meanwhile, Karl Ritter had arrived in Zurich to place himself under Wagner's guidance and tuition—a mixed blessing, as it turned out. An entertaining and affectionate but difficult young man with a strangely lopsided face, Ritter combined literary and musical talent with great powers of perception, but was incapable of throwing off his inhibitions and applying his talents to a life of solid endeavor. It seems likely that he was a homosexual who sought the proximity of a dominant male presence. Stressing the need for absolute secrecy, Wagner summoned him to Villeneuve, where he arrived during the second week in May.

On May 8, when Wagner's ship was well on the way from Marseille to Malta, Minna wrote him a pathetic letter whose draft is preserved in the Burrell Collection. It implies that she was as uncertain of her suspicions as Jessie still was of her determination to elope. In advance of her husband's birthday, Minna wished him enduring good health and the best of good fortune on his impending hazardous journey. Had it not been for providence, she wrote, this latest blow would have driven her out of her mind. "I beseech you, what is going on inside you again *this* year? Nothing is sacred to you, nothing more remains for you to destroy but our *conjugal happiness*. That is why you guard yourself against reproach by fabricating the meanest, most unjust and contemptible accusations; why you persuade yourself of things that have *never* existed between us; and why you ultimately deceive yourself in order to excuse the abominable treatment to which you are once more subjecting me." Never in fourteen years had she heard a single word from him on the subject of their incompatibility. It was only in the past two years, since his unhappy preoccupation with politics, "which have already destroyed so many happy relationships," that she had unwisely become embroiled in violent scenes with him. That was the only respect in which she had failed to understand him, but it had been apparent to her simple mind that "no good would come of your revolutionary activities." She had striven to be all things to him, and he himself had written her, even from Bordeaux, that he knew of no greater happiness than to lead a tranquil and untroubled life with her in the Alpine countryside. She had not been serious in her recent allusion to the formal mode of address and begged his pardon for having teased him so stupidly. "If you will but grant me this one *last* request," she wrote, "look back once more on our entire life, quietly and without rancor, and you will find that I was right, and that we were *both* happy and content with each other." She did not now insist on their being reunited, but would go into service or rejoin the theater.

Minna's letter was still in the mail when events overtook it, though another letter dated the same day, this time to her from Jessie's mother, indicates that Mrs. Taylor still had no inkling of the conspiracy. Because her "children" were not in a position to pay it, she trusted that Frau Wagner would accept the annual allowance of 2,500 francs from herself, this to be guaranteed for two years, and added that she had already entrusted Herr Wagner with the first quarterly installment of 625 francs. She would rejoice if the wife of the man whose talent she so much admired would accord her the title with which she signed herself: "Your friend, Ann Taylor."

After this interlude, which Wagner spent on tenterhooks at Villeneuve, the curtain rose on the last act. Word reached the Hôtel Byron from Bordeaux that all was lost. Jessie wrote to say that she had confided in her mother, who had betrayed the whole plan to her husband, and that Eugène was hell-bent on putting a bullet in Wagner's head. She had reluctantly undertaken not to see him for a whole year.

Jessie had been mistaken in her mother. Ann Taylor naturally had no intention of giving her money up for lost or admitting that she had made a bad investment. Eugène Laussot's humiliation would reflect on her entire family, so she made up her mind to forestall the "abduction" of her daughter by a little German conductor whose music she did not, in any case, understand.

Wagner was unwise enough to write at once to Laussot advising him what a "mistake" it was for any husband to try to hang onto a wife who did not love him. He also announced that he was coming to Bordeaux and foolishly mentioned that his passport might land him in trouble with the authorities because he would not have time to obtain a French visa. He said good-bye to Karl and set off for Geneva, where he again became obsessed with thoughts of death. That night he wrote to Julie Ritter in Dresden, describing the turmoil he was in. On May 12, he left Geneva for Lyon and Bordeaux, where he arrived three days later, resigned to his fate.

Next morning, after spending the night at the Hôtel Quatre Soeurs, he sent word to Eugène Laussot that he would await his pleasure there. Instead of a reply, he received a summons to police headquarters, where he was questioned about his passport. When he uneasily admitted that he had no valid visa because the journey had been undertaken in haste, on urgent family business, it was conveyed to him that this urgent family business was the very reason why he could not be permitted to remain in Bordeaux. He was asked to quit the city at once, no attempt being made to deny that proceedings had been taken against him at the request of the family concerned. Wagner begged the police inspector's permission to rest for a couple of days and was granted it all the more willingly because the aforesaid family had left Bordeaux at noon that day.

Eugène Laussot had, in fact, retreated to the country with his wife and mother-in-law. Wagner wrote Jessie a letter describing what had happened. He did not disguise from her that he took such a poor view of her husband, who had "sacrificed his wife's reputation" by denouncing him to the police, that he would be unable to enter into any kind of communication with her until she had released herself from "this shameful relationship." It only remained to see that Jessie got the letter.

An eerie little episode followed. Going to 38 cours du Jardin Public, Wagner rang the bell and the door swung open of its own accord. He walked up to the first-floor suite and tiptoed from room to room until he reached Jessie's boudoir. Then he put the letter in her sewing basket and retraced his steps, still without seeing a soul. We do not know when Laussot came back, but he must have been careful to ensure that Jessie never got the letter.

On May 19, after a brief tour of Lyon, Wagner returned to Villeneuve, where Karl Ritter greeted him with the unexpected news that his mother and his sister Emilie would be arriving very shortly. To Wagner their visit seemed heaven-sent. He brought them up to date on the latest developments and reassured Frau Ritter, herself a rather nervous person, about his own state of mind. She and her daughter remained at Villeneuve for a week and helped him to celebrate his birthday.

It was now that Julie Ritter first displayed her virtues to the full. She was one of those uniquely unselfish women to whom Wagner owed his professional advancement and survival. Not a word of reproach escaped her lips, even though her friendship with the Taylor-Laussots must have made the whole affair extremely painful to her. There was no hope of further financial assistance from Mrs. Taylor, and Julie Ritter's own resources were too limited to guarantee Wagner complete independence. She not only stood by her original offer, however, but earned his heartfelt gratitude by providing him with sufficient funds to cover his immediate expenses.

Before leaving, Frau Ritter commended her son to Wagner's continued care. He and Karl then set off through the Visper-Tal to Zermatt, at the foot of the Matterhorn. Karl found this desolate part of the Valais "horrid," so they moved on to Thun, where Wagner refreshed himself by rereading the *Odyssey*. Drawn together by the solitude that surrounded them, the composer and his twenty-year-old acolyte developed a close personal relationship of which *My Life* provides a vivid though possibly incomplete picture: "Despite my young friend's extreme reticence, which still betrayed some of his former shyness, I always found his conversation agreeable and enlivening, especially after I saw how communicative, exuberant, and vivacious the young man could sometimes become when he squatted down beside my bed before retiring to rest and gave free rein, in the pure and pleasant dialect of the German Baltic provinces, to whatever had aroused his interest."

That Wagner was entirely without homosexual tendencies is beyond dispute.* No hint of any such inclinations can be detected in his boyhood or his literary works, his letters or recorded remarks, nor does anything in Cosima's diaries point in that direction. It is nonetheless noticeable—and here we are straying far ahead—that he more than once became the object of ardent and inordinate male "crushes," invariably on the part of sexually disturbed young men of whom Ludwig II and Nietzsche were only two. This seems less surprising or ludicrous if we dissociate Wagner's appearance from the portraits and caricatures made of him in old age. Until well into his forties, but especially during his early days in Zurich, he was a slim, fiery man with big bright eyes, a pale, transparent complexion, and soft, almost girlish features that contrasted in a strangely attractive way with his firm jaw and lofty brow.

Far from puny by contemporary standards, Wagner captivated those around him with his mental agility and volatile temperament. Although Carl Schurz, who met him at Zurich in the fall of 1849, described him as "an exceedingly arrogant, domineering fellow" whom no one could abide, few were able to resist the charm of his conversation and personal appearance—least of all Karl Ritter, who, like Hans von Bülow not long after him, fell completely under Wagner's spell.

The idyll at Thun was disagreeably marred on June 21 by a letter from Jessie Laussot to Wagner's young companion. "He did not know whether to show it to me," writes Wagner, "because he could not help concluding that Jessie had gone mad." She informed Ritter that she was turning her back on the recent past, and that any future letters from Wagner would be thrown into the fire unread.

The key to the mystery lay in an exchange of letters between Minna and Jessie's mother. Mrs. Taylor had shocked and offended Minna by writing her a letter based on a grotesque misunderstanding. Apparently, Jessie had once remarked to Wagner at Bordeaux that her father had belonged to a religious sect that rejected both the Protestant and the Catholic forms of baptism, so she herself belonged to no recognized denomination. Wagner's jocular response was that he had come into contact with other, far shadier sects because he had discovered, after getting married at Königsberg, that the ceremony had been performed by a "*Mucker*" [religious bigot]. Whether or not this remark had been wrongly reported to Mrs. Taylor, her understanding of it was that Wagner had pronounced his marriage invalid, and she duly wrote as much to Minna. Minna, who was outraged, felt fully entitled to send her unwitting correspondent a detailed account of her married life, together with Wagner's latest letters to her and other material. Mrs. Taylor had used this documentary evidence to persuade Jessie of her lover's mendacity and of the futility of entering into a liaison with such a man. She succeeded to the extent of eliciting a promise from Jessie that she would sever all contact with him.

The Burrell Collection contains a letter from Ann Taylor to Minna that confirms the accuracy of Wagner's suspicions, most of which were later verified by Julie Ritter. Mrs. Taylor's letter opens with the words: "I return herewith the two letters and the documents [or document; the faulty German wavers between singular and plural] which you had the kindness to send me, thanking you very much for the trouble you have gone to in this unpleasant affair; and also for your very dear letter, which I shall keep as a sacred token of our friendship, loyalty, and sympathy." This correspondence between Bordeaux and Zurich formed the background to Jessie's letter of rejection. Because of her allusion to the wrong he had done his wife, Wagner at once sent Karl Ritter to Zurich to acquaint Minna with the "true" state of affairs. At the same time, he informed Mrs. Taylor that he would be repaying the 625 francs remitted to his wife with thanks for her "recognizably generous intention, which has now become void."

As for Julie Ritter, the worthy woman received a seventeen-page jeremiad in which Wagner complained that all Jessie lacked was the revolutionary strength to emancipate herself. His love for her had been wonderfully, radiantly returned. "Had you only been able to see the exultation of love that burst from every fiber of that richly endowed and blessed woman when she not so much confessed as revealed through her whole being, through the spontaneous, clear, and naked manifestation of love, that she was mine!" All had been destroyed by human cowardice. Mother and husband had conspired to cure his weak-willed beloved of her "unseemly" passion. "May they be proud of themselves, those artful physicians: It is a beautiful corpse they have acquired!"

Karl returned from Zurich with a letter from Minna which, although it contained fresh accusations, conveyed that she might be open to a rapprochement. Wagner responded with a lengthy missive whose vague but favorable account of recent events drove Minna to adorn it with marginal notes such as "A downright lie!" "Outrageous!" and "So that's why!" Nevertheless, her husband was coming around at last. He now realized, he said, that her love for him was stronger and more potent than all her errors. He attached no conditions to his return, merely trusted that she would in future be more open with him and more amenable to his whole personality. "I hope that we may yet live together in serene contentment to our lives' end."

Karl also brought news of Sulzer and Baumgartner, those two loyal friends—"sensible people," he called them, unlike "the mad Englishwoman." When Wagner asked if he would like to return to Zurich with him, Karl jumped at the chance, and they set off on July 3.

The Wagners never discussed the Jessie Laussot affair, any more than they mentioned Minna's adultery with Dietrich, the Königsberg businessman. Each knew the other's story but both held their peace. As for Jessie, she eventually left Eugène Laussot and went to live in Florence with the essayist Karl Hillebrand. It proved to be a lifelong liaison.

Writing on July 10 to Julie Ritter, whom he vainly urged for years to settle in Switzerland, Wagner added a touching postscript: "Mother, what do you think? Surely, no such beginning should have turned out like *this*? Alas!" He had addressed her as "Mother" ever since their reunion beside the Lake of Geneva. It is Siegfried's cry as he bends over Brünnhilde: "Mother! Remember me!" Wagner had neither stridden through the flames nor woken the sleeper for long, but he was still making his way in the world and had yet to learn the meaning of fear. That he was taught by stronger women.

The Jewish Pamphlet

The name of Wagner's house in Sterngasse, in the suburb of Enge, was Abendstern. What Wagner's friends had rechristened "Villa Rienzi" was a modest little suburban house with a view of the city, the lake, and the Glarner Alps. It had a small lakeside garden and a rowboat to go with it, so Wagner was able to stroll down in his dressing gown when he felt like a dip. Sulzer, Baumgartner, and Spyri, who were delighted to have him back, came to lunch the very first Sunday. Liszt received a reassuring letter, and it seemed that Wagner was regaining his emotional equilibrium. He even began, on August 12, 1850, to sketch some music for *Siegfrieds Tod*, a surprising fact that has remained almost unknown to this day and is not generally included in this context.* Curiously enough, Wagner never referred to these early experiments. He gave the manuscript away, probably to Jakob Sulzer, and was not to know that it would one day turn up at the Bibliothèque Nationale in Paris. One assumes that he was inhibited from continuing along these lines by three factors: The drama was not explained in terms of its mythical origins; the motifs had not developed beyond their original form; and the composer had yet to complete his design for a new theory of opera.

Wagner was also distracted by some self-imposed reading matter intended to bring him up to date with current topics of discussion in the world of music. Among other things, he read the first half-year's issues of *Die Neue Zeitschrift für Musik*, now edited at Leipzig by Franz Brendel. That August, his prejudices kindled by the phrase "Hebrew artistic taste," he wrote *Judaism in Music*, a piece that Brendel published in two installments on September 3 and 6, 1850, under the transparent pseudonym "K. Freigedenk." By perpetrating these twenty pages of atrocious prose, Wagner jeopardized Brendel's academic position, alienated friendly critics, forfeited the trust of his friends, and incurred the implacable resentment of posterity. But that was not all. We can only deplore the zeal and marvel at the blindness with which he whipped him-

self into such a disastrously misguided lather of mock-revolution-
ary extremism. It was his first betrayal of the "liberalism" which
he now regarded merely as an "abstract principle" and a "not very
perspicacious intellectual game." He conceded that people had
striven without enthusiasm for the emancipation of the Jews,
as for so many other things, when they should really have been
emancipating themselves from the Jews because the latter were
"repellent."

To Liszt, who was dismayed, he explained his views as follows
in a letter dated April 18, 1851: "I nursed a long-suppressed grudge
against these Jewish goings-on, and that grudge is as essential to
my nature as bile is to the blood. An opportunity presented itself
when I was most annoyed at their accursed scribbling, and so I
eventually let fly. It seems to have caused a tremendous stir, which
suits me well, because all I really wanted was to give them a fright
of that kind." Besides, he went on, he had been compelled by
"inner necessity" to proclaim his opposition to Meyerbeer (whose
name was not mentioned). He was driven to this by "genuine
desperation" whenever he encountered the mistaken belief, to
which even a number of his friends subscribed, that he had something in common with that composer.

Well, there it is. We who have followed Wagner's career thus far
may be tempted to shelve such a painful subject, all the more so
since it will recur, but the century that has elapsed since his death
demands a more patient and detailed explanation. Honesty and
sincerity are called for, even if they only paint a warning picture
of the fruits of hatred.

Anti-Semitism has many different roots and manifestations, as
everyone knows, and some of them can sound like enlightened
social economics. During the nineteenth century, anti-Jewish prejudice and invective were still unassociated with the moral oppro-
brium that now attaches to them. After *Tannhäuser* had caused a
rumpus at Paris in 1861, even a man like Herwegh could confuse
a critics' conspiracy with a Jewish plot when attacking corruption
in the French and, sometimes, the German press: "The same bird
squawks in the *Kölnische Zeitung*. There he even signs his name,
Szarvady, in plain German Hirsch or Hersch, so that *the big Jew*
can keep watch on the little one. Moses and his Prophets are
everywhere—or rather, Moses and *Le Prophète!*" Such remarks
were considered elegant and witty at a time when anti-Semitism

was neither exclusively right-wing nor exclusively German. The early French socialists, Proudhon included, voiced anti-Semitic sentiments. Written in 1843, an article entitled "On the Jewish Question" appeared in the following year's *Deutsch-Französisches Jahrbuch*. Its author was Karl Marx. "What is the worldly basis of Judaism?" he demanded. "Practical necessity and self-interest. What is the worldly religion of the Jew? *Haggling*. What is his worldly god? *Money*."* He went on: "The god of the Jews has secularized himself and become a worldly god. Barter is the worldly god of the Jew." For Marx, therefore, there was no emancipation of the Jew, merely an emancipation of the human race through the abolition of plutocracy.

Similar ideas are also to be found at the beginning of Wagner's tract. The Jew held sway and would continue to do so for as long as "money remains the power that deprives all our activities of their effect. It is unnecessary to mention here that the Jews' historical tribulations and the rapacious brutality of Christian Germanic rulers were responsible for placing this very power in the hands of the sons of Israel."

Wagner's contention that people must emancipate themselves from the Jews is startlingly paralleled by Marx, whose article stated that the social emancipation of the Jews connoted "the emancipation of society from Judaism."

If Wagner was really so eager to lash out at the banking world, Paris, Meyerbeer, Mendelssohn, and music critics, he could have made these forays into a delicate subject of which he understood nothing—made them and left it at that. Anti-Semitism hung in the air, and it is hard for posterity to gauge the spirit of a bygone age, but there can be no excuse for Wagner's surrender to the malevolence that drove him to brand the Jews as "repellent."

All his other conclusions followed from that. Given to vulgar "babbling" and spuriously cultured, the Jew was incapable of expressing himself in German in a lively and spirited fashion—indeed, he made himself ridiculous. Being unable to use the language, he had equally little talent for singing and was therefore unsuited to music. How, in that case, had he gained access to the contemporary musical scene? "No art affords a more abundant opportunity to speak in it without really saying anything than music, because the greatest geniuses have already said all there was to be said in it as an absolute art in its own right."

Wagner succumbed to the temptation to denigrate the Jews. He needed them because they alone could help him denounce contemporary music. Religion and politics did not arouse his ire: In religion, the Jews had "long ceased to be foes worth hating," and in politics no conflict existed, but he could oust them from art only by an appeal to the emotions—by mobilizing the basest of instincts against that which was "spontaneously repellent" in the Jew.

Only one Jew had realized, while seeking redemption, that it could be found only in conjunction with "our own redeeming attainment of true humanity," and that was Ludwig Börne. Why did Wagner pick on Börne? Probably because he recalled his talks with August Röckel, the Börne disciple whom he now betrayed in twenty printed pages. Börne, he declared, had known that "becoming socially humanized with us" meant ceasing to be a Jew. But his example had also demonstrated what that process cost in terms of effort, distress, fear, sorrow, and suffering. Were the Jews to take part in the "regenerating task of redemption through self-destruction," everyone would be united and "undifferentiated."—"But remember," Wagner concluded, "that your redemption from the curse laid upon you can take only one form: the redemption of Ahasuerus—decline and fall!"

Wagner's tendency to wallow in heady rodomontades must have been fostered by implacable hatred and deep emotional scars for him to have channeled his destructive and redemptive urges into the eternal surrogate-aggression of anti-Semitism. What did it all signify? Was anti-Semitism—were his writings on art as a whole —an attempt to replace lost illusions with a new ideology?

The Shape of Things to Come

On September 18, 1850, Wagner voiced his mistrust of all reform in a foreword to his Dresden memorandum on theatrical reorganization, which had never been printed. All he still believed in now, he declared, was revolution. He was even more explicit in a letter to Uhlig dated October 22, which warned his friend against trusting in politics, parties, or democratic leaders. People had had enough of them, he said. The spoon-fed, downtrodden masses had merely fuddled themselves with political schnapps instead of being and doing what they "really are and will do." Hitherto, the only known manifestation of enslaved human nature was crime, which shocked and disgusted people, "but how will it seem to us if the immensity of Paris is burned to rubble, if the flames spread from city to city, and if we ourselves, wild with enthusiasm, set fire at last to these uncleansable Augean stables in order to gain some healthy air? I assure you, quite deliberately and without deception, that the only revolution I now believe in is that which will commence with the burning of Paris." Strong nerves would be required, he wrote, and only the staunch would survive. "Let us see how we shall rediscover ourselves after this healing conflagration. I could picture this, at a pinch: I could even imagine, here and there, some enthusiast summoning together the survivors of our old world of art and saying to them, 'Who would care to help me stage a drama?'" No money would be available for this enterprise, and those who volunteered would assemble in a makeshift timber building and present people with a sudden demonstration of true art. "When? I cannot say, for nothing is being done here. I only know that the next storm will surpass its precursors in exactly the same measure as the February Revolution surpassed our expectations in 1847. There is only one more step to be taken, and it is imperatively necessary."

That winter, Wagner readdressed himself to the definition of opera. What was intended to be an article on the nature of opera developed into his chief theoretical work on the subject, *Opera and Drama*. The most voluminous of his Zurich prose works, it culminated in the Sibylline pronouncement: "The creator of the future work of art is none other than the artist of the present, who senses the life of the future and yearns to be embodied therein." Wagner completed his first draft on January 10, 1851, and the final version on February 11. Papo the parrot, whom he had neglected during these exertions, fell dead in his cage on the day the fair copy was finished. His master sent out some elaborate obituary notices and submitted the manuscript of *Opera and Drama* to Uhlig with the words: "Here you have my testament: Now I can die."

Wagner read his latest work in twelve installments to a circle of friends at Haus Abendstern. Those present included Adolph Kolatschek, who had emigrated from Stuttgart, and the poet Georg Herwegh, also of Stuttgart, who had become editor of the journal *Europa* in 1837, when he was only twenty. Herwegh had first fled to Switzerland in 1839 to escape military service. In 1842, after gaining early fame with his *Gedichte eines Lebendigen*, he went on a triumphal tour of Germany, only to be expelled because of a pamphlet hostile to the king of Prussia. Returning to Switzerland, he moved in 1843 to Paris, where he became an intimate of Countess Marie d'Agoult, the mother of Liszt's children. He set off to aid the Baden insurgents with a volunteer corps recruited in France, but was defeated by weight of numbers and took refuge again in Switzerland. Now that his wife had marched across the Rhine at the head of a band of freedom fighters, attired in a black velvet costume complete with hunting knife, Herwegh led a bachelor existence at the Hôtel du Lac, where he made a rather languid and blasé impression on his fellow guests.

Opera and Drama was new and unfamiliar territory. Kolatschek fell asleep during the readings; Herwegh was bored and eventually stopped coming. It was not until later that he came to appreciate Wagner's "extremely daring schemes and opinions."

While at work on *Opera and Drama*, and even more so while listening to his own torrent of words during those evening readings, Wagner had developed an awareness of how far he must travel to become, at long last, what he really was. He would have to concentrate on his grand design and detach *Siegfrieds Tod* from the traditional operatic framework into which *Lohengrin* had fitted. Insofar as it had ever existed and had not been demolished by Devrient's objections, his old Siegfried scheme inevitably collapsed. To enable everyone to grasp the beginning at the end, he would have to retrace his steps and show Siegfried's origins. Between May 3 and 10, 1851, he wrote the preliminary draft of *Der Junge Siegfried*. Fully fleshed out for the first time, the hero emerged in all his radiant youth. According to George Bernard Shaw, this Siegfried is "a totally unmoral person, a born anarchist, the ideal of Bakoonin [sic], an anticipation of the 'overman' of Nietzsche. He is enormously strong, full of life and fun, dangerous and destructive to what he likes. . . ." The tale of one who went forth to learn the meaning of fear was still fresh in Wagner's memory. "Imagine my fright," he wrote to Uhlig, "when I suddenly realize that this fellow is none other than young Siegfried, who wins the Hoard and rouses Brünnhilde."

He committed the prose version to paper at the end of May and, encouraged by Liszt, produced the entire text of *Der Junge Siegfried* between June 3 and 24. He also made a musical note of the boyishly cheerful "Forth into the forest, into the world!" in the margin. Unless our ears deceive us, the motif seems even now to be a trifle at odds with its musical context, but he retained it with good reason. It was a sigh of anticipation.

No change had yet occurred in Wagner's politically unpolitical ideas. "I hanker fiercely after revolution," he wrote to Kietz on July 2, "and all that really gives me courage is the hope that I shall witness and take part in it."

He had written the text of *Der Junge Siegfried* while suffering from a rash and overtaxing his strength by taking useless sulphur baths whose poisonous residue he later felt obliged to sluice away with water. He was plagued by an unremitting sense of unease, as if forcibly prevented by body, blood, and nerves from executing and completing what had yet to mature. He never succumbed to the dangers of premature productivity—except when theorizing, and even that was more a craze for diverting his creative energy into displacement activities and surrogates of an inferior nature.

Then came some distraction in the shape of Theodor Uhlig, who paid a long-planned visit to Switzerland. On meeting his Dresden friend at Rorschach, Wagner was shocked to see that tuberculosis had already left its mark on him. Youthfully pale, with the gentle fervor of a reincarnate Schiller, Uhlig insisted on hiking to Zurich in Wagner's company. Together with Karl Ritter, they went by way of Heiden and tramped across Appenzell to the Säntis, where the snowfields lay at well over 8,000 feet.

In July, Wagner read Uhlig the beginnings of *A Communication to My Friends*, designed not only as a foreword to the poems of *Holländer*, *Tannhäuser*, and *Lohengrin* but as the signpost that would mark a turning point in his career. Snatches of music, too, haunted him that summer; and on July 23, he noted down the theme of the Ride of the Valkyries on a sheet of manuscript paper. He also thought he had the opening of *Der Junge Siegfried* in his head—a few descriptive motifs such as Fafner's.

Then, on July 30, he and Uhlig set off alone on their last excursion together. They visited the scene of the Tell legend and stayed at the Gasthof Goldner Adler in Brunnen. Proceeding by way of Grütli, Beckenried, Stans, and Engelberg, they reached the Surennen Pass, where Uhlig fell into an icy torrent at over 7,000 feet but "made no fuss" because he was a devotee of water cures. After a night at Amsteg, they trudged up the Maderaner Valley to the

Hüftli Glacier, eagerly discussing politics, Dresden, the theater, and Wagner's plans for the future. It was a future in which Uhlig, one of his shrewdest and most faithful friends, had no part. When they said good-bye on August 10, it was forever.

Wagner completed his autobiographical *Communication* soon after Uhlig's departure. In it he declared that he had concentrated the whole of his artistic resources on what had to be expressed, "to the extent of gradually but completely abandoning my received ideas of operatic structure." His final corrections prior to printing, which were added early in December, included a reference to his intention of presenting three dramas and a prologue "at a festival especially devoted to that end."

He now had a conceptual grasp of everything, but everything remained to be done.

Genesis of a Religion in Disguise

On September 16, 1849, while still at the outset of his essays on the theory of art, Wagner defined their purpose to his friend Theodor Uhlig. "I consider it absolutely essential, however, to write these pieces and send them out into the world before proceeding with my more immediate artistic activities. I must deign to engage in precise communication, and so must those who are interested in the nature of my art, or we shall all grope around forever in a loathsome twilight that is worse than the sort of utter, hidebound darkness in which people see nothing at all and merely continue to cling devoutly to the familiar old banister rail." But no one deigned to engage in any real communication, or even to read him properly.

During the years 1849–51, Wagner produced a series of essays on art that occupy 650 pages in the German edition of his collected works. They remain strangely unexplored to this day. Few have fought their way through the jungle of his prose and brought to light anything more than a handful of his wide-spaced statements of principle, programmatic pronouncements, slogans, and catch-words—for example, the much-cited *Gesamtkunstwerk* [universal work of art or synthesis of the arts].* It would appear, in fact, that only two instances of the latter term occur in Wagner's major essays. One of them can be found in *The Artwork of the Future*, in a very woolly and rhetorical phrase intended to show that Wagner was aiming, not only at collaboration among the various arts, but at a community and association of all artists, a "communal genius" that would create a *"Gesamtkunstwerk* of the future." This should probably be construed simply as a future efflorescence of art; in other words, yet another of the author's hazy and ill-defined utopias.

We are left with no choice but to reexamine Wagner's writings on art. Concealed in the undergrowth of his theoretical prose, like the Hoard in Fafner's cave, lies the key to his conception of himself and to a century-old fallacy on the grand scale. It may be possible to arrive at the truth by translating the gist of his major essays, wherever necessary, into readable, intelligible language. This should be done, moreover, without engaging in the abstractive glorification and indulgent suppression practiced by his apologists, and also without adopting the disdainful approach typical of impatient modern observers who have hitherto been understandably reluctant to swallow the indigestible, thumbtack-studded porridge of Wagner's theoretical jargon.

If we begin by discarding all his superfluous frills—all the cant about sincerity, purity, and the redemption of society by love of mankind—every one of his essays on art will be found to contain a firmly held, central idea. Closely related to his concept of redemption and doctrine of regeneration but discussed here in historical terms, this comprised Wagner's assumption that mankind had undergone a gradual decline since the golden age of Greek antiquity, losing "drama" in the process, and his vision of a new, art-induced communal experience based on a postrevolutionary society. This linking of art and revolution does not at first sight seem so irrational, particularly if we listen to Wagner's arguments in favor of his theory of decline. It could readily have found a place in some section on art in the Communist Manifesto, had not the latter been written by Marx and Engels. All Wagner's aesthetic axioms and postulates are suspended like puppets from this central idea, an unbroken thread running from the ancient world to his vision of the future. It was the same basic idea that organized the whole of his material in the field of art theory, down to and including the minutiae of literary and musical composition, alliteration, and harmony.

Wagner explained his mode of procedure in *A Communication to My Friends. Art and Revolution* was designed to reveal the connection between the nature of art and the sociopolitical state of the modern world; *The Artwork of the Future* to point out the lethal influence of that connection on the arts, which had become incapable, in their egocentric disjunction, of producing the real and "only valid" work of art (a telltale phrase in itself); and *Opera and Drama* to show how opera had hitherto been mistaken for "that work of art in which the germs, or even the consummation, of my intended artwork of the future has already become manifest," when, in reality, "only a reversal of the existing artistic procedure in opera could enable the proper thing to be achieved."

So how did he proceed from there? Gingerly, at all events, when it came to showing his hand. His hymn to the Greeks possessed a charm and initial innocence that must later have endeared him to Nietzsche on the spot. "Once it had surmounted the crude, natural religion of its Asiatic homeland and placed the *beautiful, strong, free human being* at the apex of its religious consciousness, the spirit of Greece, as revealed during its golden age of politics and art, found suitable expression in *Apollo,* the real paramount and national god of the Hellenic tribes." This Apollo had been the agent of Zeus's will on Greek soil. The great tragedian Aeschylus represented him as a blend of the grave and the gay; the Athenians had seen him as such; and now came Wagner, dispensing the fruits of his Dresden-acquired knowledge with remarkable self-assurance. There is no doubt that he had a richly imaginative conception of Greek tragedy, even if he tended to transfigure and harmonize it with the best of intentions. Inspired by Dionysus, he declared, Greek playwrights had made it the exalted task of every ingredient in the arts, which human life had begotten "of intrinsic, natural necessity," to bring forth that most sublime of all imaginable works of art, the drama. Such was the Greek work of art, and such "the Greek nation in its supreme truth and beauty." But the decline of tragedy was associated with the dissolution of the Athenian state. "Just as the sense of community flew apart in a thousand egoistic directions, so too did the great *Gesamtkunstwerk*"—a harmless recurrence of the term—"of tragedy disintegrate into its separate artistic components: The comedian Aristophanes wept, frantic with laughter, on the ruins of tragedy, and all artistic activity halted at last before the earnest musings of philosophy, which debated the reason for the impermanence of human beauty and strength."

But *Art and Revolution* does more than celebrate Greek drama and collaboration among the arts in a single human mode of expression, nor does it simply mourn their passing. It also reveals that Wagner was thinking of a sociopolitical ideal, present in early prehistoric communities, which the Greek city-state had ceased to fulfill—hence its decline. The work of art had disappeared from human history, not only in Greece but elsewhere, because—and this argument lies buried in a subsequent passage—the ancient world sickened and died as a result of slavery. The slave, claimed Wagner, had become a disastrous and universal hinge of fate. "By reason of his mere existence as a slave, which was deemed to be necessary, the slave revealed how futile and impermanent were all the beauty and strength of Greece's special breed of man. He also demonstrated for all time that *beauty and strength, as fundamental characteristics of public life, can happily endure only if they belong to all men.*"

With the decline of tragedy, art gradually ceased to be "the expression of public consciousness. Drama dissolved into its component parts: rhetoric, sculpture, painting, music, and so on." Christianity, described in Wagner's minor writings as an essential moral stage in human progress, had not permitted the emergence of true art but actually obstructed it by means of an antisensualism that deprived life of pleasure. Bourgeoisie and royalty had then abused art by employing it for ornamental and decorative purposes, nor had "real, true art" been reborn during the Renaissance. Art had become an acquisition and was now on a par with arts and crafts, lacking all ideal content. "Its real nature is industry, its moral purpose the acquisition of money, its aesthetic pretext the entertainment of the bored. Our art sucks its lifeblood from the heart of our modern society and the focal point of its circular movement, which is wholesale financial speculation. It borrows an unfeeling charm from the lifeless remains of medieval chivalric convention and descends from there, with a speciously Christian lack of disdain even for the mite of the poor, to the depths of the proletariat, enervating, demoralizing, and dehumanizing wherever the venom of its lifeblood flows." The trend toward entertainment had deprived drama of music and opera of the essence and supreme purpose of drama, which was to stir and move. But just as the ancient world had foundered on the problem of slavery, so the new world could be created only by the abolition of slavery in its most demeaning form, namely, industrial and financial servitude. Only then would it be possible to found a new artistic age. In Greece, art in its prime had been *conservative* "because it presented itself to the public mind as a valid and appropriate form of expression." Now, however, "genuine art" was "*revolutionary* because it exists only in opposition to what is generally accepted"—for the present. Wagner drew a careful distinction between revolutionary art and the art of the future. Revolution was essential to the rebirth of art. "If Grecian art embraced the spirit of a fair nation, the artwork of the future must embrace the spirit of a free mankind transcending all the barriers of nationality; its national character must be no more than an ornament, the charm of individual diversity, not an inhibiting limitation." Only on "the shoulders of our great social movement" would art attain its due place of honor. The better things of the past related to the beginnings of a better future: an attractive idea, or merely an unhistorical utopia?

The last thing Wagner wanted was a universal "reversion to Greekdom." His watchword was "Forward!"—not to a differently organized society, but to "the new man." In *The Artwork of the Future*, he strove to define the nation as a community in collective need and excluded those who, though living in luxury, created needs for themselves, above all "the need for luxury, which is luxury itself." This sounds modern and socialistic, but its prime prerequisite was the new, unselfish man who reconciled himself to equality of needs. The history of the Greeks from ancient times to the present day was the history of egoism, and the end of that period would bring "redemption in communism." Wagner's footnote: Anyone ashamed of being thought an egoist would have to accept being "called a communist." He needed a political theory of redemption at this stage because his exposure of false needs had to encompass false art and, above all, fashion. Art as a means to enjoyment? To the wealthy it was a luxury. And to the poor? The sole concern of "popular reformers with a mania for instructing others"—it is not quite clear whom he meant by this—was to "trickle the honey of music into the vinegar-sour sweat of the mistreated factory worker, it being all that can alleviate his sufferings." He passed a similar judgment on landscape painting, admissible though it might be from an aesthetic standpoint. A "sad affinity" existed between the "pretty-sounding music" of the day and the "nice views" purchased and mindlessly goggled at by philistines. What connected them was "certainly no thoughtful idea, but that sloppy, abject *Gemütlichkeit* which selfishly averts its gaze from the sight of human suffering all around and rents a private little heaven in the blue haze of natural vulgarity." So far, so good, but these are merely critical skirmishes preceding the gradual establishment of a counterposition.

Passion music, oratorios, and operas, said Wagner, were steps leading up to the artwork of the future. Reverting to Beethoven, he characterized his Seventh Symphony as "the apotheosis of the dance itself" (though only to contrast it in "shape" with previous symphonic music) and described the Ninth Symphony as music's redemptive transformation into "universal art." Only now did earlier statements of this kind become building blocks in Wagner's dogma. His musical article of faith was that Beethoven's last symphony was a *ne plus ultra*—not only was but had to be, or his doctrinal edifice would collapse. Absolute music had reached the end of the road: It lacked moral determination and would be absorbed into the still more absolute music of drama. *The Artwork of the Future* and *Opera and Drama* betray Feuerbach's influence in defining as "absolute" any partial art that had become divorced from the *Gesamtkunstwerk*. "Wagner's exposition of Beethoven's 'absolute music,'" writes Dahlhaus, "is precisely analogous to Feuerbach's exposition of 'absolute philosophy.'" This was an allusion to Hegel's speculative ideas, whose metaphysical dimension was to be lowered into the realm of experience and secularized for the sake of man. Wagner's treatment of the absolute in music was less a "lowering" than an exaltation, or so he believed, because he released it into quite another realm of infinity—that of endless melody. But the vehicle of endless melody was the orchestra. In the course of its long history, music had evolved the orchestra as "the basis of infinite, communal emotion." In contrast to Greek drama, the artwork of the future would be unable to dispense with this supreme vehicle of human emotion—the orchestra—because it made possible a new communal experience. Thus the supreme communal art was (musical) drama.

The art of writing in isolation—absolute writing, so to speak— was merely a product of sick times. The healthy person did not describe and contemplate what he desired and loved (in other words, did not write novels and poems) but represented the same in drama. Representation alone could, as it were, humanize the poet. It would be for the writer of the future to subordinate the three sister arts of music, speech, and dance to the plot or "action" [*Handlung*]. There is no doubt that Wagner did not yet see himself as this ideal musical poet, portrayer, and universal artist of the future, just as he distinguished between "revolutionary" and "future" art: He did not incorporate dance (pantomime) in his dramatic conceptions, nor did he ever allow music to assume the purely collaborative role he required of it in theory. He remained too much of a musician, and he knew it. Nevertheless, all his pronouncements combined so well to form a single great theory that Glasenapp and other Wagnerites marveled at its brilliant unity and "lack of antecedents." They labored under a definite delusion in the latter respect, for Wagner's grand design did not spring from nothing, nor did it lend itself to painless implementation. His disciples prudently forgot that his avowed prerequisite for the artwork of the future was the destruction of the existing order. "Dearest friend," he wrote to Liszt on June 5, 1849, "without engaging in political conjecture, I feel bound to state, quite frankly, that no art can grow in the soil of antirevolution; it might not grow at first in the soil of revolution either, unless timely steps were taken to ensure that it did." Wagner was eager to forge ahead.

His initial requirement of the drama of the future, which must also have been inspired by Greek tragedy, was that the plot should culminate in the death of the protagonist—a "necessary" death determined by actions rooted in the entirety of the protagonist's nature. No dramatic denouement could be regarded as complete until the principal character had ceased to be subject to arbitrary assumptions about what he might do in the future—until his life was over and could therefore be reviewed in full. This laid the foundations for the mythical cosmology of the *Ring*. The celebration of such a death, which concluded the drama, was the noblest that could be undertaken by man: "The nature of this *one person* having been revealed to us by death, it discloses the rich content of human nature in general."

And here Wagner makes a revealing digression: The theater of the future would have to be of novel design because the present opera house's social stratification and surrender to love of ostentation precluded an aesthetically satisfactory solution.

On the one hand, too much superfluous art was produced; on the other, society was divided into the supremely cultivated and "the rabble." Just as absorption by love would transform the egoist into a communist—once society had overcome its selfish stratifications —so the arts would be delivered from their isolation and transformed into the artwork of the future. Though little more than a metaphorical phrase, this set an important seal on Wagner's chain of evidence: The indivisible artwork of the future would stem directly from human nature itself.

"Art and Climate" was written in rebuttal of the charge that his assessment of human nature was mistaken and ignored the effect of climate. One did not, he said, have to look to climate "to perceive what has made the modern European artistically incapable"; the cause lay in "civilization, which is quite indifferent to all climatic factors." The following passage contains his argument in a nutshell: "It was not our climate that caused the spiritedly robust peoples of the North, who once destroyed the Roman world, to degenerate into servile, dull-witted, idiotic-looking, neurasthenic, hideous, unclean human cripples; not that which took the happy, enterprising, self-assured, heroic races and changed them past recognition into our own hypochondriacal, cowardly, groveling citizenries; not that which turned the radiantly healthy Germans of old into our own scrofulous linen weavers, themselves woven from skin and bone, or turned Siegfried into Gottlieb and spearsmen into paper-bag twisters, court councillors, and feeble imitations of Jesus Christ. No, the credit for that glorious achievement belongs to our *sanctimonious pandect-civilization* with all its splendid consequences, among which pride of place must go not only to our industry but to our unworthy, heart- and soul-stunting *art*— consequences directly traceable to that civilization, which is altogether foreign to our nature, but not to natural necessity."

Discounting Wagner's Feuerbachian criticism of religion, anti-Christian sentiments, glorification of the ancient Germans, and vehement attacks on civilization, all these remarks served to prepare the reader for his development in *Opera and Drama* of an alternative world, an art-world of the future founded on a "new principle."

Opera and Drama was undoubtedly Wagner's most intelligent prose work, containing many readable and, in matters of detail, exceptionally well-argued passages. It was also his most dangerous work because its vision of the future extended to artistic technique and developed into a *complete ideology*, making excursions into the history of music, linguistics, and political philosophy.

Opera and Drama, too, tackles subjects of a generally political and social complexion. After citing the tragedy of Oedipus and Antigone's opposition to the state,* Wagner claims that the state's decline can possess no rational significance other than "the fulfilling of society's religious awareness of its purely human nature." He goes on: "The social religion of the future will thus be founded on the unhampered self-determination of individuality." Which, being interpreted, means that society as a whole will find fulfillment, according to Wagner's (anarchistic) ideas, in the freedom of all its component parts. This must also be mentioned, if only to guard Wagner against recruitment by collectivists of all colors.

This time, he comes quickly to the point. To summarize the antithesis between opera and drama in a single sentence: The error committed by the artistic genre known as opera consists in its having promoted a means of expression—music—into an end in itself (as, for example, in the "melodic beauty" of Italian opera); whereas the end or purpose of expression—drama—reappears in the guise of a means, reduced to the status of a crutch supporting an inescapable operatic plot. How can the drama of the future be attained by reversing this process?

The renewal of art must be preceded by the renewal of life—that much has already been established. Just as art has become ossified in art criticism,* so "life" has congealed in politics. In Wagner's view, therefore, the political rationality of contemporary civilized society is more or less matched by the contemplative criticasterism of a "professorial" culture. The contemplative superstructure must therefore be stripped of its power before the writer-composer and dramatist can again create in freedom—unselfconsciously, or, to be more accurate, spontaneously, impelled by the universal desire and instinct that lies at the root of all life and is being smothered and vitiated by deliberation and contemplation. Wagner then takes violent exception to Meyerbeer's work, which seems to him to typify the degenerate, "unspontaneous" operawriting in which means and end have been reversed with an eye to pure effect. The essence of this art, he says, is effect without cause.

Wagner conducts separate examinations of the evolution of melody and verse. The poet-composer of the future, that "purposeful portrayer of the spontaneous," can employ neither traditional, "patriarchal" melody nor strict verse with rhymed endings and mechanical rises and falls if he wishes to convey emotion in a natural and intelligible manner. Wagner therefore advocates a free form of verse with a *new* emotional linkage which the readily confusable *vowel* cannot supply. This the consonant is able to do. Because the effect of a consonant *preceding* a vowel greatly clarifies the meaning of a word and, consequently, the meaning of uniform, related, and mixed emotions, *alliteration* provides the poet with a boundlessly effective means of linking the expression of one emotion with that of another in so sensuous a way that the connection becomes perceptible to the ear. Wagner explains this with reference to the sung word. His long-winded dissertation on consonance and assonance, on the correspondence and noncorrespondence of speech and musical rhythms, and on emotional intelligibility, may be summarized as a plea that the transmission of content from poet-composer, via actor-singer, to listening audience should be as simple as breathing in and out. Wagner's alliteration theory acquires significance only when related to his musical analyses, which shed an entirely new light on the method of composition he adopted when starting to write the *Ring*, and therefore merit closer examination here.

Wagner claims that the old-style composer, whose sole aim was to appeal to emotion through music, could do this only by "tuning down his infinite resources" to a very restricted level. Beethoven's reversion to the "patriarchal" melody of "Freude schöner Götterfunken" had also been, like the melody itself, artificial and "tuned down. . . . But the mere construction of this melody was not Beethoven's artistic purpose. We see instead how he deliberately tunes down his capacity for melodic invention, if only briefly, far enough to reach the natural basis of music on which he can proffer the poet his hand, but can also grasp the poet's." Writing to Liszt in 1855, Wagner said that he considered the finale of the Ninth Symphony to be its weakest movement—as bold an assertion then as it would be today. The difference between the "patriarchal" melody and one that grows out of poetic intent on a natural verse foundation, he went on, is that the former manifests itself only in the most limited family relationship between notes, whereas the latter breaches the more intimate key relationship by associating with keys that are in their turn related, so as to "extend it to the basic affinity of notes in general by expanding the firmly transmitted emotion into infinite, purely human emotion." The key in which a melody is written presents its constituent notes to the human ear and sensibilities in a related series. The need to break up and extend this series arises from the *poetic* intent inasmuch as certain keynotes are made vehicles of special expression by the verse, or words. "These keynotes are, in a sense, young adult members of a family who yearn for unsupervised independence outside the wonted family circle: They gain this independence not as egoists, however, but through contact with others that are also situated outside the family." Here we see the macrocosm of Wagner's sociology, the surmounting of selfishness by human love, invading the microcosm of his theory of composition. "The maiden succeeds in emerging from her family and gaining independence only through the love of the youth who, being the scion of another family, attracts her to himself. Thus the note that emerges from the confines of its key is one that is already attracted and governed by another key, and it is into the latter key that it must consequently flow pursuant to the essential law of love. The keynote that thrusts itself from one key into another, and by this process alone discovers its kinship with the latter, cannot but be thought of as motivated by love." According to this remarkable line of argument, a keynote becomes wedded to another key purely because it yearns to do so—a truly "natural" explanation of the keynote-governed splendor of *Tristan*'s score.

But how does poetic speech compel other notes to leave the family circle of their key? This is where alliteration comes into its own. We have already seen, Wagner goes on, how alliteration can couple words of contrasting, as well as kindred, emotive force, for instance "*Wohl und Weh*" [weal and woe]. "Musical modulation can render such a connection perceptible to the senses with a far greater measure of expression. To take an alliterated line of wholly uniform emotional content, '*Liebe gibt Lust zum Leben*' [Love imparts delight to living], for example, the musician would here [in a passage where alliteration betokens no emotional change] have no occasion to venture outside his chosen key, but would keep the musical rise and fall, which is emotionally quite adequate, in that same key. Contrasting this with a line of mixed emotional content such as '*die Liebe bringt Lust und Leid*' [Love brings delight and sorrow], we should find that here, where alliteration couples two opposing emotions, the musician would feel impelled to pass from the struck chord corresponding to the first emotion to another that corresponds to the second. . . ."

Pursuing his theme, Wagner cannot resist taking this sample modulation, together with its verse content, and neatly reverting to the first emotion. If the line *"die Liebe bringt Lust und Leid"* were followed by *"doch in ihr Weh auch webt sie Wonnen"* [yet into its woe it weaves things blissful], *"webt"*—"weaves"—would become a keynote leading into the first key because the second emotion has reverted to the first, now enriched, emotion. This is a reversion which the poet, "by dint of alliteration, could represent to sensory perception only as a development of the emotion *'Weh'* into that of *'Wonnen,'* but not as a resolution of the generic emotion *'Liebe,'* whereas the composer becomes intelligible for the very reason that he quite perceptibly returns to the first key and firmly defines the emotional genus as uniform—a course not open to the poet, who was compelled to change the root initial for alliterative purposes." What Wagner means is that the consonant does not possess a related key, so the poet must here make use of music. Conversely, the musician derives justification for his modulating procedure from the content of the verse.

It is therefore possible to distinguish between thematic primary keys and motif-governed attendant keys, and the farther the poet-composer pursues his psychological art by equipping a character with an abundance of human motives, the more his modulation technique must develop. Such is his incentive and compulsion to change key that he is driven almost to the point of breaking it down altogether. Wagner does not, of course, say so as baldly as that. Instead, he sticks to his original example. If the first line, *"die Liebe bringt Lust und Leid,"* and the second line, *"doch in ihr Weh auch webt sie Wonnen,"* were separated by a longish series of lines whose emotional content was partly corroborative and partly restrictive of theirs, it could readily be imagined that the composer would have to modulate into a diversity of keys until the primary key disclosed its ultimate kinship with all others. This would constitute a poetic and musical "period," or cycle, derived from a single primary key. The most consummate work of art must therefore be that in which many of these cycles evolve from each other, jointly and intelligibly proclaiming the nature of man. Perfect drama depicts the human disposition by presenting its audience with a series of logically self-determining emotional factors, with the result that the plot unfolds spontaneously.

By setting forth his entire program in this way, Wagner had skillfully diverted his readers' attention from an abstract concept —the artwork of the future—and focused it on methods and principles that gave some inkling of his own future course. But he was not content with hints alone.

It was inevitable that, having once evolved his theory of "verse melody" and buttressed it with examples, he should go on to discuss his own most personal absolute quantity, orchestral melody. Related to verse melody "as a *presentiment,*" he said, "is the preparatory, absolute orchestral melody; from it, as a *recollection,* derives the 'idea' of the instrumental motif." This one sentence presents a perfect description of the leitmotif technique.

But what of the chorus? The chorus present in ancient Greek tragedy had bequeathed its dramatic significance to the modern orchestra—meaning, no doubt, the Wagnerian orchestra. It was consistent with this view that, as Cosima noted in her diary on September 29, 1871, Wagner should have described the funeral music following Siegfried's death as a Greek chorus "to be sung, as it were, by the orchestra"—a statement illustrative of the incomprehension displayed by numerous devotees who regretted, after Wagner's death, that he had not written more choral operas. In the drama of the future, he said, the stage would have no place for a mere harmony-producing mass like the chorus in traditional opera, which was losing its proper function and would have to disappear. Because distinguishable personalities alone had the power to involve an audience, the drama's "more numerous surroundings"—a euphemism for the anonymous crowd—must be assigned "the character of individual participation in the motifs and actions of the drama." As Wagner saw it, only the orchestra in its capacity as a vehicle of endless melody, as something that eschewed meaningless utterances and clung strictly to the overall poetic purpose, could continuously convey every detail of the drama's content and purpose to the receptive ear. From this he surprisingly inferred that traditional spoken drama, with its artificially upheld laws, was encompassing its own end. Only in the unity of the ever-present whole, in other words, of orchestral melody, was it possible to resolve "the problem posed till now by the unity of time and space." This was an implicit dig at the endeavors of French and German dramatists, both classical and modern, whose products could not, from this standpoint, be anything but artificial and unsatisfying. The drama of the future would surmount the problems besetting less healthy periods of artistic history. The laws of dramaturgy would accord with the spontaneous expression of human emotion, thus enabling the ancient promise of early drama, drunk as it was with beauty, to find fulfillment in a new communal experience. Music would accomplish what words could not.

The quintessence of Wagner's theory of drama may be summarized as follows: Only that which is wholly fused with musical expression, or singable and comprehensible in terms of motif, is poetic; only that which helps to fulfill and convey the poetic intent is musical;* all else is superfluous and consequently bad. So much for *Opera and Drama.*

A Communication to My Friends contains a further brief account of Wagner's fusion and ramification of thematic motifs in his own music dramas of that web which he not only wove over individual scenes but spread, "in intimate connection with the poetic intent," across the drama in its entirety. His last major essay ends with the assurance that, next time he communicated with the world, it would be through the medium of his completed magnum opus.

What did all this amount to?

A conception of the world that proceeded straight from ancient Greece to a suspended dissonance in a classless society to end all societies. Or, to put it another way, from Zeus-Wotan to Richard Wagner himself.

*   *   *

Wagner's writings on art between 1849 and 1851 constitute a complete theoretical system that seems both logical and coherent but suffers from one disadvantage: It is a religion in disguise.

Thanks to psychoanalysis and behavioral research, we now have an informed understanding of unconscious psychical "inflation," and the role of undirected mental energy in individual and collective psychology. This awareness was lacking at a time when the sectarian doctrine latent in Wagner's artistic treatises exerted a direct or indirect influence on society, arousing hysterical extremes of partisanship and hostility that now strike us merely as absurd but then provoked an endless succession of factional groupings and misunderstandings. We cannot gloss over such things and pretend that Wagner's sole concern was operatic reform—that all the other theses and concepts in his prose works were cranky excrescences, lovable eccentricities, aberrant or "extravagant" whims unworthy of serious consideration. It would be equally improper to dismiss his essays on art as the dilettantish and essentially trifling products of a musician-writer, and thus to underrate their symptomatic importance. Genius must be accepted as a whole or not at all, even if it suffers from mental elephantiasis.

Disguised religions—the term was coined by Carl Bry in 1924— are associated with the image of the monomaniac who harnesses his doctrine to the postulate of a new world, an artificial paradise of eschatological complexion. They manifest a will to power that motivates men drunk with the heady wine of their own preconceptions. Anything that comes their way serves to confirm their monomania. They reduce the world to whatever dimensions may be required to underpin their single fixed idea. Partially correct or not—and it usually contains a germ of truth—this idea seeks to explain and cure the world's ills from a particular point of view that must be defended against all comers and held at all costs. In Wagner's case, his fixed idea was the drama of the future, a thing created more or less by himself.

Surrogate religions, both crude and subtle, tend to emerge at times when nostalgia for the past commingles with hopes for the future, when the sluggish pace of events frustrates what is long overdue, and when an age is riven with irremediable conflicts. This applied as much in the middle of the last century, when terms like "modernity" and "progress" were gaining ground in defiance of entrenched opposition, as it did in the 1920s or does today. When reformism loses momentum, its place is taken by utopian formulas and unpolitical, escapist dreams.* There is no doubt that the failure of the 1849 revolution was instrumental in arousing and intensifying Wagner's titanic urge to bestow his favors on the world. It was not a random or fortuitous process.

How this urge developed within him, matured there, and took possession of him, can only be explained—and then only in part —if we constantly bear in mind the principal features—the leitmotifs—of his career to date. Biographical prose being incapable of disjunction into words and orchestral melody, our account of the factors governing this process must call in turn on "presentiment" and "recollection." They include his belated surmounting of failure in childhood and youth, which fostered a tendency toward escapism (a tendency shared, be it cautiously noted, by other would-be "redeemers"); the disproportion between his brilliantly inventive mind and lack of self-fulfillment at many stages in his life; the twin goads of aggression and missionary fervor; his often fanciful and unrealistic response to extraneous conditions and the opposition of others; and, last but not least, fear. We already know of Wagner's childhood fears. These had been sublimated and replaced by others. Wagner the man sought refuge in illusion because of a deep existential dread.

Psychical "inflation" can attack individuals or whole groups. Religious sects have gone far by steeping their adherents in a single idea for which all others may, if necessary, be sacrificed; but they are not alone. Similar successes have been scored by Freud and Marx, the flat-earth theory and nudism, the Shakespeare-was-Bacon movement (to which Nietzsche subscribed), and those who claim that the Jews are the root of all evil. In every case, a part is substituted for the whole, a surrogate solution for some unmastered human or social problem. Whatever the causes and beliefs that lie at the root of each, the conclusions drawn are transferred to a plane on which experience fades and facts that do not fit the jigsaw puzzle are trimmed to size or discarded. Not even Wagner's anti-Semitism can be divorced from this context, given that it was never shaken by his lifelong debt of gratitude to members of the Jewish race.

In Wagner's scheme of things, this coupling of the particular with the general—a process sometimes carried to the lengths of total confusion and substitution—must be closely studied alongside his identification of art theory with social utopianism. Why? Because it symptomizes the salvationist nature of his approach.

All disguised religions are doctrines of salvation that attempt to found their entire system on a monocausal basis. Partially blind to past and present historical developments, they ascribe an effect to a single cause. In so doing, they refashion reality for their own convenience, for it goes without saying that any such order of artistic precedence as Wagner devised and founded on "historical" evidence, so called, must be a false and arbitrary premise that fails to do justice to the development and role of the individual arts. Partial views, hypothetical assumptions, and auxiliary constructions, accurate and useful though they may be individually, are assigned an inflated value and placed on a par with the theoretical system in its obfuscated entirety. Wagner's theory of alliteration is as much a hypothetical abstraction as dodecaphony: serviceable, but not the only key to salvation.

Being arbitrary in one's premises, deriving effects from a single cause, and explaining the world from a single standpoint constitute a method that lends itself to boundless eclecticism and random presentation. Reconciling opposites presented Wagner with no difficulty whatsoever. His philosophical dabblings positively predisposed him toward the fusion of incompatibles, just as he also resorted, when logic and reality failed him, to etymology. He found it quite easy to reconcile anti-Semitism and emancipatory ideas, revolutionism and contempt for parliamentary institutions, Hellenism and Germanism. This explains the apparent conflict between his political activities and his own assertion, or that of his conservative apologists, that he had never been a "political person," had participated in the revolutionary movement for "purely humanitarian" reasons, had been a revolutionary for art's sake alone, or—as an even more revealing passage in *A Communication* puts it—had never been able to abandon his spontaneous support for all that was revolutionary "in favor of a politically constructive idea." How could he, when politics itself had to be subordinated to his all-embracing explanation of the world from a single standpoint and incorporated in a single, all-embracing, eschatological construction that had as little to do with art as it did with politics?

A disguised religion is bold enough to promise something total and final. Richard Wagner sought to prove, not only that his own method of composition was better and more modern, fulfilled the articulatory needs of the day, was psychologically more effective and contributed to the understanding of human nature, but that it spontaneously and inevitably sprang from a kind of cosmic will —from human nature itself—and was intimately related to the regeneration of society. This claim gave him the right to present his contemporaries with a choice: They could either become champions of goodness and truth, human progress, salvation, love of mankind, and so on—in which case they must lend him their support—or espouse the evils of this world by opposing him and his work.

How deep the disappointment when his outstretched hand was

brushed aside! How keen the self-inflicted anguish when his claim was rejected! Even so, he clung to his all-or-nothing approach. This alone explains the remarkable statement of principle in his *Communication* of 1851: He could not regard anyone as a friend who unthinkingly divorced the artist from the human being; comprehension of his art was restricted to those who also loved him as a man.

Just as Kant held that there could be only one philosophical system because there was only one form of reason, so Wagner held that there could be only one conception of art. He made himself irrefutable by definition. Did he succumb to the obsession that prompts real transformers of the world to believe in their own infallibility? To a limited extent, and where the higher reaches of Wagner's artistic pretensions are concerned, the term disguised religion may be replaced with that of Titanism.*

Wagner was a Titan—a rival god who sought to conquer the world. This was no hubris but a desire for totality that is far from uncommon in German idealistic philosophy and constitutes an almost integral part of its most important doctrinal edifices. With their flawed relationship to authority and their not oversuccessful history, the Germans were quick to exchange action for intellectual Titanism. Wagner's system ranks—not intellectually, perhaps, but in its aspirations—with the ideological structures of Hegel and Marx. The artist added his self-contained system to the store of philosophical and economic thought. By presenting a unified scheme embracing art and society, he furnished the last component of a *cultural revolution* whose failure was as much preprogrammed from the outset as that of Wotan's gamble on the expiation of the world by a free race of men: He planned without people.

For what kind of people, whether they called themselves communists, wore reformist attire, or even crowded around the artwork of the future, would have permitted major spheres of their existence to atrophy for the sake of a monolithic ideology or a resounding program? Advocates of disguised religions always undertake to build a world in which the human being, though not better off, will be transmuted into an ideal person. The campaigns waged by all such ideologists, not excluding Richard Wagner the artist of the future, are unconcerned with the happiness or freedom of individuals whose enjoyment of life is to be enhanced by art; they aim at concepts that cannot be realized until the human being adapts himself to them. The attainment of this utopia presupposes renunciation: a diminished life characterized by diminished human requirements.

Obsessive preoccupation with a "self-contained system" breeds a sense of superiority vis-à-vis all who have not been smitten by the thunderbolt of revelation. Any such system divides the world into initiates and noninitiates, producing an insufferably know-it-all attitude in the former. Only initiates could converse with Wagner. He could be engaging, unselfish, and touchingly solicitous about his friends, but there was no communicating with him from a theoretical position other than his own. His missionary fervor was allied with an intolerance not wholly to be explained as the natural blindness of genius to anything alien. If genius were fair, and fair to all the other creative forces of the day, it would probably be incapable of accomplishing its task. As Jakob Sulzer put it in a letter written to Mathilde Wesendonck after Wagner's death: "Wagner was extremely subjective by nature. His knowledge of the world was unique to himself, and he wanted that knowledge to conform solely to the spontaneous image of it he carried in his consciousness." Nevertheless, the friend-or-foe syndrome that existed in his imagination cannot altogether be ascribed to the subjectivity of genius.

Disguised religions are recognizable by their very claim to be at odds with a world populated by demons or dunces. They are antisystems, properly speaking, and their deepest impulse consists in an antiemotion. Were the object of that antiemotion to disappear because everyone had been converted, all that remained on the morrow of doomsday would be an emotional hangover. That was why Wagner did not address himself to the world at large. He was not interested in the masses, whom he referred to as the "rabble" [*Pöbel*]. His memorandums and proclamations were addressed to outstanding individuals, just as his *Communication* was produced for consumption by friends. He would have liked nothing better than a worldwide league of disciples whose faith in him was even greater than his own. And, remarkably enough, the sectarian antiprinciple did attract numerous sectarians to the Wagnerite ranks, from anthroposophists to eurhythmics, fanatics, and faith healers.

Wagner toyed very early on with the idea of founding an exclusive "fan club" designed to enhance the feeling of security he derived from his small band of active patrons. On November 19, 1849, he startled and disconcerted his Dresden friend Ferdinand Heine by appealing to him to recruit a circle of friends from among "those who love me—that is to say, love me, my works, and my artistic aims and endeavors so much that they think it important to sustain me for the sake of my art and my artistic endeavors." Although his chief concern was money, the idea of a sect had been born. He urged his friends not to regard him simply as someone in need of help but as "an artist and an artistic trend that they desire to preserve for the future and not see come to grief." Being still compelled at this stage to shun publicity, he intimated to Heine that the Dresdeners should assist him by confining recruitment to genuine sympathizers and passing the word among friends. This was asking a great deal of people who had yet to recover from the effects of revolution. Wagner eventually apologized and dropped the idea, but not for good.

His friends had no inkling of his world-encompassing ideas. Even before it properly existed, however, the Wagnerite sect had already been tainted and its members disastrously branded as a coterie that aspired to redeem the world.

Water, Mountains, Nibelungs

———————◆———————

D ebilitated by chronic constipation and plagued by facial
erysipelas, Wagner went to take a cure at the Albisbrunn
hydropathic institute near Zurich. For a time, hydrotherapy, dieting, and teetotalism became his new religion. Theodor Uhlig had
brought him a copy of *Wasser tut's freilich* [*Of Course Water Works*]
by J. H. Rausse,* a pupil of Priessnitz, whose radical belief in the
curative powers of Nature seemed to Wagner to contain a Feuerbachian element. For nine weeks he submitted to a Spartan regi-
men of wet packs and cold compresses, cold baths and long walks,
and restricted himself to a diet of dry bread and cold soup—no
beer, wine, coffee, or tea allowed. It is not surprising to learn that
his initial sense of well-being and inner cleanliness gave way, as
time went by, to baffled disappointment at his loss of weight,
growing irascibility, and nervous twinges.

After his departure for Albisbrunn on September 15, 1851, Minna
supervised their removal to rather more comfortable quarters at 11
Zeltweg, the journey into town from idyllic Abendstern having
become too inconvenient. Their guests of late had included Wilhelmine Schröder-Devrient's former lover, the expatriate Saxon
officer Hermann Müller, who was embarking on a new military
career in Switzerland. Müller was persuaded to join in the cold-
water cure, so Wagner had at least one congenial companion dur-

234

ing his walks and dismal evenings in the austerely appointed sanitarium.

At Stuttgart, Karl Ritter had been devoting himself to a highly unbalanced form of hydrotherapy which consisted of drinking excessive quantities of water. Wagner soon contrived to lure him, too, to Albisbrunn, but his missionary zeal was sadly frustrated when Karl mitigated the rigors of the cure by purchasing illicit snacks from "cheap confectioners' shops in the neighboring village." Karl did, however, cheer him with the unexpected news that Frau Ritter had inherited a considerable fortune from a wealthy uncle—considerable enough to enable her to make Wagner an annual allowance of 800 thalers. This he continued to receive until 1859.

With the bleak Alpine landscape spread out before him, sometimes shrouded in mist, sometimes surmounted by an icy sky of crystalline blue, Wagner took advantage of his partial relief from money worries to ponder on the Nibelungs. Feeling that *Der Junge Siegfried* had been an inadequate vehicle for what he wished to convey, he delved back into the origins of the myth. As regards *Siegfried*, he wrote to Uhlig on October 12, he entertained some "ambitious ideas: three dramas plus a three-act prologue." In drafting the first prose sketch for *Der Raub des Rheingoldes* between November 3 and 11, he intended merely to comply with the structural dictates of his subject. There could, however, be no question of an independent "subject" in the strict sense. Where did the Rhine Gold occur in the saga, and what had the citadel of the gods to do with the curse of the gold? Here Wagner came upon the bedrock of his own conception, the factor that governed all else. He reread Hagen's edition of *Die Völsungsage*, which Uhlig had borrowed for him from Dresden Library, but it told him nothing new. The first prose sketch for *Die Walküre* took shape between November 11 and 20.

He was breaking away from the contemporary theater and its public—"breaking with the formal present, definitely and forever," he wrote to Uhlig on November 12. He could imagine a performance "only after the revolution, for revolution alone can provide me with artists and audiences. The next revolution will inevitably put an end to our whole *theatrical goings-on*. They must and will come crashing down, all of them—this is inescapable. I shall then summon together what I need from the ruins; *then* I shall find what I need. I shall erect a theater beside the Rhine and issue invitations to a great dramatic festival. After a year of preparation, I shall present my entire work over a period of *four* days. With it I shall convey to the people of the revolution the *significance* of that revolution in its noblest sense. *That audience* will understand me; the present one cannot." Such were the inferences he drew from his writings on art.

Wagner returned to Zurich on November 23 and proceeded to cram the new apartment with all kinds of cozy little knickknacks. Despite his growing doubts on the subject, he continued to preach the virtues of hydrotherapy until everyone was exasperated, even Sulzer, who once walked out in a huff.

Still counting on France, he had secretly hoped that the great purge—the overthrow of the existing order—would be initiated in Paris during 1852. When Louis Napoleon's coup d'état shattered his expectations and predictions at a stroke, he renounced his attempts to "combat prevailing stupidity" and "galvanize the corpse of European civilization." As far as he was concerned, he told Uhlig, the calendar had stopped at December 1851.

The historical fact of the matter was that Napoleon Bonaparte's nephew, Charles Louis, had become a member of the National Assembly in 1848, after sundry attempted coups, expulsions, and spells of imprisonment, and had then, on December 20, 1848, been elected president of the Republic. On December 2, 1851, when friction between himself and the country's legislators came to a head, he assumed dictatorial powers, bloodily quelled armed resistance in Paris, and sent the opposition leaders into exile. He was proclaimed Emperor Napoleon III a year later.

It has been surmised that this blighting of republican hopes in the home of revolution led to a "resigned" hiatus in Wagner's *Ring*, to its profoundly "pessimistic," self-destructive ending, and to a radical change in his political ideas. This is not so. No causal nexus has been convincingly demonstrated, nor does the theory of a politically motivated hiatus in the *Ring*'s conception really hold water.

Where the *Ring* is concerned, the idea implicit in the *Nibelungen* story of 1848—that the gods should expiate their guilt through the exercise of a mortal man's free will—is logically bound, on closer examination, to entail the downfall of those same gods. There are also signs that Wagner glimpsed this solution very early on, even before producing the final version of *Siegfrieds Tod*. He brought a copy of the latter from Dresden and presented it to Jakob Sulzer in Zurich. Inscribed in the margin in German script, probably at the end of 1848,* are the lines: "Perish ye in joy at the man's deed,/ at the hero whom ye begot!/ Out of your dread fear/ I proclaim your blessed deliverance through death!" He must, therefore, have known how the *Ring* would end by the time he wrote to Uhlig from his hydropathic sanitarium, exultantly announcing that he had decided to present it as a tetralogy.

As for his political ideas and activities, the French coup d'état had a contrary effect, at least to begin with. On December 17, "in the presence, and with the participation, of Karl Ritter," Wagner and Herwegh arrived at a "decision" that was, so he wrote to Uhlig the following day, to introduce a turning point in history. "We undertook to devote all our energies and all our available powers of persuasion to disseminating this decision among an ever-wider circle of people, so that it will finally—not too far hence, one hopes —be put into effect. It is to this end, except when I write poetry and music, that I shall henceforth devote all my literary activities, whose purpose shall for once be a very definite, practical goal of incalculable effect, and, at the same time, a goal beyond the power of any reactionary force in the world to obstruct." He conceded that his decision had been materially influenced by recent political events, "but only in a positive way."

No hint of resignation there, but what exactly was this mysterious "decision"? The world was never told, nor did history take a new turn. We can only surmise that Wagner and his two friends planned to form a revolutionary cell—the politicophilosophical nucleus of an international conspiracy. Wagner's invitation to Feuerbach to join him in Switzerland, which was not accepted, seems to point in this direction. Central Europe was a political desert, so it would at least have been a "definite, practical" policy to concentrate all its progressive forces in one place. The scheme may well have foundered on objections from Wagner's Swiss friends, who were realistically concerned for the preservation of political peace, and on Herwegh's and Ritter's notorious lack of drive. This time, at least, Wagner had chosen the wrong allies.

Writing to Ernst Kietz on December 30, 1851, Wagner summarized his reactions to the setback in France and the experiences he had undergone during the three postrevolutionary years: "The whole of my politics is nothing more, now, than the most sanguinary hatred for our entire civilization, contempt for all that springs from it, and a yearning for Nature. . . . I am now paying dearly for the fact that I ever cared a jot for the workers. With their workers' clamor, they are wretched slaves whom anyone can hoodwink with promises of plenty of 'work.' Servility is deeply rooted all around us. No one in France save Proudhon (and he only vaguely!) realizes that we are *human beings.* Throughout Europe, I prefer dogs to these doglike people. I do not despair of a *future,* but only the most terrible and destructive revolution can again make 'human beings' out of our civilized beasts."

Anyone devoid of patience for humanity must hate it. Though understandable after what had happened in France, Wagner's disdain for the masses may be ascribed not only to exasperation but also to the disastrous sentiment that always manifests itself when intellectuals and artists play midwife to the dictatorship of the proletariat.

The winter, his least productive time of year, passed easily and agreeably in Zurich. His letters contain references to the women for whom he had become an object of admiration. Alert to the gaze of one pair of eyes in particular, he saw them grow moist beneath trembling lids, detected tears of emotion and adoring glances. Whose they were he told no one at this stage. He did not admit, even to himself, how different he had felt since the same pair of eyes—at least, one presumes they were the same—encouraged him to give his *Tannhäuser* Overture at Zurich on March 16, 1852.* The effect was "tremendous," he told Uhlig—indeed, it drew tears as heartfelt as those that had greeted the preceding rehearsals.

"A woman has solved the riddle for me," he confided enigmatically. "People see me as an iconoclastic preacher of repentance against the sin of hypocrisy." People, or just the woman in question? Marschall von Bieberstein, with whom he had left revolutionary Dresden and who now earned his living in Zurich as a journalist and insurance agent, had introduced him to a visiting couple named Wesendonck.* The Wesendoncks came from the Rhineland. Mathilde, née Luckemayer, an industrialist's daughter, was twenty-three when she first met Wagner. Otto Wesendonck, who was thirteen years older, had made a substantial fortune as a partner in Loeschigk, Wesendonck & Co., a firm of New York silk importers. After moving to Zurich in April 1851, the couple spent the remainder of the year settling in. They did not make an appearance on the cultural scene until early in 1852. Wagner not only kindled Mathilde's senses, poetically inclined as she already was, but introduced the glamorous Muses into her husband's sober, business-oriented world. We do not know if Mathilde Wesendonck contributed to the friendly chorus that persuaded Wagner to stage *Der Fliegende Holländer* at Zurich, but its four ambitious and successful performances between April 25 and May 2 cost him a full month's toil and nervous tension. It also interrupted his sporadic attempts to work that spring. "My nerves are still bad," he wrote to his niece Franziska on March 21, "and I doubt if I shall last much longer."

In the hope that a change would do him good, he and Minna left on May 12 for Fluntern on the Zürichberg. Here they stayed at the Pension Rinderknecht, which gave a fine view of the lake, the mountains, and the Limmat Valley.

One weekend, Georg Herwegh lured Wagner off to Mariafeld to see some friends named Wille. François Wille was a journalist who had championed constitutional democracy in his role as a Schleswig-Holstein delegate to the Frankfurt assembly, so the collapse of the German unity movement had compelled him to quit Hamburg. Eliza Wille, a shipowner's daughter, was wealthy enough to afford the expense of their early retirement to Switzerland.

This was the first of Wagner's numerous visits to the Willes' handsome country house, whose terrace and garden looked out over the Zürichsee, and his newfound friends were soon to attend a memorable first performance.

"I am more than ever stirred by the sweeping grandeur and beauty of my subject," he wrote to Uhlig on May 31, 1852. "In it, my entire view of the world has found its most consummate artistic expression."

Wagner's stay at the Pension Rinderknecht was blighted by incessant rain and permanently overcast skies. He toiled at the original poem of *Die Walküre* between June 1 and July 1. On the very morrow of its completion, he realized what it entailed. "The two Siegfrieds will now require thorough revision," he told Uhlig, "notably as regards everything to do with the divine myth, because the latter has now assumed a far more precise and moving physiognomy." But there was time enough for that. Back in Zurich on July 7, all he wanted was to recuperate from his working holiday at Fluntern. Not for the first or last time, he sought escape in sheer movement. Armed with 100 thalers from Liszt, he embarked on a lengthy trek through the mountains.

Although a native of the lowlands, Wagner was an intrepid Alpine walker who blithely trudged across glaciers and anesthetized himself against fear and exhaustion by pushing himself to the limit. Setting off on July 10 from Alpnach, south of Lucerne, he tramped along the Sarner See to Lungern—a mere twelve miles or so, one of his shortest day's marches. Next day, he crossed the 3,000-foot Brünig Pass and skirted the Brienzer See, reaching Interlaken after a six-hour hike. From there, on July 12, he veered south to Lauterbrunnen and turned left across the Kleine Scheidegg, a pass more than 6,000 feet high, from which he descended to Grindelwald in the northeast. July 13 saw him climb the Faulhorn, a day's ascent of some 5,000 feet—no mean achievement, even for an experienced mountaineer. On July 14, after heading east toward the Grosse Scheidegg, he reached Meiringen.

But the most arduous and adventurous part of his trip was still to come. A further trek along the Hasli-Tal brought him to the Grimsel See. He stayed overnight at the Grimsel hospice, where the landlord recommended one of his servants as a guide for the following day, July 16. This guide turned out to be an uncouth and inconsiderate type. He raced up the Aare glacier with Wagner panting in his wake, and was so rude to him while they were climbing the Siedelhorn (9,500 feet) that Wagner vowed to get his own back. They barely had time to enjoy the distant prospect of Mont Blanc and Monte Rosa before the man was off again, sliding down the snowfields at such a breakneck speed that Wagner avoided a fall only by subsiding onto the seat of his pants and digging his heels into the icy surface.

At Obergestelen he rested for a day, but not because he had run out of steam. On the following day, he overhauled his guide while climbing to the Gries glacier and set a pace that left the man gasping. For two hours they toiled across the glacier, fresh snow making it difficult even for the guide's trained eye to detect the hazards in their path. Then they made the steep descent to the riverbed of the Toce and Formazza, where Wagner paid off his companion and sent him back.*

He later discovered that his aversion to this sinister guide from the Grimsel hospice had not been unfounded. Two tourists from Frankfurt had recently perished while crossing a glacier in his company. In November of the same year, he was bribed by his master to set the inn ablaze. The landlord drowned himself when detected in this insurance fraud; the arsonist was arrested and jailed.

Racked by the mental and physical torments that always assailed him during a spell of literary or musical gestation, Wagner set to work on the last—or, rather, the first—component of his tetralogy. The original version of his *Rheingold* poem was written between September 15 and November 3, 1852. He visited Mariafeld only once during these weeks, accompanied by Herwegh, who had introduced him to the works of Byron and Shelley. Hafiz, too, delighted him, but all these excursions into poetry brought a rallentando in the progress of his work. Eliza Wille and her sister were entranced by his rendering of Beethoven's Ninth Symphony on the piano, and Eliza declared that she never again heard it so lucidly performed.

After finally and laboriously dredging the *Rheingold* libretto from his imagination, Wagner paid another brief visit to the mountains. During the first week of November, he and Herwegh went on a three-day tour that took in Glarus, the Glärnisch, the Klöntal, and the Wallenstädter See.

Wagner's relations with Herwegh were growing steadily closer and more intimate. In seeking to discover what topics they discussed, we must revert to the fragmentary and imprecisely dated additions to Wagner's essays on art, with their Marxian affinities.

Herwegh, the revolutionary bard and poet of the proletariat, had first met Marx at Cologne in 1842, while on his triumphal tour of Germany. Herwegh drew closer to Marx in Paris during 1843, and their friendship flourished to such an extent at this crucial stage in Marx's life that Jenny Marx sought refuge with the Herweghs for two days after her husband's expulsion from France in 1845. Bakunin, too, saw a good deal of Herwegh at this period. On his return to Paris in 1848, Marx broke with Arnold Ruge, his friend and comrade-in-arms, because the latter had called Herwegh an idle rogue. Though warned by Marx against invading Baden, Herwegh did not become a renegade in defeat. He continued, albeit impotently, to profess his socialist beliefs after the

Bismarck era dawned, and he remained true to them to the end of his days. He even wrote the workers' anthem for Ferdinand Lassalle's Deutscher Arbeiterverein, which was set to music by none other than Hans von Bülow, and Cosima became godmother to Herwegh's son Marcel. Herwegh got himself appointed honorary correspondent of the First Socialist International and persisted in his unyielding devotion to the cause. Are we to take it that he concealed his beliefs from Wagner over the years? He cannot have failed to speak of Marx and expound his theories on their long mountain rambles or at supper in Swiss country inns. To suppose otherwise would be absurd.

After his excursion with Herwegh, Wagner jotted down another three lines of music for his "brides of the wind," daughters of god, Wotan's brood—a Valkyrie motif that was probably his very first and dated from the Dresden period. He then proceeded to revise the two Siegfrieds, which did not acquire their final titles—*Siegfried* and *Götterdämmerung*—until 1856. Because he had dramatized the prior history of his characters and remotivated them, the last two dramas did not quite fit their precursors. Deletions, modifications, and additions were made, though these amounted to an extraordinarily small percentage of the whole. The gods met their end and Valhalla went up in flames.

On December 18, 1852, three days after the last words were written, Wagner called on the Willes at Mariafeld, once again with Georg Herwegh. That night he read the entire poems of *Rheingold* and *Walküre* to an audience consisting of his hosts, Eliza Wille's sister Frau von Bissing, and Herwegh. They retired to bed at midnight, tired but eager to hear the rest of a work that so far exceeded the compass of a normal libretto. Wagner read them *Der Junge Siegfried* on the morning of December 19 and the concluding part of the tetralogy that evening. "I felt I had reason to be satisfied with the effect," Wagner remarks in his autobiography. "The ladies, in particular, were so deeply moved that they abstained from all comment. I, unfortunately, was left in an almost alarming state of agitation. I could not sleep, and was so averse to conversation the next morning that no one grasped the reason for my precipitate departure. Only Herwegh, who escorted me back, seemed to divine my mood and shared it by preserving a similar silence."

Wagner ordered and paid for a private edition of fifty copies, which appeared in February. One person never received the copy intended for him. After long weeks of mounting anxiety, the news smote Wagner like a blow in the face: Theodor Uhlig had died in Dresden on January 3, 1853, at the age of thirty-one.

Know Ye What Is to Come?

O n four successive evenings—between February 16 and 19, 1853
—Wagner read *Der Ring des Nibelungen* to an invited audience
of friends, and friends of friends, at the Hotel Baur au Lac. It was
his greatest success in the field of recitation. The listening Zurich-
ers sat there enthralled, even though he did not claim that his
poems were independent works of art. He read out stage directions, sketched histrionic gestures, indicated unseen mountains
with his outstretched arm, raised one slender hand above his head
like a blazing torch and gazed heavenward, transformed himself
into a sorrowful god, and murmured softly to a kneeling Brünnhilde. Strange and novel though his audience found it all, they
remained spellbound for four sessions of three hours each—the
women especially.

It may have been the success of these readings, coupled with his
previous guest appearances as a conductor at subscription concerts, that prompted him to embark on a costly and unprofitable
venture. This series of three special concerts may fairly be regarded as the first Wagner festival.

Rehearsals began on May 9. Seventy-two musicians converged
on Zurich from other parts of Switzerland and western Germany,
most of them skilled instrumentalists. Zurich itself provided a
choir of 110 singers. Wagner's neighbor, Emilie Heim, wife of the
conductor Ignaz Heim, sang Senta's Ballad from *Der Fliegende Hol-*

länder—the only outstanding solo performance. At one morning rehearsal, Wagner heard his *Lohengrin* Prelude for the very first time, with its divided violin choir. On May 14, he gave a reading of the prologue to his three operatic poems, and all who proposed to attend his concerts were invited to further readings free of charge. One enthusiast walked for six hours to be present. The Ritter daughters turned up, as did the young composer Robert von Hornstein, and local newspapers referred to the occasion as a congress of musical notables.

The first concert, which took place on May 18, was an unparalleled success. The ovation that greeted it was surpassed in volume and duration only by that which followed the last in the series, timed to coincide with Wagner's fortieth birthday. He was presented with a silver goblet and a laurel wreath, and an actor recited a poem in his honor. It had been written by a lady who chose to remain anonymous—possibly Mathilde Wesendonck. Applause surged around him, and the musicians at his back produced flourish after flourish. He could scarcely contain his emotions. Nothing of the kind had ever happened to him before. The Swiss were honoring him in a truly exceptional fashion, and it is probable that, had they persisted in their enthusiasm, musical reformism, and financial openhandedness, Wagner would have settled on Zurich as the site of his festival, not provincial little Bayreuth. The press paid due homage to his concerts—even the *Neue Zürcher Zeitung*, which could hardly ignore them. Wagner's works were described as "miraculous." To Liszt, who had been compelled to defer a promised visit until July, Wagner wrote: "I laid the whole festival at the feet of *one* lovely woman!" Other considerations apart, her husband had underwritten half the financial risk!

In June, Wagner dedicated a sonata* to this "one woman"—the first piece of music he had written for a long time. When it reached Mathilde Wesendonck at Bad Ems, where she was staying, she found that he had written something "Nornish" at the head: "Know ye what is to come?" She confessed in a letter to Minna that she found the words hard to interpret. Obviously, she didn't know him yet.

Wagner had moved on April 15 to a new apartment on the second floor of 13 Zeltweg. It was more luxuriously appointed than his previous quarters, with heavy velvet curtains, velvet chairs, and a general air of comfort that betokened, not only that he had overestimated his future income, but that he intended to start composing again. Composition and an agreeable semblance of prosperity always went together in Wagner's case, and it is a fact that, until he moved to Tribschen and Wahnfried, he never turned out as many sheets of manuscript as he did at this apartment, whose bourgeois ostentation surprised all who visited it.

Liszt arrived at last on July 2, and the turbulent, "well-nigh intoxicating" days of enjoyment that followed their reunion set the seal on what had long been a momentous personal relationship. Those who gathered at Wagner's apartment to partake of a gargantuan feast in Liszt's honor included Georg and Emma Herwegh, now reconciled, Sulzer, Müller, Baumgartner, Carl Eschmann, Theodor Kirchner, and François Wille. Liszt played the first of his symphonic poems, a musical stimulus to which Wagner proved exceptionally responsive at this juncture. He also immersed himself in Wagner's scores, bringing them to life on the piano with tears of admiration in his eyes.

Wagner strove to persuade Liszt that nothing really stood in the way of his returning to Germany because he had abandoned all interest in politics, but Liszt retorted that no one would believe him. It had not escaped notice that he spent most of his time with politically undesirable friends, of whom Herwegh was accounted one of the worst, and that since 1852 he had been in correspondence with Giuseppe Mazzini's close friend, Malwida von Meysenbug, who described herself as a "complete revolutionary." This being so, Liszt could hold out little hope of rehabilitation.

On July 6, Wagner set off on a brief excursion with Liszt and Herwegh. They took a boat from Zurich, walked across the Sattel Pass into Schwyz, and spent the night at Brunnen. Wagner's pleasure was only slightly marred by his companions' habit of conversing in French, which sometimes made him feel excluded. Next morning, they crossed the Lake of Lucerne by boat and visited the Rütli, where legend has it that the Swiss League was formed against Austria. There in the famous meadow, the trio drank a toast from its three springs to fraternal friendship.

On July 13, three days after Liszt's departure, the musical societies of Zurich provided an epilogue to the May concerts by assembling in Zeltweg and paying homage to the composer. Surveying the torchlit scene from his window, Wagner was moved to hear the following plea: Since he had been cast out by his native land, would he remain—to the pride and joy of all present—in the fair and freedom-loving land of Switzerland? There followed a thunderous burst of cheering. The *Eidgenössische Zeitung* reported next day that Wagner was visibly affected and delivered a short speech in which he declared that he had "chosen Zurich, which had received him so kindly, to be the focus of his immediate artistic activity to an even greater extent than before." This, not that anyone knew it, was a reference to his projected *Nibelungen* festival, and he preserved an intermittent belief in its feasibility until 1856.

He left Zurich with Georg Herwegh the very next day. Was he fleeing from the prospect of getting down to work? Was it fear, or merely disinclination, that underlay his sense of unease? In all probability, it was the same intense depression that had overwhelmed him at Meudon, before he started on the music for *Holländer*—the feeling that, after so many fallow years, he would be unable to string two notes together.

He had prescribed himself a cure at St. Moritz, but he and Herwegh were delayed by bad weather at Chur, which gave him time to immerse himself in Goethe's *West-östlicher Divan*. When St. Moritz proved uncomfortable and the cure had no effect, the two men ascended the Julier Pass, where visions of Wotan and Fricka were summoned up by the vast walls of rock that flank its summit as though thrust aside by giant hands. Then as now, it was a truly primeval sight.*

They took a carriage to the Maloja Pass and to Samaden and Zuoz to see the Bernina, but it was veiled in cloud. On July 23, when the weather improved, they enlisted the schoolmaster from Samaden as a guide and climbed the Rosegg glacier. They scrambled over rocks and trudged across ice and snow for eleven solid hours. Wagner, who kept having to show Herwegh what route to follow, was so sublimely impressed by the "sanctity of that desolate spot" (echoes of Siegfried breasting the summit of Brünnhilde's rock) that he forgot his fatigue. He suffered for this later, even though he had spent the previous week resting and studying Goethe's *Elective Affinities* with an intensity that was to leave its mark on many of his conversations with Cosima. August 10 found him back in Zurich.

Eager for a real break, he decided to undertake a relatively long trip to Italy, for which funds had been promised him by Otto

Wesendonck. On August 24, he journeyed back across the Alps via Berne, Geneva, and Chambéry, whence he traveled to Turin in a hired carriage over Mont Cenis—a three-day marathon. From Turin, where he stayed for two days, he took a train to Arquate, reaching Genoa on August 31. His initial impressions were "a dream of delight." From the sixth floor of his hotel, which we now know comprised the upper stories of the Palazzi Grimaldi and Fiesco, he caught his first glimpse of the Mediterranean.

But "rash indulgence" in ice cream proved his undoing. He took the overnight steamer to La Spezia on September 3, arrived there next day, stricken with diarrhea and seasickness, and booked into the Hotel Nazionale, not really knowing why he had bothered to come. After a restless, feverish night, he went for a long tramp through the nearby hills. That afternoon, the afternoon of September 5, he lay down on the sofa in his hotel room and tried to sleep. Instead, he lapsed into a somnolent state in which he felt as if he were being borne along by a fast-flowing stream. "The rushing sound soon presented itself to my mind in musical form as the chord of E-flat major, which surged along endlessly in figurated arpeggios. These broken chords manifested themselves as melodic figurations of increasing mobility, yet no change occurred in the pure E-flat major triad, whose persistence seemed to impart some infinite meaning to the element into which I was sinking." Wagner came to with a sudden start, as though the billows were closing over his head: He was in mid-composition and wanted to go home.

Wagner's account of this inspirational experience in *My Life* surrounds it with an aura of mystery which his biographers have happily perpetuated, almost as if the "vision" at La Spezia presented him with such a complete picture of the *Rheingold* Prelude that he rushed straight home and committed it to paper. However attractive, any such notion must be repudiated.

It means little that he said nothing of his experience to Minna —they never referred to such matters in correspondence—but others were left just as much in the dark. Further doubts are raised by Wagner's own account of the journey home. Back in Genoa, he was dissuaded from carrying out his original plan to travel along the Riviera to Nice only by a recurrence of his "former condition, with all the symptoms of diarrhea." We should not, above all, ignore the way he qualifies his description of the incident by telling us that he at last recognized the orchestral prelude to *Rheingold*, which he had been "carrying around" inside him without exactly pinning it down. Last but not least, there is the fact that the "figurations of increasing mobility" underwent considerable changes when he came to record them in writing, even as regards their all-important rising intervals, and that this musical nucleus continued to absorb new and significant elements until the final version became crystallized.

What is certain, however, is that something irrevocable had occurred—something that had merely been bottled up and suppressed by all Wagner's distractions and peregrinations. Rightly sensing that he had reached a watershed in his career, he longed to get down to work. He returned to Zurich on September 10, "unwell, out of sorts, ready to die," as he wrote to Liszt. To begin with, nothing happened. The only new development was the purchase of another parrot, Jacquot, which Minna taught to say, "Wagner is a naughty man!"—an apt indication of the prevailing domestic atmosphere.

On October 6 (via Baden, where Minna was taking the waters) Wagner went to Basel for a prearranged meeting. He was greeted at the Hotel Drei Könige by a group of celebrated confreres who had been attending the Karlsruhe Music Festival. Those who saluted him in the foyer with a choral rendering of the royal fanfare from *Lohengrin* included Franz Liszt, Hans von Bülow, who was just launching his career as a concert pianist, the violinist Joseph Joachim, and the composer Peter Cornelius. They were joined next day by Princess Carolyne von Sayn-Wittgenstein and her daughter Marie, a budding beauty of barely sixteen, and Wagner read them some extracts from the *Ring*.

Like many of his contemporaries, Wagner was promptly captivated by the charms of Princess Marie. The poet Emanuel Geibel called her a fairy-tale flower with a dawning secret in its cup. To Ernst Rietschel, who made a bust of her in 1854, she was an "Indian fairy tale," and the dramatist Friedrich Hebbel declared that he had never encountered so wondrous a blend of culture and nature in any one young girl. Wagner christened her "The Child," honored her early in 1857 with an open letter "On Franz Liszt's Symphonic Poems," and was deeply disillusioned when she defected to his enemies after marrying Prince Konstantin zu Hohenlohe-Schillingsfürst, Steward of the Household at the Court of Vienna.

The party decided to travel on to Paris, though the younger

musicians went their separate ways at Strasbourg. Joachim, one of the greatest Jewish virtuosi of his day, had been rather ill at ease with the author of *Judaism in Music,* so Wagner felt constrained to embrace him warmly and bid him "an especially cordial farewell."

In Paris, Wagner continued his readings from the *Ring* at Princess Marie's request. He, Liszt, and the ladies arrived there on October 9. The following day was to become a red-letter day in his life. Invited by Liszt to dine en famille with the children of his liaison with Marie d'Agoult, who had been reared in Paris by two elderly governesses, Wagner sat down to table with Blandine, nearly eighteen, Cosima, almost sixteen, and Daniel, the youngest by eighteen months. The two sisters bore a strong resemblance to each other, and Wagner was struck by their extreme shyness. After the meal he continued his reading of the *Ring,* some of which was "endured with admirable patience" by Berlioz, who turned up later.

October 19 brought a meeting with the Wesendoncks. Liszt and the princesses having by then left Paris, Wagner invited Minna to join him there on October 20 for a week-long reunion with Kietz and Anders. Thus, as the month drew to a close, all the women in Wagner's life—all the Graces, Muses, and Fates—flitted past each other in a sort of round dance, none of them aware what the future held in store.

*   *   *

On November 1, 1853, four days after returning from Paris, Wagner began to write the music for the *Ring.* Interrupted only by a feverish cold, he completed his composition sketch for *Das Rheingold* on January 14, 1854, after nine weeks' work.

At the age of forty, he had changed course once more, bent on creating something unprecedented—something which, although it entailed and embodied music, drama, art, and philosophy, was none of these things alone. He was carrying revolution into art by revolutionizing the language of art. "Believe me," he wrote to Liszt, "no one has ever composed like this before. I conceive of my music as a slough of the horrific and the sublime." It was an almost Nietzschean definition, and many who prefer to shun his music have failed to perceive its innovative qualities to this day.

Wagner drafted the *Rheingold* score between February and May 1854. Before watching him start to sketch the first act of *Walküre,* however, we must turn our attention to the kindred spirit whose hour had now struck. To her he dedicated the brief *Walküre* Prelude with the initials G. S. M. [*Gesegnet Sei Mathilde*; Blessed Be Mathilde], as well as with numerous marginal ciphers intelligible to her alone. She was his echo, his willing ear, and he needed her when he came to tackle the great love scenes between the Wälsungs. "Whatever he had composed in the morning," Mathilde Wesendonck recalled, "he used to perform and try out on my piano in the afternoon. The hour was between five and six; he called himself the Twilight Man!"

Wagner was overcome by a sort of creative frenzy. On May 11, he played and sang passages from *Das Rheingold* to the Wesendoncks, Herweghs, and Willes. As soon as he started on *Die Walküre*, whose first and second acts he had fully sketched by September 1 and 18 respectively, he began to spend whole evenings alone with Mathilde. She presented him with an "everlasting" gold pen, and it was for her that he wielded it so tirelessly. Their relationship took on a more genuine resemblance to a Flaubert novel than his affair with Jessie ever did. Mathilde became the embodiment of all his yearnings, all that was feminine and fraught with mystery.

*   *   *

The Wesendoncks were still staying at Zurich's best-known hotel, the Baur au Lac. At thirty-nine, Otto Wesendonck lived in unflamboyant luxury, combining wealth with refinement. Extremely sensitive, he was susceptible to neurotic and rheumatic ailments. He had lived in New York, knew the world, loved music and painting. He had also benefited from the great boom of 1853, when German banks recorded the biggest economic upswing in many years. New companies mushroomed as fast as the soil of California was yielding up its treasures. Mines, railroads, industrial corporations, and banks came into being, and all these developments profited a middle class whose exploitation of labor gave a fillip to the theory that capitalism connoted the impoverishment of the masses. Otto Wesendonck, a businessman with cultural pretensions, had been quick to dissociate himself from the productive process. He enjoyed and spent the money he had made.

Mathilde, now a ripe twenty-six, had the soft, velvety features of those whose beauty is quick to fade. Her small round chin and big, wide, pellucid eyes displayed a flawlessness seldom associated with women of letters—and she wrote a great deal in later years. Endowed with more soul than character, she had an extremely malleable and impressionable disposition—a natural sympathy that captivated her male admirers because they tended to see more in her than was actually there. What fanned the flames of Wagner's passion, in particular, was her infinite receptiveness to his music and ideas.

Middle-class refinement, feminine charm, and a good education combined to render Mathilde more than merely pretty. Her immaculate appearance, with its gilding of youth, could not but make poor Minna seem old, homely, and commonplace by comparison.

The disharmony between Minna and her husband, which was becoming more and more evident, only intensified his new obsession. Not that she neglected her duties or her efforts to keep him at home. What she wanted from him was tranquillity, civic responsibility, and the sort of concessions to the public he could never have made. The result, as Malwida von Meysenbug rightly observed, was a conjugal existence notable for its "almost daily distress and torment" and devoid even of that "ultimate conciliating and mitigating element" that children might have introduced into the marriage.

Minna's heart disease, which had wrought a perceptible change in her looks, was growing worse. At the end of June, she went to take a "whey cure" at Seelisberg, overlooking the Lake of Lucerne. On July 3, Wagner left for Sion in the canton of Valais, having agreed to conduct at a music festival there. He went by way of Montreux, where Karl Ritter had gone to live with a recently acquired wife—an imprudent acquisition, as Wagner was quick to note. Karl accompanied him to Sion, and they were joined at Martigny by the young musician Robert von Hornstein, to whom Karl, who was clearly more at home with his own sex, promptly transferred his affections. Arrangements for the music festival left much to be desired, and Wagner was so disappointed by the scanty orchestra that he quit Sion without having conducted at all. He then joined Minna at Seelisberg and spent most of the rest of July with her, doubtless chafing at the waste of time and money.

Meanwhile, unpaid debts were piling up in Zurich. Furnishing the new apartment had badly overtaxed his slender resources and left him in grave financial straits. He had hoped for some theater royalties, but they failed to materialize. Two notes of hand fell due, each for 1,500 francs—and 3,000 francs approximated to the whole of Julie Ritter's annual allowance. Otto Wesendonck, who had more than once helped Wagner out with small sums and borne the incidental expenses of his fortieth-birthday concerts, grew impatient. On July 26, while Wagner was still away, he wrote to Sulzer that his "sheer good nature" had reached its limits. "This much is clear: No money must be handed to Wagner himself. . . . I had originally thought of giving the funds to Madame Wagner, but thought it too humiliating."

Fending off his creditors with difficulty, and wrestling with a mood of depression that had peculiarly little effect on his creative processes, Wagner resumed work on the first act of *Walküre* and completed the composition sketch during August. He wrote the composition sketch for the second act between September 4 and November 18. The fair copy of the *Rheingold* score, which he had started in February, was completed—partly in parallel with his work on *Walküre*—by September 26. Meanwhile, on September 2, Minna left for Saxony—her first visit in five years.

Whatever her shortcomings, Wagner must have thought her competent to undertake complicated errands and negotiations on his behalf. He instructed her to secure the good offices of Botho von Hülsen, the Berlin intendant; visit Röckel at Waldheim (a delicate mission); and call on Liszt at Weimar to discuss the possibility of their settling in Thuringia. "In my estimation," he exhorted her by letter at the beginning of October, "the only thing to be done is that the grand duke should immediately seek the present king of Saxony's permission for me to live freely in his country, in return for which I should undertake not to quit the grand duke's territory without his consent. I should at the same time be prepared to give a formal pledge never again to engage in politics: Only in respect of the past would I have to be absolved by him from making any humiliating and readily misinterpreted statement." He had never gone so far before—an indication of how poorly he rated his prospects in Zurich—but he was proud enough not to recant.

Not for the first time, he had wrongly gauged the political situation in the German states and the strength of his own reputation. At Dresden, Minna addressed a humble petition to the new incumbent of the Saxon throne, King Johann, in terms that had obviously been inspired by Wagner but arbitrarily modified by herself: "May it please Your Majesty to grant clemency and pardon to my misguided husband, Richard Wagner, and suffer him to attend performances of his own works so as to promote his more distant activities by Your Majesty's grace and generosity." She could not have known what view was taken of her allegedly penitent, "guilty and erring" husband by the civil servants who studied her petition and eventually rejected it.

On March 28, 1854, for example, the Dresden authorities had received a confidential memorandum dated March 23 from the Vienna police.* "Strange reports," it announced, "are once more circulating about Richard Wagner. He not only lives in Zurich in the most sumptuous splendor but purchases extremely valuable articles, gold watches and so forth, at enormous prices. His apartment is adorned with the finest furniture, carpets, silk curtains, and chandeliers. This arouses suspicion, surprise, and curiosity among simple republicans, who cannot but wonder where this man, who arrived in Zurich so poor, obtains his money from. It is thus thought highly probable that he is being secretly supported by some princely German house. But people find this all the more surprising because they know, not only that he set fire to the entire theater wardrobe during the Dresden Revolution, but that he is even now seeking to effect a revolution by means of art, both orally and in writing, and that he keeps in touch for this purpose with all the leading literary and artistic propagandists. Confidence in his music of the future is definitely on the wane. There is a growing belief that the sole merit of his pieces reposes in their brilliant orchestration, but that they possess neither soul nor melody. If any of the latter be present in them, so it is said, he has stolen it."

The most extraordinary feature of this mixture of truth and falsehood, covert admiration and brazen cynicism, is that a police report should have presumed to pass artistic judgments.

No one knew better than Wagner himself how desperate his predicament was, though his friends had formed a rough idea of the extent of his indebtedness since that summer. Wesendonck and Sulzer now resolved on a risky financial rescue operation. On September 14, Wagner informed Sulzer that his debts totaled 10,000 francs, including a sum of 3,800 francs that he had borrowed from Karl Ritter and would gradually repay out of Julie Ritter's annual allowance. He therefore needed a little over 6,000 francs in cash if he were to pay all his bills and redeem all his notes of hand. His expected receipts from *Tannhäuser* and *Lohengrin*, optimistically computed at 21,000 francs, would accrue to Wesendonck provided he settled his debts and paid him an annual allowance. Wesendonck agreed, and entrusted the administration of receipts and payments to Sulzer. But it would have taken more than this to plug the leaks, old and new, in Wagner's sinking ship. The whole system of assigning future receipts in return for the settlement of present debts was eyewash, and devoid of anything but a symbolic significance that Wagner had yet to grasp: He was in pawn to King Mark. All the makings of a still-unwritten drama were there.

The World Is My Idea

The Black Flag

Georg Herwegh played an important mediatory role in Wagner's life. Like Samuel Lehrs, Gottfried Anders, Heinrich Laube, and August Röckel, he introduced Wagner to dramatic themes, books, people, and currents of political and philosophical thought that directed his ideas and activities into new channels.

Late in September or early in October, 1854, Herwegh brought him a copy of Arthur Schopenhauer's *Die Welt als Wille und Vorstellung* [*The World As Will and Idea*]. During the previous year, a piece in the *Westminster and Foreign Quarterly Review* had exhumed the philosopher's principal work from three decades of oblivion and begun to popularize it in Europe.* Herwegh's attention had been drawn to the book by an article on the English piece by Frauenstädt, a disciple of Schopenhauer's. There is something paradoxical in the fact that Wagner, a music dramatist hovering between reformism and resignation, should have been introduced by the most "progressive" and militant of his friends to a profoundly pessimistic philosophy that eschewed all forms of activism and was, in the commonly accepted sense, "reactionary." He opened the book and was taken aback by its very first sentence: "The world is my idea."

Having swiftly grasped the essentials of the work, Wagner was somewhat disconcerted by its philosophical conclusion. He did not relish the total annihilation of the will and the renunciation of the world because they seemed to conflict with his forward-looking theory of art and, no doubt, with certain other things to which he had devoted less thought. Herwegh, however, was quick to warn him against precipitately dismissing Schopenhauer's ideas, pointing out that all tragedy derives from a perception of the futility of the external world. This cogent argument does credit even to a failed revolutionary who, like Herwegh, clung doggedly to his original aims.

"On reviewing my *Nibelungen* poem, I recognized to my surprise that I had long been familiar in my own poetic conception with that which now so disconcerted me in theory," Wagner claims in *My Life.* * "Enabled at last to understand my Wotan, I was startled into resuming my study of Schopenhauer's book." By the summer of the following year, he had read it no less than four times.

Wagner's enthusiasm for the Frankfurt philosopher knew no bounds. "What charlatans, compared to this man, all the Hegels, etc., are! His cardinal idea, the ultimate negation of the will to live, is terribly solemn but uniquely redeeming. It was not new to me, of course, and cannot be entertained at all by anyone in whom it does not already reside."

Schopenhauer became Wagner's sedative. In his unhappiness, both real and imagined, he had at last found the moral right and courage to acknowledge his yearning for death or something like it. Did he really mean to throw in his hand? He had already condemned himself to political inactivity and was doubtless temporarily in earnest on the subject. Schopenhauer is the philosopher of those who need vindication, not incitement. Wagner felt cured, above all, of self-delusion. He had no wish to go on pretending to himself. The world was "rotten to the core," and he scornfully refused to deny this any longer. On January 15, 1854, or nine months before encountering Schopenhauer's philosophy, he had confided to Liszt that what he sought was "a sleep so profound that all sense of life's afflictions ceases" or "a woman's tears" that would redeem the world from its curse.

And then, quite suddenly, a new subject burst on the scene. To what extent was Mathilde Wesendonck the second factor that drove him to vent his emotions and translate them into an ecstatic drama of love and death? He certainly did not write *Tristan und*

Isolde on her account, still less in her image, for their relationship had yet to overstep the bounds of propriety. Conversely, it would not be altogether true to say that he loved Mathilde on Isolde's account. Mathilde had been there before he came across Schopenhauer—before he devoted a single thought to Tristan—but from this point on he loved her all the more fiercely because of two obvious equations: I am Tristan, you Isolde. And just as Schopenhauer held that the entire world was an object only in relation to the subject, so Isolde-Mathilde was "the perception of the percipient, in sum, an idea." She had only to play her allotted role and be a stimulus, a spur to supreme endeavor.

The third and most superficial incentive to Wagner's *opus metaphysicum* verged on the trivial: Karl Ritter had abandoned music in favor of literature. He had already surprised Wagner on the way to Sion by showing him the manuscript of a drama entitled *Alkibiades*. Now he drew his attention to the Tristan theme by submitting a dramatic outline whose main defect was that it concentrated on the "lighter phases" of the romance. Wagner, who recalled the German version by Hermann Kurz and Friedrich von der Hagen's edition, immediately saw that the essence of the legend was profoundly tragic and should not be obscured by incidentals.

He sketched out the contents of the three acts on returning from a walk in October 1854, though he subsequently cut an episode from the last act in which Tristan is visited on his deathbed by the Grail-seeking Parsifal. He identified Tristan, languishing from the effects of a wound but unable to die, with the Amfortas of the Grail romance—another anticipatory element that was later omitted.

"Never in my life having enjoyed the true happiness of love," Wagner wrote to Liszt on December 16, 1854, "I shall erect a memorial to this loveliest of all dreams in which, from first to last, love shall for once find utter repletion. I have devised in my mind a Tristan and Isolde, the simplest yet most full-blooded musical conception imaginable, and with the 'black flag' that waves at the end I shall cover myself over—to die."

With a single sentimental gesture, this sentence marvelously summarizes the essentials of the theme and ends on a death-laden metaphor. The "black flag" occurs in medieval versions of the romance. The dying Tristan has sent for Isolde, and the approaching ship is to signal, by means of a white or black sail, whether his beloved is on board. Tristan's legitimate wife falsely asserts that the sail is a black one, and Tristan expires before Isolde can reach his side.

By cutting out a profusion of subsidiary incidents and characters, Wagner also eliminated the jealous intrigue and Tristan's original manner of dying, which was untypical in terms of *Opera and Drama* and too thematically bald. The black flag gave way to a *"Liebestod"*—a love unto death.

"For the present," says Wagner in *My Life*, "I contrived to wrest myself away from this idea rather than permit it to disrupt my great musical work." He was at a crucial stage in *Die Walküre*, being in the throes of composing Brünnhilde's Death Song to Siegmund and Wotan's great monologue of resignation.

Die Walküre, Tristan, and Schopenhauer were the trinity that ruled Wagner's world of stimulation and self-oblivion at the end of 1854, and it would have been out of character had he failed to externalize this pleasurable, painful awareness of his own existence, his own powers, by diverting it into self-dramatization and missionary fervor.

All were now to be converted to the black flag and acquainted with his state of mind. All were to have the philosophical key to existence rammed down their throats, as it were, with the enthusiasm that had once been reserved for hydrotherapy. Wagner preached Schopenhauer to Ritter, the Willes, and the Wesendoncks, sent a copy of *Die Welt als Wille und Vorstellung* to August Röckel in Waldheim Jail, and discreetly conveyed to Liszt, a Catholic, how close he felt in spirit to the prophet of pessimism.

The London Concerts

From the Valkyries' joyous "Hoyotoho!" to Wotan's vengeful outburst of wrath, the musical torrent sped on. Wagner made Sieglinde anticipate the redemption motif from the finale of the *Ring* in gratitude for the miracle of Siegfried's conception, plunged Brünnhilde in deepest slumber, and enclosed her rock with a flickering curtain of fiery semiquavers. In little more than five weeks, from November 20 to December 27, 1854, he sketched the whole of the third act of *Walküre*, thereby completing one of the boldest and most exuberant musical ventures he ever undertook—a work still regarded by many as central to his entire *oeuvre*.

There were distractions in plenty, however. He agreed once again to conduct the Zurich Musical Society's winter concerts, coached the Quartet Society in Beethoven's great C-sharp Minor Quartet, and promised to assist the Zurich Theater with its *Tannhäuser* rehearsals in February. On December 24, he received an invitation from the "Old" Philharmonic Society to conduct eight concerts in London during the spring of 1855.

Despite Wagner's skepticism, Wesendonck and Sulzer felt certain that these guest appearances in England would prove financially as well as artistically rewarding. Two hundred pounds sterling was a substantial fee, and they had heard that life in London was cheap. Wagner, who had long regretted their refusal to settle his debt to Karl Ritter because its repayment was depriving him of Julie Ritter's annual allowance, fell in with the idea, though largely for financial reasons.

On March 5, 1855, he took lodgings at 22 Portland Terrace, Regent's Park, only fifteen minutes' walk from the Old Philharmonic Society's concert rooms. There he became acquainted with the islanders' puritanical artistic conventions, which extended to the wearing of gloves, stocks, and black or white ties. The concert programs were monstrously long and indiscriminate. Wagner was expected to conduct eight to ten items—sometimes including two symphonies—in a single evening. Meyerbeer, Potter, and Lucas were interspersed with Mozart and Haydn; Paer's *Ave Maria* followed hard on the heels of Beethoven's Eighth; and the Ninth was preceded at Wagner's second concert on March 26 by a medley of Weber, Cherubini, Mendelssohn, and excerpts from his own *Lohengrin*. He only just managed to prevent the performance of a Lachner symphony by throwing a tantrum during program discussions.

Two rehearsals were allowed for Beethoven's Ninth. In every other case, Wagner was limited to one per concert. That the orchestra fulfilled any of his intentions was due solely to the good offices of one or two musicians who talked their colleagues into attending extra rehearsals. Wagner's approach to familiar works was quite unconventional. The critics, whom he had neglected to woo by inviting them to the customary reception, were lukewarm at best, hostile at worst. They did not understand his rubati and found his tempi either too fast or too slow. Worse still, journalists, headed by the music critic of the *Times*, James Davison, had read his anti-Jewish pamphlet and found it—in the best English tradition—incomprehensible. Felix Mendelssohn-Bartholdy was the darling of the London musical scene and the favorite composer of Queen Victoria, to whom he had dedicated his Scottish Symphony, while Meyerbeer reigned triumphant in the realm of opera.

Mendelssohn was represented in no less than five of Wagner's eight London programs by the *Hebrides* Overture, the Violin Concerto, the Italian Symphony, the A Minor Symphony, and the *Midsummer Night's Dream* Overture. A letter to Minna dated April 17 seems to imply that Wagner publicly expressed his contempt for this fact by wearing white kid gloves—an implication pounced on with glee by Wagnerites and all the more fiercely condemned by the composer's enemies. But this is a partial misunderstanding. Did he don the gloves on purpose? No, he simply forgot to remove them. It was de rigueur for a conductor to wear kid gloves. The unusual feature was not that he wore gloves, but that he removed them *after* Mendelssohn's Italian Symphony so as to set off the earthy German romanticism of Gluck's *Euryanthe* Overture that followed it—a minor act of spite. It was said that he made an exhibition of himself in London, but this is untrue. He endured a four-month ordeal and ended by convincing the Londoners of his abilities.

What is true is that London did not appeal to him. He disliked its musical tastes and conventions and had no time for the British parliamentary and political system. It became clear that he also disliked the enshrinement of party-political representative democracy and nursed his own conception of freedom. Finally, London was far too expensive to suit his pocket. It was nonetheless a boundless exaggeration to imply, as he did in *My Life*, that the atmosphere of the British capital had taught him to appreciate the full horror of Dante's *Inferno.* *

After the fourth concert on April 30, he wanted to leave right away and was dissuaded only by consideration for Prosper Sainton, the leader of the orchestra, who had engineered his invitation to London. It was not until May 14 that he finally managed to rouse an audience from its lethargy with his *Tannhäuser* Overture, which was warmly applauded in a quite un-English manner.

The overture received another hearing at the seventh concert on June 11, officially at the request of Queen Victoria, who proposed to attend. It is more probable, however, that the royal command stemmed from her consort, Prince Albert, who was himself a composer and usually selected the Philharmonic Society's programs. Mendelssohn apart, Victoria disliked orchestral music.

This repeat performance of the *Tannhäuser* Overture drew great applause, the queen and her consort having firmly signified their approval by taking the lead. During the intermission, the "amiable and good-natured" royal couple received Wagner in the refreshment room. It undoubtedly gratified him that he, a proscribed revolutionary "wanted" by German monarchs, should have been so courteously received by the rulers of Britain, just as it must secretly have amused Prince Albert to spite his Wettin kinsfolk by honoring Wagner in this fashion. Wagner wrote to Minna that the queen was not fat "but very short and far from pretty, with a regrettably reddish nose." Then thirty-six years old, the woman who was to give her name to an entire era struck him as pleasant and kindly rather than imposing. She affably inquired whether he might not arrange his works for performance at the Italian Opera, Covent Garden. Prince Albert knowledgeably objected that Wagner's libretti were unsuited to such treatment, and that Italian singers would be unable to interpret them, whereupon Victoria retorted that the majority of the artists at the Italian Opera were German anyway and need only sing in their mother tongue. Wagner jocularly remarked that German singers, too, were spoiled.

That was the high-water mark of his London visit. While saying good-bye to Hogarth, the secretary of the Philharmonic Society, he came face to face with Meyerbeer. Flummoxed by this chance encounter, the two men astonished Hogarth by exchanging not a word. When Hogarth asked Wagner if he did not know Meyerbeer, Wagner replied that he had better address the same question to Meyerbeer. Hogarth later did so, and assured Wagner the same evening that Meyerbeer had spoken of him in terms of the highest esteem. Somebody, one assumes, was being tactful!

Wagner's last concert on June 25 (at which, incidentally, he conducted a duet from Meyerbeer's *Prophète*) was rewarded with an ovation. Even the musicians dropped their reserve and gathered around him in a cheering throng. Berlioz, who had been present at this farewell concert, also attended the last-night party at his lodgings.

On June 30, after an absence of four months, Wagner arrived back in Zurich. He had spent four-fifths of his £200. All he had left was 1,000 francs.

Masquerade

On July 13, 1855, Wagner set off with Minna for Seelisberg on the Lake of Lucerne. Here he started fair-copying as much of his *Walküre* score as was complete, but his zest for composing and orchestrating remained dormant.

He returned to Zurich on August 15, unrefreshed by his month's absence. Although he resumed orchestrating the second act of *Walküre* and had completed the task by September 20, he was as out of tune as an instrument. He lacked music and would happily have read anything, even some scores by Berlioz, but Berlioz had run out of spare copies. Writing to Liszt, Wagner complained that everything around him had been "mute" for nearly two years, and that his contacts with the outside world brought him nothing but disquiet.

One bright spot was a visit on August 24, 1855, from the fifty-year-old Danish writer Hans Christian Andersen. Andersen had heard the *Tannhäuser* Overture conducted by Mendelssohn in 1846 —and had clapped in defiance of surrounding opposition. He had also seen *Lohengrin* in 1852 and been encouraged by Liszt to visit Wagner in Zurich. Andersen gives an account of their conversation in the latter part of his biography. Wagner, whose knowledge of Danish composers was limited to Niels Gade, not only gave him a friendly reception but questioned him on the entire range of Danish operas and Singspiele. After listening attentively, he said, "It is as though you have told me a fairy tale from the world of music—as though you have raised a curtain for me on the other side of the Elbe." Andersen concludes: "It was a happy and unforgettable hour, the like of which I have never experienced since."

Shortly afterward, Wagner suffered the first of thirteen attacks of a painful allergy. This ailment, which he identified as facial erysipelas, confined him to bed for days and weeks over a period of six months. It grew steadily worse, and visitors less fortunate than Andersen were often rebuffed.

Though engaged in scoring the third act of *Walküre* from October 8 onward, Wagner made the following note in his skeleton diary during December: "Tristan more definitely conceived." Either he felt that his nerves were unequal to the burden of his huge tetralogy, or he was susceptible to other outlets and still-keener temptations.

The gloom of these wintry six months was somewhat relieved by his growing circle of Zurich friends. Gottfried Semper, who had secured a teaching post at the Federal Polytechnic, was very hurt when his wife was excluded from invitations to the Wagners' parties, and protested to Wagner that she was "no more stupid" than the others. The aestheticist Friedrich Vischer, formerly a moderate left-wing delegate to the Frankfurt assembly, was awarded a professorship at Zurich, and Ritter and Hornstein also settled there temporarily. The Swiss writer Gottfried Keller, whose literary standing had steadily risen since the publication of the first version of *Der grüne Heinrich*, returned to Switzerland from Berlin and joined the Wille-Wagner set. Before long, references to Keller's close relations with the poet-composer, who was six years older, began to appear in letters to his friends. "Wagner occasionally provides a hearty midday meal at which everyone drinks with gusto," he wrote to Lina Duncker on January 13, 1856. "I see a great deal of Richard Wagner, who is a good man as well as a brilliant one," Hermann Hettner was informed in a letter dated April 16, which went on to deliver a surprising appraisal of the *Nibelungen*: It was "German through and through, but purified by the tragic spirit of antiquity." That, at least, was the impression it made on him at the time. Later, on April 30, 1857, Keller gave the poet Ferdinand Freiligrath a teasing description of the whole Zurich set, qualified at the end by a piece of self-mockery. Wagner, he wrote, was "an extremely talented person, but also something of a hairdresser and charlatan. He has a bric-à-brac table on which can be seen a silver hairbrush in a crystal bowl, etc., etc." It would, however, be obtuse to misconstrue this as Keller's sole and definitive verdict on Wagner.

Their esteem was entirely mutual. Although Wagner found Keller prickly and treated him with remarkable condescension in *My Life*, he had the highest regard for his short stories. He enjoyed reading aloud from *Die Leute von Seldwyla* and told Cosima that no one in Germany had written anything like *Der grüne Heinrich* since Goethe.

On the evening of March 20, when the Wesendoncks came to congratulate him on completing the score of *Walküre*, Wagner had a stand-up row with Otto. Fine words were no use to him, he complained, so why not step up his monthly allowance? The Wesendoncks walked out in dismay, and it took all his powers of persuasion, plus Minna's help, to repair the breach.

Three days later, on March 23, he completed the fair copy of the score as well, but it was not given its first hearing until April 26, when he invited his friends to hear the first act. He doubled in the parts of Siegmund and Hunding while Emilie Heim sang Sieglinde, and Theodor Kirchner, a Schumann enthusiast from Winterthur, provided the piano accompaniment.

To many of those present, it seemed the most dramatic performance they had ever attended. Wagner himself found this sample a poor substitute for the real thing. He was tired of living on written music alone, and there were reasons for this which, unbeknown to him, far transcended any nostalgia for the theaters of Germany. He was producing "big-city" art. Its technical subtlety, dense orchestral texture, and middle-range polyphony were unsuited to provincial Swiss audiences and music festivals, however worthy. According to Ernst Bloch, they were socially conditioned by "a broad metropolitan bourgeoisie, with its desire for amorphous nervous stimulation." Even though Wagner aimed far beyond that, he felt drawn toward the society that had produced him, and his impatience with exile was not a product of homesickness alone.

There was nothing for it but to follow Liszt's advice and address a personal plea for pardon to the king of Saxony. This he wrote on May 15. He offered no denials, simply made light of his activities —as he later learned to do in such a practiced way—by seeking to dissociate himself from "party politics." He now recognized the "falsity" of his earlier views, he declared; indeed, he had undergone an "inward conversion" of the kind already intimated to Liszt.* He sent a copy of this petition to Liszt himself, adding that it had caused him much soul-searching, and that he had profaned his "inward conversion" even by hinting at its existence to the king of Saxony and his ministers. "But I felt able to go thus far if absolutely necessary."

On June 4, the king of Saxony referred Wagner's petition to his Ministry of Justice. In July, having copied out long extracts from the depositions made by those involved in the revolt, the Ministry of Justice recommended that it be rejected. Wagner heard the news in August.

In the middle of September, he put the following words into Mime's mouth: "Wearisome labor! Purposeless toil!" He was embarking on the composition sketch for the first act of *Siegfried.* He began the orchestral sketch on September 22, the scoring on October 11.

Meanwhile, he had lately been distracted in his Zeltweg apartment by noisy neighbors: five pianists and a flautist, not to mention a tinsmith with whom he regularly crossed swords until the man was persuaded to keep to certain working hours. One bonus was that the smith's hideous hammering inspired the motif for Siegfried's furious outburst at Mime, the childishly petulant theme in G minor.

Wagner and Zurich were now awaiting some distinguished visitors, and the whole town plunged into a veritable whirl of social and artistic functions, almost like a fashionable spa frequented by the elite of the concertgoing world. Franz Liszt arrived on October 13, to be followed soon afterward by Princess Carolyne von Sayn-Wittgenstein and her daughter Marie. They moved into the largest suite at the Baur au Lac, which had been vacated by its regular occupants, the Wesendoncks, because Otto had gone to Paris to consult his architect on the design and décor of a villa he proposed to build in Switzerland. Marie von Wittgenstein, "The Child," had suffered the fate of so many precocious young beauties: Her charms were already beginning to wilt, and it was only when she engaged in animated conversation that Wagner was sentimentally reminded of the angelic, ethereal creature she had so lately been.

For the first few evenings, he had Liszt all to himself. Blood-brother Franz played him the completed piano version of his *Dante* Symphony, which greatly impressed Wagner with its novel freedom of approach to structure and harmony. Many things could be conceded in private, he said in 1859, but there was no need to advertise them, and one of these was that he had been "quite a different fellow, as a harmonist, since becoming acquainted with Liszt's compositions." At Zurich in 1856, however, he was perceptive enough of their musical affinities to suggest that Liszt might have written a different finale—one that drew gently to a close instead of ending in a noisy coda. Quite so, said Liszt; Princess Carolyne had wanted it that way, but he would change it. He naturally did nothing of the kind, and Wagner drew his own conclusions about Liszt's dependence on the lady in question.

This reinforced his existing dislike of her. He soon began to find her letters aggressive and inimical to any free expression of opinion. In the end, the "princess" became a disruptive and emotive keyword in conversations between Wagner, Liszt, and his daughter Cosima.

Even at Zurich, Wagner took exception to her imperious manner, obtrusive enthusiasms, and social activities. She was a domineering, garrulous know-it-all. Gottfried Keller, too, poked fun at her and her Zurich courtiers. Puffing at cigars and filling her suite at the Baur au Lac with smoke, her entourage consisted of doctors and professors—a motley band of academics including Semper, Köchly, and the physiologist Jakob Moleschott—to whom she gave audiences separately and en masse. On one occasion, she summoned Wagner for a personal elucidation of the complex "plots" in his *Ring des Nibelungen*. He found them hard to explain, and ended by feeling as if he had just recounted the plot of a French play.

On October 20, escorted by both masters of the "music of the future," Princess Carolyne attended a performance of Halévy's opera *La Juive*. Two days later, Liszt's forty-fifth birthday was celebrated "with due pomp" at the Baur au Lac. The party was attended by every member of Zurich's artistic and academic upper crust, including Herwegh, Wille, Semper, Vischer, Moleschott, Ettmüller, Sulzer, Köchly, Heim, Baumgartner, and their various wives. Georg Herwegh read a poem by Hoffmann von Fallersleben, telegraphed for the occasion from Weimar, which was followed by a scratch performance of the first act of *Walküre* with Wagner as Siegmund and Hunding, Emilie Heim as Sieglinde, and Liszt at the piano. Even the *Neue Zürcher Zeitung* paid tribute to this musical offering.

On November 23, Wagner and Liszt shared a concert at St. Gallen. The latter conducted his symphonic poems *Orpheus* and *Les Préludes*, the former Beethoven's *Eroica*. Wagner stamped during the rehearsal like a horse kept too long in its stable. He needed an orchestra as a man needs air to breathe, though the results he extracted from the St. Gallen musicians left him dissatisfied. He later described this memorable gala concert as "a brilliant monstrosity." The princess and her hangers-on, the Willes, Kirchner, and others, had also traveled to St. Gallen, and the festivities lasted for two days.

On December 1, Wagner resumed work on the first act of *Siegfried*. "Once a woman lay whimpering, out there in the wild wood. . . ." It was only when he had come to compose the music, he wrote to Liszt, that the true essence of his poem dawned on him. Secrets were continually revealing themselves, and everything was becoming fiercer and more urgent. The work did, in fact, change during its musical development, for that was when it acquired its psychological—indeed, psychoanalytical—modernity. Was this an introspective period? That would have been uncharacteristic of Wagner, so we should not be surprised by Gottfried Keller's assertion to Lina Duncker in a letter dated March 8 that Liszt's presence had again made Wagner "very irascible and self-centered."

Minna, too, was irascible. When her neighbor Emilie Heim, the wife of the conductor Ignaz Heim, began to cast languishing glances at Richard, her jealousy revived to such an extent that "Heimchen" was banished from the Wagners' musical gatherings. Her place was taken by Frau Pollert, who had sung Isabella in the one and only Magdeburg performance of *Das Liebesverbot* and was now under contract to the Zurich Theater.

Wagner had lately been showing a perceptible interest in Johanna Spyri, wife of the editor of the *Eidgenössische Zeitung* and future authoress of children's books, who was newly married. Had she not been so wrapped up in herself and suspicious of her husband's idol, the creator of the sentimental and sugary world of Heidi might easily have stolen the role of Isolde from Mathilde Wesendonck. Wagner's relations with the Wesendoncks had temporarily cooled a little, partly because of their long absence but also because Mathilde was preoccupied with a new addition to the family.

He was just about to compose the forging scene in *Siegfried*, abrim with sensational ideas, when some all-important news arrived from Otto Wesendonck: After purchasing a plot of land for his villa in the Enge suburb of Zurich, he had discovered that a doctor named Binswanger planned to build a lunatic asylum next door, so he had bought the neighboring plot as well. There, in a cottage close to his own future abode, Wesendonck proposed that the creator of the *Ring* should complete his great work, exempt from material concerns, for an annual rent of 800 francs.

From February onward, Wagner supervised the conversion and refurbishing of his little house. On March 31, while still at Zeltweg, he finished scoring the first act of *Siegfried*. The final notes were penned during a visit from Mathilde Wesendonck, into whose eyes he now gazed with hope rekindled. As for the last two acts, he wrote to Princess Carolyne on April 7 that he expected the rural tranquillity of his new home to engender the mood and incentive he needed for their composition. All his thoughts and feats of ingenuity were now devoted to renovating the house at Enge, on the green hill that beckoned like some Canaan when he walked down from Zeltweg to the lake for his morning constitutional. On April 20, he and Minna bridged the gap between moving out and moving in by spending a week at the Hotel Sternen, a rather squalid establishment.

What lay ahead? Minna felt uneasy; Wagner, looking back down the years, could see nothing but a succession of masquerades. Any change was preferable to none, but would this one prove to be an end or a beginning? His magnum opus was in the doldrums and temptations were crowding in on him. Schopenhauer, Buddhism, his plea for clemency, his spirit of resignation—had all these made a different man of him? He might have been saying amen: farewell to the world and hail to a permanent resting place.

But just as a person can continue to dream of better things while seemingly turning his back on reality, so Wagner's renunciation of change in the material world entailed no renunciation of the impulses absorbed by his world of expression. If there were things that could no longer, perhaps, be discerned in his ideas and actions, they insinuated themselves, albeit sometimes veiled in obscurity and not as purposefully as he would have wished, into the fabric of his music, where they became an early intimation of a new freedom of expression and perception.

The House on the Green Hill

The Good Friday Legend

On April 28, 1857, after prevailing almost by force over their builders' delaying tactics, the Wagners moved into the little house that Mathilde Wesendonck, writing from Paris, had casually christened Asyl [Refuge]. The weather was cold and damp, the new heating equipment proved inadequate, and Minna and Richard both retired to bed with colds. It was only by degrees that their new home took on the elegance and comfort proper to what was this time intended as a permanent abode. The building had three main rooms on each of two floors and an attic guest suite overhead. In the workroom on the first floor, Wagner's desk was installed beside a large window with a view of the lake and the Glarner Alps. The garden was large enough to stroll in and contained a vegetable plot for Minna. It also boasted a rose hedge that acquired special significance. Toward the end of Wagner's tragicomic romance at Asyl, he used to pick a rose each morning and place it on his desk. In later years, the scent of roses never failed to conjure up memories of the time when his passion was in full flower.

His assertion that *Parsifal* was conceived at Asyl on Good Friday is an example of Wagnerian self-dramatization. Good Friday fell, in 1857, on April 10, or eighteen days before he moved in. He did not resolve the mystery until 1879, in conversation with Cosima.

He had been thinking, he said, of the impression made on him by the magic of Good Friday. Laughing, he added that it was "all as far-fetched as my love affairs, for it wasn't Good Friday at all—nothing, just a pleasant, countrified atmosphere that made me tell myself, 'This is how it ought to be on Good Friday.' "

He had never felt as secure and at home in a rural setting as he did at that time. "Peace and tranquillity surround me," he wrote to Liszt on May 8. He was still undistracted by neighbors, however congenial, because the Wesendoncks' villa, a coldly sumptuous building in Renaissance style, was as yet unfinished and unoccupied.

On May 12, he began fair-copying the score of such parts of *Siegfried* as he had already completed, and on May 22, his birthday, he embarked on the music for the second act, the *Ring*'s most idyllic episode. Mathilde Wesendonck came to wish him many happy returns, and that evening he was surprised to hear the garden of Asyl resound to the song of the Rhine Maidens, alias Frau Pollert and her daughters Pauline and Mina, who had been studying the roles with his permission. His idyll seemed complete. In the weeks that followed, he often walked over the Gabler, which he called the Green Hill, into nearby Sihltal. He was so enchanted by the birds that sang to him on these rambles that, "in artistic imitation of Nature," he borrowed their voices for the forest scene in *Siegfried*.

Yet his reluctance to proceed with the *Ring* was steadily growing. Although he reached Fafner's "I lie here in possession—let me slumber" on May 30 and started the orchestral sketch for the second act on June 18, he made the following note on the manuscript sheet: "*Tristan* already resolved on." On June 27, he stopped work altogether. Writing to Liszt the next day, he announced that he had conducted his Siegfried into the solitude of the forest, left him under a lime tree, and "taken leave of him with heartfelt tears." He now intended to execute *Tristan* on a smaller, more manageable scale, hoping that a "thoroughly practicable opus" of the sort he envisaged would keep him solvent for some time to come.

On August 20, with the poem already in his head, he started on the prose sketch for *Tristan*. Two days later, the Wesendoncks moved into their villa, which had at last been vacated by Parisian plasterers and paperhangers. Thus the new phase in Wagner's relations with them coincided, almost to the day, with the inception of *Tristan* in its original form. "We had drawn so close," he says in *My Life*, "through being such near neighbors in a country place, that our contacts were bound to multiply considerably, if only because of our routine daily encounters."

Before the Wesendoncks' villa could attain full social splendor —one of their first visitors was the composer Robert Franz—the Wagners entertained some guests of their own. One was the music critic and conductor Richard Pohl, who arrived from Weimar at the end of August. Originally an admirer of Liszt, Wagner, and Berlioz in equal measure, Pohl was the first to gain an impression of this artistic and financial symbiosis on the hilly outskirts of Zurich. At soirees in the Wagners' home, which were also attended by their neighbors from the big house next door, Pohl clearly perceived the influence exerted on Wagner by that "lovely appari-tion" Frau Wesendonck, a "charmingly feminine and poetically thoughtful soul" beside whom his rapidly aging and "homely" wife paled into insignificance. Pohl could not help noticing how wide a gulf separated the Wagners. Minna pinned no hopes on the *Nibelungen;* indeed, she found the Rhine Maidens' song outlandish and asked Pohl if he really considered it so beautiful. This made the visitor think twice, not unnaturally, but he preserved agree-able memories of some lively evenings at the Wagners' home and walks in the neighboring mountains. Meanwhile, more guests were expected. Hans von Bülow and his bride had announced their intention of paying a visit. Writing to Ludmilla Assing on August 26, Gottfried Keller mischievously referred to the "newly-weds" whose forthcoming stay would doubtless provide an occa-sion for "little episodes in the cult of the future." Bülow had married Liszt's second daughter at Berlin on August 18.

Enter Cosima. . . .

The Bülows' honeymoon took them via Geneva to Lausanne, where Hans visited his boyhood friend Karl Ritter. On August 31, the young couple arrived in Zurich. Wagner had booked them into the Hotel Bellevue. As soon as Hans had recovered from an attack of the nerve-induced rheumatism that always afflicted him at cru-cial junctures in his life, Wagner persuaded the Bülows to move to Asyl on September 5, two days after attending a soiree there. Their fellow guests included Emma Herwegh (Georg was away), Robert Franz, Hermann Müller and Gottfried Keller. The latter, who found Cosima von Bülow "an admirable and singular young woman," declared that it was a long time since any member of her sex had appealed to him as much.

Though not really pretty, Cosima had an unusual face with strongly defined features, a prominent nose and pale, thin, taut-skinned cheeks, large, lustrous eyes and handsome light-brown hair which she usually wore braided low on the neck. She was a tall, gaunt, distant figure of a woman. Bülow, on the other hand, had eyes that radiated a sort of cold, dark fire. His face seemed imprinted with morbid unease and hypersensitivity—a half-appealing, half-disquieting nervous excitement. It was almost the face of his late middle age.

The Bülows' first encounter with Emma Herwegh, which quickly blossomed into friendship, was to cause much ill feeling. She aroused Wagner's ire by inviting them to Falkenburg without him. This provoked him into outbursts against her for luring his guests away. Cosima informed Emma in elegant French how much embarrassment it had caused her that "*notre gracieux Maître et Seigneur*" had not been invited too. Later on, when the Bülows had returned to Berlin and no word came from Cosima, Wagner regretfully concluded that he had offended her. He wrote to Hans that he was saddened by Cosima's long silence. "If she found my manner unduly strange, or if she was affronted by an occasional brusque remark or little gibe (on account of the Herweghs, etc.), I should have just cause to regret having been rather too confiding —something I readily appreciate and deplore whenever it happens. . . ." Then, when Cosima still made no response: "I feel I am still a little silently at war with her, God knows why. Plain jealousy of the Herweghs—isn't that allowed?"

But the cause of their estrangement was more deep-seated. Wagner had no idea what a field of tension he was in, for Cosima had promptly perceived, when he introduced Frau Wesendonck to her as "Saint" Mathilde, that the Muse's place at the Master's side was already occupied. It was a musical gathering. Hans von Bülow played excerpts from Klindworth's piano arrangements of *Die Walküre* and picked his way brilliantly through the orchestral sketches for *Siegfried*—the first time this music had been heard. Wagner himself sang all the parts. Meanwhile, the trio of women who spanned the whole of his artistic career—Minna Wagner, Mathilde Wesendonck, and Cosima von Bülow—sat listening like figures in a group photograph. Mathilde sat there proudly, doubtless remembering the dedications and marginal notes that adorned the *Walküre* manuscripts. "Cosima," to quote Wagner's own recollection of the scene, "listened with her head bowed, saying nothing; if pressed for an opinion, she began to weep." Cosima confirmed the accuracy of this description by recording it at his dictation in *My Life*.

It is hard to conceive of these women together, and just as hard to imagine what they felt, but it was near them and surrounded by them that Wagner devoted the morning hours of the ensuing three weeks to writing the libretto for *Tristan*. He finished the original version of the poem on September 18 and presented it to Mathilde Wesendonck, saying that he owed its completion to her. This thoroughly ambiguous remark may well have referred to his outward circumstances—to the peace and quiet of his new abode—but her response to it was more extreme than prudence dictated. She led him to a chair in front of the sofa, embraced him, and declared that all her wishes were fulfilled. If we are to believe what Wagner wrote to his sister, Klara Wolfram, in the following year, she even said it was time for her to die.

Though taken aback by the elemental vehemence of this avowal, Wagner was not unresponsive to it. As for Cosima, whether or not she knew of this dedicatory scene or guessed at it, she retreated even farther into her shell.

There was another occasion when Minna, Mathilde, and Cosima met as a group of listeners: Wagner's first reading of *Tristan und Isolde*. On that September evening, he read of love's sweet bliss and broken faith, of virtue abandoned and a tragic passion culminating in death. The ladies were breathless with emotion. Mathilde was so moved by the last act that Wagner had to console her by remarking that no one ought to grieve over the denouement because "in a matter so grave, things generally turned out this way," and Cosima "wholeheartedly agreed."

Otto Wesendonck and Hans von Bülow sat quiet throughout. At this stage, none of those present could have defined what he or she was feeling. The atmosphere was charged with jealousy, both baseless and well founded.

Bülow set off for Berlin on September 28, taking a complete copy of the *Tristan* poem with him. He thought he had observed a kind of "transfiguration" in Wagner, and felt certain that the *Ring* would dominate the musical scene until well into the next century.

Johanna Rosine Wagner, Richard's mother. *Painting by Ludwig Geyer, 1813*

Adolf Wagner, Richard's uncle and mentor. *Drawing, 1832*

'Brühl in Leipzig." Richard Wagner was born in the house farthest to the right. *Watercolor, 1840*

Minna Wagner, *née* Planer. *After an engraving by Weger*

Uprising in Leipzig, September 1830. *Watercolor by G. E. Opiz*

Franz Liszt.
Portrait by Miklós Barabás, 1846

King Ludwig II of Bavaria.
Painting by F. Dürck, 1864

Cosima von Bülow, Baron Augusz, Franz Liszt, and Hans von Bülow in Budapest, 1865

Richard Wagner. *Painting by Franz von Lenbach, 1871*

Rheingold.
Drawing by Theodor Pixis, 1869

Tannhäuser, Act II, Scene 3. *Drawing by M. Rouargue, 1861*

Festspielhaus, Bayreuth, during a production of *Rheingold*, 1876

Götterdämmerung, Act I, Scene 2.
Sketch by Professor Josef Hoffmann for Bayreuth Ring *production*

Cosima, Siegfried, and
Richard Wagner. *Photo by
Adolph Gross, 1873*

Richard Wagner while playing
the piano, Palazzo Vendramin,
February 12, 1883. *Pencil
drawing by Paul von Joukowsky*

Herwegh, who had since returned to Zurich, presented Cosima with a farewell poem whose closing lines carried the message: "To a world out of tune thou shalt ne'er thyself resign. . . ."

At the end of October, Cosima wrote to Emma Herwegh: "*Mes amitiés à Minna, si vous la voyez; et pour le Kapellmeister, il sait ce que je lui suis* [My regards to Minna if you see her; as for the Kapellmeister, he knows what I am to him]." But did he really?

Tristan and Emma Bovary

The Wesendonck saga began in earnest in 1857, the year that saw the publication of Gustave Flaubert's *Madame Bovary*. The husband in the case gets little mention, though it was Otto Wesendonck who owned the houses, threw the parties, and footed the bills for everything. Wagner found Otto tiresome, as he concedes in his memoirs, in a passage whose obliquity does nothing to disguise the brazen presumption of his conduct. "I had often noticed," he says, "that Wesendonck, in his honest, unrefined way, felt disturbed by my making myself at home in his house. In many matters, such as heating, lighting, and the hours appointed for meals, I was deferred to in a way that seemed to encroach on his rights as master of the house."

The incubation period was over, both for *Tristan* and for the affair that now entered its acute phase. October 18 brought another communal excursion to the Willes at Mariafeld. Everyone strolled arm in arm, notably Wagner and Mathilde, who were celebrating the month that had elapsed since the poem's dedication. Lovers are quick to celebrate, perhaps because they fear that their opportunities to do so may be numbered.

The musician in Wagner had begun a metamorphosis—one that merits special note: On October 1, he had begun to compose the music for *Tristan*.

This "birth of the modern" was an explosion of energy. In retrospect, Wagner told Cosima on September 28 and October 1, 1878, that he had been possessed by a desire to "vent his frenzy," and on December 11 of the same year he added that what had driven him to write *Tristan* was an urge "to go completely symphonic for once." This is an inadequate account of its motivation. He had a tendency to explain his music's anguished yearning for solitude in terms of the motifs "that express a world of emotion alternating between extreme desire for bliss and the most resolute longing for death." But this might mislead one into supposing that the real novelty of the work lies on the surface, in a metaphysical inter-weaving of pleasure and pain, in "unfleshed passion," in the "soar-ing ascent of the violins, which surpasses all reason," or in "perfumed torments pierced by flashes of light" (Thomas Mann). As ever, Wagner presents us with a dualistic combination of differ-ent levels, of superficial and fundamental causes and effects.

Tristan's chromatic conflict, its soulful, painful descent from one key to another, is a "literary" device that transcends the bounds of music and expresses disenchantment with a real world whose fixed points of reference are steadily disappearing. As a resort to artistic means, it characterized the decadent aspect of romanti-cism, which attained its last and most mature consummation in *Tristan*. Bourgeois ideals had withered in the outside world and resistance could be offered only in art itself, by revolutionizing its means. Flaubert and Wagner were confronted by the same prob-lem. *Tristan* and *Madame Bovary* both presuppose a real world in the throes of instability: King Mark is not alone in his weariness. The conventions are mocked with a candor that would have been unthinkable only a decade earlier. The outrage felt by both men's contemporaries, or those of them who upheld the conventions, was not surprising. That *Tristan* did not cause a far greater stir requires some explanation. Given the nature of the second act, Wagner was just as open as Flaubert to a charge of "offending against public morals, good manners, and religion." Minna, who found the li-bretto "disgusting" and "almost indecently passionate," loathed the whole opera because she was aware of its "instigation." But it was the music that brought its lasciviousness and "immoral" ten-dencies to life. If this did not sink in at once, it was because Wagner overtaxed the ears of his audience, and because the urge for release and resolution was confined to a deeper level by a self-imposed framework and carefully calculated intervallic tension: in short, by the dialectic of subtlety.

Wagner offered the unheard and unheard-of work to Breitkopf & Härtel as a "practicable opus" for a fee of 600 louis-d'or, an obsolete form of coinage worth twenty francs and containing just over seven grams of gold. Hermann Härtel, a prudent business-man, replied that *Tristan*, though worth considering, was not an easy work to stage. If Wagner were prepared to drop his original demand, he could open the enclosed sealed envelope. Inside was an offer of 200 louis-d'or. Wagner accepted it and delivered the manuscript for engraving act by act.

While engaged on the first act of *Tristan*, which took six months including orchestration, Wagner wrote four of the five *Gedichte für eine Frauenstimme* [*Poems for a Female Voice*], his only settings of someone else's lyrics that bear comparison with his major works. These have passed into musical history as the *Wesendonck Lieder*. Mathilde recalled in her memoirs that he took each of her poems as it was completed and invested it with "supreme transfiguration and consecration" by means of his music. She was granted an opportunity such as few adoring dilettantes have ever enjoyed.

How glorious was physical propinquity when transfigured into spiritual communion; when two beloved faces encountered one another almost daily by common deceit and mutual arrangement, either behind the villa's slender colonnade or in the half-timbered Asyl nearby, where Mathilde, to Minna's chagrin, strode briskly past her and up to the composer's first-floor workroom, there to polish a syllable of verse or drink in the next sixteen bars of immortality. How glorious, too, the delusion that it could all go on forever: he, seated at the piano, conjuring forth the iridescent harmonies of *Tristan* as a setting for her poem *Träume*; she, at the window of his workroom, gazing past the villa's putti-adorned terrace at the lake (just as he was later to picture her gazing from the terrace in the direction of her vanished love); or in the music room of her husband's sumptuous mansion, when Richard sang and played her what he had written, reveling in the fuller, undamped acoustics and his freedom from the constraints of home, or improvised on Isolde's narrative with the rich but delicate touch for which he was famed, sometimes merely sketching the music with fleeting fingers. "I who silently restored his life, and silently protected him from foe's revenge . . . !" Mathilde, too, had her great moments. The *Wesendonck Lieder*, all but one of which were orchestrated by Felix Mottl, preserved the *Tristan* tone, although only *Träume* (December 4) and *Im Treibhaus* (May 1)—the latter written between the first and second acts—were expressly described by Wagner as studies for *Tristan*, while *Der Engel* (November 30) is clearly based on a passage from *Das Rheingold*. Together with *Schmerzen* (December 17) and *Stehe still* (February 21), they constitute a cycle of which Wagner proudly noted, in the diary he kept for Mathilde in Venice, "I have never produced anything better than these songs, and very few of my works will be able to stand comparison with them."

On December 23, while Otto Wesendonck, anxious to secure his fortune against a financial crisis in America, was away on business, Wagner marked Mathilde's birthday by serenading her in her villa with an arrangement of *Träume* for small orchestra and solo violin. On December 31, he presented her with the composition sketch for the first act of *Tristan* and some dedicatory verses proclaiming that "what Tristan and Isolde lamented, their tears and their kisses" he laid at her feet "that they may extol the angel who has raised me so high."

Whatever Otto Wesendonck may or may not have learned of all this on his return, it proved too much for him. Although he had recovered his spirits and faced the future with renewed optimism —he had emerged from the financial crisis even wealthier than before—the atmosphere at the villa suddenly deteriorated to such an extent that Wagner had no recourse but flight. He applied for a passport to Paris.

He left Zurich on January 14, 1858. For some mysterious but providential reason, he missed his connection at Basel and was obliged to spend a night in Strasbourg. On reaching Paris he booked into the Hôtel du Louvre. Here he found that Orsini's attempt on the life of Napoleon III had plunged the capital into such a ferment that he feared his revolutionary past might land him in trouble with the authorities. But for his delayed arrival, he would have stayed at a hotel on rue le Pelletier—the very place from which the assassins had launched their abortive attack. As always in such razor-edged moments, he felt called upon to "confer with the daemon" that ruled his destiny.

The outward face of Paris had changed a good deal, thanks to the modernization undertaken by Georges Haussman, prefect of the Seine, and Wagner felt less at home there than ever. He would have felt even lonelier had it not been for Cosima's brother-in-law, Emile Ollivier, a man of endearingly republican views who assisted Wagner in the matter of his French proprietary rights. As for Blandine, Ollivier's wife, she impressed him favorably with her "gentleness, gaiety, and a certain droll composure." She was so quick on the uptake that "the slightest intimation sufficed to create

a mutual understanding on any subject of interest to us both."
Physical resemblance made her Cosima's more cheerful counterpart, and Wagner was not the first man to be surprised and
charmed by this duplication of her sister's image.

Berlioz, whom he found "kindly disposed" on the whole, read
him the libretto of his opera *Les Troyens,* but Wagner was
thoroughly disappointed by its striving for theatrical effect. Most
of his other Paris acquaintances were widows, for the ranks of the
previous generation were thinning fast. Hérold's widow he met at
an orchestral concert. At the home of Madame Erard, widow of the
piano manufacturer, he played excerpts from his operas in the
presence of yet another musical relict, Signora Spontini, with such
success that his hostess promised him a piano.

Back in Zurich on February 6, he promptly invited his friends
to Asyl to tell them about his highly successful trip. After that, all
seemed to go on much as before. Mornings were devoted to scoring
the first act of *Tristan,* afternoons to walking on the slopes of the
Gabler or in nearby Sihltal, evenings to reading or reading aloud
from Calderón, Cervantes, and Lope de Vega—if Wagner had not
already visited Mathilde's salon in his role as the "Twilight Man"
or exceeded the quota of their "working visits." Minna, whose
reaction to these visits became increasingly resentful and suspicious, was now plying herself simultaneously with remedies for
heart trouble and insomnia.

Richard and Mathilde now became enmeshed in a crisis of their
own making. Mathilde had lately been taking Italian lessons from
Francesco de Sanctis, a handsome, hot-blooded, forty-year-old Ne-
apolitan who lectured on aesthetics and Italian literature at Zurich
Polytechnic. Although he published a dialogue entitled *Schopenhauer e Leopardi* in 1858, de Sanctis had little time for Wagner or
music and much preferred taking tea or going for drives with his
pupil to any involvement in German romantic complications.
Wagner was so consumed with rancor after the Italian's visits that
he sometimes lay awake half the night. Meanwhile, Otto Wesendonck seemed quite unaware of his rivals' mutual jealousy.

By way of compensation for Wagner's birthday serenade in
Mathilde's honor, Otto's own birthday was celebrated on March
31 with a house concert whose timing, venue, and magnitude
caused a considerable stir. That over thirty musicians should have
gathered to perform selections from Beethoven in the Wesen-

doncks' residence—during Holy Week, too—was socially unprecedented. The guests were reported to have numbered more than a
hundred, though the extant guest list identifies only about seventy
of them. They included the patrician Stockar-Eschers and the
Köchlys, Sulzer, Hagenbuch, and the Herweghs, Alexander
Müller, Hermann Müller of Dresden, who was now a Swiss railroad official, Gottfried Semper and the Willes, Robert Marschall
von Bieberstein and his wife, and numerous Zurich notables. Gottfried Keller, that fervent admirer of *Tristan*, was too ill to attend
this unique social function. Wagner himself was presented with an
ivory baton carved from a design by Semper, but the whole affair
left him feeling depressed, "as though the potential climax of a
vital relationship had been reached" and "the bowstring was over-
stretched." Mathilde's friend Eliza Wille, who had become Wagner's confidante in matters of the heart, felt the same.

Wagner had scarcely completed the first act of *Tristan* on April
3 and conveyed the news to his delightful neighbor when the tune
went wrong. He saw Mathilde only briefly on April 5. Their evening communion was disrupted by the arrival of Francesco de Sanctis and Robert Marschall von Bieberstein, and Wagner retired in
high dudgeon. Mathilde did not come out into the garden next day.
That evening, Wagner flared up over Goethe's *Faust*. Not that he
failed to share Mathilde's admiration for the work, but he thought
—quite rightly—that to stylize the tormented figure of Faust into
an ideal was to misconstrue the author's intention. It must have
been a dismal evening. Wagner began hectoring and lecturing his
beloved in an intolerable manner. In the end, perhaps because she
had cited the Italian in support of her argument, he vented his fury
on the absent de Sanctis.

The very next morning, April 7, he sent Mathilde a letter of
apology headed "Morning Confession" rolled up in a pencil sketch
of the *Tristan* Prelude. "Ah, no, no!" the missive began. "It is not
de Sanctis whom I hate, but myself, for catching my poor heart
unawares in such frailty, again and again!" Having spent the night
before last brooding, he was rational again by morning and able
to pray wholeheartedly to his "angel."—"And this prayer is Love!
Love! The profoundest spiritual joy resides in this love, the source
of my inspiration!" There it was at last, in black and white. He
then tried to dispose of their foolish quarrel over Goethe. "Any
attempt to adjust Goethe for the philistine convenience of the

world rests ultimately on a misunderstanding of the author; but that this is possible at all makes me wary of him and, more especially, of his interpreters and adjusters." After another admonition against "trying to turn Faust into one of the noblest human types," Wagner concluded: "Today I shall come into the garden; as soon as I see you, I shall hope to find you undisturbed for a moment. Take my entire soul as a morning salutation!"

Minna, who must have suspected that something was afoot, intercepted the messenger—a gardener named Friedrich—and opened the letter. Outraged by its preamble and concluding words, she burst into her husband's workroom. She was further enraged by his lack of response to the "vulgar" construction she placed on what he had written. He kept completely silent until her fury had abated a little. Then he strove to explain that her view of the matter was mistaken, and that foolish and precipitate action on her part could only do harm to all concerned. Minna appeared to accept this.

It was not all Minna's fault that the bubble eventually burst. Strangely enough, the advice to "have it out" with Mathilde came from Emma Herwegh, who resented Wagner's having made Eliza Wille, and not herself, his confidante in affairs of the heart. Now there were two candidates for the role of Minna's Brangäne. Having waited until Wagner had gone for a walk one day, Minna called on her neighbor. "If I were any ordinary woman," she said, "I should take this letter to your husband." Mathilde, who prided herself on having no secrets from Otto, was deeply offended—so much so that she promptly told him what had happened.

Wagner returned from his walk to find the Wesendoncks setting off for a drive in their carriage, Otto smiling strangely, Mathilde pale and distraught. He guessed the truth as soon as he walked into Asyl and noticed Minna's "cheerful" expression. Warning her of "unpleasant consequences," he reminded her that the doctor had long been prescribing a cure for her heart trouble and urged her to comply with his advice at once.

On April 15, he accompanied her to Schloss Brestenberg on the Hallwyler See, a sanitarium run by a Dr. Adolf Erismann. Through Eliza Wille, whom he visited at Mariafeld the following week, Wagner learned that Mathilde now declined to have anything more to do with his wife. She was offended, not because he had loved her, but because she had been obliged to deny the fact.

Both the Wesendoncks were affronted at his having cloaked their relations in such "mystery," it seemed, and they went off to Italy for several weeks.

Wagner had been reproached by Otto for leaving Minna insufficiently informed of "the purity of these relations." Taking this rebuke to heart, he wrote to her on April 23 and told her to forget whatever aspects of the affair she found hard to understand. It is clear from his letters to Minna at Brestenberg that he genuinely meant to placate and appease her, not least because their reconciliation might enable him to stay on at Asyl. It must also have been during these weeks that he revived the idea of adopting a child to make Minna's position easier and give her life new meaning.

On May 3, he received the piano promised him by Madame Erard, which he later took to Venice and Lucerne. Inspired by the instrument's mellow tone, he started next day on the composition sketch for act 2 of *Tristan*, whose first sheet bears the note "Still at Asyl." This peaceful interlude could not last, however, for the day had to come when Minna and Mathilde both returned to Zurich.

Wagner's first distraction came on May 20 with the arrival of a young man whom Liszt had recommended to him. Though not yet seventeen, Karl Tausig was an amazingly precocious pianist who combined prodigious musical talent with an engaging blend of youthful impudence and sophisticated conversation. Wagner put him up at the nearby Hotel Sternen, where he stayed for two months. Tausig reluctantly accompanied Wagner on walks whose length he soon tired of, carried messages to the villa when the Wesendoncks returned, and proved such an entertaining companion that Wagner became genuinely fond of him. He treated Tausig like a son, scolding him gently for his boyish misdemeanors but delighting in his technical proficiency and keen intelligence. Wagner's affection for Tausig was remarkable, if only because the angelic young virtuoso happened to be Jewish. Suddenly remembering that *Judaism in Music* required all Jews to be repellent, he hastened to inform Minna that Tausig's father was "an honest Bohemian and a thoroughgoing Christian."

On Wagner's forty-fifth birthday, Karl Tausig and Hermann Müller accompanied him to Brestenberg to visit Minna, who was suffering from an irregular heartbeat. At the end of May she returned to Asyl to ensure that all was in order there. She now seemed to attach little importance to recent events. As Wagner puts it in *My Life,* her view of the matter was simply that there had been "a minor love affair" which her shrewd intervention had disposed of. One night, since she persisted in referring to it with "a certain distasteful levity," he resolved to define their position "clearly and firmly," regardless of her state of health. If ever they were compelled to leave Asyl, he said, it would mean a final parting of the ways. Minna, who shrank from the idea of a separation because it would degrade her socially, deplored this in a "gentle, dignified" fashion and kissed his hand when they parted for the night—"the first and only occasion on which she gave me any token of loving humility." Still believing in the possibility of a change of heart, he expressed the hope that they might continue the life they had resumed. Minna, however, gave quite another account of the scene to Emma Herwegh, who was now on her side: "I wished I had not been there; dear Richard vented his spleen on me until two o'clock in the morning."

On June 2, the day after he returned from Italy, Otto Wesendonck requested an interview with his neighbor, tenant, debtor, and faithless friend. We can only guess at its nature, but the upshot was that Wagner tried to sever personal contact with the Wesendoncks while remaining on amicable terms. How could he have hoped to succeed when everything, the recent past included, was crowding in on him? He was in the process of devising the music for those *Tristan* "sophisms" that conduct one from life at its most ebullient to the death wish at its most intense—his "greatest masterpiece in the art of subtle, gradual transition," as he had called it in an earlier letter to Mathilde. What followed this "great scene" in the second act was something too close to home for comfort: the entrance of King Mark, "that upholder of the moral world order and, thus, harbinger of death" (Wagner to Cosima on June 17, 1874). Mark's grief at his friend's disloyalty called for music imbued with the deepest, most agonizing sorrow, and Wagner produced it without a single false undertone, a single hint of insincerity.

On July 6, he wrote to tell Mathilde that they would be seeing each other less often in the future. "How could they have ended, those great battles we won, save in victory over every wish and desire?"

Renunciation, which did not come easily, had been preceded,

probably the night before, by his last and perhaps most violent outburst of passion. He had renounced her, he said, but not yet completely enough. The feeling that they must part was still opposed by thoughts of a possible union between them. "I came to you," he recapitulated, "and there was a clear and definite understanding between us that any other course entailed an iniquity that could not even be contemplated." In other words, when her anger against Minna had erupted once more, he had suggested that they leave their partners and marry. She, it seems, had replied that this would be "sacrilege." He found the word foolish and incongruous enough to laugh at it in later years. Recounting the scene to Cosima on March 14, 1873, he said that it was really quite an apt description of his proposal because he had not, in his heart of hearts, meant it seriously. The fact remains that he made it.

Mathilde was no Emma Bovary. Like Jessie Laussot, she either lacked the courage or was too well off and well drilled in the conventions to take the plunge. Temporarily preoccupied with a young child, as Emma was, she had no energy to spare for strenuous extramarital adventures. But did that justify Wagner in belittling her and the part she played in enhancing his emotional sensitivity during the writing of *Tristan?* "Nothing the Wesendonck woman does surprises me," he told Cosima on April 5, 1872. "She is irrational and has never known what's what." But he came closer to the truth in a letter to Eliza Wille dated June 5, 1863: "That is why I tell you: she is still my first and only love! I feel this now with ever-increasing certainty." That was before he set a final seal on his union with another woman who permanently readjusted the picture he retained of his past. It was not Mathilde's fault that until July 5, 1858, he cast her in an exalted role which she could never have sustained indefinitely.

The Grand Finale

The evil day was postponed by another succession of visitors. On July 10, to Wagner's faint annoyance, the tenor Joseph Tichatschek turned up and moved into the guest room. On July 11, Asyl's door was darkened by the gigantic figure of yet another tenor, Albert Niemann, who came accompanied by his actress fiancée Marie Seebach. Tichatschek and Niemann were wary of each other, so neither would consent to sing. Tausig's entertaining company and helping hand in the household made life tolerable until Wagner fetched Minna back from Brestenberg on July 15. They found on arrival that their Saxon gardener had erected a sort of triumphal arch over the front door. Minna, who was determined to make the most of her victory over her rival in the neighboring villa, insisted on keeping this floral tribute up for several days. Mathilde was duly enraged and hit back.

In despair, Wagner wrote to his confidante Eliza Wille regretting that ignorance of Mathilde's true wishes had prevented him from burning his bridges after the first contretemps. "I cannot but pardon her refusal to see that all my renewed consideration for my wife derives first and foremost from consideration for herself, because I realize how mistaken her notions are in this respect. But that she could further torment me, a few days after I last took leave of her, with childish and nonsensical reproaches about my supposed relations with my wife—reproaches which she has communicated to my friend in the form of an opinion thereon—makes me painfully aware that she can, after all, have little appreciation of what I am suffering on her account." The friend in question was Hans von Bülow, and the Bülows had announced their intention of coming to stay, so Cosima's information about the latest disastrous developments on the Green Hill came from both sides of the fence.

First, however, the young musician Wendelin Weissheimer turned up with a letter of introduction from Wagner's longtime friend Louis Schindelmeisser. It was not the last time Weissheimer's path crossed Wagner's at a dramatic juncture in the older man's career. Wagner was at Brestenberg on the day of Weissheimer's arrival, so he did not welcome his youthful admirer in the garden of Asyl until July 17. In response to Weissheimer's compliments, Wagner replied that "the age had brought forth these works through him." The conductor and composer Franz Lachner, who was in Zurich for a music festival, left his card but did not, it seems, have any conversation with Wagner. The Bülows, who booked into a Zurich hotel on July 16, soon got the measure of the situation. On July 19, Hans von Bülow witnessed a frightful scene in the course of which Wagner made it plain to Minna that their time at Asyl was up, though he did not pin the blame on her alone. The die was cast, therefore, but how were they to dismantle their home with so many visitors around? Tichat-schek left at last, and Hans and Cosima, who had been looking forward to a few quiet weeks beside the Zürichsee, moved into Asyl's guest suite in an atmosphere pregnant with doom. To crown everything, the Wagners received a visit from Countess Marie d'Agoult, who had been staying in Zurich since June 22 to make the acquaintance of the great, see her daughter again, and get to know her son-in-law. Hans, who was greatly taken with Marie, thought her a beauty still, despite her snow-white hair. He also found her so like Liszt in profile that the resemblance put him in mind of Siegmund and Sieglinde. Meanwhile, the Zurich scene was suspiciously viewed from afar by Princess Carolyne. After Wagner's departure, which regrettably forestalled a long-planned visit by Liszt, she accused Marie d'Agoult of having persuaded Wagner to miss his friend on purpose.

Liszt apart, the entire cast seemed to have assembled on stage for the finale. It was not quite complete, however. Karl Klindworth arrived from London at the end of July, and Bülow has left a description of him playing the piano while Wagner, "expending every ounce of energy," sang passages from *Rheingold* and *Walküre*. Finally, on August 3, there came a guest appearance by Karl Ritter, whose company Wagner always welcomed on awkward occasions. The Wesendoncks steered clear.

In all this turmoil, Wagner was vividly aware of the cameolike face of Cosima, the silent observer. She not only recognized his genius at this time—many did that—but perceived his weakness. Leaving Zurich for a few days, she escorted her mother home to Geneva in the company of Karl Ritter. There, tragedy almost struck. Karl had decided to leave his wife. Alone with him, Cosima realized how badly they both had blundered in their choice of partners. Under the lingering influence of the Asyl atmosphere, she asked him to help her commit suicide. They took a boat out on the Lake of Geneva, and Cosima announced that she was going to drown herself. She abandoned her intention only when Karl vowed to follow suit if she did. On her return to Zurich, she alarmed Wagner with her "morbid, passionate endearments." He was too busy severing one Gordian knot to feel inclined to tie another.

Wagner packed for a trip to the south—just where in the south he still had no precise idea. On August 16, Hans von Bülow accompanied him on a farewell visit to Mathilde Wesendonck in the house next door. Then the Bülows departed. Hans wept when they said good-bye, and Wagner felt that the man truly loved him; in other words, that any sacrifice could be demanded of him.* Cosima preserved a somber silence. One day years later, Wagner was to tell her, "You should have come away with me then."

Minna, who had decided to supervise the removal from Asyl after her husband left, attracted public attention by selling off their unwanted household effects. "Sale on account of departure," she proclaimed, "at Frau Wagner's on the Gabler in Enge, next door to Herr Wesendonck." Thanks to this indiscreet advertisement in the press, tradesmen and creditors of all kinds flocked to claim their due, and the Wagner scandal became the talk of the town.

Wagner spent his last night at Asyl sleeplessly recalling how he had once hoped to die there with Mathilde's lips on his. He rose, shut the last of his valises, and lay down once more to await the break of day.

Tuesday, August 17, 1858, dawned at last. Minna silently prepared her husband's breakfast and made him some tea. Then she accompanied him to the station, kneeling before him in the carriage and covering his hands with tears and kisses. He remained unmoved, exhorting her "to be gentle and noble and gain Christian consolation for herself." Instead, she flew into a rage and reviled him until they reached the station. With the weight of the world on his shoulders, he disappeared from view.

Peregrinations Resumed

Venice

In the train on that warm and sunny day, Wagner was overwhelmed by a boundless sense of relief, although he knew that his escape was only temporary and that no final solution had yet presented itself. At Geneva, where he heard that the Viennese had given *Lohengrin* an enthusiastic reception, he decided to consult Karl Ritter on which Italian town or city would suit him best. Still in the process of leaving his wife, Karl sang the praises of Venice and offered to accompany him there. Wagner left Geneva on August 25, picking Karl up at Lausanne on the way. They traveled across the Simplon to Lake Maggiore, spent a halcyon day on the Isola Bella, and finally reached Venice by train on August 29. Karl was so excited that he lost his hat while they were steaming along the newly constructed embankment; and Wagner, equally carried away by the sight of their destination, hurled his own hat after it.

Venice was a peaceful place in those days, and undisturbed by the sound of traffic. What struck Wagner most of all was its close conjunction of grandeur, beauty, and decay. He found the black gondolas sinister and was apprehensive of cholera. After spending a night at the Hotel Danieli, he rented an apartment at 3228 Campielli Squillini, one of the Giustiniani palaces on the Grand Canal.

This fifteenth-century building was redolent of decaying splendor and lurking mildew. The plaster walls were painted gray, the badly upholstered furniture was covered with shabby red plush, and the doors would not shut. Writing to Minna in his old, familiar, husbandly style, he recounted his daily routine and described his surroundings as "rather dilapidated." His salon, which looked out on the Grand Canal, had an elaborately painted ceiling and a fine mosaic floor. The walls he covered with dark-red hangings; the doors, which were out of period, he concealed behind red portieres. He worked every morning, went walking in the afternoons, ate at the Albergo San Marco, and spent his evenings reading and playing the piano in the company of Karl Ritter, or sometimes of Prince Peter Vladimirovich Dolgoruki, an exiled Russian writer.

Wagner relished his solitude. Venice was the source from which the world would hear "lamentations of the most anguished bliss," he confided to the exhibitionistic journal he kept for Mathilde's benefit from August 21, 1858, until April 4 of the following year. It contained all he felt about the object of his ill-starred adoration. Mathilde did not read this diary until Eliza Wille had persuaded her to forgive its author for the scandal he had caused. His effusions provide our most eloquent indication of what the whole affair was worth: It had paralleled *Tristan* by transporting him into a frenzy that became the receptacle for all his unfulfilled and sublimated sexuality.

On October 15, he resumed work on the orchestral sketch for *Tristan*, albeit laboriously and plagued by various ailments that convinced him he did not have many years to live. He developed gastritis, together with an ulcerated leg so painful that it prevented him from walking for some time and made sitting at his desk a torment.

The second act of *Tristan* very nearly sustained another dramatic interruption. Wagner's seven-month seclusion in Venice was not quite as relaxed as his daily routine and his journal for Mathilde might lead one to suppose. The sole tenant of the Palazzo Giustiniani had been under police surveillance from the outset. Wagner's sojourn in Venice, which did not go unreported by the Austrian press, gave rise to some brisk and wide-ranging political activity by government and police authorities at work behind the scenes.*

Though not itself a part of the German Confederation, Venezia had been administered by Austria ever since the defeat of Napoleon Bonaparte, who had ousted the last of the doges. The head of the supreme Viennese police authority, Baron Johann Kempen von Fichtenstamm, had urged the Austrian premier and minister of foreign affairs, Count Karl von Buol-Schauenstein, to do Saxony a favor by expelling the "political refugee" from Venice at once. Rebuffed, he notified the Dresden authorities of his correct procedure in this matter and sent an official directive to police headquarters in Venice. This drew a soothing response from the music-loving Venetian police superintendent, Angelo Crespi, whose acknowledgment of September 5, 1858, referred to Wagner's "artistic genius" and reported that the exile was devoting himself entirely to his profession.

Crespi could not, however, prevent Kempen from gaining a free hand in consequence of wider political developments. As tension increased between Austria on the one hand and Sardinia-Piedmont on the other, Buol-Schauenstein became too preoccupied with the international situation to care whether the letter of the law was observed in the case of a runaway conductor. On February 3, 1859, Kempen decreed Wagner's expulsion. Again the local police came to his rescue. Wagner was advised to obtain a medical certificate and apply to Archduke Maximilian, governor general of Lombardy and later emperor of Mexico, for permission to extend his stay. The request was granted, and Wagner, who was among the crowds that welcomed Maximilian when he visited Venice soon afterward, raised his hat from afar in gratitude for this act of indulgence.

Alarmed by the activities of Garibaldi and Cavour, who aimed to unite and liberate their country, the Austrians massed half a million men in northern Italy. Some of their units disembarked at Venice, so Wagner's peaceful strolls became a thing of the past.

If he were not to get caught between the opposing forces, Wagner's departure could be delayed no longer. On March 24, he said good-bye to Karl Ritter for the last time. Traveling by way of Milan, Como, and Lugano, he reached the snowy St. Gotthard, which he crossed in an open sleigh. He arrived in Lucerne on March 28. The Austrian police promptly reported his change of residence through diplomatic channels, and the Saxon Foreign Ministry transmitted this information to the ministries of the Interior and Justice in the following terms: "With reference to his communication dated September 24 of last year, the undersigned most humbly begs to report that, as recently advised by the Imperial and Royal Austrian Legation here, and notified by the head of the Imperial Supreme Police Authority, the fugitive Richard Wagner departed Venice on the 25th of last month and has gone to Lucerne. Dresden, April 13, 1859. Ministry of Foreign Affairs. Beust."

Lucerne

Wagner moved into the annex of the Hotel Schweizerhof, which was deserted at this time of year. There, being the only guest, he was pampered by the hotel housekeeper. Then twenty-seven, Verena Weitmann saw to his creature comforts and ensured that no one disturbed him. Wagner, in his turn, kept "Vreneli" informed of the progress of his work and resolved to employ her himself when circumstances permitted.

On April 2, he paid a one-day visit to Zurich and the Wesendoncks. He was "in no way abashed" to be their guest. As he kissed his beloved's hand under the eyes of her husband, he felt as if he were in a dream—as if everything had become "quite insubstantial." His last entry in the journal for Mathilde is dated April 4. It gives the following description of his sense of dreamlike unreality dissolving into the realm of pure imagination: "Where we are, we do not see each other; only where we are not do our eyes dwell on each other." All he still loved was the image he retained of her.

Sometimes, even in the midst of his most inspired work, a mood of chill dread overcame him. It was a rainy spring, and his favorite lake was shrouded in mist. Isolated from the world and dependent on newspapers alone for word of what was going on, he experienced a resurgence of interest in politics. In northern Italy, French and Italian troops had forced the Austrians onto the defensive. Writing to Mathilde on April 30, he confessed: "Just imagine, I am afraid of losing all my patriotism and might secretly rejoice if the Germans took some more hard knocks. Bonapartism is an acute but passing ailment from the world's point of view, whereas Austro-German reaction is chronic and lasting." In June, the Austrians were decisively defeated at Magenta and Solferino. More than three hundred thousand men took part in the second of these battles, which began on June 24. Harking back to Leipzig and the year of Wagner's birth, the *Times* of London pointed out that it had been forty-six years since Europe had witnessed as great a battle as the one that had just strewn the plain of Lombardy with corpses.

Georg Herwegh poured out his fierce derision in political articles published by the *Intelligenzblatt*. Wagner was delighted with them and their author. Writing to Cosima von Bülow in 1858, he told her that in recent years at Zurich, Georg Herwegh had been his "dearest person in masculine form." He now found the tone of Herwegh's articles "capital" and expressed a wish to discuss them,* but we do not know if Herwegh ever took up his invitation to visit Lucerne.

Finally, at the end of May, the weather turned sunny and summery. Wagner had been taking strenuous morning walks—a self-prescribed aid to his chronically sluggish digestion. These he now abandoned in favor of rides on Liesi, the hotel's twenty-year-old nag, which headed for home without being asked as soon as it grew tired.

Tristan was entering its final phase. The closer he came to completing it, the more Wagner missed the company of knowledgeable friends. He would, for instance, have welcomed a visit from Tausig. Instead, he was visited at the end of July by another young protégé of Liszt, the twenty-four-year-old composer Felix Draesecke. He bored Wagner at first with his incessant chatter, then realized that his reports on the German musical scene were unwelcome and ended by gaining the older man's confidence. Other callers at Lucerne included Wilhelm Baumgartner and the composer and critic Alexander N. Serov, who was the first to champion Wagner's music in Russia. On the afternoon of August 6, Wagner summoned Draesecke to his hotel room and invited him to look through the score of *Tristan*. It was almost finished. At half-past four, in Draesecke's presence, he wrote in the final bars. That evening the Wesendoncks arrived to help him celebrate the Dresden premiere of *Lohengrin*.

But *Tristan*'s completion seemed bleakly disenchanting compared to the elation that had gripped him while at work on it. Only then did he become conscious of the void that faced him on awakening from a long dream filled with music.

"So Germany wants to serve me up to the enemy by force!" Such had been Wagner's response to Liszt when the latter advised him in May to go to Paris. He declined to waste another word on the subject of an amnesty, but his decision to try Paris was made with a heavy heart. On September 9, 1859, he went to Zurich and spent three luxurious days at the Wesendoncks', where he enjoyed a reunion with Herwegh, Keller, and Semper. Conversation that evening turned to Magenta and Solferino, and a fierce exchange developed between Keller and Semper, who asserted that the defeat of Austria betokened "the defeat of the German national principle," whereas Louis Napoleon's France represented "Assyrian despotism." Wagner set absolutely no store by the national principle at this time, and it would be wrong to conclude, as one might from *My Life*, that he took no part in the argument. The letters he wrote to Mathilde from Paris tell a different story. He had thoroughly soured Semper's spirits by first attacking him and then appeasing him. Semper felt deserted by his Dresden comrade-in-arms and accused Wagner of luring him into a trap, but the two hotheads eventually made up.

On September 10, after paying a visit to Sulzer, who had moved with his family to Winterthur, Wagner set off for Paris.

Paris

The ensuing tale of woe has often been told. It presents us with the picture of a man who seemed to lose all touch with reality, who made enemies where none had previously existed, who tried to correct one mistake with another by obtaining money from any and every source in order to pay off his swiftly mounting debts. It would be as absurd to reproach the world for maltreating a "sore-pressed Master"—to add to the torrents of tears that have been shed for him ever since Glasenapp—as it would be to follow Robert W. Gutman in accusing him of plain theft, as if the man concerned had been a scoundrel intent on lining his pockets by fraud and deceit. Wagner was a faultfinder and breeder of resentment, true, but the peaks and troughs of his emotional life in the following three years of mischance, miscalculation, and misdirected effort reveal him as a man who, having lost touch with the world while under the Wesendoncks' aegis in small-town Zurich, now believed that his hour had struck and would pass him by unless he staged his works at once. With the bulk of his music dramas already written, he had seen none of them performed save *Holländer* and *Tannhäuser.* His plan was to raise the necessary funds by giving concerts in Paris, prepare the French public for productions of *Tannhäuser, Lohengrin,* and *Tristan,* procure a suitable theater and company, and then emerge triumphantly self-sufficient—in need of nothing and no one, not even the theaters of his native Germany. "I think I am entitled to count on a great success," he wrote to Minna, who was to rejoin him, but he was blind to the enormous risks he was running. His scheme gave birth to French *wagnérisme* but ended in complete financial disaster.

Incorrigible in his good-natured impulses and illusions, he made yet another attempt to salvage his marriage, at least outwardly, though he prefaced Minna's move to Paris by getting Dr. Pusinelli to convey to her that it was subject to one proviso: "Out of regard for her state of health," they would have to abstain from sexual intercourse.

One of the first people to provide him with an entrée into influential Parisian musical circles was Auguste de Gaspérini, a music-loving physician to whom he had been recommended by Hans von Bülow. Wagner describes Gaspérini as "young, enthusiastic, brimming with vitality and confidence, and—notwithstanding all his theories—very far removed from Buddha and his sterile contemplations." Wagner was to be seen everywhere in Paris, impatiently pushing ahead with his concert plans. To save the expense of hiring a hall, he requested the free use of the Grand Opéra. When an approach to Napoleon III's private secretary failed to yield results, he dropped the idea and rented the Théâtre Italien instead. Three major concerts were planned, each comprising selections from his works, and Hans von Bülow came to assist him with rehearsals. He at first had trouble with the musicians, who could not follow his signals and complained, when called to order, that they were not "Prussian soldiers." They only gradually became aware, through his music, of the sort of man they were dealing with.

Wagner's first rehearsal of the *Tristan* Prelude was like a leap in the dark. With no points of reference or previous experience to guide them, the instrumentalists were obliged to learn his new musical language letter by letter. Feeling as if he had to lead them "from note to note," he suddenly saw how far he had come in the past eight years—how far removed he was from the contemporary world of art. It was natural that he should want to fill "the frightful gulf" behind him before reapplying himself to composition. This sentiment, which he expressed in a letter to Mathilde, made all his future tribulations, both musical and theatrical, a foregone conclusion.

It should not, however, be thought that his hard work went entirely unrewarded. At the first concert on January 25, 1860, spontaneous applause greeted the melodic development of a *Tannhäuser* theme after sixteen bars, and selections from *Lohengrin* and the *Holländer* Overture, for which he had written a new ending earlier that month, were also warmly received. The audience seemed enthralled, though they were somewhat puzzled by the *Tristan und Isolde* Prelude, which had been given a concert-hall ending in December. Those present included Auber, Berlioz, Gounod, Meyerbeer, Ernest Reyer, the Belgian musicologist François Gevaert, and the French novelist Jules Champfleury, who wrote an encomium on Wagner two days later. The second concert on February 1 was poorly attended—the French were fonder of the theater than concerts—and Wagner had to paper the hall by distributing free tickets. On the third night, February 8, someone had the effrontery to hiss after the *Tristan* Prelude. This called forth such a storm of applause that Wagner was taken aback, but his soothing gestures only unleashed a further ovation. It was as unprecedented an experience for the composer as his music was for ears that had never heard its like before. Tired out by his exertions, mental and physical, he had his hand kissed by newfound devotees and was besieged by unknown French intellectuals who had attended all three concerts. He had triumphed indeed, but at a price.

The extent of the loss is attested by a recently discovered letter dated February 10, 1860,* in which Wagner tells an unknown correspondent: "My three concerts have lost me 11,000 fr. The second cost 7,000 fr. and took 3,300 fr., the third cost almost as much and took 4,400 fr. In the certainty of having the emperor at a fourth concert (14 days from now), and in view of other favorable prospects, I have resolved on another performance, and shall surely then be in a position to repay Madame Erard's loan of 2,000 fr. Do you think you can now arrange this extension for me?" The fourth concert never took place. Whether or not Madame Erard sanctioned the delay, Wagner had no money left to pay the orchestra.

Reactions to his concerts varied widely. Having deliberately omitted to invite the press, he was savaged by those critics who bore allegiance to Meyerbeer and the musical taste of the day. "Fifty years of this music, and music will be dead," lamented one, and another: "Wagner makes music without melody, without rhythm, without system."

But that was only one side of the coin. He had endeared himself to those members of the younger generation of French writers who considered him a "democrat"—Théodore de Banville, for example, acclaimed him as a revolutionary artist—and to the Symbolists, who were captivated by the aesthetic charms of his musical idiom. On February 17, 1860, Charles Baudelaire wrote Wagner a letter that anticipated the basic ideas in his pamphlet, *Richard Wagner et le Tannhaeuser à Paris*, and may thus be regarded as the original manifesto of French *wagnérisme*. Baudelaire declared that he blushed with shame at the sight of so many absurd and undignified articles and wished to demonstrate his gratitude by dissociating himself from "all those imbeciles." He "knew" Wagner's music. "It seemed to me that this was my music, and I recognized it as every person recognizes the things he is destined to love. . . . You have led me back to myself in my hours of melancholy, to that which is great." Baudelaire omitted his address for fear that Wagner might think he wanted a favor of some kind, but Wagner sought him out and invited him to his Wednesday receptions, which attracted a growing circle of adherents.

Among other visitors to his "salon" were the composers Camille Saint-Saëns and Charles Gounod, the illustrator Gustave Doré, the Louvre curator Frédéric Villot, Jules Champfleury and his youthful confrere Catulle Mendès, the musicians Louis Lacombe, Ernest Reyer, and Léon Kreutzer, the Hungarian pianist and composer Stephen Heller, the Czech painter Jaroslaw Czermak, the painter, critic, and future director of the Grand Opéra, Emile Perrin, the Leibniz translator Comte Foucher de Careil, the politician Jules Ferry, the music critic Léon Leroy and his brother Adolphe, who taught at the Conservatoire, Malwida von Meysenbug, and Emile Ollivier and his wife, Blandine.

Wagner's relations with Blandine became the subject of certain rumors in Paris, and it is true that he saw a great deal of her. Minna had cause for concern, even though neither of them transgressed the bounds of propriety, because Wagner might easily have succumbed to the spontaneous gaiety that distinguished her from her younger sister. When he left Paris, he presented her with his desk.

Hans von Bülow greatly furthered Wagner's theatrical plans, to which he now devoted himself with vigor, by introducing him to Count Pourtalès, the Prussian envoy, and his attaché Count Hatzfeld. They smoothed his path to the French Court and launched a high-level diplomatic campaign in which Wagner's cause was championed with the emperor by Princess Pauline von Metternich, an exceedingly silly and excitable woman whose enthusiasm for the arts was as pronounced as her lack of real artistic appreciation. Even Empress Eugénie was brought into play. The diplomatic corps of the German Confederation, the body that had been hounding Wagner for his allegedly treasonable activities, did its utmost to prevail on the man who had dashed Wagner's hopes in the early 1850s to decree that *Tannhäuser* be performed in Paris. By the middle of March 1860, it had succeeded, and Napoleon ordained that funds be made available for the opera's production. The resulting friction between the court and the legitimist aristocracy was to have fateful repercussions. Just as it had in Dresden, *Tannhäuser* got off on the wrong foot.

One day, Count Hatzfeld invited Wagner to accompany him to the home of Madame Marie Kalergis, who made him a present of 10,000 francs. This would have been a substantial help had his rent and living expenses not already put him so much in debt that he was unable either to put Schott's advance aside or to fulfill his obligations to Otto Wesendonck. He was in the red with Baron Emil Erlanger, the banker, and had accepted 3,000 francs from a Madame Salis-Schwabe. This "gift," for which he insisted on signing a note of hand, was later to cause him great embarrassment. In token of his gratitude to Marie Kalergis, he presented a quasi performance of the second act of *Tristan*. Early in May, this "eccentric fragment" was premiered at the home of Pauline Viardot-Garcia, who sang Isolde. Wagner took the part of Tristan, and Karl Klindworth came specially from London to accompany at the piano. Hector Berlioz, whom Saint-Saëns called "a human paradox," insisted on attending despite his prejudices against the composer. Of the audience of two, Marie Kalergis "remained silent" and Berlioz looked bewildered. At a musical soiree at Wagner's lodgings not long afterward, Klindworth accompanied a performance of the first act of *Die Walküre*. Among the guests were Marie Kalergis and the tenor Albert Niemann, who had just arrived from Hanover and signed his *Tannhäuser* contract, which guaranteed him over 60,000 francs.

Madame Kalergis was related to the wife of the Saxon ambassador in Paris, Baron Albin Leo von Seebach, who eventually succeeded in persuading the Saxon Court to amnesty Wagner in return for a series of rather humiliating admissions on the subject of his misguided involvement in the political movements of the 1840s. Dresden seemed disinclined at first to listen to its ambassador in Paris. In the early summer of 1860, however, various German princes forgathered at Baden-Baden for a meeting between Napoleon III and the king of Prussia. When even Princess Augusta of Prussia pleaded Wagner's cause, the obdurate king of Saxony found himself in an increasingly difficult position. Johann's change of heart came none too soon, for Wagner had almost abandoned hope of recognition in Dresden and Germany at large. Writing to Julie Ritter on June 8, 1860, he expressed delight at his reception in Paris, at the admiration and sympathy he had found there, and at the importance attached to the forthcoming production of *Tannhäuser*. He also wondered "whether the arrogant, illusory specter of the self-styled German intelligentsia may not also be a bit of a fairy tale." On July 22, he was informed by Ambassador Seebach that the Royal Saxon Government had resolved on July 15 that he should be permitted to reenter German territory—with the exception of Saxony itself—provided no objections were raised by the German states concerned. It was not even a partial amnesty, merely a waiving of extradition rights.

On August 12, for the first time in eleven years, Wagner crossed the German border on his way to Bad Soden, where Minna had been taking a cure since the beginning of July. On the following day, he accompanied her on a brief visit to his brother Albert in Frankfurt. On August 16, after an intermediate stop at Darmstadt, he traveled by way of Heidelberg to Baden-Baden to thank Princess Augusta of Prussia for her help in securing the concessions he had been granted. Augusta, who received him in the pump room next morning, on a wet and cheerless day, expressed scant interest in his concerns and fobbed him off with empty promises.

Wagner returned to Paris on August 19, after a steamer trip from Mannheim to Cologne. To Otto Wesendonck he wrote: "I experienced—I regret to say!—not the slightest emotion when I again set foot on German soil: God knows, I must have grown quite indifferent!" And to Liszt, in September: "Believe me, we have no Fatherland. If I am 'German,' I assuredly carry my Germany around within me."

Then the Paris hurly-burly got under way. Rehearsals began at the Opéra on September 24, with Albert Niemann in attendance. The casting process had dragged on for months. Madame Fortunata Tedesco, a Jewess, had been engaged for the role of Venus. Elisabeth was sung by Marie Sax, daughter of Adolphe, the instrument maker, who helped the hunting scene along with saxhorns and saxophones—French horns were at a premium in Paris—and Lucien Petipa, the celebrated ballet master, choreographed the bacchanal, which had still to be written. Wagner was utterly confident of success; indeed, he championed France and the French at this period with more verve than he would ever again expend on any culturally advanced nation including his own. Writing to Otto Wesendonck on October 20, in the thick of rehearsals, he declared that he had never felt so at home and would never feel so again in Germany. Every detail of the production, he said, would meet his requirements to perfection. Unfortunately, he underestimated the magnitude of the calamity that had been foisted on him in the person of the conductor Pierre Dietsch, a *"Schöps* [chump] *d'orchestre,"* as Wagner punningly christened him. After the first rehearsal he attended, Bülow called Dietsch "one of the most abject fools" he had ever come across—"an old man destitute of intelligence and memory, utterly ineducable and lacking in ear." To Joachim Raff he wrote that Dietsch was "the most asinine, insensitive, and unmusical of all conductors."

But danger threatened the work from quite another direction. The press was undermining it in advance with those who opposed the rise of anyone too confident of royal favor, and Wagner made the worst mistake anyone can make in a closed society: He behaved arrogantly. Enemies poked fun at his receptions and accused him of flaunting a reputation he had yet to earn. Who, they demanded, was this German who proposed to teach the musical French a lesson? *Tannhäuser* anecdotes began to circulate in the capital, and newspapers ascribed derogatory remarks about Wagner's music to the veteran composer Rossini, one of them being that it needed melody as roast meat needs gravy. When Rossini publicly repudiated this canard, Wagner called on him to express his gratitude. He also had frequent encounters with Auber over ice creams at the Café Tortoni. The elderly composer questioned him about *Tannhäuser* and was particularly interested to know if it would offer a feast to the eye as well as the ear. Wagner gave him an outline of the plot, whereupon Auber rubbed his hands. "*Ah,*" he exclaimed, "*il y aura du spectacle; ça aura du succès, soyez tranquille!*" But Wagner found it impossible to rest easy, and the burden he had shouldered soon proved too much for his constitution.

At the end of October, worn out by rehearsals, he contracted a form of typhoid fever that confined him to bed for several weeks. Because people thought him likely to die, rehearsals were suspended altogether. Nursed by Gaspérini and Minna in the more modest establishment on rue d'Aumale to which he had recently moved—his original lodgings on rue Newton had been menaced by a road-widening scheme—he raved deliriously for days on end. Still in a frail condition, he finally resumed work at the Opéra on November 20. The score for the Venus scene was completed in December, but it was not until January that he put the finishing touches to the new bacchanal for the Paris version of *Tannhäuser*.

The management had asked him to write a ballet for the second act because Parisian socialites, who seldom turned up at a theater before the first intermission, liked to round off a good meal by watching their favorite danseuses perform. Wagner not only refused on artistic grounds but threatened to withdraw his work from production. Instead, he devised the scenario and music for a mythologically extravagant Venusberg bacchanal, which turned out to be one of the most imaginative, daring, and sensitive ideas he ever conceived for the stage, and which only his previous experience of *Tristan* enabled him to write.

The new Venus scene invested the work with greater dramatic depth. Many have since called the pleasure-grotto music stylistically incongruous, though the very conflict between parts stemmed naturally from Wagner's continuing perception of the work. The Paris addition provided a link between his earliest and latest auditory experiences and was, in the words of Ernst Bloch, "a master-piece of lust and of nothing else on earth, an abyss of satyriasis down-daemonized out of *Tristan* sounds; and from far away in that abyss, from its nonexistent shore, there drifts across the song of nymphs, the brothel splendor of a higher order. . . ."* Such was the music to which the Symbolists responded most of all.

Wagner was determined to put Dresden in the shade. He took Malwida von Meysenbug to the first full rehearsal on February 19, 1861. It ended at half-past midnight, but not before the members of the orchestra had risen to their feet in mid-rehearsal and applauded the composer. Malwida pronounced it a tragedy that he was not to conduct the work himself. On February 20, Albert Niemann requested the omission of a high and demanding passage that had allegedly earned him ridicule from the rehearsal audience. Unless Wagner were prepared to make this cut, he would have "no recourse but to find himself another Tannhäuser." This was not the only contretemps. The energies of all concerned were flagging after five months of rehearsals, and French composers who had been waiting in vain for an Opéra production resented it that the Ministry of State kept granting Wagner additional funds. The premiere was repeatedly postponed.

The doors of the Opéra finally opened on March 13, after 164 rehearsals in whole or part. Parisian high society turned out in force. Outside the theater, Théophile Gautier ran into Hector Berlioz, who harshly criticized Wagner's music. The scene was witnessed by Gautier's fifteen-year-old daughter Judith. Something impelled her to retort, with a forwardness incredible in a girl of her age, "One can easily tell that you're speaking of a confrere—and, no doubt, of a masterpiece!"

The performance opened. The bacchanal proved a spellbinder, and the first scene passed off in comparative quiet. Just when the cast thought victory was assured, however, the long-rehearsed attack was launched—and launched at one of the loveliest moments in the entire work: the transition from bacchanal to morning hush, when the shepherd's pipe is heard. Laughter and jeers rang out, and entrances were ruined by interjections such as *"Encore un pèlerin!"* The *"péchés Venusbergeois"* were loudly ridiculed, and even the emperor's applause was drowned. It is untrue that the Jockey Club merely took exception to the defeat of sensual passion by sacred love (something the French admittedly found hard to comprehend) or to the absence of a ballet in the conventional place. This was a planned and coordinated political demonstration.* Indeed, there were Jockey Club members at the second and third performances who, when reproached by friends who wanted to enjoy the music in peace, pleaded that they must "get back to work" and went on whistling. The painter Czermak almost came to blows with some hecklers, and Ambassador Seebach was hoarse the next morning. As for Princess Metternich, she retired in fury to the back of her box. "Madame," a marshal of France told her as she was leaving the theater, "you have cruelly repaid us for Solferino." Wagner wanted to withdraw the work at once, but Malwida von Meysenbug dissuaded him. He had stood his ground, if nothing more. The premiere could not be called a defeat. Encouraged by the applause they had received from the impartial section of the audience, the artists adjudged the contest a draw.

The management requested some cuts, which were duly made, but those among the cast who thought that resistance would wane —that the Jockeys had had their fun and would leave it at that— were sorely disappointed. On the night of March 18, the aristocratic rowdies of the Jockey Club came to the theater equipped with dog whistles and flageolets. The emperor and empress put in a second ostentatious appearance, but in vain. Blowing little silver whistles required far less effort than cheering and clapping, so the majority fought a losing battle against the minority's din, which assumed unimaginable proportions during the second and third acts. Niemann became so infuriated that he hurled his pilgrim's hat at the audience. Despite everything, the singers soldiered gamely on, consoling themselves with the thought that the next performance would take place on a Sunday, when subscribers usually offered their tickets for sale to the general public.

During this third performance on March 24, which Wagner did not attend, the uproar reached such a pitch that it more than once interrupted the proceedings for periods of up to fifteen minutes. Nothing could be heard at times but the Jockeys' shrill whistling. Prince Sagan, one of the ringleaders of the mob, justified his behavior in later years by pleading total incomprehension. "We were told there would be a row," he said, "so we went as a matter of course." The rest of the audience were torn between anger and sorrow. Little Olga von Herzen, Malwida von Meysenbug's foster child, filled the air with outraged cries of "*A la porte! A la porte les*

Jockeys!" When she visited the Wagners late that night, Malwida found them drinking tea. Although Wagner jokingly accused Olga of having hissed him, Malwida felt the tremor in his hand when he bade her good-night and realized how hard he had taken it all.

This time he did withdraw the work. It was probably his greatest mistake, because advance bookings augured a box-office success and the Jockeys could not have gone on whistling forever. Bülow felt that *Tannhäuser* would have won after six performances, though the artists' stamina might not have been equal to another three. Wagner, who was unwilling to expose them to further rough treatment, dismissed the venture as a total disaster.

The French press reacted with cynical regret, if not satisfaction. Paris coined a new verb based on *tanner*, to tan or thrash. This was *tannhauser*, and the March 28 issue of one periodical conjugated it for its readers as follows: *je tannhause, tu tannhauses.* . . . But the reaction of the musical and literary modernists was very different. Baudelaire wrote in *Richard Wagner et le Tannhaeuser à Paris:* "What will Europe think of us, and what will they say of Paris in Germany? This handful of boors is bringing us all into disrepute!" And Stéphane Mallarmé's *Hommage*, a sonnet of somber and mysterious beauty, paid tribute to Wagner's art in every line.

Wagner was one of the first composers to benefit, as well as suffer, from public uproar. Indeed, he may well have been the very first to find his growing reputation unimpaired by adverse criticism. For the first time, a sizable section of the German music-loving public ranged itself pointedly behind him. At Dresden, where his official status was still that of a rebel on the run, theatergoers gave him a spontaneous ovation in absentia.

After all expenses had been deducted, the Paris production of *Tannhäuser* earned him 750 francs.

Via Karlsruhe to Vienna

Bloody but unbowed, Wagner set off for Karlsruhe. On April 21, 1861, he was received by Grand Duke Friedrich I, who was then thirty-four and had ruled Baden since 1852, and Grand Duchess Luise. His *Tristan* project was again discussed during this private audience, but under less auspicious circumstances. Eduard Devrient put a brake on Wagner's expectations by pointing out that the illustrious Schnorrs, Ludwig and his wife, Malvina, had moved to Dresden and that it would be difficult to find singers of comparable quality. Accordingly, Wagner fell back on Vienna, the only present source of favorable reports.

After a few days in Paris and another brief visit to Karlsruhe, where he was again received by the grand duke on May 9, Wagner headed for Vienna in quest of soloists for a Karlsruhe production of *Tristan*. On May 11, seated in a chair on stage at the Vienna Opera, he heard a full rehearsal of *Lohengrin* for the first time ever. He was so moved at the end that he could barely get to his feet. When the tenor Alois Ander took advantage of a break in the proceedings to introduce Eduard Hanslick, who had merely wished to pay his respects, Wagner greeted him curtly, "like someone quite unknown to me." Ander pointed out that they knew each other of old, whereupon Wagner replied that he remembered Herr Hanslick perfectly well—and turned his attention to the stage again. Since he resisted all further attempts by members of the company to dispel this budding and ultimately disastrous animosity, it was hardly Hanslick's fault that the two men have passed into musical history as irreconcilable enemies.

The Vienna management showed no inclination to release any soloists for Karlsruhe, arguing that *Tristan* might just as well be produced in Vienna. If the singers were good enough for Karlsruhe, what possible objection could Wagner have to the Vienna Court Opera? It was a cogent argument, the more so because conditions in Vienna were socially favorable too. Wagner had acquired a sincere admirer in Dr. Josef Standhartner, the empress's personal physician, a music lover of handsome appearance and upright character. Karl Tausig and the composer Peter Cornelius, whom Wagner had not seen since Basel in 1853, were also in Vienna, as was Heinrich Laube. Now established as director of the Burg Theater, Laube was the center of a motley social set which he entertained in his cramped apartment, wreathed in cigar smoke and surrounded by dogs, at late-afternoon gatherings prior to curtain.

On May 15, Wagner was rapturously acclaimed at a performance of *Lohengrin* given in his honor. The warmth of his reception seemed almost beyond belief. The audience turned to his box and applauded him after the prelude, and he was summoned to the stage after every act by "a cry of delight like a thousand trumpets," to cite his own description. He concluded the performance by delivering a few words of thanks from his box. *Der Fliegende Holländer* earned him a similar reception a few days later. He tried to hide but was constantly recalled to the stage. "An incredibly cordial, lively audience," he exulted in his letters. "Princes and counts in their boxes, too—everyone joined in the shouting and applause." Success was such balm to his battered soul that he indiscriminately praised every aspect of the production. The spurned Hanslick, who naturally persisted in his aversion to the composer and his work, gave a demonstration of integrity. "From the purely human standpoint," he wrote, "we also sincerely rejoiced."

Wagner left Vienna on May 20 and resumed his lifelong habit of tracing petallike ellipses on the map of Europe. He just missed Sulzer at Winterthur, which left him free to devote the day to Goethe's *Wilhelm Meisters Wanderjahre,* an apt choice of reading matter. He celebrated his birthday in Zurich at the Wesendoncks' with his old cronies Sulzer, Herwegh, Semper, and Keller. By way of Karlsruhe, where he apprised Grand Duke Friedrich of the new situation, he returned on May 26 to Paris, for which he now cherished no love at all, and prepared to strike camp.

It was the Parisian aristocracy that eventually came to the homeless composer's aid. Count Hatzfeld, the Prussian attaché, offered help on behalf of friends "who wished to remain anonymous," and Princess Metternich was requited for her luckless involvement in the *Tannhäuser* project with a rather un-Wagnerian Albumblatt in C major. By the time Minna departed to take the waters at Bad Soden on July 11, all the Wagners' household effects had been mothballed and crated. The Paris venture was at an end. Wagner stayed on temporarily at the invitation of the Prussian ambassador, Count Pourtalès. The embassy guesthouse, 78 rue de Lille, overlooked a garden in which two black swans inscribed melancholy circles on the surface of an ornamental pond. On July 29, Wagner composed an Albumblatt in A-flat major, "Arrival at the Black Swans'," and dedicated it "In remembrance of his noble hostess, Countess von Pourtalès." This second piece sounds more Wagnerian. It combines the *Tristan* mood of the *Wesendonck Lieder* with an allusion to *Tannhäuser* and closes on a somewhat abrupt concert ending—a song without words like the so-called "Porazzi Melody" of his later years, which attains an extreme degree of formal abstraction.

Wagner left Paris for Bad Soden next morning. Minna accompanied him as far as Frankfurt, where Arthur Schopenhauer—he recalled—had died a year earlier, and then returned to Bad Soden. She later went on to Dresden while her husband attended a music festival at Weimar before heading back to Vienna. The final part of *My Life* opens with the words: "And so I again crossed Thuringia and passed the Wartburg, which thus, whether visited or seen from afar, became strangely associated with my leaving Germany or returning thither." He was probably thinking less of 1849 than of 1842, when he had likewise limped home from Paris with his hopes in ruins. What had changed in the interim? He had completed another five and a half scores, but he was confronted by a broken marriage and a mountain of debts.

Between Vienna and Paris

"Wagner's here!" So saying, young Wendelin Weissheimer burst in on a rehearsal of the Weimar Musicians' Association. Liszt broke off at once and called on the orchestra for a flourish. There was universal rejoicing when the door opened to reveal the unmistakable figure of Wagner, with his small build, short stride, and curiously large, impressive head. Everyone clustered around, and Liszt embraced him with tears in his eyes. Wagner's eyes, too, were moist. It was his first real homecoming after twelve years of notoriety and exile.

He was little interested in the festival as such, which had attracted some six hundred musicians, and spent most of his time with Liszt and Ollivier. Blandine never stirred from his side. Speeches were delivered at gala banquets, mostly by Liszt and Wagner himself. At long last, the exile had a chance to air his experiences, and this put him in a mellow mood. Often close to tears, he sought an outlet in boisterous high spirits.

To his great delight, he did not have to travel to Vienna alone because Blandine and Emile Ollivier had decided to visit Cosima at Bad Reichenhall, where she was recuperating from the aftereffects of her first confinement on October 12 of the previous year. Wagner's farewell conversation with Liszt included a reference to Hans von Bülow, who had conducted with distinction at the festival and returned to Berlin the day before. "We sang his praises," Wagner recalled, "though I added with jocular familiarity, 'There was no need for him to marry Cosima as well.' To which Liszt replied, with a little inclination of the head, 'That was a luxury.' "

Wagner traveled with the Olliviers to Nürnberg, where they toured the town and visited the Germanisches Museum. Blandine, who was again in that state of "excitable gaiety" which Wagner found so attractive, continually capped his jokes. They spoke German together and laughed at her husband's good-natured incomprehension. In Munich, they ran across young Robert von Hornstein, whom Wagner knew from Switzerland, and joined him for the evening at a beer cellar. Rather the worse for wear, they caught a night train to Bad Reichenhall and arrived there at daybreak on August 12.

The two sisters spent the day conversing in private. On one of the few occasions when Wagner gained access to their room, he seriously suggested adopting them both—"a proposal greeted with more mirth than confidence." He once complained to Blandine of Cosima's wild ways, which Blandine defined as *"la timidité d'un sauvage."* He had previously written to Bülow on April 4: "Cosima's temperament is her health's worst enemy. She comes of far too exceptional stock, and is therefore hard to look after." On September 19, 1861, shortly after the Reichenhall reunion, he wrote again to reassure Bülow, who had poured out his troubles to him: "She is a wild young thing, I repeat, but she possesses great nobility. You must cling to that if you are to render her capable of any sacrifice, even the sacrifice of her harmful little habits. She must become equable and serene out of pride in herself."

As he was saying good-bye to Cosima in the hall of her boarding-house on August 13, he caught "a look of almost timid inquiry." Then he climbed into a one-horse carriage and drove to Salzburg, reaching Vienna on the following day.

Reality turned out to be harsher than his recent experiences in the Austrian capital had led him to expect. He had taken everything and everyone too literally. An apartment lent him by the journalist Adolph Kolatschek proved quite unsuited to his needs, and the local theater magnates, Intendant Count Lanckoronsky and Director Matteo Salvi, left him completely in the dark as to when rehearsals of *Tristan* could commence.

By a fortunate last-minute coincidence, Wagner bumped into Dr. Standhartner, who was on the point of taking his family abroad. Standhartner offered him the use of his Seilerstätte apartment for several weeks, complete with the services of his pretty niece, Seraphine Mauro, who lived in the same house and could therefore attend to his creature comforts. Half-Italian and half-Viennese, Seraphine had a doll-like face framed by a wealth of dark ringlets that hung down to her ripe young bosom. Wagner could hardly have remained indifferent to the charms that had already enslaved Peter Cornelius, who was tortured with jealousy. For a short while, "Seraphinchen" or "Dolly" became the sole focus of Wagner's interest in the opposite sex—so much so that he shunned the company of everyone save Cornelius and Tausig.

He soon paid a call on the tenor Alois Ander, who was proving the main impediment to preparations for *Tristan.* Ander had lost his voice after allegedly catching cold during a visit to the crypt of Speyer Cathedral, though knowledgeable observers claimed that his affliction of the vocal chords was psychosomatic. Wagner was assailed by a feeling of utter futility when Frau Dustmann, his Isolde, declared that Ander had been "studying" the role of Tristan for months without memorizing a single note. Like the plan for a *Tristan* production at Karlsruhe, this one seemed likely to be thwarted by vocal incompetence, and the work began to be regarded as unperformable. Wagner was so disheartened that he wrote to Minna on October 19 asking her to help him "bear the misery" of their separation instead of treating him with suspicion. "My earlier operas are all over the place; my new works are presenting me with almost insuperable difficulties. In my new works, I have pressed on far, far ahead of my time and that which our theaters are capable of. . . . No one cares about me. I must begin all over again."

But then a miracle happened: At this of all times, he determined to write *Die Meistersinger.* It was not in Venice a short while later, as he picturesquely states in *My Life,* but in Vienna, in the thick of his fears and misgivings about *Tristan,* that he resurrected the idea of a lighter work for the stage. This considerably devalues subsequent speculation about the "inspirational" significance of his stay in Venice. Wagner communicated his *Meistersinger* plan to Schott in a letter dated October 30, 1861, together with a number of hard-luck stories and requests for money. He intended, he said, to tackle the subject right away. After his many disappointments in the matter of *Tristan,* he had decided to write a popular work designed to take the theaters of Germany by storm. It was to be based on his vague and one-dimensional Marienbad sketch of 1845. But could *Die Meistersinger* remain no more than a cheerful travesty of the song contest, composed around a brawl in Nürnberg? Since then, Wagner had plumbed the depths of disappointment and humiliation. Life had taught him a bitter lesson in self-denial, and that, for all Sachs's mischievous pranks, was the essence of the *Meistersinger* character with whom Wagner came—after all his sad experiences and his renunciation of Mathilde—to identify himself more and more.

It was after this decision that the Wesendoncks invited him to join them in Venice for a brief spell of relaxation. He traveled by train to Trieste and by steamer to Venice, where he disembarked on November 7 and booked into the Hotel Danieli. He may well have been impelled by a faint hope of reacquiring Asyl, but a single hour in Mathilde's company sufficed to destroy the illusion that he could ever live on her doorstep again. He found the Wesendoncks "in very flourishing circumstances" and dared not ask them any favors. Mathilde was once more pregnant. The sight of her was intolerable to him. The truth was that Isolde had never betrayed King Mark, nor was the subject of *Die Meistersinger* broached by Mathilde, who was in possession of the Marienbad prose sketch, but by Wagner himself, who asked for it back.

With characteristic indifference, he accompanied the Wesendoncks on sightseeing tours of Venetian churches, palaces, and picture galleries. For once, though, he found himself dazzled by a masterpiece whose dimensions—twenty-two feet by twelve feet—were as great as its artistic merit: Titian's *Assumption of the Virgin.* It was not in the Doge's Palace but in the Accademia, where the picture hung between 1818 and 1919, that he set eyes on the *Maria Gloriosa dei Frari,* or "Glorification of the Assumption of the Virgin Mary." Looking at it, he felt a resurgence of his "old powers." At this point, his memoirs abruptly state: "I resolved to proceed with *Die Meistersinger.*"

Why did he associate his decision, made previously, with that particular moment, and what fact, if any, did he suppress? Every form of masterpiece stimulates the creative urge: His account of the incident means no more than that. All else is speculation, but could this have been the moment when his conception of the theme changed course toward Hans Sachs's redeeming act of renunciation*—toward artistic mastery rather than indulgence in the joys of love? In fact, Titian's Virgin bears a significant facial resemblance to Mathilde, with her small round chin and rosebud mouth, and one of the figures left behind on earth is reaching after her ascending figure with a conspicuously outstretched arm.

Wagner's return trip to Vienna, which ended on November 13, took two full nights and a day. "Pinned between Then and Now," he wrote to Mathilde, "I journeyed off into drabness." This time he took the overland route, and it was on the train that he allegedly conceived, "with the utmost clarity, the Overture in C Major" for *Die Meistersinger von Nürnberg*. He qualifies this statement a few pages later by telling us that the music had come to him "like a distant vision" glimpsed in a mood of despondency. His idea of the *shape* of this overture must of necessity have been vague because important components of the prelude, such as the guild motif, were only devised during his subsequent study of Wagenseil in Vienna. Was it simply that he abandoned himself to C major euphoria on the journey, or did the whole thing amount to even less than that? Wagner's letter to Mathilde of December 21, 1861, which was previously quoted, provides a far more convincing account of how and why he lighted upon the *Meistersinger* during his return journey. Insensitive to outward things and preoccupied with his private visions, he had found himself thinking, once again, of his beloved Nürnberg. "And then I heard what sounded like an overture to *Die Meistersinger von Nürnberg*." *Like* an overture. . . . For once, we can take the composer at his word.

Peter Cornelius, who was highly enthusiastic about Wagner's new venture, saw to it that the Imperial Library lent him the principal works on the subject. These were Jacob Grimm's *Über den altdeutschen Meistergesang* and Johann Christoph Wagenseil's *Nürnberger Chronik* of 1697, together with its appendix, *Von der Meistersinger holdseligen Kunst,** a title familiar to Wagner from his boyhood reading of Hoffmann's *Serapionsbrüder*. From this he derived the *Meistergesang* terminology, and he promptly drew up detailed lists and tables for future reference. Between November 14 and 16, he wrote a new prose sketch in which the comedy became more deeply colored by his philosophy of art. Another, almost identical, version followed on November 18. At this stage the Marker was called Veit Hanslich.

On November 20, Wagner sent a fair copy to Franz Schott in Mainz. "You will see from this what it is about, and will surely concur with me if, in executing this task, I expect it to be one of my most original, or at any rate popular, works." The composer's timetable was ambitious, if not audacious. He proposed to complete the libretto by January 1, 1862, the first act of the score by the end of March, the second by June, and the third by September. A full score would be sent to every German theater during October, and the premiere would take place at Munich in November. He was further prepared to incur a contractual penalty for each and every delay. Apart from the reference to Munich—he aimed high and eventually hit the mark—everything in the letter was remote from reality. Self-deception can be a boon. Even Wagner must have known, in his more objective moments, that he was getting absolutely nowhere in Vienna as things now stood. The Metternichs, who were staying there and had attended a morning audition of passages from *Tristan* with Luise Dustmann and the theater orchestra, held out hopes of offering him a suite in the guesthouse of the Austrian embassy in Paris. On the strength of this, and in view of his continuing frustrations in Vienna, Wagner prepared to leave for France.

At a soiree given by Frau Dustmann before his departure, he was again accosted by Eduard Hanslick, who strove to convince him—sobbing as he did so, according to Wagner—that his musical judgment was untainted with malice. Wagner soothed the critic's ruffled feelings but squandered this final chance to win him over.

Although the Metternichs hinted vaguely that their offer of accommodation in Paris might have to be postponed, Wagner girded himself for departure. Cornelius, who saw him off at the station on November 30, murmured an encouraging snippet from the *Meistersinger* sketch in his ear: "The bird that sang today, full fair its beak had grown. . . ." Like all the vicissitudes in Wagner's eventful life, this one, too, cried out for an apt quotation.

Princess Metternich was unable to keep her promise because her mother had died. More precisely, she needed the rooms earmarked for Wagner to house her mentally deranged father, Count Sandor, who had become quite ungovernable since his wife's death and required concealment from the public gaze. Wagner took a room at the Hôtel Voltaire, where, almost unconscious of his bleak surroundings and dependent for company solely on Charles Truinet, his devoted translator, he started on the libretto for *Die Meistersinger*.

Writing to Malwida von Meysenbug in January 1862, Wagner told her that his four weeks' work in Paris had been the happiest period in all his recent experience of life. Countess von Pourtalès, who had lost her husband a few weeks earlier, was the first to hear the full text read aloud. He had become a solo entertainer to the aristocracy, but none of them offered to help him or give him shelter. For the first time, friends and acquaintances shrank from his written requests for accommodation, among them Cosima von Bülow in Berlin. He even suggested that Cornelius move in with him and bring Seraphine Mauro as housekeeper to them both. He, Wagner, would find nothing amiss with this arrangement, though the "social term" would be hard to define. Cornelius, covetous of Seraphine's exuberant bosom, declined his offer of a *ménage à trois* with thanks.

Unable to remain in Paris and mindful, no doubt, of Schott's function as a source of ready cash, Wagner decided to move to the vicinity of Mainz. Blandine Ollivier, whom he was never to see again, took leave of him "with a look of infinite sorrow."

Early in February, he traveled to Karlsruhe and plied Grand Duke Friedrich of Baden with renewed tales of woe for a full hour. From Karlsruhe he went to Mainz, where he had arranged to give a full reading of his *Meistersinger* libretto at Schott's home, 5 Weihergraben, on the evening of February 5, 1862. He had previously written to Vienna to tell Peter Cornelius that he would revert to the formal *"Sie"* unless Cornelius came to Mainz posthaste.

Cornelius was still missing when the handful of guests assembled, one of them being Wendelin Weissheimer, but Wagner refused to start without him and swore that he would appear at any moment. He turned up on the stroke of seven, even though he had been delayed by floods and lost his fur coat while crossing the Rhine.

Everyone who heard this reading found it unforgettable. Wagner read so expressively that he was soon able to omit the characters' names because his capacity for vocal inflection made it impossible to confuse them. His audience might have been listening to an entire company. According to Weissheimer, the reading was "a brilliant feat of rhetoric," and interrupted only by loud applause from all present. He recalled how enchantingly Wagner delivered Sachs's *"Wie duftet doch der Flieder"* in the second act and his allusion to King Mark in the third. He also praised the tenderness with which Eva's lines in the quintet—*"Selig, wie die Sonne meines Glückes lacht"*—flowed from his lips. *"Ein Kind ward hier geboren. . . . "* Wagner's little audience knew that they were standing beside the cradle of an epoch-making work.

Cornelius left at once so as to underline the exceptional nature of the occasion. He had not accepted Wagner's "proposal of marriage" orally any more than he had by letter. For reasons that were perfectly clear to him, he preferred to remain independent.

Where to now? Wagner decided against Mainz and Wiesbaden and took a fancy to Biebrich, a small town across the Rhine from Mainz, where he spent a week at the Europäischer Hof before taking lodgings at the home of an architect named Frickhöfer. Feeling temporarily forlorn, he left it up to Minna whether or not she would rejoin him. "I shall probably remarry my wife in the near future," he wrote to Bülow on February 16. Dr. Pusinelli had more or less managed to stabilize her condition, though Dresden friends such as Gustav Kietz were appalled to see how rapidly she was aging. Money, at least, was no problem. Wagner had undertaken to pay her an annual allowance of 1,000 thalers, and he kept his promise.

Minna arrived in Biebrich on February 21, 1862, unannounced. She and Wagner had an unpleasant scene the very next day, while unpacking the crates from Paris. Relations between them became even more strained a few days later, when some belated mail and Christmas presents arrived from Mathilde Wesendonck—"that dirty bitch [*Mistweib*]," as Minna called her in a letter to Natalie. While Minna was still at Biebrich, Wagner received news of August Röckel's release from Waldheim and, via Malwida von Meysenbug in London, of Bakunin's successful escape from Siberia—names and subjects whose awkward associations caused constant friction. On March 3, after more intolerable scenes, Minna departed. Wagner described her visit to Cornelius as "ten days of hell."

Late in May, he attended a performance of *Lohengrin* at Karls-ruhe. Although it was given in the version abridged by Julius Rietz for Leipzig, it did present Wagner with a discovery. Ludwig Schnorr von Carolsfeld, who was guesting in the title role, proved to be a singer-actor who enjoyed Wagner's unrivaled admiration from then on. After all he had heard about him, Wagner was slightly disconcerted by the tenor's squat and corpulent physique. As soon as he heard Schnorr sing, however, he was so enchanted by the youthful verve and demonic fire in his magnificent voice that he invited the singer to his hotel after the performance. They took to each other at once, and it was arranged that Schnorr and his much older wife, Malvina—he himself was only twenty-six— should pay a lengthy visit to Biebrich.

Two women entered Wagner's circle at this period, one a bird of passage and the other a friend for life. He first met twenty-eight-year-old Mathilde Maier at one of the Schotts' grand soirees. A notary's daughter from Alzey, she was sitting at table that evening between Wendelin Weissheimer and a lawyer named Städl, until they abandoned her to join Wagner, who had turned up late and was eating his dinner alone in an adjoining room. In revenge for this act of desertion, she monopolized Wagner for the rest of the evening. What most impressed her on first acquaintance was the element of "profound suffering" in his nature—something she was destined to alleviate. Not long afterward, Wagner formed a less-enduring relationship with Mathilde Maier's near namesake Friederike Meyer, the actress sister of Luise Dustmann, his pro-spective Isolde in Vienna. In the creative mood that was now descending on him, these two conquests were more than enough to satisfy his need for female companionship.

Weissheimer records how, during their walks along the Rhine, Wagner used to hum the motif that introduces *Die Meistersinger* like an exclamation mark in C major. At the end of March 1862, within a day or so of being amnestied by the king of Saxony, he embarked on the music for the *Meistersinger* Prelude and, thus, for the entire opera. Thanks to his newly awakened zest for work, the early stages of composition proceeded smoothly. According to *My Life*, the *Meistersinger* Prelude finally came to him in its entirety while he was gazing at the magnificent view from his balcony: "golden" Mainz, with the majestic sweep of the Rhine in the foreground. Months had passed since his "seminal" visit to Venice.

Biebrich

Wagner was scarcely into his stride when a succession of ailments overtook him. "To be dead would suit me well enough," he wrote to Minna on April 21, "but to live without ever being really healthy is no pleasure." His abdominal trouble recurred, this time accompanied by a constricted sensation in the chest and palpitations severe enough to keep him awake at night. He sent for a doctor, but: "The doctor claims to have found nothing wrong with my heart—they never do!" It was the same old story for the next twenty years.

He was always on the lookout for a new Asyl—another refuge. He even contemplated installing himself on the fourth floor of an ancient tower at Bingen, but no one would have been willing to act as his servant there. According to friends, his life at Biebrich was hectic, restless, and full of distractions, though he resolutely worked every morning. The old stream of visitors recommenced. Friederike Meyer turned up from Frankfurt to pay him a surprise visit. He was even more surprised when she promptly fell sick and was joined at Biebrich by her solicitous theatrical director, Herr von Guaita, with whom he discussed the possibility of producing one of his operas at Frankfurt. He heard after the couple had left that Friederike was rumored to be Guaita's mistress.

Alone on the morning of his forty-ninth birthday, Wagner devised the orchestral introduction to the third act of *Die Meistersinger*, its most pensive and contemplative passage. When the curtain rises to reveal Sachs silently engrossed in his book, the bass instruments break into a subdued, profoundly mournful melody characterized by "extreme resignation," as Wagner said in a letter to Mathilde Wesendonck written the same day. Then, sonorously delivered by horns and other wind instruments, comes the *"Wach' auf"* theme, solemn here but later to be joyously rendered by the chorus, and this "gospel" is delivered by the entire orchestra. "I now realize," he confided to Mathilde Wesendonck, "that this work will be my consummate masterpiece, and that I shall consummate it."

His guests that evening included the other Mathilde, the notary's daughter from Alzey. Mathilde Maier lived at Mainz with her mother, sister, and two aunts. She was a German beauty, neither stylish nor endowed with Mathilde Wesendonck's transparent pallor, but shrewd, warmhearted, affectionate, womanly, and young—a second Eva. Not for the first time, Wagner had come across a living embodiment of someone who already existed in his creative imagination. Mathilde had blue eyes, a soulful expression, wavy, shoulder-length fair hair worn over the ears, and a pretty little mouth which she sometimes pursed in a wry and mocking way. She was a good listener—Wagner once paid tribute to her agreeable capacity for silence—but suffered from incipient deafness, which not unnaturally inhibited her in the company of a musician. Though slightly apprehensive of having an affair with Wagner, she protested when his manner became too paternal because it hurt her feminine pride. Wagner may well have expected too much of her, perhaps because he began by placing her on too high a pedestal. She declined to join him on a visit to Weissheimer at Osthofen because it would, she said, have grieved her mother to see her conduct misinterpreted. Reluctant to take on Sachs but lacking any gallant young Stolzing to woo her, she remained Wagner's "good little girl" and never married. "Like this," Wagner wrote to her on June 20, 1862, "you will be all mine, even if I may never possess you." And again, to Betty Schott: "My art has continued to fare quite well with respect to women's hearts, probably because, for all the vulgarity that prevails, women still find it hard to let their souls become as hidebound as our male citizens have so amply succeeded in doing." But was this the only reason? Did they not also feel that his music dramas were exalting them into another human species, that his poetic libretti cast them in the role of redeeming angels?

Minna always seemed to sense when something was in the wind. Although he had been amnestied since March 18 and she was keeping a room free for him at Dresden, he had no intention of moving in with her. She now wrote him one of her most furious and—according to him, for the text has not survived—insane letters. This prompted him to moot the idea of a final, legal separation through Dr. Pusinelli, but she refused so curtly that Wagner quailed and pretended it was all a big mistake: Pusinelli had misunderstood him—he had merely meant to suggest that they should amicably agree to live apart.

Meanwhile, a heightening of erotic tension occurred, just as it had during the genesis of *Tristan* on the Green Hill. Early in July,

Hans and Cosima von Bülow visited Biebrich, Hans suffering so badly from liver or gallbladder trouble that the pain brought on by nervous excitement left him unable to sit or lie down in comfort. With Bülow at the piano, Wagner spent two weeks rehearsing Ludwig and Malvina Schnorr in the title roles of *Tristan und Isolde.* "My daughter," Liszt reported to Franz Brendel from Rome, "writes me wonderful things of Schnorr and his wife and the performance of 'Tristan' with Wagner at Biebrich. Would that electric telegraphs already existed in the interest of musical ubiquity!" Weissheimer claims to recall an evening when Wagner developed his ideas on *Parsifal* in considerable detail. He "talked himself into an emotional state," declaring that he had always had a premonition that *Parsifal* would be his last work. Cosima's eyes were swimming with tears. When Weissheimer retired to the balcony, Bülow quietly followed him out. "However little hope there is," he whispered, "and however little prospect of accomplishing his plans, he will attain his goal and bring off *Parsifal* as well—you mark my words."

The summer brought a constant stream of visitors. One July day, August Röckel and his daughter Louisabeth, an actress at the Weimar Court Theater, walked into the hotel dining room where Wagner was lunching with the Bülows and the Schnorrs. The two old friends and comrades-in-arms embraced each other with deep emotion. Röckel, it seemed, was on his way to the Frankfurt Riflemen's Festival and had no intention of dropping his republican activities altogether. Finally, Luise Dustmann arrived on a visit from Vienna and accused her sister, Friederike Meyer, of scandalous conduct. Wagner, who already knew of the Guaita liaison, could not have cared too much because he joined Friederike, the Schnorrs, and the Bülows on two excursions, one to Bingen and the other to the Drachenfels by way of Schlangenbad, Remagen, and Rolandseck. Their two weeks up, Ludwig and Malvina Schnorr returned to Dresden.

When the Bülows left, Wagner accompanied them on a two-day visit to Frankfurt to see Friederike Meyer play the Princess in Goethe's *Tasso.* While they were lunching with Friederike and Guaita, who invited Wagner to conduct a Frankfurt production of *Lohengrin* in the near future, the impresario picked a jealous quarrel with his mistress. Friederike defended herself against Guaita's furious onslaught with wit and sarcasm while the Bülows and Wagner, who was not entirely uninvolved, looked on in amused surprise. This time, Wagner felt, he and the Bülows would part on a cheerful note despite poor suffering Hans's "increasing and often excessive ill humor." As for Cosima, she seemed to have lost the diffidence he had noticed at Bad Reichenhall the year before. The account of this day in *My Life* contains a very significant passage whose most important sentences were deleted after Wagner's death: "All here was silence and mystery, yet the conviction that she belonged to me assumed such certainty that, feeling strangely elated, I carried matters to an extremity of high spirits. While escorting Cosima across a public square to the hotel in Frankfurt, I took it into my head to invite her to sit in an empty wheelbarrow standing there, so that I might thus convey her to the hotel. She promptly consented, whereupon, overcome once more with surprise, I lost the nerve to put my madcap scheme into effect. Bülow, who was following us, had seen the incident. Cosima, quite unabashed, explained its significance, and I fear I could not suppose his mood to be on a par with ours because he expressed misgivings about it to his wife." Wagner neglects to mention what form these misgivings may have taken, apart from ill-disguised jealousy: Cosima was in the third month of another pregnancy.

On September 21, 1862, Wagner sent Cosima a letter—one of the few that have been preserved.* "Be kind to me," he wrote, "and hold me dear." This first instance of the use of "*du*" between them was buried in a long and otherwise innocent missive.

In Mathilde Maier, Wagner saw Pogner's Evchen, snug contentment and quiet companionship; in Friederike Meyer, the lure of amorous adventure; in Cosima, the mystery of an unspoken mutual attraction. And yet, curiously enough, *Die Meistersinger* ground to a halt. Penniless since August, Wagner pursued Schott to Bad Kissingen in the hope of extracting another advance, but the publisher, who was ill, declined to see him. The Biebrich interlude seemed about to end before he could find a refuge elsewhere. Then, in September, word reached him from Vienna that the tenor Alois Ander was at last in a position to rehearse *Tristan*.

Wagner set off for Leipzig on October 29, the main purpose of his visit being to attend a concert that Wendelin Weissheimer was to conduct at the Gewandhaus on November 1. The program consisted largely of Weissheimer's own works but included the *Meistersinger* Prelude, which had been completed in June. Bülow played Liszt's Piano Concerto in A Major, and the evening ended with the *Tannhäuser* Overture. At a rehearsal, Wagner caught sight of Cosima seated in a corner of the hall "in mourning and very pale, but smiling amiably at me." Her sister Blandine had died in childbirth at St. Tropez on September 11. "All that filled us," Wagner recalled, "was so solemn and profound that only unconditional surrender to the pleasure of seeing each other again could help us to bridge that gulf." Unfortunately, the absurdity of some of Weissheimer's compositions lent the occasion "a ghostly touch," and the concert, which was notable inasmuch as it included the first performance of the *Meistersinger* Prelude and celebrated Wagner's return to his native city, was very poorly attended. Wagner said he had never seen a hall so empty. Although the *Meistersinger* Prelude was encored in response to loud applause from his supporters, Weissheimer's ensuing pieces failed so disastrously that Wagner, seated with Cosima at the back of the deserted auditorium, scandalized his relatives by persistently laughing and whispering.

On his return to Biebrich, where his landlord had given him notice to quit, he again went looking for lodgings with Mathilde Maier. Although he had far from abandoned the idea of settling in the neighborhood, the imminence of his departure seemed to fill him with a zest for adventure—a deceptive sense of freedom that drove him into the arms of Friederike Meyer. The actress had terminated her engagement at Frankfurt and was on the point of leaving for Vienna, where she hoped to make some guest appearances at the Burg Theater. Whether or not she had carefully contrived this plan for Wagner's sake, they turned up in Vienna together. Friederike's presence there at once aroused the ire of her sister, Luise Dustmann, who regarded her as the black sheep of the family. After all his troubles with Alois Ander, alias Tristan, Wagner had now succeeded in alienating his Isolde as well. To crown everything, Friederike's audition at the Burg Theater was a flop and her hopes of guest appearances came to nothing. Wagner, who was beginning to find her tedious, urged her to take a holiday in Venice. After a few vain attempts to resuscitate their former relationship, Friederike returned to Herr von Guaita and never reappeared on Wagner's horizon.

Unsure of his feelings, with a new work bogged down in the first act and no support from publishers or impresarios, Wagner resumed his involvement with Vienna. Thus began the last and most depressing phase in his lonely flight from himself.

How Will It End, My Friend?

———————————

It is difficult to guess how the Viennese reacted when Wagner set out, late in 1862, to build a livelihood in their city on the threadbare promises of a theater manager, and how *Tristan und Isolde* would have sounded to Viennese ears had it been performed there. Ander persistently forgot the first act as soon as he turned his attention to the second, and Luise Dustmann, when asked by the conductor, Heinrich Esser, how she managed to memorize her part, is reputed to have answered that his guess was as good as hers. Torn between hope and despair because the singers proved incompetent or were unavailable for rehearsals, Wagner looked for other ways of endearing himself to the Viennese.

On November 23, 1862, he gave a reading of the *Meistersinger* libretto at the home of Dr. Standhartner. The latter, obviously with Wagner's consent, had included Eduard Hanslick in the guest list. Hanslick, who left in high dudgeon when the reading was over, is widely reported to have done so because he recognized himself in Beckmesser or thought the character a deliberate travesty of himself. A more likely assumption is that someone in the know tipped him off to the fact that Beckmesser's name had originally been Hanslich. No one would admit to this indiscretion, of course, and the critic was cynically congratulated on having sat through the reading without losing his temper. Although Hanslick disclaims any annoyance in his memoirs, it is true that most of his subsequent pronouncements on Wagner contained some element of malice.

While at Biebrich, Wagner had laboriously excised pieces from the *Ring* and *Die Meistersinger* and furnished them with endings designed for concert performances in Vienna. His copyists there included Cornelius, Tausig, Weissheimer, and Johannes Brahms, then twenty-nine, who wrote out part of *Die Meistersinger* during these weeks and also studied the score of *Tristan*. Brahms was highly impressed by Wagner's ability, and the following testimony to his admiration—which Wagner never reciprocated—comes from no less a person than Hanslick: "I often heard him vigorously defend Wagner when hidebound or presumptuously arrogant people subjected him to derision and abuse." Tausig had rented the Theater an der Wien for a series of three concerts, and the empress herself attended the first of these on December 26, 1862; the program included first performances of Pogner's Address, the Gathering of the Mastersingers, and the orchestral version of the Ride of the Valkyries. Wagner's appearance on stage signaled a deafening ovation lasting several minutes. Even the empress leaned out of her box to applaud—an unprecedented mark of favor. Wagner humbly acknowledged this tribute with his arms spread wide, just as he did the equally tumultuous applause that followed the Ride of the Valkyries. Presumably, it was experiences of this kind that so often blinded him to his true predicament. He had a baffle erected prior to the second concert, which unhappily fell on New Year's Day. This improved the acoustics of the hall but augmented the loss he could hardly fail to incur on so ill-attended an evening.

Still awaiting the resumption of rehearsals for *Tristan* and disinclined to pick up the threads of his work on *Die Meistersinger*, Wagner felt sorely in need of the care and companionship of a woman who would be more to him than a maidservant. Mathilde Maier, who had accepted his kisses, was afraid he might break her heart and cast her aside, and he well knew why. He could not marry her while his wife was still alive, he wrote to her on January 4, 1863, but he had no desire to give Minna the coup de grace. "I need a woman who will resolve, despite everything and everyone, to be to me what a woman could be, under such miserable circumstances—could and must be, I tell you, if I am to prosper further." He paid a visit to Biebrich during February, still in search of somewhere to live, but failed to change Mathilde's mind.

Then, after financing his traveling expenses by giving a concert in Prague on February 5, which earned him 1,100 gulden, he embarked on a Russian tour arranged for him by Marie Kalergis, his longtime friend and admirer.

Wagner's Philharmonic Society concerts at St. Petersburg on March 3 and 10, 1863, which were warmly received by appreciative audiences, must have given him unique satisfaction. The orchestra, comprising 130 musicians drawn from all the imperial theaters, produced a tonal effect such as he had long imagined but never actually heard before. All that marred the proceedings was that Prince Dolgoruki, head of Section II of the Security Service, imposed police surveillance and insisted that the concert be prefaced by the imperial anthem, whereupon many members of the rebellious student elite walked out.

Wagner was so physically exhausted after two weeks that he set off for Moscow in low spirits, suffering from a heavy cold, and had to cancel the first of his three scheduled concerts there. The strain of rehearsals brought on violent chest pains—renewed symptoms of incipient heart disease.

Back in St. Petersburg, he wrote to Minna: "I am boundlessly overworked and have already been ill twice. . . . I shall be unable to repeat such ventures without killing myself in the process." On April 5, he began a series of readings from *Der Ring* and *Die Meistersinger* at tea parties given by Grand Duchess Helena Pavlovna, whom he sounded out on the possibility of an annual invitation to Russia and—more important still—an annual allowance.

Via Berlin, where Cosima had given birth to her second child, Blandine, on March 29, he returned to Vienna. All at once, he recalled Proudhon's maxim: *"Le génie est sédentaire."* Wistfully, he wrote to Liszt in Rome that he would someday love to abandon himself to pure enjoyment in those lovely southern climes, but what good were new impressions to someone who had failed to cope with all that he had gained from earlier ones? After discharging his most pressing debts and bringing Minna's allowance up to date, he was left with 4,000 thalers, and with these he proposed to settle down. Genius is sedentary. . . . He was still wavering between a country house at Biebrich, a summer residence at Bingen, a country house in Switzerland, and an apartment in Vienna. "If he starts a love affair in every town where he happens to be staying," Esser wrote to Schott, "that is his own concern, and none of mine." However, the conductor of the Vienna Opera went on to warn Schott not to throw his money away, and his misgivings turned out to be well founded.

Wagner opted for the most expensive solution. For 1,200 gulden a year, he rented the upper floor of a large house at Penzing, half an hour's walk from the opera house. This apartment, which comprised an imposing suite of rooms spacious enough to have accommodated a large family, was luxuriously appointed. In a fit of *horror vacui* that can only be attributed to extreme loneliness and a desire to work on *Die Meistersinger* in surroundings worthy of a masterpiece, he furnished the apartment with hangings and carpets, cushions and plush armchairs, frills and furbelows; ordered velvets, silks, and lace, new linen and quilted dressing gowns; engaged a housemaid; and took over his landlord's married couple, Anna and Franz Mrazeck. The whole venture proved too much by far for his purse and was soon to have dire results.

True, he got down to orchestrating the first act of *Die Meistersinger* and spent his fiftieth birthday more pleasantly, in the company of his staunch friend Standhartner, than he had its immediate predecessors. True, the local glee clubs and choral societies celebrated the occasion with a belated torchlight procession and serenade on June 3, and their written dedications referred to him for the first time as "honored Master," but the master lacked a mistress and his happiness was incomplete.

His request to Mathilde Maier to join him and "supply the deficiency in a seemly manner"—in other words, by becoming his housekeeper—was met with a curt demand that he should divorce his wife and marry her, so he temporarily dropped the subject. He consoled himself for the lack of a suitable partner with the sister of a seventeen-year-old housemaid who had tired of him and given notice. Mariechen, who took her place, became his "sweetheart." Writing to her while away on a concert tour, he adjured her to keep her little room well warmed and scented. "God, how I look forward to relaxing there again with you at long last! (I hope the pink drawers are ready too???)—Yes, yes! Just be nice and sweet. I deserve a really good time again."

But his craving for celestial love persisted, and he continued to hanker after Mathilde Wesendonck. "Ah, my dearest," he wrote to Eliza Wille, "we love but once, however much we may be intoxicated and flattered by what life parades before us: Yes, I realize only now that I shall never stop loving her alone." At Budapest, where he gave two concerts at the end of July, he met a young and beautiful Hungarian singer, a soulful and unsophisticated creature who sang excerpts from *Lohengrin* and—so he informed Mathilde Wesendonck—fell passionately in love with her "awakener."

Wagner would have found this all very enjoyable had he not been so constantly dogged by money worries. Of the 1,000 gulden he earned in Hungary, 500 were expended on the return journey, and a promissory note for another 1,000 gulden fell due when he got back to Vienna. Because Austrian law prescribed relatively severe penalties for debt and default, he was forced to borrow still more heavily. This put him at the mercy of moneylenders whose rates of interest were so high that he lost as much as 200 percent on each such transaction.

Calmly and dispassionately, Mathilde Wesendonck pinpointed his problem in September 1863: "You seize on each new illusion in haste, apparently to blot out the dissatisfaction engendered by past illusions, and no one knows better than yourself that it cannot be, nor ever will be. How will it end, my friend? Are not fifty years experience enough, and should not the moment come at last for you to be completely honest with yourself?" It was wonderfully put and covered everything, but the moment of truth was still a long way off.

Wagner's work that fall was hampered by fatigue, lethargy, and ill health. Viennese deadlines proved unrealistic because singers let him down and the management made no real effort to secure guest artists. On November 21, he left at short notice for Zurich, where he stayed with the Wesendoncks for the last time. At his own request, breakfast and lunch were served in his room and communal meals "saved up for special, festive occasions." He kept his distance to avoid complications. Although he still hoped against hope for financial assistance, the visit turned out to be an utter failure in this respect. He painted a grim picture of his position to Wesendonck but soon gathered that no more help would be forthcoming.

On the way back to Vienna, he spent a day and a night at Mainz as a guest of Mathilde Maier's family. He had turned down a concert in Dresden but accepted an invitation from Prince Hohenzollern-Hechingen to conduct his private orchestra at Löwenberg in Silesia. He broke his journey there at Berlin, where Hans von

Bülow persuaded him to stay for a concert he was giving the same night. November 28 proved to be a momentous day for them both.

Wagner lunched with Bülow and covered some of his traveling expenses by selling a gold snuffbox, a gift from the Grand Duke of Baden, for ninety thalers. Later on, while Bülow was rehearsing, he and Cosima went for a carriage ride through Berlin. "This time hilarity deserted us. We gazed mutely into each other's eyes, and a fierce desire to acknowledge the truth prompted us, without need of words, to confess the boundless unhappiness that weighed us down." The original version of *My Life* goes on: "With tears and sobs we sealed the avowal that we belonged to each other alone. It came as a relief to us both." Because the last and most important part of this passage was suppressed after Wagner's death and did not appear in any edition of *My Life* until 1963, doubts were expressed in some quarters whether Cosima could really have "defected" from her husband so early on. Since then, her diaries have fully borne this out. November 28 was always celebrated as one of the red-letter days in their life together.

Wagner spent the night at the Bülows' home. Although Cäcilie Avenarius, his younger half-sister, had been bitterly hurt when she learned of his failure to call on her during his visit to Berlin that March, he again neglected to see her before traveling on to Löwenberg. Here he earned a fee of 1,400 thalers from Prince Hohenzollern-Hechingen, an elderly and gout-ridden patron of the arts, for conducting one concert before an invited audience.

He returned to Vienna on December 9, more than usually fatigued by his excursion, and spent the ensuing days in world-weary inactivity. He also spent the rest of his ready cash on sundry social functions. Despite his alarming burden of debt, he invited Porges, Tausig, and Cornelius, who was celebrating his thirty-ninth birthday, to a Christmas Eve party at which lavish gifts were displayed for them beneath a candlelit tree. Cornelius alone received so many presents that he gave half of them away to his friends the next day. They included a tinderbox, a cigar case, a set of gold shirt studs, and an elegant pen wiper.

Early in 1864, purely with an eye to replenishing his coffers, Wagner tried to arrange another concert tour in Russia. The response to his letters, which took weeks to get there, was negative. The route to St. Petersburg had been cut by insurgents in the

Polish provinces. His Hungarian friends held out equally little hope of profitable concerts in their part of the world. Meanwhile, tradesmen were dunning him and creditors protesting his notes of hand.

Wagner's fortunes were going steadily downhill. Few of his letters to Cosima have survived, thanks to Eva Chamberlain's destructive zeal, but the few we possess suffice to show how much valuable information about this period of his life has been lost. One of them, dated March 10, 1864, employs the familiar *"du."* "You sensed the final convulsion with which I took leave of life. Since then I have entered on a final phase of suffering: I feel sure that it will soon be past. One last, sad effort, and it will be over." Was he contemplating suicide? This was the month when the Vienna production of *Tristan* was finally shelved, and disgrace and imprisonment for debt loomed large. Wagner's attorney, Dr. Eduard Liszt, a younger uncle of Franz, urgently advised him to leave Vienna. We can calculate the precise extent of his indebtedness from a letter written to Eduard Liszt after his departure. He had issued checks to Emanuel Kellner for 7,400 gulden, to Joseph Glauber for 4,500, and to the hired servant Franz Goltsch for 200. Tausig had underwritten his debts to Schweikart, an interior decorator. In all, the liabilities listed in his letter to the lawyer amounted to 12,100 gulden [very approximately, $35,000, or £20,000].

He hurriedly sold whatever he could to raise a few thalers and wrote to Eliza Wille asking her to sound out the Wesendoncks on the possibility of taking refuge with them. His request came at the worst conceivable moment: Mathilde Wesendonck's brother had just died. Eliza's negative response reached Vienna too late to catch him. He fled from the city on March 23, having asked his friends—in vain, as it turned out—to sublet the apartment and store his furniture, not sell it, because he intended to return.

By March 25, 1864, he was in Munich. Only two months short of his fifty-first birthday, homeless and in poor health, he roamed the streets on a raw, gloomy Good Friday. Displayed in the window of a shop near Brienner Strasse he saw a portrait of Ludwig II, who had succeeded Maximilian II as king of Bavaria on March 10. Struck by the eighteen-year-old monarch's "soulful features," he reflected that, were Ludwig not a king, he would like to make

his acquaintance. As he pensively made his way to the Hotel Bayerischer Hof—broke or not, he insisted on lodging in comfort—he
composed himself a grimly humorous epitaph.

On March 26, he crossed the Lake of Constance. "Once more a
refugee in need of asylum," he traced yet another of his ellipses on
the map. From Zurich he drove out to Mariafeld, where Eliza
Wille offered to put him up—in some embarrassment, because her
husband, François, was away in Constantinople. The Wesendoncks declined to reestablish contact with him and confined
themselves to sending over a few pieces of furniture. His temporary quarters, a house next door to the Willes', were hard to heat.
Ill and wretched though he felt, he chose this moment to play the
maestro, and Eliza Wille preserved a vivid memory of him in his
black beret, looking like a figure by Albrecht Dürer. His reading
matter ranged from Johann Tauler, the fourteenth-century German mystic, to Jean Paul's *Siebenkäs,* works by George Sand and
Walter Scott, and even *Felicitas,* a novel by his hostess. He busily
wrote letters and issued decrees like a king without a kingdom.
Vague references to long-term plans served only to disguise how
much at a loss he felt and how little able to justify his continued
presence at Mariafeld. He was at the end of his tether—a tolerated
but unwelcome guest in the Willes' bourgeois circle, bereft of
courage and with scant prospect of reviving his former connections. He seemed to be staring into a fog that refused to lift—a
void. He sat in his room reading Schopenhauer and drinking
Vichy water. "I must find a really good, beneficial water, or I'm
done for," he wrote to Cornelius on April 8.

Eliza did her best to cheer him up. Admiringly, she looked
through his portfolio of manuscripts and sketches and spoke of the
glorious future ahead of him. He listened with only half an ear, as
usual, then said impatiently, "Why speak of the future when my
manuscripts are locked away in a shrine? Who will perform the
work of art that I, and I alone, can bring forth with the aid of
propitious daemons, and perform it so that everyone will know:
There it is—that's how the Master saw his work and meant it to
be?"

He paced up and down the room before coming to a halt in front
of her. Then, with a ferocity incongruous in a beaten man, he
summarized what he expected of life. "I am differently constituted," he announced, "—highly strung. I must have beauty,

brilliance, light. The world owes me what I need. I cannot live in a miserable organist's post like your Master Bach. Is it so outrageous of me to believe that I deserve the modicum of luxury I like—I, who bring enjoyment to the world and to thousands?"

So saying, he slumped into his chair beside the window like a general waiting vainly for reinforcements. *How will it end, my friend?* He may well have been thinking of Mathilde across the lake in Zurich, and of her latest admonition. His sleepless nights he spent *à la* Lear, roaming the nearby heath.

At some stage, possibly at someone else's suggestion, he hit on the idea of marrying a wealthy wife. Although he had sworn never to do so again, he asked his sister Luise Brockhaus to see if Minna could, after all, be persuaded to grant him a divorce. Luise, who flatly refused to put pressure on her, pointed out that the kapellmeister's job at Darmstadt was vacant and urged him to apply for it. He would, she told him, be better advised to concentrate on his profession.

One feverish night, when his brain was overstimulated by reading, he dreamed that Frederick the Great had summoned him to join Voltaire at his court. Something inside him gave him no peace. François Wille returned from his trip to the East and was "rather dismayed" to find Wagner in residence, soaking up all the attention he could get. When Wille explained, amiably but firmly, that a man liked to be "something more than a cipher in his own house . . . not a mere foil to someone else," the eternal fugitive decided to move on. Vaguely intimating that he planned to inspect some theaters in Germany, he announced his intention of leaving. "My friend," he told Eliza on his last evening, "you do not know the extent of my suffering or the depth of the misery that lies ahead of me."—"No," she replied staunchly. "Something will turn up."

He left her a sealed letter for Mathilde Wesendonck, but she got it back unopened and returned it to him. He wrote to Eliza from Basel, angling for another invitation to Mariafeld. Her reply reached him at Stuttgart: She disapproved of the plan and told him that his destiny lay elsewhere. That line of retreat, too, had been cut off.

He arrived in Stuttgart on April 29, having arranged to see Karl Eckert, formerly kapellmeister in Vienna and now director of the local opera. Eckert, who was well-disposed toward him, was to introduce him to Baron von Gall, the Stuttgart intendant. Wagner also telegraphed Weissheimer to join him. He proposed, he said, to bury himself somewhere in the Rauhe Alb and complete *Die Meistersinger*, and Weissheimer was to make the piano arrangement. Never had his plans for the future been so vague—or so modest. When Weissheimer reached Stuttgart on April 30, a Saturday, Wagner greeted him at the Hotel Marquardt with the words, "I'm done for!"

Staying in the room next to Wagner's was Angelo Neumann, the singer who later became an impresario. Robbed of sleep because his next-door neighbor kept pacing up and down in squeaky shoes, Neumann summoned a waiter and inquired the identity of the caged lion. On expressing his surprise and delight to the owner of the hotel, Neumann was informed that the celebrated Herr Wagner was in such dire financial straits that he could not afford to come down for meals. Herr Marquardt would have been glad to waive the charge, but how to convey this tactfully?

Wagner did not, in fact, go hungry because Kathi Eckert, a rich and beautiful woman who had sacrificed her position in Viennese society for the sake of her talented but ailing conductor husband, kept open house. Wagner and Weissheimer decided to attend a performance of *Don Giovanni*, with Angelo Neumann in the title role, before leaving for the Rauhe Alb—or wherever—on Tuesday, May 3. On Monday evening, while Wagner was dining with the Eckerts, he was handed a card: *"Le secrétaire aulique de S. M. le roi de Bavière"* requested a word with Herr Richard Wagner. Suspecting a ruse on the part of some creditor who had tracked him down, Wagner sent word that he was not on the premises. While packing his bags the next morning, he was further depressed to receive some letters from Vienna urgently requesting his presence. The idea appalled him. Where to now, Vienna or the Rauhe Alb? If the truth be told, he could not afford either. It was enough that Frau Eckert had discreetly settled his hotel bill. Then, at ten o'clock, came the unexpected information that Hofrat Franz Seraph von Pfistermeister of Munich wished to see him. After hesitating for a while, Wagner asked Weissheimer to leave him alone with his visitor.

There were no witnesses to the lengthy interview that followed. King Ludwig's cabinet secretary informed Wagner that he had been trailing him at the monarch's behest for two full weeks—he had even paid abortive visits to Vienna and Zurich. He brought with him a ring, a portrait of Ludwig, and a message to the effect that His Majesty, being an admirer of Wagner's work, had resolved to save him from an unjust fate by keeping him "forever at his side in friendship." Pfistermeister, the divine messenger who was to become a bitter personal enemy, invited Wagner to accompany him to Munich. Wagner sat down and wrote Ludwig a letter of fervent gratitude: "These tears of the most heavenly emotion I send you, to tell you that the marvels of poetry have now entered my poor, loveless life like a divine reality. And that life, its last words and music, belong henceforth to you, my gracious young king: Dispose of them as you would of your own property!"

By the time Pfistermeister left the room and Weissheimer returned, the world had undergone a complete transformation. Wagner flung his arms around Weissheimer's neck and wept. Later, while they were lunching with the Eckerts, news came that Meyerbeer had died the previous day. Weissheimer burst into "coarse laughter." The coincidence of Meyerbeer's death and Wagner's change of fortune was indeed an occasion for malicious glee, and Wagner could not forbear to make this point at the end of his autobiography.

At five that afternoon, he and Pfistermeister boarded the train to Munich. The mail from Vienna, which was still in his pocket, had lost its terrors for him.

PART THREE

1864-1882

THOMAS MANN: "*Anguished and great, like the nineteenth century whose consummate expression it is, the disembodied figure of Richard Wagner stands before my eyes. I see it physiognomically furrowed by all his propensities, overburdened with all his impulses, and I can scarcely distinguish between love for his work, one of the creative world's most magnificently questionable, equivocal, and fascinating phenomena, and love for the century of which most was filled with his life—that restless, harassed, tormented, obsessed, and unappreciated life that ended in a glow of world renown.*"

A Farce with a First-Class Cast

Act 1: The Appointment

Munich, May 4, 1864. The curtain rose at last on a royal comedy whose ceremonial make-believe proved too much for every member of the cast. Wagner had been very nearly crushed by "the abject cares of everyday life." He was to be spared them from now on, but at the cost of a living lie which it took him years to face. His friendship with Ludwig II has often been hymned as the fulfillment of a dream and the pinnacle of a career. In retrospect, this ostensibly magical, brilliant, and triumphant episode turns out to be an intermezzo of the most shameful and insidious kind. With the exception of a few peripheral figures, all concerned lost face and then tried to save it, either by camouflaging their self-deception or by ascribing the disastrous outcome of the fairy tale to the machinations of a court cabal. In reality, they all proceeded on false assumptions and became so hopelessly entangled that we can perceive their tragic stature only with the benefit of hindsight: Ludwig, who mistook dreams for reality; Wagner, who overstepped his allotted bounds for the first and last time; and Cosima von Bülow, who lost her innocence, not because of religious ambition and erotic passion, but by foisting another man's child on her husband and deceiving a gullible young king.

Handsome, dark-eyed, and homosexual, a brooding and solitary

young man of disquietingly melancholic and unsociable temperament, Ludwig had been deeply affected by the first opera he ever
saw, which happened to be Wagner's *Lohengrin*. Gottfried von
Böhm, the senior civil servant who later wrote Ludwig's biography, recalled that the fifteen-year-old crown prince shed tears of
delight on this occasion. He promptly learned the libretto by
heart, read the rest of Wagner's dramas, and showed a special
interest in *The Artwork of the Future*. There is much evidence to
suggest that it was not music at all that so attracted him to Wagner's world of drama, but that the subjects and characters themselves were idealized by his poetic fancy into a combination of all
the arts. He was susceptible to auditory stimuli and fond of mythology. His taste was haphazard. The Lohengrin Grotto with its
elaborate machinery, built at his command; his childish and mawk-
ish love of swans; his penchant for private performances devoted
not only to Wagner's operas but to commissioned works on historical subjects, mostly of an amateurish nature—all these things cast
as much doubt on the authenticity and profundity of his appreciation of art as did his fondness for listening to random selections
of "numbers" from Wagner's stage works.

Writing to Cosima von Bülow on June 4, 1865, shortly before the
first performance of *Tristan*, Pfistermeister reported that the king
had taken a bath one night after going for a longish ride. Standing
naked in the big royal bathroom, he had struck the surface of the
water with each palm in turn. The sound produced by these blows
had reminded him so vividly of the final motif from *Tristan* that
the whole scene—Isolde beside Tristan's corpse—had come to life
in his mind's eye. "Isn't that odd?" Pfistermeister concluded. Luise
von Kobell, who later married Cabinet Secretary Eisenhart, wrote:
"Ludwig was not really musical. His former piano teacher called
the day he gave him his last lesson as crown prince a 'lucky day,'
on account of his exalted pupil's lack of talent." Embassy Secretary
von Leinfelder once told Ministerial Councillor von Völderndorf:
"Do not imagine that it was music that endeared Wagner to the
prince's youthful mind. It had a truly demonic effect on him, but
not a pleasant one. . . . At the point where Tannhäuser reenters
the Venusberg (the passage also occurs in the Overture), for example, his body would go into positive convulsions each time. They
were so severe on one occasion that I feared he would have an
epileptic fit. The composer would never have conquered him; it

was the poet who enthralled the young prince's dreamy disposition." Ignaz von Döllinger, Ludwig's mentor, declared in 1865 that he found the young king's predilection for Wagner inexplicable because Ludwig had no ear for music. Even if one does not go so far as to describe Wagner's compositions as music for the unmusical, their dramatic impact and appeal to the senses as well as the musical intellect render them art for the many and the few alike. Although Ludwig was certainly no member of the latter category, he confided to Wagner at the outset that he, Wagner, had long been his "real teacher and educator."

Wagner was granted his first audience late on the afternoon of May 4. He was deeply impressed by the tall young monarch's outward appearance, his noble bearing and fiery gaze. Writing to Eliza Wille the same day, he declared: "Unhappily, he is so handsome and intelligent, soulful and splendid, that I fear his life will evanesce in this base world like some fleeting dream of the gods."

Ludwig told him that he must complete his *Nibelungen* cycle and undertook to finance its production. He was to be relieved of all material concerns. Wagner bowed low over the royal hand and remained in that position for a long time, unspeaking. "Had you but seen how his gratitude shamed me," Ludwig wrote to his cousin, Archduchess Sophie Charlotte. Wagner to Eliza Wille: "My happiness is so great that I am quite shattered by it." Ludwig again to Sophie Charlotte: "I felt as if we had exchanged roles." He bent over Wagner—he was several inches taller—and drew him to his breast "with the feeling that I myself was swearing an oath of eternal fealty." It was a rash and precipitate vow.

No less hazardous was their exchange of roles. As time went by, they forgot themselves and neglected to keep their distance. "My dearest Beloved!" wrote Ludwig. "My beloved, most glorious Friend!" replied the composer—but that was relatively mild compared to some of the king's terms for him: "One and All! Embodiment of my happiness . . . Exalted, divine Friend . . . Source of the light of my life . . . Supreme Goodness . . . Savior who makes me happy . . . Dearly beloved Adored One, Lord of my life. . . ." Wagner's replies were neither more nor less deferential, but the embarrassing aspect of their correspondence—and the possibility of a homosexual relationship between them can be ruled out—reposes less in these verbal embraces than in the fact that their high-flown phrases betokened a departure from reality and a resort to self-deception, if not deception itself. "How ardently I yearn for some tranquil, solemn hours that will grant me another glimpse of the long-missed countenance of the dearest person on earth!" wrote Ludwig on January 5, 1865. "Whatever I have dreamed of, hoped and longed for, will soon come to life. Heaven is descending to earth for us. O Holy One, I worship you!" And the dearest person on earth replied in kind to his "adored, angelic Friend." At Bayreuth on July 10, 1878, when Cosima mentioned that she had been reading some of his letters to the king, Wagner commented, "The tone wasn't good, but I didn't set it." Earlier, on December 27, 1873, after writing Ludwig yet another letter in which he had "perished" on paper, he told her that, when he used such language, he could not "lay it on thick enough" and called it a senseless convention. This shows that his perfervid epistolary style was deliberate playacting. If he had ceased to be dishonest, he would have had to cease being himself—and what then?

Wagner and Ludwig fell in love with their roles. Worse still, they forgot they were playing them. So far from glorifying their authors, the letters that passed between them disclose what Pierre Boulez has called "the mechanics of guile." He goes on: "Their exaggeration of the noble and ideal betrays the artificiality of the roles they were playing and reveals the parodistic nature of this exchange of ideas, which posed as an exchange of notes between Pope and Emperor in the days of the Holy Roman Empire, transforming it into a dialogue between masked players of whom each strove to convince the other that his disguise was authentic." Himself a great dramatist and composer, Wagner saw through the charade in retrospect—that much is certain. The realization left a deep scar and a big residue of shame.

There was something childlike about Ludwig's passion for Wagner, and it was that very quality in him which proved so detrimental to them both. Ludwig's politically hazardous fondness for living cocooned in fantasy came as a positive challenge to Wagner, the unpolitical artist: Not content with marching his blindly devoted disciple toward the Grail, he felt driven to mobilize the entire Kingdom of Bavaria as well. For the first time ever, he sought to manipulate the keyboard of practical politics and exert an influence on appointments. Early in 1865, an elderly clairvoyant named Frau Dangl endeavored to persuade him that he had a mission to save Ludwig from his enemies. Wagner's first thought

—like the king's—was for himself, and that was his natural right. It could hardly have been otherwise, after all the depths he had plumbed and the humiliations he had undergone. Unfortunately, to quote the painter Friedrich Pecht, Wagner's natural egoism was anything but a benign influence on the king "because it could not fail to enhance his own."

Ludwig reigned for 296 days in 1864, the year of his accession. Of these he spent only 68 in his capital. The fact that he failed to attend so many political and public functions was not in Wagner's interest. The Ultramontanists took advantage of his weakness to extend their influence. It was not the king who ruled, but his ministerial bureaucrats. For the moment, they refrained from commenting on the Wagner mania that had overcome their youthful monarch, who controlled a portion of his civil list but not the national exchequer.

The miracle had occurred at last: Wagner was free of his debts. On May 9, Ludwig authorized an initial payment of 4,000 gulden. Wagner promptly went to Vienna to conclude an armistice with his creditors, but not without bitterly reproaching his closest friends, Standhartner included, for having precipitately and irresponsibly sold off his personal property. He was particularly incensed by the loss of his Erard piano.

While Wagner was still in Austria, Ludwig assigned him, with effect from May 1, 1864, an annual stipend of 4,000 gulden—as much as a ministerial councillor or senior civil servant. On June 10, he granted him another 16,000 gulden as an outright gift, together with 4,000 to cover removal expenses. On October 18, the royal exchequer concluded a contract with Wagner under which he was to receive a fee of 30,000 gulden for composing the *Ring*. Of this sum, 16,500 gulden were paid out, 6,000 being an advance on his now increased salary, which was finally, on December 6, set at 5,000 gulden a year. The total sum disbursed by the royal exchequer was 131,173 gulden, 46 kreuzer. This represented one-third of the annual sum freely available to the king, or one-tenth of his entire civil list.

After his first visit to Vienna in May, from which he returned with Anna and Franz Mrazeck and the dog Pohl, Wagner moved into Haus Pellet, a villa that had been rented for him at Kempfenhausen, near Starnberg, about halfway to Ludwig's residence at Schloss Berg. The "Annals" record that he enjoyed the king's company "almost every morning." These first few weeks were the most carefree in their entire relationship. Wagner spent hours reading aloud to Ludwig, who felt that all his dreams had indeed come true. Profound affection, a concordance of ideas, and a passionate devotion to art seemed to have created an enduring bond between them. On May 22, the king marked Wagner's birthday by presenting him with a specially commissioned portrait of himself in oils. Wagner's second trip to Vienna in June resulted in his first serious difference of opinion with Peter Cornelius, who was composing *Der Cid* and had no immediate intention of obeying Wagner's "summons." When he returned, sudden disenchantment set in. The king went off to Bad Kissingen and the idyll beside the Starnberger See disclosed its imperfections. Wagner was in an uneasy frame of mind—edgy, worried about his health, and unable to work. It was not misfortune that had unsettled him this time, but its opposite. He needed a woman.

"Will you come and manage my house for me?" he wrote to Mathilde Maier. Given that Hans and Cosima von Bülow were about to visit him, he was playing with fire. After his pledge of devotion to Cosima on November 28 of the previous year, one can only marvel that he continued to call Mathilde his "dearest sweetheart" and that he had, only two months after that date, urged her to hold him "unalterably dear." Now he asked her point-blank to come and keep house for him, much as if Sachs were hoping to engage Eva as a resident maid of all work. He also enclosed a letter for her mother in which he explained that, although Minna's state of health precluded a divorce, Mathilde would be "well and honorably cared for" under his roof. There followed a uniquely awful breach of good taste: "Bearing in mind" the possibility of his wife's death, he requested Mathilde's hand in marriage.

Fortunately, Frau Maier never read this letter. Mathilde declined to give it to her on the grounds that she would be "shattered" by the prospect of parting with her daughter. Wagner gave up the struggle and commended Mathilde to a kindly providence. "Fear no escapades on my part," he wrote. "For the present, some friends are coming to stay with me."

Reenter Cosima, unaccompanied by her husband, on June 29. Hans von Bülow, who did not arrive until a week later, sent her on ahead with Daniela, then three and a half, and Blandine, fifteen months. We have already spoken of Cosima's wild and erratic behavior, but what happened now bore greater testimony to her determination and sense of mission—to a fanaticism that steeped her love for Wagner in quasi-religious fervor. Although her feelings for him contained an element of idealism, action was the current order of the day. Recognizing her allotted place in life, she consummated her union with Wagner while Bülow's two small daughters slept in the room next door.

Cosima seems at once to have grasped the finality of the Starnberg decision, which gave an irreversible twist to the injured-third-party game in Wagner's life and was soon to end it forever. She wrote to Marie von Buch, later Baroness von Schleinitz: "I have been here three days, and feel as if it were already a century and will last I know not how long." This sounds sublime, though one cannot forbear to point out that her *solitude à deux* beside the Starnberger See was daring for its period. Wagner was now in a hurry to undo his precipitate efforts in another direction. Writing to Mathilde Maier on July 19, he expressed the fervent hope that she had not yet shown his recent letter to her mother. He was no longer of a mind to accept "any sacrifices that may have been offered." Let all remain as it had been: He wanted to spare himself "fresh heartaches" and begged her forgiveness. His fear of being left on the shelf had nearly ruined everything.

Hans von Bülow arrived at Haus Pellet on July 7, close to a nervous breakdown and suffering from rheumatism. Even the snug atmosphere of the lakeside house, with its tranquillity, its quietly attentive servants, and its delightful garden, failed to improve his condition. This was no time to discuss marital problems or divorce, especially as Wagner wanted to retain Bülow's friendship and render an engagement in Munich palatable both to him and the king. It was therefore thought better to leave him in the dark, and Cosima temporarily played the sensitive, ailing wife. This is apparent from Wagner's letter to Bülow on September 30, when Cosima was three months pregnant with Isolde, their firstborn: "I too am alarmed by Cosima's indisposition. All that relates to her is exceptional and unusual: She deserves freedom in the noblest sense of the word. She is at once childlike and profound —the laws of nature will never lead her on to anything less than the sublime. No one will ever help her but herself. She belongs to a special order of things—one we must learn to comprehend through her. You will in the future have more leisure and a greater measure of personal freedom in which to attend to this and find your noble place at her side. That too consoles me." It was a letter couched in obscure and ambiguous language whose true meaning was known to him alone.

Wagner's first step was to secure the precarious equilibrium of his new position. Before leaving for Kissingen, his "beloved young friend" had inquired the extent to which his views had changed since the revolutionary essays of 1849–51. Wagner duly wrote *State and Religion*, an essay designed to crystallize future interpretations of his revolutionary ideas and activities once and for all.

This piece brought him sundry visitors, among them, on August 16 or 17, Ferdinand Lassalle. At the end of May, Mathilde Maier's friend Dr. Städl had written to Wagner suggesting that his program of universal education might be supplemented by familiarizing his royal patron with some of Lassalle's socialist lectures—an absurd request, given that Wagner was intent on playing down his own socialist past. Lassalle himself had something quite different in mind. He was temporarily more concerned about his mistress, Helene von Dönniges, than with the German labor movement. Having become friendly with Hans von Bülow in Berlin, he called on him in the hope that Bülow would persuade his now "powerful friend" to intercede for him with the king. He intended to charge Helene's father, the Bavarian chargé d'affaires at Geneva, with depriving his daughter of her liberty, and needed a friend at court. It is probable that Helene herself accompanied him to Starnberg.* When presented to Wagner, Lassalle introduced her as Brünnhilde and himself as Siegfried. It seems that he rightly construed the *Ring* as a socialist work of art.

Wagner gave Lassalle a hearing but urged him not to overrate his influence, so the socialist leader returned empty-handed to Switzerland, where he challenged Prince Rackowitza, whom the Dönniges family regarded as Helene's legitimate fiancé, to a duel. On August 26, he telegraphed Wagner that he was withdrawing his challenge because of "the person's utter worthlessness." Two days later he changed his mind, and on August 31, he died from the effects of this anachronistic "affair of honor." Not unsurprisingly, Wagner remembered Lassalle with no great affection.

He did not trouble the king with such trifles. Except in Ludwig's absence, when he was obliged to communicate his "despair of art's salvation" by letter, Wagner introduced Ludwig by word of mouth to the far-reaching plans that might help to realize the vast tetralogical work whose completion he so ardently desired. He did little real composition at this period. The *Huldigungsmarsch* [*March of Homage*], the first of three Wagnerian marches that may justifiably be excluded from his *oeuvre*, was intended to be performed as a birthday gift to the king on August 25, 1864. Originally scored for military band, it was not rewritten for symphony orchestra until 1871. A very bizarre and rather incoherent piece of work, it is steeped in the atmosphere of the *Tristan* and *Meistersinger* preludes, from which trumpets emerge like sun from morning mist above the Starnberger See. Just when one expects to hear the Mastersingers' motif proper, everything subsides into a kind of hymn tune. A paradoxical and strangely premonitory reflection of the situation, it has a morbid, despairing quality and ends on a forced note.

The *Huldigungsmarsch* received its first hearing on October 5, a bleak and chilly autumn day, in the courtyard of the Munich Residenz. Ludwig looked on from a window—no members of the public were present—as the massed bands of three infantry regiments performed it under the baton of Bandmaster Siebenkäs. After that, it was promptly forgotten. There were other, more important things in the wind than expressions of mutual loyalty. Impatiently, Wagner urged the king "most graciously to ordain" that *Der Ring des Nibelungen* be completed, systematically rehearsed, and finally performed. He also undertook a variety of outflanking maneuvers that bore witness to his propensity for farsighted, though not always felicitous, essays in personnel selection. A "colony" had to be established, and its governor could be none other than Hans von Bülow. Wagner presented him to the king at Schloss Berg, and Bülow made such a favorable impression that Ludwig invited him to dinner. Writing to Mathilde Maier, Wagner preened himself on the unalloyed success of his plan to obtain Bülow a preliminary engagement as the king's "personal performer" [*Vorspieler*]. Bülow was to familiarize Ludwig, "who knows no music at all," with "good musical literature," while he himself would thus acquire a loyal associate.

Despite his initial hesitation in accepting it, Bülow's Munich appointment came at an opportune moment because he had undermined his position in Berlin by making a series of injudicious remarks. His health was the only problem. Cornelius, who saw

him a few months later, was alarmed enough by the sight of his
shrunken frame to predict that "one more storm" would "break
this noble reed." In August, Bülow left Starnberg for Munich,
where he languished in bed at the Hotel Bayerischer Hof, partially
paralyzed in both legs and one arm and—as Wagner puts it in the
"Annals"—"furious." Why was he in such a state? Did he know
more than he admitted, or was he merely offended that Cosima,
instead of remaining at his side, had chosen the very day when he
was compelled to seek medical assistance—August 19—to join
Liszt at the Musicians' Congress in Karlsruhe? Cosima had much
to tell or intimate to her father, who reproached her severely.
Downcast and despondent, she returned with him to Munich on
August 28, and they hurried to Bülow's sickbed. It was a dismal
reunion not improved by Wagner's arrival in Munich the following day. Liszt and he regarded each other with mixed feelings. It
was three years since their last meeting. In the interim, Liszt's plan
to marry Princess Carolyne had been thwarted by the machinations of her family. Having transferred the focus of her enthusiasm
from earthly intercourse to heavenly communion, she was bent on
bullying Liszt into taking holy orders. Her already disruptive
effect on him was now compounded with the threat of a cardinal's
hat—from Wagner's point of view, an unappealing prospect. Liszt,
too, looked weary. All three men were in the prime of life: Liszt
two months short of fifty-three; Wagner fifty-one; Bülow only
thirty-four, but in terrible shape.

    After conversing with Bülow and paying a joint call on the
painter Wilhelm von Kaulbach, Wagner and Liszt drove through
Forstenrieder Park—a royal route with which Wagner was soon
to become closely acquainted—to Kempfenhausen. It is clear from
the *Brown Book*, a diary that Wagner began to keep for Cosima's
benefit in the following year, that the two men had an altercation
at Haus Pellet. Liszt made an attempt to save Bülow's marriage.
He accused Wagner of not being truly in love with his daughter
and predicted that she would end by spurning him. Each of them
found it hard to keep his temper. Liszt played extracts from as
much of *Die Meistersinger* as already existed and was deeply impressed by what he termed "a masterpiece of humor, wit, and
charm." He also played the Beatitudes from his oratorio *Christus*.
Wagner, who scented Rome in the background, greeted them—if
Cosima's diaries are to be believed—with considerable reserve.

This was not the Liszt he loved and admired. He was unable to infect Liszt with the triumphant mood he had instilled elsewhere with his tidings of royal favor, even though the older man was astonished to read Ludwig's effusive letters. "Wagner's relations with the king are well-nigh miraculous," he reported to Princess Carolyne.

Liszt left for Stuttgart on the morning of September 3. That evening, the Bülows also left to make preparations for their move from Berlin to Bavaria in November. Their departure was meant to signal the start of Wagner's "workaday" Munich routine, a period of intense creativity. "For the present," he wrote to Ludwig on September 26, "I have now resolved to lay aside all other tasks, profitable to me as their greater ease of performance might make them, in order to devote myself, exclusively and forthwith, to completing the composition of my great Nibelungen work." At an audience on October 7, Ludwig finally and formally "commanded" him to complete the *Ring*. This ritual gesture, which Wagner had extracted from him, was made in imitation of seventeenth-century custom, even though the young monarch merely raised his hand to dispatch a train whose signal was already set for departure.

The train proceeded at a Wagnerian andante, its progress retarded—as the laws of Wagner's life dictated—by numerous hazards and obstructions. At the end of September, he tried to resume fair-copying the score of the second scene from act 1 of *Siegfried*. On October 15, he moved to Munich and installed himself, supposedly for good, at 21 Brienner Strasse. This handsome house, which was situated in a select residential quarter near the Propyläen, had a rectangular ground plan and a central portico surmounted at first-floor level by a loggia. The Italian flat roof was enclosed at the front and rear by a wall topped with stone urns. Wagner's new home adjoined the property of Count Adolf Friedrich von Schack, who had erected a special building in the garden to house his private collection of paintings. The two men developed a good-neighborly relationship because Wagner had long known the cultivated art collector as an editor, translator, and adapter of Spanish and Persian literature, and their relations were further cemented by discussions on Calderón, Firdausi, and August Platen.

The house on Brienner Strasse, which the king made over to

Wagner, and which Wagner restored to the civil list after leaving Munich, was run by a staff comprising the Mrazecks and Verena Weitmann, whom Wagner summoned from Lucerne. His enjoyment of this imposing and luxurious abode was marred, soon after he moved in, by a severe and protracted hemorrhoidal indisposition, as well as by a series of annoying setbacks that multiplied the closer he seemed to come to his objectives.

On November 26, the king decided to have a festival theater built for the purpose of staging the *Ring* in Munich. At an audience on November 29, he commissioned Gottfried Semper, who had been recommended to him by Wagner and hurriedly sent for, to design this new building. It was to be commandingly sited on Gasteig hill, at the end of an extension road running from Brienner Strasse, through the Hofgarten, and over a new bridge spanning the Isar —in other words, a Wagnerian slash across the face of the Bavarian capital.

As soon as the plan for a festival theater became known, opposition reared its head in the cabinet. Munich's artists and writers, too, felt not unnaturally resentful. Although they were not old-established Bavarians, men like Paul Heyse, Friedrich von Bodenstedt, Franz Lachner, and Moritz von Schwind constituted a privileged elite in the capital, which then had 166,000 inhabitants, and disliked having to share their fame and popularity with such a shady royal protégé. How much, they asked, did Munich know about him? Only that he used to be a wanted revolutionary who had publicly professed his allegiance to Feuerbach, that he wrote unperformable works and had several times fled from other cities, leaving mountainous debts behind. What was more, Bavaria had just acquired a new prime minister in the person of Ludwig von der Pfordten, the clerical conservative who had already crossed swords with Wagner in Saxony and was consequently prejudiced against him, so there could hardly fail to be a clash between opposing forces. It was Pfordten's firm conviction that if only the princes would stick together like the democrats—among whom he numbered Wagner, Semper, and Bülow—Wagner's music would never be performed anywhere. He now exploited mounting hostility toward Wagner's "luxurious" habits and attacked his presumption in wanting a theater of his own as well as the run of the royal exchequer.

The tolerant citizens of Munich had no immediate quarrel with

Wagner. They were inured to the vanities and vagaries of artists and traditionally cool toward bureaucrats. With a little tact and self-restraint, Wagner could have won and retained their favor. He could even have indulged with impunity in scenes like the one at Augsburg on August 24, when the stationmaster complained that his baggage was ten pounds overweight. Wagner called him a "stupid fellow" and was later fined twenty-five gulden, plus costs, for insulting a government official—at that time, a grave misdemeanor. The Bavarians merely laughed. Wagner paid his fine with the king's money, and the king was popular.

In the long run, however, conflict was unavoidable. Wagner and Bavaria were as incompatible as Lohengrin and Brabant. Carl Amery calls the Bavarians a tribe whom Kant and Hegel passed by. In other words, they have no eschatological or synoptic conception of history. Their approach to life is timeless, their religious faith devoid of chiliastic elements and expectations of salvation. The Bavarian conservative is nonplussed by "saviors of the people," not because they are left-wing, but because he simply fails to understand them. Wagner, with his eschatological fixation, his notions of redeeming and rejoicing the world, was bound to strike the Bavarians as alien. He wanted salvation, but they had no wish to be saved by him or anyone else.

To the locals, one of the most immediate and obvious grounds for annoyance was Wagner's "colony," to which uninvited outsiders also flocked. Everyone scented favoritism. Wagner made a mistake in recommending the appointment of Friedrich Schmitt, whom he knew from his days at Magdeburg, to train his new breed of singer-actors. Schmitt's German bel canto method proved inadequate, and Wagner found it hard—even though he hurled his beret at him during a rehearsal of *Tristan*—to get rid of the man.

Wagner's appointees did not find life a bed of roses, for he enveloped and devoured them like a ravenous reptile. A few independent spirits such as Peter Cornelius resisted his call to the last. On June 24, 1864, while still in Vienna, Cornelius confided to a friend: "I am to become a complete Kurwenal to him. Wagner fails to understand that I possess many qualifications for the role, down to and including doglike devotion, but that I also, unfortunately, have a trace of independence in my character and too much talent to be merely the zero after his one." Serfs, he added, did not write works like *Der Cid*. Having received the offer of a royal appointment in October, Cornelius vacillated until Christmas before accepting employment as "Wagner's friend." Then, enticed by assurances of important work in prospect, he submitted to the Wagnerian yoke. He arrived in Munich on December 30.

Rightly fearing the worst, Cornelius did not believe that the new arrangement would last. If he left his Karlstrasse lodgings and lunched with Wagner at two o'clock, he would still be at Brienner Strasse when darkness fell—nor could he voice his feelings because the master would have found them incomprehensible. His relations with Wagner could not be justified to the world at large, he wrote to Josef Standhartner on January 24, 1865. "Wagner has no idea how *tiring* he is. . . ."

Cornelius went on to give a graphic description of what he meant. "The other day we were at Frau von Bülow's! Wagner promptly picked up a copy of Schack's *Firdausi* and read a number of cantos from *Rustam and Suhrab*. By now, Bülow had finished his lesson. Before a dozen minutes were up, we were in the thick of *Tristan und Isolde*—the first act being sung in full. Meantime, tea was served. We had barely drunk half a cup before Wagner was deep in the story of *Parsifal*—and that continued throughout the evening until we broke up. Just think of the poor little Heintz girl, an extremely talented pupil of Bülow's from Berlin. She hears (a girl of sixteen or seventeen) *Tristan* for the first time—then the story of *Parsifal*—then Bülow gives her copies of *Die Meistersinger* and *Tristan* and she reads them till three or four in the morning, both libretti in succession, though luckily fourteen pages of *Die Meistersinger* are missing, which makes her task a little easier. Our great friend has to talk, read, and sing about *himself*, otherwise he feels out of sorts." In March, Cornelius sneaked off to Weimar to prepare for the first performance of *Der Cid*. He did not return till August, thereby missing the premiere of *Tristan* and widening the rift between himself and Wagner.

Wagner was now at liberty to make heavy demands on his contemporaries. He also enjoyed the devoted protection of a king and could look forward to the imminent fulfillment of his wishes, but was he happy? On the contrary, he seems to have been more than ever fearful that destiny might fell him with an avenging thunderbolt. On February 1, he worried the orchestra by standing perilously close to the edge of the podium. "Gentlemen," he declared, "I am used to standing on the brink of the abyss." Protestant interloper at a Catholic court, musical revolutionary, and pet aversion of powerful enemies, Ludwig Geyer's erstwhile "Cossack" and "brigand" was even closer to the abyss than he thought. The satirical magazine *Punsch* had already christened him "Herr Rumorhäuser." Now a Munich innkeeper coined yet another sobriquet for him: "Lolus," a play of words on Lola Montez, the adventuress who had cost Ludwig's grandfather his throne.

On February 6, Wagner had his first taste of the king's capricious side. That morning he was visited at Brienner Strasse by Cabinet Secretary Pfistermeister, who must have hurried straight back to his royal master. Instead of being admitted when he turned up for a prearranged audience at one o'clock, Wagner was dismissed and ushered down into the courtyard on the grounds that the king was displeased with him. There were two possible reasons for this rebuff. A note in the "Annals"—"*Mein Junge*" ["My boy"] —suggests that he had spoken with undue familiarity to the king's secretary—or even to the king himself—and that Pfistermeister had stirred things up. Another charge against him was that he had wrongfully demanded payment from the royal exchequer for a portrait of himself by Friedrich Pecht, having originally intended it as a gift to the king. Although he managed to dispel this misunderstanding, Ludwig's temporary absence from the theater gave rise to a rumor that Wagner was in disgrace. Every newspaper splashed the story, which was greeted with jubilation by a wide variety of mutually hostile cliques. Then, on February 14, 1865, Ludwig allayed Wagner's fears with a letter castigating "wretched, shortsighted people who can speak of disfavor, who have no idea, nor ever can have, of our love!"

On February 19, the Augsburg *Allgemeine Zeitung* advanced to the attack with an anonymous article entitled "Richard Wagner and Public Opinion." Its source, which soon leaked out, was Oskar von Redwitz, author of the narrative poem *Amaranth*, who had lived in Munich since 1861 and had temporarily served as a liberal member of parliament. The article sought to drive a wedge between Wagner and the king by accusing the former of extravagance and the latter—obliquely—of gullibility. It charged the "erstwhile man of the barricades" with abusing his privileged position. His pretensions to comfort in everyday life were "of so exquisitely sybaritic a nature that an Oriental potentate would not disdain to lodge at his abode in front of the Propyläen." Wagner was distinguished not only by ingratitude for the favor shown him but by an exaggerated opinion of himself. He and the friends he had summoned to Munich should modestly learn "not to come between Bavaria's people and her king by persisting in their brutal disregard for local conditions, which merit great esteem in musical as well as other respects."

It was sometimes hard to tell which Wagner aroused most hostility: the exrevolutionary, the monarchist, or the newcomer. The press attack was also directed at his "colony" and included Bülow, who at once issued a public counterblast in which he pronounced its author an "infamous calumniator." Wagner's response was temperate and discreet. He drew attention to the meritorious way in which Bavarian monarchs had traditionally summoned men of art, science, and letters to their courts, thereby turning Munich into an artistic metropolis. He felt entitled to regard himself as an artist who was being paid for his achievements. He aspired to be no more than that, and his relations with his gracious lord and king were of no other kind.

"You are acquainted with my reply," he wrote to Eliza Wille on February 26. "It is less than candid in one respect: its account of the limited nature of my relations with the king. For my own peace of mind, I wish it were so. The king's affection for me is marvelously profound and fatalistic. If, for my own tranquillity's sake, I renounce the rights this affection grants me, I still do not know how I can begin to justify it to my heart, my conscience, to evade the obligations it imposes on me." What was he driving at? What was the source of his anxiety? He had previously, on February 23, stated in a letter to Schott that "a strange quirk of fate" had burdened him with the destiny of "almost an entire nation, or certainly of a king."

He was referring to the rival factions which, having so far failed to discredit and eliminate him, were temporarily trying to court him and use his influence with the king to their advantage. Wagner had never wanted this to happen. We owe our first intimation of which party was involved—the house of Thurn and Taxis—to Julius Fröbel, a reliable political observer. Prince Maximilian Karl von Thurn und Taxis, who employed a widespread network of agents in the hope of carving out a kingdom for his eldest son comprising the Westphalian Rhineland and part of Belgium, was putting out feelers to the Bavarian court. Operating there on behalf of the house of Thurn and Taxis and a banking consortium was the diplomat Georg Klindworth, a notorious double agent of the pre-1848 period whom Wagner had met at Brussels and could not simply cold-shoulder in Munich. The plan was to get Klindworth appointed cabinet secretary with Wagner's assistance, for which the composer would be rewarded with shares in an agricultural bank. Klindworth paid several visits to Brienner Strasse, escorted at first by an aide to Prince Taxis, a Baron von Gruben of Regensburg, who suggested that Wagner might care to participate in one of the prince's financial ventures. Wagner feigned incomprehension. The two emissaries returned, this time with some bait in the form of Klindworth's "daughter" Agnes Street, who was on close terms with Liszt and other highly placed and influential men at various European courts. Klindworth made Wagner an outright offer of help if he prevailed on the king to replace Pfistermeister with himself.* "Again I remained obtuse," Wagner wrote to Mathilde Maier. "The Jesuits proposed to give me two festival theaters, two schools of art, villas, securities— anything I wanted—as long as I proved compliant." The king's aide-de-camp and intimate, Prince Paul von Thurn und Taxis, a youthful scion of the Regensburg house, learned of this diplomatic activity and warned Pfistermeister that attempts were being made to oust him. Pfistermeister underwent a sudden transformation. Remarkably accommodating all of a sudden, he now promised Wagner all the funds and credit he could wish. Temptations crowded in, almost suffocating Wagner with the dust stirred up by these backstage battles. "I am fearful in the depths of my soul, and I ask my daemon: 'Why this cup to me?' " he continued in his letter to Eliza Wille of February 26. "Why, when all I desire is peace and undisturbed leisure in which to work, should I be charged with responsibility for the welfare of a divinely endowed man, if not the welfare of an entire country?" He should swiftly have renounced this putative "responsibility" and retired from the arena if he wished to avoid disaster. Instead, he felt that his first move should be to assure himself of the king's devotion. Writing to Ludwig on March 9, 1865, he requested a vote of confidence. He could not, he said, find it in his heart to say, "My king, I bring you disquiet; let me go."* This echo of Tannhäuser in the Venusberg was followed by a simple question: "What shall I do?" On March 10, Ludwig sent him a temporizing reply: "I am obliged to inform my One and

Only that circumstances over which I have no present control—that the iron constraints of necessity—make it my sacred duty not to speak to you, at least for the present." There were signs that the dowager Queen Marie had intervened in person. Dissatisfied, Wagner wrote back on March 11: "Shall I go? Shall I stay? . . . One word, and I shall gladly accept my fate. But the decision must be taken, and today!" Ludwig replied before the day was out: "Dear Friend, *remain, remain* here, and all will be glorious as before. I am much occupied. Till death, your Ludwig." To which Wagner replied on March 12 that the story that he was to unveil *Tristan* to the world must now come true. "From the truest of hearts, with sweet tears. Loving you forever and beyond the grave, Richard Wagner."

Act 2: A Fleeting Dream

"There was a brief period when I truly thought I was dreaming: It was the time of the *Tristan* rehearsals," Wagner wrote to Mathilde Maier. "That was how it had to be someday: an artistic workshop, noble, spacious, free, and lavish in its whole design; a wonderful, heaven-sent pair of artists, intimately known and tenderly devoted to me, astonishingly talented. Like an enchanted dream, the work developed into an undreamed-of reality."

Ludwig Schnorr von Carolsfeld had already proved himself an exceptional Tannhäuser at a royal command performance in March. On March 31, encouraged by his experience of working with the singer, Wagner sent the king a "Report on a German Music School to be Founded in Munich." With Schnorr's assistance, he felt confident of realizing the new style of presentation he had originally conceived in Paris. From this aspect, his experiences while working on *Tristan* surpassed anything he had ever known. During rehearsals, Schnorr sculpted his portrayal of the title role in response to Wagner's whispers and gestures with such swiftness and assurance that the composer was soon reduced to silence; indeed, he was so moved by the third act that he could only avert his head. Once, when Tristan was lying on his sickbed on stage, Wagner bent down and told him quietly that, confronted by the ideal embodiment of his work, he had run out of praise to offer.

He and Schnorr became intimate friends and had no further need to confer on problems of interpretation.

The day of the first orchestral rehearsal—Baron von Perfall, the intendant, had introduced Hans von Bülow to the orchestra as its new conductor—coincided with the birth of Isolde, Cosima's first child by Wagner. Bülow, who was either unaware or pretended not to know that the baby was Wagner's, always acknowledged her as his own. Wagner owed his cuckolded friend the second of the musical miracles he experienced at this period: Bülow, who was so familiar with the score that he "knew every last fragment of it by heart," had assimilated Wagner's intentions "down to the most delicate nuance." He and Wagner were at one, and a feast of art and artistry beckoned. The miracle had its price, however, for Bülow knew even less of the local mentality than Wagner.

Although the people of Munich were good-natured enough to swallow many of the liberties taken by these artists and outsiders, condescension was another matter, and they could not abide being treated as stupid or inferior. On May 3, when the orchestra pit was to be enlarged by the removal of a row of stalls, the theater engineer, Penkmayr, objected to this loss of seating capacity. Bülow's tactless retort—"What does it matter if the stalls seat a couple of dozen *Schweinehunde* more or less?"—unleashed a storm of protest, and the press declared that his position in Munich had become untenable. Premier von der Pfordten advised the king to remove Wagner and Bülow from the capital for a considerable period once *Tristan* had been performed. On May 9, the *Neueste Nachrichten* published an apology by Bülow to the effect that he had been referring only to those theatergoers who were suspected of having plotted against "the honored master" and vilified him by word of mouth and in writing. This the *Neuer Bayerischer Courier* dismissed as inadequate. For four successive days, it carried the stock announcement "Hans v. Bülow is still here!" in letters of increasing size. Wagner himself was finally obliged to issue a public plea, at one of the last rehearsals, that everyone should consign recent events to oblivion and concentrate on the matter at hand, not on personalities.

The dress rehearsal, which took place on May 11 before an invited audience of six hundred, went without a hitch. The impossible had been accomplished.

On May 15, the day appointed for the premiere, Wagner's enemies struck. Bailiffs descended on Brienner Strasse with the promissory note he had given Madame Salis-Schwabe, whom Malwida von Meysenbug had persuaded to help defray the cost of his Paris concerts in 1860. Dr. von Schauss, her legal representative in Munich, had already warned him by letter on March 20 that failure to settle his debt might interfere with the production of his "grandiose opera," but he had cast this unvarnished threat to the winds. Now, the provisional distraint on his personal effects could be lifted only by emergency help from the royal exchequer, which promptly shelled out 2,400 gulden. That afternoon Malvina Schnorr, his Isolde, went hoarse and was unable to sing. The premiere had to be canceled. Crowds gathered in front of the notices outside the theater, and the city buzzed with rumors. Was the work unperformable after all? *Punsch* published a series of caricatures, and the Münchner Volkstheater rehearsed *Tristanderl und Süssholde,* a skit on the "opera of the future."

Some of the friends who had assembled in Munich—Klindworth from London, Gaspérini from Paris, Porges, Uhl, Draesecke, Damrosch, Pohl, and Kalliwoda—had to go home. Others returned when the Schnorrs came back from a spell of relaxation at Bad Reichenhall, where Malvina regained her voice. On May 22, *Der Landbote* reported: "Röckel, Herr von Beust's last May prisoner, has been in Munich for some days at Richard Wagner's request. Yet another man of the barricades!" Georg Herwegh, whom Wagner had specially invited, stayed away, as did Semper, Liszt, the Willes, and the Wesendoncks. When the curtain finally rose on June 10, the audience included ex-King Otto of Greece, the pianist Anton Rubinstein, and Wagner's brother Albert. Many members of the public who had waited in line for cheap seats were turned away at the door for fear of demonstrations against Bülow.

Brussels lace and satin muffs were much in evidence. Aristocratic ladies wore crinolines and fringed silk jackets. Cosima turned up with a wreath of pink rosebuds on her head. The twenty-two-year-old king appeared in his box at six o'clock, an imposing figure despite his civilian clothes. Tall and slender, with his grave face framed by dark, wavy hair, he was generally considered by the ladies to be "devilishly handsome." During the fanfares and cheers his dark-blue eyes gazed into space, heedless of the subjects whose love he never truly returned. On May 22, he had chosen *Tristan* to be the name of the steam yacht in which he sailed the narrow waters of the Starnberger See.

It was a memorable moment in the history of music, and one that was favored by fortune. There was no uproar, no first-night fiasco. The audience not only listened but preserved a portentous hush during intermissions—a tribute both to the musicians and singers who did *Tristan* justice and to those who were hearing it for the first time. Wagner himself said to Cosima on March 26, 1879, that people would come to think it a remarkable era when such works could be presented to the public. At eleven o'clock it was all over. Tumultuous applause drowned a scattering of hisses from those who were critical of Wagner's music or ill-disposed toward him personally. Hand in hand with the composer, who looked pale and exhausted, the singers stood on stage and wept.

Edouard Schuré, who helped to popularize Wagner's work in France, was studying in Munich at the time. Like many connoisseurs and confreres, he was dumbfounded not only by *Tristan* but by Wagner's adamantine faith in himself; the composer, he said, reminded one of Faust and Mephisto in turn. The Bavarian newspapers—to be fair to them—wrote respectfully and grandiloquently of the "profound solemnity," "noble endeavor," and "immense creative power" evinced by Wagner's work. In short, they were better at sensing the opera's epoch-making significance than defining it. Many foreign critics spoke of "dissonance" and "indecency." Eduard Schelle passed the following judgment: "The poem is in every respect an absurdity; the music, with the exception of a few passages, a subtle brew concocted by a dissipated, morbid imagination." Leipzig's *Allgemeine Musikalische Zeitung* declared on July 5, 1865, that Wagner had paid tribute to Gottfried von Strassburg's "lubricious French outlook on life," disclosing "the glorification of sensual pleasure, with all its titillating devices." He was guilty of "the most deplorable materialism" and his music had become "a color-grinder for immoral painting."

The second performance achieved an even greater success, for "Parsifal, too, is one of us," as Wagner remarked to the Schnorrs. By Parsifal he meant the king, who traveled to Munich by special train for the occasion. His ministers, being glad to get hold of him, took advantage of the intermissions to confer on affairs of state. At the third performance on June 19, which was attended by Anton Bruckner, Wagner's conception of the work was so fully and triumphantly realized that he half-seriously proclaimed, "Never again!" It seemed to him too perfect to repeat. In fact, the king requested a fourth performance on July 1, together with a private hearing of pieces from nearly all his idol's music dramas including *Das Rheingold* and *Die Meistersinger.* The cast then dispersed, among them Anton Mitterwurzer, who had sung Kurwenal. Wagner said an almost casual good-bye to Schnorr in the street. Both men hoped to meet again soon, and both were filled with a joyous sense of achievement.

"That was the climax," Wagner wrote to Mathilde Maier. "From then on, all was unadulterated anguish."

Act 3: Paradise Lost

After a turbulent first act and an idyllic centerpiece illumined by the gentle flicker of summer lightning, the final act of the Munich farce unfolded. While attention was focused on the alarums and excursions on stage, a messenger arrived with sad and shocking news: Ludwig Schnorr von Carolsfeld had died of a lightning fever at Dresden on June 21.*

His death blighted many of Wagner's hopes. Paradoxically, it coincided to the very day with the royal command that closed down the old Munich Conservatoire, sent its staff packing, and paved the way for Wagner's new music school. Wagner and Bülow set off for Dresden as soon as they heard the news of Schnorr's death but were two hours too late to attend his funeral. They returned via Prague the same night.

Wagner seemed suddenly to have aged. While walking with Edouard Schuré in Munich's public park, the Englischer Garten, he talked incessantly of Haydn, Calderón, Shakespeare, and himself, referred to Berlioz with admiration, and complained that death was hemming him in on every side—stalking his most loyal supporters. Dr. Lapommeraie, one of his Parisian devotees, had recently been guillotined for poisoning his mistress. "They all come to a bad end," he concluded darkly.

Early in August, accompanied by her husband but not by her children, Cosima went to Hungary to attend a performance of her father's oratorio *The Legend of St. Elizabeth.* Wagner was annoyed because he felt sure that Liszt would make another attempt to separate them, and that Cosima would return as browbeaten as she had from Karlsruhe the year before. And so it went on. He sought relaxation at a hunting lodge on the Hochkopf, overlooking the Walchensee, a retreat placed at his disposal by the king, but the main result of this rather imprudent foray into the mountains with Franz Mrazeck was a feverish cold that left him feeling worse than before. On August 10, the day after he got to the lodge, he began making entries in the *Brown Book*, the leather-bound diary in which he communed from afar with Cosima as he had once done at Venice with Mathilde Wesendonck. "We must never part again, do you hear?" he insisted. The *Brown Book* discloses what a strange double life his beloved was leading—pledged to him but sustaining her pseudomarriage to Bülow. She now proved herself a difficult and demanding mistress, and was not slow to heap reproaches on his head. His diary reveals that a jealous missive had reached him on August 18. "And now poor M[athilde] M[aier] has to catch it again: God, what designs on her I'm supposed to have—yes, the way I'm supposed to have kept company with her—what endearments I squander on her!" Cosima was not quite as wide of the mark as he implied, but later on August 18 he wrote: "O Cosima, you're the soul of my life! Utterly and completely!"

On returning to Munich, Cosima ran Wagner's house and her own, looked after her children, entertained her friends, and acted as her new lord and master's minister plenipotentiary—his secretariat. Cornelius saw more clearly than most how Wagner abdicated one sphere of responsibility after another in her favor. Although the couple kept their relationship a secret, little escaped the notice of their tactful friends.

"Wagner is wholly and absolutely under her influence," wrote Cornelius. "With or without children she is . . . daily at his house. One can no longer speak to him alone. Every letter that arrives for him she opens and reads aloud." Was she an Amazon intent on seizing power? That would be too facile a picture of the situation. Cosima yearned to sacrifice herself to a worthwhile cause. In entering Wagner's service, she assumed the burdens of a regency that Wagner voluntarily, if precipitately, relinquished to her. She dealt with the king on his behalf. Her true status can be inferred from Wagner's few extant letters to her. They differ in tone from all his missives to other women—his companionable familiarities to Minna, his romantic ballads to Mathilde Wesendonck, his artless courtesies and confidences to Mathilde Maier. Here, from the very first, we detect a conspiratorial note, a joining of hands for all eternity.

Cosima had the strength to withstand the rigors of this double life. She now spent less time at home than at Wagner's house on Brienner Strasse, where a study and a living room were set aside for her use. Arriving at midday, she would stay until late at night —a white-gowned figure stretched out exhausted on the sofa, dreaming and muttering in her sleep—while her husband was working at the theater or teaching his pupils. The atmosphere between the Bülows was extremely tense. Wagner not only heard tell of Bülow's violent outbursts but was dismayed to witness them in person. Reviewing this period, Cosima noted in her diary on July 11, 1869: "He [Richard] recalls scenes, at which he was present, when Hans struck me, and says he was horrified at the serene indifference with which I endured this." It is clear that her marriage to Bülow was an utter disaster. After escaping from her governesses in Paris, she had plunged into matrimony with someone of unstable temperament and constitution. Liszt's illegitimate daughter acquired a noble name and became a baroness, but at the cost of tying herself to a moody, irascible man who should never have married at all. She could have tolerated Bülow's moods had he been her superior in every respect; but he, in his turn, was merely the servant of a master who had long ruled her heart.

Wagner was alive to the cyclical nature of life. Music expressed a similar tendency toward repetition, he confided to his *Brown Book*. The ordinary person's life took the form of a canon; his own he compared to a fugue whose indeterminable course would end in death. He and Cosima were living "in a Bach double fugue." This renewed preoccupation with Bach suggested a definition of the German spirit which he committed to a journal kept for Ludwig II between September 14 and 27, 1865, but not published until 1878, when excerpts from it appeared in expanded form under the title *What Is German?* Bach, he declared, was an aid to understanding the German spirit in that the latter manifested itself wherever beauty and nobility came into being without an eye to profit. His journal for the king, be it noted, was as much a mixture of the right and the true, the suspect and the erroneous, as his treatises on art in the 1850s. He recommended the establishment of a political newspaper to be edited by Heinrich Porges and Dr. Franz Grandauer. The barriers between people and princes were to be dismantled in every sphere of life. The Germans were menaced by two dangers: oppression by a military caste, and international isolation resulting from "a system of national arming" against the rest of Europe. Prophetically, Wagner went on: "I have no hesitation in regarding the maintenance of huge standing armies, which have become the paramount interest of the ruling dynasties, as a conceivable and possible reason for the downfall of the monarchies in time to come." In accordance with his plan for a military system on the Swiss pattern—originally Röckel's idea!—Wagner envisaged that the monarch and his citizen army or militia would hold grand public musters "on the Lechfeld, for example, in a Frankish plain." One would have to be blind not to recognize a distorted reflection of this idea in the Nazi rallies of our own century; but then, all manner of things can be distilled from the writings of this conservative anarchist who perceived no fundamental difference between left and right, revolution and royalism. He even went so far as to suggest that Ludwig form a people's militia, place himself at the head of the German Movement, and get himself elected emperor.

All this constituted active intervention in politics. Peter Cornelius, who seemed to sense this, saw it as the beginning of the end and, in his letters, likened Wagner to a "Marquis Posa" [a character in Schiller's *Don Carlos*]. To make matters worse, Ludwig had Wagner's outline proposals copied and submitted them to his ministries "for implementation." This may have been what led to the "break with Pfistermeister" referred to in the "Annals" on October 11, for the cabinet secretary and Premier von der Pfordten were pursuing a policy of mediation between Prussia and Austria. Their only real opponent was Max von Neumayr, the Minister of the Interior, but his liberal stance inside the cabinet had already been shaken by some rioting at Munich on October 8 and 9.

Where cultural policy was concerned, Wagner wanted to bring about a substantial reduction in Pfistermeister's influence by engineering the appointment of an intendant to control every aspect of the court's sponsorship of the arts. He wrote Ludwig a letter deploring Munich's cultural status quo and requesting long-term financial security for himself. In the latter regard, he asked for a life tenancy in the sum of 200,000 gulden, of which 40,000 were to be administered by himself and the remaining 160,000 invested for him at 5 percent interest by the royal exchequer. This correspondence, which dragged on into October, was conducted by Cosima with Pfistermeister and Secretary Johann Lutz, an appeals court judge. Wagner was eventually granted an annual salary of 8,000 gulden—precisely what he had asked for—but not a guaranteed life interest in the capital sum referred to above. He also got his 40,000 gulden in cash. When Cosima went to collect this on October 20, treasury officials informed her that no paper money was available, only silver coin. After some hesitation, she decided to take all 40,000 gulden in silver. The bags were loaded into two hackney cabs and escorted to Brienner Strasse by government officials. This incident, coupled with rumors of Wagner's affair with his conductor's wife, helped to undermine his public reputation still further.

Half of the 40,000 gulden he spent within four months. However inexplicable this may sound, his "profligacy" seems in retrospect to have been a simple and transparent form of displacement activity. Whenever his personal relationships were at their frailest and most insecure—at Paris, Penzing, and Munich, in that order—he surrounded himself with the plumpest possible cushions swathed in plush, velvet, and silk. Society at large saw only the grotesque side: a parvenu losing his sense of proportion and yielding to the pride that precedes a fall.

November 1865 brought a last emotional climax. After touring Switzerland incognito at the end of October, Ludwig invited Wagner to Schloss Hohenschwangau, where a bedroom and music room had been specially prepared for him. His week there—from November 11 to 18—was one long round of celebration, though Ludwig did confess that his dreams were occasionally haunted by premonitions of farewell. On the morning of Sunday, November 12, Wagner roused his royal host with a musical offering performed by ten bandsmen posted on the turrets of the castle. At seven o'clock precisely, they launched into the reveille from the second act of *Lohengrin*. Ludwig greeted his guest each morning with a few lines of verse on a slip of paper. Wagner's manservant, Franz Mrazeck, was astounded by their intimate tone and bemused by the sight of his master driving with the king in a four-horse carriage, complete with outriders. He began to wonder if he were dreaming—if he himself had become a member of the royal entourage. Wagner inscribed professions of love for Cosima in the *Brown Book*, together with an injunction to "Pray for poor Hans!" He also read Ludwig the opening pages of his memoirs. The king was beside himself with joy. "I am in heaven!" he wrote to Cosima, whom he regarded as a species of secretary to his new cultural cabinet, but not as Wagner's mistress.

At some stage, conversation at the castle turned to politics. Wagner maligned Pfistermeister to Ludwig for having spoken ill of him to Julius Fröbel and questioned his future value to Munich. He was hurt and surprised when, despite his complaints, the king engaged too long in conferring with court officials to invite him to join the royal table. Inevitably, the visiting cabinet secretaries came into contact with Wagner, and the talks he had with them sowed the seeds of a fatal temptation: He resolved on an attempt to overthrow the government.

As he informed his confidant in a subsequent intrigue, Dr. Oscar von Schanzenbach, on January 17, 1867, his decision was prompted by a conversation at Hohenschwangau with Cabinet Secretary Lutz. In the hope of securing Wagner's cooperation, Lutz had explained the government's policy as being "that, since it could not depend on Austria and wanted even less to do with a German parliament, it was pursuing the idea of an accord with Bismarck and the new Prussian tendency, with the object of restoring the Bavarian constitution to its pre-1818 form." Wagner naturally repudiated this policy, but it was his interview with Lutz that finally encouraged him to throw caution to the winds and urge Ludwig to appoint a new cabinet: "Pfi" and "Pfo," as he called his pet aversions Pfistermeister and Pfordten, must this time be ousted at a stroke.

Ludwig made Wagner a farewell present of a watch with a picture of Lohengrin inside the lid. He consoled himself for Wagner's departure with a special treat: his aide-de-camp, Prince Paul von Taxis, reenacted the operatic hero's arrival. Attired as Lohengrin and drawn by an ingeniously constructed and illuminated swan, he glided across the lake to the strains of *Lohengrin* music performed by some royal musicians. Ludwig was so enchanted by this piece of nonsense that it was repeated the following night. He even wrote to Wagner seeking detailed information about an authentic Lohengrin costume, but his inquiry remained unanswered in the ensuing uproar. Wagner's proposals were meanwhile being scrutinized by senior government officials.

All hell had broken loose by the time he returned to Munich. Cosima promptly reported to the king that journalists had resumed their malicious campaign against his protégé. The *Neuer Bayerischer Courier* wrote: "In view of his insatiable appetite, the least of the evils visited on our country by this outsider can be likened only to swarms of locusts that darken the sun for months on end. But this fearful picture of a national scourge from Pharaonic times is as nothing to the mischief wrought by this boundlessly conceited person when he is enabled to practice the politics of the future instead of the music of the future. . . . The paid music maker, the barricade-man of Dresden who once aspired to blow up the royal palace at Dresden at the head of a gang of murderous arsonists, now intends gradually to estrange the king from his loyal henchmen, replace them with men of his own political complexion, isolate the king and exploit him in the interests of the treasonable idea espoused by an indefatigable party of subversion."

Wagner responded by urging Ludwig to remodel his cabinet— as though the replacement of Secretary Pfistermeister and State Treasurer Hofmann would have achieved anything—and implied that he was dealing with a Mime and a Fafner whom it was his duty, as an incarnation of Siegfried, to destroy. Ludwig seemed to agree with him. "Rejoice!" he replied. "I must get a new secretary at all costs; I spurn the impotence of Mime and Fafner. The Dragon will rear up and succumb with a whimper." In the sober light of official routine, however, the picture looked quite different. After careful consideration, Ludwig left everything as it was. The persons concerned, who had naturally discovered what was afoot, hit back with a deliberately provocative article in the *Volksbote* on November 26. Pfistermeister and Hofmann, it stated, were to be "set aside in order that certain hankerings after the exploitation of the royal exchequer may be readily satisfied."

Wagner then made a crucial mistake. In a letter dated November 27, he vigorously urged the king as follows: "Immediate dismissal of Pfistermeister and simultaneous appointment of Neumayr to form a new cabinet." In other words, Pfordten was to be replaced by the liberal minister of the interior who had previously been ousted from the cabinet. "But, my king, be swift and resolute!" Cornelius, a reliable observer, knew something else: Wagner had taken Dr. Grandauer into his confidence, and Grandauer had recommended a friend, Emil Riedel, to succeed Pfistermeister. Wagner had mentioned Riedel's name to the king at Hohenschwangau, and Ludwig, in turn, had been ingenuous enough to mention it to Pfistermeister himself. This meant that Pfi and Pfo already knew their potential successors, and Pfi and Pfo knew how to fight back. In the event, Riedel declined the post of cabinet secretary because he had no wish to be regarded as Wagner's creature. Grandauer, too, backed out, and the plan burst like the soap bubble it was.

On November 27, the king informed Wagner that the time was not yet ripe to dismiss Pfistermeister and the other members of his cabinet. "I say this most positively," he added. "I have my own good reasons, believe me." On the following day, Cosima saw to it that an article signed "fr" was delivered to the editorial offices of the *Neueste Nachrichten*. This anonymous piece, which appeared in its 333rd issue on November 29, defended Wagner and advised the king to deliver himself from burdensome anxieties "by removing two or three persons who enjoy not the smallest esteem among the Bavarian people." Cornelius detected Cosima's hand in this disastrous article, and few were in doubt about its authorship. In fact, a draft of it still exists in Wagner's own handwriting.

Premier von der Pfordten, resolutely seizing the initiative, made it plain to the king that public indignation might sweep him from the throne as it had once deposed his grandfather. Writing to Ludwig on December 1, he said: "Your Majesty stands at a fateful parting of the ways, and must choose between the love and esteem of your loyal subjects and the 'friendship' of Richard Wagner." The latter was "despised by every section of the community . . . despised . . . for his ingratitude and treachery toward benefactors and friends, for his overweening and vicious luxury and extravagance, and for the shameless way in which he exploits Your Majesty's undeserved favor." Talebearers can expect no gratitude, so Pfordten eventually received his comeuppance. Meantime, Ludwig continued to pine for his favorite. "Be of good cheer," he wrote on December 3. "Your Friend will never desert you."

Ludwig arrived in Munich on December 5, and his ministers

met the next morning. On each of these days, the king took counsel at greater length than he had ever done in the previous course of his reign. He conferred with his mother, who was firmly opposed to Wagner; with his great-uncle Prince Karl, who stressed the danger of a revolution; with the archbishop of Munich; and with academics and representatives of the nobility. All his relatives, advisers, civil servants, and ecclesiastical dignitaries cast their votes against Wagner. A committee had collected nearly four thousand signatures on a petition to the king from the citizens of Munich—butchers, bakers, and purveyors to the court who scarcely knew what all the fuss was about. Even Dr. Gietl, Ludwig's personal physician, added his drop to the bucket. When he confirmed that the Bavarian people were losing faith in their sovereign because it was feared that Wagner might gain influence over him "in other matters too," the king conceded that Wagner had indeed "taken certain liberties." A mirage was dissolving, an illusion fading. For a moment Ludwig saw things as they really were. "Feel my pulse," he told Gietl, "—see how shocked I am." When his cabinet threatened to resign, he wrote to Pfordten: "I have reached a decision. R. Wagner must leave Bavaria."

Ludwig acted swiftly. He instructed Lutz, the second cabinet secretary, to call on Wagner that evening and communicate his decision by word of mouth. Wagner turned pale, then vented his wrath on Pfistermeister and called him an abominable schemer. "Control yourself," Lutz is said to have retorted. "I am here in an official capacity."

Next morning Wagner had it in writing: "Much as it grieves me, I must ask you to comply with the request I conveyed to you yesterday through my secretary." That evening he read a newspaper report to the same effect. For two days and nights he conducted a correspondence with the king in which he vainly sought a public repudiation of the misleading facts and figures broadcast by his detractors. Though privately of the opinion that Ludwig had lost his head, Wagner refrained from turning on him. He preferred to maintain an appearance of friendship, partly to avoid weakening the king's position still further, and partly, no doubt, to preserve his annual stipend of 8,000 gulden.

Shortly after five o'clock on the morning of December 10, he drove to the station accompanied only by Franz Mrazeck and his dog Pohl. He looked pale and wraithlike—gray as the hair on his head. After saying good-bye to Porges and Cornelius on the plat-form, he spoke in a low voice to Cosima, who had also come to see him off. "Silence" was the only word that could be distinguished. When the train pulled out, Cornelius felt as if a vision had faded. Cosima was completely shattered. Instead of going home, she went to the house on Brienner Strasse.

Between Munich and Tribschen

Deaths and Burials

Expelled with courteous apologies and exiled on full pay. . . . It is hard to gauge precisely how depressed Wagner was by this peculiar form of disgrace. Ludwig held out the possibility of rehabilitation for months until his banished favorite lost all desire to return. On December 23, Wagner moved into Aux Artichauts, a two-story country house near Geneva whose comparative discomfort was only partly offset by a distant view of Mont Blanc. Here he proposed to resume work on *Die Meistersinger von Nürnberg.*

Although the press was still making capital out of recent events in Munich, Wagner's ignorance of the relative strength or weakness of his position deterred him from replying in kind. The progressives had engaged in fruitless petitions on his behalf, protested against his removal, and lectured the king on the quality of his advisers. In January, Herwegh published a satirical poem about the people of Munich—long rather than good—in which he derided the savage Bavarian, with his beer-cellar mentality, for failing to recognize the musician of the future. The musician himself was debarred from giving tongue because he had no wish to place the king in a position that might jeopardize his own plans. Ludwig had already broached the idea of abdicating, and a king without a country would have been useless to an artist without money.

Back in Munich, gossip centered not only on Cosima, the "carrier pigeon," but also on poor Minna, whose venomous letters Wagner had ceased to read since early in 1865. The *Volksbote* reported that Wagner had left his wife to starve in penury while he himself wallowed in luxury. It even produced an anonymous "witness" to testify that Frau Wagner had been compelled to seek assistance from the Dresden poor law authorities. Dr. Pusinelli prevailed on the said authorities to rebut this allegation, and Minna herself sent the editor of the *Volksbote* a similar rebuttal written in her own shaky hand—a last pathetic token of love and gratitude. Two weeks after these excitements, on January 25, 1866, she died of a heart attack.

Wagner heard the news at Marseille, whither he had gone via Lyon, Toulon, and Hyères, still on the lookout for a new abode, after a fire at Aux Artichauts had precipitated his intention of moving on. Minna's death left him mute and dazed. He did not go to Dresden for the funeral, merely asked Pusinelli to make the necessary arrangements. All he requested from his wife's estate were his letters to her, some of which were withheld.

Returning to Geneva on January 29, he was told that his old dog Pohl had also died and been buried in the garden by the tenant of the house. In a paroxysm of grief, he dug the animal up, put a collar around its neck, wrapped it in its blanket, and reburied it in a nearby copse overlooking the lake. The stony, silent stupor induced in him by the news of Minna's death had found release in this frenzied outpouring of emotion—this ritual interment of the past.

Then he resumed work on *Die Meistersinger*. On February 20, he wrote to Bülow: "I wish the king would present me with one of the Schloss Bayreuth pavilions as a retreat; Nürnberg close at hand, Germany all around me." It was his first allusion to Bayreuth before dictating his recollections of 1835 to Cosima. Next day, he completed the orchestral sketch of the first act of *Die Meistersinger*, with its multivoiced finale. Cosima saluted him as follows: "Hail to Nürnberg's beloved Sachs. David." They soon devised some new telegraphic code names. His was "Will" and hers "Vorstel," an abbreviation of the last word in the title of Schopenhauer's magnum opus. Cosima had now taken over all the female roles in his life, those of "Eva" Maier and "Isolde" Wesendonck included. On March 8, 1866, she and her five-year-old daughter Daniela set off for Geneva and her first experience of Wagner's company uninhibited by the presence of her husband, who was away on a concert tour. Earthly love became united with celestial: The two forms of paradise were one at last, and Parnassus lay ahead.

The House beside the Lake

Taking little Daniela with them, Cosima and Wagner traveled to Lucerne by way of Lausanne and Interlaken. They arrived there on March 30. "The term is up, and yet again have passed another seven years!" It was seven years, almost to the day, since Wagner had booked into the Hotel Schweizerhof on returning from Venice. Another cycle in his eventful life was complete. It was Good Friday when he and Cosima crossed the Lake of Lucerne to the Rütli and first caught sight of Tribschen, a house on a promontory south of the town. Here in the solitude of this headland on the open side of the lake, with a view of the mighty mountains opposite, they felt they could live in peace.

While Cosima returned to the Bavarian capital, Wagner concluded a tenancy agreement with Lieutenant Colonel Walter Amrhyn, Tribschen's owner. "All I am counting on," he wrote to both the Bülows, "is that you should occupy it with me for as long as possible." On April 10, the king instructed Lutz to send Wagner 5,000 francs, a year's rent, and on April 15, 1866, Wagner moved in —once again, "for good."

He christened his new home "Triebschen," from *angetriebenes Land* ["jetsam land," or land formed by silt], a version adopted by Wagnerites although the name of the property and headland was originally spelled "Tripschen." Situated on a gentle rise, flanked by trees and easily visible from the lake, the house was of square design but pleasing proportions, with three floors and a lofty roof. A rowboat lay moored below it on the lake, whose waters were seldom disturbed by more than a ripple, starlings congregated in the trees, and cows grazed the meadows behind the house. Wagner was so determined to leave his bones there that he made preparations for his demise—much to the distress of Verena Weitmann, who had faithfully followed him to Lucerne from Munich.

His lonely walks and bouts of self-pity were of short duration. Cosima joined him on May 12, this time accompanied by all three daughters: Daniela, Blandine, and Isolde. Wagner met them at Romanshorn. Three days later he started to compose the second act of *Die Meistersinger*, with its rapturous midsummer atmosphere, and soon came to Sachs's evocation of the scent of lilac [*Flieder*], which gently relaxes a man's limbs and brings words thronging to his lips. Even if lilac had existed in Germany in Sachs's day, which it did not, it would certainly not have blossomed on Midsummer's Eve. Are we to assume that Wagner blundered twice over? Not at all. By *Flieder*, he meant the common elder [more properly *Holunder*, which does not lend itself to use in a rhyming libretto], and elder was an aphrodisiac, seductive as the music of an act that enchants, excites, and culminates in a brilliant musical curiosity: the cudgel scene, whose tumult is curbed and disciplined by its strict fugato structure.

On May 15, the day when Wagner embarked on this second act, he received a telegram from Ludwig reiterating his desire to abdicate. He would, he said, be happy to retire to Switzerland as a private citizen, provided always that he could live at the Dear One's side. Wagner was horrified—what good to him would Ludwig be in Switzerland? In reply, he urged the king to be patient and devote himself to affairs of state. Ludwig, however, was not so easily dissuaded. On the morning of May 22, Wagner's fifty-third birthday, he left Munich secretly, caught the Lindau express at Biessenhofen, and crossed the lake by steamer to Romanshorn. Before the day was out he presented himself at Wagner's door, where he gave his name as Walther von Stolzing. It was a blissful reunion—novel, too, in that Sachs was playing host to Ludwig the German. The king slept downstairs, never far from the side of his aide and personal friend, Paul von Taxis, who was by now on the same sort of terms with Wagner and Cosima as his master. The puzzled citizens of Munich thought their sovereign had absconded. While the members of the German Confederation prepared to make war on each other, Ludwig went off on a family outing to Alpnach and Stans with Wagner and Baroness von Bülow. Then, escorted by his aide-de-camp, he returned to Schloss Berg—not forgetting, while still en route for home, to send the Glorious One an exultant telegram: "Fortified by our happy time together, firmly resolved to tear up the weed by the roots." By this time, Wagner himself had ceased to believe in such nonsense. Ludwig's escapade brought him to the brink of disaster for a second time. In view of the tense political situation, the fact that he had gone off to stay with the "debt contractor" caused widespread public anger.

Immediately after the royal visit to Tribschen, the Munich press came out with its first overt reference to the relations between "Madame Hs. de Bülow" and "her 'friend' (or what?)." Bülow characteristically challenged the *Volksbote* editor, Dr. Zander, to a duel, but the bearer of his challenge, who turned up armed with a riding crop, was shown the door. Bülow thereupon made matters worse by publishing a scornful tirade in the *Neueste Nachrichten*. Shuttling between Tribschen, Zurich, and Munich, the Bülows eventually requested the king himself to write Bülow a personal letter repudiating press attacks on the integrity of all concerned.

It should here be pointed out that Cosima's influence over Ludwig had grown by leaps and bounds since Wagner's departure. She was the recipient and transmitter of official communications from the court and handled all financial problems arising between Wagner and the exchequer. She also recommended appointments and dismissals. All this she did in what was, for a woman of her time, an unusually direct and self-assured tone—a tone, moreover, that was shrewdly attuned to the king's transsexual proclivities. The compliance or uncertainty it induced in him was such that he ultimately lent himself to a fraud of unparalleled effrontery.

Meanwhile, on June 6, Bülow submitted his resignation. From behind the scenes, Wagner drafted a letter which the king was to send Bülow as an earnest of his faith in the irreproachable conduct of the conductor's wife and friend. Ludwig, who took several days to make up his mind, received a heartrending appeal from Cosima. "I fall on my knees before my king and beg, in humility and distress, for the letter to my husband," she wrote on June 7. "My royal Lord, I have three children to whom it is my duty to transmit their father's honorable name untarnished. For the sake of these children, so that they may not someday despise my love for the friend [Wagner], I beseech you, my most exalted friend, to write the letter." On June 8, Ludwig telegraphed the following assurance to the Hotel Baur au Lac in Zurich: "Parsifal will not desert his own."

He duly signed the letter and sent it off. The crucial passage in this profession of faith, which Bülow published in two newspapers on June 19, read: "Being acquainted with your disinterested and most honorable conduct, as well as with your incomparable artistic achievements in regard to the musical public of Munich; and having furthermore been enabled to acquire the most thorough knowledge of the noble and magnanimous character of your esteemed wife, who has sympathetically assisted her father's friend and her husband's exemplar [i.e. Wagner], it remains for Me to inquire into the inexplicable nature of those criminal public calumnies, in order that, having attained a clear insight into such outrageous goings-on, I may ensure that justice is meted out to the culprits with ruthless severity." Aside from the use of capital initials for all personal pronouns, Wagner's draft had been left unaltered. Cornelius and his friends were too familiar with the style to be in any doubt as to who had guided the royal pen. Although this suspicion was widespread, to have questioned the king's statement in any way would have been tantamount to lese majesty. Ludwig had innocently but publicly perjured himself, and Zander was fined by a Munich court.

From that point on, however, the fire continued to smolder until it burst into flames at Tribschen later that summer. By this time, Cosima was pregnant with another child whose paternity could hardly have been a secret from her husband. The violent quarrels that ensued between Wagner and Bülow drove the latter to the verge of a nervous breakdown but did not detract from his admiration for Wagner as an artist, nor for what he had already written of *Die Meistersinger*.

On September 15, Bülow went into self-imposed exile at Basel, and on September 28, Cosima returned to Tribschen. Wagner was just composing the music for the Prize Song. On October 30, on the recommendation of Heinrich Esser and Joseph Hellmesberger, he engaged the young Viennese horn player and conductor, Hans Richter, as his secretary and copyist. By then, in addition to Richter, the Tribschen household numbered no less than twelve: Wagner and Cosima; Daniela, Blandine, and Isolde; Agnes the governess and a children's nurse; the housekeeper, Verena Weitmann, who added to the list in January 1867 by marrying Jakob Stocker from the Schweizerhof at Lucerne; the menservants Peter Steffen and Jost; Marie the parlormaid; and a French cook.

The *Meistersinger* idyll had scarcely attained a degree of stability when a storm blew up. On November 10, 1866, Ludwig Schnorr's widow appeared at Tribschen with a pupil named Isidore von Reutter. Malvina Schnorr, who on Wagner's recommendation had been granted an annuity by the king and appointed to the new school of music at Munich, came bearing sensational tidings from the spirit world. Fräulein von Reutter, a charlatan of guardsman-like physique and low intelligence, laid claim to mediumistic powers. According to nocturnal messages received from the late Ludwig Schnorr, she, Isidore, was the predestined bride of King Ludwig while Malvina was to marry Wagner. Alarmed by the amorous glances of Malvina, whom he had imprudently addressed as *"du"* during rehearsals for *Tristan,* and whom he now recognized as a hysteric of the first order, Wagner fought hard to remain calm and composed while at table with his two unwelcome visitors. The disembodied Schnorr had further ordained, so Wagner was informed, that his future compositions must be less vocally demanding—from the widowed Malvina's point of view, a singularly convenient request!

As soon as the ladies had returned to their hotel, Wagner gave orders that Fräulein von Reutter was never to be admitted to his house again. According to a record of her supernatural visitations, which she left behind at Tribschen, he was to sow the seeds of love for her in Ludwig's heart. As for Malvina, she persisted in her efforts to convince Wagner of her mission; indeed, she became so importunate during the next few days that he was compelled to warn her off by letter. She then returned to Munich and complained of the Wagner-Cosima relationship to the king—she had, after all, seen Cosima playing mistress of Tribschen in an advanced state of pregnancy. Wagner had no recourse but to petition for Malvina's immediate expulsion from Bavaria.

Ludwig proved strangely dilatory. Late in the following year, 1867, we find him venting his annoyance in writing to Düfflipp, his new court secretary: "I have become thoroughly disgusted with the everlasting wrangles and complaints of Wagner, Bülow, Porges, Fröbel, and the rest. I have been so lenient and patient with these people, and conferred so many benefits on them, that they should have good cause to be satisfied and grateful. My patience is at last wearing thin." When Düfflipp pronounced the whole situation "suspect" [*nicht koscher*], Ludwig voiced his own first private suspicion that there might be some truth in the sorry rumor which he had never been able to bring himself to believe: "Is it really a case of adultery? Then alas!" The affair dragged on for nearly two years until the fall of 1868, when, after numerous royal admonitions, Malvina left Bavaria.

German Politics

If the preceding incidental reference to a new court secretary seems abrupt, this is because of its connection with the far-reaching changes that occurred in the political landscape during 1866. It was the consequences of a fratricidal war—between Austria and Prussia—that prompted Wagner, cozily ensconced at Tribschen on the doorstep of the German Confederation, to undergo an important change of political alignment. This process, which went hand in hand with his work on *Die Meistersinger*, simultaneously destroyed the illusions he had nursed in regard to Ludwig's potential role in German history.

As late as April 29, 1866, Wagner was still endeavoring to persuade Ludwig of the greatness of his mission and warning him against Bismarck. "The destinies of the noblest, greatest nation on earth" were being gambled with in a "horribly frivolous" manner. Bismarck, characterized as "an ambitious Junker," was "deceiving his feebleminded king in the most shameless fashion and making him play a dishonorable game"—audacious language indeed to use to another monarch! Before long, Wagner declared, no one would be able to distinguish between true and false, and his "Germany" would perish forever. Clearly influenced by Constantin Frantz, the conservative federalist with whom he was then conducting a brisk correspondence, Wagner drafted a political program for submission to Ludwig in June 1866. Under the terms of this program, Bavaria was to become the savior of Germany. "It is given to Bavaria alone to determine the fate of Germany and impart an entirely new direction to the international politics of Europe."

Then the guns gave tongue. In Bohemia, the needle gun invented by Johann von Dreyse of Sömmerda shattered the already crumbling self-confidence of Austria's military commanders. The scales must have fallen from Wagner's eyes, for by June 23 he had bowed to the inevitable. "God has passed sentence on the German Confederation," he wrote to August Röckel. "Nothing could have perished more miserably. . . . My friend, if you must continue to engage in politics, cleave to Bismarck and Prussia. God help me, I know of no alternative." Soothingly, he added that no centralized state could emerge even now. Prussia, too, would learn that the only possibility was a German federation.

Even before the conclusion of the Treaty of Prague, which strengthened Prussia's position but, thanks to Bismarck's political acumen, treated the South German states with exceptional leniency, Ludwig II not only revived the idea of abdicating but sought Wagner's permission to do so. "Oh, secure me the Dear One's assent," he wrote to Cosima. Once again, he toyed with the thought of quitting Munich. He could no longer endure "having to be parted from Him who is my All." Wagner, who at this period showed more political acumen than the king, sent him a brief note on July 26. "Send for Prince Hohenlohe at once," he wrote. "Unbosom yourself to him thoroughly and confer with him."

Wagner realized that the moment had come to rid himself of his old enemies at court. Ludwig, who needed an excuse for his own political failure, would recognize their utter uselessness without further prompting. Pfistermeister resigned in October 1866. On October 3, the king wrote to Wagner: "Today I spoke with Neumayr and persuaded him to assume the post occupied by Mime and his gang." Mime and his gang. . . . Ludwig's sarcastic references to his politicians and court officials carried certain dangers, for it soon became clear that the letters and telegrams passing between Munich and Tribschen were being intercepted and read. Was the royal family keeping Ludwig under surveillance? Were government officials plotting against him? Could a foreign intelligence service be involved? Because of these suspicions, much of the correspondence was conducted by Cosima and Paul von Taxis, while important telegrams and messages of devotion were ostensibly exchanged by servants: Franz Mrazeck to Jakob Stocker and vice versa.

On March 9, 1867, Wagner went to Munich to negotiate Bülow's recall with the king, not for reasons of conscience, but because he wanted to be assured that the *Meistersinger* production and the Royal School of Music were safely in Bülow's expert hands before Cosima dragged the whole truth out into the open by leaving him for good. On March 12, after talking to Röckel, he went to Prince Chlodwig zu Hohenlohe-Schillingsfürst and presented another exposition of his ideas on Bavaria's role as a German state. Whatever the opposition to him, Wagner said, it was essential that Hohenlohe remain in the cabinet. The prince replied that this depended on the king, not on himself.

It was not until the end of 1867 that Wagner suffered his bitterest disappointment at Ludwig's hands. In September, he had begun to write a series of fifteen articles entitled "German Art and German Politics" for the *Süddeutsche Presse,* a semiofficial journal jointly subsidized by the state and the king and founded by Julius Fröbel at Hohenlohe's instigation. These articles, of which the first appeared in the very first issue, were not dissimilar in tone from Wagner's letters to Ludwig. "Even Prussia must and will acknowledge that it was the German spirit that, in its upsurge against French dominion, gave her the strength she now employs solely in the cause of expediency; and here will be the proper point at which—for the common weal—a well-managed Bavarian state can join hands with her. But at this point only: There is none more beneficial."

Wagner ended by sharply criticizing what Maximilian II of Bavaria, Ludwig's predecessor, had done for belles lettres. The epigones had been encouraged to close ranks and "gad along as 'inoffensively' as possible." The Munich articles even alluded to the "deterrent" effect of literary prizes—an oblique reference to Paul Heyse, who had been awarded the Maximilian Prize in 1857.

The whole of Munich's literary colony could recognize itself in Wagner's caricature of journalistic and theatrical degeneracy. He went on to lament the decline of the theater, castigate art critics, and pillory his confreres—not excluding "rivals in the Nibelungen field." We are told that, years later, the veins on Emanuel Geibel's forehead still used to bulge at the very mention of Wagner's name. Wagner also launched a renewed attack on the philistinism of the German middle classes and their susceptibility to French influence.

Although Wagner's name was not appended to these essays in cultural dissection, the public scented that a new clique of "forty-eighters" was at work. On December 19, after the thirteenth article had appeared, the series was discontinued. Fröbel claimed that the king himself had banned the publication of any more such "suicidal" pieces. Ludwig must either have been alarmed at the tone of the last article to appear or had his attention drawn to its potentially damaging consequences, for he had lavished praise on the earlier articles as recently as November 21.

Wagner paid a visit to Munich on December 23 but failed to settle matters to his satisfaction. It seems that the king had caught wind of Fröbel's strictures on Cosima's way of life. Already annoyed by the Wagner colony's petty complaints, and with Malvina Schnorr's scandalous tittle-tattle still ringing in his ears, Ludwig had Cosima formally "admonished" by Secretary Düfflipp. Although he granted Wagner a placatory audience and went so far as to tender Cosima an apology, Wagner declared in January that he had suffered enough in the way of "harsh and distressing" treatment. He returned to Tribschen on February 9, 1868, his relations with the king at their lowest ebb.

Decisions

Many things were not progressing as they should have, and Wagner's affair with Cosima was entering a crucial phase that remained unresolved until the fall. When she visited him at Tribschen in May, the "Annals" record that he was overcome by "a wilderness of emotions."

Cosima returned to Munich on May 20. Wagner followed next day to supervise the *Meistersinger* rehearsals. He again stayed with the Bülows—a voluntary exercise in self-control that imposed an additional strain on everyone's nerves. On May 22, he joined Ludwig aboard the steam yacht *Tristan* and sailed to Roseninsel on the Starnberger See, where "Junker Stolzing" treated "Hans Sachs" to a birthday lunch.

In June, visitors from all over Europe attended the first performance of *Die Meistersinger von Nürnberg*. Given under Bülow's direction on June 21, 1868, it proved to be the composer's most incontestable and unqualified success since the Dresden premiere of *Rienzi*. During the prelude, he was summoned from Cosima's side and invited into the royal box, where Ludwig's retinue regarded him with raised eyebrows. When the audience clamored for him at the end of the second act, he stood to acknowledge their ovation at the king's request. Stepping to the front of the box, he bowed—an unprecedented breach of etiquette and infringement of court convention. Hanslick's review in the *Neue Freie Presse* declared that there were some who expected the king to take a bow too. As for the performance itself, his verdict showed that he had not forgotten his discomfiture at the Vienna reading: "Herr Betz is doubly deserving of our praise for his Hans Sachs because the immense efforts devoted to it go unrequited and the part is thoroughly unrewarding. Sachs has numerous monologues and dialogues with which he bores his listeners to distraction." Wagner's "ingenious musings" had produced a system that was "erroneous in principle and unlovely and unmusical in its steadfast implementation. We account the *Meistersinger* an extremely interesting musical oddity or pathological symptom."

Hanslick was probably the first critic to extend Goethe's definition of classicism and romanticism—that the former is healthy and the latter sick—to a product of supreme musical maturity, in this case by employing the concept of disease as an aesthetically pejorative criterion. Setting aside his subjectively disparaging overtones, he was not entirely wrong. *Die Meistersinger* is not, as undiscerning ears are inclined to believe, a work that belongs to, or even portrays, the intact world of music and history. The Prize Song itself is shown as something ossified and obsolete, nor is it regenerated by Stolzing's invocation of the knights and minstrels of old. The music presages the end of an era. When interpreting the *Meistersinger* Prelude in *Jenseits von Gut und Böse* almost twenty years later, Nietzsche wrote: "It has fire and courage and, at the same time, the flaccid skin of fruit that ripen too late." Summing up, he went on: "This music admirably expresses what I think of the Germans: They belong to the day before yesterday and the day after tomorrow—*they still have no today.*"

The *Meistersinger* music is an extreme expression, though not in Hanslick's sense, of this tension between past and future: *It is ambivalent "late" art.* The critic Truhn described the opera as "a monstrous great beast" and declared that the music savored of unripe gooseberries. Nothing could have been more characteristic of Wagner and the reception of his work. A structurally perfect masterpiece rich in musical architecture, vibrant with subtlety and lyricism, *Die Meistersinger* was accused of being discordant nonsense. Then everyone changed tack. Once the work had been euphorically identified as "the" German opera by an age that consistently ignored its democratic in favor of its national components, all that people detected in it was a sort of chauvinistic bombast. This reputation has stuck, but *Die Meistersinger* does not deserve it. Anyone who has not been moved to laughter and tears by its humanity, its mischievous charm, its musical subtlety, its gravity and gaiety, is guilty of listening with half an ear, unacquainted with the finer points of its libretto and musical idiom, and insensitive to artistic perfection.

*   *   *

While returning to Lucerne on June 24, still flushed with success, Wagner devised the exultant theme for the finale of *Siegfried*. Then illness confined him to his bed for ten despondent days. He had been obliged to leave Cosima behind in Munich. Was he once more doomed to play Sachs—condemned to renounce his Eva? Nothing was settled, and he had found it impossible to speak with Bülow, his principal assistant at the birth of *Die Meistersinger*, about their complex personal relations. In August, by which time Cosima had rejoined him at Tribschen, he sketched out a play, *Luthers Hochzeit* [*Luther's Wedding*], in which the monk-and-nun theme paralleled the daring and unconventional nature of their own relationship. If he was Luther, he felt, nothing must deter him from fighting for their eventual union. This theme, so fraught with personal significance, recurred to him throughout the rest of his life.

On September 14, 1868, Wagner and Cosima left for Italy with the manservant Jakob Stocker, Vreneli's husband. They spent a night on the St. Gotthard en route. Describing an evening with Wagner a month before his death, Cosima records in her diary how they congratulated themselves on their only son's talent and good looks. "The Gotthard was good for him," Wagner observed—an oblique reference to the fact that young Siegfried had been conceived high in the Alps. On September 17, after visiting Stresa and the Borromean Islands, they reached Genoa, where Wagner had caught his first glimpse of the Mediterranean fifteen years earlier. In warm but not oppressive weather, they strolled the city's streets and admired its palaces. Wagner proposed that Cosima should stay with him from then on, that she should send for her children and damn the consequences, but Cosima counseled prudence. Then they traveled by way of Milan and Como to Lugano, where they heard on September 28 that storms were ravaging Ticino. At Bellinzona the next day, they debated whether to wait or press on regardless. They decided to head for Biasca, where floods compelled them to continue their journey to Giornico on foot. Just as they were leaving Biasca, they were overtaken by a sudden thunderstorm. After wading through mud and debris for a solid hour, incessantly lashed by torrential rain, they reached Faido.

Here they spent two days almost cut off from the outside world. Cloudbursts had carried away bridges and devastated whole villages. On October 3, while still at Faido, Cosima wrote her husband a letter, presumably stating her intention of leaving him for good. On the following day, after braving the elements and negotiating more mountain torrents for upward of four hours, the little party trudged into Airolo. Jakob Stocker was deeply impressed by the "Frau Baronin's" courage and stamina. By the time Wagner and his companions got back to Tribschen—via the St. Gotthard, Andermatt, Amsteg, and Flüelen—he could not help wondering whether fate had meant them to survive at all.

On October 14, Cosima left for Munich to have it out with her husband. Wagner accompanied her and the four little girls as far as Augsburg before returning to Switzerland. There followed a fierce exchange of letters. In the interests of a divorce, Cosima proposed to visit Rome. Wagner, who firmly opposed this plan, annoyed her by enlisting the help of her half-sister, Claire de Charnacé, whom he summoned from Paris to dissuade her.

At long last, albeit in devious language, he apprised the king of the significance of his newfound relationship with "the Friend." Not long afterward, on November 1, he set off for Leipzig. A letter written in October to his sister Klara Wolfram goes some way toward explaining the strange sense of restlessness that impelled him to make this trip: "My sole knowledge of the concept of the family stems from my former relations with my brothers and sisters, but life has done much to diminish that knowledge. Without wishing to arrange a regular family conference, I often toy with the notion of visiting you all in turn."

At Munich, where he stopped on the way, the king predictably declined to grant him an audience. Traveling on to Leipzig, he stayed with Ottilie and Hermann Brockhaus. The press was not informed of his visit because he wanted it to be a family affair— an opportunity to tell his relatives something of his recent experiences and compositions. He played to them and was astonished to learn from Ottilie's friend Sophie Ritschl, a distinguished academic's wife, that she already knew Walther's Prize Song. It appeared that she had been introduced to it by one of her husband's students, a budding philosopher and ardent music lover of twenty-four. Wagner pricked up his ears and expressed a desire to meet this young man, whose name was Friedrich Nietzsche.

Nietzsche had studied under Ritschl at Leipzig and done his military service the previous spring. Released on account of a fractured breastbone, he had recuperated at home in Naumburg and returned to Leipzig in October. On October 8, before leaving his little home town on the Saale, he had written a letter to Erwin Rohde, a fellow student and kindred spirit. It contained two key sentences that anticipated his whole future attitude toward the composer he had yet to meet. Wagner, he said, was "representative of a modern dilettantism that absorbs and digests all artistic interests." He was nonetheless amazed, from this very aspect, at the extent to which every artistic aptitude was present in the man. "I like in Wagner what I like in Schopenhauer: ethical fresh air, a whiff of Faust, the Cross, death, the tomb, etc."

The introduction was arranged by one of Nietzsche's friends and contemporaries, Ernst Windisch, an Indologist and Sanskritist. "If you wish to meet Richard Wagner," wrote Windisch, "come to the Café Théâtre at a quarter to four." They duly set off, but the first appointment came to nothing. Wagner had sallied forth "with a huge hat on his big head"—his "Wotan hat." A second appointment at the Brockhauses' on November 8, 1868, was preceded by an unfortunate scene. Nietzsche's tailor refused to part with the evening suit he had ordered because the young man could not produce any ready cash. After a halfhearted struggle, Nietzsche stormed off into the dark and rainy night. He entered the Brockhaus drawing room without a tailcoat but in an "exalted, novelistic frame of mind."

Little guessing what spiritual torment and bliss lay in store for him, the young philosopher was introduced to his senior by thirty-one years. "I am presented to Richard and address a few reverential words to him," he reported to Rohde the next day, his intimate tone implying that the two of them—Richard and Fritz—had long been wedded in spirit. "He inquires very closely into how I come to be acquainted with his music, heaps frightful abuse on all performances of his operas except the celebrated Munich ones, and pokes fun at conductors who genially call to their orchestras: 'Gentlemen, now it gets passionate! A touch more passion, my dear fellows!' W. loves imitating the Leipzig dialect."

Nietzsche had, in fact, become acquainted with Wagner's music in 1861, as a seventeen-year-old schoolboy, when introduced to the piano arrangement of *Tristan und Isolde* by Gustav Krug. Even in *Ecce homo*, in the section *"Warum ich so klug bin"* ["Why I am so clever"], he wrote: "All things considered, I should not have endured my youth without Wagner's music." Written shortly before his mind gave way and after years of striving to shake off Wagner's influence, *Ecce homo* also contained an admission that he was still searching vainly in every field of art for a work possessed of "the same dangerous fascination, the same horrible, sweet infinitude" as *Tristan*. His final conversion to Wagner's music occurred on October 28, 1868, when he heard the *Tristan* and *Meistersinger* preludes. "Every fiber, every nerve within me quivered," he wrote to Rohde the same day. Defenseless against the temptations of the extraordinary, he had encountered a music with Hegel and Schopenhauer in its bones. Incapable of love in the commonly accepted sense, he was overcome by a passion for which no cure existed. Just this once, he fell genuinely in love, and he did so with all the uncompromising extremism that characterized his life and ideas and ultimately drove him to issue the century's most blatant challenge.

The two men had many things in common from the first. They came from the same part of the world. Nietzsche's place of birth was Röcken, a village on the road from Weissenfels to Leipzig, only a few miles from Johanna Wagner's home. Both men felt deeply rooted in the Central German cultural area bounded by the Harz, the Thüringer Pforte, and Elster—the home of Martin Luther, Heinrich Schütz, and Novalis—without ever quite mastering their aversion to its endearing but provincial atmosphere. Wagner had never visited his mother's birthplace and severed nearly all his ties with the family and Saxony after her death, returning only briefly when compelled to do so for professional reasons. Nietzsche criticized every quality in his sister that reminded him of Naumburg and detested the Naumburg vernacular, a cross between South Saxon and the more melodious dialect of Thuringia. He preferred to forget the days when he had marched stiffly through the rain, filled with childish punctilio, because school rules ordained that pupils should walk home in a decorous fashion. He outgrew Naumburg just as Wagner had outgrown his Leipzig adolescence, except that Wagner cloaked his checkered background in a bourgeois life-style, whereas Nietzsche tried to obliterate the memory of his bourgeois childhood in a Lutheran parsonage by blaspheming against the traditional virtues—Christian humility most of all. Seldom did men of genius dissociate themselves so utterly from their origins without occasioning any real break in their development. Their paths crossed at a juncture that seemed to augur well for both of them. That the intersection occurred at Leipzig was purely fortuitous.

They took to each other on the spot. Both before and after dinner, Wagner played the principal passages from *Die Meistersinger* in his own inimitable way, taking all the parts himself. He was in a very exuberant mood, Nietzsche told Rohde. "He is, in fact, a marvelously vivacious and high-spirited man who speaks very rapidly, is very witty, and brings great gaiety to a party of this most intimate kind." They both enthused about Schopenhauer. Wagner then read a passage from his own autobiography—a scene from his days as a student in Leipzig, which Nietzsche found exceedingly amusing. Wagner shook the younger man's hand warmly when the party broke up and invited him to continue their conversation at Tribschen. The next day, he left.

A week later, on November 16, 1868, Cosima finally moved to Tribschen with her two youngest daughters, Isolde and Eva. She was deeply distressed at having to leave Daniela and Blandine behind in Munich. For the present, her cohabitation with Wagner remained a secret and she lived in strict seclusion. Her newfound happiness was at first alloyed with melancholy, and she wept a good deal. Wagner himself was out of sorts—plagued with abdominal trouble and depressed by so many reports of friends and acquaintances dying that he started to keep a register of deaths. And yet, for the very first time, an element of stability and continuity entered his life. He resumed work on the score of *Siegfried*, dictated some more of his autobiography,* and recorded his impressions of Rossini, who had just died, for the *Allgemeine Zeitung*. At the turn of the year, in advance of a new edition of *Judaism in Music*, he wrote a letter of justification and explanation to Marie Muchanoff, the widow of Kalergis. "The theaters belong to the Junkers and the theatrical pranksters, the concert institutes to the music-Jews:

What is there left for us?" Jewish became synonymous with all that displeased him in art.

Cosima was "filled with dread" by his decision to preface *Judaism in Music* with a new introduction in which he complained of persecution "on the part of the Jews." Her forebodings were fully justified. It was the most gratuitously foolish thing he could have done, and made it seem to his friends that he was deliberately turning his back on the world. "God Almighty," Bülow wrote to Pohl on March 6, when he received a copy of the pamphlet, "what a hullabaloo there'll be!" And there was. Some 170 counterblasts were published, Mannheim operagoers hissed *Die Meistersinger* to a standstill, the Viennese construed Beckmesser's serenade as a parody of synagogue singing, and *Rienzi*'s Paris premiere was preceded by an uproar in the press. Berthold Auerbach was not the only one of Wagner's former friends and acquaintances to be deeply hurt. The most dignified retort to be written by a nonmusician, Gustav Freytag, appeared in No. 22 of *Der Grenzbote*. Freytag declared that he considered it wholly inopportune to attack the Jews because Jewish fellow citizens had long been "allies to good ends." Even in the days of their servitude, the Jews had produced a large number of eminent figures under highly disadvantageous circumstances. Now, however, non-Jews had lost the right, in music as well as elsewhere, to accuse Jewish artists of being limited. Wagner himself had displayed qualities in his own works that were often censured in Jewish artists. "In the light of his pamphlet, he himself appears more Jewish than anyone." His gift for the subtle handling of effects, his delight in the outlandish and far-fetched, and, last but not least, "the unmannerly presumption of a willful dilettante who avidly oversteps the bounds of his art"— this aspect of his talent ought to be interpreted "on his own submission, as peculiarly Jewish." "Since Herr Wagner would on no account agree that he himself belongs to Judaism in music, the rest of us have indubitably lost the right to talk about the limitations of Jewish musicians."

Freytag was only half-correct, for Wagner naturally felt misunderstood; but then, where *could* he have hoped to find true understanding? Cosima pronounced him an anomaly—a figure born out of his time. In conversation with Edouard Schuré on October 4, 1869, she said, "He ought to have graced the world in the days of Aeschylus. He now believes he can resolve the insoluble misunderstanding between himself and the world by means of occasional explanations, and the more he talks the deeper the rift becomes." Wagner was still seething with fury at retorts such as Freytag's when, on July 3, 1869, Deputy Eduard Lasker persuaded the Prussian Landtag to pass a law banning religious discrimination—the statutory basis of a regrettably short-lived trend toward Jewish emancipation in Germany.

Wagner's self-induced afflictions were compounded with distress at his real or supposed betrayal by sundry friends. Laube had made mock of *Die Meistersinger*, and the New Year's issue of the *Süddeutsche Presse* contained a malicious piece by Julius Fröbel on *Opera and Drama*, the second edition of which had appeared in 1868. Fröbel, who continued to give politics precedence over art, described Wagner as the founder of a "sect" whose aim was to replace the state and religion with an opera theater and thereby control them. Perceptive as it was, the timing and semiofficial nature of Fröbel's diatribe came as a shock. Few things so embittered Wagner as this particular attack, but one disappointment followed hard on the heels of another. "Worst of all," noted Cosima, "his experience with the king. We discussed the possibility of going to live in a Parisian garret. A living room and two small bedrooms for ourselves and the children."

This should not be taken too seriously. At long last, on February 10, 1869, Ludwig wrote Wagner a conciliatory letter, though it did contain an awkward request: He looked forward to a Munich premiere of *Das Rheingold* in the near future, this being one of the joys he needed if he were not to perish in "the vortex of mundane existence." Very reluctantly, Wagner assented to its being put into rehearsal: "You have done as much to facilitate such performances in the past two years as you possibly could, under prevailing circumstances, and I thank you for that from the bottom of my heart. At all events, you have thereby earned, as you have by all the benefits conferred on me, the indisputable right to act entirely as you think fit in regard to my works and their performance."

Trials and Tribulations

The Munich Rheingold

On April 5, 1869, after making an exhaustive study of *Das Rhein-gold*, Hans Richter left Tribschen to relieve Bülow in Munich. On April 8, Bulow sent the two remaining children, Daniela and Blandine, to Tribschen and prepared to quit the Bavarian capital. For weeks on end, Cosima's diary records her preoccupation with death and Wagner's heartache over the work that had been "wrested" from him by Ludwig.

On Whit-Saturday, May 15, a young man paused at the gate of Tribschen and stood listening to "an anguished chord" being played, over and over again, on the piano. Appointed to a chair of classical philology at Basel University on February 13, Friedrich Nietzsche had been in the city since April 19. Now, on the strength of Wagner's invitation, he had traveled to Lucerne at the first opportunity and walked along the lake to Tribschen. Diffidently, he made his presence known. Cosima was not at home, having gone into town with Blandine on some errand connected with Wagner's birthday. Jakob Stocker took Nietzsche's card to his master, who was evidently at work, and returned to inquire if he were the Herr Nietzsche from Leipzig. If so, would he come to lunch on Monday next? On Whit-Monday, Nietzsche caught the morning steamer to Tribschen. "A peaceful, agreeable visit," says

Cosima's diary. They sat in the drawing room under the apt gaze of *Dionysus with the Muses of Apollo,* the painting which had so impressed Wagner in his youth and which Cosima had since acquired from the estate of Friedrich Brockhaus.

The young philologist's first visit to Tribschen must have been a somewhat formal occasion. Wagner was not in the best of moods, and by four that afternoon Nietzsche found himself being driven back to town "through a drizzle" by his host and hostess. A few days later he sent Wagner a birthday letter thanking him for "the best and most uplifting moments" of his life, which for him were associated with Wagner's name. On May 28, he delivered his inaugural lecture at Basel University.

From then on he became a regular visitor to the Wagner home. His next visit fell on June 5—rather awkwardly, because Cosima was expecting a baby at any moment. Wagner wanted to put him off, but Cosima thought it better if he came. After a "tolerable" evening, she withdrew to bed at eleven. Then the labor pains began. At midnight, so as not to disturb anyone, she carried her bedclothes downstairs to the lower bedroom. Two days earlier she and Wagner had quarreled violently over her refusal to move down into the bedroom next to his. Double standards indeed! She was bearing his child but they slept apart. She was still living in sin; he was not.

When the baby was born at four in the morning—the midwife did not arrive until after three—Wagner was tormented by Cosima's cries in the room next door. Hearing Vreneli give an exclamation in response to some remark from the midwife, he rushed out onto the landing, panic-stricken, only to be told that Cosima had been delivered of a son. The Rigi was bathed in the first rays of the sun. That morning his head was filled with Siegfried's paean of joy in the third act—"*Heil dem Tage . . .*"—and on the third morning after his son's birth he came to Cosima and recited the lines he had just set to his satisfaction: "*Leuchtende Liebe, lachender Tod!*" The music for them he inscribed in her diary. By June 14, the composition sketch for *Siegfried* was complete, and the orchestral sketch for the third act took shape between June 25 and August 5.

Hans von Bülow was kept in ignorance of his wife's confinement. He had suffered the tortures of the damned in Munich, remaining there only in the vain hope of averting a public scandal.

Writing in French to Countess Charnacé, Cosima's half-sister, on September 15 of the following year, 1869, he told her that he had shrunk from suicide only because he could not see a shred of honor to be gained by it. The letter goes on: "Last November, when I asked Cosima an almost indelicate question about the reason for her abrupt departure, she saw fit to perjure herself in reply. That was how, a few months ago, I first learned from the newspapers of the master's happiness at having at last been presented by his mistress (full name supplied) with a son who had been christened Siegfried as a good omen for the completion of his new opera. My cuckold's edifice has thus been rounded off in the most splendid fashion. I was unable to quit Munich at once, but you cannot imagine the hell I endured during the last few months of my employment there." On June 15, 1869, Cosima asked him to grant her a divorce and allow her to keep their two daughters, Daniela and Blandine. Hans agreed by return. "It must be so," he wrote in English. He was a broken man.

Cosima recovered more quickly from her latest confinement than she had on previous occasions, though she needed rest and suffered from periodic fits of depression. Tribschen received numerous visitors that summer, but few of them heard tell of the infant who was thriving upstairs in the care of a nursemaid, nor could anything be discerned of their hosts' spiritual crises, their "remorse," or Wagner's paroxysms of weeping.

On July 16, 1869, three French Wagnerites arrived in Lucerne— one female, two male, and all endowed with a charm, intelligence, and imagination that welded them into a bright and brilliant major triad. They were Judith Mendès-Gautier, Théophile Gautier's twenty-one-year-old daughter; her husband, Catulle Mendès, an up-and-coming novelist six years older than his wife; and their thirty-year-old friend Philippe-Auguste Villiers de l'Isle Adam, a late romantic poet much influenced by Edgar Allan Poe.

Wagner met his visitors at the station and conducted them to the Hôtel du Lac. He was surprised and enchanted. The little girl who had so brusquely interrupted Berlioz outside the Opéra in Paris had grown into a beauty with a classical profile and a shapely figure—outwardly, perhaps, not unreminiscent of Leah David. She also retained the temperament that had earned her the family nickname "Hurricane." Judith was the product of a Franco-Italian marriage. Her mother, Ernesta Grisi of Milan, was a sister of the famous soprano Giulia Grisi. Liszt called Judith "extremely beautiful" and Théodore de Banville described her as follows: "The line of her nose continues that of her brow, as in those blessed days when the gods still walked the earth. . . . Dark hair curling softly in a way that makes it look disheveled, complexion dark ivory, teeth white, small, and not too close together, lips red as coral, eyes small and somewhat deeply set but extremely lively and brimful of mischief when they light up with laughter, nostrils full, eyebrows fine and straight, ears entrancing, neck on the plump side but admirably poised—every feature appropriate to a serene, godlike Sphinx or a female warrior of Thyatira whose simple, perfect, flawlessly ideal beauty could serve as a model for the illustrator of the *Comédie Humaine.*" In short, Judith took Wagner's breath away. "We are united by a noble emotion," he confided on the way to the hotel. Then he hurried on ahead to tell Cosima all about their unusual trio of visitors.

The next few days were devoted to excursions, readings, and conversations on art, music, and religion. Judith was thrilled to the core—drunk with admiration. Wagner caught her standing shyly, reverently at the door of his workroom. "How enthusiastic you are!" he cried, torn between delight and amusement. "One shouldn't be unduly so—it's bad for the health." Judith persuaded him to play passages from his composition sketches, thereby annoying the Serovs, who were also visiting Tribschen but had not so far dared to make such a request. Nothing was denied to Judith, whose wishes Wagner could read in her eyes. During a boat trip on the lake, she gazed, not at the surrounding scenery, but only at his profile, which seemed to her transfigured by reflected sunlight. He even told her about *Luthers Hochzeit,* a project he never discussed with anyone but Cosima, and was so filled with exuberance that he clambered around in the trees of his magnificent garden like a schoolboy. Cosima was obliged to ask the young woman not to gaze at her husband with such rapture because there was no knowing what folly he might commit. To Cosima, the *"gamine"* with the Roman brow and nose remained a rather uncanny creature, like someone from another world. Her diary for July 17 contains the entry: "That woman says out loud all the things I believe in my innermost heart; that she can utter them at all makes her alien to me." Even so, Judith managed to win her over. Cosima, so outwardly cool and aloof, so different in temperament, confided her most intimate concern of the moment: her desire for a divorce, to which Liszt, her own father, was said to be stubbornly opposed.

The three French visitors left for Munich, where Bülow had bidden farewell to the Court Theater by conducting a repeat performance of *Tristan* in Liszt's presence. Liszt, who later met Judith at the home of Countess von Schleinitz, drew her aside and inquired how Cosima was. She retorted with a temperamental outburst: "Don't say a word against your daughter. I'm so much on her side that I won't let anyone reproach her." Wagner was beyond the scope of human laws, she sternly proclaimed with her head held high; in Cosima's place she would have done just the same. "It is your duty as a father not to place any obstacle in the way of the admirable solution that Cosima rightly expects!" Liszt apparently replied that he shared her opinion but could not, as a man of the cloth, be heard to say so publicly. He too desired a legal solution and had never intended to delay matters. Judith thereupon asked if she might write to Cosima and tell her so. Her letter reached Tribschen on August 28, in the midst of a controversy over the forthcoming premiere of *Das Rheingold*.

Two days before the date appointed for the dress rehearsal—on August 25, which happened to be Judith's birthday as well as the king's—Hans Richter had submitted his resignation as conductor on the grounds that the mise-en-scène, and the stage machinery in particular, threatened total disaster. Richter's move, which had been approved in advance by Wagner, was originally meant to bully Ludwig into postponing the premiere. But the king, who had no idea what was afoot, remained adamant. The dress rehearsal, with Richter still at his post, eventually took place on August 27 in the presence of Ludwig and four or five hundred invited guests. A prosaic Valhalla, a wooden rainbow, the Rhine Maidens attired in everyday clothes in front of the curtain—every one of these abominations was promptly relayed to Tribschen, where all was aflutter in the dovecote. Wagner, who had met his sister Ottilie Brockhaus while out walking on August 27, had invited her and her husband to lunch the next day, and Nietzsche was hurriedly summoned to complete the party. Dinner that evening was interrupted ten times by the arrival of letters and telegrams. For good measure, Cosima had spent the entire morning sobbing and weeping because Hans von Bülow had quit Munich without leaving an address. She was somewhat consoled by Judith's account of her conversation with Liszt. The French couple telegraphed from Munich that the *Rheingold* orchestral playing had been magnificent in rehearsal, but that the scenery and scene changes were "absurd, ludicrous, impossible." A telegram from Richter, urgently requesting that Wagner prevail on Ludwig to postpone the premiere, reached Lucerne at 1:40 P.M. Wagner's appeal to the king went off only forty-five minutes later, presumably because he had kept the post office messenger waiting at Tribschen.

Franz Betz, who was cast as Wotan, wrote to say that one glimpse of "this demented chaos" would suffice for Wagner to "prohibit" the performance on the spot. Rather unfairly, Wagner forwarded this letter to the king. That evening, while Cosima was writing Judith a letter of thanks, Wagner telegraphed to Richter asking whether the king's command still stood. Richter's reply arrived the next day: The premiere had been postponed, but he had been dismissed. Baron von Löen, the intendant at Weimar, asked if his kapellmeister Eduard Lassen might conduct instead, but Wagner rejected the offer. "In the midst of all this," wrote Cosima, "Pr[ofessor] Nietzsche, unfailingly pleasant. Dismal day, what will come of this affair? The king's behavior puzzling."

Ludwig responded to Richter's "impertinence" and Betz's complaints with a letter dated August 29 to Düfflipp—a missive whose exaggeratedly regal tone reminds one a little of Nietzsche's last deranged jottings. If "the people at the theater" continued to disobey orders, "the weeds must be mercilessly uprooted." Düfflipp was to take the sternest measures against "these worthless creatures." The letter concluded: "This is my will. Amen." On August 30: "Truly criminal and brazen, the behavior of 'Wagner' and the theater rabble; it is an open revolt against my commands, and that I cannot tolerate. . . . If 'Wagner's' abominable intrigues succeed, the whole rabble will become more and more presumptuous and impertinent, until they are past curbing; that is why the mischief must be torn up by the roots—'Richter' must go and 'Betz' and the rest be brought to heel."

"Wagner" only rated quotation marks now. As for Betz, he could not be coerced: His contract expired on August 31, so he simply returned to Berlin. Ludwig's fury was unabated: "The vile and unpardonable intrigues of 'Wagner' and associates must be stopped forthwith," he decreed on August 31. "I hereby command that the performance take place on Sunday. 'Richter' is to be dismissed at once. If W. dares to offer any more resistance, he is to be deprived of his salary forever, and not another work of his will ever be performed on the Munich stage." Ludwig himself decided to withdraw to Hochkopf and await developments. Wagner, who hurried to Munich on September 1, either to supervise rehearsals or prevent a public performance altogether, was again obliged to submit his proposals in writing. The king found them quite reasonable but insisted on the appointment of a new conductor. Most of Richter's potential successors got in touch with Wagner and declined. Meanwhile, Ludwig continued to vent his wrath on paper. Here he is writing to Pfistermeister from Hochkopf on September 2: "Just to crown the poor management of the 'Rheingold' affair, which has become intolerable to me, I learned today that R. Wagner has come to Munich in complete defiance of my wishes. It would serve him right if there were an unpleasant demonstration against him, now that the Bülow scandal is *au comble. J'en ai assez.*"

Together with Hans Richter and the young composer Franz Servais, Judith and Catulle Mendès called on Wagner during his brief stay in Munich. This he spent, for reasons of privacy, at a small apartment in Neue Pferdestrasse belonging to Reinhard Schäfer, an engineer friend of Richter who later founded the Munich Wagner Society. It was also at Schäfer's apartment, while Judith waited in the street below, that Wagner had a largely abortive interview with Intendant von Perfall and Court Secretary Düfflipp.

He returned to Tribschen next day, having secured nothing save a postponement. "Hands off my score!" he menacingly enjoined Franz Wüllner, the new conductor appointed by Perfall. "That's my advice to you, sir, or may the devil take you! Beat time for glee clubs and choral societies, or—if you must tackle operatic scores —get them from your friend Perfall. And tell that fine gentleman that, unless he frankly confesses to the king that he is personally incapable of presenting my work, I shall light a candle that cannot be blown out by all his scribblers for local rags, paid for out of the leavings from the *Rheingold* expenses. You two gentlemen will need a lot of schooling from a man like me before you learn how ignorant you are!" If the gentlemen swallowed such abuse and remained on speaking terms with its author, it was only because they could not offend the king by resigning their posts. Although

Wagner accomplished nothing by behaving in this way, everything turned out far less badly than he had feared. Karl Brandt, the head machinist imported from Darmstadt, wrought such miracles within a few weeks that Wagner never lost touch with him thereafter.

Rheingold's first public performance on September 22 was ostentatiously boycotted by the composer. It was not a total disaster. Those who had ears to hear, heard, even though the scenic significance of the work and its musical-dramatic exposition of what was still to come could not at first be fully apprehended from this isolated "prologue" to the rest of the *Ring*, and even though its allusive qualities aroused widespread derision. The editor of the Munich *Vaterland*, who described the Rhine Maidens' scene at the bottom of the Rhine as a "whores' aquarium," was promptly sued by Heinrich Vogl for libeling his wife, Therese (Wellgunde).

Seemingly unmoved by the fate of his score, Wagner continued to work on the *Ring*. No more illusions about the king were cherished at Tribschen. Whoever was to blame, the cock had long since crowed thrice. No one with Ludwig's invective on the *Rheingold* affair still ringing in his ears could have been blamed for dismissing his written assurance of October 22—"I shall never lose faith in you, in no way, you understand"—as specious. Wagner replied, "I *cannot* write to you!" Suspecting more than he knew, he was honest enough to make no secret of his disappointment. On November 20, 1869, he again protested against the debasement of the *Ring* in Munich "to the level of a miserable operatic repertory," and asked, "Do you want my work as I want it, or do you not want it so?" But all in vain.

Whenever Ludwig relapsed into his former style, Cosima found it impossible to express the sorrow that overcame her on reading such "expressions of love and rapture." On November 5, while she and Wagner were musing aloud at Tribschen on things in general, Wagner declared that they would one day have to send "Fidi"— their son Siegfried—out into the world. "When he approaches manhood, he will have to mix with people, become acquainted with adversity and the world's contradictions, gad around and misbehave himself, or he will become a dreamer, perhaps a *crétin*, such as we see in the king of Bavaria." This remark should be borne in mind from now on.

The Young Professor

The Nietzsche affair was only an episode in Wagner's life. To Nietzsche himself, it meant far more. It became a source of impulsion and passion: the revelation of a world of art which he fervently espoused until it proved too much for his constitution; until it proved, like any form of art, too earthbound and inadequate to satisfy him; until his path diverged from Wagner's; until his pride no longer permitted him to tolerate the demands on his patience made by an older man who was set in his ideas; until the absolute nature of his philosophy—the genius that spurred him on—transformed their unequal relationship into a fatal choice between himself and Wagner.

To the composer, Nietzsche began by seeming merely amiable and useful. How knowledgeably he spoke! What pure delight to listen to him—to know that one was appreciated and interpreted by a musical philosopher! To one who felt himself a victim of intrigue in the lifelong struggle for existence, what could be more welcome than a kindred spirit—than comprehension as well as enthusiasm? When the young professor held forth on Greek tragedy, he might have been talking about the *Ring* itself.

And yet, viewed in the light of their correspondence and of Cosima's diaries, the relationship between Wagner and Nietzsche seems "privatized" and diminished. It loses the mythical dimensions ascribed to it in retrospect. The two men were separated by a generation gap of thirty-one years. Proud as he was of this first "professor" to take his artistic objectives seriously and interpret them, and highly though he valued his opinions, Wagner had no inkling that this young man was likewise destined to challenge their century after his own fashion. All he perceived in Nietzsche was a misfit with inchoate ideas and a talent for propounding them.

Humanly speaking, they were worlds apart. On the one hand, an ebullient artist and man of the theatrical world who would gladly—health and wealth permitting—have been an epicurean, a go-getter whose life flowed past like a dream, a sensualist involved in the everlasting drama of existence, laughing and weeping as his emotions dictated. On the other, a brilliant but austere pedant who *procured* experiences and exaggerated what life had not granted him—a capacity for fun and enjoyment—into the strident laughter of the Superman and Zarathustra. Once she realized how this human paradox appeared to other people, Cosima was puzzled in the extreme. "God, Nietzsche!" she told Richard Strauss in 1901. "If only you had known him. He never laughed and always seemed taken aback by our jokes. He was shortsighted, too, to the point of weaksightedness; a poor night bird, blundering into things right and left—one whom it is strangely touching to encounter as an advocate of laughter."

And laughter abounded in the Wagner household. Nietzsche listened gravely whenever someone cracked a joke, thereby prompting Wagner to be more outrageous still. Flushed cheeks and shining eyes were the professor's sole reaction, almost as if he were ashamed on the others' behalf. Even as a student, he had derived chill ecstasy from mortifying his flesh in various ways. Now, in 1869, he assumed the additional burden of vegetarianism, a form of self-denial whose futility Wagner had personally sampled during his early years at Zurich. Encouraged in these dietetic experiments by his friend Carl von Gersdorff, Nietzsche determined to obey Gersdorff's further commands to the letter. This gave rise to his first tiff with Wagner at Tribschen in September, when he proclaimed his conversion to vegetarianism. "You're an ass!" retorted Wagner, who remained "extremely vexed" throughout the meal by Nietzsche's refusal to abandon his principles in the face of reasoned argument.

None of these differences in outlook, nor even what he later termed Wagner's theatricality, detracted from Nietzsche's boundless admiration for the composer and, more particularly, for Cosima. He already adjudged Baroness von Bülow a "most influential" woman and later numbered her among "the rare instances of superior cultivation" he had known, these being—in his experience—invariably of French origin.

All was sweetness and light at this stage. "Dearest friend," Nietzsche reported to Erwin Rohde, "what I learn and discern, hear and apprehend there is past describing. Schopenhauer and Goethe, Aeschylus and Pindar live on, believe me." And from Naumburg on October 7: "Wagner is beneficial to me in the highest sense, of course, principally as a model that cannot be comprehended in terms of existing aesthetics."

To Nietzsche, Tribschen was an incubation period, a never-to-be-disavowed phase of sublime inspiration and intellectual delight. The Dionysian idea—the twofold face of rapture and destruction —was already stirring within him. For the moment, however, he was enlisted in shopping expeditions and commissioned to choose presents for the children in Basel. Like any adopted "uncle" and friend of the family, he unprofessorially helped Cosima to set up the puppet theater on Christmas Eve, the first to be spent at Tribschen by Wagner's growing brood of offspring. The proscenium arch was adorned with the Order of Iftekhar, which Wagner—hitherto deprived of any such hardware—had just been awarded by the Bey of Tunis.

On Christmas Day itself, Wagner gave a reading of his lengthy Munich sketch for *Parsifal,* which disposes of the claim that Nietzsche was later surprised by his alleged change of heart and obeisance to the Cross. To Rohde, Nietzsche described his visits to Tribschen as "the most beautiful and uplifting memory" and made no reference to any objections or misgivings on the subject of *Parsifal.* Cosima's diary mentions a "sublime conversation" on the philosophy of music that may well have been associated with Schopenhauer's reflections on the metaphysics of music. Both men's subsequent writings disclosed the effects of this.

Ineluctably compelled, either to relinquish the *Ring* entirely to Munich, or to delay its completion by factitious means, Wagner now gave more definite thought to the idea of founding a festival of his own. The name Bayreuth must often have cropped up, notably when he came to dictate his autobiographical reminiscences of 1835. He had first seen that idyllically situated little town in Upper Franconia on the way from Karlsbad to Nürnberg, but only in passing. On the evening of March 5, 1870, he once more turned his attention to *Die Walküre.* Cosima noted: "Later, when we were discussing the production of these works, I told Richard he ought to look up the article 'Baireuth' [sic] in the encyclopedia, this being the place Richard had mentioned as the one he would choose. To our delight we found a splendid old opera house listed among its buildings!" During the next few weeks, more literature on Bayreuth was procured by the Lucerne bookseller Prell, who happened to come from neighboring Wunsiedel.

On June 15, 1870, Wagner made another attempt to persuade Ludwig to have *Die Walküre* performed in private for his own delectation, but in vain: The premiere took place on June 26. Prior mistrust and hostility notwithstanding, it proved to be a great success. Franz Wüllner again conducted, and Karl Brandt worked wonders from the technical aspect. After a second performance on June 29, *Rheingold* and *Walküre* were given alternately three times in succession. Among those who traveled to Munich for the occasion were Johannes Brahms, Franz Liszt, Camille Saint-Saëns, and other loyal French Wagnerites. We are told that Liszt sobbed throughout the Brünnhilde-Siegmund scene, and no wonder. Having been privy from the first to the genesis of the work and its deepest levels of significance, he knew more about it than anyone else in the audience.

Ludwig did not attend the dress rehearsal or the first two performances, either because his conscience was pricking him or because the threat of war intensified his natural urge to shun the public gaze. Rumors of an impending conflict between France and Prussia, which conjured up the specter of Bavaria's involvement as an ally of the latter, were rife during the early part of July. They also carried to Wagner's Swiss retreat, where his French friends' return from Munich was awaited with scant enthusiasm. On July 10, almost as if he wanted to flee the world, Wagner headed for the mountains.

A veritable caravan drove to Hergeschwyl and set off up the Pilatus: Wagner and Cosima; Hans Richter; the children's student tutor; Jakob Stocker; the two eldest girls; guides and porters. After a "merry ride" they were greeted at the summit by "sublime impressions of silence and solitude." Even here, however, Wagner and Cosima did not escape tidings of mobilization and diplomatic exchanges, and their fears were unallayed by views of the Bernese Oberland and the metallic glint of moonlight on rock. Cosima was too agitated to sleep a wink during their last night in the mountains, and the forthcoming proclamation of papal infallibility reminded her of "the tinkle of bells on a fool's cap." After five days, the party returned to the lowlands and Tribschen, where Cosima heard on July 18 that her marriage to Hans von Bülow had been legally dissolved in Berlin. It was the eve of the Franco-Prussian War.

*   *   *

Although Wagner and Cosima dreaded the prospect of war until the last minute, the Ems Dispatch and reports of French "effronteries" sent them into a chauvinistic frenzy—the same frenzy whose eruption throughout the German states impelled the French to mobilize. On July 16, between *Rheingold* and *Walküre*, Ludwig II of Bavaria proclaimed that an "alliance contingency" had arisen and decreed the mobilization of the Bavarian Army. This scattered the last of Wagner's wits. The French declaration of war on July 19 was announced at Paris by none other than Emile Ollivier, Cosima's brother-in-law. In this sense, the war became a family matter, and all the more ironic because its outbreak coincided with a visit from the French Wagnerites.

Judith and Catulle Mendès, Villiers, Camille Saint-Saëns, Henry Duparc, Edouard Schuré, René Joly—all were fresh from the Beethoven festival and model performances of Wagner's works at Weimar, and all had just seen *Walküre* in Munich. Under the circumstances, Wagner wanted to put them off. He discussed the matter with Cosima, who agreed that "to see a Frenchman now would be very disagreeable." Once the visitors were in Lucerne, however, he felt bound to entertain them. Although political topics were avoided by common consent, Wagner could not resist harping on differences in national "character." The "noble emotion" that had united them was gone. In an undisguised allusion to Villiers de l'Isle Adam, Wagner drew his French guests' attention to "the objectionable nature of their rhetorical poetry," speaking with such vehemence and conviction that even Catulle Mendès was "much affected." While Moltke prepared to defeat MacMahon's and Bazaine's armies with his strategy of encirclement and annihilation, Camille Saint-Saëns accompanied his German host at the piano in the Norns' Prologue from *Götterdämmerung*: "Know ye what is to come?" The French party had trouble getting home across the frontier.

On July 28, Nietzsche stopped at Lucerne en route to the mountains. He left his sister Elisabeth, who was accompanying him, at the home of some friends on the promontory opposite Tribschen, clearly nervous of an unheralded encounter between her and the lady of the house. Cosima might have found it embarrassing, he thought, just as Elisabeth might have shown what she thought of an adulterous relationship blessed with such an abundance of children. Elisabeth was thoroughly middle class, not only in the floral patterns with which she furnished her brother Fritz's house, but in her moral judgments. She observed Tribschen through a telescope until the next day, when she was rowed across the lake for her first introduction to the Wagner household.

Two years younger than her brother, Elisabeth was a sentimental creature and—like Cosima—easily reduced to tears. Everything about her was demure and dainty—her ringlets, her gentility, her sensibilities. She preserved her looks into old age, thanks to a naturally fine, pale complexion, and she used her engaging appearance and manner to establish a corrupt dominion in the hearts of those with whom she ingratiated herself. After this first meeting, which prompted Cosima to record that Elisabeth, then twenty-four, was a "nice, unassuming girl," brother and sister set off for the Maderanertal.

Although Nietzsche had been granted a Swiss resident's permit, patriotism impelled him—quite needlessly, in Cosima's view—to go to war. He could only obtain a dispensation to join the medical corps. Of the period between August 22 and September 7, he spent a week at the front and the remainder of the time tending gravely ill and wounded men. Sobered by the sight of blood and filth and prostrated with diarrhea and diphtheria, he was discharged on September 14 "with the most dismal memories, especially of the battlefield at Wörth."

The sympathies of the Swiss, who feared that a dominant power in the north might enfold them in the Reich's unwelcome embrace like prodigal sons, lay with the French. However, Wagner was at least—and at long last—able to silence his Swiss neighbors' strictures on the sink of immorality in their midst. Tribschen ceased to be a love nest and became a matrimonial home. On August 25, Ludwig's birthday, Wagner and his mistress were married by Pastor Tschudi at the Protestant church in Lucerne. Their witnesses were Malwida von Meysenbug and Hans Richter. On Sunday, September 4, the faithful Willes turned up for Siegfried's christening. King Ludwig, whom Wagner had precipitately named as a godfather for inclusion in the parish register, was as ignorant of this honor as had been François Wille, who stood proxy for him. A neighbor, Countess Bassenheim, was the child's godmother. In the interim between MacMahon's surrender at Sedan, which signaled the end of the empire and encouraged the Italians to occupy the Papal States, and the encirclement of Paris by German forces, Siegfried Helferich Richard Wagner was baptized at the church where his parents had been married ten days earlier.

The Road to the Reich

Cosima declared that the French were getting their just deserts for every bar of *Tannhäuser* they had hissed. On August 18, 1870, she recorded her husband's devout hope that Paris, "that kept woman of the world," would be burned to the ground. The destruction of Paris would be symbolic of "the world's final release from the pressure of all that is bad."—"I spell ruin to the Napoleons," Wagner told her on September 4, shortly after Sedan. "When I was six months old there was the Battle of Leipzig, and now Fidi is pulverizing the whole of France." He longed for Paris to be bombarded and dreaded the possibility of a premature armistice, yet his patriotism ended where bad taste began. When he heard that German soldiers were singing *Die Wacht am Rhein,* he said he hoped the French would win. "We have sunk too low," he exclaimed, moved to tears by the thought that Germans should march to do battle in a sacred cause with such a song on their lips.

But the musical magician of Tribschen could also suffer from patriotic flatulence. In honor of the "grapeshot prince" of 1849— "the feebleminded monarch," as he had called the king of Prussia only four or five years earlier—he composed a *Kaisermarsch* whose empty pomp was self-contradictory. Such is the fate of artists who have long outgrown themselves: whenever someone parodied Wagner, he picked on the Wagner of the *Kaisermarsch.* That the composer himself did not take it too seriously is evident from his own parody of the final chorus. This he devised for the girls to sing while parading in honor of Cosima's birthday at the end of 1871. "*Heil! Heil dem Kaiser! König Wilhelm!*" became "*Heil, Heil der Mutter! Unserer Mama!*" As for little Fidi, he produced his own version at table: "*Heil Kuchen!*" ["Hail cakes!"] An anarchist and federalist who had long ago passed sentence on authority in *Der Ring des Nibelungen,* a royal bard and herald of the German Confederation, a revolutionary and author of sternly patriotic verses, Wagner was neither a political tub-thumper nor an opportunist, but a frustrated redeemer: Lohengrin the Second, endeavoring to ally himself with a world to which he did not truly belong. He lacked the skill to do so, and his advice was rejected. When he suggested to Berlin that he might compose some music in honor of the fallen, to be performed on the "august occasion" of the victorious Army's return to the capital, he was informed that it was not proposed to revive painful memories in any such special manner. It was further intimated to him by an editor of the *Norddeutsche Allgemeine Zeitung* that he should beware of supposing that he had acquired a monopoly of the German spirit.

Wagner let matters rest and resumed work on the score of *Siegfried*, which was nearly finished. He also told Ludwig of his intention to advertise the plan for a festival of his own. If all went well, this might result in the establishment of a "German national enterprise whose direction must, of course, be placed entirely in my hands alone." Entirely in my hands alone. . . . The king made no response to this pleonasm. He did, however, sanction a meeting between Wagner and Düfflipp, which took place at Augsburg on April 15.

It was Wagner's first visit to the newly constituted Reich, where he and Cosima spent precisely a month. Accompanied by Peter Cornelius and Richter's friend Reinhard Schäfer, Court Secretary Düfflipp met them on their very first evening at an Augsburg hotel called the Drei Mohren—a name that inspired Cosima to remark in her diary that an attempt was made there to "wash the Moors white" [i.e., milk the pigeon]. The amiable Düfflipp, who was well disposed toward Wagner and always kept a foot in both camps, brought dire news: Because the third act of *Siegfried* was still incomplete, the king had been thinking of presenting the first two acts on their own. Wagner replied that he would rather burn his score than relinquish it under such circumstances, and Düfflipp left empty-handed next morning.

At five o'clock on the afternoon of Monday, April 17, Wagner and Cosima reached Bayreuth. The town, which then had 17,000 inhabitants, made an extremely favorable impression on them, even though Wagner woke up shivering that night and a doctor had to be summoned to the Hotel zur Sonne. On Wednesday, they inspected the margrave's opera house, only to find it too small and florid for a production of the *Ring*. Because the town's location and special characteristics suited his requirements, however, Wagner decided to settle there. He even inspected a possible theater site near the Hofgarten, which turned out to be too low-lying. Although no formal negotiations took place at this stage, his presence caused a great stir among the local inhabitants.

Moving on to Berlin via Leipzig and Dresden, Wagner discussed the practical aspects of the festival venture. A sum of 300,000 thalers would be needed: one-third for the building itself; one-third for technical installations, costumes, and scenery; and the balance for artists and other personnel. This would be raised by an issue of 1,000 "patrons' certificates" at 300 thalers apiece, the right to a free seat being priced at 100 thalers. Management of the patrons' fund was provisionally entrusted to Karl Tausig, the curly-haired and capricious young virtuoso whose charms vanquished everyone, especially the ladies. Bülow was alone in feeling a deep aversion to Tausig's character, though he esteemed him so highly as a pianist that he considered him Liszt's equal, if not his superior. Already a sick man, Tausig set off in July for Leipzig, where, devotedly nursed to the last by Countess Krockow and Marie Muchanoff, he succumbed to typhus at the age of twenty-nine. The infant organization had sustained a blow. But for the vigorous and imaginative efforts of Marie von Schleinitz, wife of the minister of the Prussian royal household, who placed herself at the head of the Berlin patrons' movement, Bayreuth might never have become a reality.

Lothar Bucher, who had been a friend of the Bülows during their Berlin days and had remained loyal to Cosima, secured Wagner an invitation from Bismarck for the evening of May 3. He was largely satisfied with his visit to Bismarck's home, an informal occasion that ended in an exchange of parliamentary gossip, and left with the feeling that he had met "a great and simple personality." When he conveyed his respect for the chancellor, Bismarck replied, "My sole achievement worthy of the name is to have obtained an occasional signature." And again: "I merely discovered the hole in the crown through which smoke can travel." Wagner was greatly taken with Bismarck's candor and charm: not a hint of reticence, an easy tone, and the most cordial and communicative manner, all of it inspiring trust and sympathy. "But we can only observe one another, each in his own sphere. To have dealings with him, to win him over, to ask him to support my cause —that would never cross my mind. I nonetheless regard our meeting as extremely valuable." Bismarck is reported to have told Lothar Bucher that he had never met anyone so self-assured. He may really have meant conceited.

Wagner wrote to Düfflipp on the way back to Switzerland telling him that Ludwig's behavior contained the seeds of a distressing "estrangement." On May 12, as though to punish the erring monarch and make his own position clear, he announced from Leipzig that the first festival would take place in 1873. Without consulting anyone in advance, he also stated publicly that the venue would be Bayreuth. "Your plan relating to the performance of your *Nibelungen* work at Bayreuth is divine," Ludwig wrote to Wagner on May 26, but he had written the contrary to Düfflipp on April 19: "The Wagner plan displeases me greatly. . . ."

The Last Year in Switzerland

While visiting Tribschen on his way from Lugano to Basel early in April 1871, Nietzsche had read Wagner extracts from a manuscript provisionally entitled *Origin and Aim of Tragedy*. Wagner seemed faintly surprised and disappointed that the essay made no mention of his own work, and Nietzsche was anxious not to offend him. Even at the expense of his reputation for scholarship, he resolved to insert an unmistakable reference to Wagner and change the title.

Rumors reached Switzerland in May that the Louvre had been burned, and Nietzsche was deeply shocked by the news. During another visit to Tribschen on May 28, Nietzsche remarked that "for the scholar such events mean the end of all existence." Wagner, who disputed this, retorted, "If you aren't capable of painting pictures again, you aren't fit to possess them." Nietzsche had brought his sister Elisabeth with him. That evening, they all strolled along the picturesque lakeside road. The sun subsided into a sea of flame and the moon floated wanly above the lake in a pale-blue sky. Everyone was overcome by a presentiment of farewell.

Cosima by now regarded Nietzsche with mixed feelings. The professor had given her a copy of his inaugural lecture on Homer. She had since been told in Leipzig by Wagner's nephew Clemens Brockhaus that Nietzsche had also presented a copy to his sister with an identical dedicatory poem. "I had to laugh at first, but now . . . see it as a suspicious trait, a sort of addiction to deceit, as if he were seeking to avenge himself for some strong impression." Whether because of this venial sin or in consequence of the rather disappointing reading in April, Cosima was convinced by July 17 that Wagner had "squandered" more love than he had received. "[Nietzsche] is undoubtedly the most gifted of our young friends," she wrote on August 3, "but most displeasing in many respects because of his not entirely natural reticence. It is as if he were resisting the overpowering effect of Wagner's personality."

Dark thoughts, but not as somber as the music her husband was engaged in composing. The second act of *Götterdämmerung* took shape between June 24 and October 25, 1871, the orchestral sketch between July 5 and November 19. This is Hagen's act, the *Ring*'s grand portrayal of treachery—the blackest thing Wagner ever wrote, and unfailing in its operatic drama. It opens with Alberich's "Sleepest thou, Hagen my son?" At Bayreuth, Wagner once played the scene between Alberich and Hagen on the piano, rejoicing at the effect it would produce. "It will seem as if two strange animals are conversing with each other; *nothing* is intelligible and all is interesting." This was operatic, but its operatic quality acquired still greater depth from Wagner's power of artistic expression.

There were times when the inspiration that had fired him while working on the second act of *Götterdämmerung* struck sparks in the third. "I have composed a Greek chorus," he exclaimed to Cosima on the morning of September 29, "but a chorus that will be sung, as it were, by the orchestra after Siegfried's death and during the scene change; the Siegmund theme will ring out, as if the chorus were saying, 'He was his father'; then the sword motif, and finally his own theme; then the curtain will rise and Gutrune enters, thinking she has heard his horn. How could words ever convey the impression these solemn themes will evoke in their new form? Music always expresses the immediate present." Wagner had perfected his technique: He could now express everything by means of orchestral melody alone. In its wordless recapitulation of the whole vast tragedy, Siegfried's funeral music anticipates the formal conclusion of the *Ring*.

The closer he came to completing his sketch for the end of the *Ring*, however, the more depressed Wagner was by the still unaverted threat posed by Ludwig's rights in his work. On July 20, Cosima found her husband in tears at the thought that the king, who had known and shared all he felt, should have abandoned him in this way. He had striven to be honest in every respect; he stood there in all simplicity, and now, with this one lie, he would go to his grave. "He wept passionately," Cosima noted, and on July 27 she recorded the following outburst: "The humiliation of being dependent on this king is outrageous and intolerable. Were he only to make something of a stand, had he only supported my cause, I could justify myself and him, but as things are . . ." On September 1, Wagner went so far as to predict that, someday "we shall undoubtedly get news from there [Bavaria] of sudden insanity or death." He was right, but fifteen years premature.

For his birthday on August 25, the king received the *Siegfried* piano arrangement only, not the score, so that none of the vocal parts could be extracted from it. All assurances to the contrary, it seemed clear that Wagner had completed the work. Ludwig was so incensed that he tore up the covering letter.

On November 1, 1871, Wagner wrote to Friedrich Feustel, a Bayreuth banker and chairman of the municipal council, to acquaint him with his festival plans and explain why his choice had fallen on Bayreuth. "The place should not be a capital city with an existing theater, nor one of the largest and most frequented spas, which would, especially in summer, bring me a thoroughly unsuitable public. It should be situated in the middle of Germany and in Bavaria, since I propose to settle there for good and naturally think it fitting, while I continue to enjoy the favors shown me by the king of Bavaria, to settle nowhere but in Bavaria itself." His suggestion met with a remarkable response. Only one week later, on November 7, Bayreuth's municipal council was empowered to place at the disposal of Richard Wagner—not a note of whose music the city fathers had yet heard—"any site he might consider suitable" for the construction of a festival theater.

Wagner arrived in Bayreuth on December 14. Next day, he inspected a site the council had offered him near the Stuckberg, in the suburb of St. Georgen. He broke his journey home at Mannheim, where the music dealer Emil Heckel had founded the first local Wagner Society that summer. Although Wilhelm Riehl, a respected but ultraconservative novelist and cultural historian at Munich University, called for the establishment of "anti-Wagner" societies, nothing came of his proposal. The Mannheimers had invited Wagner to give a promotional concert on December 20. Cosima arrived from Basel on December 17, and Nietzsche followed the next day.

Wagner was loudly cheered at the banquet after the concert, which went well. Nietzsche, who sat forlornly among the staunch Wagnerites of Mannheim, was forced to endure what Cosima described as a "doleful" serenade by the local glee club.

The Wagners then left for Switzerland with a party including Hermann Levi, the Karlsruhe kapellmeister, whom Nietzsche greatly admired and Wagner remembered with gratitude for having declined to conduct at Munich in Richter's stead. A small, silent, and introverted man, Levi was the son of a rabbi. He had the helpless charm and lively intelligence of many great musicians, and his reserved manner and sensitive, meditative face, which was framed by a massive beard, captured Wagner's interest. After Levi had left the train, Wagner declared that he respected the kapellmeister "if only because he calls himself plain Levi, not Löwe or Lewin, etc." The evening was spent at Basel with Nietzsche and Fritz Brockhaus, a nephew. Wagner spoke a great deal about Bayreuth. He had been presented with the Stuckberg site by the town, and the laying of the foundation stone was set for May 22, 1872. Theodor Muncker, the mayor, had called for three cheers in honor of Cosima and Fidi. "It will be our creation," Wagner told Cosima. "You will be the margravine of Bayreuth!"

The Mannheim concert served to reinforce Nietzsche's views on art. "What do the rest of my artistic recollections and experiences amount to, beside this latest one?" he wrote to Erwin Rohde. "I felt like someone whose presentiment had at last been fulfilled. For music is precisely that and nothing else, and that—and nothing else—is precisely what I mean by the word 'music' when I describe the Dionysian."

On January 2, 1872, Nietzsche sent Wagner an unbound advance copy of his book, now entitled *The Birth of Tragedy from the Spirit of Music*, as "a token of goodwill and friendship." Great enthusiasm reigned at Tribschen, and Wagner now returned the talented young author's affection in a way that went beyond mere self-interest. He was happy, he said, to have lived to read the book. Everything seemed to be nearing a climax—a meeting of minds such as modern times had never before witnessed. Many of the ideas to which Wagner had undoubtedly given livelier expression in conversation than in his essays on art—and he had entertained a vivid conception of Attic tragedy since 1847—recurred in an intensified and spiritualized form in Nietzsche's sublime prose.

It was his meetings with Wagner at Tribschen that prompted Nietzsche, late in 1871, to consider devoting himself entirely to the Bayreuth project. When Emil Heckel hit on the idea of arranging promotional lectures in every major German city, he offered to relinquish his professorial chair to Rohde. "I myself propose to spend next winter roaming the German Fatherland, that is to say, invited by the Wagner Societies in the larger towns to lecture on the Nibelungen stage festivals." Wagner thought little of this idea. Instead of roaming the country like an itinerant preacher, he said, Nietzsche would do better to mount a campaign against the contemporary educational system in his capacity as a professor of philology.

The Bayreuth project nearly came to grief again when Friedrich Feustel and Mayor Muncker paid an unheralded visit to Tribschen on January 8 and announced that the owner of the proposed site at St. Georgen had refused to sell it to the council. On January 2, however, the council had selected another plot at the foot of the Bürgerreuth. Wagner was so upset by these teething troubles that he declined to negotiate further. All that prevented a breakdown in the proceedings, according to Muncker, was Cosima's "shrewd and amiable persuasion."

After a detour to Berlin, where he found the Patrons' Association flagging badly, Wagner inspected the Bürgerreuth site on February 1 and was at once impressed by its greater suitability. Situated on a gentle incline, with a panoramic view of Bayreuth and the Sophienberg, it was easily accessible yet suitably distant from the center of town. He promptly acquired some land for his future home, a plot adjoining the Hofgarten priced at 12,000 gulden, and appointed Feustel and Muncker to form a festival management committee, the latter to serve as a focal point for the still-uncoordinated Wagner Societies.

And yet, as he resumed work on the composition sketch for act 3 of Götterdämmerung and embarked, in parallel, on the orchestral sketch, he felt far from confident and was more than once tempted to throw in his hand. Tokens of spontaneous support were few, and correspondence relating to preparations for the stone-laying ceremony not only fatigued him but spoiled his appetite for work. Misunderstandings and empty promises abounded; money did not.

But what else did he expect? Revolutionary in original intent, the *Ring* was coming to fruition in the wrong age. It was meant to seem regenerative—radiant as the brand-new Reich—but no amount of rich showpieces for brass sufficed to promote this belief. It remained what it was, and the bitter taste came through. Nowhere did it glorify authority and power, and its only really exultant passage—the *Siegfried* finale—spoke, albeit still inaudibly, of death. Such was the work for which this presumptuous composer was demanding money from the public of the *Gründerzeit*, the heyday of German industrial expansion: money for a gigantic musical dragon and a theater of his own in which gold would be expressly anathematized. The Patrons' Association found it hard to explain this to prospective subscribers.

Understandable though Wagner's disappointments seem, it was naive of him to suppose that the primary manifestation of the "German spirit" was a readiness to pay for the things of the spirit, and that material prosperity would automatically enhance the welfare of art. The nonfulfillment of this belief continued to provide him with food for thought.

The Tribschen years were drawing to a close, and with them his work on the *Ring*. All that remained was its laborious completion, but there were no more changes in its substance. That the *Ring* was consummated at the same time as the German Empire may fleetingly have struck him as an omen, but he did not see any very obvious connection between the two events.

*   *   *

Wagner departed for Bayreuth on April 22, 1872. Nietzsche, who paid his last visit to Tribschen three days later, was sad to have missed him. He found Cosima sorting papers and tidying up, the house littered with packed bags and crated belongings, the dog off its food, the servants in tears. Confronted by this bleak and cheerless prospect, he grasped the full extent of what was coming to an end. "What they mean to me," he wrote to Carl von Gersdorff, "these three years spent near Tribschen, which I visited twenty-three times! Without them, what should I be? I am happy to have crystallized that Tribschen world for myself in my book [*The Birth of Tragedy*]." And in *Ecce homo*, written shortly before his mind gave way, he added a postscript: "I would surrender the rest of my human relationships cheaply; the Tribschen days I would not relinquish from my life at any price. Days of trust, of gaiety, of sublime occurrences—of *profound* moments. . . . I do not know what others may have experienced in Wagner's company, but no cloud ever crossed *our* sky."

Settling in at Bayreuth

No National Theater

Franconia was Wagner's last stop but not, even now, his last address. He began by moving into the Hotel Fantaisie at Donndorf, southwest of Bayreuth on the road to Bamberg. Owned by Duke Alexander of Württemberg, it was bounded immediately to the rear by the spacious grounds of Schloss Fantaisie. On April 30, after a tiring journey, Cosima and the children joined Wagner in this "dreamy, enchanted world." She found the "splendid park," which rang with the shrill screams of peacocks, "even more remote than Tribschen."

Excavation work for the festival theater had begun on April 29, concurrently with the building of the Siegesturm, a victory monument which the patriotic citizens of Upper Franconia had voted to erect on a wooded eminence not far from the Bürgerreuth in memory of those killed in the Franco-Prussian War. Based on Semper's original design, detailed plans for the theater had been worked out since the previous August in consultation with Karl Brandt and the Leipzig architect Otto Brückwald. Brandt, the machinist from Darmstadt, contributed a surprising number of architectural ideas. One of his inspirations was to bring the proscenium forward still further, a feature which Wagner regarded as the interior's crowning glory because it created the illusion of an unbroken transition from auditorium to stage.

But Wagner had little immediate opportunity to confer with Brandt or Brückwald or salute the valiant city fathers of Bayreuth. Accompanied by Cosima, he went off to conduct a concert for the Wagner Society of Vienna, where he stayed with Josef Standhartner and met the last noble Marie to adorn his lifetime's collection. This was twenty-four-year-old Countess Marie Dönhoff, née Principessa di Camporeale. Then the wife of the first secretary of the German embassy in Vienna but later, in 1886, married to Prince Bernhard von Bülow, the German chancellor-to-be, Countess Dönhoff became an enthusiastic sponsor of the Bayreuth project. At Vienna, where Wagner had once been so unhappy, he was now embarrassed enough by the extent of the applause he received to forbid any further tributes from musicians and students. His very first rehearsal on May 8 sent the students of Hellmesberger's conservatory into raptures. That night, however, when he attended a performance of *Rienzi* at the new Opernhaus am Ring, he was so infuriated by the quality of the trumpet playing that he got up during the overture and went off to eat an ice cream. After skulking at the back of his box throughout the performance, he dismayed and upset his loyal Wagnerites by buttonholing Kapellmeister Herbeck and tearing the performers and production to shreds.

Wagner's Viennese friends and critics could not help noticing how much he had aged. His hair was sprinkled with gray. Ludwig Speidel called his thinness "transcendental" and averred that his features "betrayed more markedly the doctrinaire, the pedant, the Saxon schoolmaster." Surprisingly, Eduard Schelle paid tribute to the vigor of a man "who lives out idealistic speculations in an age when the world is ruled by speculation on the stock exchange," but his extremely apt description did nothing to conciliate the press. Wagner was unwise enough not to invite any journalists to the stonelaying ceremony and brushed aside all inquiries about it.

Preparations for the ceremony disclosed an administrative snag which Bayreuth took years to overcome. How was a small and ill-equipped town to house and feed so many demanding visitors? Nearly a thousand musicians, singers, and guests had somehow to be accommodated. To prevent the arriving hordes from milling around in helpless confusion, members of the local athletic club and fire brigade were detailed to meet their trains. Although this eased the situation a little, there were times when the influx proved too much for Bayreuth's stock of horse-drawn conveyances.

On May 22, a rainy day, everyone trudged up the hill through ankle-deep mud. The proceedings opened at eleven o'clock with words of benediction and music from a military band. Wagner struck the stone three times with a hammer and turned away, moist-eyed and pale as death. Because of the incessant downpour, the rest of the speeches were to be delivered in the old opera house. Nietzsche's "Richard Wagner at Bayreuth," the fourth of his *Thoughts out of Season,* describes the drive there as follows: "When, on that May day in 1872, the foundation stone had been laid on the hill at Bayreuth, in pouring rain and beneath a gloomy sky, Wagner drove back into town with a few of our number. He said nothing, and no one word can describe his long, inward-directed gaze. He was that day entering upon the sixtieth year of his life: Everything that had gone before was a preparation for this moment."

"Insofar as artistic ability permits," Wagner declared in the course of his speech at the old theater, "you are to be offered what is most perfect from both the scenic and dramatic aspect." According to notes taken at the time, however, he also pointed out that the scheme had often of late been described as the building of "a national theater at Bayreuth."—"I am not entitled to acknowledge the validity of that description. Where is the 'nation' that is building itself this theater?" In a German parliament, a theater would at best be treated as a chimera. The soil on which the stone had been laid was his personal relationship with the friends of his art. But that was the essence of the German spirit: that it built outward from within. . . . His address was followed by the "Wach' auf" chorus from *Die Meistersinger.*

The commemorative concert, which opened with the *Kaisermarsch* and included Beethoven's Ninth Symphony, did not begin until five o'clock that afternoon. Hans von Bülow took it very much amiss when he heard that Cosima had allowed Wagner to fetch her and the children from their box and range them beside him on the stage. At seven, the guests assembled for a banquet at the Sonne, where places were laid for three hundred people, and two neighboring hotels. Wagner delivered a lively tribute to the king of Bavaria but made no mention of the Reich or emperor. Betz and Niemann retired to bed at half-past nine, their pride doubtless injured because they had not been seated at the celebrities' table. That was another of Bayreuth's burdensome legacies: Everyone there wanted to be more privileged than the privileged, nearer the Grail, admitted to the inner circle of initiates.

It was late when Wagner left his friends and mingled with the artists. "No one present during the dedicatory hours of that day," he wrote later, "could fail to gain the impression that the further fulfillment of my enterprise had become the common concern of widespread artistic and national interests." This was not so, however. The same autumn—Wagner had by then moved to a spacious town house on Dammallee—he stridently complained in a letter to Nietzsche that no help at all was forthcoming from princes and aristocrats. "I, at all events, have reached the stage where I would speak my mind to anyone, and Empress Augusta herself would get an earful if she crossed my path. For one thing is certain: Any form of compromise is out of the question."

Nietzsche's admiration for this uncompromising attitude was tinged with deep spiritual distress. Not only was he feeling intolerably restricted by his academic duties, but his first major treatise on art—a work whose unique qualities he proclaimed with his own brand of Messianic fervor—had cost him dear.

Art reposes on imponderable foundations, as anyone will discover who attempts to measure its marvels. In May 1872, Ulrich von Wilamowitz-Moellendorf had published *Zukunftsphilologie* [*The Philology of the Future*], a riposte aimed at Nietzsche's *Birth of Tragedy*. Trenchant and original, radical and individualistic in its orthography and the use of lowercase initial letters for nouns, it was a pamphlet from the pen of a youthful scholar who later won distinction but never felt altogether happy about this product of his youth because it wounded his opponent more deeply than was customary in a traditional academic dispute—in this case between adherents of the Berlin and Leipzig schools of philology. The main charge against Nietzsche was that he had distorted scientific and historical truth for his own unscientific ends. In fact, neither the "tragic individual" nor the "tragic nation"—still less the genesis of tragedy itself from originally discrete Apollonian and Dionysian elements—was a scientifically demonstrable hypothesis. Philologists could not accept such a theory. Even Nietzsche's tutor, Friedrich Ritschl, pronounced *The Birth of Tragedy* "ingenious claptrap" and fell out with his former pupil. Hermann Usener told his students at Bonn that anyone guilty of writing such stuff was "scientifically defunct." In June, Wagner sprang to Nietzsche's defense in the *Norddeutsche Allgemeine Zeitung* with an open letter in which he expressed his familiar aversion to "professorial culture"—a sentiment that availed Nietzsche little. Erwin Rohde came to his friend's assistance not only by discussing Nietzsche's book but also by publishing a pamphlet of his own entitled *Pseudophilology: . . . A Philologist's Open Letter to R. Wagner.* The damage to Nietzsche's reputation was such, however, that his lectures were poorly attended for some time.

Wagner implored him to come to Bayreuth, but the younger man resisted the temptation to expose himself to the elder's overpowering influence. With a strange flash of clairvoyance, Wagner once predicted in a letter to Nietzsche that the time was coming when he would have to defend *The Birth of Tragedy* against its author.

On the Brink of Ruin

Although Wagner's relations with Liszt were slowly and laboriously normalized, they never quite attained their former intimacy. Wagner was filled with deep suspicion and unfounded jealousy whenever Cosima spent too much time in her father's company. On May 28, 1873, he traveled with her to Weimar for the first complete performance of *Christus,* which was given—contrary to Princess Carolyne's wishes—in the city's Protestant church. Wagner came away with very mixed impressions of the work but persuaded Liszt to come to Bayreuth for the topping-out ceremony at the festival theater site.

The next phase of construction was in jeopardy, however. Only 340 patrons' certificates had been issued by the summer of 1873, and total revenue—inclusive of £500 sterling contributed by the khedive of Egypt—amounted to 154,540 gulden. On June 24, 1873, Wagner dispatched a copy of his brochure, "The Festival Theater at Bayreuth," to Prince Bismarck. A brief covering letter stated that it was sent for information only, not as part of a fund-raising campaign. It did, at the same time, convey the author's "profound anxiety" at the thought that his enterprise should be put into effect without the participation of "the sole ennobling authority." He would have to console himself by reflecting on the fate that had befallen the literary revival of the German spirit during the latter half of the eighteenth century, a process to which Frederick the Great, "albeit the true hero of that revival, remained cold and indifferent." Wagner's letter was never answered, though Bismarck is said to have referred his brochure to a committee.

Flawless weather, a reverential atmosphere, and an architectural design of striking originality were not, therefore, enough to banish every cloud from the horizon when the festival theater was topped out on August 2, 1873. To the strains of the march from *Tannhäuser*, Wagner himself and representatives of the Wagner Societies ascended the building, which was nearly a hundred feet high and decked with German and Bavarian flags. On reaching the platform where Cosima and the children were awaiting him with Liszt and a group of workmen, Wagner delivered a humorous response to the "baptismal" address. Then, after *Nun danket alle Gott* had been sung at this dizzy altitude, everyone repaired to the Malersaal for a gala banquet while the local inhabitants amused themselves on the Bürgerreuth until a display of fireworks brought the day to a close.

On August 30, Wagner was regretfully obliged to confirm a rumor that "the proposed performances cannot take place before the summer of 1875." Bills remained unpaid and construction companies were threatening to suspend work.

Work on the villa adjoining the Hofgarten proceeded with relative speed despite the usual aggravations. In September, while still at the rented house on Dammallee, Wagner received a visit from Anton Bruckner, who had sent him his Second and Third symphonies, in C minor and D minor respectively, in the hope that Wagner would allow one of them to be dedicated to him. Although he had looked at neither score and was eager to get rid of the gauche Austrian, Wagner gave him a cordial welcome. Of course he would accept a dedication, he said. Despite Bruckner's protests that he had just come from Marienbad and was unused to anything but mineral water, he plied the poor man with glass after glass of strong beer. Gustav Kietz, who was engaged on a bust of Cosima, records that Bruckner came to him next morning in a terrible state: Thanks to all the beer, he could not remember which of his symphonies Wagner had chosen. Kietz vaguely recalled an allusion to the key of D minor, but had been so busy modeling that he thought the other two were talking about Beethoven's Ninth. Overjoyed at this solution to his dilemma, Bruckner embraced Kietz warmly. We are left to wonder what Wagner thought when he came to study the score. Did he perceive any element of affinity or continuity? Ernst Bloch's *Geist der Utopie* refers to Bruckner's "clarification" of Wagner; and Dahlhaus writes: "Where Wagner claimed the Beethoven symphony's musical power of speech for the music drama, Bruckner appropriated the musical language of the music drama on behalf of the symphony." Wagner himself affords us no deep insight into his own musical impressions.

Time passed, and still no royal assistance came from Munich. On November 21, 1873, Wagner conferred there with Councillor Düfflipp, who undertook to influence Ludwig in favor of underwriting the theater's construction costs. "But of the king himself," Cosima noted after Wagner's return, "alarming news. Every day he has some new idea, and has hardly been talked out of it when he reverts to it again. He no longer goes out, takes his midday meal at seven in the evening, has sixty candles lit in one small room, and only emerges at eleven to eat again until after midnight. . . . He sees no one but his equerry, who conveyed a reprimand to his aide, Count Hohenstein, whereupon the latter resigned his post!" It was all very worrying indeed.

Back in Bayreuth on November 28, Wagner had a meeting with Karl Brandt and Professor Josef Hoffmann of Vienna, who submitted scenery sketches for the *Ring*, Arnold Böcklin having declined the commission. In quest of artistic "nobility," Wagner had approached painters of historical and mythological subjects, not stage designers. An obstinate and cantankerous man, Hoffmann proved an unfortunate choice and was eventually eased out, but not before he had inflicted a wound from which Bayreuth took half a century to recover. Like the costume designer Carl Doepler a year later, he failed to grasp that a superabundance of perfect illusion is self-defeating.

Wagner was dissatisfied, but what exactly did he want? For one thing, he wanted no pseudo-Germanic portrayals of characters from the medieval *Nibelungenlied* done in the style of Peter von Cornelius and Julius Schnorr. Nor, he wrote to Doepler, would it be suitable to modify examples drawn from classical antiquity. Insufficient attention had hitherto been paid to descriptions of the ancient Germans' dress by Roman authors who had come into contact with them, but would these fill the bill in any case? To conjure up events from a cultural epoch outside human experience, and to do so "with appropriate vividness," was a fascinating challenge to anyone's inventive powers, but it called for a genius who did not exist in the field of scenic design. The Germanic image had been firmly monopolized by trash or ultraromanticism. Although Wagner himself sensed what ought *not* to be, he lacked the visual imagination required to translate his hazy dreams into tangible form.

Early in 1874, the court secretariat formally declined to guarantee funds for the completion of the festival theater. Wagner did not know what he had done to forfeit the king's favor yet again, but rumors of the probable reason finally came to his ears. The poet Felix Dahn had composed an ode to Ludwig, who had well-meaningly suggested that Wagner set it to music. Wagner's refusal to do so, partly because Dahn's metrical system did not lend itself to a musical setting, and partly because he always preferred to supply texts of his own, had upset the king. Ludwig disclaimed any resentment, saying that he could well understand that Wagner had "higher things" to do than set "fulsome poems" to music, but his court officials claimed to know better.

Whatever the precise truth, the festival project was on the brink of ruin. Visiting Wagner on January 8, Emil Heckel found him in utter despair. "He proposed to write me an open letter," Heckel recalled, "explaining that the venture had failed and that better times must be awaited before work on the building could be resumed. He said, 'I shall have the open sides of the festival theater boarded up so that owls will not nest in it, at least, until building can proceed.' " Heckel, who refused to abandon hope, replied that this must not be allowed to happen.

After Heckel's departure, Wagner had another idea. As a last resort, he wrote him a letter for the grand duke of Baden proposing that the emperor himself should crown his enterprise by subsidizing it, and that "in return for a guaranteed subvention of one hundred thousand thalers, or one-third of the total cost, three complete performances of my festival drama *Der Ring des Nibelungen* shall be given in the summer of 1876 at the festival theater constructed especially therefor, on the fifth anniversary of the peace treaty concluded with France." Promptly informed of this plan by Wagner's Mannheim devotee, the grand duke of Baden thought it so unlikely to bear fruit that he declined to act as an intermediary.

Writing to Rohde in January 1874, Nietzsche said, "It has been a cheerless state of affairs since the New Year—one from which I have at last contrived to rescue myself in the strangest way. I began, as coolly and objectively as possible, to examine why the venture has failed. I have learned a great deal in the process and feel I understand Wagner far better than before." But how does one best understand a person in the throes of failure? Only by inward dissociation. Nietzsche's friends would have been amazed if, two years before the great Wagner essay that linked his name forever with the composer's, they had read his jottings on Wagner the "actor and tyrant," the Germans' crudity of form, and a Counter-Reformationist art designed to dominate the theatrical masses. Overbeck alone claimed to recall having heard Nietzsche pass an extremely unfavorable verdict on *Lohengrin*, but Nietzsche kept his coldly analytical aphorisms to himself. As recently as May of the preceding year, he had written the following tribute to Wagner on his birthday: "What should we be if we did not have you, and what should I, for example, be but a stillborn creature! I always quail at the thought that our paths might never have crossed: Life would then be truly not worth living, and I should have no idea at all what to do with my next hour." Now, however, the Dionysian festival, the birth of the heroic from the spirit of music, the "workshop" (Nietzsche's own term for Bayreuth), the "colossal four-towered Nibelungen edifice," the place where dramatic art was to be "ennobled and purified"—as Nietzsche himself had put it in his "Admonition to the German Nation"—all this was coming to grief. The whole enterprise had proved to be an unromantic forceps delivery, and who was to blame? Wagner the "actor."

"His strength and honesty of character," Nietzsche wrote in a draft essay on Cicero in 1874, "is manifest in his capacity as an artist. But his purity of taste is not so great that he can imitate Demosthenes, however much he emulates him. (Wagner—Beethoven.)" The theatrical world was impure, as Nietzsche must have known. The philosopher set himself above the artist, but what if the artist did *not* come to grief? On April 1, Nietzsche wrote to Gersdorff: "If only you knew what an essentially despondent and melancholy view I take of myself as a productive being! All I continue to seek is a little freedom. . . . I can offer nothing in the way of achievements, as the artist or ascetic can. . . ." Conscious that the sole fruit of his great ability was a work whose scholarship had been impugned on account of Wagner's influence, he naturally felt despondent. On April 4, Cosima noted the receipt of a very woebegone letter "from our friend Nietzsche, who is fretting. Richard exclaimed, 'He should either marry or write an opera, though the latter would be such that it would never get performed, and that would not bring him to life either.' " When Nietzsche heard that Wagner and Gersdorff had been toying with the idea of getting him married, he was extremely hurt and shocked by the whole idea. To make matters worse, he was dogged by poor health. His eyes caused him so much pain that he had to undergo a preliminary course of atropine treatment. Nietzsche's long purgatory was beginning.

The Turning Point

Meanwhile, tidings of salvation had reached Bayreuth. On January 25, 1874, Ludwig had a change of heart. "No, no, and again no! It must not end like this; help must be given! Our plan must not fail!" His help, which consisted of an advance secured by royal guarantee, ruined the original festival idea because it necessitated the sale of tickets and turned a theater for all into a theater for the privileged. The contract with the court secretariat provided for a loan of 100,000 thalers. The actual sum guaranteed, 216,152 marks, was gradually repaid by Wagner and his heirs out of the festival theater revenues.

"Oh, my gracious King!" Wagner wrote back on February 3. "If you will but cast an eye at all the German princes, you will see that you are the only one to whom the German spirit still looks in hope." It was true. Whatever had gone before, and whatever else may tarnish our view of this royal friendship, Ludwig for once surpassed himself. But for him, the composer's idealism would ultimately have been thwarted by reality. Wagner was now able, in a letter to Muncker and Feustel dated March 7, to announce that the festival had been postponed for the last time and would definitely take place in 1876.

The villa next door to the Hofgarten was likewise nearing completion in the spring of 1874. Ludwig had made Wagner a gift of 25,000 thalers toward it and granted him permission to build a gateway giving access to the Hofgarten itself. Wagner moved into his new home on April 28, 1874. He experimented with various names before christening it Wahnfried [translatable only by some such approximation as "Illusion's Repose," though *"Frieden"* means peace or tranquillity and *"Wahn"* can connote delusion— even mania or obsession]. It was there, on June 26, that he finished scoring the second act of *Götterdämmerung*. Emil Scaria was auditioned for the part of Hagen the following day.

Nietzsche paid his antepenultimate visit to Bayreuth early in August 1874. Wagner would gladly have kept a room free for him at Wahnfried, but this time Nietzsche stayed elsewhere. He came bearing the piano arrangement of Brahms's *Triumphlied*, which he had heard at a concert in Basel. Scored for choir and orchestra, this was Brahms's musical tribute to the Reich and, as such, a companion piece to Wagner's *Kaisermarsch*. Wagner laughed loudly at the thought of anyone setting the word *"Gerechtigkeit"* [justice] to music.* It was August 8, or two days later, before he decided to give the *Triumphlied* a hearing. Cosima records their great dismay at the "poverty" of the music and mentions that Wagner was extremely irate, calling it "Handel, Mendelssohn and Schumann enveloped in leather." Nietzsche, who had been quite impressed by the work, was nonplussed, but it is improbable that Wagner was being deliberately provocative. In any case, Nietzsche himself did not remain a Brahms enthusiast: When taking leave of his former idol's world in *Der Fall Wagner*, he simultaneously launched a fierce attack on Brahms. He must also have played his own recently completed *Hymnus an die Freundschaft* on the piano before leaving Bayreuth on August 15, for Cosima notes that everyone was dismayed by Nietzsche's musical dilettantism.

Bayreuth settled into its own peculiar kind of daily routine, with artists arriving for auditions, domestic worries, servant problems, and attendances by Wagner at regular Thursday gatherings devoted to historical and political topics. The society of Franconian worthies must have been in sharp contrast to life at Wahnfried, but then, did he ever fit into the world he had created for himself?

He had always made it clear to Cosima that his background was modest, and that much of his life had been spent in socially unacceptable company, but did she really understand this side of him? Cosima disliked his Saxon jokes and imitations of friends from Dresden, not to mention the faces he pulled while sitting for a bust by Gustav Kietz. She once froze with embarrassment to find him with his fingers in his mouth and his eyes crossed, gargoyle fashion.

Wagner was no paragon of gentility or would-be social charmer. Almost defiantly, he informed anyone who cared to listen that his grandfather had been a humble exciseman stationed at the gates of Leipzig. His language at home could be rough and ready, though Cosima not unnaturally refrained from recording many of his pet expressions and turns of phrase. Only in one instance has she left us a phonetic reproduction of his Saxon dialect in full flower.

He was so devoted to the children that he wept on one of the rare occasions when he chastised them in support of Cosima's strict disciplinary code. Cosima herself was a stern parent capable of slapping her offspring hard and sending them supperless to bed—insistent, too, on their kissing her hand whenever they entered the room. The children were well mannered, certainly when their mother had her eye on them, but no amount of discipline could altogether quench their natural exuberance. Wagner, who cracked jokes with them, enjoyed playing paterfamilias to four daughters and a son—a bigger brood than he had ever dreamed of presiding over. It would have cut him to the quick to know that Cosima later repudiated Isolde, the first fruit of their love, and denied that he had fathered her. He could never bring himself to be harsh toward his nearest and dearest, just as he never drew a distinction between his own children and Bülow's, who fondly addressed him as "Father Richard."

This was finality, but was it fulfillment? Was it happiness? Did Wagner ever know contentment? Cosima's record of the early years at Bayreuth is one long succession of crises. Wagner felt genuinely, gravely ill, but no one—not even the doctor—took his symptoms seriously. On August 8, 1872, he had complained of severe palpitations, and on September 17 of the same year he confided to Cosima that he thought there was "something amiss" with his heart. On May 12, 1873, he again felt unwell and spat blood. What alarmed him almost more was his sudden inability to remember words—even the word "death" eluded him while in conversation with the doctor. Names, too, slipped his mind, and his voice would trail off into brooding silence.

Dr. Landgraf, the physician who had been summoned to the Wagners' hotel on their first visit to Bayreuth, could find nothing specifically wrong. He prescribed dieting, mineral water, and long walks, and left it at that. Other doctors whom Wagner consulted on his travels put his chest pains and insomnia down to pressure exerted by the generation of gases in the stomach. This was not so wide of the mark, except that a close relationship exists between the vascular system located above the stomach and the action of the heart, so that excessive pressure gradually destroys the cardiac musculature, a pathological process known today as Roemheld's Syndrome. It was a fatal condition. Modern cardiac therapy would undoubtedly have prolonged Wagner's life. He did not, however, take due care of himself, so a rupture could have occurred at any time. One can only marvel that his heart withstood the strain to which it was subjected in the years that remained to him.

It had been a wearisome, harrowing year, his first at Wahnfried and second at Bayreuth—a year dogged by nightmares and bouts of ill health, financial worries and tidings of death. And yet, for all his anxieties and disappointments, he finally completed the *Ring* on Saturday, November 21, 1874. Cosima's diary gives us a detailed and graphic description of that "thrice sacred, memorable day." Toward noon she heard him calling for the newspapers. Since he had complained the previous day how tired he felt and doubted that he would be finished before Sunday, she thought it meant he was too exhausted to work anymore. Thinking to distract him, she gave him a letter she had just received from her father about their projected visits to Vienna and Budapest. A few minutes later she came upon him reading the letter, and he asked her to explain various points. She told him what she proposed to write in reply, averting her eyes deliberately from the score so as not to annoy him. "Offended, he showed me that it was finished and then said bitterly that, whenever a letter arrived from my father, it banished all my concern for him." She managed to conceal how hurt she felt, but later, when he harped on the subject, emotion got the better of her. She was still weeping when she wrote the following words: "So I have been robbed of this supreme joy, and certainly not because of any reprehensible impulses on my part! 'That a woman should learn to know' ['*Das wissend würde ein Weib*'—Brünnhilde in the final scene of *Götterdämmerung*]. That I have dedicated my life to this work in suffering did not earn me the right to celebrate its completion in joy. Therefore I celebrate it in sorrow, bless the sublime and wonderful work with my tears, and give thanks to the evil god who enjoined that I should first atone for its completion with my suffering."

That night, after she had written the above, Wagner came and embraced her. They loved each other too fiercely, he said; that was the cause of their anguish. It was two weeks before she made another entry in her diary—her longest intermission ever.

*   *   *

With the festival theater's budget temporarily unsecured and Wahnfried swallowing up sums so enormous (15,000 marks a quarter in 1877) that Cosima flinched to record them, Wagner was forever compelled to look for new sources of income. On February 8, 1876, he agreed to a proposal from the German-born American conductor Theodore Thomas that he should write a march to commemorate the hundredth anniversary of the Declaration of Independence. This he had sketched by February 20, though by February 14 he was unashamedly complaining that all he could think of while working on the piece was the $5,000 he hoped to get for it. Not to mince matters, the *Centennial March* turned out to be a musical uproar orchestrated on the scale of *Parsifal*—empty music, like Mendelssohn's *Lorelei*, Bruckner's *Helgoland*, or Brahms's *Academic Festival* Overture. It opens with a thrice-repeated motif that appears to have been borrowed from the overture of Gluck's *Iphigenie*. Why try to conceal this plagiarism when Wagner himself did not? One day in the summer of 1876, during rehearsals for the *Ring*, everyone went up to the festival theater for a performance of the march conducted by the composer. Someone in his party remarked that it was Gluck's birthday. Wagner, who may have detected the insinuation, said nothing at the time. Once in front of the orchestra with baton poised, however, he said for all to hear, "Gentlemen, today is Gluck's birthday. Let us play the new march in his honor."

Plagiaristic or not, the *Centennial March* earned him 9,000 marks from Schott in addition to his fee of $5,000. However indirectly, it also gave a fillip to his musical imagination. It was during February that he sketched the melody for "Komm, schöner Knabe," the Flower Maidens' chorus in *Parsifal*—"trying to be American," as he wrote on the manuscript sheet in question.

On March 1, he traveled to Vienna, where he had promised to conduct *Lohengrin* for the benefit of the chorus. It was his last visit to the capital of the Dual Monarchy. From then on he avoided the city where, as he wrote to Franz Jauner, the director of the Vienna Opera, "any blackguard can attack me with impunity." After Vienna came Berlin and the supervision of rehearsals for a production of *Tristan* to be conducted by Karl Eckert with Albert Niemann in the title role. At the first performance on March 20, which was attended by the emperor, the empress, and their entire court, seats in the stalls fetched 150 marks apiece. Wilhelm I not only received Wagner during the interval but promised to come to Bayreuth for the *Ring*. He further decreed that the net proceeds of the performance, some 5,000 thalers, be remitted to the Bayreuth festival fund.

These successes should have recompensed Wagner for all his self-imposed burden of strain and stress in regard to the festival organization. Ever since *Die Meistersinger* embarked on its triumphal progress, and ever since the Bayreuth project was first announced, his international standing had risen by leaps and bounds. He was a weird and wonderful figure, but the price of glory was high. He had physically overtaxed himself. Writing to Karl Brandt on January 3, 1876, he said that the preliminary rehearsals had left him feeling thoroughly ill. "Hemmed in by cheats, promise-breakers, and rogues of all kinds, I have long been deprived of light relief." The enthusiasm he aroused among fellow artists contrasted strangely with the response he evoked from the public. An object of alarm rather than affection, he could only console himself with the forthcoming production of his magnum opus. Although he was not indifferent to the world's opinion of him, it would have been too late then to correct it.

The First Festival

―――――◆―――――

The Rehearsals

The last page of *Götterdämmerung* was engraved at Schott's on May 9, 1876. On the same day, Richard Fricke, ballet master and assistant director at Dessau, arrived in Bayreuth to begin rehearsals. A grizzled little man with a keenly observant eye, Fricke kept a record of his weeks there. He was alarmed to note the extent of the difficulties that beset the whole venture. He also found it hard to please Wagner, who demanded the impossible of him, and it was several days before he learned to understand him at all. "He speaks rather like someone talking to himself for his own benefit, then blusters in such a way that one can only roughly piece together what he means. He bursts out laughing, turns irritable, then promptly laughs again, sarcastically railing against whatever happens to annoy him." There were incessant conferences, altercations with singers, difficulties with scenery. The head of the enormous dragon, which had been made in London, turned up late and was only sewn on during the first act of *Siegfried*—upside down, with the result that the head and neck did not fit properly. The budget came under severe strain. Little money was coming in, and by early June each day of rehearsals was costing 2,000 marks. Feustel reported that the festival coffers would be empty before the month was out. Faced with disaster, Wagner angrily declared that the Bayreuthers lacked esprit de corps and regarded the festival merely as a chance to line their pockets.

Just when rehearsals began, Wagner developed a gumboil so severe that it temporarily kept him away from the theater with agonizing pains in the cheek and jaw. Fricke confided to his diary that Wagner wanted to be his own producer but had lost his eye for detail, under the circumstances, and forgot his instructions from one day to the next. "Wagner speaks quietly, indistinctly, gesticulates a great deal with his hands and arms; the final words of a sentence convey approximately what he wants, and one has to pay attention like mad. I think I shall soon get the hang of it."

Much of what followed was the product of daring improvisation. This applied equally to Brandt's feats of technical ingenuity, not the least of which were the Rhine Maidens' swimming machines. It was still uncertain, when the first run-through was held on June 3, whether the underwater scene could be presented at all. "The sisters Lilli and Marie Lehmann and Fräulein Lammert had arrived. Friendly salutations. They looked at the machines and the gymnasts [locally recruited stand-ins] swimming in them. 'No,' said Lilli, 'nobody can expect that of me. I won't do it at any price.'" She added that she had been confined to bed until recently and was still feeling light-headed. To reach their elevated cradles, which could be propelled to and fro as well as raised and lowered, the ladies had to climb a ladder. Brandt and Fricke helped them up. "With 'Ach's and 'Oh's, squeals and squeaks, we strapped them in, and the voyage began quite slowly." One man sat at each vehicle's steering wheel while another operated the mechanism that raised and lowered the passenger—who had to sing reclining on her stomach—and a musical coadjutor synchronized her evolutions with the score. Lilli Lehmann preserved a horrific recollection of the final rehearsal, at which someone hit on the idea of "attaching to the footrest a train gummed to wire mesh whose tremulous movements communicated themselves to us as well as our machines and never let us come to rest. I can still hear Flosshilde calling, 'Mottl [her musical coadjutor], I'll spit on your head if you don't hold me still!'" When the scene was over, the machines were pushed into the wings and berthed alongside small timber platforms. It took some time to release the singers from their harness. Suspect as they had seemed at first, however, these contraptions proved theatrically effective in the highest degree.

"At all these preliminary rehearsals," Fricke wrote on June 8, "I am nonetheless becoming concerned about Wagner's health. He darts between the singers, stands beside them, and demonstrates gestures. His volatile temperament makes him forget yesterday's remarks and instructions in regard to scenes, positions, and changes of position. When someone comes up to him and says, 'Dear Meister, yesterday you said such and such,' he promptly and vehemently retorts, 'No, no, today I want it like this.' And the next day he says, 'You can leave it like that.' " Wagner's vacillations were a symptom of his uncertainty in the face of something totally untried. He was acting for the first time ever as his own director, producer, chief administrator, and designer. Musically, too, Hans Richter—who was uncertain of the composer's preferred tempi— did no more than wield the baton as his viceroy on the podium. On the stage itself, Wagner demanded—according to Heinrich Porges—absolute realism. Complaining that the stage direction "Mime rubs his back" in scene 3 of *Rheingold* had not been carried out vigorously enough, he told the singer, Schlosser, to extend the scope of the gesture and "give his ass a good rub" as well. "The piccolo gives some suggestive little trills there anyway." Cosima, who had been watching the rehearsal from the rear of the auditorium, silently left the theater.

At a *Walküre* rehearsal on June 17, Wagner urged Josefine Scheffsky (Sieglinde) and Albert Niemann (Siegmund) to kiss each other more ardently. To demonstrate what he meant, he launched himself at Niemann, who was so tall that he could only reach him by standing on tiptoe. "It was positively alarming," wrote Fricke, "to see how energetically Wagner conducted the battle on the mountaintop. Niemann averted his gaze: 'Great Heaven, if only he would get down! If he falls, it's all over.' But he didn't fall; with a swollen cheek still swathed in cotton wool and a thick cloth, he sprang like a chamois into the valley. Wagner is, and remains, one of the oddest figures imaginable. To the young musicians who had settled themselves behind the scenes with their piano arrangements, he said in passing, 'Must you really have those old books in your hands—don't you know it by heart yet?' When Betz (Wotan) asked him, so as to know where to stand, 'Where does Fricka enter?' Wagner said, 'Left, the devil always enters from the left.' "

He almost reduced Fricke to despair with his eternal second

thoughts. While rehearsing *Walküre* on June 20 and 21, he altered all the arrangements he had made on June 19. "He went still further—he even varied the orchestral tempi and demanded a complete change in Brünnhilde's passage, '*Lebe, Weib, um der Liebe willen,*' which he had caused to be taken quite slowly the day before. He was terribly agitated, leaping around and stamping his feet in a way that made one turn hot and cold. The Valkyries, armed with big, heavy shields and spears, were bathed in sweat. Sieglinde had quite pleased him yesterday in her difficult passages, '*Rette mich, Kühne, rette mein Kind,*' et cetera, but today nothing was good enough for him. With an angry gesture, he turned away from her and muttered irately to himself. I had never seen him like that before."

The strain began to tell. On July 22, with his final goal in sight, Wagner's thoughts turned to death. Going to the window that night, he saluted his natal constellation, the Great Bear, and said, "Protect my wife and children, good star. Do with me what you will."

Almost the only bright spot in these weeks of excessive nervous tension was the arrival of Nietzsche's "Richard Wagner at Bayreuth," the fourth of his *Thoughts out of Season.* To this Nietzsche had devoted every good waking hour in a nightmarish six months during which his health had dramatically worsened. Christmas 1875 brought him to the verge of total collapse, smitten with violent headaches and fainting fits that led him to fear he was suffering from a brain disease like his father, who had died at the age of thirty-six. "In my case," he told Carl von Gersdorff, "it may be even quicker."

We possess a graphic description of Nietzsche's ailments. They included stomach trouble, spells of remorseless pain experienced at intervals of weeks or only days, "a sensation closely akin to seasickness lasting several hours in a day," outbursts of insensate fury, nights spent retching on an empty stomach, pressure in the head, and a recurrent fear of blindness. This condition did not cloud his mind; it simply rendered him incapable of leading a normal life, and a lesser mortal would have been silenced long before he actually was. Provisionally relieved of his academic duties on February 6, 1876, he was thereafter able to complete the fourth of his *Thoughts out of Season* only by husbanding his strength with extreme care. That he did not wish to complete it at all is only one myth among many, but there were certainly times when he thought it too private for publication.

The truth is enshrined in the draft of a letter addressed to Wagner in July: "If I thought only a little differently of you, I should not publish this piece." An earlier letter marking Wagner's birthday on May 22 had avowed Nietzsche's "eternal disquietude" at the composer's hands and declared that "the dearest hopes I pin on the events of this summer are that *many* shall be similarly disquieted by you and your work and thus gain a share in the greatness of your nature and career." Far from being an outdated and insincere tribute to a master at the height of his fame, "Richard Wagner at Bayreuth" was a final hymn to a friendship that Nietzsche himself would not long be able to sustain—a tribute instinct with the sadness of farewell. But was ever an artist extolled in this way by a philosopher? "Wagner has devised a style that signifies infinity; he has become heir to Hegel, music as an idea. . . ." What Nietzsche adduced from his youth and life in explanation of Wagner's specific genius for expression and theatrical rhetoric was music in the ears of the master of Bayreuth. "Friend," he wrote back, "your book is stupendous! How ever do you come to know so much about me?" On July 11, Cosima telegraphed her thanks for "the sole refreshment and edification" vouchsafed her apart from her overwhelming impressions of the *Ring*. Malwida von Meysenbug had been urging Nietzsche since July 3 to make the trip to Franconia. He finally set off on July 23, although a letter to Gersdorff dated two days earlier described his state of health as "lamentable."

Nietzsche sat in on rehearsals of *Götterdämmerung* from July 24 to 26. On July 25, he wrote to his sister: "From noon Sunday until Monday night, headaches; today, exhaustion. I simply cannot wield a pen. I was at the rehearsal on Monday. It did not please me at all, and I had to leave." In view of the frequent interruptions, which prolonged each act interminably, even a fit man would have felt taxed beyond endurance—and Nietzsche could see almost nothing in poor light. The reality of these evening rehearsals was more than a little depressing: faulty tempi, which Wagner furiously criticized, tottering scenery, a general air of theatricality. As *Nietzsche contra Wagner* puts it: "It is clear that I am fundamentally antitheatrical by nature. For the theater, that mass art par excellence, I nurse in the depths of my soul the profound contempt that every artist now feels." And, in the midst of that mass art, Nietzsche now had his first experience of the artist qua dictator. It was a Wagner such as he had never known before: a lion tamer, a man of action, an autocrat viewed with fear as well as admiration, a chieftain who kept his tribe of singers, instrumentalists, and machinists sweet with coarse jests. What could such a man know of a philosopher's solitude, of the pain that afflicts a seeker after truth? Nietzsche sat there alone in the gloom, suffering torments of alienation; Wagner stood in the limelight that betokened illusion—and happiness. Whatever element of falsity this happiness contained, and whatever distress Wagner may have felt at the artistic flaws in his dream come true, he was enjoying a kind of fulfillment and triumph: The emperor and empress had graciously consented to come.

Nietzsche's disillusionment, which went deeper than his impressions of the Bayreuth public, is echoed by concurrent entries in Cosima's diary. "Realize more and more how imperfect the representation is," she noted on July 26. "The performance will fall as far short of the work as the work itself is removed from our time!" And on July 28: "In the evening, costume tryout. When I asked Professor Doepler to make Siegfried's costume somewhat less tight-fitting and those of Gutrune's women less gaudy, the poor man became so incensed and rude that it dawned on me for the first time what a bungler we're dealing with. All the costumes are reminiscent of Red Indian chiefs and, apart from their ethnographic absurdity, bear the impress of small-town-theater tastelessness." Alberich, in his cloak and epaulettes, looked positively ludicrous.

Here again is Nietzsche on July 28: "I have now seen and heard the whole of *Götterdämmerung*. It is a good thing to get used to it, and I am now in my element." On July 31, during *Die Walküre*, he found the light unbearable and had to listen with his eyes shut. On August 1: "Persistent headache . . . I long to depart; remaining here is too nonsensical. I quail before each of these lengthy art-evenings, yet I do not stay away." Elisabeth, to whom these querulous letters were addressed, deleted all reference to illness from the first edition of *Der junge Nietzsche*. This made it seem that her brother had defected or worse, but his own *Fröhliche Wissenschaft*, Book 5, conceded that his objections to Wagner's music were "physiological" and demanded, "Why disguise them in aesthetic formulas?"

Silent and gloomy during rehearsals, Nietzsche fled Bayreuth on

August 2 or 3—before the final run-through—for Klingenbrunn near Regen in the Bavarian Forest, where he had another bad spell at the Gasthaus zum Ludwigstein. His exhaustion was so great that he could not shake it off. *"Incessant* pains in the head, as at certain times in Basel," he wrote to Elisabeth. Pondering on the desecration of his idol, he forged some aphorisms that developed into the makings of another book, originally entitled *The Plowshare.* They warned against the cultural idea which he had only just proclaimed in "Richard Wagner at Bayreuth." But Nietzsche did not make things easy for himself. He proposed, after all, to return to Bayreuth for the opening of the *Ring.* Meanwhile, other visitors had arrived there.

It was widely rumored that King Ludwig would come, but he did not wish to be seen. The peculiar circumstances of his arrival were elicited by only one Berlin newspaper reporter, who stationed himself on the open section of track near the Rollwenzelei, where Ludwig's train was expected during the night of August 5–6. Cosima accompanied Wagner to the railroad station and then drove home. Wagner, attired in a dark suit and white waistcoat, paced up and down with Georg the manservant at his heels. Only the railroad director and a few local peasants had assembled in the brilliant moonlight. It was after midnight when the train, consisting of three cars for Ludwig and his entourage and one each for servants and baggage, halted at the signalman's cabin above the Rollwenzelei. The royal carriage drove up a specially prepared farm track preceded by a mounted servant bearing a storm lantern. Ludwig alighted and walked to his carriage, where Wagner's diminutive figure awaited him. They shook hands in silence and drove off together to the Eremitage. Wagner did not get back to Wahnfried until three in the morning.

Before the *Rheingold* dress rehearsal on August 6, which had to be postponed for an hour on his account, the king sent for Cosima and told her that she should never have doubted his abiding loyalty. That night, when the performance was over, Ludwig and Wagner drove through the festively illuminated streets. Fricke, who happened to be just behind the royal carriage, noted: "The king, of course, had declined everything [in the way of public appearances]. He adhered to this resolve until he drove through Bayreuth after all, though in a closed carriage. A remarkable king indeed!" On Monday morning, August 7, Ludwig sent a letter to

Wahnfried: "No mere words can adequately convey my enthusiasm and sense of deepest gratitude."

August 7 was *Walküre* day. This time, for acoustics' sake, every seat in the house was filled. After the first act Wagner left the royal box and thanked Albert Niemann, who had sung superbly, in a faltering voice choked with tears. Turning to address the orchestra, he was still so affected that he could hardly get a word out. When the king returned to the Eremitage after attending this dress rehearsal, so Fricke was told, he went for a walk on the grounds with his retinue, singing the while. He then gave orders for the fountains to play to an accompaniment of Bengal lights.

Ludwig set off for Hohenschwangau after the last dress rehearsal on August 9, again by night. Wagner, who saw him off, thought he detected a hint of annoyance in his manner: Having forbidden any kind of public demonstration at Bayreuth, he seemed surprised that none had taken place. Nevertheless: "You are a god-man," Ludwig wrote on August 12, "—the true artist by God's grace who has brought the sacred fire from heaven to earth to purify, beautify, and redeem it! The god-man who in truth can neither fail nor err!"

On the same day, Saturday, August 12, Nietzsche returned from Klingenbrunn to Bayreuth and Wilhelm I arrived by special train. After being greeted at the station with cheers, the emperor told Wagner, "I never thought you'd pull it off."

The Performances

The *Ring* attracted four crowned heads to Bayreuth: the emperors Wilhelm I of Germany and Dom Pedro II of Brazil; the king of Bavaria, who only returned for the third series of performances because he had no wish to meet any of his fellow monarchs; and the king of Württemberg. "It seemed true indeed," Wagner wrote in his "Retrospect of the Stage Festivals of 1876," "that never had an artist been thus honored; for though it was not unknown for such a one to be summoned before an emperor and princes, no one could recall that an emperor and princes had ever come to him." Grand Duke Carl Alexander of Saxony-Weimar was greeted at the station by Franz Liszt, who had been in Bayreuth since August 1. The town teemed with noblemen and notabilities. Visitors to the festival included the grand duke of Schwerin and the Prussian princesses, Household Minister Count von Schleinitz and Countess Marie, the countesses Dankelmann and Usedom, the Dönhoffs and diplomats Robert von Keudell and Joseph Maria von Radowitz. The Austro-Hungarian nobility was represented by Prince Rudolph Liechtenstein, Count Julius Andrássy, and counts Salm, Csáky, and Apponyi. Of the three German parliamentarians sighted—Franz Duncker, Heinrich von Marquardsen, and Cornelius Heyl—none belonged to the Social Democratic or Center parties.

No bizarre and novel occasion of this kind could fail to be seized on by the souvenir industry, which brought out Nibelungen caps and Wagner cravats. Restaurants became unbearably crowded, patrons waited in vain for service, and waiters were run off their feet. During the first cycle, music was a less frequent topic of conversation than sausages, beer, schnitzels, and fried potatoes. The mental strain imposed by long nights of concentration on unfamiliar operas and daily delvings into voluminous libretti was compounded, thanks to the torrid and sultry weather, with physical exhaustion. On August 13, in default of sufficient carriages, many of the audience tramped through the dusty streets for their first visit to the "red barn" of a theater on the hill.

The house was jam-packed by six-thirty that evening. Surveying the auditorium, the Berlin critic Isidor Kastan spotted all the "music-of-the-future Amazons, Valkyries out of uniform, so to speak," wallowing in rapture. He also noted the "Berlin aura" emanating from various big-time writers and critics, who swapped repartee until the emperor entered his box in unwonted civilian dress.

The prelude came to an end, and the curtain—the newfangled "Bayreuth Lens," gathered at the top and sides—rose on the Rhine scene, with Karl Hill as Alberich. What happened after that episode, which went quite well, was less gratifying. *Rheingold* seemed dogged by misfortune. Franz Betz, who had mislaid the ring, made two quick dashes into the wings during the curse, and a stagehand raised the backdrop too soon during the first scene change, disclosing the rear wall of the theater and a group of fellow stagehands standing around in their shirt sleeves. Fricke summed up: "Many of the scene changes went wrong, and it is fair to say that none of these mistakes had occurred at any rehearsal. Wagner was called for half an hour at the end, but did not come. He sat in his room, beside himself with rage, cursing all the performers except for Hill and me, who were with him. There was no pacifying him." He left his place of torment looking distraught, and his spirits did not revive until the emperor of Brazil paid a late-night visit to Wahnfried.

Paul Lindau, who has been quite unjustly vilified by Wagner's literary devotees for his "*Nüchterne Briefe aus Bayreuth*" ["Down-to-Earth Letters from Bayreuth"], wrote of this first performance: "To sum up the evening right away, I shall begin by remarking that my own impression of it was that Wagner's confirmed supporters were not as satisfied with the performance as they had hoped, and that Wagner's opponents were not as disappointed as they had feared." This hit the nail on the head, and everyone waited eagerly to see what the next day would bring forth.

To observers who were not of Wagner's inner circle, *Die Walküre's* three acts seemed, first and foremost, too long. Lindau wrote: "Wagner says all that is in his heart, and sometimes, unless I am mistaken, a trifle more." The enormous dimensions of the work became all the more noticeable because the sets were comparatively poor. During the interval, Wagner was summoned to the emperor's box. Wilhelm said jocularly that, had he been a musician, Wagner would never have lured him down into the orchestra pit. He also regretted being unable to attend the last two works in the cycle. He said good-bye, took a pace backward, failed to notice the step, and stumbled so badly that it was all Wagner could do to save him from falling. He remained convinced that a backward fall would have spelled the old man's death.

In *Siegfried,* which had to be postponed until August 16 because Betz was indisposed, Georg Unger—in the title role—was always overshadowed by Carl Schlosser's Mime and Amalie Materna's Brünnhilde. Lilli Lehmann sang the Forest Bird and Louise Jaide made an intelligent Erda. Paul Lindau gives a graphic account of his very diverse impressions of the three acts of this memorable first performance. He was utterly enthralled by the forging scene: "What Wagner here attempts and achieves with the orchestra is indescribable." Atmosphere and action were enhanced by "irresistibly thrilling" music of a kind unheard before. "In reality, the orchestra here becomes the sole agent of the plot, the true hero. It works the puffing bellows and makes sparks fly on the hearth. It

smelts and casts and welds and hammers and files—it does everything. Less brilliantly executed, it would be puerile; the way Wagner does it is magnificent, wonderful. The forging scene is
admirably authentic. The orchestra is no less important in the
poetic second act. The whole of this long act is pervaded by a
rustling sound, an indeterminate humming and wafting that
moves one most strangely. An Eichendorff lyric on the grandest
scale."

This passage has been purposely cited in rehabilitation of its
author. An Eichendorff lyric. . . . Who else would have hit on such
a comparison but Paul Lindau, a man still decried to this day for
his allegedly malicious and denunciatory pamphlet.

But then came the dragon, for so long a topic of conversation
and object of speculation throughout Bayreuth. "It is a big monster that bears not the slightest resemblance to the lindworm of
our German imagination: no wings, a cross between a lizard and
a porcupine, bunches of hair—a great ugly beast that can roll its
eyes, open its jaws, and lash its tail. As soon as it is propelled onto
the stage, its great size and singular appearance claim our whole
attention. We no longer listen to the music, we no longer listen to
the singing, we gaze at our lindworm. Anyone who can, with an
easy mind, give an assurance that he even momentarily took an
interest in the words and music throughout the lindworm scene
—anyone able to claim that he felt anything during this scene but
frivolous curiosity—let him stand forth and have the courage to
utter that quite unbelievable statement in the presence of fifteen
hundred spectators. . . . Into the wings with the lindworm!" And
so thought everyone.

Despite this, Lindau described the first performance of *Siegfried*
as Wagner's real triumph. "Think what you may of the artistic
trend itself that Wagner represents, all who emerged from the
festival theater yesterday took with them the profound conviction
that they had there been treated to a magnificent work by a magnificent artist."

The premiere of *Götterdämmerung* on August 17, with Gustav
Siehr as Hagen, caused all concerned much toil and anxiety. "Final
scene beneath all criticism!" Fricke noted in his diary. "Wagner is
feeling from day to day how differently his work can be staged; he
senses all the things that must be banished and cast aside. 'Next

year we shall do everything differently,' he told me in confidence."
But there was no next year.

After the final ovation, Wagner joined the whole cast on stage.
"The Muses," wrote Lindau, "have denied Wagner the blessed gift
of eloquence. Whenever he opens his mouth some mishap occurs."
Tonight was no exception. "You have now seen what we can do,"
he said. "Now it is for you to *want*. And if you want, we shall have
an art!" So saying, he bowed and walked off. To those who had
made so many sacrifices on his behalf, it sounded churlish and
ungrateful. What more did he expect? What had they had until
now, if not art? As usual, Wagner was compelled to explain and
apologize. Addressing the artists at a banquet in the festival restaurant on August 18, he denied having meant that art was still lacking
in what they had achieved together; what they lacked was a national art such as that of the French and Italians. Then he para-
phrased *Faust:* the transient was symbolic in art, too; but what they
had offered the public, however inadequate it might have been in
many respects, should nonetheless be accounted an event. The idea
had brought them to the summit of their ability, so it would probably be fair to say that he had the beginnings of a *new* art to offer.
With a strangely tearful smile, he concluded, "I really mean that,
believe me. I really mean it." Later in the evening he rose to deliver
another short address. With a sudden gesture at his father-in-law,
he declared that, but for Liszt, they might never have heard a note
of his music. Then he went over and embraced him.

Wagner attended the third cycle, which spanned the period
August 27–30, in the company of Ludwig II. Recalling these occasions on November 5, he told Cosima that "his uppermost thought
during the performances was 'Never again, never again!' He had
winced so much that the king asked what ailed him, and he had to
restrain himself by main force." On September 9, Cosima noted:
"Richard is very sad, says he wishes to die!" Was it a Pyrrhic
victory?

"Wagner has achieved what no artist before him even ventured
to aspire to," wrote Paul Lindau. "Bayreuth—to use his own description of the sum of all these efforts and results—Bayreuth
is not a 'national undertaking'; indeed, its eminently personal
character renders it the complete negation of the national. But
undoubtedly, it is the most potent individual achievement imagin-

able." Those who had come to Bayreuth for art's sake alone found it all the harder to endure the side effects of this individual achievement: an intolerant band of devotees, faith instead of understanding, arrogance and proselytism—in short, a cult. "What prevails here," Lindau reported, "is a menial subservience such as can scarcely be imagined. Anyone who does not quite belong to the orthodox feels as isolated and uneasy as a liberal reporter at a Lassallean workers' rally." The Wagnerite Alfred Pringsheim—future father-in-law of Thomas Mann—menaced a non-Wagnerite with his beer glass in the taproom of an inn. The majority of these arguments centered on form and formlessness and that questionable concept, the universal work of art [Gesamtkunstwerk].

The art historian Conrad Fiedler declined to be misled by disputes between supporters and opponents over faults in production and Wagner's artistic pretensions. Though not among those who believed that Wagner had reinvented music, he pointed out that "A truly novel production based on content will . . . always seem revolutionary, and will at first have an appearance of formlessness." Form was not a finite quantity, he went on, and he discerned in the *Ring* a striving after something new in the way of form. "In Wagner, dramatic occurrence and music are not in any way contrasted; instead, the dramatic occurrence first comes to life in the music. So far from being independent of and separate from the occurrence, the music never relinquishes the occurrence, as it were, and is not relinquished by it, so that the latter finds ever more concentrated expression."

The professional newspaper critics seemed incapable of such discernment. Eduard Hanslick did at least praise the scenic marvels and technical tricks. He also acknowledged Wagner's musical stature but questioned whether it ought to be an opera composer's ambition to "make music to a series of magical machines." Wilhelm Mohr's verdict was that, even if the whole affair had been a fiasco, Wagner had carried the day: His work of art had won the battle for him, not his ideas. Musically, he had triumphed. Reviewing the "musical drudgery" of the first two festival evenings on August 20, 1876, Ludwig Speidel wrote in the *Wiener Fremdenblatt* that Wagner imitated real occurrences, and that his music was "the most skillful aping of reality." Isaac Moses Hersch sarcastically asserted in "Herr Richard Wagner, the Musical Struwelpeter" that Wagner was "confused and shaky"—a "buffoon" of a composer. Renewing his attack in the *Wiener Fremdenblatt* on October 15, Speidel demanded to know "What is national about Wagner's libretto for *Der Ring des Nibelungen?*" The German nation had nothing in common with such an outrage, he went on, and "should it ever take genuine pleasure in the fool's gold of the 'Nibelungen Ring,' it would, on that sole account, be stricken from the ranks of the civilized nations of the West." Descriptions such as "shoddy work" and "folly" were not infrequent.

Something alien had appeared on the scene. Writing in our own century, when the clouds of poison gas and incense had to some extent dispersed, Ernst Bloch declared: "Satan's angel is the splendor of baroque amid the bourgeoisie, in its German alliance with stale, refurbished, romantic feudalism." Nietzsche, too, had spoken of baroque—as of so many other things—and the word has lately cropped up elsewhere. Though not entirely irrelevant, it is not entirely apt, for quite another angel presided over this encounter between the newly rich, newly refurbished, and art in the grand manner presented in a provincial German town. This angel was not only alien but stimulating, and thus capable of an extremely powerful and enduring effect such as the splendor of baroque could not have produced on its own. It was the reappearance of the High Renaissance in a German *Gründerzeit* environment, and Guido Adler and Albert Schweitzer were the first to point out that no one stands closer to Wagner than Claudio Monteverdi.*

Once art and society have drawn apart and lost their points of congruence, there exists in this "long-winded" art on the grand scale an undeniable, irrevocable antinomy that poses a problem to art of almost any kind—the conflict between the culinary process and the actual ingredients. Art is an extremely delicate confection.

What radiated from this Renaissance pageantry of the *Gründerzeit?* "The splendor emanating from Valhalla is an illusion sustained by the music, provided one does not listen to it too closely," writes Carl Dahlhaus. "The dead gods return to die again." The myth demonstrates how everything decays and perishes, to be replaced by something different. But this is lost on the audience. Confronted by Germany's only socialist work of art prior to the advent of naturalism, the Reich's upper classes were enchanted!

Anticlimax

One man had remained and said nothing. After returning to Bayreuth for the start of the festival, Nietzsche hung on there for another two weeks. He was generally to be found in the shady garden behind Malwida von Meysenbug's house, depressed and brooding darkly with his head bowed beneath its smooth thatch of brown hair and his mouth concealed behind an ever more luxuriant mustache. Simply but neatly dressed, Nietzsche had what Lou von Salomé describes as "a quiet, almost inaudible way of speaking and a cautious, pensive gait." He shunned the crowds—Wagnerites included—and found it hard to endure the mediocrity of the petty scribblers whom he categorized as "Nohl, Pohl, and Kohl." When addressed on the subject of his Bayreuth pamphlet he responded almost coolly. The heat exacerbated the headaches that drove him to periodic outbursts of temper.

"My error," Nietzsche sorrowfully confessed, "lay in coming to Bayreuth with an ideal, so I had to suffer the keenest of disappointments. I was strongly repelled by the superabundance of all that was ugly, distorted, and overwrought." Wagner had so little time to spare that Nietzsche seldom exchanged a word with him. On one occasion, Nietzsche chanced to visit the Bayreuth lunatic asylum. We are told that the angst-ridden visitor was given some poems by inmates to peruse, one of them entitled *Christ as a Butterfly's Proboscis.* *

On August 27, Nietzsche returned to Basel with Edouard Schuré, who happened to be traveling on the same train. He devoted some of the journey to telling Schuré about his few conversations with Wagner: "He told me he proposed to reread world history before writing the poem for *Parsifal.*"

Other friends departed one by one, Mathilde Maier last of all, and peace descended on Wahnfried. Wagner, who wanted to put some distance between himself and Bayreuth, was feeling the pull of the Mediterranean. He still spoke with remarkable confidence of repeating the cycle the following year, dominated solely by the thought that he must remedy the remaining defects in the *Ring*'s staging and presentation. "My work is still incomplete," he wrote to August Förster, codirector of the Leipzig Theater, on September 6. "The performances have shown me that much remains to be done. So give me time to present my work again next year, here at Bayreuth, in a carefully corrected form." He did not deliver his most scathing verdict on the first series of performances until two years later. "It was all wrong!" he told Cosima on July 23, 1878. One cannot but marvel at the perseverance and success with which the Bayreuth set not only denied Wagner's awareness that the first *Ring* performances had missed the mark but actively strove to perpetuate their shortcomings.

Soon after Wagner and his family left Bayreuth on September 14, Feustel's preliminary computation of the festival's financial deficit reached him at Verona. This deficit rose by degrees to 148,000 marks, banishing any prospect of repeating the venture on the existing basis.

At Naples, Wagner received a letter from Nietzsche, who was also casting southward glances. "After *this* summer, the autumn seems to me, and doubtless not to me alone, more autumnal than any previous one. Underlying great events is a streak of blackest melancholy from which one certainly cannot escape fast enough to Italy, or work, or both." When he thought of Wagner in Italy, he recalled that that was where the inspiration for the beginning of the *Rheingold* music had come to him, and he wished Wagner nothing but beginnings. "You know, perhaps, that I too am going to Italy next month; but less, I think, as I would to a land of beginnings than to one that will end my sufferings. These have reached another peak. It really is high time. My [university] authorities know what is entailed by granting me a whole year's leave of absence, disproportionately great though this sacrifice is for a small community. They would lose me one way or the other unless they offered me this means of escape. In recent years, thanks to my long-suffering temperament, I have endured unceasing pain as though born to it and nothing else."

Leaving Naples for Sorrento on October 5, the Wagners moved into an annex of the Hotel Vittoria, situated well over a hundred feet above the sea on the edge of a cliff. They swam, went for donkey rides, and made an excursion to Capri, whence they returned "amid shooting stars and phosphorescent waves." In the middle of the month the weather changed. The sea was lashed by a tempest complete with hail and thunder—an inauspicious prelude to Nietzsche's sojourn in Italy. At Genoa, he was confined to bed with a headache and nausea—"duration of condition, forty-four hours," he wrote to Elisabeth. Malwida von Meysenbug, who had rented the Villa Rubinacci at Sorrento, urged him to come and recuperate there under her motherly supervision. Nietzsche accepted the invitation and asked if he might bring two friends with him. These were Albert Brenner, a law student, and Dr. Paul Rée, a young Jewish philosopher of recent acquaintance. As soon as he reached Sorrento on October 27, Nietzsche called on the Wagners at their hotel, which was only five minutes from the villa, accompanied by Malwida and Rée. This first reunion was followed by an exchange of visits that lasted until November 6. Cosima found Nietzsche "very run down and much concerned about his health." He was in his least talkative mood and often retired to the solitude of his room when the weather became too much for him.

It was on All Souls' Day, November 2, that Wagner and Nietzsche are alleged to have had their fateful talk about *Parsifal* while strolling on the cliffs at Sorrento. We are told that Wagner spoke of the profound religious experience that was inspiring him to write the work, whereupon Nietzsche strode off, disillusioned by Wagner's sudden "conversion," and broke with him for good. This story is one of those time-honored falsehoods in which the beloved subject has been shrouded—to whose advantage it is hard to tell —by writers down to the present day. Elisabeth Förster-Nietzsche produced not a scrap of evidence to support her touching version of the end of this "friendship written in the stars," which Ernest Newman exploded half a century ago. Today the whole thing strikes one as a downright lie. First comes the assertion that Nietzsche countered Wagner's religious fervor by preserving a defensive silence; then he excused himself and strode off into the dusk, never to see the composer again. Cosima, who would not at this stage have had the slightest reason to fabricate anything about Nietzsche, made the following succinct entry in her diary on the day in question: "Thursday, 2nd. All Souls' Day, weather fine again. We went for a nice walk and spent the evening with our friends Malwida and Professor Nietzsche." So nothing occurred on the walk that would have impelled Nietzsche to say good-bye forever. Why, in any case, should the *Parsifal* "revelation" have provoked a breach at all? Nietzsche had been acquainted with the prose sketch since Christmas 1869, but that is far from the end of the matter. On July 1, 1877, without betraying the least hint of his "traumatic experience" at Sorrento eight months before, Nietzsche wrote to Malwida: "My best wishes and salutations to the indefatigable Bayreuthers (I marvel at their courage three times a day)." Malwida, too, knew nothing of any incident at Sorrento. Last but not least, further food for thought is provided by a letter from Nietzsche to Cosima dated October 10, 1877: "The splendid promise of *Parcival* may console us whenever we stand in need of consolation." Nevertheless, the two men's meeting at Sorrento was their last. As for what separated them forever, that will be discussed in due course.

The Wagners left Sorrento on November 7. They traveled by way of Naples to Rome, where Wagner was only temporarily distracted from his paramount concern by artists' receptions, embassy soirées, and sightseeing tours. On October 21, while still at Sorrento, he had written to King Ludwig suggesting that the Reich government should take the festival theater into national ownership on condition that Bayreuth guaranteed to mount annual festivals on the lines of the first. This resolution was to be proposed either by a Reichstag deputy, or by the chancellor's office, or by the king himself in the Bundesrat. Expenses would be defrayed by the sale of 1,000 seats and by an annual subvention of 100,000 marks from the Reich government, which would retain the right to allot the remaining five or six hundred seats gratis to those who could not afford to pay for them. That, more or less, should be the burden of the proposal. "It suffers from only one defect," wrote Wagner, "which is that I should have to entrust its implementation to the 'Reich.' It would be better, seemlier, and far more natural were Bavaria and her king to carry it out on their own."

His letter remained unanswered. In December 1876, he considered selling out and turning Bayreuth over to the Munich Court Theater; indeed, he even proposed to declare the enterprise bankrupt and relinquish the whole of his personal property and income for the benefit of creditors. Back home on December 20, however, he took heart again. Undaunted, he drafted a circular advocating "the establishment of a patrons' association for the care and maintenance of the stage festivals at Bayreuth." It would then be left to this body to address a request for support to the Reichstag. With the zeal proper to an incorrigible founder of institutions, he even considered establishing a "College of Musical and Dramatic Interpretation," which would supply the Bayreuth festivals with trained personnel. He was later to rue the efforts he devoted to this idea as much as he regretted having founded the *Bayreuther Blätter*, which he only kept afloat for the sake of its editor, Hans von Wolzogen.

Thus the year that had witnessed the first Bayreuth festival closed on a note of somber uncertainty. To Cosima, one of the few bright spots was Nietzsche's Christmas letter. He wrote that "what was formerly bleak and cheerless is still so now, and what was great remains so—indeed, *is* so now more than ever." Although Wagner proposed a "very moving" toast to Cosima on her thirty-ninth birthday, her own verdict on the occasion was a sad one: "I sense how much of me is dead, and how little I must concern myself about myself."

Treasured Kisses

How much of Cosima had died? How much did she suspect or know? Unnoticed by all but a few, the festival had coincided with one of the most enchanting, surprising, enlivening, thrilling episodes in Wagner's life. To convey what happened in words of full orchestral resonance: He had once more encountered the angelic Judith Gautier, once more experienced a celestial love that transcended earthly consummation, once more immersed himself in the sight of two dark eyes and a beautiful face. He did so with the ardent abandon peculiar either to a young man tormented by his first taste of love, or to an old man whose hopes and dreams are —or seem to be—fulfilled by a resurgence of youth in the sunset glow of his declining years.

Cosima cannot have known much. The most she may have noticed was a change in him during respites from his arduous festival commitments: stray glances questing for a creature sculpted in amber and bronze; not this time for a stately Brünnhilde, but for a ripely seductive woman who seemed the perfect embodiment of all that had attracted him in Leah David, Jessie Laussot, and Mathilde Wesendonck. Judith had aged not at all, or only to the extent that her looks were enhanced by every passing year. To a man of sixty-three who yearned for relief from the turmoil around him, the golden sheen of her complexion, dark eyes, and radiant smile —to quote Rémy de Gourmont—seemed the most entrancing reward that life could have offered. He took her on unchaperoned tours of the festival theater and clambered with her among the scenery, hand in hand. They met and embraced in secret, exchanging glances and kisses which Wagner described in retrospect as the proudest and most rapturous he had ever known. He visited her at the house where she was staying, only a few minutes' walk from Wahnfried, and sat enthralled at the feet of the woman whose love of luxury and Parisian perfumes seemed to him to smack of voluptuous, quasi-Oriental elegance. Judith still worshiped and admired him as she had in the Tribschen days. Surprising though she may have found his ardor, she did not deride his boyishly maladroit advances but sat in her corner of the sofa and let him pour out his heart to her. As for Wagner, he succumbed to the lure of her shapely breasts, drew her to him, and smothered her with passionate kisses.

"Was it for the last time that I put my arms around you this morning?" he wrote to her on September 4, shortly before she left. "No, I shall see you again. I want to because I love you." These words occur in his only extant letter of the Bayreuth period. His subsequent letters to her, written in an idiosyncratic French that disguised more than it disclosed, alternated between the formal and informal modes of address.

Judith later denied having yielded to Wagner's advances at Bayreuth. According to Henri de Regnier, Wagner urged her to elope with him. This, however, is nonsense: He merely asked her to join him in London. One cannot but agree with Willi Schuh that, since he loved her, the question of whether or not she became his mistress is fundamentally irrelevant. At the same time, he loved her in an almost unreal fashion that reversed their former relationship: he, the devotee, the suppliant who devoured her with his eyes, embraced her body, and drew strength from her lips for a work that had yet to be wholly revealed to him; she, the stern, bewitching Muse who gently returned his kisses with girded bosom and blessed his endeavors in respect of *Parsifal,* or whatever.

Judith was embarrassed by Wagner's letters and protestations of love. Although she had parted from Catulle Mendès, she had no intention of leaving her current lover, a not exceptionally talented musician named Benedictus. Where Wagner was concerned, she had kindled a fire but was unprepared to quench it. For him, the whole affair served to create a false aura of passion and conspiracy which he continued to sustain when all hope had died—an illusion designed to keep him in a creative frame of mind. "How glad I should have been to receive a few lines from you!" he wrote. "I still see you here before me from my desk, to my right, on the chaise longue, looking at me (God, with such eyes!), while I write down reminder slips for my unfortunate opera singers." He asked her to send him a coverlet for the said chaise longue. This he proposed to call Judith and recline on. From London in May 1877: "And you still haven't visited me here!" And again: "Precious soul! Sweet friend!" Later still: "Oh, how I long to kiss you once more, dearest sweetheart!" Parts of this correspondence—the more personal and compromising items—were sent poste restante via Bernhard Schnappauf of Ochsengasse, a Bayreuth barber who acted as factotum to the Wagner household. If he were to be separated from Judith for an indefinite period, Wagner at least wanted some seductive reminders of her presence. Nothing can better illustrate the nature of his sexual attachment to her than his requests for silks and satins from Paris. He was not entirely satisfied with chamois, a flesh color, because it did not match her complexion. He sent her a sheet of the Communion music—"*Nehmet hin mein Leib . . .*"—and asked her to procure him various perfumes that doubtless conjured up the scent of her skin. Milk of iris, white rose powder, ambergris, *rose de Bengale,* balm of Arabia, Turkish slippers—all these helped to maintain a sensual rapport between Judith in Paris and Wagner in the throes of composition.

"Love me," he wrote on October 1, 1877, "and let us not wait for the Protestant kingdom of heaven: It will be terribly tedious! Love! Love! Love me forever!" On November 9, 1877: "Ah, I make music, I don't care a jot for life and the world at large. I feel loved, and I love." On November 15, 1877: "Let's wait for [the advent of] the telephone!" And, for once in German: "*Du!* Precious, beloved soul!!!" Unhappily, Judith now asked him to look at some of Benedictus's scores. Wagner was appalled that his beloved soul could have given herself to a man who hoped to advance his career in this way. Benedictus went down considerably in his estimation, but he pulled himself together and refrained from offending the man. On December 5, 1877, he telegraphed his publisher to send Judith the libretto of *Parsifal* without delay. "O precious soul!" he wrote before the month was up. "Dearly beloved soul! Everything is so tragic, everything that is real!" One of his last cries from the heart is dated January 4, 1878: "I embrace you, my beautiful love, my

precious, adored soul. My child, my Judith!" Nowhere does reflected beauty shine with greater sadness or intensity than in the
love letters of an aging man.

"My precious love," he wrote once more on February 6, 1878, "I
have completed the first act." Then: "Why in heaven's name didn't
I find you in my Paris days, after the failure of *Tannhäuser*? Were
you too young at the time? Let us be silent, let us be silent, but let
us love! Your Richard."

How much, to repeat, did Cosima know of all this? Discounting
an article published by Louis Barthou in 1932, all our written
sources state either that the Wagners never quarreled over the
affair, or that Cosima was wholly ignorant of it. Although her
diaries seldom mention Judith's name from this point on, the
younger woman has been positively identified as the cause of the
sigh that escaped her on February 12, 1878: "The misfortune I
dreaded did not pass me by; it burst in on me from without! God
help me!" Two days earlier, on February 10, Wagner had coolly
written to inform Judith that he had asked Cosima to "undertake
the commissions with which I have bothered you for so long."
Business matters were distracting him from his work on the music
for *Parsifal*. "But do not worry on my account. All that is preying
on my mind will soon be over. Be kind to Cosima: Write her some
nice, long letters." No man could more tactfully have entrusted his
wife with the aftermath of a love affair. Judith had served her
purpose and put him in the mood for *Parsifal*. Either Cosima had
discovered a sample letter, or she had caught Schnappauf playing
the go-between, or her husband had made a clean breast of the
whole affair. Whatever the truth, she never referred to the subject
and kept up a "friendly, businesslike" correspondence with Wagner's old flame. Of her few subsequent references to Judith, one
is dated September 1881. It seems that Judith turned up at Wahnfried "in a rather revealing outfit" and Cosima could not decide
whether Wagner found her presence welcome or "as he puts it,
embarrassing."

Wagner's relationship with Judith was the only thing that ever
threatened the bond between himself and Cosima. The place at his
side was hers, and she filled it to the full.

The Open Wound

---•◆•---

Siegfried Meets Parsifal

"There's something I don't want to tell you." Cosima's reaction to this tantalizing statement, which she recorded on January 25, 1877, was not unnatural: She pressed her husband for details. "I'm starting on *Parzival*," he replied, "and I won't give up until it's finished." At this, so the diary tells us, she "laughed aloud for joy."

However long the decision may have taken to mature, the impression created is of a desperate, almost frantic burst of activity induced by pressure of debts and the unlikelihood of further Bayreuth festivals—a burden of worry that would have overwhelmed a lesser man. Whenever dominated by a creative idea, Wagner was immune to qualms of any kind. At the same time, he could not deny how the land lay. On March 28, he wrote to Dr. Strecker, the Schott's director: "I do not propose ever again to produce the *Ring des Nibelungen* at my own expense and under my personal management at Bayreuth, as my mood and energies are no longer equal to it."

So he turned instead to *Parsifal*, which spelling had superseded "Parzival" by March 14. According to Görres, the name was derived from the Persian *fal parsi*, meaning "foolish innocent."

Wagner converted this into "guileless fool." When informed of this, Judith Gautier pointed out that *fal parsi* did not occur in Arabic, but Wagner brushed her objection aside. Görres probably had no Arabic, he wrote back, and must have heard it from an Orientalist. "Besides, that doesn't matter either. I don't care what the Arabic words really mean, and I very much doubt if there will be many Orientalists among my future audiences!"

He began his draft on March 14, 1877, and read the entire poem aloud to Cosima on April 20. This reading was followed by others delivered to his friends and contemporaries, including, on one occasion, an entire delegation from the Wagner Societies. Their fervent enthusiasm is hard to understand, and can only be ascribed to his histrionic skill. However poetic the libretto's conception, however brilliantly devised and adapted the characters and mythical framework, and however intrinsically profound the treatment of this epic piece, which, though static, embodies the theatrical in its purest form—that is to say, as a festivity and celebration—the poetic texture itself is brittle, stiff, and indigestible. The language is so abstract that it almost defies comprehension. Gone is the elemental freshness of the early dramas; gone are the often grating but always gripping, crude but forceful sonorities of the *Ring* idiom, the sweetly mysterious susurrations of *Tristan*, the crisp and woodcutlike verses of *Die Meistersinger*—gone are all these, to be replaced by an old man's disjointed verbal set pieces, scraps of speech, obliquities laboriously uttered.

That the Parsifal legend should have entered the literary panorama of the years around 1880 "like a belated inheritance," as Pierre Boulez so aptly puts it, was not attributable to its linguistic form alone. More than two decades had elapsed since Wagner's first encounter with the theme. It was probably this aging process that transformed the Knights of the Grail into a merciless elite who can be delivered from their constraints only by a "free" spirit, just as the gods of the *Ring* are by Siegfried: Siegfried, the naive man of action, recurs in Parsifal, the naive man of faith. The exclusive nature of the "lodge" is destroyed by Parsifal's dramatic gesture in the final act, and the redeemer introduces a social transformation too: Not only is a woman—Kundry—shown the Grail and released from her curse by death, but light is brought to all by a noninitiate. "No more shall it be locked away. Uncover the Grail, open the shrine!" This ritualization and externalization of the underlying theme cannot be interpreted from a purely Christian point of view because the Grail itself has been divested of its Eucharistic function.

The orthodox complaint that Wagner misappropriated Christian symbols and profaned them for theatrical purposes is just as artistically obtuse as the assertion, current since the publication of Nietzsche's later essays, that Wagner made obeisance to the Cross by presenting Christian mysteries on the stage.

To Wagner the music dramatist, Christian symbolism was only one revelatory language among others. The para-Christian world of *Parsifal* contains elements of Indian, Germanic, and Moorish mythology. Wagner himself expounded the problems posed by the religious theatrical language of his "Stage Dedication Festival Play" in the opening words of "Religion and Art" (1880), his last major essay. The crucial passage reads as follows: "It might be said that, where religion becomes artificial, it remains for art to salvage the essence thereof by capturing the figurative value of the mythical symbols that religion would have us believe in the literal sense, so as to disclose, by means of ideal representation, the profound truth concealed in them." This applies in the fullest measure to *Parsifal*. As for the objections to its Catholic flavor, these may be countered by pointing out that Wagner still contemplated producing *Luthers Hochzeit* and the Buddhist-inspired *Sieger*. What advertises *Parsifal*'s redemptive mysticism is its fervent negation of the will—a form of symbolic extinction. It was the only Wagnerian work to spring from the unadulterated spirit of Schopenhauer (long after Schopenhauer had been deserted by Nietzsche). *Parsifal* deputized for *Die Sieger* and rendered the latter superfluous with its hugely overstylized rejection of a materialistic and culturally optimistic era. To that extent, it may accurately be described as Wagner's "farewell to the world."

Yet the financial realities of that world continued to plague him even now, at the age of sixty-four. Under pressure from the treasurers and trustees of the festival theater, he signed a contract with the London agents Hodge & Essex. This committed him to a series of concerts in the newly built Royal Albert Hall, which could accommodate some 10,000 people, in ignorance of the fact that 2,000 of the most expensive seats belonged to shareholders and were consequently not for sale. Wagner's life seemed dogged by such miscalculations. He threatened that if everything went awry despite his efforts—if a renewed appeal for subscriptions failed to cover the Bayreuth deficit—he would sell Wahnfried and sign up for an American tour.

Accompanied by Cosima, he arrived in London—which he likened to "Alberich's dream"—on May 1, 1877. He conducted eight concerts between May 7 and 29, sharing each program with Hans Richter. Wagner himself seemed depressed and overtired, his singers were afflicted with hoarseness, and his expectations, both artistic and financial, were not fulfilled despite large audiences and an imposing orchestra of 169 musicians. Queen Victoria, who preferred lighter music, received the German composer at Windsor Castle on May 17. "After luncheon," the widowed queen wrote, a trifle mockingly, "the great composer Wagner, about whom the people in Germany are really a little mad, was brought into the corridor by Mr. Cusins. I had seen him with dearest Albert in '55, when he directed at the Philharmonic Concert. He has grown old and stout, and has a clever, but not pleasing countenance. He was profuse in expressions of gratitude, and I expressed my regret at having been unable to be present at one of his concerts."* Wagner's opinion of Victoria was no more flattering. On January 18, 1880, he told Cosima of his "annoyance with the queen, the silly old frump, for failing to abdicate and thereby condemning the Prince of Wales to an absurd existence; in earlier times, he said, sons became their mothers' guardians when they came of age." Wagner also met George Henry Lewes, Goethe's English biographer, his mistress George Eliot, and the poet Robert Browning. Cosima visited art galleries and sat for a portrait. They left London on June 4. All Wagner earned for his pains was £700, or one-tenth of the Bayreuth deficit.

On June 6, Cosima urged her husband to make use of the 40,000 francs she had recently inherited from her mother. He wanted nothing more to do with the Munich Court Theater because Ludwig was pressing for the repayment of his loan. This last major financial crisis in Wagner's life had repercussions on the history of the stage. By precluding a second production of the *Ring*, to which he himself might have made authentic amendments, it condemned posterity to worship at an unfinished shrine.

To recuperate from the rigors of London, Wagner spent a month taking the waters at Bad Ems with Cosima and the children. Apart from meeting his two Mathildes, Wesendonck and Maier, he consorted with no one. "He rises soon after 5 A.M.," a newspaper reported, "takes a stroll, attends the morning concert, breakfasts, and works. At 4 P.M. the whole family can be seen at the spa orchestra's concert; the conductor always has a few pretty pieces by Wagner in his program. They dine in the garden. At 9 P.M., general withdrawal." On June 16, Siegfried presented Emperor Wilhelm with a bouquet on the promenade. Physically, Wagner's cure at Bad Ems did nothing to alleviate his main problems: sluggish bowels, abdominal distension, painful flatulence. "Everything seems to be going wrong with me," he wrote to his doctor.

After a stay at Heidelberg, an excursion to the house of Justinus Kerner, and a sentimental journey to Tribschen, Wagner had another fruitless interview with Düfflipp in Munich. "Ah, now I know where I stand," was his reaction to the news that Ludwig had given no firm instructions with regard to the *Ring*. "So I have nothing left to hope for!" His plan to emigrate to America assumed more definite form, at least in correspondence.

On August 2, 1877, Cosima was surprised to hear the first notes of *Parsifal* issuing from her husband's workroom. The Communion melodies he played her on August 10, and the principal passage —*"Nehmet hin mein Blut"* ["Take ye my blood"]—was complete by the following day. Amfortas's sufferings, Wagner remarked, were embodied in it.

In September, he told Cosima that, whenever he wrote music, he felt he was starting completely afresh. *Parsifal* imposed a musical shape of its own. Wagner was already experimenting with vocal texture. In order to convey their spiritual, immaterial quality, the words of the Communion had to be "neither male nor female, but neuter in the highest sense of the word." For this purpose, he decided to use a mixture of voices. In October, he had trouble with the Knights' processional but spurned any resort to "artificial" devices. Gurnemanz's interpolated words must sound, he said, as if they "had to be."

At the turn of the year, while the musical outlines of *Parsifal* were taking shape, printed editions of the libretto were sent to various people including Ludwig II and Franz Liszt. Nietzsche received his copy on January 3, 1878.

The Mortal Insult

Among the most incomprehensible features of the Wagner-Nietzsche literary corpus are the legend of the *Parsifal* dedication and the suppression or dismissal of certain vital correspondence. The legend, a venial sin, was broadcast by Nietzsche himself with one of those inexactitudes so dear to him for reasons of effect. According to him, the inscription on his copy of *Parsifal* read simply: "To his dear friend Friedrich Nietzsche from Richard Wagner, Senior Church Councillor [*Oberkirchenrat*]"—but more of that later. As for the suppression of correspondence, this concealed the real reason for Nietzsche's public and posthumous repudiation of his erstwhile friend. *Parsifal*—Wagner's alleged obeisance to the Cross—stood proxy for Nietzsche's underlying motive, and posterity accepted the deception at face value. Both these lies—the legend and the concealment of Nietzsche's underlying reason—seem permanently etched into the public mind, even though the truth has been staring us in the face for a century. Regrettably, C. P. Janz's recent biography of Nietzsche pays only shamefaced and halfhearted deference to the facts. He does not cite the scandalous letters in question and may not (since he relies solely on Curt von Westernhagen) have been acquainted with their full wording. Westernhagen himself, who brought the unsavory documents to light in 1956,* was so eager to expose Nietzsche and protect his hero Wagner that he sidestepped a number of important passages. Such is the correspondence that must now be discussed without fear or favor, for it dealt Nietzsche the incurable wound—the mortal insult—that could not be healed by the spear that had inflicted it.

Those involved in the correspondence were as follows: a Frankfurt physician and Wagner devotee who flagrantly broke his pledge of professional secrecy; Richard Wagner, who began by being genuinely concerned about Nietzsche's health but carried indiscretion to embarrassing and impermissible lengths, even by modern standards; and Nietzsche himself, who brought the other two together.

Founder of the Frankfurt Wagner Society and author of a well-meant essay on the *Ring*, Dr. Otto Eiser had invited Nietzsche to lecture at Frankfurt in 1877. Although Nietzsche declined on grounds of ill health, Eiser made his acquaintance in Switzerland that summer. Astonished to hear that his long and painful illness had never been submitted to thorough clinical investigation, Eiser invited him to Frankfurt, where he and an ophthalmologist friend, Dr. Krüger, examined him between October 3 and 7, 1877. Both doctors diagnosed changes in the fundus oculi, very severe damage to the retina, and a chronic inflammatory process that contributed to his violent and paroxysmal headaches, though these were further ascribed to hypersensitivity of the central nervous system. Eiser warned Nietzsche against all experimental cures, prescribed rest, and forbade him to do any reading or writing.

On October 13, Cosima noted the receipt of a letter from Nietzsche enclosing Eiser's *Ring* manuscript but reporting "bad things" about his health. Through Hans von Wolzogen, who had just moved to Bayreuth as editor of the *Bayreuther Blätter*, Wagner conveyed his thanks for Dr. Eiser's essay and asked for news of his friend's condition.

Replying to Wolzogen on October 17, Eiser disclosed that the results of Nietzsche's recent examination were not encouraging. So appreciable were the changes in the fundus of the eye that his headaches could be traced to this pathological process. Even though this divested them of some of their sinister significance, it did not render the doctors' findings in respect of his eyesight any less depressing. He, Eiser, had acquainted Nietzsche with the full facts and had no need to describe the distressing choice "that faced our poor friend in consequence of this information."

Wagner now took a personal hand in the correspondence. Firmly and succinctly, he voiced his fears. "In assessing N.'s condition, I have long been reminded of identical or very similar experiences with young men of great intellectual ability. Seeing them laid low by similar symptoms, I discovered all too certainly that these were the effects of masturbation. Ever since I observed N. closely, guided by such experiences, all his traits of temperament and characteristic habits have transformed my fear into a conviction." He thought it highly significant that the physician whom Nietzsche had consulted in Naples, a Dr. Schrön, had advised him first and foremost to marry. To put backbone into him, Wagner thought it important that "some firm action be taken"—for example, that he be prescribed a course of hydrotherapy. He urged Eiser to advise Nietzsche at his own discretion without glossing over the primary cause of his complaint. "The friendly *doctor* undoubtedly possesses an authority denied to the doctoring friend."

Dr. Eiser, who revered Wagner and Nietzsche in equal measure, was so flattered at being addressed in such terms by the great composer, and so dazzled by the confidence reposed in him, that he forgot himself. (The italicized passages in his reply are here published for the first time.) Although his examination of the patient had not disclosed any immediate grounds for an assumption of this kind, he wrote, he was far from inclined to dispute the accuracy of Wagner's observations on that score. What militated against them were statements made by the patient himself.

"In discussing his sexual condition, N. not only assured me that he had never been syphilitic but replied in the negative when I questioned him about strong sexual arousal and the abnormal satisfaction of the same. I only cursorily touched on this latter point, however, and cannot therefore attach too much weight to N.'s remarks on the subject. As against this, I find it more cogent that the patient speaks of gonorrheal infections during his student days, and also that he recently had intercourse several times in Italy on medical advice. These statements, whose truth is certainly beyond dispute, do at least demonstrate that our patient does not lack the capacity for satisfying the sexual urge in a normal manner; a circumstance which, though not inconceivable in masturbators of his age, is not the general rule." Furthermore, Nietzsche evinced a definite inclination to marry, which would be surprising in a *"confirmed masturbator."* "I concede that my objections are all far from watertight and open to rebuttal by your long and exhaustive observation of our friend. I am bound to accept your assumption all the more readily because I, too, am led by many aspects of N.'s comportment and behavior to regard it as only too credible. The more I accept the accuracy of your conjecture, however, the less I can concur with the favorable conclusions you draw, in your sympathy and friendship for him, with regard to N.'s possible recovery." Nietzsche's eyesight was past restoring, Eiser emphasized; the most that could be done was to maintain his present level of vision. Instances did occur in which *"neurotic, hysterical patients debilitated by masturbation or otherwise"* could be cured of profound disorders, but not when such serious changes had taken place in the fundus of the eye. Nietzsche's eye complaint precluded any definite mode of treatment or change in prognosis *"since the specific of syphilis can be just as definitely ruled out*

as the chronic nephritis that so often lies at the root of the trouble."* Eiser went on: "*Masturbation, if genuinely present, can be construed as a cause only in the broadest sense—to the extent, let us say, that those debilitated by self-abuse are always less resistant and, like anyone suffering from exhaustion, more prone to all pathogenic states of fatigue and irritation.*"

Nietzsche's headaches and their paroxysmal intensification were quite another matter. "*Such pathological irritability of the nerve centers can most certainly be brought into a direct causal nexus with the sexual sphere, so the solving of the masturbation question would here have a most important bearing on diagnosis—although, given the well-known tenacity of the vice, I myself would be dubious of any method of treatment and its success.*" There was room for hope that Nietzsche's general condition would improve a little—eyesight apart—but only if "*the patient addicted to the vice of masturbation*" could rid himself of it, perhaps by contracting a happy marriage. "My quickest and best means of elucidating the sexual situation will be to question N. openly."

Even discounting contemporary fallacies in regard to masturbation and the undue importance attached to it as a catalyst and cause of diseases, the habit carried an undoubted stigma. Nietzsche himself seems to have felt this, as a sentence in *Zarathustra* implies: "In solitude there grows what a man brings into it, the inner beast as well." Worst of all, Wagner now had it medically attested in black and white that Nietzsche had infected himself in youth, that he was incurably sick and had "had intercourse" in Italy—in other words, that he had summoned Italian streetwalkers to his bed. Wagner may well have learned this in Naples from Dr. Schrön or Malwida von Meysenbug. If not, he would certainly have questioned Malwida about it at the earliest opportunity. At all events, no serious biographer of Nietzsche dares to dispute that his subject was stricken with the aftereffects of youthful experiments in sex.

Being well aware of the potentially explosive nature of what he had divulged, Dr. Eiser took out some insurance: "Meanwhile, I leave it to you, in your kindness, to decide whether I may inform N. that I have told you about his state of health, or whether not only the details of our discussion but the discussion itself shall remain undisclosed." Wagner's sole response on October 29 was as follows: "Not another word about our friend. I know him to be in the best of care, thanks to your love. I cannot do anything for him now. If he fell on really hard times, I could assist him, for there is nothing I would not share with him." That sounded sincere enough, granted, but he was never given a chance to prove it.

Wagner's letter left the doctor's question unanswered. To anticipate the denouement of the sorry affair, somebody talked. Nietzsche found out about the correspondence, though when and from whom remains uncertain. Did Eiser speak to his patient after all? Josef Hofmiller claimed to have heard as much from one of Eiser's friends, or so, at least, we are told by Westernhagen. What possibly supports this theory is Nietzsche's first attack on Wagner in *Human, All Too Human*, but it was mild and in contrast to the many friendly things he found to say about him during the years succeeding its publication in 1878. What is more likely is that the letters were not kept securely enough, and that their existence was advertised by someone with access to Wahnfried. Not, in all probability, by Wagner himself, whom the first signs of Nietzsche's estrangement and defection reduced to absolute silence on the subject of his former friend, but by someone else at his court—someone whom he very soon tired of but never discarded. That person was the philologist Hans von Wolzogen, his poor literary substitute for Nietzsche. Having started the correspondence with Eiser on Wagner's instructions, Wolzogen would almost certainly have seen and read the doctor's replies.

Whatever the truth, rumors were rife at the latest during the festival of 1882, when Nietzsche's sister Elisabeth and Lou von Salomé found Bayreuth's hotels and private houses buzzing with gossip. Lou von Salomé made friends at this time with the young Russian painter Paul von Joukowsky, and Joukowsky, who had become a member of the Wahnfried set, may also have been in the know. However Nietzsche learned of the correspondence, there can be no doubt that it came to his ears. On February 22, 1883, shortly after Wagner's death, he wrote to Franz Overbeck: "Wagner was by far the *fullest* person I ever knew, and in *this* sense I have suffered great deprivation for the past six years. But there is something between us like a mortal insult, and it could have become terrible had he lived any longer." What this was he explained to the musician J. H. Köselitz, whom he renamed Peter Gast, on April 21, 1883: "Wagner is rich in malicious ideas, but what do you say to his having exchanged letters on the subject (even with my doctors) to voice his *belief* that my altered way of thinking was a consequence of unnatural excesses, with hints at pederasty?"*

That, of course, was one of Nietzsche's inexactitudes, and less shameful than the truth. Writing to Ida Overbeck in July 1883, he said that instances of an *"abysmal* treachery of revenge" had come to his ears in the preceding year.

Wagner knew too much, and Nietzsche knew that he knew. Malwida von Meysenbug, too, had learned too much, and Nietzsche broke with her for little apparent reason. Above all, however, Nietzsche's sense of shame was heightened by the knowledge that Cosima, the woman he most revered, was also privy to his secret. The barb implanted by Wagner's correspondence with Eiser had penetrated too deeply for the wound to heal, even after Wagner's death.

Beside that, what did *Parsifal* matter?

Nietzsche worked off his resentment at Wagner's "abysmal treachery" by dint of subsequent revisions, and it was not until years later, in *Ecce homo,* that he publicized the fateful inscription in his copy of *Parsifal,* reproducing it in an incomplete form that lent it a provocative tenor never intended by the author. It should first be mentioned that Franz Overbeck, the friend of Nietzsche's whom Wagner liked best, had in 1873 published "On the Christianity of Our Present-Day Theology," a controversial pamphlet in which he postulated a genuinely critical theology with an entirely independent approach to the Christian religion. Wagner, who denied that *Parsifal* possessed any Catholicizing tendency and did not identify the Grail with the tabernacle or a sacrament, had actually inscribed Nietzsche's copy of the libretto as follows: "Cordial greetings and regards to his dear friend Friedrich Nietzsche. Richard Wagner (Senior Church Councillor: for kind transmission to Professor Overbeck)." If we therefore accept that Wagner's aside was addressed, not to Nietzsche, but to Overbeck, whose pamphlet he was gently deriding, it takes on a significance quite different from that imputed to it by Nietzsche and his readers.

On January 4, 1878, within a day of receiving the *Parsifal* libretto, Nietzsche wrote a letter to Reinhart von Seydlitz. He made no reference whatsoever to Wagner's dedication, merely regretted that the whole poem was too limited by its Christian and period setting. Much that was acceptable to the mind's eye would be unendurable in performance. "All these fine inventions belong to the epic and are, as I say, for the inner eye." The language, he not unfairly commented, read like a translation from some foreign tongue. "But the situation and its sequential development—is this not poetic in the highest degree? Is it not a final challenge to music?" From now until the end of his life, Nietzsche's constant acknowledgment of the fascination Wagner's work held for him betrays how little hope he had of ever healing the trauma that Wagner had inflicted on his psyche.

Musically fastidious though he was, his compulsion to contradict the Wagnerite in him drove Nietzsche to descend to the level of Franz von Suppé. Then, at a concert in—of all places—Monte Carlo, he heard the *Parsifal* Prelude. "From the purely aesthetic aspect," he wrote to Peter Gast on January 21, 1887, "did Wagner ever produce anything better? Supreme psychological assurance with regard to what is intended to be said, expressed, *communicated*; the most succinct and direct form for the purpose; every shade of emotion reduced to the epigrammatic; music as a descriptive art so full of clarity that it calls to mind an embossed shield; and, last of all, a sublime and extraordinary feeling, experience, spiritual happening at the heart of the music that does Wagner the greatest credit: a synthesis of emotional states which many people, even 'superior people,' would consider incompatible; music imbued with judicial severity, with 'sublimity' in the awesome sense of the word, with a cognizance and perception that cut through a soul like knives—and with compassion for what is seen and judged. Such things exist in *Dante*, but nowhere else. Did ever a painter portray so melancholy a loving gaze as Wagner does with the final accents of his prelude?" Could anyone improve on the precision, beauty, and aptness of Nietzsche's description? Has anyone ever had a better understanding of Wagner?

But renegades can never escape their past; a sense of loss tends to increase their love. Obedient to this rule, Nietzsche continued to wrestle with his former ideals and argue for and against them —a form of debate whose positive and negative emphases need not impair its descriptive precision. Long after Wagner's death and shortly before Nietzsche's mental extinction—right up to *Der Fall Wagner* and *Nietzsche contra Wagner*—this one-man debate retained its subjective truth and was conducted with such keen discernment that the seeds of contradiction were always inherent in it.

Nietzsche prefaced his most scathing indictments with the words: "I shall treat myself to a little relief." Even *Ecce homo* ("Why I am so clever," Section 6) conveys how fiercely the battle raged within him to the bitter end. "I think I know better than anyone the prodigy Wagner could be, the fifty worlds of strange delights to which none but he possessed the wings to fly; and being what I am, namely, strong enough to turn the most dubious and perilous things to my own advantage and, thus, to grow stronger, I name Wagner my life's great benefactor." Although this passage is sometimes quoted, the full truth emerges from the following sentence: "That wherein we are related—that we have suffered more deeply, at each other's hands as well, than people of this century are capable of suffering—will link our names forever; and as surely as Wagner is a mere misunderstanding among Germans, so surely am I and shall ever be."

In other words, Wagner was his one and only love.

The German Spirit
and the West

———◆———

In his latter years, Wagner no more possessed a coherent, self-contained outlook on life than Nietzsche did a systematic philosophy. Any attempt to construct one, undertaken for whatever purpose, belongs in the realm of pious fiction. Wagner's disguised religion, which was simply a functional structure and working hypothesis, had long ago been shed like an empty chrysalis and tossed to his devotees and detractors to squabble over. Just as Nietzsche's works, and his late works in particular, were a battlefield disputed by the most antithetical evaluations and extreme contradictions, so Wagner, at once a representative and adversary of his age, played out a drama in various roles. There are times when he seems, as Joachim Fest puts it, like "the synthetic product of an anthropological puzzle which, for all its incompatibilities, is far from disparate and held together by an elemental personality that roughly bonds the cracks." If Nietzsche's allusion to the "actor" in Wagner means anything, it is this: He picked up cues and delivered his lines as they came. Relating all the conflicts of the age to himself and his work, he gave utterance to reaction and revolution, continuity and innovation, the real and the ideal.

His conception of the ideal was based on a past, predominantly transfigured by myth, which was sometimes at odds and sometimes in harmony with the present. This is borne out by an entry in Cosima's diary dated May 4, 1870: "When our breakfast conversation turned to Richter and his stay in Paris—he did *not* see Notre Dame and in the Louvre *only* Napoleon's boots—Richard said: 'Anyone who has learned nothing of the "ancient Greeks" in childhood is blind to beauty. All my subsequent feelings about the ugliness of our present-day world come from looking at the illustrations in Moritz's *Mythology*. Perseus in his handsome helmet, but otherwise naked, delighted me and filled me with abhorrence of our whole military system, tightly buttoned and laden with medals. When I read that crowned poets received no prize apart from an olive wreath, I was thrilled and despised the people who went around wearing ribbons. It was respect for the olive wreath that inspired my contempt for decorations, not democratic conceit or plebeian crudity, as your father, for one, doubtless imagines.' "

Wagner's ideal of beauty was founded on archetypes, even though he succumbed temporarily to the martial fever of the Franco-Prussian War. Even then, however, his execration of *Die Wacht am Rhein* shows that his instinct had not entirely deserted him. It would be fair to say that all his political passions ended where bad taste began. Everything, the heroic included, had to be at once natural and human yet larger than life-sized, aesthetic in form but not conventional. Few things measured up to this criterion. On October 16, 1869, he said he would like a room "expressly devoted to honoring every single genius such as Cervantes" and stressed how the latter's genius "created exactly like Nature, and that he and Shakespeare were among the poets whose art, like Homer's, was quite imperceptible; whereas, for example, the Greek tragedies, Schiller, Calderón, seemed like high priests and constructed their edifices, as it were, out of a single idea." This brought Wagner back to his ideal of art. Reverting to *Don Quixote*, he said that "in *Werther*, Goethe had created something similar, that is to say, a book whose art is quite unnoticeable. Whenever Cervantes tries to be an artist he becomes academic and conventional—his genius [on the other hand] is quite unconscious and resembles an elemental force." Beethoven melodies and Shakespeare scenes were everything to him, Cosima noted on December 4, 1880.

Wagner's admiration of the natural vigor inherent in the great creative personalities of the West—an admiration that forever attracted him to Beethoven and often inspired him to deliver grotesquely unfair verdicts on other figures in musical history, the great J. S. Bach excepted—was coupled with his rejection of everything contemporary as symptomatic of decadence, with a blind professional jealousy and antiprogressive rancor that had dogged him since his Paris days and colored all his thinking. He detested big cities for producing nothing but "rabble" and blamed undesirable developments on every revolutionary movement since 1789, including the one to which he himself had belonged. He doubted if the world owed anything to the French Revolution. "An emphatic no. It has diverted us from our proper course of development along alien paths—parliamentarism, freedom of the press—whereas all interests should be represented by corporations, and once these interests are satisfied, decisions should be announced without any quibbling from people who know and understand nothing about them" (September 10, 1873). Wagner's article "Modern" (1878) discerned the negative origins of the civilizatory-modernistic trend in the Young German movement and identified the triumph of false up-to-dateness with "victories of the modern Jewish world." As he saw it, Europe had the French to thank for all these iniquities. To him, Parisian "bustle" and theatrical corruption became as synonymous with civilization as, eventually, did France and French rationalism.

We must not overlook the disconcerting effects on Wagner of an incipient and impending age of psychology, technology, drawing-room comedy, social criticism, Impressionism—in short, of an age that he himself had helped to introduce with the modernisms of his artistic idiom but simultaneously feared: he, who indicted decadence but called himself a "plenipotentiary of decline." We now understand how technological and economic development, together with the intellectual and artistic transformation of the world, can evoke cultural criticism as well as progressive euphoria, and how they were bound to engender those politicoeconomic and philosophical systems and ideologies that permeated and fought each other during the second half of the nineteenth century, foreshadowing the disasters of the twentieth. For us, too, many aspects of progress are turning into their opposites. Wagner anathematized the civilization he hated for its preoccupation with money. He cursed the objectivization of political reality and intellectual and artistic "modernity"—all spheres of which contained distinguished Jewish representatives—for being a "Latin-Semitic" corruption of human existence. He despised the press, whose power he ascribed to French influence. In 1873, he expressed the hope that another war with France would annihilate the industry of that "wicked country" and thereby destroy its influence as well. "If only we could hope for a big, powerful dynasty, but I fear that our dynasties are heading for destruction!"

These quotations and the even less admirable remarks that follow are not strung together in any spirit of denunciation. Their purpose is to show how Wagner's attitudes could veer from one position to its diametrical opposite—an ever-surprising process that persisted until his dying day. Even his attacks of intemperate nationalism were usually succeeded by resignation. Would there really be nothing left, he asked himself, but republicanism and America? At first he took refuge in Prussian ideals of discipline and duty as embodied in the victorious army. "Europe now admires France again! And Richard says, 'There are definitely two opposing principles involved here: The Romance peoples, bedazzled by the French Revolution, have reawakened memories of the ancient world and expect the Republic to bring them heaven on earth; the Republic, so they imagine, will banish all evils including their own [need for] exertion and self-sacrifice. Germans, on the other hand, do not indulge in illusions; being more level-headed, they instinctively recognize that no shibboleth can bring the world's salvation. In the Prussian officer's "When my king commands, I obey," which must seem terribly stupid and blinkered to the French, there lies a deeper meaning and a deep realization that certain matters cannot be discussed with the half-demented. Having passed through all these illusions myself, I have now reached the stage where I can see the point in a blinkered sense of duty.' " But on October 24, 1870, when Nietzsche wrote of his fear that militarism and pietism would bring pressure to bear on every sphere of existence, Wagner exclaimed that he would tolerate any form of suppression save obscurantism. "The one thing man can take pride in is freedom of the spirit, the one thing that raises him above the beasts. To curtail or deprive him of this freedom is even worse than castrating him."

Impaled on the horns of a contemporary dilemma whose complexity he failed to master or even apprehend, he abruptly turned the page back to Luther and Gustavus Adolphus—to the spirit of Protestantism. The older he became the more fiercely he inveighed against the third "J" in his rogues' gallery—Jews, journalists, and

Jesuits—and, after the Vatican Council, against the Catholic Church in general and the Vatican in particular. "We turned to so-called cultural topics," noted Cosima on July 21, 1871, "and Richard agreed with me when I disclaimed any hint of approval for the bestowal of Christianity (Charlemagne and the Saxons), and said that I would give up the whole of discovered America in exchange for the poor natives' not having been burned at the stake and persecuted. He recounted the story of Radbod, the Frisian prince who, with one leg already in the font, jumped out when he learned that he would not meet his heathen father in heaven (Siegmund!); that was why he had made his Ortrud, an ill-converted heathen, come of Radbod's line. The Romans' conquest of countries was much more humane, he said—they imposed no form of religion. . . . Shakespeare, the triumph of the oppressed but ultimately resurgent Anglo-Saxon spirit, describes (so to speak) the downfall of the Normans, those cunning, ferocious, and powerful adventurers. This spirit culminated in Protestantism, just as the Normans always continued to be associated with the Catholic Church."

Within the context of this historical outlook, three names continually recur: Luther, Gustavus Adolphus, and Bernhard von Weimar. Wagner would have liked to write historical plays about them but did not consider the literary drama a medium suited to his own talents. These three great names in the history of Protestantism were joined, though only temporarily, by another: Bismarck, too, was incorporated in the German-Latin, Protestant-Catholic conflict. "Richard regrets that Bismarck does not express himself as forcefully as he should in regard to Catholicism."

Wagner's excessive emphasis on the interdenominational conflict of the time must be viewed against the background of the first Vatican Council (October 8–20, 1870), whose declaration of papal infallibility sowed the seeds of a dispute that temporarily split the college of cardinals and the German episcopate. This gave birth to the Old Catholic movement in southern Germany, France, and Switzerland—a reformist movement similar to that of the Saxon German Catholics of the 1815–48 period. Although it was headed by eminent German theologians such as Ignaz von Döllinger of Bavaria, they did not wish to go to the lengths of founding denominational communities of their own. The gauntlet was picked up by political Catholicism, so it might be said that the strengthening of the Ultramontanists in Bavaria and the clerical controversies on

Wagner's doorstep helped to drive him onto the side of Prussia and Prussian policy in the Kulturkampf—in short, onto Bismarck's side.

His vacillation stemmed also from an impractical and fundamentally unpolitical approach to politics. Forever prone to the hopes, expectations, and demands he associated with every change in the political situation, he was always doomed in the end to disappointment, whether by the king of Saxony, by Bavaria and Ludwig II, or by the men who to him personified the Reich and the portentous "German spirit."

What, though, was "German"? Nietzsche's Europeanism; the conservative federalism of a man like Constantin Frantz, whose opposition to Bismarck after the founding of the Reich earned Wagner's temporary disapproval on the grounds that it betrayed his typically German failure to recognize greatness when it emerged; or the martial spirit of the Prussians, who also aroused Wagner's ire for refusing the Bavarians the right to march under their own colors during the war against France? Who were more German, Goethe and Mozart or Bismarck and Field Marshal Roon?

One of Wagner's letters to Nietzsche (October 24, 1872) contains a notable passage: "I ponder more and more on 'what is German' and am finally, on the strength of recent studies, developing a remarkable skepticism that reduces 'being German' to something purely metaphysical, yet makes it seem, as such, boundlessly interesting and at any rate quite unique in history, paralleled perhaps by Judaism alone, if Hellenism, for example, does not properly qualify as a companion piece." And to Ludwig II on August 23, 1874: "This 'German spirit,' too, is doubtless an idea that enables something to be dangled with loathsome irresponsibility before the vain and shallow mass of the people: But where does this spirit manifest itself in solemn truth? Certainly not in our great poets."

On the one hand (July 30, 1871): "At breakfast Richard asked me if I knew the epic of Walther and Huldigunde. When I said yes, he went on, 'I find in it the traits I call truly German, the composure verging on humor, as in Walther's fight with the Gibichungs and then with Hagen, whose eye he hacks out and who hacks off his hand, whereupon they joke together about it. I imagine these traits to be present in the Prussian Army.' " On the other (February 28, 1872): "Richard sang something from Die Zauberflöte and said to me, 'You see, Sarastro—that's German: that gentle aura of humanity wafted toward one for all the absurdity of the operatic genre.' " Elsewhere he mentions Sarastro's "spiritual dignity" and the "fine humanity" in the priest's words.*

A gentle aura of humanity. . . . That would have been unthinkable without Latin influence, but anyone who rooted his ideal too deep in myth and neglected his sense of history was bound to find it hard to achieve a synthesis. "At table he inveighed against the Renaissance, claiming that it had greatly impaired Germanic development. That age had no more understood classical antiquity or taken it seriously than it had Christianity. Immensely gifted people had been in the service of an all-corrupting authority, and, as ever, the naive German had allowed himself to become so impressed by foreign culture that his own feelings were almost annihilated. Remarkably enough, however, though all had set out to destroy what was German, they had not entirely succeeded." Was that a foretaste of Houston Stewart Chamberlain or an interpretation of history based on current conditions in the theater: rule by impresarios, art in the service of an "all-corrupting authority," alias the Grand Opéra—Meyerbeer, Spontini, and Anton Rubinstein, who had no understanding of Christianity and were vitiating German taste? Wagner's Jewish pamphlet sprang from very similar origins.

But what developed in him during the 1870s went far beyond *Judaism in Music*, which could still be explained in artistic and sociological terms. Wagner's anti-Semitism needs analyzing more thoroughly because its personal, economic, and racist ingredients mingled to form a dangerous pseudoideology. Evil equals property, property equals Jew; therefore the Jew is the basic evil. There were times when Wagner completely succumbed to this iniquitous identification of the Jew with all that was evil. Cosima reproduced his remarks on the subject without embellishment. On April 7, 1873, he had an argument with Dean Dittmar of Bayreuth. The dean held that intermarriage was the answer to the problem. "But Richard maintained that the Germans would cease to exist because the fair German blood was not strong enough to withstand this 'dishwater.' We had seen, after all, how the Normans and Franks became French, and Jewish blood was far more corrosive than Latin. He, Richard, could only hope that 'those fellows' would become so arrogant that they entered into no more misalliances with us. They might even give up speaking German. We should then learn Hebrew, so as to get on well, but remain German. On this joke, the conversation ended." But that was not Wagner's last word on the subject. Integration was impossible, he asserted, and the Germans would not allow themselves to be subjugated. On April 2, 1874: "Richard was very annoyed today at the Jews walking the streets here in their best clothes, it being their Easter festival. 'I shall put my foot in it again if I ever become a town councillor. Fancy offending public sentiment like that by flaunting their festive garb on our days of mourning! It's a relic of Lessing, the idea that all religions are good, including stupid Mohammedanism."

Toward the end of the 1870s, he modified his views: Personally, he had had some excellent Jewish friends, but their emancipation and equality, granted "before we Germans amounted to anything," had been pernicious (December 27, 1878). By October 11, 1879, he was in favor of "total expulsion," and news of a fire at the Vienna Court Theater in 1881 prompted him to remark that all Jews should be burned to death during a performance of *Nathan der Weise*—Lessing's play on religious tolerance. Compare "Sarastro—that's German: that gentle aura of humanity. . . ."

Spectral analysis of Wagner's anti-Semitism discloses a number of facets. There was, to begin with, his personal grudge against Mendelssohn for losing the score of his youthful C Major Symphony, and against Meyerbeer, the unloved patron who had always waddled home first like the tortoise beating the hare. The recurrence of their names in Cosima's diaries suggests that Wagner suffered from something akin to a complex where both men were concerned. On April 19, 1879, he told her that he had dreamed of conversing with Mendelssohn in the [familiar] second-person singular, and on April 3 of the following year she made the following entry: "Richard slept well but dreamed of Meyerbeer, whom he had reencountered at a theater, and who said to him, 'Yes, I know, my long nose'—as if Richard had poked fun at his nose, whereupon Richard more or less apologized and the audience applauded their reconciliation." Did he feel uneasy? Verbal anti-Semitism has always been a product of fear on the part of the weak and inferior, the "fatherless" and ill bred, whose lack of manners impels them to seek refuge in defiance. (In 1918, when his position was at its weakest, Thomas Mann railed against Jewish intellectuals in his diary.) In the second place, however, Wagner's early dealings with Jewish moneylenders had inspired him with the hatred of the poor for the rich and influential—a hatred that stems from a similar source and intensifies the blind reaction of those unable to fathom the ways of the world. (As Goethe says, vehemence is a favorite substitute for truth and strength.) Even in his own enlightened century, Wagner found no friend of equal stature who might have been in a position to explode his pseudoideology. This, coupled with the first two factors, engendered the fury that comes of a bad conscience—the delight in abuse that is born of double standards. If the truth be told, he attracted Jews like a lodestone. His double standards were such that he never "purged" the Bayreuth set of its Jewish members. They sat at his table and partook of his hospitality. No friends were dearer to him than Samuel Lehrs, his companion in misfortune, and Karl Tausig, the young and divinely inspired pianist—in other words, the weak whom he could never bring himself to hate. As for his dearest work, *Parsifal*, he entrusted it to Hermann Levi, a rabbi's son.

It was a love-hate relationship. This alone explains why he compared "being German," regarded as a purely metaphysical state, to being Jewish—an idea revived by Thomas Mann when writing *Doktor Faustus*. In "Know Thyself" (1881), Wagner predicted that it would someday be possible to coexist with the Jews because they were, fundamentally, "the noblest of all." It is also significant that he had no time for anti-Semites such as Bernhard Förster and Eugen Dühring.

The hollowness of his whole attitude became apparent whenever quality was concerned. He once had a "wild and comical dream." In need of 4,000 thalers, he had gone to borrow them from some Jews, "one of whom, in the midst of the transaction, sang him the aria from *La Dame Blanche*, and Richard could not help remarking that he had a good tenor voice!" Toward the end of his life, Wagner passed some remarkable comments about Mendelssohn. On September 22, 1878, he told Cosima that he often sang Mendelssohn themes to himself; two months later he expressed particular pleasure in *Calm Sea and Prosperous Voyage* and called Mendelssohn "a fine musician"; and on June 6, 1879, as on several other occasions, he pronounced the *Hebrides* Overture "truly masterly." *Fingal's Cave*, he declared on June 17 of the same year, was "undoubtedly M[endelssohn]'s masterpiece." In 1880, he refused to sign Förster's rabid "Mass Petition against the Rampancy of Judaism." On December 22, 1880, he explained his attitude by remarking that all such measures were useless while property existed. "World peace" would help, but at present the Jews were the only free people, "for it is only through money that I can prevent my son from becoming a slave to the state." When the impresario Angelo Neumann, himself a Jew, suspected that his Berlin plans for Wagner were being jeopardized by rumors of an anti-Semitic campaign at Bayreuth, Wagner wrote to him on February 23, 1881: "I wholly dissociate myself from the present 'anti-Semitic' movement: An article by me, soon to appear in the *Bayreuther Blätter,* will proclaim this in such a way that it should be impossible for *persons of intelligence* to associate me with that movement." It did, however, require considerable intelligence to discern what he meant when he also wrote articles urging Jews to steer clear of Germans until the latter had found and recognized their own identity!

Everything was later ascribed to Gobineau's influence, but this conjecture should be treated with the utmost caution. As our chronological account of Wagner's last few years will show, the belief that he fell prey to the Frenchman's racial theories is scarcely tenable: He met him far too late in life for that. Although he "initially" (in 1881!) saw merit in Gobineau's *Essai sur l'inégalité des races humaines,* and although he himself had entertained the most questionable ideas about miscegenation between "superior" and "inferior" races and the redemption of the latter, *Parsifal* had long been completed and remained quite unaffected by any such theories. So far from satisfying him, the fatalistic doctrine of the decline of the "civilizing" Aryan race aroused his opposition. From this point on, both in conversation and on paper, he mooted the possibility that the races might have run their course, and that only the blood of Christ could avail the world. Abstruse though it may be, the idea that the redeeming blood of Jesus was intended to purify all races (in "Herodom and Christianity," 1881, his earliest possible reaction to Gobineau) can hardly be reconciled with the Frenchman's theories.

Wagner never came to grips with the problems of decadence and regeneration, Judaism and Germanism, because he persistently confused religious, social, and political factors. Nothing better illustrates this deep-seated confusion than his attempt to write a "History of the German Character" and pick up the thread of his earlier ideas in "What is German?" (edited in 1878 for publication in the *Bayreuther Blätter*). In 1870, he had still identified this "German character" with that of Prussia—with the military might and determination of these Nordic Spartans. "Only now did he understand the Prussians and their austere, tight-lipped character: 'French uniforms are all far too baggy; our men resemble inflexible machines.' " But did their cultural strength match their military victories? "Of the Germans, Richard says humorously that Moltke has made something of them, but out of uniform they are not worth their salt" (November 3, 1877). On February 10, 1878, he wrote to Ludwig II: "Certainly, few people imagined that the dreary Prussian conception of the state would be so soon thrust on us in the guise of German imperial wisdom." And on July 15, 1878: "I am so disgusted by this new Germany. Is this supposed to be an empire? 'Berlin' an imperial capital? It is simply contempt from on high, which is now being reciprocated from below." Prussian Junkers as guardians of German culture? In June 1878, he encouraged Constantin Frantz to write an article critical of Bismarck for the *Bayreuther Blätter*, whereupon some of his staunchest supporters—even Jews who had failed to take offense at his anti-Semitic utterances—left the Patrons' Association because their national pride had been hurt. "What does a Junker of his [Bismarck's] sort know about Germany?" he demanded on December 16, 1878. A month earlier he had complained that Bismarck saw the world only through the eyes of a diplomat and was incapable of recognizing an outstanding personality, "only the wretched people he has to deal with. . . . He is a man of the people and guided by popular instinct, not reflection or concern. He is creating German unity but has no conception of its nature." On August 7, 1879, he confessed to feeling ashamed that he had dismissed his French friends' warnings in 1870—ashamed "even vis-à-vis Herwegh" for having expected so much of people like the emperor. Bismarck lacked dignity and poise, he said, so on whom or what could one rely to reduce the German ethos to a common denominator?

"Richard passed a tolerable night, so our breakfast time was very cheerful, cheerful and serious, for Richard spoke again about the ten years that will follow the production of his dramas. During these, he proposes to explore his 'What is German?' theme and investigate everything from Provençal influence in the Middle Ages down to the latest developments—even including the element of youth—at the risk of ending up in a mood of utter despair." Despair? "My dear friend," he told Edouard Schuré on September 4, 1873, only six months later, "I am not to be numbered among the patriots of today, for I am suffering all that anyone could possibly suffer, as things now stand in Germany. I am hanging, as it were, on the Cross of German thought." As for what remained of the German ethos, Cosima noted the following observation by Wagner: "Is it not conceivable that, if the Northerners spread throughout the South and finally founded a nation, German would assume the place of Sanskrit in India and become the cultural language, as it were, and English that of Prakrit, the vernacular. In studying this, I am thinking of my own enterprise as well. Have I been a sort of mirage, or should my appearance on earth and the ideas I brought with me be regarded as a portent?"

At all events, doubts had arisen within him—doubts not only about the feasibility of his artistic utopia but about the Reich in which he would have liked, for want of anything better, to realize it. His hopes for the German spirit vanished after the festival of 1876, and not only because they had proved to be a cultural mirage. On November 13, 1879, Cosima noted: "In the evening, our friend Gersdorff's presence turned conversation to the subject of war, and Richard recalled how utterly astounded Garibaldi had been to see Germans advancing through shellfire in 'passo di scuola' [marching in step]. 'You can't wage war on donkeys like these,' he must have said to himself, '—they aren't a bit nervous.' And Richard remarked how hard it was to decide whether a private soldier was heroically courageous or simply frightened of his sergeant. He had always championed military organization and was convinced that our officers possessed the said heroic courage, but the present state of affairs—national exhaustion, more and more taxes, and continuous military expansion—was barbarous. Conquering new provinces and never stopping to wonder how to win them over, never debating how to make friends with Holland, Switzerland, etc., nothing at all but the army!" Wagner was thinking in particular of Alsace-Lorraine, where the arrogance of Prussian military administrators was doing incalculable harm. His own travels had convinced him of this, and he reverted to the subject again and again. Only a few days later, on November 19, 1879, he declared that the army of which he had had such high hopes now struck him as "so much barbarism and cretinism."

As Wagner became disillusioned with reality and disenchanted with the original aims of the Franco-Prussian War, so he ceased to believe that the common man had been drawn into the war for an exalted purpose. "Then he reverted to the army," Cosima noted on December 10, 1881, "and said that he would like to get Siegfried exempted from military service. When someone remarked that soldiers die for glory, he exclaimed, 'Because they're more afraid of their sergeant than a bullet—sometimes a bullet is merciful. Ask yourself whether the soldiers at Spichern died for glory's sake.' " The war had not long been over when he questioned the permanence of Germany's military might. History showed, he said, that such superiority was often ephemeral. The future belonged to America and Russia. Years later, on December 1, 1881, he condemned rearmament as senseless in view of the Reich's widespread poverty. "Over coffee, I read that another 20 million marks or so are to be spent on the army. Richard said jokingly, 'Germany is a beggar armed to the teeth. It's better not to meet us in the street.' "

This prompted him to reconsider his attitude toward the Social Democrats and the multiparty state. (Feustel, it should be noted, held a Reichstag seat for the National Liberals.) In 1873, according to an entry in Cosima's diary dated March 27, Wagner had maintained that Bismarck ought simply to "dissolve the provincial diets and all, then enact laws and enforce them with the help of the army." When the *Sozialistengesetze* [Bismarck's antisocialist laws]* were passed, however, he described their suppression of press freedom and freedom of association as "childish and inane" (May 24, 1878). A few days later, on May 30, he deplored the "narrow-mindedness" betrayed by these measures. Reaction was always a bad thing, he added on May 31. True, the leaders of the movement were a muddleheaded and possibly scheming bunch, but "the future belongs to the movement itself, and doubly so because we can devise no better means of checking it than stupid repressive measures." Two attempts on the life of Emperor Wilhelm I, both of them unconnected with the Social Democrats, gave Bismarck the pretext he needed for outlawing all members of their party save those in the Reichstag itself. This he did although Germany had experienced only a feeble tremor of the earthquake that was convulsing her neighbors to the east, south, and west: Russia scarred by anarchist bombs, assassinations in Venezia and Serbia, and the first miners' revolts and strikes in France. All of these occurrences were likewise attended by what Zola called "the stupidity natural to disasters"; in other words, by all the blunders the various governments could possibly have committed. Wagner was outraged when the police gunned down a tipsy student in the streets of a Franconian town. He was horrified when Bismarck's legislation spawned a multitude of informers and pronounced him incompetent to handle domestic affairs. He even, on July 5, 1879, expressed disgust at Frederick the Great for having founded the Prussian monarchy, which had caused so much misery. Frederick himself was comprehensible and interesting only as an individual, he said; in other respects, he was a kind of caricature. Wagner now believed that Germany was heading for "a complete political breakdown" and that social problems, though "held in check by wars," would become more and more pronounced (July 13, 1879). He was impressed by the rudiments of the socialist movement in England but betrayed his private uncertainty by remarking that "efforts will probably be directed, not against property, but toward property for all" (December 4, 1878).

"We are drifting with all sails set into an age of reaction whose beginnings can doubtless be foreseen, but not its course or culmination," declared the *Frankfurter Zeitung* on June 7, 1878. Considering how rigorously the *Sozialistengesetze* were being applied to publications at this period, even some of Wagner's remarks in "Religion and Art" (1880) may be accounted daring. "The worker's resentment," he wrote, sprang from "a recognition of the profound immorality of our civilization." He went on: "Careful consideration discloses that any demand which so-called *socialism* may make on the society evolved by our civilization, however seemingly just, at once casts doubt on the justification for that society." The socialists' postulates were vague and ill conceived, however, and contemporary socialism was deserving of note only when it entered into "genuine and intimate association with groups of vegetarians, animal protectionists, and preachers of moderation." What accounted for this sectarian note was Wagner's recent contact with Ernst von Weber, author of the pamphlet "Torture Chambers of Science," whose antivivisectionist campaign had gained him a lot of publicity.

In "Know Thyself" (1881), Wagner stated that " 'Property' has attained almost greater sanctity in our politicosocial conscience than religion: Offenses against the latter are treated leniently, damage to the former implacably. Property being regarded as the basis of all social endeavor, it cannot fail to seem all the more pernicious that not everyone owns property; indeed, that most members of society are born disinherited. Obviously, in virtue of its own principle, society is thereby thrown into such a dangerous turmoil that it has to frame all its laws so as to resolve this insoluble conflict; and the protection of property, for which armed force, in the broadest terms of international law, is primarily maintained, cannot in truth be described as other than the protection of the haves against the have-nots." Was it only his contacts in the upper reaches of the Berlin aristocracy that saved Wagner from relapsing into disgrace, as in 1848? Was it because of such statements that the Patrons' Association failed to persuade the "haves" to contribute any more money to the Bayreuth festivals after 1878? Although this question has never been raised, its elucidation a century later is precluded by the silence of all concerned.

Unpublished until 1975, some of Wagner's jottings in the *Brown Book* reveal that the anarchist in him moderated his views and evolved some very reasonable sociological ideas—thus becoming dangerous again. "If property and its inviolable possession be regarded as essential to the continuance of a moral society, it surely becomes evident that this can be so only if no one is debarred from it and all partake in it." He went on: "If people still fail to grasp how the old (barbarous) abuses—inequality of property, etc.—are to be avoided, history will have to begin all over again, so as to instruct us afresh and more forcefully."

Where did these ideas originate? Wagner was appalled by the poverty of the weavers of Hof and Bayreuth. He heard tales such as are still recorded in the village chronicles of Lower Bavaria. The peasants were so desperately poor that many of them could not afford to pay the village schoolmaster his kreuzer. One teacher with fourteen children requested assistance from the royal district inspector of schools. All he got was some advice on birth control: He should pray and fast more assiduously. Wounded veterans roamed the countryside, begging if they could find no employment in their ungrateful Fatherland. Wagner castigated the wealthy for ordering furniture and dress lengths from Paris and London instead of giving work and bread to their needy fellow citizens. On March 24, 1881, Cosima aroused his ire by asserting that the Russian nihilists were more remote from the people than the czar. "When I said that these conspirators had no right to act in the peasants' name, Richard exclaimed, 'No right? What right has the czar? This is a question of authority, of right as *jus*—power, as the Romans called it. There is no such power in the rulers, but there is in the conspirators.' In the evening, he related how his brother-in-law General Meck used to have his Cossack [orderly] flogged and then make him kiss the knout! These people could not, he said, have changed so quickly."

Did he recall his adolescence and early manhood? When rereading the letters he had written between 1849 and 1853 to his Dresden friend Theodor Uhlig, Cosima—who sanctioned their publication after her husband's death in censored, abridged, and doctored form!—thought his pleasure in them showed how "consistent" his character had remained throughout his life. "He still expects socialism to come, as he did then, except that he does not foresee its coming at any particular juncture" (June 2, 1879). He may have clung, not only to the shattered illusions of yore, but to Schiller's worthwhile exhortation: "Tell him to respect the dreams of his youth when he becomes a man." But what form did this "lifelong consistency of character" take? It can best be described, perhaps, as unity in diversity—the natural condition of a man whose breast became a battlefield for all the warring tendencies of his age. In his work, these conflicts were resolved; in his life, they remained disjunct and antithetical. If Wagner's *oeuvre* is seen as a self-portrait and self-criticism of the German character, his life may be regarded as the time of trial that produced it. He was not one of those who content themselves with a single opinion on any particular subject. Failure to notice the self-contradictory nature of this approach depends on an ability to prevent one's right hand from knowing what the left is up to, and Wagner evidently needed the relief that this and other forms of self-deception brought him. To put it another way, Wagner could not have borne to know who Wagner really was.

He incorporated his youthful and revolutionary essays in his collected works, by which time he was little suited to playing the prophet of the German ethos. As for his everyday remarks, some of these remained unpublished for a century. On October 16, 1873, petulantly: "No Richard for you, Germania!" To Emil Heckel on February 4, 1876: "The world, and 'Germania' in particular, is becoming more and more repugnant to me." The Germans, he said, were obtuse and insensitive. "The German brain can only be reached through a sort of head cold," he declared on January 23, 1881. The Prussian state was one big lie* (September 28, 1881), and he would never be able to bring himself to utter another word about politics or even mention a name such as Bismarck (December 1, 1881). And on March 18, 1880: "I don't have any remaining illusions. When we left Switzerland I thought it a remarkable coincidence, the victories and the conclusion of my work. I inquired if there were a thousand people in Germany with three hundred marks to spare for such an enterprise, and what a wretched response I got! I arrived at the most miserable time Germany has ever known, with that beastly agitator at its head."

Wagner was the Germans' most ambivalent genius. On the one hand, he proposed the establishment of a *Faust* theater (November 7, 1872)—a kind of Shakespeare memorial theater with exciting new features. Many things would be only hinted at. "During the walk, the ground should revolve and various landscapes be shown; Faust and Mephisto should seem to be walking. . . . It wouldn't matter if things went on behind the audience. Spectators turning around to look would enliven the scene—they would be participants." We do not have a record of Wagner's exact words, only their echo in Cosima's diary, but he clearly envisaged a theater that would involve its audiences—enhance their self-discovery and purify them with the aid of a humanity which he himself found nowhere but in *Faust*, Beethoven's Ninth, and *Die Zauberflöte*. On the other hand: "Better barbarism than this present state of affairs" (July 25, 1878). Wagner advocated the death penalty on the grounds that those guilty of capital offenses did not deserve to live. He more than once debated methods of execution and condemned "false humanitarianism, a way of hushing things up that stems from society's own bad conscience" (August 7, 1878).

The divide between humanitarianism and barbarism is knifeedged. Cosima recorded one Wagnerian pronouncement—a singular kind of anthropology-in-a-nutshell—in which the transition becomes almost imperceptible: "Phlegmatic people he likened to the earth's ice crust, which creates an impression of solidity, 'but they will burn along with the rest. People of our sort stand there like a volcano that reveals from time to time what goes on inside it; I wish I could threaten destruction' " (May 11, 1873).

But always, even in the depths of despair, the cry for redemption and deliverance rang out. "Yes," said Wagner on November 10,

1872, "certainly the whole world is blind, but it also contains the urge for truth, for knowledge, for light. However this blind urge expresses itself, even by persecuting the truth, it exists nonetheless. All the good there ever was still exists. We need only disregard time and space to know that eternity is ever present, and not be too attached to forms. Greatness is forever reappearing, and while light exists it cannot be extinguished—it must continue to shine."

Redemption for the Redeemer

Prolonging the Magic

"The happiest time of my life. . . ." Thus wrote Wagner to King Ludwig, while composing the music for *Parsifal*. His letter carried the ring of truth, as did his one-word reply to Cosima on March 25, 1878, when she asked if he felt content: "Boundlessly." Although his health was deteriorating, no terminal illness could mar the satisfaction he derived from hours of productive endeavor at his desk. Every day prolonged the magic of achievement, of consummation, while Cosima looked on, half dreading the possibility that *Parsifal* might never be completed. Her diary, which charts its composition almost bar by bar, reveals that the creative process was far more complex than in previous works. The text had to be tailored to the many changes that intervened between Wagner's preliminary pencil sketches and their emergence in fully orchestrated form. Motifs were rearranged, modulations expanded, abbreviated, refined, and simplified. In quest of a concentrated musical idiom, the aging composer strove to express himself with the utmost pregnancy and precision. His steady progress deluded him into looking beyond the work in hand. On Friday, January 11, 1878, Cosima noted: "Before lunch he told me he was getting on so well that he intended to compose *Die Sieger* immediately after *Parsifal*, so as to prolong his present condition."

The orchestral sketch for act 1 was completed on January 31. In February, Wagner started on act 2, the orchestral sketch for which occupied him between March 13 and October 11. On Monday, September 23, 1878, lunch at Wahnfried was enlivened by a jocular reference to Karlsbad wafers and Communion. "This is the sort of fare my Knights of the Grail must get," Wagner observed. "I can't give them bread and butter, or they'll end by tucking in and not wanting to leave." That afternoon he reverted to *Parsifal*. " 'Ah,' he said, 'how I dread the whole idea of costumes and greasepaint! When I consider that characters like Kundry will have to be dressed up, I'm immediately reminded of those dreadful first-night parties. Having created the invisible orchestra, I'd like to invent the invisible theater as well! And the inaudible orchestra,' he added, ending his sorrowful reflections on a humorous note."

It was this same fear of contact with theatrical reality that inspired the central passages in "Public and Popularity," published as a series of three articles in the summer of 1878. "Only supreme purity in the relationship between a work of art and its public can provide the requisite basis for its superior popularity." This was the real argument underlying his festival idea. It reveals him as a purist who was blind to the fact that even model performances are subject to the same practical problems as any others.

Wagner finished composing act 2 on September 30 and launched straight into the orchestral sketch. October 30 saw the start of act 3, and Christmas Day brought Cosima a surprise that left her at a loss for words. Siegfried came skipping into her room that morning with the whispered news that a violinist was playing something from *Parsifal*. The something turned out to be the prelude and the violinist an entire orchestra—the Meiningen Court Orchestra, which Wagner had been secretly rehearsing for the previous three days. That evening there was a house concert: Beethoven's *Zur Weihe des Hauses* Overture, the F Major Symphony, the *Siegfried Idyll*, the Andante and Presto from the A Major Symphony, the *Egmont* Overture, and, once again, the prelude to *Parsifal*. "He stands there," Cosima rhapsodized, "he calls forth these wonders, and he loves me. He loves me!" It was a unique occasion, even for Wahnfried, and never to be repeated.

On March 27, 1879, Wagner wrote to inform King Ludwig that he was nearing the end of his work on the music for *Parsifal*. Impatient though he was to prevail over his physical infirmities sufficiently to complete the composition sketch and thus produce a permanent record of the music he had devised for his poem, "another emotion" was simultaneously holding him back. " 'Fool!' I tell myself. 'Are you really so eager to chase away the thing that masks all your miseries, the profound satisfaction that is all that keeps you, while engaged on this task, soaring above the world and its woes?' "

The composition sketch was finished on April 16, 1879, the orchestral sketch on April 26. The work was complete, the creative process at an end.

Those who hear this music for the first time—and one always hears it "for the first time"—tend to feel that everything has been put together with excessive rigidity and attention to form, that Wagner's ideas have lost their freshness, and that artistic inspiration has given way to the practiced skill of the expert. As the work unfolds, however, every succeeding bar enhances its novelty value, modifying our appreciation of what we hear until *Parsifal*'s peculiar idiom comes to seem like an old man's avant-gardism for which no counterpart exists in the fiery musical language of the composer's youth—like boldness in the guise of sovereign serenity.

"In its [*Parsifal*'s] very ponderousness," wrote Theodor Adorno, "which alarms the unsuspecting operagoer, there lurks the ever surprising element of novelty." Few in number, the allegorical motifs are transposed and arranged in a seemingly austere, ascetic manner. Many things are deliberately left uninflected with a simplicity that foreshadows Mahler. The blending of wind instruments, too, with its subdued luminescence, is quite unprecedented. The music conjures up pale colors that glow with brilliant intensity in moments of crisis, only to fade into obscurity once more.

We can already discern a hint of art nouveau in *Parsifal*—floral decoration in hues ranging from olive drab to russet. In startling contrast is its Passion language, some of whose melodic expressions are undoubtedly modeled on J. S. Bach.* Wagner never came closer to Bach than he did in *Parsifal*, and the publication of Cosima's diaries has disclosed how familiar he was with the master's works. His intimate knowledge of the *St. Matthew Passion* was based on the same thorough study he devoted, during his *Parsifal* years, to the choral preludes and fugues, cantatas and motets. In the works of Bach, whom he considered the musician par excellence, he discovered the world's basic musical language. Bach's music, he said, was to that of other composers what Sanskrit is to other languages: a thing complete in itself. His assimilation of it could not have failed to influence the musical development of *Parsifal*.

Italy Again

On August 23, 1879, while Liszt was paying a visit to Bayreuth, Wagner started work on the score. Wahnfried's chief acquisition that fall was a handsome young Franconian aristocrat of twenty-two, who arrived there on October 20. Employed to tutor Siegfried on Malwida von Meysenbug's recommendation, Heinrich von Stein was one of the most promising and independent-minded members of the Wahnfried set. Slim, blond, and blue-eyed, he soon shook off his initial reserve and endeared himself to the whole family. Wagner's admiration for him would have known no bounds had he not been a pupil of his pet aversion Eugen Dühring, the pugnacious academic who must be credited with having invented the German anti-Semitic vocabulary. Wagner persistently derided Stein's penchant for Dühring's anti-Christian, antisocialist doctrines, which were based on mechanistic scientific positivism, until the young man ceased to mention his professor's name.

Another cloud of gloom had descended on Wagner as soon as he finished his composition sketch for *Parsifal*. The weather, his state of health, his heavy financial expenditure—all these combined to depress him. Doctors recommended a change of climate, so he resolved on a lengthy visit to Italy.* After celebrating New Year's Eve at the Hotel Marienbad in Munich with Lenbach, Hermann Levi, and Ludwig von Bürkel, Düfflipp's successor as court secretary, Wagner and his entire household left Germany. They were not to return until late in the fall of 1880.

Reaching Naples on January 4, Wagner moved into the Villa d'Angri on Posilipo, a seaside eminence overlooking the city and its bay. The colonnaded villa, which was approached by way of a long, winding road, contained a handsome suite of rooms. Beyond it, a footpath led through the picturesque garden and grounds to the palm tree that marked the highest point in the vicinity. "Naples is the city for me," Wagner exclaimed. "Be damned to the ruins. Everything's alive here!" At the end of January, however, his sense of well-being was marred by an attack of erysipelas, probably allergic in origin, and he made no headway with his work.

Naples soon got wind of his presence. Paul von Joukowsky, who was staying nearby with Henry James, a personal friend, paid his first visit to the Villa d'Angri on January 18. March 9 brought another visitor in the person of Engelbert Humperdinck, then twenty-five and touring Italy on a Mendelssohn Scholarship. Wagner invited him to call in again on his way back from Sicily. Once Joukowsky had deserted Henry James and, to the latter's incomprehension, joined Wagner's court in company with his young Italian friend Pepino, the Wahnfried circle was complete. Wagner, who was no more offended by the Russian painter's proclivities than he had been by those of other homosexuals in the past, recruited Joukowsky as his designer for *Parsifal*.

For the present, music took second place to the written word. Wagner continued to dictate his autobiography and prepared some articles for the *Bayreuther Blätter*, almost as if his infant work needed swaddling in print. To Feustel, the Bayreuth banker, he lamented his "entire lack of hope for Germany and conditions there," and on March 31, in a letter to King Ludwig, he vented his annoyance at the entanglement of his *oeuvre* in things mundane: "My own achievements, creations, and schemes pursue me everywhere like gnawing serpents, encircling and constricting me like some Laocoön. It was my misfortune to devise the idea of a Bayreuth ideal!" He was, he said, so utterly exhausted that no concessions or efforts on his part could any longer accomplish what needed to be done. "Reports of performances of my works cause me nothing but sorrow. I wish I were able to withdraw permission for them everywhere. That is why I have already thought seriously about emigrating to America, because there I would obtain the funds required to buy back all the performing rights I have assigned."

This plan went back a long way. American interest in a series of concerts had been voiced as early as 1854, and offers reached Wagner in the following year. More proposals for an American trip were made in 1859. Ever since then, probably encouraged by his impressions of Wesendonck's wealth, Wagner had entertained the fixed idea that America was a Canaan whose streets were paved with gold. Negotiations were now put in hand through Newell S.

Jenkins, a Dresden-based American dentist who had more than once treated Wagner at Bayreuth. On February 1, 1880, Wagner informed the family circle that he proposed to move to Minnesota, build a house and drama school there, and dedicate *Parsifal* to the Americans. The situation in Germany had become intolerable, he said. (He went even further on August 20, when Cosima reports him as saying, quite seriously, that Bayreuth had been an act of folly.)

Writing to Jenkins from Naples on February 8, he announced: "I consider it not impossible that I may yet decide to emigrate to America for good, taking my entire family and my last work with me." In return, he demanded a million dollars. Half of this sum would enable him to settle in a climatically favorable part of the Union; the other "would be employed as capital, to be placed on deposit in a state bank at 5 percent. America would thereby have purchased me from Europe forever." On the other hand, he said, the festivals must also be held and financed. This was asking a bit too much. On April 1, when Jenkins called at Naples on his way from Dresden to Constantinople, he found Wagner "so full of illusions about conditions in America that arguments against the plan carried no weight with him." It was all Jenkins could do, with the aid of friends, to talk him out of the whole idea. In fact, Wagner would probably have lacked the energy to make a fresh start at the age of sixty-seven. The issue was ultimately decided by the children, who were too attached to Wahnfried and Bayreuth for him to want to uproot them. It was the children, too, who entertained him most in Italy. He relished their delight in the bustling Italian scene and marveled at Siegfried's swiftness of perception, his talent for languages and drawing.

On May 26, Wagner drove with his family and Joukowsky to Amalfi. From Amalfi, he rode in a donkey cart to Ravello, where he toured the Palazzo Rufolo. From this half-ruined castle in twelfth-century Moorish style, a flight of marble steps led down to a little rose garden which the visitors found enchanting. With its wealth of color, its niches and benches picturesquely wreathed in greenery, its Saracen pavilions nestling beneath cypresses and aloes, its intoxicating scents and air of seclusion, it might have been a set designed by Nature itself for the second act of *Parsifal*. "Klingsor's magic garden is found!" Wagner wrote in the visitors' book. After a boat trip to the Villa Portiglione on May 29, Joukowsky produced a sketch for the act in question. All that was missing was the temple of the Grail.

On three successive evenings, from June 23 to 25, Wagner read Aeschylus's *Oresteia* aloud to Cosima and Joukowsky. Cosima felt that she had "never before seen him like this," so completely at one with what he was reading. Cassandra's grim admonitions were "heartrending," and Joukowsky preserved a lifelong recollection of the cry, "Apollo! Apollo!"

If compassion for suffering humanity and the knowledge that man is unconscious of his fate inspired Wagner with the ideas, some abstruse, some merely odd, propounded in "Art and Religion," which he completed on July 19, 1880, it cannot now be ignored that he was genuinely moved by "the tragedy of mundane existence" and felt that mankind was doomed to disaster by its failure to live in harmony with Nature and the moral law. Man was burdening himself with guilt by engaging in violence and brutality, by waging war and slaughtering animals; indeed, by torturing them. Both now and in subsequent essays, Wagner would have liked nothing better than to overturn the globe and its inhabitants and stand them on their head. This urge stemmed from his blind Titanism, which was not content with simple contemplation and averse to looking for philanthropic solutions. That left only one recourse: by advertising man's need for redemption, art would have to do what religion had lost the power to accomplish. To exist at all, art must be founded on morality. That Wagner genuinely felt this cannot be doubted.

On August 8, alarmed by a severe allergic rash which he took to be a recurrence of his dreaded erysipelas, he fled the maritime climate of Naples and left for Rome. By way of San Marcello, Pistoia, and Florence, the Wagners and Joukowsky traveled to Siena, where they were to be rejoined by the rest of the household. They visited the cathedral as soon as they arrived on August 21. Wagner was "moved to tears" by the interior, with its sixteen columns of layered marble. No building had ever made a greater impression on him, Cosima noted, which seems strange until we learn that he immediately identified it with the temple of the Grail and asked Joukowsky to sketch it for the Bayreuth production of *Parsifal*.

Cosima set up house at the Villa Fiorentina, a palazzo with its own garden, and Wagner installed himself in a spacious bed once occupied, so the story ran, by Pope Pius IV. Its dimensions prompted him to remark that there was room in it for the entire Schism. He whiled away the time at Siena by reading bound volumes of an illustrated weekly magazine, *Fliegende Blätter*, which seemed to him to recapture the spirit of the age. Before returning to Germany, it was decided to spend a week or two in Venice. On October 4, Wagner, Cosima, and the children booked into the Hotel Danieli. Two days later, they moved to the Palazzo Contarini, on the Grand Canal. Wagner had already, while staying at Sienna in September, annoyed King Ludwig by hinting that he planned to spend six months in America. What had alarmed him most of all—and inhibited his work on the orchestral score—was the prospect of having to surrender *Parsifal* to Munich. His formal renunciation of the Court Theater's services on September 28 was thus a dramatic gesture.

Ludwig's response to it was soothing. On October 15, 1880, he decreed that the orchestra and chorus of the Munich Court Theater should be made available for festival performances, and on October 24 he consented to *Parsifal*'s production at Bayreuth alone.

It was at the Palazzo Contarini on October 22 that Wagner renewed his acquaintance with someone who has already appeared on the scene. Count Joseph Arthur Gobineau, author of *La Renaissance, Nouvelles asiatiques,* and *Essai sur l'inégalité des races humaines,* enjoyed a reputation for literary and stylistic brilliance but was physically and mentally past his prime and had become something of a captious eccentric. Wagner, who found him an estimable and interesting personality, invited him to Bayreuth in the coming year, but he was still ignorant of Gobineau's theory that the Aryans constituted an "elite race." It was not until February 13, 1881, that a work by the philologist August Pott drew Wagner's attention to *Essai sur l'inégalité des races humaines* and prompted him to study the original French text.

Leaving Venice on October 30, Wagner and his party reached Munich the next day. He found his stay there largely enjoyable, though, in retrospect, it was not without its disagreeable moments and provoked another succession of restless, dream-haunted, pain-racked nights. The family lodged with Fräulein Schmidt, a former landlady of Wagner's, at 8 C Brienner Strasse. Relatively congenial company was provided by Hermann Levi, the painter and draftsman Wilhelm Busch, the sculptor Lorenz Gedon, Lenbach, Heckel, Pohl, and Michael Bernays, a professor of literature at Munich University. On November 6, everyone met at Lenbach's studio for a Saturday soiree that started well but ended in disaster. Wagner became so "agitated and enraged" and spent "such a terrible night" in consequence that Cosima had seldom felt more conscious of "life's miseries and original sin."

What had happened? As Lenbach later described the incident, Wagner heaped curses on every monarch in the world—emperor, kings, and Lenbach's idol Otto von Bismarck. "Don't talk to me about Bismarck!" he fumed. "He should have made peace with the French after Sedan. By pursuing the war to the gates of Paris he divided the two nations for a century." Although this version of the quarrel has always been disputed by (conservative) Wagnerian authorities, who represent it as a malicious fabrication on Lenbach's part, Cosima obliquely confirmed a few days later that Bismarck had been at the root of it. If the words attributed to Wagner are authentic, he must have forgotten that he himself had called for the bombardment of Paris.

A private, late-night performance of *Lohengrin* had been arranged for King Ludwig on November 10. Wagner watched it from the royal box while Cosima and a handful of others looked on from the back of the otherwise deserted auditorium. Wagner's last meeting with the king on November 12 ended on a sour note. The *Parsifal* Prelude was to be performed for Ludwig at half-past three in the afternoon, after due rehearsal, but he kept the orchestra waiting for nearly half an hour. Some thirty people, including the publisher Ludwig Strecker, Kapellmeister Fischer, Rubinstein, Lenbach, and the singer Franz Nachbaur, secreted themselves in various boxes so that the king would think himself alone in the theater. The prelude was received with rapt and silent attention. Then Levi came to the orchestra pit with the news that Ludwig wanted it repeated. Wagner complied. When Ludwig further requested the *Lohengrin* Prelude for purposes of comparison, Wagner handed the baton to Levi and left the orchestra looking pale and angry. He summoned Cosima to his dressing room and greeted her cheerfully, having meanwhile recovered his composure. The *Lohengrin* Prelude came to an end. The orchestra rose and Levi turned to face the royal box, only to find that Ludwig had already left. Toward half-past five, the subdued gathering broke

up. That night the king and his equerry attended a private performance of Hermann von Schmid's play *Aus dem Stegreif.* Wagner
never saw him again.

Later the same evening, in Lenbach's presence, Wagner unleashed another furious attack on Bismarck, "that bulldog face
which is always being painted." After apologizing—unsuccess-
fully, by all accounts—he read the death of Falstaff from Shakespeare's *Henry V.* Cosima records that he was "greatly struck by the
passage about kings having curious humors."

The Final Score

Wagner returned to Bayreuth on November 17 and at last resumed
work on the score. For the moment, however, he remained listless
and discontented, slept badly, and flew into rages at the slightest
provocation. On December 1, 1880, he publicly informed his patrons that the next festival would be held in 1882—and this at a time
when the score of the relevant work did not yet exist. It was not
until shortly before Christmas that he began to orchestrate in
earnest. He invited Joukowsky to live at Wahnfried until he had
set up a studio of his own; and on January 8, 1881, Engelbert Humperdinck arrived. There were times in the ensuing race between
composer and copyist when Humperdinck failed to keep pace with
Wagner's output.

In January, Wagner told an astonished Hermann Levi that he
was to conduct *Parsifal,* but first they would run through an act
together. "I hope I shall succeed in finding a formula that will
make you feel quite at home with us and one of us." The previous
year he had been reluctant to let Levi touch *Parsifal* unbaptized,
and recently at Munich he had told him that he "fussed over his
soul too much." There is no doubt that Levi was alive to Wagner's
many inner contradictions, his blend of kindly and sinister ideas,
and that he agonized over his personal position. It is, however,
clear from the conductor's letters to his father, the chief rabbi of
Giessen, that this inner conflict left his love for the master unimpaired. Although Wagner remarked to Cosima on July 24, 1882, that
"as a member of the orchestra he would not care to be conducted
by a Jew," his treatment of Levi evinced an unusual degree of
affection, trust, and artistic appreciation. He ended by making

him, to all intents and purposes, musical director of the 1882 festival, but first their relationship had to stand an acid test.

From April 12 to 14, 1881, Levi spent "three glorious days" at Bayreuth discussing the next year's rehearsal plans with the composer. The first act was orchestrated by April 25. Then came another intermission because Angelo Neumann had persuaded Wagner to supervise some rehearsals of his Berlin *Ring* production. Encouraged by the respectable success of his Leipzig production in 1878, Neumann had rented Berlin's Viktoria Theater with a "free" Wagnerian ensemble and carried out some effective promotional work among the higher echelons of the capital's social hierarchy.

Wagner and Cosima traveled to Berlin on April 29. Casting problems apart, the Berlin *Ring* was an undoubted triumph. After attending various rehearsals and the first performance of the cycle, which spanned the evenings of May 5, 6, 8, and 9, the Wagners returned to Bayreuth on May 11. Here they found Count Gobineau, who had arrived in their absence and been pampered by the girls. Although Gobineau's visit lasted nearly four weeks, it was not the occasion of a conspiracy between two elderly racial fanatics. To judge by Cosima's diaries, they seem to have spent most of the time talking at cross purposes. On May 15, for example, Wagner read Gobineau some passages from his autobiography relating to Bakunin. His obvious pleasure at having written them can hardly have been shared by his listener. On May 18, Wagner and his guest quarreled over the Irish, whom Gobineau pronounced "incapable of working." Wagner lost his temper and castigated the English, retorting that he would not work under such conditions either. "The count goes so far in his ideas as to reproach the Gospels for championing the poor"—not a sentiment calculated to appeal to an exrevolutionary who had written *Jesus of Nazareth* in 1848! Finally, at lunch on June 3, Wagner "positively exploded in favor of Christianity as compared to racial theory." Gobineau's alleged influence and all its corollaries appear even more tenuous in the light of these ideological differences. One cannot help feeling that a certain school of Wagnerian criticism has seized on a construction devised by Glasenapp and Chamberlain with altogether different ends in view. The best ammunition against Wagner has always been supplied by his devotees.

Once Gobineau had left Bayreuth, Wagner started orchestrating the second act of *Parsifal*. Levi returned to Wahnfried for more consultations at the end of June. At lunch on Wednesday, June 29, Wagner came to the table with an anonymous letter accusing Levi of having an affair with Cosima, exhorting Wagner to preserve the purity of his work, and urging him not to let a Jew conduct it. Reluctant to keep any secrets from a trusted associate but little guessing how the sensitive conductor would react, Wagner gave Levi the letter to read. Levi departed the following day and wrote to Wagner asking to be relieved of his duties. On Friday, July 1, Wagner recalled him in the following terms: "For God's sake come back at once and get to know us properly at last! Lose none of your faith, but acquire some fortitude as well. Perhaps—there'll be a great turning point in your life—but, come what may, you're my *Parsifal* conductor." Lose none of your faith. . . . In other words, the Mosaic faith was at liberty to preside over *Parsifal*. Levi returned to the fold on Sunday, July 2. "The atmosphere at lunch extremely relaxed—indeed, very merry. Richard called for some *Hebrew* wine!"

In August, a young English soprano presented herself at Wahnfried and secured an engagement as one of the solo Flower Maidens in *Parsifal*. Carrie Pringle by name, she sang Agathe's aria "very tolerably." Nothing more is known about this evening audition and little more about the singer herself, though she must have been an attractive creature. The mystery that surrounds her role in the last act of Wagner's life has never been completely dispelled. More visitors arrived toward the end of September, one of them Liszt and the other a woman, this time from the past. With pounding heart, Judith Gautier crossed the threshold of the man who had loved her so ardently. Some music making and a few excursions followed, but Cosima says little more about this reunion. Pleading work, Wagner took leave of Judith with the words, *"Ma chère enthousiaste, prenez pitié de moi"* ["My dear devotee, have pity on me"].

It was a static time with few landmarks to record: the essay "Herodom and Christianity," occasional visitors, readings from Goethe and Shakespeare, Cervantes and Scott, and, with the third act of *Parsifal* in prospect, reminiscences on the subject of *Tristan* and its creative excitements. A static time, but with it came the desire for space and movement. "We are thinking of far-off places," Cosima wrote on October 5, 1881, "—of Palermo. He reads about it in Baedeker and then goes back to work in a cheerful sort of mood." The second act was completed on October 19.

The Wagners left Bayreuth early in November. After traveling by way of Munich, Bolzano, Verona, and Naples, where they boarded a steamer, they reached Palermo on November 5. Here they took three adjoining rooms, with a terrace overlooking the garden, at the Hôtel des Palmes. The first page of the score for act 3 was written on November 8. Young Fidi practiced his Sicilian dialect and spent much time drawing in the street while his sisters consorted with the local aristocracy. Wagner would have liked to finish *Parsifal* before the year's end, but abdominal pains and cardiac spasms conspired to thwart him. He felt ill, unhappy, and indifferent to future success. All his works, he said, were merely pearls cast before swine. Having correctly paginated the manuscript sheets in advance, he was able to skip a few and orchestrate the last bar in time to add the "finished" score to Cosima's birthday presents on Christmas Day, but it was still incomplete.

On January 13, 1882, he spoke at lunch of his fear "with this, as with all his other works," that death would cut him short. That evening the chorus and overture from *Die Feen* were played to mark Joukowsky's birthday. Wagner slipped quietly away, and Cosima, who followed him out, found him putting the finishing touches to his score. "It was giving me no peace," he told her. A little later: "The glorious strains of the *Tannhäuser* march ring out. He comes in, and—it is finished!"

Christ's words on the Cross, perhaps unconsciously employed to signify completion—but did they mean that all had been accomplished, that the wound was healed and death the only merciful release? It is the music that discloses what was meant: sorrow tinged with happiness as the end draws near. Wagner's whole *oeuvre* may genuinely be, as Wapnewski surmises, a "monument to the erasure of a lifelong illusion," guilt surmounted and torment extinguished in art, with its twofold illumination of the artist and the world at large. If so, these final bars were a cry from one grown weary of his mission, a redeemer's plea for redemption. Little more remained to be done.

Genius, Work, and Character

———◆———

W agner, in contrast to other men of genius, was lucky enough to evoke a reaction this side of the grave. Most of his obituaries were published in his lifetime. Scholars devoted to the study of aesthetics chimed in half a century late, insofar as they deserve to be taken seriously, but they have contributed almost nothing to our overall knowledge of the man. He became, in his day, a model of notoriety whose name was on everyone's lips and whose reputation extended far beyond the frontiers of art. As a leading light of the "modern age" he detested so profoundly, he attained a prominence that assured him of privileged treatment in later life. He traveled by rail in "saloon" cars, a V.I.P. whose approach was signaled ahead by railroad authorities as far afield as southern Italy. He was meat for literature, caricature, and satire. A Viennese farce by Bauernfeld featured a character named Richard Faust who appeared in a Wagner mask. The same author wrote that Wagner was "the goblin of publicity" personified. As one who aired his views on all and sundry, he was forever being quoted. Without even wanting to, he constantly became embroiled in public controversies that made him the subject and object of journalistic debate—and, coincidentally, "good box office." He once wrote to Peter Cornelius from Tribschen: "Of myself there's nothing much to tell, since so much is said about me. If a man pondered from dawn till dusk how to set about making a scandal of himself, he couldn't set about it one whit better than I. I think I'm very much envied for my skill in that respect." In August 1876, Karl Marx confessed himself astonished that the "Bayreuth fools' festival of that state musician Wagner"—a misnomer—should hold such appeal for the masses. He enlarged on this theme in a letter to his daughter Jenny the following month: "Wherever one goes these days, one is pestered with the question: 'What do you think of Wagner?' " It may readily be imagined that Eduard Hanslick found the topic just as irritating. He is reputed to have said that, were the Holy Ghost to descend on the twelve Apostles in the guise of a dove, its first act would be to inquire their opinion of Richard Wagner. Not since the appearance of Goethe's *Werther* had feelings run so high and the general public become so involved. In more recent times, only Picasso and the Beatles have enjoyed comparable exposure.

Wagner was not only aware of his personal impact on others but concerned about it. "I know," he told Cosima on September 20, 1879, "I was persuasive. I drove people mad and then ran away from them—it has been the same story all my life." He never held a low opinion of his art or balked at making the most immodest pronouncements. Even the self-doubt that haunts every artist was to some extent a by-product of his belief that he was an epochal figure. On September 4, 1881, he wondered "if he would, perhaps, be entirely forgotten, displaced by someone who would make things easier for the audience. 'However,' he concluded, 'it won't be easy to make them easy.' " Knowing this, he lamented the imminent demise of music itself.*

But this does not answer the question of how Wagner's attributes can be reconciled with the image of genius. Although Shaftesbury's theory—that genius is the incarnation of a quasi-divine movement and sustained thereby—influenced an entire age, it does not help to provide a simplified explanation of Wagner's rise to prominence. No one was awaiting a Messiah, a spirit through which the universal spirit would reveal itself, a god who would lay down new rules. No one was waiting for rules at all, and nothing can disguise the isolation and profane nature of the epochal phenomenon called Richard Wagner—neither the misguided Wagnerite sect nor the sectarian doctrines of its idol, which were merely an aid to defining Titanic aims, not Titanic themselves, and which he himself grew out of and discarded in later years. Wagner was not the great consummator of a movement such as *Sturm und Drang* or romanticism or expressionism, nor was he borne along on the shoulders of a multitude. He did not accomplish what hundreds of composers aspired to and would have liked to achieve themselves.

Kant's more cautious definition of genius was "the talent for invention," a natural gift that laid down rules for art—but only, be it noted, for art. (He also questioned whether geniuses were particularly useful, given that they created disorder.) Schopenhauer held that genius was "supreme intellect endowed with complete objectivity and love of truth"—a definition that would disqualify Wagner on more than one count. Albert Wellek says that persons of genius seldom represent a type, and then only to a very limited degree. "The fundamental characteristic of genius has rightly been perceived in its universality"—an interior universality from which it shapes the world. Wagner was not a type but an exception—above all, as Nietzsche correctly discerned, in the psychological sphere.

Wellek, citing Weininger, bases his remarks on the psychological factor comprising the inner tensions that envelop the world like a net: "That he should carry the whole world within his breast, contradictions and all—that is the nature, destiny, and tragedy of the genius. No one can encompass the world without inner tension." This applies in full measure to Wagner. In his unsuccessful attempt to encompass the world, Wagner once more stands revealed as the tragic artist who, in contrast to the harmonious, produces like an "elemental force"—one of his own invariable requirements.

Wagner dreamed, very early on, of being a dramatist as well as a musician. This made things harder for him than for most, calling as it did for a combination of talents seldom found in one person. The story of his boyhood, and even the early works that show no signs of a specifically Wagnerian musical idiom, demonstrate that he grasped the laws of musical structure and articulation with exceptional speed and intuition (the word is apt here, for once), and that, despite inadequate teachers and courses of instruction, he mastered them with an ease that immediately surpassed mere craftsmanship. Musically speaking, nothing was beyond him, but what of the other arts?

His multiple gifts were problematic. In other words, we are dealing with a man whose highly developed talents were *stylisti-*

cally asynchronous. Wagner was an artistic innovator of the first rank, but only in regard to music and the specific theatrical talent that conjoined his music to other things. It cannot be denied that his capacity for sculptural realization—even his taste in pictorial design and talent for production—lagged far behind his other gifts and abilities. The stage directions interpolated in his libretti belong to quite another category: Being projections of the inner eye, they are virtually impracticable except on film. They proved obstructive to his stage works and remained so for a long time. Stylistically, they were out of period. (It should nonetheless be pointed out that even the most questionable aspects of a work of art can seem modern to posterity. As patina builds up and the level of audience appreciation changes, many ineptnesses take on the character of art.) Wagner's conception of the "theatron" was also fully consonant with his inner eye and cinematic approach, as he revealed in his speech at the stonelaying ceremony in 1872. There was to be "nothing clearly discernible" between the audience and the stage. What went on there must have "the unapproachability of a dreamlike apparition" and be accompanied by ghostly music that would present the spectator with "an authentic facsimile of life"—in other words, with total illusion. Disappointed by what he saw on stage, Wagner ended by favoring "suggestion" instead. Realism versus illusion was a dilemma he never really resolved.

In addition, Wagner himself could never quite determine how far his various talents shared in the totality of his work. He wavered between them in youth, as we have seen, and his numerous pronouncements on whether he should be regarded as a poet or a musician are conflicting. "I'm no poet," he declared on January 22, 1871, "and I don't care a jot if people criticize my style. In my work, action is all. It doesn't much concern me whether people understand my verses—they'll certainly understand my plot." It is all the more nonsensical to malign Wagner's libretti because the words alone are not what constitutes their poetic quality—though it must be conceded that the *Meistersinger* libretto was more poetic than any of its predecessors in the entire corpus of operatic literature. A dramatist reveals his poetic gifts not only in language but in plot, in arrangement of material, dramatic construction, and psychological depth. This emerges strongly from Thomas Mann's essay on the *Ring* (1937): "I have always thought it absurd to question Wagner's poetic stature. Poetically speaking, what could be

more beautiful and profound than Wotan's relationship with Siegfried, the god's paternally derisive, condescending affection for his
destroyer, the loving abdication of old authority in favor of eternal
youth? The wonderful sounds the musician devises at this point he
owes to the poet." The same applies to many passages from *Holländer* onward. No matter how far the libretti fall short of literature in its own right, the music is literary in conception. Thomas
Mann called "the unquenchable chromaticism" of the Liebestod "a
literary idea" and the *Rheingold* Prelude "an acoustic thought." In
his own writings, Wagner claimed that he had become a poet
through his capacity for musical expression. And a musician? "I'm
a fine musician," he told Cosima on January 13, 1878. It was only
when he composed without thinking that he had full command of
all he required; as soon as he started wondering how to transpose
a theme into another key, he became confused. "In my case," he
explained on August 16, 1869, "emphasis should be laid on the
combination of poet and musician. As a pure musician I should not
amount to much."

By arranging his collected writings in purely chronological
order, he meant to show—albeit in a manner too complicated for
general understanding—that he had no literary pretensions. His
middle-aged penchant for writing, a task he found easy and agreeable compared to the laborious process of composition, was another matter. It is a curious fact that most people prefer to do what
they do least well: Wagner the author, Nietzsche the composer.
Wagner wrote with great facility—excessive facility, which is why
failure attended almost everything he wrote after 1848 with the
exception of parts of his autobiography, which he dictated. He
took more trouble with his dramatic texts, making things harder
for himself the more he strove to comply with a preconceived
theory (except in *Die Meistersinger,* where the poet vanquished the
theorist) and allowing himself to be guided as best he could by his
musical powers of imagination. Very little had to be altered in the
course of composition, and then usually on account of a modified
word order, not because the text militated against the music. This
form of procedure is hardly indicative of textual primacy—a fact
that long went unrecognized. Wagner's music was so all-absorb-
ently dominant that it devoured his libretti like a carnivorous
plant. On the other hand, it lends itself to use as an atmospheri-

cally stimulating background to the most unrelated dramatic occurrences in a way that has made Wagner the most versatile film composer of all time.

Attractive though parts of them seem, the Zurich commentaries on his musical-dramatic creative process are largely negated by what has just been said. The vast compass of his theoretical writings was, perhaps, a necessary consequence of his long breathing space before tackling the *Ring* and the intense artistic strains imposed by his method of composition. Even toward the end of his life he could not describe what happened when, half-consciously following the thread of an idea, he made his way through the intricate ramifications of his musical web. Ideas came to him, often at very long intervals. He would walk through a gate, round the corner of a building, straighten a cushion, stand musing at a crossroads, turn down a path in the Hofgarten at Bayreuth—and be struck by an idea, a theme, a motif, or just a phrase. Fragments meaning little by themselves, these were jotted down or memorized, and he could usually associate them with the exact spot where they had come to him. But it was only the process of composition itself that recalled them to his mind and brought them into an organized harmonic relationship. That was why he never had to rack his brains for an idea while working. He composed with a strangely indifferent attitude toward his surroundings, unaffected by the turmoil that reigned in his private life.

This is remarkable, given that the substance of what he composed, so far from leaving him cold, moved him deeply and often reduced him to tears. (It occurred to him late in life that he pursed his lips while composing, like someone in the throes of giving birth.) In November 1854, he reported to Princess Carolyne von Sayn-Wittgenstein that composing the music for *Die Walküre* was an "exceedingly painful" task. He was being punished for artistically trifling with the sorrows and sufferings of the world, he said, and had "time and again become quite ill" in consequence. Composing the first half of the third act of *Tristan* caused him "hypochondriac distress," and on May 18, 1869, while producing the composition sketch for *Siegfried*, he described it in a letter to King Ludwig as a "solemn and most exhausting" task; the "melancholy, painfully emotional" passages he found particularly fatiguing. This did not apply to private circumstance. Turmoil could rage around him unnoticed; his work never suffered. Were the sorrows of the world essential to him? Wasn't it necessary for him to suffer and cause suffering? What bearing had this peculiarity on a creative process which, insofar as we can survey the course of Wagner's life, was not appreciably impaired by it? What with all the disasters, feuds, and emotional outbursts, the grotesque and irksome incidents that pursued him, he sometimes marveled at his ability to produce anything at all. Discounting the *Parsifal* years, he nearly always lived in the shadow of depressing or alarming developments. "And, in the midst of this chaos, I am finishing *Die Meistersinger!*" he wrote to Ludwig in January 1867. "Who would believe it of me? What kind of person am I? What is so special about me?"

*　　*　　*

In 1872, the Munich psychiatrist Dr. Theodor Puschmann published a curious study purporting to prove that Wagner was an insane megalomaniac. Though not to be taken seriously, it ran through two editions at once. Puschmann was the pioneer of a specialized Wagner literature that has spilled over into the twentieth century and now occupies a shelf of its own. Psychologists, whose observations are often confined to what is diagnosable, have detected all kinds of insanity and mental illness in Wagner. All that emerges from the less naive and biased of their pathographies is the following string of assertions: Wagner was neurotic, hysterical, neurasthenic (overstrung by physical exhaustion—a statement for which some evidence can be adduced), and temperamentally hypomanic (egocentrically pugnacious). Some of these traits were undoubtedly sublimated in his work, with its sensual blend of color and excitement, its kinetic and erotic qualities. We know that he was volatile and capricious, arrogant and quick-tempered, but that he could also be witty, sensitive, gentle, and a charming companion.

What is so special about this? Nothing, on the face of it, except that the effect of Wagner's life story on outsiders, as compared with that of other men of genius, has a troublesome peculiarity that requires explanation: Observers of his career experience no shared sense of exaltation, or only in a vague and questionable way. They cannot identify with his propensity for the great and

Titanic, only—and to a limited extent—with the more human aspects of his joys and cares, his efforts to be less of his own worst enemy.

Genius would probably be deprived of its finest qualities if its weakest points—and Wagner had some very vulnerable ones—were not exceptionally pronounced, if no inadequacies were present. "He told me recently," Cosima noted in her diary on December 16, 1877, "that his vehemence had been given him to offset his softness."

His emotional nature contrasted strangely with his punctilious manner of working. Never has such an effervescent and impatient genius written in so perfectly formed a hand. Wagner's scores are masterpieces of painstaking calligraphy. But both aspects of the man—passionate involvement in life's battles and extreme, almost pedantic precision where his work was concerned—were rooted in the same fundamental urge for self-assertion. "Paradoxical as it may sound," writes Hans Gal, "the sublime ethos of the artist and the complete unscrupulousness of the man are expressions of the same basic instinct that leads him, on the one hand, to seek artistic perfection and the highest level of attainment open to his talent, and, on the other, to make unlimited use of every conceivable advantage in the struggle for existence. Nothing could be more absurd than to try to separate the man from the artist." To a radical artist like Wagner, everything served the same single end.

But he had a palliative that never failed to ease the strain and pain of his relations with the world around him. Without a sense of humor, Wagner would have been wholly intolerable to himself and others. "Ah, that's my salvation," he told Cosima on August 6, 1878, "to have been endowed with this gift for turning the utmost gravity into absurdity from one moment to the next. That's what has saved me from going over the edge."

A few examples may serve to illustrate this. Droll ideas were forever bobbing up in his mind—while dressing, for instance, which he called a productive occupation, or taking a bath, or walking, or lying awake at night between two dreams. Unfavorably impressed by the size of his cabin and bunk aboard the steamer that was taking him back across the Channel after his London concerts in 1877, he wryly observed that "the latitude here must be very narrow." Noting that Goethe and Lord Byron were said to have had skin as soft, white, and hairless as his own, he added, "Byron was the link between the human being and Shelley." When reminded at table how well he had looked at a particular time in the past, he agreed: well enough, he said, to have sat for a painter—as a still life. He once reproved young Siegfried for lolling around with his mouth open. "Beethoven," he told him, "would have composed much more if he'd kept his mouth shut." On the evening of December 21, 1879, Josef Rubinstein came and played Beethoven's Piano Sonata in A-flat Major, Opus 110. It was a glorious moment, noted Cosima, "when Richard, who was seated opposite me (on the little sofa beside the piano), suddenly crawled toward me across the floor and tried to kiss my feet. I seized his head and he tiptoed back to his seat, whispering, 'He didn't notice.' " And on May 19, 1880: "It would be my greatest triumph ever if I made you all laugh in my final hour." All these anecdotes convey something of Wagner's compulsion, often engendered by profound melancholy, to pull faces at the world around him.

The modern artist runs a risk of becoming neurotic in isolation. Wagner would firmly have denied this, though he did have certain misgivings. Referring to Robert Schumann, he declared that the true artist does not go insane; he knows what he wants. Wagner was fortunate in possessing an expansive temperament. He saw his peculiar mask for what it was: a form of self-protection. "I only see," he wrote to Röckel in January 1854, "that exaltation is the normal state of my nature, whereas ordinary repose is its abnormal state. I do, in fact, feel well only when I'm 'beside myself': then I'm quite at one with myself. If Goethe was different, I don't envy him for it."

Genius, or what we call by that name, remains a gamble on the part of Nature. It is associated with nervous high tension, with an apparatus of thought and imagination so flexible and mobile that it surprises itself, with a sensitivity to phenomena and interrelationships that pass unnoticed by others, with an instinct for the moment when the exceptional will succeed—a moment to be patiently awaited but not missed—and with an ever-possible and sometimes essential incomprehension of the uncomprehending. "This marvelously organized nature," wrote Judith Mendès-Gautier in her recollections of Wagner, "endowed with such exquisite sensibility, nervous and impressionable in the highest degree, suffered from terrible outbursts that left one wondering how he could possibly withstand them. One day of grief aged him ten years, but by the morrow he was even younger than before."

These eruptions of grief, this distraught and distressing mode of behavior, were the price exacted by his nature for the inordinate experiments conducted by his artistic will.

POSTLUDE

———◆———

1882-1883

THEODOR W. ADORNO: "*The consoling feature of great works of art reposes less in what they express than in their having managed to wrest themselves from existence.*"

Parsifal: The Farewell

W agner's physical appearance and state of health fluctuated at
Palermo. Fit and lively one day, he looked pale, puffy, and
exhausted the next. Having learned of his presence in Sicily from
some French friends, Auguste Renoir requested a sitting at the
Hôtel des Palmes and was granted one on January 15, 1882. Wagner
wore a wide-sleeved velvet jacket lined with heavy satin. His conversation with Renoir, conducted in a mixture of French and
German, was strange and erratic. Renoir, grimacing excitedly as
he worked, produced a full-face portrait of him in thirty-five minutes flat. "Of the exceedingly curious pink-and-blue result, Richard says it resembles an angel's embryo swallowed by a gourmet
in lieu of an oyster."

In February, he moved with his family to a villa owned by a local
admirer, Prince Gangi, in the Piazza dei Porazzi. Here, on March
2, he unearthed a melodic fragment recorded while engaged on the
second act of *Tristan* and rounded it off into a short piano piece
(later christened the "Porazzi Melody"). But the Villa Gangi, too,
proved a failure in the long run because the weather turned un-
pleasantly cool and the sunless rooms were hard to heat. Siegfried
developed a feverish cold, and Wagner grew more and more irritable. He complained of boredom, was upset by the mail he received,
and resented being a burden to those around him.

It was during these weeks that the family became acquainted

with a cultured young member of the Catanian aristocracy, Count Biagio Gravina, who formally requested the hand of Blandine, Cosima's second-eldest daughter, in marriage. After Gravina's somewhat obscure financial prospects had been clarified to Wagner's satisfaction, his proposal was approved and accepted. On March 20, with Blandine's fiancé in attendance, the family moved to the Hôtel des Bains at Acireale. Here Wagner unexpectedly witnessed yet another piece of nineteenth-century history. On March 27 the special train carrying Garibaldi, then seventy-five and close to death, rumbled slowly through the town. The inhabitants turned out to line the track and bid farewell to Italy's national hero, who was venerated like a saint. Garibaldi did not appear, being bedridden, so the occasion had a funereal flavor. Gravina wept, and Wagner paid tribute to the revolutionary who had wrought so many changes in his lifetime.

On April 1, after a recurrence of Wagner's cardiac spasms, the family set off for Germany again. Preparations for the Bayreuth festival had meanwhile begun under Levi's supervision. On May 11, Arthur Gobineau turned up at Bayreuth and spent another five weeks at Wahnfried before taking a cure for his various ailments, which included severe arteriosclerosis, atrophy of the liver, and heart disease. Cosima recorded very little of the aging invalids' conversation during these weeks. Wagner did not get much out of their last reunion. His sixty-ninth birthday was celebrated in style on May 22. Blandine, whose fiancé had arrived unannounced that morning, greatly affected everyone by honoring her stepfather with a warm and affectionate birthday tribute in verse. Up in the gallery, Humperdinck conducted a boys' choir in the chorus from the first act of *Parsifal*, and the evening was enlivened by *Schnadahüpfln* [humorous impromptu songs] sung to guitar accompaniment. Wagner laughed until the tears ran down his cheeks at an account of a peasant brawl, crying, "An *Iliad!*" while Gobineau sat in a corner muttering, "*C'est affreux, puéril!*"

Then it was back to the same old troubles—scenery, costumes, scene changes—that always afflicted Wagner's stage productions. He complained of bungling on the part of his staff, was aghast at the "dissipated women" in the magic garden, where "all should be innocence," and could not endure the "authentic" armor worn by the Knights of the Grail. After a costume tryout on June 19, Cosima remarked that it fell under three headings: "(1) horror; (2) absolute absurdity of the figures showing off the things for our benefit; (3) earnest and anxious attempts at alterations. I ended up believing that we shall pull it off after all, but oh, how let down we feel!"

Stage rehearsals began on July 2 under Levi and Fischer, with Heinrich Porges and Julius Kniese recording all the composer's stage directions in their piano scores. At this point, Wagner received formal notification that King Ludwig would not be coming to Bayreuth for *Parsifal*. On July 8, he wrote Ludwig a querulous letter: "Nothing could have dealt me a harder blow than the news that my exalted Benefactor has resolved to attend none of the performances of the Stage Dedication Festival Play. *Who* inspired this supreme and ultimate upsurge in all my mental energies? In constant recognition of *Whom* was it that I accomplished everything and looked forward to success? Though now assured, that success is turning into my life's greatest failure. What does anything matter to me if I cannot rejoice *Him* thereby?" He added: "This is the last thing I shall do. I know, from the immense fatigue that today grants me only enough strength to pen these few lines, what the state of my energies is. *Nothing* more can now be expected of me."

On July 25, the day between the dress rehearsal and the premiere, an artists' banquet was given at the theater restaurant. It was attended by Liszt and Wagner's closest friends, among them Judith Gautier, conspicuously attired in a sailor-boy blouse, and the ever-faithful Mathilde Maier. Wagner delivered a short speech in which he recalled 1876 and regretted that his words on that occasion had been misunderstood. "Now," he whispered haltingly, three times in succession, "now—now I have learned to hold my tongue." But his newfound reticence deserted him. He went on to call the Wagnerites foolish blockheads. Although this was said in front of Wagnerite witnesses, Glasenapp—who was among them—felt that the only unforgivable sin lay in retailing these remarks and exposing them to the incomprehension of the world at large.

Wagner slept badly on the eve of the premiere. Cosima heard him muttering in his sleep, "Children, I am going, suffering. . . ." At half-past three on the afternoon of July 26, a gusty, rainy day, they drove to the theater. Wagner promptly took exception to being gaped at when they walked in, but his only criticism of the first act, which passed off almost to his satisfaction, was its "histrionic" quality. When Gurnemanz (Emil Scaria) conducted Parsifal to the Grail Castle, many of the audience were overcome with dizziness as the panoramic backcloth glided past, so perfect was the illusion of movement. Then the castle appeared and was flooded with light as the C major chord rang out. Klingsor's magic garden, on the other hand, proved a failure, its sensual impact ruined by garish colors. The Flower Maidens' costumes were tasteless, though they sang delightfully. Wagner fell vicariously in love with one of them and shouted "Bravo! Bravo!" from his box after her diminuendo, causing some of his own supporters to hiss him in ignorance of who the interrupter was. Kundry, he had said on January 4, 1881, "should really be lying there naked, like a Titian Venus." Since this was impossible, her costume was modeled on Makart's painting of Charlotte Wolter as Messalina. Visual splendor supplanted dramatic intention. When the second act was greeted with prolonged applause despite these irremediable defects, Wagner came to the front of his box and announced that, by common consent, "no curtain calls would be taken" so as not to break the spell. This little speech marked the start of a century-old controversy over when, and when not, to applaud. Wagner was exasperated when the audience, who had misunderstood him, sat silent at the end of the performance. "Now I don't know at all," he complained. "Did the audience like it or not?" Another short address from the composer brought a belated storm of applause. He was eventually obliged to step out in front of the curtain and announce that, although he had tried to reassemble his artists, they were already disrobing. "The drive home," Cosima noted, "being taken up with this subject, was a vexed one."

After the performance, some of the artists, patrons, and critics drove through pouring rain to the Hotel Fantaisie at Donndorf. Angelo Neumann's table companion was Eduard Hanslick. "The dreaded Viennese critic," he recalled, "had grown noticeably silent under the immediate and powerful impact of Parsifal." That night, August Förster was suddenly moved to say, with tears in his eyes, "Wagner is dying, you mark my words." Everyone was startled, and Neumann asked his Leipzig codirector what he meant. Förster replied that no one who had created such a thing could live much longer—that he was finished and would very soon die. The dismay occasioned by this remark was slow to subside.

The second performance on July 28 was likewise reserved for

members of the Patrons' Association. Thanks to Wagner's misconstrued intervention at the premiere, it too passed off in total silence, and those who tried to applaud after the second act were hissed. When the performance was over, Wagner stepped in front of the curtain and addressed his patrons. Raising his hat, he said with perceptible coolness, "I hereby take leave of you."

On the third night, July 30, for which every seat cost thirty marks, Wagner addressed the audience yet again. He was anxious, he said, to dispel a misunderstanding. Though opposed to clapping between scenes, he had no wish to deprive his artists of their due reward when the curtain fell. But it was no use: Even after his death, devout Wagnerites persisted in their adherence to an already hallowed tradition.

Among those who attended the second performance were Lou von Salomé and Elisabeth Nietzsche. Elisabeth subsequently regretted not having spoken to Wagner that summer—not that this deterred her from fabricating a conversation with him for inclusion in her suspect recollections of Nietzsche. Lou von Salomé stayed at the same house as Malwida von Meysenbug, Heinrich von Stein, and Paul von Joukowsky. She struck up a friendship with the Russian painter, thereby causing a lot of gossip which Elisabeth duly relayed to her brother. "Long live Cagliostro!" Nietzsche wrote to Peter Gast on July 30, and on August 1: "The old sorcerer has scored another huge success, with old men sobbing, etc." But the old sorcerer was sad. Having wept before the August 1 performance, all he said at the close was, "I'm tired." He was utterly exhausted, listless, despondent, bereft of hope. After the fifth performance, Emil Scaria found him having one of his attacks in a small room backstage, gasping and flailing his arms as if warding off an invisible assailant. "This time I escaped," he told Scaria when he had recovered full consciousness, and begged him not to mention the incident. A contemporary letter from Wagner to Cabinet Secretary Bürkel ends with the words: "An extraordinary lassitude has come over me." After a lifetime of tension, the bowstring was growing slack. He was so apathetic that August that Neumann almost persuaded him to relinquish the world rights of *Parsifal*. Then, just before signing the contract, Wagner hesitated and asked for time to consider.

Of the ensuing performances,* Wagner saw little but the Flower Maidens' scene in the magic garden. On August 3, during a reception at Wahnfried, he sat joking with them beside the drawing-room stove. A mysterious accident occurred during one of the later performances. One of the six solo Flower Maidens—none other than Carrie Pringle, who had just secured an engagement at Milan's La Scala—dashed out of Klingsor's enchanted garden and fell. Whether or not she had tripped over a cord, as someone claimed, she was slightly hurt and had to be driven by cab to her lodgings on Wahnfriedstrasse, near the Hofgarten. Had the accident been engineered by some ill-wisher? The fact is, we know as little about it as we do about Wagner's strange predilection for the "blossoms" in Klingsor's garden, a shadowy subject only hinted at by his daughter Isolde and a few cryptic remarks in Cosima's diary. On September 6, when the festival was over, Cosima noted that her husband still missed the Flower Maidens. "He had been unable to show sufficiently how pleased with them he was, even though, at every performance, he had loudly called 'Bravo' over the heads of the entire audience." His allusion to "Undine creatures" on the eve of his death undoubtedly related, not only to the Rhine Maidens, but also to them, the creatures who, for all their innocence, present an image of temptation to man. Glasenapp's assertion that he turned to Cosima and added, "Are you one too?" was a brazen fabrication.

Wagner's disappointment at Ludwig's failure to attend the festival persisted throughout these weeks. On August 24, he sent the king a birthday greeting in the form of a rueful little poem. Liszt, who had left for Weimar on August 5, returned to Bayreuth on August 24 and stayed for a week. Other visitors included Bruckner, Delibes, and Saint-Saëns, whose opera *Samson et Dalila* had been performed by Eduard Lassen at Weimar in 1877, years before it was premiered in France. Bülow, married for the second time on July 29, had meant to visit Bayreuth, in part for his daughter Blandine's wedding, but the plan was thwarted when Brahms, for whom he now conducted, declined to attend the festival. He went instead to Klampenborg, near Copenhagen, the scene of his very first vacation with Cosima. There, unable to shake off old and painful memories, he brooded on Bayreuth from afar.

On August 25, Ludwig's birthday, after a delay occasioned by ecclesiastical red tape, Blandine was married to Count Biagio Gravina at a civil ceremony held in Wahnfried itself. Twenty-seven people sat down to the lunch that followed, and fireworks were set off during intermissions in the evening's performance of *Parsifal*. The young couple were married again in church the next day and left for their honeymoon in a saloon car provided by the railroad management. Wagner, who attended the evening reception at Wahnfried, waxed so irate over everything and everyone that his ill humor persisted long after the guests had left. Cosima had gone to him that afternoon, while he was sitting at his desk, and asked him how he felt. "He told me then," she wrote, "that he wished himself dead."

On Tuesday, August 29, the day of the final performance, a "great effusion" occurred between Wagner and Liszt, probably in regard to the latter's intention of leaving on the morrow. Cosima and her father left for the theater at four o'clock. Wagner, who did not appear until the first intermission, found everything on stage to his liking. During the last act he sneaked into the orchestra. Unseen by the audience, he took the baton from Levi at the twenty-third bar of the Transformation music and conducted the rest of the work himself.

The singers said later that no finale had ever made such demands on their lungs. The applause that followed it beggared description, or so Levi told his father, but Wagner did not show himself. He remained seated among the musicians, cracking bad jokes. After ten minutes, when the uproar still refused to subside, Levi called for silence at the top of his voice. The applause died away and Wagner began to speak from the conductor's stand, at first to Levi and the orchestra. Then the curtain rose to reveal the cast and technicians assembled on stage. Wagner spoke, wrote Levi, "with such warmth and sincerity that everyone began to weep. It was an unforgettable moment."

Death in Venice

—◆◆—

V enice, a place to die in. . . . Once upon a time, on each Ascension Day, the doge would board the *Bucentaur* in solitary state and sail out into the Adriatic escorted by a procession of sumptuously decorated ships. As he passed the Lido, he tossed a wedding band into the sea and proclaimed, "We espouse thee, Sea, in token of our firm and abiding dominion." But Venice lost her dominion, and the wedding of city and sea became a funeral rite. Not that he knew it, Wagner's own bond with Venice was already sealed.

The family arrived there on the afternoon of September 16, 1882, after a journey made hazardous by violent storms. The railroad bridge at Ala and the magnificent bridge over the Adige at Verona collapsed only half an hour after they crossed them; in fact, they were the last people to traverse the second of the two. Their first two nights were spent at the Hôtel de l'Europe, where they learned of these terrible disasters and heard rumors that the floods were bringing a virulent fever in their wake. September 17 was devoted to arranging more permanent quarters in the Palazzo Vendramin-Calergi, situated at the extremity of the Grand Canal's northern arc, on the Cannaregio side; and on September 18, the Wagners and their staff installed themselves on the palazzo's mezzanine floor.

Their landlords were the della Grazia family, relatives of the duke of Bordeaux, and their fellow tenants for part of the time were Count Bardi and his wife, Adelgunde of Braganza. Count Bardi was the son and heir of the duke of Parma and a nephew, through his mother, of the French Pretender, Henri V. The lobby of the mezzanine was adorned with Bourbon lilies.

Fifteen rooms in the entresol had been reserved for the Wagners' use. The red-papered drawing room in the side wing had a double window overlooking the Grand Canal and was furnished in Louis Seize style. Adjoining it on the left was Wagner's study, a room lined with gold-blocked Venetian leather. It had a dressing area and oriel, an escritoire, a couch, and, beside the curtained window, a cozy working area furnished with its own desk and armchair. Cosima was assigned a yellow silk "tea salon," which connected with the children's rooms, bedrooms, and guest rooms.

The palazzo, one of the loveliest buildings in Venice, has a garden at the rear with an ornamental pool in white marble. From this garden, which is accessible from the entresol, Wagner went for walks to the Cannaregio. He also made frequent excursions on foot to the Rialto, which he always confused with the Lido. Moored at ground-floor level and ready for use at all times was the gondola presided over by Luigi, Wagner's favorite gondolier. Luigi used to ferry him to St. Mark's Square, where he liked to sit on the stone bench in front of the basilica, unrecognized and unnoticed by the strollers and tourists who gazed up at the four bronze horses on the portico. He would sit there hunched with his elbows propped on his knees, a pose in which he half-humorously predicted that his corpse would someday be discovered.

Delving back into the past, immersing himself in his childhood and adolescence, contemplating his early career, conjuring up all the joy and anguish of a lifelong quest for fulfillment—all the errors and delusions, too—Wagner was inundated with a profusion of mental images during his weeks and months in Venice. He lived off the past and was haunted by it. He dreamed of going skating with Herwegh, recalled scenes from his childhood and described them to Cosima, was once more addressed in his dreams as Richard Geyer, thought of his little sister Cäcilie and how he had scared her by pretending there was something horrible in her bed. Was she still alive, the sister who, like all his family, had grown so remote from him? Leipzig and Dresden might have been on another planet and Wagner himself a relic of some bygone age. Sometimes he yearned to live to be ninety, or at least to survive for another ten years, so as to see his son reach man's estate, but when Daniela begged a lucky coin from him, he told her sadly, "You will soon be getting other things from me, dear child."

The equilibrium he had maintained since completing *Parsifal* was deserting him. His thoughts revolved around Bayreuth. He could have busied himself with plans for another festival, but for Ludwig's tiresome determination to have *Parsifal*, of all his works, privately staged in Munich. The fact was, Wagner had no desire to relinquish *Parsifal*—he wanted to wrest it away from the world on behalf of his own theater, his own creation. "Though that will pass away," he wrote to Angelo Neumann on September 29, "for who would maintain it in keeping with my intentions I do not know and cannot tell." That excluded Cosima, among other people! "If my strength, which I overtax on such occasions, were to decline before my death to such an extent that I could no longer occupy myself with these performances, I should certainly have to consider ways and means of preserving my work for the world in as pure a form as possible." Under these circumstances, he went on, he would be prepared to entrust *Parsifal* to Neumann's touring company.

He did not look to the future, merely expressed desires. Writing to Ludwig on November 18, he informed him that he wished to present all his works at the festival theater, one by one, in such a way that these Bayreuth productions could serve as models of correctness, if only for the benefit of immediate posterity. "For this I shall require some ten more years of vigorous life, during which my son will attain his full majority. I shall entrust the spiritual and ethical preservation of my work to him alone, knowing of no one else to whom I could relinquish my office."

Reviewing what he had composed, Wagner looked for unity in its totality and diversity. *Tannhäuser, Tristan,* and *Parsifal* were all of a piece, he said. He was not entirely happy with *Der Fliegende Holländer* and *Tannhäuser,* both of which existed in too many versions.* His declared intention of revising these two works—an intention expressed only weeks before his death—sprang less from a desire to "salvage" something imperfect than from a proper recognition of what any work should possess, namely, a living thematic unity that transcends the work itself and must be imbued with meaningful structural coherence. He wished to make it clear

that his works should be received with discernment and understanding, not merely enjoyed.

He lived in a mood of "optimistic resignation," pinning all his
hopes on "the utter downfall of this world of property." The best
that could happen to anyone, he declared, was exile to Ceylon. On
October 9: "To endure life, one would have to be dead." Although
October proved a wet and dismal month and St. Mark's Square
was flooded, he felt no desire to head back north. Bayreuth, he said,
had little to offer him, and he confided to Joukowsky how much
he regretted having built his "lovely house in such a foul climate."
Sometimes he gave vent to wryly humorous remarks. Hermann
Oldenberg's *Buddha* did absolutely nothing to inspire him with
calm acquiescence and peace of mind. His cardiac spasms recurred
with increasing frequency, causing him terrible pain. Slowly and
laboriously now, he walked the lanes and squares of Venice, often
pausing with his hand on his chest or hastily sitting down, overcome with pain and fatigue. "Harlequin, thou must perish," he
played on the piano—a popular song he had learned from Minna
in the old days.

Visitors came and went: Hermann Levi, the newlywed Gravi-
nas, and the lanky Countess Usedom, who always amused the
children by bending down to kiss their father's hand, in return for
which she received a peck on the cheek. On the afternoon of
October 12, Daniela's twenty-second birthday, the family received
a visit from Dr. Henry Thode, her husband-to-be. Thode noted in
his diary that Wagner came out to greet him "on his wife's arm,"
followed by children and guests like a prince with his retinue. A
sick prince, Thode might have added, though the rest of the proceedings were anything but regal. Wagner was in his postprandial
mood. They all sat down in the drawing room overlooking the
Grand Canal, Wagner with the light in his eyes. He disliked this,
he said, but Tristan and Isolde had suffered likewise before him.
He was wearing a quilted black satin jacket and a white waistcoat.
Thode expressed the hope that he was well. "Yes," he replied gaily,
"I lie there all day long, suffering the most violent spasms, and
don't recover until the evening, and along comes this heartless
family of mine and says, 'What a pleasure it is to see Father doing
so well here!'" On hearing that Thode hoped to qualify for a
university lecturership in the coming year, he exclaimed, "Not

another of them!" and proceeded to criticize Florence, the youthful art historian's favorite city, for being "starchy." Then, after surmising that Thode must have formed a "pretty" opinion of him, he added, "I'd better go before the worst happens."

The atmosphere was just as unconstrained during the festivities that evening, when the party was joined by Rubinstein, Hausburg, and Heinrich von Stein. Thode alarmed everyone by predicting that incessant rain would cause an epidemic of fever in the near future. Wagner kept harping on the subject, as though fascinated by it, but eventually took refuge in jest. Having sung Hagen's Vigil with Rubinstein at the piano—"A splendid bass, don't you think?"—he further astonished all present by performing Brünnhilde's Farewell. "Which did you prefer," he demanded as Thode was leaving, "my bass or my soprano?"

His nature was such that he retained his agility and his singular capacity for impish humor. On one occasion he cavorted around like a boy. On another, when psychic phenomena were under discussion, he abruptly tapped the supper table with his foot while seated. Comparing himself with Liszt, he disclaimed all *noblesse* and decorum. "I suffer," he said, "from the disease of incivility."

Heinrich von Stein, of whom he had cherished high hopes, left on October 15 for Halle, where he planned to qualify for a university lecturership with a dissertation on Giordano Bruno.* On October 25 came the news that Gobineau had died at Turin twelve days earlier. Wagner left Cosima to compose an obituary for the *Bayreuther Blätter*. The next day he wondered aloud where Nietzsche was.

In the small hours of October 31, he woke Cosima and called her to a window to see the comet over Venice. That afternoon, they visited St. Mark's Square, where they enjoyed the spectacle of a splendid sunset on one of the few fine autumn days since their arrival. The same evening Wagner read several scenes from *Romeo and Juliet* aloud, deeply affecting his listeners and reducing himself to tears. "But who," asked Cosima in her diary, "could ever describe, still less paint him during readings of this kind? His countenance illumined, his eyes remote yet shining like stars, his hand magical both at rest and in motion, his voice gently girlish, yet plumbing the depths and soaring through space."

Still in October, he embarked on "The Stage Dedication Festival at Bayreuth, 1882." This article contained some shrewd and perceptive comments on producing musical works for the stage. Its emphasis on the need for simple gestures and movements, for underplaying rather than overplaying operatic roles, and, last but not least, for simplicity in costume and décor, makes it well worth reading today. Wagner expressed satisfaction that his audiences had been "removed from their wonted world." Then, quite unheralded, came the following cry from the heart: "Who can spend a lifetime looking, with senses alert and a heart untrammeled, at this world of murder and robbery organized and legalized by fraud, deception, and hypocrisy, without sometimes being compelled to turn away in horror and disgust? Where does his eye alight then? Very often, I suspect, on the abyss of death." Wild outbursts such as these can only have been triggered by Wagner's preoccupation with that last dread word.

He continued to write between spasms—four of them on November 10 alone. Once he lay prostrate for nearly two hours, racked with pain and almost unconscious. Another night he got his pills mixed up and had to sedate himself with opium drops.

Liszt's arrival on November 19 only aggravated matters. Although the two men's personalities were mutually attractive, proximity did not suit them. They tended to speak simultaneously and at cross-purposes. If one of them wanted to play cards, the other felt an urge to talk. When Wagner got up in the middle of a game of whist and went to the piano to demonstrate an idea that had just occurred to him, Liszt paid no attention. After they had said goodnight, Wagner angrily censured him to Cosima. Neither man had any understanding of the other's way of life.

All else apart, Liszt disturbed the even tenor of the palazzo's daily routine. He was forever surrounded by a swarm of acquaintances, forever talking of matinees, dinners, and soirees. Wagner remarked at table that widows—and widowers—should either move in with their children or enter a convent. His worst quarrel with Cosima, who probably never forgave herself, occurred on November 30, only eleven weeks before his death. She sprang to her father's defense, whereupon he jumped out of bed, remarking that she obviously thought herself virtue incarnate. Although they made up, he returned her kiss without warmth—the first time such a thing had happened in all their years together.

On December 8, Wagner greeted Joukowsky with the words, "My friend, we have now been through fire and water with you

—now only death can separate us." When Humperdinck arrived on December 18, Joukowsky came into the room to greet him. Wagner flared up at this intrusion and sent Joukowsky home. It was not long, however, before he called on Joukowsky and begged his forgiveness, kneeling in the middle of the room—some measure of the anguish he felt at having lost the ability to control his fits of temper.

Then came more hours with Liszt, "Brother Franz," illumined by a lifelong friendship, exalted and made magical by love: Liszt pricking up his ears at the "Porazzi Melody" and marveling at its beauty, Wagner musing on the one-movement symphonies they both aspired to write. "If we write symphonies, Franz, let's not set off theme against theme—Beethoven exhausted that idea—but spin a melodic thread until it's spun. No drama, though!" But their paths had diverged. Liszt had long since abbreviated the thematic material in his piano pieces with intervallic motifs. He no longer spun threads out but was experimenting on the frontiers of traditional harmony. Liszt's was an ascetic avant-gardism. His setting of *La lugubre gondola* for two voices—funereal music composed, on some strangely prescient impulse, in Venice itself—is technically reminiscent of Stravinsky in his middle period, half a century later. Wagner listened with only half an ear. He owed Liszt a great deal and fully realized that he was closer to him than to most of his contemporaries. He had derived much from the symphonic chromaticism of Liszt's middle period and admired the vast dimensions of such poetic symphonies as *Dante*, though he never cared for the concluding apotheoses of Liszt the optimistic and devout Catholic. As for Liszt's brittle late style, which was ahead of its time in a way that differentiated him from the composer of *Tristan*, Wagner greeted it with incomprehension and described what he heard of it sketched on the piano as "dissonance."

For his own part, he had no desire to be adventurous or experimental; he wanted to rest and contemplate the past. On December 14, with the violinist Raffaele Frontali and the musicians of the Liceo Benedetto Marcello, he started rehearsing his C Major Symphony, which had not been revived for fifty years, with the intention of performing it as a birthday treat for Cosima at the privately rented Teatro La Fenice on Christmas Eve. The final rehearsal was held on December 22. "Richard had a spasm," noted Cosima, "but conducted the first movement and then, after quite a long intermission, the others. I sat hidden away from him, and was touched to reflect that, having performed this work fifty years ago for his mother, he was doing so now for me. I also took pleasure in the straightforward, outspoken work. I told Richard, 'That was written by someone ignorant of fear.' "

Two days after the rehearsal, the hall was festively illuminated. This time the first two movements followed one another in quick succession. After the second, Wagner went over to Cosima and Liszt and said a few cheerful words. At the end, he murmured in Liszt's ear, "Do you love your daughter?" Liszt looked startled. "Then sit down at the piano and play." To everyone's delight, Liszt complied at once. "Then Richard recounted the history of his symphony in French. Toward one o'clock we rode home, Venice looking blue and transfigured." It was the eve of Cosima's forty-fifth birthday.

Then solitude closed in and the farewells began. Humperdinck, who stayed on until January 3, saw Wagner's face "bathed in a transfiguring glow by the sunset of his life," but what he described in retrospect as transfiguration was only dissolution—a look most nearly to be found in Renoir's portrait: an anguished smile of distaste and weariness that rent and blurred his subject's features. No one realized how close the end was.

"Harlequin, thou must perish. . . ." Wagner toyed with this tune on the Ibach piano whose arrival in Venice he had greeted by remarking that, from then on, he would only write "soft" music. He improvised an intrada to *O du lieber Augustin* and kept breaking into a popular song from the Seven Years' War, which also contained a reference to death. When he playfully addressed Cosima as "Phylax," from Gellert's poem *Der Hund*, he recalled what an impact the line "Phylax came to die!" had made on him as a child. Visited one evening by the painter Vassili Volkov and the authoress Ada Pinelli, he ended with—yet again—"Harlequin, thou must pe-e-rrr-ish!" "He only flares up inside from time to time, like a half-extinguished fire," noted Cosima. He had even stopped flinging accusations at the world. Instead, a strange uneasiness came over him. He developed a sudden distaste for the Palazzo Vendramin, which he now associated with physical pain and farewells, as well as with a sense of estrangement, even from the beloved woman who was proving stronger than himself and would outlive him. In relentless detail, Cosima recorded his sufferings and dreams—even those aspects of him that still defied her comprehension. During the early hours of January 11, she heard him say in his sleep, "If He created me, who asked Him to? And if I am made in His image, it remains to be asked whether I welcome the fact."

Still no transfiguration. . . .

Despite Wagner's efforts to dissuade him, Liszt departed for Budapest on January 13. Joukowsky, whom Wagner had urged to return to Russia for the centenary of his father's birth, which was to be marked by the official tributes due to a distinguished poet, translator, and tutor to the czars, insisted on remaining at his side, a prey to dark forebodings.

Hermann Levi's last visit on February 4 was slightly marred by his own poor state of health and an allusion to Nietzsche's having introduced him to a so-called "young Mozart" named Peter Gast, who had proved to be an utter incompetent. During the evening, Wagner remarked to Cosima that Nietzsche had no ideas of his own. Next day they all discussed the future casting of *Parsifal*. It is not only possible but probable that Carrie Pringle's name cropped up. She was by then studying in Italy, chaperoned by her parents, and there is a distinct likelihood that Wagner—at first unbeknown to Cosima—asked Levi to invite her to Venice for an audition.

On Shrove Tuesday, February 6, the whole family turned out to see the carnival celebrations in St. Mark's Square, which was lit by a double row of more than three hundred gas lamps. From the Capello Nero, they watched Prince Carnival borne in procession around the square to meet his death by fire beside the columns of the Piazzetta. *Harlequin, thou must perish.* . . . Once, Wagner strolled over to the raised wooden dance floor with the children, only to return looking saddened. Poor workmen, he said, were prancing around there without knowing why. Midnight struck and the flames were extinguished. Toward one o'clock they all rode back to the Vendramin in their gondola. It was Ash Wednesday. Before she fell asleep, Cosima heard her husband say, "I am like Othello. The long day's task is done." The words were misattributed but apt.

Wagner's penultimate prose work was an open letter to Heinrich von Stein on the subject of his dramatic colloquies *Helden und Welt*. It is a laborious and stylistically marasmic piece of writing, except for one passage. Drama, he declared, was not a species of literature but "an image of the world reflected by our silent interior." Here we have a wonderful reappearance, lustrous as crystal held up to the light, of his lifelong conception of an inner dramatic thread—something he had derived from the Greeks and Calderón and contrasted with the superficial operas of his day. He went on to brand parliamentarians, academics, state, and Church as "deterrent object lessons" and inveigh against the "Semitized Latin world" (an expression of Gobineau's). It was a last feeble outburst by the exanarchist and anti-Semite, though he had recently given Cosima a not inaccurate explanation of the whole anti-Semitic problem: The threat of socialism, he said, was being turned against the Jews.*

The sight of shuttered and unoccupied Venetian palazzi started him on another train of thought: "There's property for you—the root of all evil. Proudhon took a far too material view of it, because property causes people to marry for its own sake and thus promotes racial degeneracy. That's what I liked about Heinse's *Glückselige Inseln*—his statement that they [the inhabitants of the Isles of the Blest] refrained from owning property so as to avoid the many evils associated with it." It seems that Wagner ultimately chose to discard all theories that attributed human decadence to purely biological factors, and that, with the cessation of his demands on the world, his ideas underwent another change—or at least showed signs of turning a corner.

At the very period when August Bebel was writing *Die Frau und der Sozialismus*, Wagner devoted himself to the emancipation of women in love. This was not a new departure. His *Brown Book* already contained some ideas on the subject jotted down at Acireale on March 27, 1882: "As long as our judgment of natural and human matters takes sole cognizance of sexual division in its varying efficacy, the genus will remain far removed from what is ideal. Culture and art, too, could attain perfection only if they were a consequence of the act of that elimination of the divided unity of male and female." Divested of its tangled genitives, the gist of Wagner's statement was that humanity would never attain its ideal state until men and women played an active part on equal terms. Marriages devoid of mutual affection, the *Brown Book* continued, had been more detrimental to the human race than any others.

Wagner tried to develop this theme in Venice, but his strength was failing too fast. Entitled "On the Feminine in the Human," his last and uncompleted article was intended as an epilogue to "Religion and Art." Even in its unfinished state, it betrays a loss of concentration, not only as regards handwriting but in style and argument. "In reviewing such essays as are known to me on the decline of the human races, I find that only perfunctory and, as it were, incidental attention is paid to the nature of marriages and their influence on the characteristics of the various breeds." Though trivial at first sight, the theory that follows seems on closer examination to open a door into another world of ideas. Wagner ascribed the decline of the human races to marriages of convenience. Property and the abuse of marriage were the real reasons why man had sunk lower than the beasts, but polygamy could not produce a "significant individual." Man was superior to natural generic law; what ennobled him was love—a view outlined in Wagner's conversations since 1881. It was not, he said, a question of racial vigor. If one did not posit time and space, there would be no decline; perhaps, in the last analysis, everything ultimately tended toward the preservation of morality. Was this an attempt to overcome the influence not only of Gobineau but of Darwin, whose *Descent of Man* he had read in September 1877? As recently as November 29, 1882, in alluding to a paper by Emil Haeckel on Goethe, Darwin, and Lamarck, he had stressed the absurdity of "proceeding from effect to cause to monad, or always remaining entrapped in the idea of time, space, and causality." Was all his yearning for redemption, all his urge to redeem the world, becoming submerged in the desire for snug security and an emotional haven? Did the regeneration of mankind consist solely, after all, in its ethical improvement, its moral exaltation and self-preservation? "Faithfulness in love: marriage," wrote Wagner, "—here lies the power of man over Nature, and we call it divine."

Three nights before his death, he dreamed of meeting his mother at the Brockhauses', looking young and attractive and altogether unlike his early recollections of her. Other dreams brought encounters with the women in his life. He dreamed of Wilhelmine Schröder-Devrient and of Minna, received dream letters from Mathilde Wesendonck and Friederike Meyer but laid them aside unopened, saying, "What if Cosima is jealous?"

On Monday, February 12, Hermann Levi bade him an emotional farewell. Wagner did a little work on his article before lunch and went for an outing with Eva in the afternoon. At supper he spoke of prisons and punishments—all of them, he said, a consequence of property. Then, as he had the evening before, he read aloud from Friedrich de la Motte-Fouqué's *Undine,* using a copy whose interleaves bore a handwritten Russian translation by Joukowsky's father. Joukowsky sketched him while reading on a sheet from his ruled note pad. In this last portrait, the angle of Wagner's downward gaze was such that his eyes seemed shut.

Cosima was already in bed when she heard him talking loudly and volubly. She rose and went into his room. "I was talking to you," he said, and gave her a long, tender embrace. "Once in five thousand years it works!" He explained that he had been speaking of the "Undine creatures" who yearn to possess a soul. Going to the piano, he played the mournful "Rheingold, Rheingold" theme. Then came a self-quotation: " 'False and base are those that rejoice above'—to think I knew that then with such certainty!" And, when he was lying in bed: "I am kind to them, these creatures of a lower order, these wistful creatures of the deep." That was all.

On the evidence of their daughter Isolde, Wagner and Cosima had a fierce altercation next morning, probably over Carrie Pringle's summons to Venice. Nothing else can account for Cosima's enigmatic behavior in the next few hours, or for Dr. Keppler's strange aside in his report on the cause of death.* The end had been hastened, he said, by "mental excitements." He went on: "The actual attack that so abruptly terminated the master's life *must* have been similarly occasioned, but it is not for me to engage in conjecture on the subject." Why did Keppler underline the word "must"? Had some member of the family or household staff let slip what everyone by then preferred to forget?

Wagner rose very late that morning. "I must take care of myself today," he told his manservant, Georg, while getting dressed. Despite his malaise, he took coffee with Cosima—and that, it seems clear, was when they quarreled over Carrie Pringle's forthcoming visit. Wagner eventually retired to his room to work until lunchtime. Siegfried, then a boy of thirteen, was practicing on the drawing-room piano when his mother entered, seated herself at the instrument, and began to play—the first time he had ever heard her do so. He inquired what the piece was, and she replied, "Schubert's *Lob der Tränen.*" That was how Joukowsky found her when he arrived for lunch at a quarter to two, weeping as she played Schubert's *In Praise of Tears.*

At two o'clock, Wagner sent word by Georg that the others were to start lunch without him. Cosima told Joukowsky that he had suffered several more spasms, quite severe ones, but that he would be better left to himself. She sat down to lunch looking reassured, and the meal proceeded in a relaxed and cheerful atmosphere.

The housemaid Betty Bürkel, who had remained within earshot of Wagner, was the first to hear him groaning. He was seated at the desk with his beret lying in front of him, apparently waiting for a spasm to subside. The pen had fallen from his hand. "The process of women's emancipation is under way," he had written, "but only amid ecstatic convulsions. Love—tragedy. . . ." At the sudden and insistent sound of his bell, Betty hurried in. "My wife," he told her, "—and the doctor." Georg helped him over to the dressing alcove and removed some of his clothes while Betty ran off to tell her mistress to come at once. Siegfried never forgot the sight of his mother hurrying from the room. "It conveyed a violent access of impassioned anguish; as she went, she collided so hard with the half-open door that it almost splintered."

Cosima found her husband slumped in a chair, exhausted. His eyes, which were shut, had ceased to see the things of this world. The long battle was drawing to a close: He had suffered enough. Death, the ultimate solitude, had come to Richard Wagner. No last wish, no look of transfiguration was discernible in his pain-racked features. They laid him on the couch. Cosima sank down beside it, clinging to his knees. By the time Dr. Keppler arrived at three o'clock, no pulse could be detected.

The others were in the drawing room, numb with apprehension, when Georg came in.

"It's all over," he said.

Lament for the Dead

The same day, tidings of Wagner's death were conveyed to a shocked and respectful world. "Terrible, frightful!" exclaimed Ludwig, the luckless monarch who had always hoped to die before him. "*Triste, triste, triste! Vagner è morto!*" Verdi wrote to Giulio Ricordi on February 14. "I was almost distraught when I heard the news yesterday. Enough said! A great personality is gone from our midst! A name that leaves a powerful impress on history —*una potentissima impronta,*" he amended. "It was hard," Friedrich Nietzsche wrote to Peter Gast, "to have to be, for six long years, the adversary of the man I most revered, and for that I'm not roughhewn enough." The draft of his letter of condolence to Cosima, which she did not keep, contains the following passage: "You have lived for a goal and sacrificed everything to it; and, over and above your love for that man, you comprehended the supreme invention of his love and hope: that you served: to that, you and your name will evermore belong—to that which, though it is born in a man, does not die with him." Hans von Bülow falteringly declared that his spirit had perished with Wagner's own fiery spirit. "*Soeur,*" he telegraphed to Cosima, "*il faut vivre.*" Anton Bruckner was composing the Adagio of his Seventh Symphony and had reached Letter W in the score when he heard the news from Venice. He wept—"Oh, how I wept!"—then brought the tubas' grand lament to a tranquil major-key conclusion.

Cosima sat beside her husband's corpse for twenty-five hours, stiff and silent, until Dr. Keppler, with Joukowsky's assistance, persuaded her to leave the room. Then he set to work, and the palazzo soon became filled with the penetrating aroma of arsenical embalming fluids. Adolf von Gross, Feustel's son-in-law, who had been appointed the children's guardian, arrived in Venice from Bayreuth on Thursday, February 15. He and his wife went down on their knees before Cosima—from then on, the pose most commonly assumed by the master's initiates. The younger children stared curiously at the fast-emptying rooms. The servants were packing up, though Cosima was reluctant to leave and Keppler had to insist on casketing the body. The sarcophagus, procured from Vienna, had a metal-framed window through which could be seen the lean, wryly withdrawn features preserved for us in Benvenuti Augusta's death mask. When the inner casket was closed, Cosima took possession of the key.

The waters of the Grand Canal were palely gilded with sunlight when, on Friday, February 16, black-draped gondolas conveyed the coffin and its escorts—the family, Joukowsky, Ritter, and the Grosses—from the palazzo to the railroad station, where two special carriages were waiting. Cosima spent the journey in a separate compartment with the blinds drawn. Levi and Porges joined the train at Innsbruck. Early on Saturday morning, when it passed slowly through Munich, dim figures lining the route dipped their torches in salute.

Toward midday, after switching tracks at Munich, the train pulled into Bayreuth station. The carriage containing the coffin spent the night beside the platform with a deathwatch in attendance. Cosima, who had been taken to Wahnfried, was too overcome to escort the coffin into town on Sunday morning. A long cortege formed in the station square toward midday, with the horse-drawn hearse flanked by a dozen pallbearers—two of them Jews: Muncker, Feustel, Gross, Standhartner, Niemann, Porges, Levi, Richter, Wolzogen, Joukowsky, Seidl, and Wilhelmj. The coffin was greeted at the gates of Wahnfried and carried to the waiting vault. The children kneeled before it, excitedly nuzzled by their dogs, while the parson delivered a brief and impersonal address.

What followed is posterity and another story: Wahnfried without Wagner—a today removed from his own by a catalog of disasters more earthshaking than any he experienced in life.

APPENDIX

Notes, Comments, Documents

Alarums and Excursions

4   Richard Wagner's nine brothers and sisters in order of age: (1)
Albert (March 2, 1799–October 31, 1874) was a serious artist who
never enjoyed great success in any capacity, whether as a singer,
actor, or theatrical producer. His daughter Johanna, a well-known
soprano, married Alfred Jachmann, a lawyer and district administrator, in 1859. She also did some acting after 1862 and ended her
career as a teacher at Munich's Royal School of Music. (2) Gustav
(August 21, 1801–March 29, 1802) died in infancy. (3) Rosalie (March 4,
1803–October 12, 1837), a talented actress, married Dr. Oswald Mar-
bach, an author and university lecturer in philosophy, in 1836. (4)
Julius (August 7, 1804–March 29, 1862) became a goldsmith. (5) Luise
(December 14, 1805–January 3, 1872) married the publisher-bookseller Friedrich Brockhaus in 1828. (6) Klara (November 29, 1807–
March 17, 1875), a singer, got married in 1828 to Heinrich Wolfram,
a fellow artist turned businessman, and retired from the stage
while still young. (7) Theresia (April 1, 1809–January 19, 1814) lived
less than five years. (8) Ottilie (March 14, 1811–March 17, 1883) got
married in 1836 to Professor Hermann Brockhaus, a classical
philologist and brother of Friedrich Brockhaus. (9) Cäcilie Geyer
(February 26, 1815–May 14, 1893), Wagner's half-sister, married the
publisher-bookseller Eduard Avenarius in 1840.

5   In the letters Wagner wrote during the late 1850s to his wife Minna, who had by then moved to Dresden, he referred to his brother Julius as a tramp and an idler, "an unpleasant, thoroughgoing boor." Julius, who made a habit of sponging off his relations, had no talent for anything else. All the other brothers and sisters were studiously respectable but devoid of family solidarity.

9   It may well be that Ludwig Geyer painted a portrait of Friedrich Wagner, just as he did of Johanna Rosine and himself. Wagner had no recollection of any such picture, however, or he would have tried to trace it.

9   Cited from *My Life*, Wagner's autobiography, which is sometimes the sole source of information about episodes of his childhood and adolescence. Whenever one of his autobiographical remarks is cited without attribution, its source is the complete [German] edition of 1976. Any excerpts from Wagner's family and private correspondence not identifiable from the list of authors in the bibliography are taken from material preserved by the Richard-Wagner-Nationalarchiv, Bayreuth.

12   Writing to Liszt on April 4, 1855, when he was badly behind with his work and in urgent need of security, Wagner abruptly came out with the following sentiment: "The way things stand with me now, I need a very soft, gently encompassing element to whet my appetite for work." Similarly, on July 20, 1881, Cosima recorded a humorous couplet expressing his love of things "gently caressable" and "agreeably soft."

23   "The practice of giving Wagner's leitmotifs rigidly identifying names is as questionable as it is unavoidable: questionable because the translation of musical expression into verbal concepts can never be adequate—if it could, the last word on music would have been spoken—and unavoidable because it is illusory to conceive of transmitting a wordless, emotional understanding of musical motifs without resorting to speech. Names that half-miss their objective are nonetheless the only way of reaching it" (Carl Dahlhaus in *Richard Wagners Musikdramen*).

23   Even Wagner's relations with Minna Planer (who was several years his senior) were mother-fixated. On April 1, 1874, he told Cosima that one of his reasons for marrying Minna was "the lack of a maternal home to which I should have been glad to return. My marriage was a form of emancipation."

A Prerevolutionary Awakening

45 An extant fragment of an orchestral work in E minor, which ends in a funeral march, should probably be identified with this overture.

49 Referring to this Fantasia in F-sharp Minor on January 18, 1878, he told Cosima with some satisfaction that it was "more him" (than the later Sonata in A Major). The Fantasia, he said, could have been "by a pupil of Spohr."

Prelude in the Lower Ranks

62 It was not until 1888 that Hermann Levi staged *Die Feen* in Munich with considerable success.

72 Together with parts of the Burrell Collection, Otterstedt's portrait of Minna was acquired in 1978 by the Richard-Wagner-National-archiv, Bayreuth.

The Serious Side of Life

79 It was a bitter disappointment to Wagner that Minna never had children. He often welcomed the young sculptor Gustav Kietz to his Dresden home by opening the door a crack and calling, "Kietz, we still have no children."

81 This episode long remained shrouded in mystery. It did not become clear that Minna had deceived him until Cosima's diaries were published (entry dated July 29, 1878).

81 Cola di Rienzo was born in 1313, exactly five hundred years before Wagner, which must have seemed an added attraction to someone who was alert to numerical correspondences and kept a lookout for them in his own life. According to his half-sister Cäcilie, Wagner was superstitious about numbers even as a child: His first name and surname contained thirteen letters, the same number as the sum of the digits in 1813, the year of his birth.

86 Cosima Wagner and Julius Kniese put together a two-and-a-half-hour version of *Rienzi* designed—in vain, as it turned out—to detach the work from the grand opera tradition and establish it as a music drama. Wagner himself recognized the impossibility of

this. His grandson Wieland produced an abridged *Rienzi,* also lasting less than three hours, for Stuttgart. A similar version scored a success at Wiesbaden in 1979.

Flight From Riga

90   See Siegfried Fornaçon, "Richard Wagners 'Thetis,' " Bayreuth Festival Program, 1971: *Der Fliegende Holländer.*

A German Musician in Paris

99   They are customarily said to number six, but this is not strictly true. In addition to *Dors, mon enfant* (anon.), *L'Attente* (Victor Hugo), *Mignonne* (Pierre de Ronsard), *Tout n'est qu'images fugitives* (Jean Reboul), *Les deux grenadiers* (Heinrich Heine), and *Adieux de Maria Stuart* (Pierre Jean de Béranger), Wagner almost completed *Extase* (Victor Hugo) and wrote the melody, though not the accompaniment, for *La tombe dit à la rose* (Victor Hugo). *La Descente de la Courtille,* also written in the winter of 1839–40, was scored for choir and orchestra. Apart from *Adieux* (March 26, 1840), all the songs with piano accompaniment were written late in 1839.

99   It was psychologically consistent that Wagner's rabid self-dissociation from Meyerbeer should have been fostered by memories of his once subservient attitude toward him, not by professional setbacks of any kind. Although *Judaism in Music* did not mention Meyerbeer by name, he was its ultimate target and inspiration. Wagner endeavored to justify his feelings in a letter to Liszt dated April 18, 1851: "There is something special about Meyerbeer where I'm concerned: I don't hate him, but I find him infinitely repellent! Because he still made a show of patronizing me, I am reminded by this everlastingly amiable, obliging person of the most obscure— I might almost say, most corrupt—period of my life. This was the wire-pulling, backstairs period in which we are taken for fools by patrons for whom we privately feel no affection whatsoever. It is an utterly dishonest relationship. Neither of the two is sincere, each feigns affection, and both make use of each other only for as long as it suits them." Meyerbeer was less hurt by *Judaism in Music* than by the far better-substantiated criticism in *Opera and Drama.* In a diary entry dated November 24, 1851, he confessed to being "demoralized" by reports that Wagner had fiercely attacked him in his latest essay on the future of opera.

103   The *Rienzi* Overture, composed after the body of the work itself, is peculiar inasmuch as it takes the form of a résumé or distillation in which every constituent motif is crowded together at the outset. Although it cannot altogether be encompassed by our verdict on the rest of *Rienzi*, which appears in the Riga chapter, it undoubtedly fostered the attempt to classify the entire work as a music drama.

On the Road to Music Drama

110   Dietsch's libretto, based on Wagner's scenario and written in collaboration by Foucher and Revoil, was clearly no better than the music. " 'The Flying Dutchman' by Dietz [sic] has since foundered badly," Heinrich Heine wrote in *Lutetia* (part two, chapter lvi). "I did not hear this opera, merely caught a glimpse of the libretto and saw to my disgust how the fine plot . . . had been botched in the French text."

112   On this subject, Gustav Kietz cites a letter from Ferdinand Heine in Dresden to his brother Ernst: "Has Wagner forgotten that they turned Domingo the father confessor in *Carlos* into Perez the chancellor, and how carefully all allusions to the Church and priesthood are avoided?"

120   Wagner described *Rienzi* thus on December 27, 1845, in a letter to Alwine Frommann, the first and staunchest of his Berlin devotees. Still earlier, on October 27, 1844, he had referred to the work as "a monster" and told her that he cherished no love for it. To this day, *Rienzi* has been steadfastly refused a hearing at Bayreuth. Even *Die Feen* and *Das Liebesverbot* were performed there in 1967 and 1972, though not at the festival theater itself, under the auspices of the Internationales Jugend-Festspieltreffen.

120   *Die Memoiren einer Sängerin*, a collection of pornographic reminiscences sometimes attributed to Wilhelmine Schröder-Devrient, are wholly unconnected with her and were long ago exposed as fictitious.

121   One of those present, Gustav Kietz, wrote: "I found it quite incomprehensible that *Der Fliegende Holländer* should, as it were, vanish from the Dresden stage after only four performances, for the work had made a far deeper and more moving impression on me than *Rienzi*." The Kassel premiere on June 5, 1843, evoked a similar

reaction from Louis Spohr. Far from reporting that it had failed there, he spoke of "universal acclaim" and remarked on the "satisfaction and interest" loudly voiced by members of the audience as they streamed out of the theater.

122   An unpublished letter to Franz Liszt dated May 2, 1852, informs us that it was not until much later that Wagner really learned, "with much trouble and toil, how important to this opera the décor is."

123   Anyone who immerses himself in the artistic sensibilities and needs of the time, and who eschews the arrogance typical of later generations, will naturally judge Meyerbeer by different and more equitable standards. Wagner knew full well where the decorative appeal of Meyerbeer's music lay. However, as George Bernard Shaw so rightly remarks in *The Perfect Wagnerite*, Meyerbeer was "no symphonist. He could not apply the thematic system to his striking phrases, and so had to cobble them into metric patterns in the old style; and as he was no 'absolute musician' either, he hardly got his metric patterns beyond mere quadrille tunes, which were either wholly undistinguished, or else made remarkable by certain brusqueries which, in the true rococo manner, owed their singularity to their senselessness. He could produce neither a thorough music drama nor a charming opera. But with all this, and worse, Meyerbeer had some genuine dramatic energy, and even passion; and sometimes rose to the occasion in a manner which, whilst the imagination of his contemporaries remained on fire with the novelties of dramatic music, led them to overrate him with an extravagance which provoked Wagner to conduct a long critical campaign against his supremacy."

Dr. Richard Faust in Dresden

133   Louis Spohr (1784–1859) not only encouraged Wagner with well-meant criticism but did a great deal for him at Kassel; as a composer, his fondness for chromatic progressions and enharmonic permutations made him an intermediate link between classical romantic harmony and that of Wagner. Although a detailed examination of his influence would be out of place here, it is worth noting that Wagner showed a marked interest in Spohr's opera *Jessonda* (1823) and often played the overture, which he had heard conducted at Dresden by Carl Maria von Weber, on the piano. (See also Wagner's remark that his own Fantasia in F-sharp Minor (1831) might have been written by "a pupil of Spohr.")

133   By this time, the Young Germans were no longer a compact group and had largely lost their scope for effective influence. The cultural and literary historian Johannes Scherr, a leading South German democrat who fled to Switzerland in 1849, had already passed the following judgment on them in *Poeten der Jetztzeit* (1844): "You may perhaps suppose 'Young Germany' to be an association like 'Jeune France,' 'Giovina Italia,' or 'Junge Schweiz.' Far from it. 'Young Germany' was not even a literary, far less a political association. The authors embraced by this collective term acquired their party designations they knew not how, and it might be hard to determine who first lit on the idea of nonsensically inferring from the opening words of the dedicatory epistle in a book by Wienbarg—from the words, 'To thee, young Germany, I dedicate this text,' which were addressed to young Germans in general—that, with Heinrich Heine at their head, the four authors Laube, Gutzkow, Wienbarg, and Mundt, to whom Kühne was subsequently added, were foremost in constituting a revolutionary, literary propaganda [association] entitled 'Young Germany.' Originally, of course, the aforesaid men had common sympathies enough. Their emergence was a reminder of the German literary 'Storm and Stress' period in the last century, and the simultaneous expression of their antipathies, which were likewise mostly shared, for some time sufficed to lend plausibility to the obscurantist clamor about a rebellious literary fraternity. Before long, however, the German spirit of separatism demonstrated, not only by driving the Young Germans along divergent paths but also by placing many of them on downright hostile terms, that any such deliberate fraternization existed solely in the mind of its denunciator." By "denunciator" Scherr meant the German novelist and journalist Wolfgang Menzel, whose venomous tirades against the "sick and effete" Young Germans had appeared in the *Stuttgarter Literaturblatt* in 1835.

147   Reproduced in full by Helmut Kirchmeyer in *Das zeitgenössische Wagner-Bild. Wagner in Dresden.*

148   Wagner's comments and Trützschler's original remark were recorded by Cosima on July 6, 1878.

The Revolutionary

155   Behind this, as in nearly all Wagner's historical themes, lay the idea of a revolution initiated by a national hero or redeemer. Such

was the utopian dream that he transferred, once his hopes had been dashed by the king of Saxony, to Ludwig II of Bavaria.

164   Comments on Bakunin may be found in *Cosima Wagner's Diaries* (July 7 and October 16, 1878).

166   Privates in the Academic Legion included professors Ernst Rietschel and Ludwig Richter and the sculptor Gustav Kietz. Professor Bendemann was a platoon commander, professors Hübner and Ehrhard commanded sections, and Grüder the portrait painter belonged to the officer corps, in which Professor Heine held the rank of captain. Gottfried Semper was a sharpshooter in the regular Communal Guard.

167   It has often been maintained that the Oehme affair was a product of rumor or fabrication, but this is not so. All depositions on the hand-grenade incident are recorded in the volume entitled "Acta wider den vormaligen Kapellmeister Richard Wagner, wegen Betheiligung am hiesigen Maiaufstande i. J. 1849," Central State Records Office, District Court, Dresden, no. 1219, and in the Justice Ministry's Dossier no. 545, vol. 46. This information was transmitted by Dr. Woldemar Lippert, director of the Saxon Central State Records Office, in his book *Richard Wagners Verbannung und Rückkehr, 1849–1862* (1927). Wagner's "Annals" are reproduced in full in the *Brown Book*.

168   According to the Roll Book of 1848, Richard Wagner formally enlisted as a guardsman in the Friedrichstadt Division on June 2, 1848. On March 21, 1849, citing an ailment from which he had already been suffering in the previous year (a double inguinal hernia whose existence was confirmed postmortem by Dr. Friedrich Keppler, his personal physician), he applied for a discharge on the additional grounds that he had never undergone military training. On the strength of a medical certificate dated May 1, 1849, from his friend Dr. Anton Pusinelli—not, be it noted, from the physician assigned him by the Communal Guard—his application was granted and the word "Resigned" inscribed beside his name. It is therefore unlikely that he attended the preliminary Communal Guard muster at the Manteuffel Brewery in Friedrichstadt on May 2—or so Dr. G. H. Müller, Dresden's Council Archivist and Municipal Librarian, rightly concluded in *Richard Wagner in der Mai-Revolution 1849* (Dresden, 1919). Although Dr. Müller had access to the files, his other conjectures about Wagner's involvement in the events of May are not invariably reliable.

168   When giving an autobiographical account of these revolutionary happenings in *My Life*, Wagner not only omitted all kinds of important details but telescoped events and jumbled his dates and days of the week. This chapter presents the first complete chronological reconstruction ever published.

169   Among other eyewitness accounts in the Burrell Collection is a statement dictated by Frau Baumgarten, the daughter of Wagner's friend Gustav Zocher, and taken down by Mrs. Burrell herself. It reads [verbatim]: "The Baumgartens lived in the Neumarkt. Salomonis apothecary, second (third) floor, at the corner of the present Landhausstrasse, then Pirnasche Strasse, next to Hotel de Saxe, corner of Moritz-Str., Hotel de Rome, then small Schuhmacher Gasse, wherefrom most shooting came. Frau B. first saw from her window a young miner, then an old one in the same miner attire; he stood on the pedestal of a lamp post opposite to her and addressed the crowd. The people went to get the key from the town hall to the town-council house in order to collect arms there. One cortege from the town hall marched past her. An athlete in gray dress with a red feather in his hat carried the saber aloft with the key attached to it. They found no weapons there and then marched in anger to the armory. She heard the first shot and soon afterward she saw a big crowd surrounding an open van pulled by proletarians, a corpse half-naked lying there on his stomach so that the bloody wound was visible; thus the corpse of the same old gray-haired miner who shortly before had harangued the crowd was exhibited."

170   Mrs. Burrell recorded Frau Baumgarten's account of the Schröder-Devrient incident as follows: "Commander of the Communal Guard Charles Napoleon Lenz married to Medizinalrath Baumgarten's sister, lived 1st floor, corner of Altmarkt & Wildsruffer Strasse, Pariser Mode Geschäft. Ground floor was 'Löwenapotheke' Besitzer Otto Schneider. When the victim of the first shot was drawn past on a *Leiterwagen*, lying on his face, Schröder-Devrient called out of the first-floor window 'Rächt Euch an der Reaction'; the insurgents took it to mean the contrary, rushed up and threw all the '*Waaren*' [merchandise] out of the windows, and made a barricade of them in the Wildsruffer Strasse."

171   The classical philologist Hermann Köchly (1815–76) was a royal tutor and a member of the Landtag. He continued to instruct Prince Georg until May 2, when the revolution supervened. With

a warrant out for his arrest, he fled via Hamburg and Brussels to Zurich, where he obtained a chair in 1850 and became rector of the university in 1856. Wagner, who was not overfond of Köchly, avoided mentioning his name as far as possible. For his part, Köchly was unmusical and thought nothing of Wagner's work from *Tannhäuser* onward. Once in Zurich, the two men steered clear of each other.

173   When word came that the old Dresden Opera House was on fire, one of the rebels is reported to have called out to Wagner, "Herr Kapellmeister, the divine spark has ignited!" Wagner's mnemonic jottings for his autobiography, the "Annals," contain the following entry: "Opera House now burned down: strangely contented."

179   On May 19, 1849, the following announcement appeared in no. 139 of the *Dresdner Anzeiger: "Warrant.* The Royal Kapellmeister Richard Wagner, of this place, being somewhat more closely described below, is wanted for questioning on account of his material participation in the rebellious activities that took place in this city, but has not so far been found. The attention of all police authorities is therefore drawn to him, and they are requested, should he enter their jurisdiction, to arrest the said Wagner and advise us accordingly without delay. Dresden, May 16, 1849. City Police Commission. [Signed] von Oppell. Wagner is 37 or 38 years old, of medium height, has brown hair and wears glasses." The extant draft of a personal description that was never printed contains some interesting particulars: "Wagner is 37–38 years old, of medium height, has brown hair and a high forehead. Eyebrows: brown. Eyes: gray-blue. Nose and mouth: well proportioned. Chin: rounded. Wears glasses. Special characteristics: *movements and speech abrupt and rapid.* Clothing: overcoat of dark green buckskin, trousers of dark cloth, velvet waistcoat, silk cravat, ordinary felt hat and boots."

Crisis in Exile

184   Even Wagner's height became the object of persistent controversy after his death because some people preferred to think of him as a dwarf while others regarded any such notion as sacrilege. The present author was himself misled, when compiling his *Wagner-Chronik* of 1972, by differing conversions of the height given in Wagner's Swiss passport into modern terms. The answer is, in fact, quite simple. In keeping with the Baden foot, which had been adopted a few years earlier as the standard intercantonal unit of

measurement, the Swiss foot measured 30 cm. and was, unlike the Saxon or Prussian foot, divided into 10 instead of 12 inches. 5 feet = 150 cm.; 5 inches = 15 cm.; half an inch = 1.5 cm. Total: 1 m. 66.5 cm., or—as the passport stated in the first place—5 feet 5 1/2 inches. (It is significant that the lowest estimate of all—153 cm., or barely 5 feet—appears in Robert W. Gutman's biography.)

188 The following quotations may serve to convey the strength of Feuerbach's abiding influence on Wagner in other realms of philosophical speculation. "Truth, reality, and sensuality are identical. Only a sensual being is a true, real being, and sensuality alone is truth and reality" (Feuerbach). "Truth is a concept and nothing else by nature than objectivized veracity; but the actual content of this veracity is reality alone, or rather: the real, the really existent; and that alone is real which is sensual" (Wagner to August Röckel on January 25, 1854). In 1851, under the spell of Feuerbach's philosophy, he went so far as to "abolish" Christmas and give out presents on New Year's Eve instead!

190 The first and, so far, only person to speak of Wagner and Marx in the same breath was George Bernard Shaw in *The Perfect Wagnerite:* "Both of them prophesied the end of our epoch; and, though in 1913 that epoch seemed so prosperous that the prophecy seemed ridiculously negligible, within ten years the centre had fallen out of Europe. . . ."

197 At Bordeaux, carried away by a false report that Bakunin and Röckel were about to be executed, he had sent them fraternal greetings couched in incredibly silly and tasteless language. The "joyful heroes" were enjoined to "die happy in the gladsome knowledge of the high esteem in which we hold you!" Wagner further consoled them against death by reassuring them of his own survival. He looked to the future "in freedom and cheerfulness" and was carrying on the work for which they were laying down their lives. "Die well, then, envied, admired, and—loved!" Fortunately, this embarrassing aberration never reached the two prisoners. Wagner sent it to them via Frau von Lüttichau, whom he still believed to be favorably disposed toward him. Whether or not her husband threw it into the fire, as Wagner was later informed, the original has never been found.

203 Where the problem of homosexuality is concerned, Wagner's attitude is conveyed by an entry in Cosima's diary dated February 25, 1881. Referring to the relationship between the painter Paul von

Joukowsky and his Italian friend Pepino, Wagner said it was something he could understand but not appreciate.

206   This refutes a detailed account in Westernhagen's *Vom Holländer bis Parsifal,* complete with musical illustrations, and, earlier, in Newman's biography. A facsimile impression appeared in the February 1933 issue of *L'Illustration.*

208   Commenting on Karl Marx's assertion that money was the Jews' worldly god, Fritz J. Raddatz writes: "Even sociologically speaking, that was untrue. For example: In the year the article was published, 1844, more than half the 10,000-odd Jews resident and gainfully employed in Bavaria were manual workers and peasants; of the 5,000 Jews domiciled in Breslau and Oppeln, 4,000 did not earn their living by trade but were manual workers, servants, mechanics, physicians, teachers, or farmers; in 1808 there were 4 moneylenders among the more than 2,500 Jews living in Paris." Raddatz (*Karl Marx. Eine politische Biographie,* Hamburg, 1975) cites an article by Eleonore Sterling in *Deutsch-Französische Jahrbücher,* "Er ist wie Du," and Simon Dubnow's *Weltgeschichte des jüdischen Volkes,* volume 3, Berlin, 1926.

Genesis of a Religion in Disguise

214   Curt von Westernhagen regrets that Wagner has been completely misunderstood because his adepts have clung to "their master's peculiarities and excesses" (*Wagner,* 1968, p. 147). He also cites Wagner's letter to Liszt dated August 16, 1853, which deplored people's inability to read his publications properly: "It would otherwise be quite impossible that the sole fruit of all my endeavors to emerge should be this unfortunate '*Sonderkunst*' and '*Gesamtkunst.*' " At this stage, however, Westernhagen loses heart and fails to probe further. Worse still was the case of Glasenapp, who extolled Wagner's writings on art as visions of genius without communicating a single concrete idea, either accurately or in context. Ernest Newman confined himself to accurate reporting without exploring the problematic aspects of Wagner's overall scheme of things. Thomas Mann shrank from tackling the essays and stuck to the music dramas because he found Wagner's prose so unpalatable. Robert W. Gutman devotes only two pages to Wagner's publications on the theory of art. Only Hans Mayer, who has studied them in the greatest depth and puts them in the intellectual tradition of "true socialism" and classical German humanism, comes close to the

truth when he writes: "As in the case of everything written by this remarkable man, the impression one gets is ambiguous: an intermingling of the very true and the very false, supreme expertise side by side with embarrassing dilettantism, views well worthy of consideration cheek by jowl with expressions of resentment and spite that were to exert an extremely baneful influence in Germany eighty years later" (*Richard Wagner, Mitwelt und Nachwelt*, p. 95).

222   The following is an excerpt from Wagner's account of the Oedipus tragedy: "Antigone's love was a *wholly conscious* love. She knew what she was doing—but she also knew that she had to do it, that she had no choice and must act in accordance with the necessity of love; she knew that she had to obey this unwitting, compelling need for *self-destruction from sympathy;* and in this consciousness of the unconscious she was the consummate human being, love in its supreme abundance and omnipotence. Antigone told the pious citizens of Thebes, 'You condemned my father and mother because they unwittingly loved one another; but you did not condemn Laius, the deliberate filicide, and protected Eteocles, his own brother's enemy: so now condemn *me*, who act from pure humanity, and thereby fill your cup of iniquity to the brim!' And lo, *Antigone's love-curse destroyed the state!* Not a hand stirred to help her as she was led to her death. The citizens wept and implored the gods to relieve them of the anguished compassion they felt for the unhappy girl; they escorted her, consoling her with the thought that things could not be other than they were: regrettably, civil peace and good order required that humanity be sacrificed! But there, where all love is born, was also born the avenger of love. A young man became inflamed with love for Antigone; he confided in his father and begged him, in his paternal love, to spare the doomed girl. Harshly rebuffed, the young man stormed his beloved's tomb, in which she had been placed alive: he found her dead, and with his sword transfixed his own loving heart. But this was the son of Creon, who personified the state. On seeing the corpse of his son, whom love had driven to curse his own father, the monarch became a father once more. The sword of his son's love pierced his heart, cutting it terribly: wounded in its innermost depths, *the state* collapsed, becoming *human* in death.—*Sacred Antigone, I call upon thee now! Unfurl thy banner, so that beneath it we may bring destruction and redemption!*" Hans Mayer is perfectly right to stress that Antigone's love-curse cannot be compared with that of the Nibelung. It is not the curse, however, but Wotan-Brünnhilde's intelligence in "desiring what is needful and effecting it themselves" (Wagner to August Röckel on January 25, 1854) that

does, after all, seem related to an act of self-destruction that causes the state to collapse. Wagner's anarchistic rejection of the state still ran deep, as we can tell from a passage that follows barely two pages later, at the end of the Oedipus story: "Ever since the *political state* has existed, not a step has been taken in history, however deliberately it may have been designed to reinforce the same, that does not conduce to its downfall. As an abstract concept, the state has always been in process of decline; or, rather, it has never entered the realm of reality. Only states *in concreto*, forever succeeding each other like recurrent variations on an unperformable theme, have attained a violent yet constantly disrupted and disputed existence. As an abstraction the state has been the fixed idea of well-meaning but misguided intellectuals; as a concrete entity, the prey of tyranny practiced by the violent or scheming individuals who fill our historical expanse with the content of their deeds." The empty stage at the end of the *Ring* was a product of such ideas.

222   Hitler not only made a careful study of Wagner's writings on art but turned them to advantage along lines conveyed by the title and conclusion of this chapter. One of his first steps was to abolish art criticism and replace it with "art appreciation" [*Kunstbetrachtung*].

227   This explains why Wagner was never wholly himself and his music never good unless harnessed to the mighty chariot of his music dramas—never, for example, when writing occasional compositions devoid of poetic impetus. He either realized this himself or suspected it. "He played me the sonata for Math. Wesendonck," Cosima noted in her diary on August 30, 1877, "and laughed a great deal at its 'triviality,' as he put it. He had never, he said, been able to write an occasional composition. The sonata was shallow and inexpressive, the 'Albumblatt' for Betty Schott artificial; only with the *Idyll* had he succeeded. . . ." But there the impetus had come from *Siegfried*, just as the *Wesendonck Lieder* were written while Wagner was living in the world of *Tristan*.

228   By analogy with Goethe's assertion that the Christian religion was a "would-be political revolution which, having miscarried, turned moral," one might call Wagner's cryptotheology a would-be political revolution which, having miscarried, turned to the philosophy of art.

231   For an examination of Titanism in German intellectual history see C. F. von Weizsäcker's *Der deutsche Titanismus*.

Water, Mountains, Nibelungs

234   Wagner also read Rausse's *Introduction to the Practice of Hydropathy for All Who Can Read and Think* and the treatise *On Common Errors in the Use of Water as a Remedy, Together with a Dissertation on the Absorption and Sedimentation of Poisons and Medicaments in the Living Animal Body and a Critique of the Curative Method of Vinc. Priesnitz*— both of which books he recommended to Jakob Sulzer in December 1851. J. H. Rausse (the pen name of H. Friedrich Franke, who died in 1848) had opened a hydropathic center at Mecklenburg and later ran the Alexandersbad Hydropathic Sanitarium at Wunsiedel.

237   Recently published items of correspondence dated 1849–51 (in *Sämtliche Briefe*, vol. IV) show that Wagner persisted in his frequent alternations between capital and lowercase initials, Roman and German script, so the addition may equally date from that period.

238   Apart from the *Tannhäuser* Overture, the program on March 16, 1852, included Beethoven's *Pastoral* Symphony no. 6 in F Major. We also have precise details of the orchestra, which numbered fifty-two musicians and comprised nineteen violins, six violas, five cellos, twenty wind instruments, timpani, and percussion.

238   "Wesendonck" accords with the spelling used by the persons concerned. First adopted by the Wesendoncks' son Karl, the simplified spelling "Wesendonk" was introduced into published letters and became customary in Wagnerian literature.

240   How he could afford to do this remains something of a mystery. Was he carrying a rucksack? How did he transport his baggage? Did he have it dispatched in advance or forwarded to the next station on his route? He tramped the mountains in stout, calf-length, lace-up boots that were specially made for him, hence his heavy shoemakers' bills. As a child, Wolfgang Wagner found a pair of his grandfather's boots in the loft at Haus Wahnfried.

Know Ye What Is to Come?

245   He told Judith Gautier in 1877 that he had promised Mathilde Wesendonck the sonata "in return for a handsome sofa cushion," but she had clearly set her heart on a "composition" as opposed to one of his "*Albumblätter,*" or humorous polkas.

247   Anyone staging the *Ring* would do well to spend some time in the Swiss Alps. Patrice Chéreau and his designers produced a rather toylike imitation of the Julier, in both shape and coloring, for their Bayreuth production of the *Ring* in 1976, apparently without realizing it. Freud would undoubtedly have reinterpreted the Julier-Felsen as a phallic symbol.

254   Filed in Saxony's Central State Records Office, Dresden, Interior Ministry no. 299 h, Weekly Reports for March 1854, fols. 27b, 28, and published in 1927 by Dr. Woldemar Lippert.

The World Is My Idea

256   "Iconoclasm in German Philosophy" by John Oxenford, *Westminster and Foreign Quarterly Review,* April 1853.

257   Written, as it was, after a lapse of more than fourteen years, this dramatically skillful turn of phrase in Wagner's autobiography should naturally be taken *cum grano.* Cosima took it down at his dictation on January 1, 1869. We know the precise date because she began her diary the same day, every detail of which she carefully recorded.

261   Some of Wagner's biographers have, in all seriousness, entitled this relatively undramatic chapter in his life "The London Inferno." Thus do quotable clichés originate!

265   Wagner's petition for pardon (Central State Records Office, Dresden, Ministry of Justice file no. 545, vol. 46, 171a–174b, eight sheets in his own handwriting) was first published in 1927 by Dr. Woldemar Lippert. It reads as follows:
Most Serene King and Lord!
       Trusting in Your Majesty's supreme favor and indulgence, a man whose former conduct inevitably made him seem a political criminal ventures to draw Your All-Highest's attention to an endeavor to explain the said conduct, considering this necessary in order, in some measure, to support a most humble petition for pardon associated therewith.
       When, seven years ago, I resolved to flee the country rather than stand trial for the purpose of answering the charge laid against me, I was prompted less by the assumption that I should find it impossible to obtain a favorable verdict than by a fundamental lack of hope that, even were my former circumstances entirely restored,

I should be permitted to gain recognition and scope for those views that had developed within me into an ideal, in both art and life. As regards art, in its extremely disadvantageous relationship with our present-day public, I had come in the course of the foregoing years to such definite and, at the same time, dispiriting conclusions that, after sundry, invariably fruitless, attempts to gain a hearing for my views and aspirations in the post I had acquired at Dresden, my realization that this was quite impossible under prevailing circumstances ultimately impelled me toward the breach with those circumstances that had been assuming ever clearer shape in my inner consciousness, until at last my attention was focused on them alone, and not, as previously, on the persons concerned. Nothing could have given this mood a more intemperate turn than the violent upheavals then developing in the world of politics. Although I never addressed myself to any one particular political party, nor ever espoused the specific theories, plans, and aspirations thereof, the belief in a complete transformation of the political and, more especially, the social world gradually gained so strong a hold over me that I began to flatter myself with ideas of reshaping it in accordance with my needs, so as to be able to think it a fulfillment of my ideal relationship between art and life. In so doing, I drew closer to politics and current events, in their own field, only to the extent that I was concerned to impress the artistic tendency of my endeavors upon their material direction, but I never abandoned myself to serious participation in any definite political enterprise. Even this, however, sufficed in the end to deprive me of all consideration for the circumstances in which I lived, so that I lost all the circumspection essential to their maintenance and thus reached a stage where I was ultimately compelled to recognize that my personal position had become untenable.

However conspicuous my behavior must therefore have seemed during the Dresden disturbances, which were, by the by, in no way foreseen by myself, I was so little aware of having committed an actual, punishable offense, notably against my Most Gracious King, that I still failed to grasp this when the pressure of events had already prompted me to flee abroad. Although I learned that I was widely accused of the basest ingratitude toward my Exalted Benefactor, my conscious mind was so little affected by this that I could not but perceive in this consequence of my ill-considered conduct at Dresden a tragic stroke of fate that had besmirched me, seemingly beyond hope of refutation, with a crime of which I could not, however carefully I examined my conscious will, find myself guilty. But the impossibility of exonerating myself of that charge became so evident to me that I was thereby driven to abandon any attempt to justify myself at Dresden. Because of this, however, the break with my past had become complete, and all that could sustain me against the many painful impressions I received from that quarter was a peculiar and truly morbid state of exaltation to whose promptings I yielded, during the early years of my exile, with a certain desperate eagerness. As though in self-vindication, I felt impelled to take the ideas on art and life that had brought me to such a catastrophic pass, arrange them as systematically as possible, develop them in greater detail, and present them to the public in a series of literary works. It was inevitable that these very works should again cause lively offense, because they demonstrated to everyone that my behavior, which could not now be viewed in anything but the most criminal light, had been prompted by something altogether fundamental. Although those literary works could only aggravate the verdict of my judges, however, they benefited me by gradually cooling my agitation and setting me little by little, after the manner of a morbid substance pathologically excreted, on the road to recovery.

Thenceforward, I again found it possible to conceive a great and purely artistic work. The more I applied myself to its execution and at last rediscovered my artistic equilibrium therein, the more there occurred within me an inward conversion that ultimately brought me a deeper insight into the nature of things, thanks to which, in a matter of cardinal importance, to wit, the relationship of the ideal to the reality of all that is human on earth, I recognized the error of my former basic conception. It would be improper for me to elaborate here on the nature of this insight, or on the extraneous factors that have reinforced it and imparted it to my inward mind, which is now finding peace. I nonetheless hope that Your Majesty will be most suitably acquainted with the change that has occurred in me by the contents of the following most humble petition, and by the pledge which I deem it necessary to associate therewith.

I should willingly endure the consequences of the former misdemeanors that led me into exile, were it not that my art itself, on whose account I once committed such headstrong errors, and to which I owe my change of heart and my hopes of someday conciliating those offended by me, directs me back to the German Fatherland to which it indissolubly binds me, because there alone can performances of my musical-dramatic works be given such as I require in order to maintain my capacity for further fruitful production by means of the continuing artistic experience to be gained therefrom. To this end, thanks to the special favor of His Royal Highness the Grand Duke of Saxony-Weimar, and to the selfless sympathy of an egregious artistic friend, a beneficial refuge has been prepared for me in Weimar itself, and my dearest wish is to be permitted to reside there from time to time.

I therefore venture to address to Your Royal Majesty the most humble request that it may please Your Majesty, in gracious recognition of my special capacity and circumstances as an artist, to suffer my conduct as a citizen and subject to be forgotten and most graciously to rescind the measures that threaten me in the event of my reentering the German Confederated States, so that I may be permitted to travel without let or hindrance from my present place of residence to Weimar and reside there at my discretion.

In requesting this exceptional favor, I readily and frankly acknowledge the great error that once diverted me from my career as an artist and into the realm of political life. Furthermore, I profoundly regret and sincerely deplore having made myself appear, in consequence of such behavior, grossly ungrateful to my Exalted Benefactor, His Most Blessed Majesty King Friedrich August; and it is not in self-justification, but solely for my own peace of mind, that I declare myself free of any deliberate, willful intent, in that it never seriously occurred to me how my intemperate behavior could be genuinely connected with any enterprise prejudicial to His Majesty. On the other hand, I firmly and formally pledge that I wish never and in no wise to concern myself again with any form of political activity, and I shall therefore gladly submit to any kind of supervision that may be deemed necessary. Lastly, I further declare, likewise in full accordance with my own wishes, that I shall be careful to ensure that my return to Germany shall in no wise and in no place attract to my person the public attention that might be encountered, even in the most informal manner, by an artist whose works have enjoyed some currency on the German stage.

May Your Majesty perceive from this that it is only my fervent desire for reconciliation, on the one hand, and, on the other, the wish to assure my artistic activity of unimpeded progress, that emboldens me to entreat Your Majesty's royal favor. May I be granted the good fortune to find a gracious voice raised on my behalf in the heart of the inspired Partner, Sponsor, and Friend of Art and Science!

I remain, in the deepest humility and devotion,
Your Royal Majesty's
most loyal and obedient subject,
Richard Wagner.
Zurich, May 16, 1856.

The House on the Green Hill

287 He said as much to Bülow himself, though in another connection, when writing to him from Venice on September 5, 1858: "Why did you weep so when we said good-bye? Now I feel I could ask anything of you, and that you would gladly do anything for me, because you love me." It does not seem superfluous to add that, novelistically though it reads, every last twist and turn in this chapter is verified by the sources listed in the bibliography. Together with Wagner's later comments on the episode, documentary evidence left by the persons concerned provides us with a complete picture of what happened.

Peregrinations Resumed

289 Lippert, who explored the Dresden and Vienna archives, presents the most exhaustive account.

292 According to unpublished letters from Wagner and Herwegh preserved by the Richard-Wagner-Nationalarchiv, Bayreuth.

295 Extracts are reproduced in Catalog no. 215 of the Musikantiquariat Hans Schneider: "Richard Wagner, 2. Teil: Dokumente 1850–1864," Tutzing, 1978.

301 Ernst Bloch, *Gesamtausgabe*, vol. 5, p. 972, Frankfurt, 1977.

302 Wagner himself was right in surmising that machinations against *Tannhäuser* were connected with a political intrigue at court: "My greatest danger lies in the hatred of Countess Walewska for Princess Metternich." Count, later Duke, Walewski, the illegitimate son of Napoleon I and a Polish countess, had become minister of state under Napoleon III in 1860. His party was traditionally hostile to the Austrians, who got *Tannhäuser* performed through Princess Metternich.

310 One argument in favor of the renunciation theory (supported by Wapnewski) might be the association of ideas that occurred to Wagner—according to Cosima's rather imprecise account—when he renewed his acquaintance with the *Assunta* at Venice on April 25, 1882: "The Virgin's radiant head recalled to him his notion of the sexual urge; the unique force, freed now from all desire, the will enraptured and redeemed."

310   Wagenseil refers to a Petrus Paganus from Wanfried in Nieder-hessen. Wagner later used the name for his house in Bayreuth.

318   A few of Wagner's letters to Cosima, all of which were reputedly destroyed by Eva Chamberlain after her mother's death, came to light at Bayreuth in 1979. These documents, whose existence was long concealed, have been used by this author.

A Farce with a First-Class Cast

342   It was not known until 1977 that Helene von Dönniges (1845–1911) accompanied Lassalle on his last trip to Germany, though this will doubtless continue to be disputed. Our sole source is Cosima's diary for October 7, 1882, which states that Lassalle had presented himself to Wagner "as Siegfried, Frl. v. D[önniges] as Brünnhilde, so as to win him over and, through him, the King of Bavaria." In Cosima's German, *darstellen* [present, represent, portray] may—but need not necessarily—mean *vorstellen* [introduce]. What seems to conflict with the latter interpretation is that Helene transferred her affections from Lassalle to the Romanian prince and married him not long after their fatal duel.

351   Wagner definitely wanted Klindworth to replace Pfistermeister. The circumstances are fully attested by Julius Fröbel's memoirs, Wagner's own letters and "Annals," a letter from Hans von Bülow dated February 12, 1865, and Liszt's letters to Agnes Street-Klindworth.

351   Ludwig responded in kind on January 28, 1866, after sadly reflecting that Wagner was not immortal: "My Friend, O My Beloved, wilt Thou flee?"—in this case echoing Venus in *Tannhäuser*, Act I.

356   Descriptions of Ludwig Schnorr's fatal illness—"the gout" had "sprung from his knee to his brain," he "roared like a lion" and had to be restrained by three men—might lead one to suppose either that he was suffering from typhus (as his family assumed) or that he died of meningitis. Clinical features have changed so much since the nineteenth century that no accurate diagnosis is feasible. Schnorr displayed no signs of fatigue at Dresden, where he was already busy rehearsing after his appearances as Tristan in Munich. The corpulent tenor, who always sweated profusely in the third act of *Tristan*, had complained of an icy draft blowing straight at his head across the Munich stage—as Wagner himself

records in "Recollections of Ludwig Schnorr von Carolsfeld"—so perhaps he died of meningitis after all.

Between Munich and Tribschen

382   He resumed his autobiography on November 19, 1868, at the passage dealing with his visit to Paris in 1849: "During the period when all news from Germany ceased, I tried to occupy myself as far as possible with reading. . . ." The authors in question were Proudhon and Lamartine.

Settling in at Bayreuth

419   Brahms's *Triumphlied,* Opus 55 (1872), for mixed choir and orchestra, was based on a biblical text and dedicated to Emperor Wilhelm I.

The First Festival

437   Here, too, as in Wagner's relationship to Heinrich Schütz, one might speak of an antipodal affinity: Monteverdi was still ignorant of many of the formal conventions that governed the musical language of the baroque, classical, and romantic periods, whereas Wagner no longer subscribed to them.

438   This incident is recounted only by Sophie Rützow in *Richard Wagner und Bayreuth,* and should thus be treated with caution. A connection with Nietzsche does seem possible, however, because the director of the asylum was a friend of Wagner.

449   *Letters of Queen Victoria. A Selection from Her Majesty's Correspondence and Journal,* edited by George Earle Buckle, Second Series, vol. II, 1870–78.

451   Incompletely reproduced in Westernhagen's *Richard Wagner* (1956). The correspondence itself is preserved in the Richard-Wagner-Nationalarchiv, Bayreuth.

454   Unlike the physicians who examined Nietzsche when his mind gave way, not to mention the overwhelming majority of medical experts since his death, Dr. Eiser believed that his ophthalmological findings precluded a syphilitic infection. Modern diagnosticians place a different construction on Eiser's detailed account of

his patient's symptoms, but only the exhumation and examination of Nietzsche's remains could have resolved this question beyond doubt.

455   For whatever reason, Peter Gast omitted this passage from the first edition of Nietzsche's letters to him, which he edited himself.

The German Spirit and the West

465   It is highly debatable whether *Die Zauberflöte*'s all-male society is more tolerant and humane than *Parsifal*'s.

471   The statutory provisions that determined the political climate in Imperial Germany during the latter part of Wagner's life, and which remained in force until the Reichstag refused to extend them in 1890, led to the banning of 1,300 publications and the disbanding of 322 organizations. Bismarck, who was dissatisfied with the law in its second, enacted form, would have liked it to go much further. This is evident from his letter to the head of the Reich Chancellery, Christoph von Tiedemann, dated August 15, 1878: "Moreover, the law requires a rider in respect of civil servants to the effect that participation in socialist politics will entail dismissal without pension. . . . I further consider it impossible in the long term, if the law is to be effective, to continue to grant voting rights, electoral eligibility, and the privileges enjoyed by Reichstag members to citizens of whom it can be legally proven that they are socialists."

475   Wagner is almost exactly echoed by the last notes Nietzsche made before he lost his reason: "The Reich itself is a lie: no Hohenzollern, no Bismarck has ever thought of Germany— — —"

Redemption for the Redeemer

479   See the section headed "Bachs Matthäuspassion in Wagners Bühnenweihfestspiel" in Wapnewski's *Der traurige Gott*.

480   At this stage, if he has not done so before, the reader must be wondering where the Wagners got their ready cash—in other words, how they contrived to travel extensively, maintain a large household, and entertain a host of guests. The festival exchequer was kept strictly separate from the composer's private purse and supervised by the administrative committee. In addition to travel-

ing expenses sporadically granted by the royal exchequer, however, Wagner received a growing royalty income from performances of his works. The situation in regard to rights was more than a little chaotic. Some he retained himself; of the rest, most were assigned to agents and a very few to publishers. He had signed a contract at Tribschen in 1871 placing all his business affairs in the hands of the Mainz agents Voltz and Batz, who tried to pocket as much of his income as they could and charged a collection fee of 25 percent. After interminable wrangling, they offered to terminate the contract for an indemnity of 100,000 marks. Wagner's only recourse was to send them periodic letters of protest whenever he felt they were taking advantage of him.

Genius, Work, and Character

491   "But music is finished," he told Cosima on June 11, 1882, "and I don't know whether my dramatic explosions can delay its end. It has lasted such a short time."

Parsifal: The Farewell

507   A total of sixteen performances were given between July 26 and August 29, alternately conducted by Hermann Levi and Franz Fischer. Parsifal was sung by Hermann Winkelmann, Heinrich Gudehus, and Ferdinand Jäger; Gurnemanz by Emil Scaria and Gustav Siehr; Kundry by Amalie Materna, Marianne Brandt, and Therese Malten; Amfortas by Theodor Reichmann; Klingsor by Karl Hill and Anton Fuchs; Titurel by August Kindermann. The Flower Maidens, choreographed by Richard Fricke, comprised Mesdames Horson, Meta, Pringle, André, Galfy, and Belce. Paul von Joukowsky's sets were once more executed by the Brückner brothers of Coburg. The Munich Court Theater orchestra was augmented by musicians from Berlin, Coburg, Darmstadt, Dessau, Hanover, Karlsruhe, Meiningen, Rotterdam, Schwerin, Weimar, Vienna, and Würzburg.

Death in Venice

512   Cosima's diaries now enable us to form some idea of what he meant when he said he "still owed" the world *Tannhäuser*. On November 6, 1877: "In the evening went through the first act of *Tannhäuser* with Herr Seidl. Richard said he intended to shorten the new first scene

appreciably; it weighed the rest down, was lacking in proportion; this scene transgressed the style of *Tannhäuser* as a whole. I defended it by arguing that it cast the same spell over the audience as that to which Tannhäuser succumbs, thereby making the second act more intelligible; it was also fitting that the subterranean world of magic should differ from the simple world above. 'That's what I told myself,' said Richard, 'but it isn't right.' " Several years later, on September 8, 1881, he referred to his projected revision of *Holländer:* "At tea in the evening Richard spoke of *Der Fliegende Holländer* and told me it had saddened him to discover so much in it that was noisy and repetitious—in short, so much that spoiled the work." There was no more talk of replacing Senta's Ballad.

514 Heinrich von Stein was appointed to a chair of aesthetics at Berlin through the good offices of Wilhelm Dilthey. Temporarily on close terms with Nietzsche, he died of a heart attack on June 20, 1887, at the early age of thirty.

519 Adolf Stoecker, an anti-Semitic Protestant clergyman, had sought to stem the advance of the German labor movement by founding a "Christian Socialist Party" of his own in 1878. Wagner's assertion that the threat of socialism was being redirected at the Jews can only be an allusion to Stoecker and his movement. Three years earlier he had preened himself on helping to initiate Stoecker's anti-Jewish campaign.

521 Dr. Friedrich Keppler, Wagner's personal physician in Venice, described his illness and cause of death as follows:
"Richard Wagner suffered from a very advanced enlargement of the heart, notably of the right ventricle, with consequent fatty degeneration of the cardiac tissue. In addition, he suffered from a fairly extensive enlargement of the stomach and from an inguinal hernia on the right side. The latter was exceptionally difficult to hold in place and had also been aggravated over a long period by the wearing of a highly unsuitable truss, so my very first advice to him consisted in prescribing a suitable truss.
"The ailments from which Richard Wagner suffered during the final months of his life were primarily disorders originating in the stomach and intestines, in particular severe meteorism. Accompanying this, though only secondarily, in consequence both of direct mechanical constriction of the thoracic cavity induced by a massive generation of gases in the stomach and intestines, and also of a reflex action by the gastric on the cardiac nerves, were painful disturbances in the action of the heart which ultimately, by ruptur-

ing the right ventricle, led to disaster. It goes without saying that the countless mental excitements to which Wagner was daily exposed by his peculiar outlook and disposition, by his sharply defined attitude toward a whole series of burning issues in the realms of art, science, and politics, and by his notable social standing, did much to precipitate his unfortunate demise.

"The actual attack which so abruptly terminated the master's life *must* have been similarly occasioned, but it is not for me to engage in conjecture on the subject.

"The medical treatment which I had prescribed for Wagner consisted in massaging the abdomen and applying a suitable truss. I avoided medicinal treatment as far as possible because Wagner was in the bad habit of taking numerous strong medicines prescribed for him by various physicians whom he had consulted in the past, often in large doses and all at once."

Bibliography

Author's Note

No biography of this nature is conceivable in isolation from the voluminous literature that has preceded it. To this extent, I owe a debt of gratitude to authors and scholars whose views I am not always able to endorse—even to those whose findings I feel bound to repudiate. Many aspects of the subject have been elucidated for all time, however, and I trust that the foregoing text and the following particulars pay due tribute to those who have served the same cause by making their own contributions to our common store of knowledge. I have listed all the sources consulted and cited, together with the persons from whom I obtained oral information.

For the English-language edition, the author's extensive bibliography of mainly German-language material has been condensed to major sources and works available in English. For a full listing of the source material described in the Author's Note, the reader is referred to the German edition.—ED.

Autobiographical Material, Diaries

Wagner, Richard. *Mein Leben*. Complete annotated edition, edited by Martin Gregor-Dellin. Munich, 1976. English version: *My Life* (2 vols.). New York and London, 1911.
Wagner, Cosima. *Die Tagebücher* (2 vols.). Complete text of the original diaries preserved in the Richard-Wagner-Gedenkstätte, edited and an-

notated by Martin Gregor-Dellin and Dietrich Mack, published by the City of Bayreuth. Vol. I, 1869–77, Munich, 1976; Vol. II, 1878–83, Munich, 1977. English version: *Cosima Wagner's Diaries*, translated and with an introduction by Geoffrey Skelton. Vol. I, London and New York, 1978; Vol. II, London and New York, 1980.

Wagner, Richard. *Das braune Buch: Tagebuchaufzeichnungen 1865 bis 1882*, presented and annotated by Joachim Bergfeld. Zurich and Freiburg, 1975. English version: *The Diary of Richard Wagner: The Brown Book*, translated by George Bird. London and New York, 1980.

Correspondence

Wagner, Richard. *Sämtliche Briefe.* Collected correspondence edited on behalf of the Richard-Wagner-Familien-Archiv, Bayreuth, by Gertrud Strobel and Werner Wolf. Vol. I (1830–42), Leipzig and Mainz, 1967; Vol. II (1842–49), Leipzig and Mainz, 1970; Vol. III (1849–51), Leipzig and Mainz, 1975; Vol. IV (1851–52), Leipzig and Mainz, 1979.

———. *Letters of Richard Wagner: The Burrell Collection*, edited with notes by John N. Burk. New York, 1950.

———. *The Letters of Richard Wagner to Anton Pusinelli*, edited by Elbert Lenrow. New York, 1932.

Wagner, Richard and Cosima. *Lettres à Judith Gautier*, presented and annotated by Léon Guichard. Paris, 1964.

Works

Wagner, Richard. *Gesammelte Schriften und Dichtungen* (16 vols.). Leipzig, 1907 *et seq.*

———. *Sämtliche Werke*, edited by Carl Dahlhaus in collaboration with the Bavarian Academy of Fine Arts, Munich. Mainz, 1970–76.

———. *Die Musikdramen*, with a foreword by Joachim Kaiser. Hamburg, 1971; Munich, 1978.

———. *Skizzen und Entwürfe zur Ring-Dichtung*, edited by Otto Strobel. Munich, 1930.

On Wagner and His Time

Boucher, Maurice. *Les idées politiques de Richard Wagner: Exemple de nationalisme mythique.* Paris, 1948.

Bry, Carl Christian. *Verkappte Religionen: Kritik des kollektiven Wahns*, edited and introduced by Martin Gregor-Dellin. Munich, 1979.

Bülow, Hans von. *Letters of Hans von Bülow*, translated by Hannah Waller. New York and London, 1931.

Dahlhaus, Carl. *Die Idee der absoluten Musik.* Kassel and Munich, 1978.
———. *Musikästhetik.* Cologne, 1967.
———. *Richard Wagners Musikdramen.* Velber, 1971.
Deathridge, John. *Wagner's Rienzi: A Reappraisal Based on a Study of the Sketches and Drafts.* Oxford, 1978.
Eckart, Richard Graf du Moulin. *Cosima Wagner* (2 vols.), translated by Catherine Alison Philips and with an introduction by Ernest Newman. New York, 1930.
Friedell, Egon. *A Cultural History of the Modern Age: The Crisis of the European Soul from the Black Death to the World War* (2 vols.), translated by Charles Francis Atkinson. New York, 1954–64.
Gautier, Judith. *Le collier des jours.* Paris, 1902.
———. *Le second rang du collier.* Paris, 1903.
———. *Le troisième rang du collier.* Paris, 1909.
———. "Richard Wagner chez lui," in *Rappel.* Paris, 1869.
———. *Richard Wagner et son œuvre poétique.* Paris, 1882.
Gutman, Robert W. *Richard Wagner: The Man, His Mind, and His Music.* New York, 1968.
Hanslick, Eduard. *Aus meinem Leben* (2 vols.). Fourth edition, Berlin, 1911.
———. *Musikalische Stationen.* Berlin, 1885.
Liepmann, Klaus. "Wagner's Proposal to America," in *High Fidelity.* Great Barrington, Mass., 1975.
Liszt, Franz. *Briefe* (3 vols.), compiled and edited by La Mara. Leipzig, 1909.
———. *Correspondence of Wagner and Liszt* (2 vols.), translated and with a preface by Francis Hueffer. New York, 1969.
———. *Franz Liszts Gesammelte Schriften* (6 vols.). Leipzig, 1880–83.
Mann, Thomas. *Wagner und unsere Zeit: Aufsätze, Betrachtungen, Briefe,* edited by Erika Mann, foreword by Willi Schuh. Frankfurt, 1963. English translation of two essays in *Thomas Mann: Essays of Three Decades.* New York and London, 1947.
Marcuse, Ludwig. *Das denkwürdige Leben des Richard Wagner.* Munich, 1963.
Mendès, Catulle. *Richard Wagner.* Paris, 1886.
Meysenbug, Malwida von. *Memoirs of Malwida von Meysenbug,* edited by Mildred Adams from the translation of Elsa von Meysenbug Lyons. New York, 1936.
Newman, Ernest. *The Life of Richard Wagner* (4 vols.). New York, 1933–46.
———. *Wagner as Man and Artist.* New York, 1960.
Peters, H. F. *My Sister, My Spouse: A Biography of Lou Andreas-Salomé.* New York, 1962.
Pourtalès, Guy de. *Richard Wagner: The Story of an Artist,* translated by Lewis May. New York and London, 1932.
Shaw, George Bernard. *The Perfect Wagnerite.* London and New York, 1898.

Skelton, Geoffrey. *Wagner at Bayreuth.* London, 1965.
Wagner, Siegfried. *Erinnerungen.* Stuttgart, 1923.
Wapnewski, Peter. *Richard Wagner—Die Szene und ihr Meister.* Munich, 1978.
————. *Der traurige Gott: Richard Wagner in seinen Helden.* Munich, 1978.
————. "Vom mehrfachen Grund der Meistersinger," in Bayerische Staatsoper program for the new production of *Die Meistersinger von Nürnberg.* Munich, 1979.
Westernhagen, Curt von. *Richard Wagner: Sein Werk, Sein Wesen, Seine Welt.* Zurich, 1956.
————. *Vom Holländer zum Parsifal: Neue Wagner-Studien.* Zurich, 1962.
————. *Wagner.* Zurich, 1968.
Wille, Eliza. *Erinnerungen an Richard Wagner.* Munich, Berlin, and Zurich, 1935.

Catalogs, Inventories, Bibliographies

Richard-Wagner-Nationalarchiv, Bayreuth, catalogs and inventories; Nikolaus Oesterlein, *Katalog einer Wagner-Bibliothek* (4 vols.), Leipzig, 1882–95; *Bibliographie Wagnérienne Française 1851–1902,* compiled by Henri Sillège, Paris, 1902; "Bibliografia Wagneriana: Opere di e su Richard Wagner pubblicate in Italia dal 1858 al 1970," compiled by Maria Adelaide Bartoli Baccherini; Curt von Westernhagen, *Richard Wagners Dresdener Bibliothek 1841–1849,* Wiesbaden, 1966; Herbert Barth (editor), *Internationale Wagner-Bibliographie 1945–1955,* Bayreuth, 1956; Henrik Barth (editor), *Internationale Wagner-Bibliographie 1956–1960; Die Besetzung der Bayreuther Festspiele 1876–1960,* compiled by Käte Neupert, Bayreuth, 1961; Henrik Barth (editor), *Internationale Wagner-Bibliographie 1961–1966,* Bayreuth, 1968; Herbert Barth (editor), *Internationale Wagner-Bibliographie 1967–1978,* Bayreuth, 1979.

Chronology

1813   Richard Wagner born at Leipzig on May 22, there christened on August 16. October, Battle of Leipzig. Friedrich Wagner, Richard Wagner's father, dies on November 23.

1814   Ludwig Geyer marries Johanna Rosine, Wagner's mother, on August 28. Family moves to Dresden. Congress of Vienna.

1815   At Dresden. Wagner's half-sister Cäcilie born on February 16. Battle of Waterloo.

1817   Wagner's first taste of school. October, German student associations attend Wartburg Festival.

1819   Ludwig Geyer's health fails. Publication of Arthur Schopenhauer's principal work, *The World as Will and Idea.*

1821   Ludwig Geyer dies at Dresden on September 30. Wagner sent to Eisleben.

1822   December 22, Wagner enrolls at the Kreuzschule under the name Richard Geyer.

1826   Carl Maria von Weber dies on June 5. Wagner's first visit to Prague.

1827   Ludwig van Beethoven dies on March 26. Wagner's second trip to Bohemia. Spends Christmas with relatives in Leipzig.

1828   Wagner enrolls at the Nikolai-Gymnasium, having reverted to his original surname. Influenced by his uncle Adolf Wagner. Much formative reading.

1829   Wagner sees Wilhelmine Schröder-Devrient on stage and resolves to become a musician.

1830   Music lessons. Hans von Bülow born at Dresden on January 8.

Wagner joins the Thomasschule on June 16. July Revolution in France. Popular unrest in the German states.

1831   Wagner studies music with Theodor Weinlig.

1832   Hambach Festival held by democratic nationalists on May 27. C Major Symphony. Third trip to Bohemia.

1833   Wagner at Würzburg. Composes *Die Feen.* Johannes Brahms born on May 7.

1834   Fourth trip to Bohemia with Theodor Apel. Appointed musical director at Bad Lauchstädt and Magdeburg. Affair with Minna Planer. Liszt meets Countess Marie d'Agoult, Cosima's mother.

1835   Wagner works on *Das Liebesverbot.* Second season at Magdeburg.

1836   Premiere of *Das Liebesverbot* at Magdeburg on March 29. To Königsberg via Berlin. Wagner marries Minna Planer on November 24.

1837   Musical director at Riga. Wagner's sister Rosalie dies on October 12. Cosima born on December 25 at Bellagio on Lake Como.

1838   Wagner starts work on *Rienzi.*

1839   Flight from Riga, via Pillau, to London. Then to Paris via Boulogne.

1840   In Paris. Wagner makes friends with Heinrich Heine and meets Liszt for the first time.

1841   *Der Fliegende Holländer* takes shape.

1842   Wagner leaves Paris and returns to Dresden. Spends June at Teplitz-Schönau. Writes *Tannhäuser* sketch on the Schreckenstein. *Rienzi* first performed at Dresden on October 20. Liszt appointed Court Kapellmeister at Weimar.

1843   *Der Fliegende Holländer* premiered at Dresden on January 2. Wagner appointed Dresden Court Kapellmeister. Friendship with August Röckel. Political discussions.

1844   Wagner works on *Tannhäuser.* Friedrich Nietzsche born on October 15.

1845   To Marienbad in July. Wagner sketches *Die Meistersinger* and works on *Lohengrin.* Ludwig II of Bavaria born on August 25. *Tannhäuser* premiered at Dresden on October 19.

1846   Wagner embarks on music for *Lohengrin.*

1848   Wagner's mother dies on January 9. March Revolution, Metternich overthrown at Vienna. Wagner advertises revolutionary sympathies. Friendship with Liszt, who settles at Weimar. Conception of the *Ring.* National Assembly convenes at the Paulskirche, Frankfurt. Wagner visits Vienna.

1849   Friendship with Mikhail Bakunin. Revolutionary articles and participation in the May revolt at Dresden. Flees country. Zurich and Paris.

1850   Exile in Zurich. Essays on art. Affair with Jessie Laussot at Bordeaux. *Lohengrin* premiered at Weimar on August 28. *Judaism in Music* published.

1852   Poem of the *Ring* completed in Zurich.

1853   Liszt visits Zurich in July. Wagner pledges friendship with Liszt and Georg Herwegh. Visits Italy. Conceives the *Rheingold* Prelude. Visits Paris with Liszt on October 10. Meets Cosima, then fifteen, for the first time. Starts to compose *Das Rheingold*.

1854   Wagner reads Schopenhauer's magnum opus. *Tristan* conceived.

1855   London concerts.

1856   Wagner petitions for pardon. Heine dies on February 17, Schumann on July 29.

1857   The Wagners move into Asyl, next door to the Villa Wesendonck. Composition of the *Ring* interrupted. Hans von Bülow and Cosima married in Berlin on August 18, make honeymoon trip to Zurich. Wagner embarks on *Tristan und Isolde*, writes *Wesendonck Lieder*.

1858   Wagner's relations with Mathilde Wesendonck come to a head. Bülows again in Zurich. Wagner to Venice, Minna to Dresden.

1859   Lucerne. *Tristan* completed. Wagner to Paris, where Minna joins him.

1860   Concerts in Paris and Brussels. Cosima's daughter Daniela von Bülow born on October 12.

1861   *Tannhäuser* rumpus in Paris. Wagner to Karlsruhe, Vienna, Venice, Mainz, Paris. Starts work on *Die Meistersinger*. Liszt settles in Rome.

1862   Wagner with Minna at Biebrich. Final separation. Liaisons with Mathilde Maier and Friederike Meyer. With the Bülows in July. Prussian constitutional crisis. Otto von Bismarck appointed premier. Wagner to Vienna.

1863   Trip to Russia. Cosima's daughter Blandine von Bülow born on March 29. Wagner with Cosima in Berlin on November 28. They confess that they "belong" to one another.

1864   German-Danish War. Wagner flees from Vienna, is granted his first audience with Ludwig II of Bavaria on May 4. June–July, Cosima with Wagner at Haus Pellet on the Starnberger See, where they consummate their relationship.

1865   Isolde, their first child, born in Munich on April 10. *Tristan und Isolde* premiered in Munich on June 10. Wagner starts to dictate his autobiography, *My Life*, on July 17, is compelled to leave Bavaria on December 10.

1866   Minna Wagner dies on January 25. Wagner in Switzerland with Cosima. They move into Tribschen. Austro-Prussian War.

1867   Cosima at Tribschen. Eva, her second child by Wagner, is born on February 17.

1868   Munich premiere of *Die Meistersinger* on June 21. Wagner travels to Ticino with Cosima. First meeting with Nietzsche at Leipzig on November 8. Cosima arrives at Tribschen on the night of November 16, never to leave Wagner's side again.

1869   Cosima starts her diary on January 1. Nietzsche, now a professor at Basel University, becomes a frequent visitor to Tribschen. Siegfried born there on June 6. Munich premiere of *Das Rheingold* on September 22.

1870   Munich premiere of *Die Walküre* on June 26. Cosima divorced on July 18. Franco-Prussian War breaks out on July 19. Wagner and Cosima married at Lucerne on August 25. *Siegfried Idyll.*

1871   Wilhelm I proclaimed emperor of Germany on January 18. Wagner chooses Bayreuth as his festival venue and announces future plans.

1872   Wagner's sister Luise dies on January 3. He and Cosima move to Bayreuth. Foundation stone of the festival theater laid on May 22.

1873   Nietzsche suffers his first severe attacks of ill health.

1874   The Wagners move into Haus Wahnfried on April 28. Wagner's brother Albert dies on October 31. Score of the *Ring* completed at Wahnfried on November 21.

1875   Wagner's sister Klara dies on March 17. Preliminary rehearsals at Bayreuth.

1876   The first Bayreuth Festival opens with *Der Ring des Nibelungen* on August 13. Wagner infatuated with Judith Gautier. In September, visits Italy and sees Nietzsche for the last time at Sorrento.

1877   Preliminary work on *Parsifal.* Wagner visits London, corresponds with Nietzsche's physician, Dr. Otto Eiser.

1878   More work on *Parsifal.*

1879   Wagner starts scoring *Parsifal.*

1880   Wagner in Italy, meets Arthur Gobineau.

1881   Wagner to Sicily.

1882   *Parsifal* completed on January 13. Second Bayreuth Festival premieres *Parsifal* on July 26. Wagner to Venice in September. Last prose works.

1883   Wagner dies at the Palazzo Vendramin on February 13. His body is transported to Bayreuth on February 16 and buried there on February 18.

Index

Wagner's Musical Works

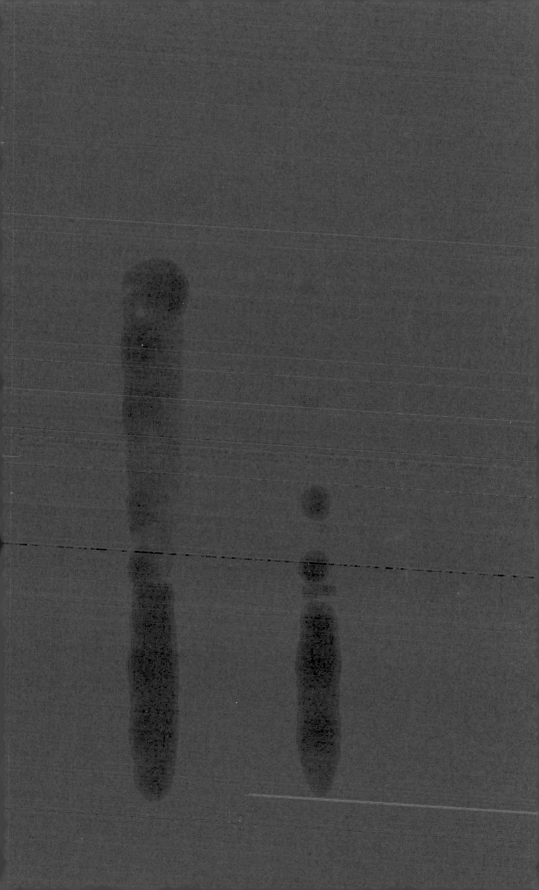